# CRITICISM

## The Major Statements

### Second Edition

# CRITICISM

## The Major Statements

### SECOND EDITION

Selected and Edited by

*CHARLES KAPLAN*

CALIFORNIA STATE UNIVERSITY, NORTHRIDGE

ST. MARTIN'S PRESS · NEW YORK

Library of Congress Catalog Card Number: 85-61246
Copyright © 1986 by St. Martin's Press, Inc.
All Rights Reserved.
Manufactured in the United States of America.
For information, write:
St. Martin's Press, Inc.
175 Fifth Avenue
New York, NY 10010

ISBN: 0-312-17527-2

# Preface

THE PRINCIPAL difference between the earlier edition of this collection of significant works of literary criticism and the present expanded version is the addition of critics representing important twentieth-century tendencies ranging from New Criticism to Deconstructionism. In response to requests for such a change from faithful users of the previous edition, many of whom suggested specific critics to be added, I have endeavored to represent these more modern tendencies by including essays or parts of longer works that either describe or exemplify them.

As in the earlier edition, I am grateful to the many instructors who have helped me with their opinions, suggestions, and objections. I would especially like to thank Helene L. Baldwin, Frostburg State College; Jane Betts, University of Wisconsin—Eau Claire; Michael M. Boardman, Tulane University; James Conley, Biscayne College; Dale Deville, Northeastern Illinois University; Bernard F. Dick, Fairleigh Dickinson University; Noel Riley Fitch, Point Loma College; Adam Frisch, Briar Cliff College; Robert J. Garrity, Saint Joseph's College; Judith Genova, Colorado College; Bruce Golden, California State University San Bernardino; Nigel Hampton, Oakland University; Eugene Hollahan, Georgia State University; Paul Hoover, Columbia College; Martin J. Jacobi, Clemson University; R.G. Malbone, SUNY College—Cortland; Gregory Mason, Gustavus Adolphus College; Fred Misurella, East Stroudsburg University; Judith Moore, Oswego State College; Raymond A. Nelson, Concordia College; John Nesselhof, Welb College; Elaine Plasberg, California State University Northridge; Bruce V. Roach, Stephen F. Austin State University; David Seal, Pacific Lutheran University; William Sharpe, Barnard College; Robert Siegle, Virginia Polytechnic Institute and State University; Lannom Smith, University of Texas—Tyler; Arlene Stiebel, California State University Northridge; Lawrence D. Stewart, California State University Northridge; Stanley Sultan, Clark University; Timea Szell, Barnard College; Thomas Tornquist, Dowling College; Clarence Walhout, Calvin College; Jay A. Ward, Thiel College.

Again, I am also indebted to my students, who continually reward and refresh me by helping me discover what can still be done profitably in the classroom. Finally, I acknowledge a particular debt of gratitude to Professor William D. Anderson, without whose knowledge, labors, and good humor this new edition could not have been realized.

*Northridge, California*                                        C. K.

# Contents

# PLATO

# *The Republic:* Book X

## ABOUT 370 B.C.

*If, as Whitehead said, the history of philosophy is a series of footnotes to Plato, then it may also be said that the history of literary criticism is a footnote to Book X of* The Republic. *Once Plato (or his* persona, *Socrates) has exiled the poets from the ideal state, the ground rules, many of the issues, and some of the terminology have been established for the two-thousand-year debate that ensues. As you read some of the critics that follow, keep in mind the issues that Plato first raises: the place of the poet in society; the relationship the form of a literary work bears to its subject matter; the effect of literature upon its audience; the proper function of literature; the relative values of literature and science; and, a crucial question, the nature of artistic imitation, or what is being imitated, how it is imitated, and what relationship that thing bears to the "real" world. In* The Ion *Plato raises the question of the nature of the artistic process, which also involves questions about the psychology of the artist. The variations on these themes that have been played since testify to the powerful effect of the Platonic dialogues on later critics, whether these critics write in support, refutation, or modification of Plato's views.*

*Because Plato's decision to ban the poets from the ideal republic follows from his basic assumptions, it is important to understand just*

From *The Dialogues of Plato,* tr. Benjamin Jowett; 4th revised edition; Oxford University Press, 1953. Reprinted by permission of The Oxford Univ. Press. The dialogue is between Socrates and Glaucon.

*what these assumptions are. The philosophical basis of a metaphysical Idealism is first carefully established, for poetry is to be seen not only in its relation to the republic but also as part of the total universe and the means of attaining true knowledge of that universe. Other frames of reference are also employed. Utility is an obvious measure of value for Plato, so he distinguishes among various kinds and degrees of usefulness; poetry is also to be contrasted with other human activities. Plato's analysis of the "parts of the soul" is a psychological model that accounts for the way human beings behave and react and learn. So, given the nature of the universe, the goal of an ideal republic, and the nature of man, where does poetry fit in? And, if you think that Plato dismisses poetry because it is merely an idle and unimportant amusement, can you imagine a political theorist today who would devote any attention to the subject of poetry?*

Of the many excellences which I perceive in the order of our State, there is none which upon reflection pleases me better than the rule about poetry.

To what do you refer?

To our refusal to admit the imitative kind of poetry, for it certainly ought not to be received; as I see far more clearly now that the parts of the soul have been distinguished.

What do you mean?

Speaking in confidence, for you will not denounce me to the tragedians and the rest of the imitative tribe, all poetical imitations are ruinous to the understanding of the hearers, unless as an antidote they possess the knowledge of the true nature of the originals.

Explain the purport of your remark.

Well, I will tell you, although I have always from my earliest youth had an awe and love of Homer which even now makes the words falter on my lips, for he seems to be the great captain and teacher of the whole of that noble tragic company; but a man is not to be reverenced more than the truth, and therefore I will speak out.

Very good, he said.

Listen to me then, or rather, answer me.

Put your question.

Can you give me a general definition of imitation? for I really do not myself understand what it professes to be.

A likely thing, then, that I should know.

There would be nothing strange in that, for the duller eye may often see a thing sooner than the keener.

Very true, he said; but in your presence, even if I had any faint notion, I could not muster courage to utter it. Will you inquire yourself?

Well then, shall we begin the inquiry at this point, following our usual method: Whenever a number of individuals have a common name, we assume that there is one corresponding idea or form[1]:—do you understand me?

I do.

Let us take, for our present purpose, any instance of such a group; there are beds and tables in the world—many of each, are there not?

Yes.

But there are only two ideas or forms of such furniture—one the idea of a bed, the other of a table.

True.

And the maker of either of them makes a bed or he makes a table for our use, in accordance with the idea—that is our way of speaking in this and similar instances—but no artificer makes the idea itself: how could he?

Impossible.

And there is another artificer,—I should like to know what you would say of him.

Who is he?

One who is the maker of all the works of all other workmen.

What an extraordinary man!

Wait a little, and there will be more reason for your saying so. For this is the craftsman who is able to make not only furniture of every kind, but all that grows out of the earth, and all living creatures, himself included; and besides these he can make earth and sky and the gods, and all the things which are in heaven or in the realm of Hades under the earth.

He must be a wizard and no mistake.

Oh! you are incredulous, are you? Do you mean that there is no such maker or creator, or that in one sense there might be a maker of all these things but in another not? Do you see that there is a way in which you could make them all yourself?

And what way is this? he asked.

An easy way enough; or rather, there are many ways in which the feat might be quickly and easily accomplished, none quicker than that of turning a mirror round and round—you would soon enough make the

[1] Or (probably better): 'we have been accustomed to assume that there is one single idea corresponding to each group of particulars; and to these we give the same name (as we give the idea).'

sun and the heavens, and the earth and yourself, and other animals and plants, and furniture and all the other things of which we were just now speaking, in the mirror.

Yes, he said; but they would be appearances only.

Very good, I said, you are coming to the point now. And the painter too is, as I conceive, just such another—a creator of appearances, is he not?

Of course.

But then I suppose you will say that what he creates is untrue. And yet there is a sense in which the painter also creates a bed? Is there not?

Yes, he said, but here again, an appearance only.

And what of the maker of the bed? were you not saying that he too makes, not the idea which according to our view is the real object denoted by the word bed, but only a particular bed?

Yes, I did.

Then if he does not make a real object he cannot make what *is*, but only some semblance of existence; and if any one were to say that the work of the maker of the bed, or of any other workman, has real existence, he could hardly be supposed to be speaking the truth.

Not, at least, he replied, in the view of those who make a business of these discussions.

No wonder, then, that his work too is an indistinct expression of truth.

No wonder.

Suppose now that by the light of the examples just offered we inquire who this imitator is?

If you please.

Well then, here we find three beds: one existing in nature, which is made by God, as I think that we may say—for no one else can be the maker?

No one, I think.

There is another which is the work of the carpenter?

Yes.

And the work of the painter is a third?

Yes.

Beds, then, are of three kinds, and there are three artists who super-intend them: God, the maker of the bed, and the painter?

Yes, there are three of them.

God, whether from choice or from necessity, made one bed in nature and one only; two or more such beds neither ever have been nor ever will be made by God.

Why is that?

Because even if He had made but two, a third would still appear behind them of which they again both possessed the form, and that would be the real bed and not the two others.

Very true, he said.

God knew this, I suppose, and He desired to be the real maker of a real bed, not a kind of maker of a kind of bed, and therefore He created a bed which is essentially and by nature one only.

So it seems.

Shall we, then, speak of Him as the natural author or maker of the bed?

Yes, he replied; inasmuch as by the natural process of creation, He is the author of this and of all other things.

And what shall we say of the carpenter—is not he also the maker of a bed?

Yes.

But would you call the painter an artificer and maker?

Certainly not.

Yet if he is not the maker, what is he in relation to the bed?

I think, he said, that we may fairly designate him as the imitator of that which the others make.

Good, I said; then you call him whose product is third in the descent from nature, an imitator?

Certainly, he said.

And so if the tragic poet is an imitator, he too is thrice removed from the king and from the truth; and so are all other imitators.

That appears to be so.

Then about the imitator we are agreed.   And what about the painter? —Do you think he tries to imitate in each case that which originally exists in nature, or only the creations of artificers?

The latter.

As they are or as they appear? you have still to determine this.

What do you mean?

I mean to ask whether a bed really becomes different when it is seen from different points of view, obliquely or directly or from any other point of view? Or does it simply appear different, without being really so? And the same of all things.

Yes, he said, the difference is only apparent.

Now let me ask you another question: Which is the art of painting designed to be—an imitation of things as they are, or as they appear— of appearance or of reality?

Of appearance, he said.

Then the imitator is a long way off the truth, and can reproduce all things because he lightly touches on a small part of them, and that part an image.   For example: A painter will paint a cobbler, carpenter, or any other artisan, though he knows nothing of their arts; and, if he is a good painter, he may deceive children or simple persons when he shows them his picture of a carpenter from a distance, and they will fancy that they are looking at a real carpenter.

Certainly.

And surely, my friend, this is how we should regard all such claims: whenever any one informs us that he has found a man who knows all the arts, and all things else that anybody knows, and every single thing with a higher degree of accuracy than any other man—whoever tells us this, I think that we can only retort that he is a simple creature who seems to have been deceived by some wizard or imitator whom he met, and whom he thought all-knowing, because he himself was unabie to analyse the nature of knowledge and ignorance and imitation.

Most true.

And next, I said, we have to consider tragedy and its leader, Homer; for we hear some persons saying that these poets know all the arts; and all things human; where virtue and vice are concerned, and indeed all divine things too; because the good poet cannot compose well unless he knows his subject, and he who has not this knowledge can never be a poet. We ought to consider whether here also there may not be a similar illusion. Perhaps they may have come across imitators and been deceived by them; they may not have remembered when they saw their works that these were thrice removed from the truth, and could easily be made without any knowledge of the truth, because they are appearances only and not realities? Or, after all, they may be in the right, and good poets do really know the things about which they seem to the many to speak so well?

The question, he said, should by all means be considered.

Now do you suppose that if a person were able to make the original as well as the image, he would seriously devote himself to the image-making branch? Would he allow imitation to be the ruling principle of his life, as if he had nothing higher in him?

I should say not.

But the real artist, who had real knowledge of those things which he chose also to imitate, would be interested in realities and not in imitations; and would desire to leave as memorials of himself works many and fair; and, instead of being the author of encomiums, he would prefer to be the theme of them.

Yes, he said, that would be to him a source of much greater honour and profit.

Now let us refrain, I said, from calling Homer or any other poet to account regarding those arts to which his poems incidentally refer: we will not ask them, in case any poet has been a doctor and not a mere imitator of medical parlance, to show what patients have been restored to health by a poet, ancient or modern, as they were by Asclepius; or what disciples in medicine a poet has left behind him, like the Asclepiads. Nor shall we press the same question upon them about the other arts. But we have a right to know respecting warfare, strategy, the administration of States and the education of man, which are the chiefest and noblest subjects of his poems, and we may fairly ask him about them. 'Friend Homer,' then we say to him, 'if you are only in the second remove from truth in what you say of virtue, and not in the third—not an image maker, that is, by our definition, an imitator—and if you are able to discern what pursuits make men better or worse in private or public life, tell us what State was ever better governed by your help? The good order of Lacedaemon is due to Lycurgus, and many other cities great and small have been similarly benefited by others; but who says that you have been a good legislator to them and have done them any good? Italy and Sicily boast of Charondas, and there is Solon who is renowned among us; but what city has anything to say about you?' Is there any city which he might name?

I think not, said Glaucon; not even the Homerids themselves pretend that he was a legislator.

Well, but is there any war on record which was carried on successfully owing to his leadership or counsel?

There is not.

Or is there anything comparable to those clever improvements in the arts, or in other operations, which are said to have been due to men of practical genius such as Thales the Milesian or Anacharsis the Scythian?

There is absolutely nothing of the kind.

But, if Homer never did any public service, was he privately a guide or teacher of any? Had he in his lifetime friends who loved to associate with him, and who handed down to posterity an Homeric way of life, such as was established by Pythagoras who was especially beloved for this reason and whose followers are to this day conspicuous among others by what they term the Pythagorean way of life?

Nothing of the kind is recorded of him. For surely, Socrates, Creophylus, the companion of Homer, that child of flesh, whose name always makes us laugh, might be more justly ridiculed for his want of breeding, if what is said is true, that Homer was greatly neglected by him in his own day when he was alive?

Yes, I replied, that is the tradition. But can you imagine, Glaucon, that if Homer had really been able to educate and improve mankind—if he had been capable of knowledge and not been a mere imitator—can you imagine, I say, that he would not have attracted many followers, and been honoured and loved by them? Protagoras of Abdera, and Prodicus of Ceos, and a host of others, have only to whisper to their contemporaries: 'You will never be able to manage either your own house or your own State until you appoint us to be your ministers of education'—and this ingenious device of theirs has such an effect in making men love them that their companions all but carry them about on their shoulders. And is it conceivable that the contemporaries of Homer, or again of Hesiod, would have allowed either of them to go about as rhapsodists, if they had really been able to help mankind forward in virtue? Would they not have been as unwilling to part with them as with gold, and have compelled them to stay at home with them? Or, if the master would not stay, then the disciples would have followed him about everywhere, until they had got education enough?

Yes, Socrates, that, I think, is quite true.

Then must we not infer that all these poetical individuals, beginning with Homer, are only imitators, who copy images of virtue and the other themes of their poetry, but have no contact with the truth? The poet is like a painter who, as we have already observed, will make a likeness of a cobbler though he understands nothing of cobbling; and his picture is good enough for those who know no more than he does, and judge only by colours and figures.

Quite so.

In like manner the poet with his words and phrases[2] may be said to lay on the colours of the several arts, himself understanding their nature only enough to imitate them; and other people, who are as ignorant as he is, and judge only from his words, imagine that if he speaks of cobbling, or of military tactics, or of anything else, in metre and harmony and rhythm, he speaks very well—such is the sweet influence which melody and rhythm by nature have. For I am sure that you know what a poor appearance the works of poets make when stripped of the colours which art puts upon them, and recited in simple prose. You have seen some examples?

Yes, he said.

They are like faces which were never really beautiful, but only blooming, seen when the bloom of youth has passed away from them?

Exactly.

Come now, and observe this point: The imitator or maker of the image knows nothing, we have said, of true existence; he knows appearances only. Am I not right?

Yes.

---

[2] Or, 'with his nouns and verbs'.

Then let us have a clear understanding, and not be satisfied with half an explanation.

Proceed.

Of the painter we say that he will paint reins, and he will paint a bit?

Yes.

And the worker in leather and brass will make them?

Certainly.

But does the painter know the right form of the bit and reins? Nay, hardly even the workers in brass and leather who make them; only the horseman who knows how to use them—he knows their right form.

Most true.

And may we not say the same of all things?

What?

That there are three arts which are concerned with all things: one which uses, another which makes, a third which imitates them?

Yes.

And the excellence and beauty and rightness of every structure, animate or inanimate, and of every action of man, is relative solely to the use for which nature or the artist has intended them.

True.

Then beyond doubt it is the user who has the greatest experience of them, and he must report to the maker the good or bad qualities which develop themselves in use; for example, the flute-player will tell the flute-maker which of his flutes is satisfactory to the performer; he will tell him how he ought to make them, and the other will attend to his instructions?

Of course.

So the one pronounces with knowledge about the goodness and badness of flutes, while the other, confiding in him, will make them accordingly?

True.

The instrument is the same, but about the excellence or badness of it the maker will possess a correct belief, since he associates with one who knows, and is compelled to hear what he has to say; whereas the user will have knowledge?

True.

But will the imitator have either? Will he know from use whether or no that which he paints is correct or beautiful? or will he have right opinion from being compelled to associate with another who knows and gives him instructions about what he should paint?

Neither.

Then an imitator will no more have true opinion than he will have knowledge about the goodness or badness of his models?

I suppose not.

The imitative poet will be in a brilliant state of intelligence about the theme of his poetry?

Nay, very much the reverse.

And still he will go on imitating without knowing what makes a thing good or bad, and may be expected therefore to imitate only that which appears to be good to the ignorant multitude?

Just so.

Thus far then we are pretty well agreed that the imitator has no knowledge worth mentioning of what he imitates. Imitation is only a kind of play or sport, and the tragic poets, whether they write in iambic or in heroic verse, are imitators in the highest degree?

Very true.

And now tell me, I conjure you,—this imitation is concerned with an object which is thrice removed from the truth?

Certainly.

And what kind of faculty in man is that to which imitation makes its special appeal?

What do you mean?

I will explain: The same body does not appear equal to our sight when seen near and when seen at a distance?

True.

And the same objects appear straight when looked at out of the water, and crooked when in the water; and the concave becomes convex, owing to the illusion about colours to which the sight is liable. Thus every sort of confusion is revealed within us; and this is that weakness of the human mind on which the art of painting in light and shadow, the art of conjuring, and many other ingenious devices impose, having an effect upon us like magic.

True.

And the arts of measuring and numbering and weighing come to the rescue of the human understanding—there is the beauty of them—with the result that the apparent greater or less, or more or heavier, no longer have the mastery over us, but give way before the power of calculation and measuring and weighing?

Most true.

And this, surely, must be the work of the calculating and rational principle in the soul?

To be sure.

And often when this principle measures and certifies that some things are equal, or that some are greater or less than others, it is, at the same time, contradicted by the appearance which the objects present?

True.

But did we not say that such a contradiction is impossible—the same faculty cannot have contrary opinions at the same time about the same thing?

We did; and rightly.

Then that part of the soul which has an opinion contrary to measure can hardly be the same with that which has an opinion in accordance with measure?

True.

And the part of the soul which trusts to measure and calculation is likely to be the better one?

Certainly.

And therefore that which is opposed to this is probably an inferior principle in our nature?

No doubt.

This was the conclusion at which I was seeking to arrive when I said that painting or drawing, and imitation in general, are engaged upon productions which are far removed from truth, and are also the companions and friends and associates of a principle within us which is equally removed from reason, and that they have no true or healthy aim.

Exactly.

The imitative art is an inferior who from intercourse with an inferior has inferior offspring.

Very true.

And is this confined to the sight only, or does it extend to the hearing also, relating in fact to what we term poetry?

Probably the same would be true of poetry.

Do not rely, I said, on a probability derived from the analogy of painting; but let us once more go directly to that faculty of the mind with which imitative poetry has converse, and see whether it is good or bad.

By all means.

We may state the question thus:—Imitation imitates the actions of men, whether voluntary or involuntary, on which, as they imagine, a good or bad result has ensued, and they rejoice or sorrow accordingly. Is there anything more?

No, there is nothing else.

But in all this variety of circumstances is the man at unity with himself —or rather, as in the instance of sight there was confusion and opposition in his opinions about the same things, so here also is there not strife and inconsistency in his life? Though I need hardly raise the question again, for I remember that all this has been already admitted; and the soul has been acknowledged by us to be full of these and ten thousand similar oppositions occurring at the same moment?

And we were right, he said.

Yes, I said, thus far we were right; but there was an omission which must now be supplied.

What was the omission?

Were we not saying that a good man, who has the misfortune to lose his son or anything else which is most dear to him, will bear the loss with more equanimity than another?

Yes, indeed.

But will he have no sorrow, or shall we say that although he cannot help sorrowing, he will moderate his sorrow?

The latter, he said, is the truer statement.

Tell me: will he be more likely to struggle and hold out against his sorrow when he is seen by his equals, or when he is alone in a deserted place?

The fact of being seen will make a great difference, he said.

When he is by himself he will not mind saying many things which he would be ashamed of any one hearing, and also doing many things which he would not care to be seen doing?

True.

And doubtless it is the law and reason in him which bids him resist; while it is the affliction itself which is urging him to indulge his sorrow?

True.

But when a man is drawn in two opposite directions, to and from the same object, this, as we affirm, necessarily implies two distinct principles in him?

Certainly.

One of them is ready to follow the guidance of the law?

How do you mean?

The law would say that to be patient under calamity is best, and that we should not give way to impatience, as the good and evil in such things are not clear, and nothing is gained by impatience; also, because no human thing is of serious importance, and grief stands in the way of that which at the moment is most required.

What is most required? he asked.

That we should take counsel about what has happened, and when the dice have been thrown, according to their fall, order our affairs in the way which reason deems best; not, like children who have had a fall, keeping hold of the part struck and wasting time in setting up a howl, but always accustoming the soul forthwith to apply a remedy, raising up that which is sickly and fallen, banishing the cry of sorrow by the healing art.

Yes, he said, that is the true way of meeting the attacks of fortune.

Well then, I said, the higher principle is ready to follow this suggestion of reason?

Clearly.

But the other principle, which inclines us to recollection of our troubles and to lamentation, and can never have enough of them, we may call irrational, useless, and cowardly?

Indeed, we may.

Now does not the principle which is thus inclined to complaint, furnish a great variety of materials for imitation? Whereas the wise and calm temperament, being always nearly equable, is not easy to imitate or to appreciate when imitated, especially at a public festival when a promiscuous crowd is assembled in a theatre. For the feeling represented is one to which they are strangers.

Certainly.

Then the imitative poet who aims at being popular is not by nature made, nor is his art intended, to please or to affect the rational principle in the soul; but he will appeal rather to the lachrymose and fitful temper, which is easily imitated?

Clearly.

And now we may fairly take him and place him by the side of the painter, for he is like him in two ways: first, inasmuch as his creations have an inferior degree of truth—in this, I say, he is like him; and he is also like him in being the associate of an inferior part of the soul; and this is enough to show that we shall be right in refusing to admit him into a State which is to be well ordered, because he awakens and nourishes this part of the soul, and by strengthening it impairs the reason. As in a city when the evil are permitted to wield power and the finer men are put out of the way, so in the soul of each man, as we shall maintain, the imitative poet implants an evil constitution, for he indulges the irrational nature which has no discernment of greater and less, but thinks the same thing at one time great and at another small—he is an imitator of images and is very far removed from the truth.

Exactly.

But we have not yet brought forward the heaviest count in our accusation:—the power which poetry has of harming even the good (and there are very few who are not harmed), is surely an awful thing?

Yes, certainly, if the effect is what you say.

Hear and judge: The best of us, as I conceive, when we listen to a passage of Homer or one of the tragedians, in which he represents some hero who is drawling out his sorrows in a long oration, or singing, and smiting his breast—the best of us, you know, delight in giving way to sympathy, and are in raptures at the excellence of the poet who stirs our feelings most.

Yes, of course I know.

But when any sorrow of our own happens to us, then you may observe that we pride ourselves on the opposite quality— we would fain be quiet and patient; this is considered the manly part, and the other which delighted us in the recitation is now deemed to be the part of a woman.

Very true, he said.

Now can we be right in praising and admiring another who is doing that which any one of us would abominate and be ashamed of in his own person?

No, he said, that is certainly not reasonable.

Nay, I said, quite reasonable from one point of view.

What point of view?

If you consider, I said, that when in misfortune we feel a natural hunger and desire to relieve our sorrow by weeping and lamentation, and that this very feeling which is starved and suppressed in our own calamities is satisfied and delighted by the poets;—the better nature in each of us, not having been sufficiently trained by reason or habit, allows the sympathetic element to break loose because the sorrow is another's; and the spectator fancies that there can be no disgrace to himself in praising and pitying any one who while professing to be a brave man, gives way to untimely lamentation; he thinks that the pleasure is a gain, and is far from wishing to lose it by rejection of the whole poem. Few persons ever reflect, as I should imagine, that the contagion must pass from others to themselves. For the pity which has been nourished and strengthened in the misfortunes of others is with difficulty repressed in our own.

How very true!

And does not the same hold also of the ridiculous? There are jests which you would be ashamed to make yourself, and yet on the comic stage, or indeed in private, when you hear them, you are greatly amused by them, and are not at all disgusted at their unseemliness;—the case of pity is repeated;—there is a principle in human nature which is disposed to raise a laugh, and this, which you once restrained by reason because you were afraid of being thought a buffoon, is now let out again; and having stimulated the risible faculty at the theatre, you are betrayed unconsciously to yourself into playing the comic poet at home.

Quite true, he said.

And the same may be said of lust and anger and all the other affections, of desire and pain and pleasure, which are held to be inseparable from every action—in all of them poetry has a like effect; it feeds and waters the passions instead of drying them up; she lets them rule, although they ought to be controlled if mankind are ever to increase in happiness and virtue.

I cannot deny it.

Therefore, Glaucon, I said, whenever you meet with any of the eulogists of Homer declaring that he has been the educator of Hellas, and that he is profitable for education and for the ordering of human things, and that you should take him up again and again and get to know him and regulate your whole life according to him, we may love and honour those who say these things—they are excellent people, as far as their lights extend; and we are ready to acknowledge that Homer is the greatest of poets and first of tragedy writers; but we must remain firm in our conviction that hymns to the gods and praises of famous men are the only poetry which ought to be admitted into our State.    For if you go beyond this and allow the honeyed Muse to enter, either in epic or lyric verse, not law and the reason of mankind, which by common consent have ever been deemed best,[3] but pleasure and pain will be the rulers in our State.

That is most true, he said.

And now since we have reverted to the subject of poetry, let this our defence serve to show the reasonableness of our former judgement in sending away out of our State an art having the tendencies which we have described; for reason constrained us.    But that she may not impute to us any harshness or want of politeness, let us tell her that there is an ancient quarrel between philosophy and poetry; of which there are many proofs, such as the saying of 'the yelping hound howling at her lord', or of one 'mighty in the vain talk of fools', and 'the mob of sages circumventing Zeus', and the 'subtle thinkers who are beggars after all';[4] and there are innumerable other signs of ancient enmity between them.    Notwithstanding this, let us assure the poetry which aims at pleasure, and the art of imitation, that if she will only prove her title to exist in a well-ordered State we shall be delighted to receive her—we are very conscious of her charms; but it would not be right on that account to betray the truth.    I dare say, Glaucon, that you are as much charmed by her as I am, especially when she appears in Homer?

Yes, indeed, I am greatly charmed.

Shall I propose, then, that she be allowed to return from exile, but upon this condition only—that she make a defence of herself in some lyrical or other metre?

Certainly.

And we may further grant to those of her defenders who are lovers of poetry and yet not poets the permission to speak in prose on her behalf: let them show not only that she is pleasant but also useful to States and to human life, and we will listen in a kindly spirit; for we shall surely be the

[3] [Or: 'law, and the principle which the community in every case has pronounced to be the best'.]
[4] [Reading and sense uncertain.    The origin of all these quotations is unknown.]

gainers if this can be proved, that there is a use in poetry as well as a delight?

Certainly, he said, we shall be the gainers.

If her defence fails, then, my dear friend, like other persons who are enamoured of something, but put a restraint upon themselves when they think their desires are opposed to their interests, so too must we after the manner of lovers give her up, though not without a struggle. We too are inspired by that love of such poetry which the education of noble States has implanted in us, and therefore we shall be glad if she appears at her best and truest; but so long as she is unable to make good her defence, this argument of ours shall be a charm to us, which we will repeat to ourselves while we listen to her strains; that we may not fall away into the childish love of her which captivates the many. At all events we are well aware that poetry, such as we have described, is not to be regarded seriously as attaining to the truth; and he who listens to her, fearing for the safety of the city which is within him, should be on his guard against her seductions and make our words his law.

Yes, he said, I quite agree with you.

Yes, I said, my dear Glaucon, for great is the issue at stake, greater than appears, whether a man is to be good or bad. And what will any one be profited if under the influence of honour or money or power, aye, or under the excitement of poetry, he neglect justice and virtue?

Yes, he said; I have been convinced by the argument, as I believe that anyone else would have been.

*PLATO*

# from
# *The Ion*

## ABOUT 390 B.C.

I CANNOT deny what you say, Socrates. Nevertheless I am conscious in my own self, and the world agrees with me, that I do speak better and have more to say about Homer than any other man; but I do not speak equally well about others. After all, there must be some reason for this; what is it?

I see the reason, Ion; and I will proceed to explain to you what I imagine it to be. The gift which you possess of speaking excellently about Homer is not an art, but, as I was just saying, an inspiration; there is a divinity moving you, like that contained in the stone which Euripides calls a magnet, but which is commonly known as the stone of Heráclea. This stone not only attracts iron rings, but also imparts to them a similar power of attracting other rings; and sometimes you may see a number of pieces of iron and rings suspended from one another so as to form quite a long chain: and all of them derive their power of suspension from the original stone. In like manner the Muse first of all inspires men herself; and from these inspired persons a chain of other persons is suspended, who take the inspiration. For all good poets, epic as well as lyric, compose their beautiful poems not by art, but because they are inspired and possessed. And as the Corybantian revellers when they dance are not in their right mind, so the lyric poets are not in their right mind when they are composing their beautiful strains: but when falling under the power of music and metre they are inspired and possessed; like Bacchic maidens who

From *The Dialogues of Plato*, tr. Benjamin Jowett; 4th revised edition; Oxford University Press, 1953. Reprinted by permission of The Clarendon Press, Oxford. The dialogue is between Socrates and Ion.

draw milk and honey from the rivers when they are under the influence of Dionysus but not when they are in their right mind.   And the soul of the lyric poet does the same, as they themselves say; for they tell us that they bring songs from honeyed fountains, culling them out of the gardens and dells of the Muses; they, like the bees, winging their way from flower to flower.   And this is true.   For the poet is a light and winged and holy thing, and there is no invention in him until he has been inspired and is out of his senses, and reason is no longer in him: no man, while he retains that faculty, has the oracular gift of poetry.

Many are the noble words in which poets speak concerning the actions of men; but like yourself when speaking about Homer, they do not speak of them by any rules of art: they are simply inspired to utter that to which the Muse impels them, and that only; and when inspired, one of them will make dithyrambs, another hymns of praise, another choral strains, another epic or iambic verses, but not one of them is of any account in the other kinds.   For not by art does the poet sing, but by power divine; had he learned by rules of art, he would have known how to speak not of one theme only, but of all; and therefore God takes away reason from poets, and uses them as his ministers, as he also uses the pronouncers of oracles and holy prophets, in order that we who hear them may know them to be speaking not of themselves, who utter these priceless words while bereft of reason, but that God himself is the speaker, and that through them he is addressing us.   And Tynnichus the Chalcidian affords a striking instance of what I am saying: he wrote no poem that anyone would care to remember but the famous paean which is in everyone's mouth, one of the finest lyric poems ever written, simply an invention of the Muses, as he himself says.   For in this way God would seem to demonstrate to us and not to allow us to doubt that these beautiful poems are not human, nor the work of man, but divine and the work of God; and that the poets are only the interpreters of the gods by whom they are severally possessed.   Was not this the lesson which God intended to teach when by the mouth of the worst of poets he sang the best of songs?   Am I not right, Ion?

Yes, indeed, Socrates, I feel that you are; for your words touch my soul, and I am persuaded that in these works the good poets, under divine inspiration, interpret to us the voice of the Gods.

And you rhapsodists are the interpreters of the poets?

There again you are right.

Then you are the interpreters of interpreters?

Precisely.

I wish you would frankly tell me, Ion, what I am going to ask of you: When you produce the greatest effect upon the audience in the recitation of some striking passage, such as the apparition of Odysseus leaping forth on the floor, recognized by the suitors and shaking out his arrows at his feet, or the description of Achilles springing upon Hector, or the sorrows of Andromache, Hecuba, or Priam,—are you in your right mind? Are you not carried out of yourself, and does not your soul in an ecstasy seem to be among the persons or places of which you are speaking, whether they are in Ithaca or in Troy or whatever may be the scene of the poem?

That proof strikes home to me, Socrates. For I must frankly confess that at the tale of pity my eyes are filled with tears, and when I speak of horrors, my hair stands on end and my heart throbs.

Well, Ion, and what are we to say of a man who at a sacrifice or festival, when he is dressed in an embroidered robe, and has golden crowns upon his head, of which nobody has robbed him, appears weeping or panic-stricken in the presence of more than twenty thousand friendly faces, when there is no one despoiling or wronging him;—is he in his right mind or is he not?

No indeed, Socrates, I must say that, strictly speaking, he is not in his right mind.

And are you aware that you produce similar effects on most of the spectators?

Only too well; for I look down upon them from the stage, and behold the various emotions of pity, wonder, sternness, stamped upon their countenances when I am speaking: and I am obliged to give my very best attention to them; for if I make them cry I myself shall laugh, and if I make them laugh I myself shall cry, when the time of payment arrives.

Do you know that the spectator is the last of the rings which, as I am saying, receive the power of the original magnet from one another? The rhapsode like yourself and the actor are intermediate links, and the poet himself is the first of them. Through all these God sways the souls of men in any direction which He pleases, causing each link to communicate the power to the next. Thus there is a vast chain of dancers and masters and under-masters of choruses, who are suspended, as if from the stone, at the side of the rings which hang down from the Muse. And every poet has some Muse from whom he is suspended, and by whom he is said to be possessed, which is nearly the same thing; for he is taken hold of. And from these first rings, which are the poets, depend others, some deriving their inspiration from Orpheus, others from Musaeus; but the greater number are possessed and held by Homer. Of whom, Ion, you are one, and are possessed by Homer; and when anyone repeats the words of another poet you go to sleep, and know not what to say; but when anyone recites a strain of Homer you wake up in a moment, and your soul leaps within you, and you have plenty to say; for not by art or knowledge about

Homer do you say what you say, but by divine inspiration and by possession; just as the Corybantian revellers too have a quick perception of that strain only which is appropriated to the god by whom they are possessed, and have plenty of dances and words for that, but take no heed of any other.   And you, Ion, when the name of Homer is mentioned have plenty to say, and have nothing to say of others.   You ask, 'Why is this?' The answer is that your skill in the praise of Homer comes not from art but from divine inspiration.

ARISTOTLE

# The Poetics

## ABOUT 335-322 B.C.

*Plato's discussion of poetry is a chapter in* The Republic, *but Aristotle devotes a separate treatise to the subject, just as he wrote other treatises on ethics, politics, physics, rhetoric, and so forth. Certain differences in their philosophical views can be gleaned from this fact, as well as from the differences in the kinds of questions that each asks. Where Plato asks, "What good is poetry compared to other things?" Aristotle asks, "What is the good in poetry considered as itself?" When Plato accuses Homer of telling lies skillfully, he stresses the noun; but Aristotle emphasizes the adverb. Of course poets lie, Aristotle grants; now let us analyze the forms and techniques of these fictions to which we respond so powerfully. For Plato, poetry has an instrumental function; for Aristotle, it has a terminal value—that is, it is not to be regarded as a competing medium for information or indoctrination but as creative art. Where Plato is analogical, Aristotle is analytical; where Plato discusses poetry in general terms, Aristotle classifies, divides, and subdivides the kinds of poetry according to their formal differences. Whereas for Plato it is important to know the similarities among all things, for Aristotle it is more crucial to know, for example, how tragedy and epic differ from one another. And, defining tragedy as the highest form, Aristotle analyzes its component elements in an order and proportion that give the relative importance of each. The process*

From *Aristotle's Theory of Poetry and Fine Art*, ed. S. H. Butcher; corrected version of the fourth (1911) edition; The Macmillan Company, 1932. Reprinted by permission of Macmillan London and Basingstoke. The editor's brackets ([ ] and ⟨ ⟩) and asterisks, which indicate reconstructed or lost text, have been retained.

21

*by which he orders the treatise is at least as significant as his conclusions, some of which have been debated and interpreted ever since. His stress on artistic form, instead of subject matter, derives from a conception of imitation that differs from Plato's: for Aristotle, it is not copying but creating. The first formalist critic, he starts into motion the concept of organic unity, which you will encounter numerous times in later critics.*

*There are also interesting differences in style between these two critics. Plato, who denounces the poets, is dramatic, eloquent, metaphorical; but Aristotle, who defends them, frequently sounds as though he is writing a technical manual. He is not prescribing a formula but describing and analyzing a form.*

*It is commonly assumed that Aristotle prescribed something called "the three unities," but where in* The Poetics *is this prescription to be found? It is worth speculating about what this student of form might say about the half-hour television drama, the comic strip, and the murder mystery novel as art forms; his approach is by no means limited to Greek tragedy.*

I

I PROPOSE to treat of Poetry in itself and of its various kinds, noting the essential quality of each; to inquire into the structure of the plot as requisite to a good poem; into the number and nature of the parts of which a poem is composed; and similarly into whatever else falls within the same inquiry. Following, then, the order of nature, let us begin with the principles which come first.

Epic poetry and Tragedy, Comedy also and Dithyrambic poetry, and the music of the flute and of the lyre in most of their forms, are all in their general conception modes of imitation. They differ, however, from one another in three respects,—the medium, the objects, the manner or mode of imitation, being in each case distinct.

For as there are persons who, by conscious art or mere habit, imitate and represent various objects through the medium of colour and form, or again by the voice; so in the arts above mentioned, taken as a whole, the imitation is produced by rhythm, language, or 'harmony,' either singly or combined.

Thus in the music of the flute and of the lyre, 'harmony' and rhythm alone are employed; also in other arts, such as that of the shepherd's pipe, which are essentially similar to these. In dancing, rhythm alone is used without 'harmony'; for even dancing imitates character, emotion, and action, by rhythmical movement.

There is another art which imitates by means of language alone, and that either in prose or verse—which verse, again, may either combine different metres or consist of but one kind—but this has hitherto been without a name. For there is no common term we could apply to the mimes of Sophron and Xenarchus and the Socratic dialogues on the one hand; and, on the other, to poetic imitations in iambic, elegiac, or any similar metre. People do, indeed, add the word 'maker' or 'poet' to the name of the metre, and speak of elegiac poets, or epic (that is, hexameter) poets, as if it were not the imitation that makes the poet, but the verse that entitles them all indiscriminately to the name. Even when a treatise on medicine or natural science is brought out in verse, the name of poet is by custom given to the author; and yet Homer and Empedocles have nothing in common but the metre, so that it would be right to call the one poet, the other physicist rather than poet. On the same principle, even if a writer in his poetic imitation were to combine all metres, as Chaeremon did in his Centaur, which is a medley composed of metres of all kinds, we should bring him too under the general term poet. So much then for these distinctions.

There are, again, some arts which employ all the means above mentioned,—namely, rhythm, tune, and metre. Such are Dithyrambic and Nomic poetry, and also Tragedy and Comedy; but between them the difference is, that in the first two cases these means are all employed in combination, in the latter, now one means is employed, now another.

Such, then, are the differences of the arts with respect to the medium of imitation.

## II

Since the objects of imitation are men in action, and these men must be either of a higher or a lower type (for moral character mainly answers to these divisions, goodness and badness being the distinguishing marks of moral differences), it follows that we must represent men either as better than in real life, or as worse, or as they are. It is the same in painting. Polygnotus depicted men as nobler than they are, Pauson as less noble, Dionysius drew them true to life.

Now it is evident that each of the modes of imitation above mentioned will exhibit these differences, and become a distinct kind in imitating objects that are thus distinct. Such diversities may be found even in dancing, flute-playing, and lyre-playing. So again in language, whether prose or verse unaccompanied by music. Homer, for example, makes men better than they are; Cleophon as they are; Hegemon the Thasian, the inventor of parodies, and Nicochares, the author of the Deiliad, worse than they are. The same thing holds good of Dithyrambs and Nomes; here too one may portray different types, as Timotheus and Philoxenus differed in representing their Cyclopes. The same distinction marks off Tragedy from Comedy; for Comedy aims at representing men as worse, Tragedy as better than in actual life.

## III

There is still a third difference—the manner in which each of these objects may be imitated. For the medium being the same, and the objects the same, the poet may imitate by narration—in which case he can either take another personality as Homer does, or speak in his own person, unchanged—or he may present all his characters as living and moving before us.

These, then, as we said at the beginning, are the three differences which distinguish artistic imitation,— the medium, the objects, and the manner. So that from one point of view, Sophocles is an imitator of the same kind as Homer—for both imitate higher types of character; from another point of view, of the same kind as Aristophanes—for both imitate persons acting and doing. Hence, some say, the name of 'drama' is given to such poems, as representing action. For the same reason the Dorians claim the invention both of Tragedy and Comedy. The claim to Comedy is put forward by the Megarians,—not only by those of Greece proper, who allege that it originated under their democracy, but also by the Megarians of Sicily, for the poet Epicharmus, who is much earlier than Chionides and Magnes, belonged to that country. Tragedy too is claimed by certain Dorians of the Peloponnese. In each case they appeal to the evidence of language. The outlying villages, they say, are by them called κῶμαι,[1] by the Athenians δῆμοι[2]: and they assume that Comedians were so named not from κωμάζειν,[3] 'to revel,' but because they wandered from village to village (κατὰ κώμας[4]), being excluded contemptuously from the city. They add also that the Dorian word for 'doing' is δρᾶν,[5] and the Athenian, πράττειν.[6]

This may suffice as to the number and nature of the various modes of imitation.

---

[1] *Komai*, villages.
[2] *Demoi*, towns, villages.
[3] *Komazein.*
[4] *Kata komas.*
[5] *Dran*, to do.
[6] *Prattein*, to do.

## IV

Poetry in general seems to have sprung from two causes, each of them lying deep in our nature. First, the instinct of imitation is implanted in man from childhood, one difference between him and other animals being that he is the most imitative of living creatures, and through imitation learns his earliest lessons; and no less universal is the pleasure felt in things imitated. We have evidence of this in the facts of experience. Objects which in themselves we view with pain, we delight to contemplate when reproduced with minute fidelity: such as the forms of the most ignoble animals and of dead bodies. The cause of this again is, that to learn gives the liveliest pleasure, not only to philosophers but to men in general; whose capacity, however, of learning is more limited. Thus the reason why men enjoy seeing a likeness is, that in contemplating it they find themselves learning or inferring, and saying perhaps, 'Ah, that is he.' For if you happen not to have seen the original, the pleasure will be due not to the imitation as such, but to the execution, the colouring, or some such other cause.

Imitation, then, is one instinct of our nature. Next, there is the instinct for 'harmony' and rhythm, metres being manifestly sections of rhythm. Persons, therefore, starting with this natural gift developed by degrees their special aptitudes, till their rude improvisations gave birth to Poetry.

Poetry now diverged in two directions, according to the individual character of the writers. The graver spirits imitated noble actions, and the actions of good men. The more trivial sort imitated the actions of meaner persons, at first composing satires, as the former did hymns to the gods and the praises of famous men. A poem of the satirical kind cannot indeed be put down to any author earlier than Homer; though many such writers probably there were. But from Homer onward, instances can be cited,—his own Margites, for example, and other similar compositions. The appropriate metre was also here introduced; hence the measure is still called the iambic or lampooning measure, being that in which people lampooned one another. Thus the older poets were distinguished as writers of heroic or of lampooning verse.

As, in the serious style, Homer is pre-eminent among poets, for he alone combined dramatic form with excellence of imitation, so he too first laid down the main lines of Comedy, by dramatising the ludicrous instead of writing personal satire. His Margites bears the same relation to Comedy that the Iliad and Odyssey do to Tragedy. But when Tragedy and Comedy came to light, the two classes of poets still followed their natural bent: the lampooners became writers of Comedy, and the Epic poets were succeeded by Tragedians, since the drama was a larger and higher form of art.

Whether Tragedy has as yet perfected its proper types or not; and whether it is to be judged in itself, or in relation also to the audience,— this raises another question. Be that as it may, Tragedy—as also Comedy —was at first mere improvisation. The one originated with the authors of the Dithyramb, the other with those of the phallic songs, which are still in use in many of our cities. Tragedy advanced by slow degrees; each new element that showed itself was in turn developed. Having passed through many changes, it found its natural form, and there it stopped.

Aeschylus first introduced a second actor; he diminished the importance of the Chorus, and assigned the leading part to the dialogue. Sophocles raised the number of actors to three, and added scene-painting. More-over, it was not till late that the short plot was discarded for one of greater compass, and the grotesque diction of the earlier satyric form for the stately manner of Tragedy. The iambic measure then replaced the trochaic tetrameter, which was originally employed when the poetry was of the satyric order, and had greater affinities with dancing. Once dialogue had come in, Nature herself discovered the appropriate measure. For the iambic is, of all measures, the most colloquial: we see it in the fact that conversational speech runs into iambic lines more frequently than into any other kind of verse; rarely into hexameters, and only when we drop the colloquial intonation. The additions to the number of 'epi-sodes' or acts, and the other accessories of which tradition tells, must be taken as already described; for to discuss them in detail would, doubtless, be a large undertaking.


V


Comedy is, as we have said, an imitation of characters of a lower type,— not, however, in the full sense of the word bad, the Ludicrous being merely a subdivision of the ugly. It consists in some defect or ugliness which is not painful or destructive. To take an obvious example, the comic mask is ugly and distorted, but does not imply pain.

The successive changes through which Tragedy passed, and the authors of these changes, are well known, whereas Comedy has had no history, because it was not at first treated seriously. It was late before the Archon granted a comic chorus to a poet; the performers were till then voluntary. Comedy had already taken definite shape when comic poets, distinctively so called, are heard of. Who furnished it with masks, or prologues, or increased the number of actors,—these and other similar details remain unknown. As for the plot, it came originally from

Sicily; but of Athenian writers Crates was the first who, abandoning the 'iambic' or lampooning form, generalised his themes and plots.

Epic poetry agrees with Tragedy in so far as it is an imitation in verse of characters of a higher type. They differ, in that Epic poetry admits but one kind of metre, and is narrative in form. They differ, again, in their length: for Tragedy endeavours, as far as possible, to confine itself to a single revolution of the sun, or but slightly to exceed this limit; whereas the Epic action has no limits of time. This, then, is a second point of difference; though at first the same freedom was admitted in Tragedy as in Epic poetry.

Of their constituent parts some are common to both, some peculiar to Tragedy: whoever, therefore, knows what is good or bad Tragedy, knows also about Epic poetry. All the elements of an Epic poem are found in Tragedy, but the elements of a Tragedy are not all found in the Epic poem.

## VI

Of the poetry which imitates in hexameter verse, and of Comedy, we will speak hereafter. Let us now discuss Tragedy, resuming its formal definition, as resulting from what has been already said.

Tragedy, then, is an imitation of an action that is serious, complete, and of a certain magnitude; in language embellished with each kind of artistic ornament, the several kinds being found in separate parts of the play; in the form of action, not of narrative; through pity and fear effecting the proper purgation of these emotions. By 'language embellished,' I mean language into which rhythm, 'harmony,' and song enter. By 'the several kinds in separate parts,' I mean, that some parts are rendered through the medium of verse alone, others again with the aid of song.

Now as tragic imitation implies persons acting, it necessarily follows, in the first place, that Spectacular equipment will be a part of Tragedy. Next, Song and Diction, for these are the medium of imitation. By 'Diction' I mean the mere metrical arrangement of the words: as for 'Song,' it is a term whose sense every one understands.

Again, Tragedy is the imitation of an action; and an action implies personal agents, who necessarily possess certain distinctive qualities both of character and thought; for it is by these that we qualify actions themselves, and these—thought and character—are the two natural causes from which actions spring, and on actions again all success or failure depends. Hence, the Plot is the imitation of the action:—for by plot I here mean the arrangement of the incidents. By Character I mean that in virtue of which we ascribe certain qualities to the agents. Thought is required wherever a statement is proved, or, it may be, a general truth

enunciated.   Every Tragedy, therefore, must have six parts, which parts
determine its quality—namely, Plot, Character, Diction, Thought,
Spectacle, Song.   Two of the parts constitute the medium of imitation,
one the manner, and three the objects of imitation.   And these complete
the list.   These elements have been employed, we may say, by the poets
to a man; in fact, every play contains Spectacular elements as well as
Character, Plot, Diction, Song, and Thought.

But most important of all is the structure of the incidents.   For Tragedy is an imitation, not of men, but of an action and of life, and life
consists in action, and its end is a mode of action, not a quality.   Now
character determines men's qualities, but it is by their actions that they
are happy or the reverse.   Dramatic action, therefore, is not with a view
to the representation of character: character comes in as subsidiary to the
actions.   Hence the incidents and the plot are the end of a tragedy; and
the end is the chief thing of all.   Again, without action there cannot be a
tragedy; there may be without character.   The tragedies of most of our
modern poets fail in the rendering of character; and of poets in general
this is often true.   It is the same in painting; and here lies the difference
between Zeuxis and Polygnotus.   Polygnotus delineates character well:
the style of Zeuxis is devoid of ethical quality.   Again, if you string together a set of speeches expressive of character, and well finished in point
of diction and thought, you will not produce the essential tragic effect
nearly so well as with a play which, however deficient in these respects,
yet has a plot and artistically constructed incidents.   Besides which, the
most powerful elements of emotional interest in Tragedy—Peripeteia or
Reversal of the Situation, and Recognition scenes—are parts of the plot.
A further proof is, that novices in the art attain to finish of diction and
precision of portraiture before they can construct the plot.   It is the same
with almost all the early poets.

The Plot, then, is the first principle, and, as it were, the soul of a
tragedy: Character holds the second place.   A similar fact is seen in
painting.   The most beautiful colours, laid on confusedly, will not give
as much pleasure as the chalk outline of a portrait.   Thus Tragedy is the
imitation of an action, and of the agents mainly with a view to the action.

Third in order is Thought,—that is, the faculty of saying what is possible and pertinent in given circumstances.   In the case of oratory, this is
the function of the political art and of the art of rhetoric: and so indeed
the older poets make their characters speak the language of civic life; the
poets of our time, the language of the rhetoricians.   Character is that
which reveals moral purpose, showing what kind of things a man chooses
or avoids.   Speeches, therefore, which do not make this manifest, or in
which the speaker does not choose or avoid anything whatever, are not

expressive of character. Thought, on the other hand, is found where something is proved to be or not to be, or a general maxim is enunciated.

Fourth among the elements enumerated comes Diction; by which I mean, as has been already said, the expression of the meaning in words; and its essence is the same both in verse and prose.

Of the remaining elements Song holds the chief place among the embellishments.

The Spectacle has, indeed, an emotional attraction of its own, but, of all the parts, it is the least artistic, and connected least with the art of poetry. For the power of Tragedy, we may be sure, is felt even apart from representation and actors. Besides, the production of spectacular effects depends more on the art of the stage machinist than on that of the poet.

## VII

These principles being established, let us now discuss the proper structure of the Plot, since this is the first and most important thing in Tragedy.

Now, according to our definition, Tragedy is an imitation of an action that is complete, and whole, and of a certain magnitude; for there may be a whole that is wanting in magnitude. A whole is that which has a beginning, a middle, and an end. A beginning is that which does not itself follow anything by causal necessity, but after which something naturally is or comes to be. An end, on the contrary, is that which itself naturally follows some other thing, either by necessity, or as a rule, but has nothing following it. A middle is that which follows something as some other thing follows it. A well constructed plot, therefore, must neither begin nor end at haphazard, but conform to these principles.

Again, a beautiful object, whether it be a living organism or any whole composed of parts, must not only have an orderly arrangement of parts, but must also be of a certain magnitude; for beauty depends on magnitude and order. Hence a very small animal organism cannot be beautiful; for the view of it is confused, the object being seen in an almost imperceptible moment of time. Nor, again, can one of vast size be beautiful; for as the eye cannot take it all in at once, the unity and sense of the whole is lost for the spectator; as for instance if there were one a thousand miles long. As, therefore, in the case of animate bodies and organisms a certain magnitude is necessary, and a magnitude which may be easily embraced in one view; so in the plot, a certain length is necessary, and a length which can be easily embraced by the memory. The limit of length in relation to dramatic competition and sensuous presentment, is no part of artistic theory. For had it been the rule for a hundred tragedies to compete together, the performance would have been regulated by the water-clock,—as indeed we are told was formerly done. But the limit as fixed by the nature of the drama itself is this:—the greater the length, the more beautiful will the piece be by reason of its size, provided that the whole be perspicuous. And to define the matter roughly, we may say that the proper magnitude is comprised within such limits, that the sequence of events, according to the law of probability or necessity, will admit of a change from bad fortune to good, or from good fortune to bad.

## VIII

Unity of plot does not, as some persons think, consist in the unity of the hero. For infinitely various are the incidents in one man's life which cannot be reduced to unity; and so, too, there are many actions of one man out of which we cannot make one action. Hence the error, as it appears, of all poets who have composed a Heracleid, a Theseid, or other poems of the kind. They imagine that as Heracles was one man, the story of Heracles must also be a unity. But Homer, as in all else he is of surpassing merit, here too—whether from art or natural genius—seems to have happily discerned the truth. In composing the Odyssey he did not include all the adventures of Odysseus—such as his wound on Parnassus, or his feigned madness at the mustering of the host—incidents between which there was no necessary or probable connexion: but he made the Odyssey, and likewise the Iliad, to centre round an action that in our sense of the word is one. As therefore, in the other imitative arts, the imitation is one when the object imitated is one, so the plot, being an imitation of an action, must imitate one action and that a whole, the structural union of the parts being such that, if any one of them is displaced or removed, the whole will be disjointed and disturbed. For a thing whose presence or absence makes no visible difference, is not an organic part of the whole.

## IX

It is, moreover, evident from what has been said, that it is not the function of the poet to relate what has happened, but what may happen,—what is possible according to the law of probability or necessity. The poet and the historian differ not by writing in verse or in prose. The work of Herodotus might be put into verse, and it would still be a species of history, with metre no less than without it. The true difference is that one relates what has happened, the other what may happen. Poetry, therefore, is a more philosophical and a higher thing than history: for poetry tends to express the universal, history the particular. By the universal I mean how a person of a certain type will on occasion speak or act, according to the law of probability or necessity; and it is this universality at which poetry aims in the names she attaches to the personages. The particular is—for example—what Alcibiades did or suffered. In Comedy this is already apparent: for here the poet first constructs the plot on the lines of probability, and then inserts characteristic names;— unlike the lampooners who write about particular individuals. But tragedians still keep to real names, the reason being that what is possible is credible: what has not happened we do not at once feel sure to be possible: but what has happened is manifestly possible: otherwise it would not have happened. Still there are even some tragedies in which there are only one or two well known names, the rest being fictitious. In others, none are well known,—as in Agathon's Antheus, where incidents and names alike are fictitious, and yet they give none the less pleasure. We must not, therefore, at all costs keep to the received legends, which are the usual subjects of Tragedy. Indeed, it would be absurd to attempt it; for even subjects that are known are known only to a few, and yet give pleasure to all. It clearly follows that the poet or 'maker' should be the maker of plots rather than of verses; since he is a poet because he imitates, and what he imitates are actions. And even if he chances to take an historical subject, he is none the less a poet; for there is no reason why some events that have actually happened should not conform to the law of the probable and possible, and in virtue of that quality in them he is their poet or maker.

Of all plots and actions the epeisodic are the worst. I call a plot 'epeisodic' in which the episodes or acts succeed one another without probable or necessary sequence. Bad poets compose such pieces by their own fault, good poets, to please the players; for, as they write show pieces for competition, they stretch the plot beyond its capacity, and are often forced to break the natural continuity.

But again, Tragedy is an imitation not only of a complete action, but of events inspiring fear or pity. Such an effect is best produced when the events come on us by surprise; and the effect is heightened when, at the same time, they follow as cause and effect. The tragic wonder will then be greater than if they happened of themselves or by accident; for even coincidences are most striking when they have an air of design. We may instance the statue of Mitys at Argos, which fell upon his murderer while he was a spectator at a festival, and killed him. Such events seem not to be due to mere chance. Plots, therefore, constructed on these principles are necessarily the best.

## X

Plots are either Simple or Complex, for the actions in real life, of which the plots are an imitation, obviously show a similar distinction. An

action which is one and continuous in the sense above defined, I call
Simple, when the change of fortune takes place without Reversal of
the Situation and without Recognition.

A Complex action is one in which the change is accompanied by such
Reversal, or by Recognition, or by both. These last should arise from the
internal structure of the plot, so that what follows should be the necessary or probable result of the preceding action. It makes all the difference whether any given event is a case of *propter hoc* or *post hoc*.

XI

Reversal of the Situation is a change by which the action veers round to
its opposite, subject always to our rule of probability or necessity. Thus
in the Oedipus, the messenger comes to cheer Oedipus and free him from
his alarms about his mother, but by revealing who he is, he produces the
oposite effect. Again in the Lynceus, Lynceus is being led away to his
death, and Danaus goes with him, meaning to slay him; but the outcome
of the preceding incidents is that Danaus is killed and Lynceus saved.

Recognition, as the name indicates, is a change from ignorance to
knowledge, producing love or hate between the persons destined by the
poet for good or bad fortune. The best form of recognition is coincident
with a Reversal of the Situation, as in the Oedipus. There are indeed
other forms. Even inanimate things of the most trivial kind may in a
sense be objects of recognition. Again, we may recognise or discover
whether a person has done a thing or not. But the recognition which is
most intimately connected with the plot and action is, as we have said,
the recognition of persons. This recognition, combined with Reversal,
will produce either pity or fear; and actions producing these effects are
those which, by our definition, Tragedy represents. Moreover, it is
upon such situations that the issues of good or bad fortune will depend.
Recognition, then, being between persons, it may happen that one person
only is recognised by the other—when the latter is already known—or it
may be necessary that the recognition should be on both sides. Thus
Iphigenia is revealed to Orestes by the sending of the letter; but another
act of recognition is required to make Orestes known to Iphigenia.

Two parts, then, of the Plot—Reversal of the Situation and Recognition—turn upon surprises. A third part is the Scene of Suffering. The
Scene of Suffering is a destructive or painful action, such as death on the
stage, bodily agony, wounds and the like.

XII

[The parts of Tragedy which must be treated as elements of the whole
have been already mentioned. We now come to the quantitative parts—

the separate parts into which Tragedy is divided—namely, Prologue, Episode, Exode, Choric song; this last being divided into Parode and Stasimon.   These are common to all plays: peculiar to some are the songs of actors from the stage and the Commoi.

The Prologue is that entire part of a tragedy which precedes the Parode of the Chorus.   The Episode is that entire part of a tragedy which is between complete choric songs.   The Exode is that entire part of a tragedy which has no choric song after it.   Of the Choric part the Parode is the first undivided utterance of the Chorus: the Stasimon is a Choric ode without anapaests or trochaic tetrameters: the Commos is a joint lamentation of Chorus and actors.   The parts of Tragedy which must be treated as elements of the whole have been already mentioned.   The quantitative parts—the separate parts into which it is divided—are here enumerated.]

## XIII

As the sequel to what has already been said, we must proceed to consider what the poet should aim at, and what he should avoid, in constructing his plots; and by what means the specific effect of Tragedy will be produced.

A perfect tragedy should, as we have seen, be arranged not on the simple but on the complex plan.   It should, moreover, imitate actions which excite pity and fear, this being the distinctive mark of tragic imitation.   It follows plainly, in the first place, that the change of fortune presented must not be the spectacle of a virtuous man brought from prosperity to adversity: for this moves neither pity nor fear; it merely shocks us.   Nor, again, that of a bad man passing from adversity to prosperity: for nothing can be more alien to the spirit of Tragedy; it possesses no single tragic quality; it neither satisfies the moral sense nor calls forth pity or fear.   Nor, again, should the downfall of the utter villain be exhibited.   A plot of this kind would, doubtless, satisfy the moral sense, but it would inspire neither pity nor fear; for pity is aroused by unmerited misfortune, fear by the misfortune of a man like ourselves.   Such, an event, therefore, will be neither pitiful nor terrible.   There remains, then, the character between these two extremes,—that of a man who is not eminently good and just, yet whose misfortune is brought about not by vice or depravity, but by some error or frailty.   He must be one who is highly renowned and prosperous,—a personage like Oedipus, Thyestes, or other illustrious men of such families.

A well constructed plot should, therefore, be single in its issue, rather than double as some maintain.   The change of fortune should be not from bad to good, but, reversely, from good to bad.   It should come about as the result not of vice, but of some great error or frailty, in a character either such as we have described, or better rather than worse. The practice of the stage bears out our view.   At first the poets recounted any legend that came in their way.   Now, the best tragedies are founded on the story of a few houses,—on the fortunes of Alcmaeon, Oedipus, Orestes, Meleager, Thyestes, Telephus, and those others who have done or suffered something terrible.   A tragedy, then, to be perfect according to the rules of art should be of this construction.   Hence they are in error who censure Euripides just because he follows this principle in his plays, many of which end unhappily.   It is, as we have said, the right ending. The best proof is that on the stage and in dramatic competition, such plays, if well worked out, are the most tragic in effect; and Euripides, faulty though he may be in the general management of his subject, yet is felt to be the most tragic of the poets.

In the second rank comes the kind of tragedy which some place first. Like the Odyssey, it has a double thread of plot, and also an opposite catastrophe for the good and for the bad.   It is accounted the best because of the weakness of the spectators; for the poet is guided in what he writes by the wishes of his audience.   The pleasure, however, thence derived is not the true tragic pleasure.   It is proper rather to Comedy, where those who, in the piece, are the deadliest enemies—like Orestes and Aegisthus—quit the stage as friends at the close, and no one slays or is slain.

<h1 style="text-align:center">XIV</h1>

Fear and pity may be aroused by spectacular means; but they may also result from the inner structure of the piece, which is the better way, and indicates a superior poet.   For the plot ought to be so constructed that, even without the aid of the eye, he who hears the tale told will thrill with horror and melt to pity at what takes place.   This is the impression we should receive from hearing the story of the Oedipus.   But to produce this effect by the mere spectacle is a less artistic method, and dependent on extraneous aids.   Those who employ spectacular means to create a sense not of the terrible but only of the monstrous, are strangers to the purpose of Tragedy; for we must not demand of Tragedy any and every kind of pleasure, but only that which is proper to it.   And since the pleasure which the poet should afford is that which comes from pity and fear through imitation, it is evident that this quality must be impressed upon the incidents.

Let us then determine what are the circumstances which strike us as terrible or pitiful.

Actions capable of this effect must happen between persons who are either friends or enemies or indifferent to one another.   If an enemy kills

an enemy, there is nothing to excite pity either in the act or the intention
—except so far as the suffering in itself is pitiful.  So again with indifferent
persons.   But when the tragic incident occurs between those who are near
or dear to one another—if, for example, a brother kills, or intends to
kill, a brother, a son his father, a mother her son, a son his mother, or any
other deed of the kind is done—these are the situations to be looked for by
the poet. He may not indeed destroy the framework of the received
legends—the fact, for instance, that Clytemnestra was slain by Orestes
and Eriphyle by Alcmaeon—but he ought to show invention of his own,
and skilfully handle the traditional material.   Let us explain more clearly
what is meant by skilful handling.

The action may be done consciously and with knowledge of the persons, in the manner of the older poets.   It is thus too that Euripides
makes Medea slay her children.   Or, again, the deed of horror may be
done, but done in ignorance, and the tie of kinship or friendship be discovered afterwards.   The Oedipus of Sophocles is an example.   Here,
indeed, the incident is outside the drama proper; but cases occur where it
falls within the action of the play: one may cite the Alcmaeon of
Astydamas, or Telegonus in the Wounded Odysseus.   Again, there is a
third case,—⟨to be about to act with knowledge of the persons and then
not to act.   The fourth case is⟩ when some one is about to do an irrep-
arable deed through ignorance, and makes the discovery before it is done.
These are the only possible ways.   For the deed must either be done or
not done,—and that wittingly or unwittingly.   But of all these ways, to be
about to act knowing the persons, and then not to act, is the worst.   It is
shocking without being tragic, for no disaster follows.   It is, therefore,
never, or very rarely, found in poetry.   One instance, however, is in the
Antigone, where Haemon threatens to kill Creon.   The next and better
way is that the deed should be perpetrated.   Still better, that it should be
perpetrated in ignorance, and the discovery made afterwards.   There is
then nothing to shock us, while the discovery produces a startling effect.
The last case is the best, as when in the Cresphontes Merope is about to
slay her son, but, recognising who he is, spares his life.   So in the
Iphigenia, the sister recognises the brother just in time.   Again in the
Helle, the son recognises the mother when on the point of giving her up.
This, then, is why a few families only, as has been already observed,
furnish the subjects of tragedy.   It was not art, but happy chance, that led
the poets in search of subjects to impress the tragic quality upon their plots.
They are compelled, therefore, to have recourse to those houses whose
history contains moving incidents like these.

Enough has now been said concerning the structure of the incidents, and
the right kind of plot.

## XV

In respect of Character there are four things to be aimed at.   First, and most important, it must be good.   Now any speech or action that manifests moral purpose of any kind will be expressive of character: the character will be good if the purpose is good.   This rule is relative to each class.   Even a woman may be good, and also a slave; though the woman may be said to be an inferior being, and the slave quite worthless.   The second thing to aim at is propriety.   There is a type of manly valour; but valour in a woman, or unscrupulous cleverness, is inappropriate.   Thirdly, character must be true to life: for this is a distinct thing from goodness and propriety, as here described.   The fourth point is consistency: for though the subject of the imitation, who suggested the type, be inconsistent, still he must be consistently inconsistent.   As an example of motiveless degradation of character, we have Menelaus in the Orestes: of character indecorous and inappropriate, the lament of Odysseus in the Scylla, and the speech of Melanippe: of inconsistency, the Iphigenia at Aulis,—for Iphigenia the suppliant in no way resembles her later self.

As in the structure of the plot, so too in the portraiture of character, the poet should always aim either at the necessary or the probable.   Thus a person of a given character should speak or act in a given way, by the rule either of necessity or of probability; just as this event should follow that by necessary or probable sequence.   It is therefore evident that the unravelling of the plot, no less than the complication, must arise out of the plot itself, it must not be brought about by the *Deus ex Machina*—as in the Medea, or in the Return of the Greeks in the Iliad.   The *Deus ex Machina* should be employed only for events external to the drama,—for antecedent or subsequent events, which lie beyond the range of human knowledge, and which require to be reported or foretold; for to the gods we ascribe the power of seeing all things.   Within the action there must be nothing irrational.   If the irrational cannot be excluded, it should be outside the scope of the tragedy.   Such is the irrational element in the Oedipus of Sophocles.

Again, since Tragedy is an imitation of persons who are above the common level, the example of good portrait painters should be followed. They, while reproducing the distinctive form of the original, make a likeness which is true to life and yet more beautiful.   So too the poet, in representing men who are irascible or indolent, or have other defects of character, should preserve the type and yet ennoble it.   In this way Achilles is portrayed by Agathon and Homer.

These then are rules the poet should observe.   Nor should he neglect those appeals to the senses, which, though not among the essentials, are the concomitants of poetry; for here too there is much room for error. But of this enough has been said on our published treatises.

## XVI

What Recognition is has been already explained. We will now enumerate its kinds.

First, the least artistic form, which, from poverty of wit, is most commonly employed— recognition by signs. Of these some are congenital,— such as 'the spear which the earth-born race bear on their bodies,' or the stars introduced by Carcinus in his Thyestes. Others are acquired after birth; and of these some are bodily marks, as scars; some external tokens, as necklaces, or the little ark in the Tyro by which the discovery is effected. Even these admit of more or less skilful treatment. Thus in the recognition of Odysseus by his scar, the discovery is made in one way by the nurse, in another by the swineherds. The use of tokens for the express purpose of proof—and, indeed, any formal proof with or without tokens—is a less artistic mode of recognition. A better kind is that which comes about by a turn of incident, as in the Bath Scene in the Odyssey.

Next come the recognitions invented at will by the poet, and on that account wanting in art. For example, Orestes in the Iphigenia reveals the fact that he is Orestes. She, indeed, makes herself known by the letter; but he, by speaking himself, and saying what the poet, not what the plot requires. This, therefore, is nearly allied to the fault above mentioned: —for Orestes might as well have brought tokens with him. Another similar instance is the 'voice of the shuttle' in the Tereus of Sophocles.

The third kind depends on memory when the sight of some object awakens a feeling: as in the Cyprians of Dicaeogenes, where the hero breaks into tears on seeing the picture; or again in the 'Lay of Alcinous,' where Odysseus, hearing the minstrel play the lyre, recalls the past and weeps; and hence the recognition.

The fourth kind is by process of reasoning. Thus in the Choëphori:— 'Some one resembling me has come: no one resembles me but Orestes: therefore Orestes has come.' Such too is the discovery made by Iphigenia in the play of Polyidus the Sophist. It was a natural reflexion for Orestes to make, 'So I too must die at the altar like my sister.' So, again, in the Tydeus of Theodectes, the father says, 'I came to find my son, and I lose my own life.' So too in the Phineidae: the women, on seeing the place, inferred their fate:—'Here we are doomed to die, for here we were cast forth.' Again, there is a composite kind of recognition involving false inference on the part of one of the characters, as in the Odysseus Disguised as a Messenger. A said ⟨that no one else was able to bend the bow; ... hence B (the disguised Odysseus) imagined that A would⟩ recognise the bow which, in fact, he had not seen; and to bring about a recognition by this means—the expectation that A would recognise the bow—is false inference.

But, of all recognitions, the best is that which arises from the incidents themselves, where the startling discovery is made by natural means. Such is that in the Oedipus of Sophocles, and in the Iphigenia; for it was natural that Iphigenia should wish to dispatch a letter. These recognitions alone dispense with the artificial aid of tokens or amulets. Next come the recognitions by process of reasoning.

## XVII

In constructing the plot and working it out with the proper diction, the poet should place the scene, as far as possible, before his eyes. In this way, seeing everything with the utmost vividness, as if he were a spectator of the action, he will discover what is in keeping with it, and be most unlikely to overlook inconsistencies. The need of such a rule is shown by the fault found in Carcinus. Amphiaraus was on his way from the temple. This fact escaped the observation of one who did not see the situation. On the stage, however, the piece failed, the audience being offended at the oversight.

Again, the poet should work out his play, to the best of his power, with appropriate gestures; for those who feel emotion are most convincing through natural sympathy with the characters they represent; and one who is agitated storms, one who is angry rages, with the most life-like reality. Hence poetry implies either a happy gift of nature or a strain of madness. In the one case a man can take the mould of any character; in the other, he is lifted out of his proper self.

As for the story, whether the poet takes it ready made or constructs it for himself, he should first sketch its general outline, and then fill in the episodes and amplify in detail. The general plan may be illustrated by the Iphigenia. A young girl is sacrificed; she disappears mysteriously from the eyes of those who sacrificed her; she is transported to another country, where the custom is to offer up all strangers to the goddess. To this ministry she is appointed. Some time later her own brother chances to arrive. The fact that the oracle for some reason ordered him to go there, is outside the general plan of the play. The purpose, again, of his coming is outside the action proper. However, he comes, he is seized, and when on the point of being sacrificed, reveals who he is. The mode of recognition may be either that of Euripides or of Polyidus, in whose play he exclaims very naturally:— 'So it was not my sister only, but I too, who was doomed to be sacrificed'; and by that remark he is saved.

After this, the names being once given, it remains to fill in the episodes.

We must see that they are relevant to the action.   In the case of Orestes, for example, there is the madness which led to his capture, and his deliverance by means of the purificatory rite.   In the drama, the episodes are short, but it is these that give extension to Epic poetry.   Thus the story of the Odyssey can be stated briefly.   A certain man is absent from home for many years; he is jealously watched by Poseidon, and left desolate. Meanwhile his home is in a wretched plight—suitors are wasting his substance and plotting against his son.   At length, tempest-tost, he himself arrives; he makes certain persons acquainted with him; he attacks the suitors with his own hand, and is himself preserved while he destroys them. This is the essence of the plot; the rest is episode.

## XVIII

Every tragedy falls into two parts,—Complication and Unravelling or *Dénouement*.   Incidents extraneous to the action are frequently combined with a portion of the action proper, to form the Complication; the rest is the Unravelling. By the Complication I mean all that extends from the beginning of the action to the part which marks the turning-point to good or bad fortune. The Unravelling is that which extends from the beginning of the change to the end.   Thus, in the Lynceus of Theodectes, the Complication consists of the incidents presupposed in the drama, the seizure of the child, and then again * * ⟨The Unravelling⟩ extends from the accusation of murder to the end.

There are four kinds of Tragedy, the Complex, depending entirely on Reversal of the Situation and Recognition; the Pathetic (where the motive is passion),—such as the tragedies on Ajax and Ixion; the Ethical (where the motives are ethical),—such as the Phthiotides and the Peleus.   The fourth kind is the Simple.   ⟨We here exclude the purely spectacular element⟩, exemplified by the Phorcides, the Prometheus, and scenes laid in Hades.   The poet should endeavour, if possible, to combine all poetic elements; or failing that, the greatest number and those the most important; the more so, in face of the cavilling criticism of the day.   For whereas there have hitherto been good poets, each in his own branch, the critics now expect one man to surpass all others in their several lines of excellence.

In speaking of a tragedy as the same or different, the best test to take is the plot.   Identity exists where the Complication and Unravelling are the same.   Many poets tie the knot well, but unravel it ill.   Both arts, however, should always be mastered.

Again, the poet should remember what has been often said, and not make an Epic structure into a Tragedy—by an Epic structure I mean one with a multiplicity of plots—as if, for instance, you were to make a tragedy out of the entire story of the Iliad.   In the Epic poem, owing to its length, each part assumes its proper magnitude.   In the drama the result is far from answering to the poet's expectation.   The proof is that the poets who have dramatised the whole story of the Fall of Troy, instead of selecting portions, like Euripides; or who have taken the whole tale of Niobe, and not a part of her story, like Aeschylus, either fail utterly or meet with poor success on the stage.   Even Agathon has been known to fail from this one defect.   In his Reversals of the Situation, however, he shows a marvellous skill in the effort to hit the popular taste,—to produce a tragic effect that satisfies the moral sense.   This effect is produced when the clever rogue, like Sisyphus, is outwitted, or the brave villain defeated. Such an event is probable in Agathon's sense of the word: 'it is probable,' he says, 'that many things should happen contrary to probability.'

The Chorus too should be regarded as one of the actors; it should be an integral part of the whole, and share in the action, in the manner not of Euripides but of Sophocles.   As for the later poets, their choral songs pertain as little to the subject of the piece as to that of any other tragedy. They are, therefore, sung as mere interludes,—a practice first begun by Agathon.   Yet what difference is there between introducing such choral interludes, and transferring a speech, or even a whole act, from one play to another?

## XIX

It remains to speak of Diction and Thought, the other parts of Tragedy having been already discussed.   Concerning Thought, we may assume what is said in the Rhetoric, to which inquiry the subject more strictly belongs.   Under Thought is included every effect which has to be produced by speech, the subdivisions being,—proof and refutation; the excitation of the feelings, such as pity, anger, and the like; the suggestion of importance or its opposite.   Now, it is evident that the dramatic incidents must be treated from the same points of view as the dramatic speeches, when the object is to evoke the sense of pity, fear, importance, or probability.   The only difference is, that the incidents should speak for themselves without verbal exposition; while the effects aimed at in speech should be produced by the speaker, and as a result of the speech.   For what were the business of a speaker, if the Thought were revealed quite apart from what he says?

Next, as regards Diction.   One branch of the inquiry treats of the Modes of Utterance.   But this province of knowledge belongs to the art of Delivery and to the masters of that science.   It includes, for instance,— what is a command, a prayer, a statement, a threat, a question, an answer, and so forth.   To know or not to know these things involves no

serious censure upon the poet's art.   For who can admit the fault imputed to Homer by Protagoras,—that in the words, 'Sing, goddess, of the
wrath,' he gives a command under the idea that he utters a prayer?   For
to tell some one to do a thing or not to do it is, he says, a command.   We
may, therefore, pass this over as an inquiry that belongs to another art,
not to poetry.

## XX

[Language in general includes the following parts:—Letter, Syllable,
Connecting word, Noun, Verb, Inflexion or Case, Sentence or Phrase.
   A Letter is an indivisible sound, yet not every such sound, but only
which can form part of a group of sounds.   For even brutes utter indivisible sounds, none of which I call a letter.   The sound I mean may be
either a vowel, a semi-vowel, or a mute.   A vowel is that which without
impact of tongue or lip has an audible sound.   A semi-vowel, that which
with such impact has an audible sound, as S and R.   A mute, that which
with such impact has by itself no sound, but joined to a vowel sound becomes audible, as G and D.   These are distinguished according to the
form assumed by the mouth and the place where they are produced;
according as they are aspirated or smooth, long or short; as they are acute,
grave, or of an intermediate tone; which inquiry belongs in detail to the
writers on metre.
   A Syllable is a non-significant sound, composed of a mute and a
vowel: for GR without A is a syllable, as also with A,—GRA.   But the
investigation of these differences belongs also to metrical science.
   A Connecting word is a non-significant sound, which neither causes nor
hinders the union of many sounds into one significant sound; it may be
placed at either end or in the middle of a sentence.   Or, a non-significant
sound, which out of several sounds, each of them significant, is capable of
forming one significant sound,—as ἀμφί,[7] περί,[8] and the like.   Or, a
non-significant sound, which marks the beginning, end, or division of a
sentence; such, however, that it cannot correctly stand by itself at the
beginning of a sentence,—as μέν,[9] ἤτοι,[10] δέ.[11]
   A Noun is a composite significant sound, not marking time, of which no
part is in itself significant: for in double or compound words we do not
employ the separate parts as if each were in itself significant.   Thus in
Theodorus, 'god-given,' the δῶρον[12] or 'gift' is not in itself significant.

[7] *Amphi*, about.
[8] *Peri*, around.
[9] *Men*, on the one hand.
[10] *Etoi*, surely.
[11] *De*, on the other hand.
[12] *Doron*.

A Verb is a composite significant sound, marking time, in which, as in the noun, no part is in itself significant. For 'man,' or 'white' does not express the idea of 'when'; but 'he walks,' or 'he has walked' does connote time, present or past.

Inflexion belongs both to the noun and verb, and expresses either the relation 'of,' 'to,' or the like; or that of number, whether one or many, as 'man' or 'men'; or the modes or tones in actual delivery, e.g. a question or a command. 'Did he go?' and 'go' are verbal inflexions of this kind.

A Sentence or Phrase is a composite significant sound, some at least of whose parts are in themselves significant; for not every such group of words consists of verbs and nouns—'the definition of man,' for example —but it may dispense even with the verb. Still it will always have some significant part, as 'in walking,' or 'Cleon son of Cleon.' A sentence or phrase may form a unity in two ways,—either as signifying one thing, or as consisting of several parts linked together. Thus the Iliad is one by the linking together of parts, the definition of man by the unity of the thing signified.]

## XXI

Words are of two kinds, simple and double. By simple I mean those composed of non-significant elements, such as γῆ.[13] By double or compound, those composed either of a significant and non-significant element (though within the whole word no element is significant), or of elements that are both significant. A word may likewise be triple, quadruple, or multiple in form, like so many Massilian expressions, e.g. 'Hermo-caico-xanthus ⟨who prayed to Father Zeus⟩.'

Every word is either current, or strange, or metaphorical, or ornamental, or newly-coined, or lengthened, or contracted, or altered.

By a current or proper word I mean one which is in general use among a people; by a strange word, one which is in use in another country. Plainly, therefore, the same word may be at once strange and current, but not in relation to the same people. The word σίγυνον,[14] 'lance,' is to the Cyprians a current term but to us a strange one.

Metaphor is the application of an alien name by transference either from genus to species, or from species to genus, or from species to species, or by analogy, that is, proportion. Thus from genus to species, as: 'There lies my ship'; for lying at anchor is a species of lying. From species to genus, as: 'Verily ten thousand noble deeds hath Odysseus

[13] *Ge*, earth. Cf. geology, geometry.
[14] *Sigunon.*

wrought'; for ten thousand is a species of large number, and is here used for a large number generally. From species to species, as: 'With blade of bronze drew away the life,' and 'Cleft the water with the vessel of unyielding bronze.' Here ἀρύσαι,[15] 'to draw away,' is used for ταμεῖν,[16] 'to cleave,' and ταμεῖν again for ἀρύσαι,—each being a species of taking away. Analogy or proportion is when the second term is to the first as the fourth to the third. We may then use the fourth for the second, or the second for the fourth. Sometimes too we qualify the metaphor by adding the term to which the proper word is relative. Thus the cup is to Dionysus as the shield to Ares. The cup may, therefore, be called 'the shield of Dionysus,' and the shield 'the cup of Ares.' Or, again, as old age is to life, so is evening to day. Evening may therefore be called 'the old age of the day,' and old age, 'the evening of life,' or, in the phrase of Empedocles, 'life's setting sun.' For some of the terms of the proportion there is at times no word in existence; still the metaphor may be used. For instance, to scatter seed is called sowing: but the action of the sun in scattering his rays is nameless. Still this process bears to the sun the same relation as sowing to the seed. Hence the expression of the poet 'sowing the god-created light.' There is another way in which this kind of metaphor may be employed. We may apply an alien term, and then deny of that term one of its proper attributes; as if we were to call the shield, not 'the cup of Ares,' but 'the wineless cup.'

⟨An ornamental word . . .⟩

A newly-coined word is one which has never been even in local use, but is adopted by the poet himself. Some such words there appear to be: as ἐρνύγες,[17] 'sprouters,' for κέρατα,[18] 'horns,' and ἀρητήρ,[19] 'supplicator,' for ἱερεύς,[20] 'priest.'

A word is lengthened when its own vowel is exchanged for a longer one, or when a syllable is inserted. A word is contracted when some part of it is removed. Instances of lengthening are,—πόληος for πόλεως,[21] and Πηληϊάδεω for Πηλείδου:[22] of contraction,—κρῖ,[23] δῶ,[24] and ὄψ,[25] as in μία γίνεται ἀμφοτέρων ὄψ.[26]

[15] Arusai.
[16] Tamein.
[17] Ernyges.
[18] Kerata.
[19] Areter.
[20] Hiereus.
[21] Poleos for poleōs.
[22] Pēleïadeō for Pēleidou.
[23] Kri, barley, for krithe.
[24] Do, house, for doma.
[25] Ops, voice, appearance, for opsis.
[26] Mia ginetai amphoteron ops, the voice of both becomes one.

An altered word is one in which part of the ordinary form is left unchanged, and part is re-cast; as in δεξιτερὸν κατὰ μαζόν, δεξιτερόν is for δεξιόν.[27]

[Nouns in themselves are either masculine, feminine, or neuter. Masculine are such as end in ν, ρ, s, or in some letter compounded with s, —these being two, ψ and ξ. Feminine, such as end in vowels that are always long, namely η and ω, and—of vowels that admit of lengthening— those in α. Thus the number of letters in which nouns masculine and feminine end is the same; for ψ and ξ are equivalent to endings in s. No noun ends in a mute or a vowel short by nature. Three only end in ι,— μέλι, κόμμι, πέπερι:[28] five end in υ. Neuter nouns end in these two latter vowels; also in ν and s.]

## XXII

The perfection of style is to be clear without being mean. The clearest style is that which uses only current or proper words; at the same time it is mean:—witness the poetry of Cleophon and of Sthenelus. That diction, on the other hand, is lofty and raised above the commonplace which employs unusual words. By unusual, I mean strange (or rare) words, metaphorical, lengthened,—anything, in short, that differs from the normal idiom. Yet a style wholly composed of such words is either a riddle or a jargon; a riddle, if it consists of metaphors; a jargon, if it consists of strange (or rare) words. For the essence of a riddle is to express true facts under impossible combinations. Now this cannot be done by any arrangement of ordinary words, but by the use of metaphor it can. Such is the riddle:— 'A man I saw who on another man had glued the bronze by aid of fire,' and others of the same kind. A diction that is made up of strange (or rare) terms is a jargon. A certain infusion, therefore, of these elements is necessary to style; for the strange (or rare) word, the metaphorical, the ornamental, and the other kinds above mentioned, will raise it above the commonplace and mean, while the use of proper words will make it perspicuous. But nothing contributes more to produce a clearness of diction that is remote from commonness than the lengthening, contraction, and alteration of words. For by deviating in exceptional cases from the normal idiom, the language will gain distinction; while, at the same time, the partial conformity with usage will give perspicuity. The critics, therefore, are in error who censure these licenses of speech, and hold the author up to ridicule. Thus Eucleides, the elder, declared that it would

---

[27] *Dexiteron kata mazon, dexiteron* is for *dexion*, down into the right nipple.
[28] *Meli, kommi, peperi.*

be an easy matter to be a poet if you might lengthen syllables at will.   He caricatured the practice in the very form of his diction, as in the verse:

$$\text{'}E\pi\iota\chi\acute{a}\rho\eta\nu \ \epsilon\hat{\iota}\delta o\nu \ M\alpha\rho\alpha\theta\hat{\omega}\nu\acute{a}\delta\epsilon \ \beta\alpha\delta\acute{\iota}\zeta o\nu\tau\alpha,^{29}$$

or,

$$o\mathring{\upsilon}\kappa \ \mathring{a}\nu \ \gamma' \ \mathring{\epsilon}\rho\acute{a}\mu\epsilon\nu o\varsigma \ \tau\grave{o}\nu \ \mathring{\epsilon}\kappa\epsilon\acute{\iota}\nu o\upsilon \ \mathring{\epsilon}\lambda\lambda\acute{\epsilon}\beta o\rho o\nu.^{30}$$

To employ such license at all obtrusively is, no doubt, grotesque; but in any mode of poetic diction there must be moderation.   Even metaphors, strange (or rare) words, or any similar forms of speech, would produce the like effect if used without propriety and with the express purpose of being ludicrous.   How great a difference is made by the appropriate use of lengthening, may be seen in Epic poetry by the insertion of ordinary forms in the verse.   So, again, if we take a strange (or rare) word, a metaphor, or any similar mode of expression, and replace it by the current or proper term, the truth of our observation will be manifest.   For example Aeschylus and Euripides each composed the same iambic line. But the alteration of a single word by Euripides, who employed the rarer term instead of the ordinary one, makes one verse appear beautiful and the other trivial.   Aeschylus in his Philoctetes says:

$$\phi\alpha\gamma\acute{\epsilon}\delta\alpha\iota\nu\alpha \ \langle\delta'\rangle \ \mathring{\eta} \ \mu o\upsilon \ \sigma\acute{a}\rho\kappa\alpha\varsigma \ \mathring{\epsilon}\sigma\theta\acute{\iota}\epsilon\iota \ \pi o\delta\acute{o}\varsigma.^{31}$$

Euripides substitutes $\theta o\iota\nu\hat{a}\tau\alpha\iota^{32}$ 'feasts on' for $\mathring{\epsilon}\sigma\theta\acute{\iota}\epsilon\iota^{33}$ 'feeds on.' Again, in the line,

$$\nu\hat{\upsilon}\nu \ \delta\acute{\epsilon} \ \mu' \ \mathring{\epsilon}\grave{\omega}\nu \ \mathring{o}\lambda\acute{\iota}\gamma o\varsigma \ \tau\epsilon \ \kappa\alpha\grave{\iota} \ o\mathring{\upsilon}\tau\iota\delta\alpha\nu\grave{o}\varsigma \ \kappa\alpha\grave{\iota} \ \mathring{a}\epsilon\iota\kappa\acute{\eta}\varsigma,^{34}$$

the difference will be felt if we substitute the common words,

$$\nu\hat{\upsilon}\nu \ \delta\acute{\epsilon} \ \mu' \ \mathring{\epsilon}\grave{\omega}\nu \ \mu\iota\kappa\rho\acute{o}\varsigma \ \tau\epsilon \ \kappa\alpha\grave{\iota} \ \mathring{a}\sigma\theta\epsilon\nu\iota\kappa\grave{o}\varsigma \ \kappa\alpha\grave{\iota} \ \mathring{a}\epsilon\iota\delta\acute{\eta}\varsigma.^{35}$$

Or, if for the line,

$$\delta\acute{\iota}\phi\rho o\nu \ \mathring{a}\epsilon\iota\kappa\acute{\epsilon}\lambda\iota o\nu \ \kappa\alpha\tau\alpha\theta\epsilon\grave{\iota}\varsigma \ \mathring{o}\lambda\acute{\iota}\gamma\eta\nu \ \tau\epsilon \ \tau\rho\acute{a}\pi\epsilon\zeta\alpha\nu,^{36}$$

---

[29] *Epicharen eidon Maraphonade badizonta.*   I saw Ipichares going to Marathon.

[30] *Ouk an g eramenos ton ekeinou elleboron.*   To be sure, I could not like his helleborе.

[31] *Phagedaina ⟨d⟩ e mou sarkas esthiei podos.*   A cancer feeds on the flesh of my foot.   The word "feeds on" is an ordinary word in the Greek of Æschylus; in the Greek of Euripides, a lofty one.

[32] *Thoinatai.*

[33] *Esthiei.*

[34] *Nun de m eon oligos te kai outidanos kai aeikes.*   I that am now little, of no account, nor attractive.

[35] *Nun de m eon mikros te kai asthenikos kai aeides.*   I that am now small, weak, and ugly.

[36] *Diphron aeikelion katatheis oligen te trapezan.*   He set a stool unseemly and a table small.

we read,

$$\delta i\phi\rho o\nu\ \mu o\chi\theta\eta\rho\grave{o}\nu\ \kappa\alpha\tau\alpha\theta\epsilon\grave{\iota}s\ \mu\iota\kappa\rho\acute{a}\nu\ \tau\epsilon\ \tau\rho\acute{a}\pi\epsilon\zeta\alpha\nu.^{37}$$

Or, for ἠιόνες βοόωσιν, ἠιόνες κράζουσιν.[38]

Again, Ariphrades ridiculed the tragedians for using phrases which no one would employ in ordinary speech: for example, δωμάτων ἄπο instead of ἀπὸ δωμάτων,[39] σέθεν,[40] ἐγὼ δέ νιν,[41] Ἀχιλλέως πέρι instead of περὶ Ἀχιλλέως,[42] and the like. It is precisely because such phrases are not part of the current idiom that they give distinction to the style. This, however, he failed to see.

It is a great matter to observe propriety in these several modes of expression, as also in compound words, strange (or rare) words, and so forth. But the greatest thing by far is to have a command of metaphor. This alone cannot be imparted by another; it is the mark of genius, for to make good metaphors implies an eye for resemblances.

Of the various kinds of words, the compound are best adapted to dithyrambs, rare words to heroic poetry, metaphors to iambic. In heroic poetry, indeed, all these varieties are serviceable. But in iambic verse, which reproduces, as far as may be, familiar speech, the most appropriate words are those which are found even in prose. These are,— the current or proper, the metaphorical, the ornamental.

Concerning Tragedy and imitation by means of action this may suffice.

## XXIII

As to that poetic imitation which is narrative in form and employs a single metre, the plot manifestly ought, as in a tragedy, to be constructed on dramatic principles. It should have for its subject a single action, whole and complete, with a beginning, a middle, and an end. It will thus resemble a living organism in all its unity, and produce the pleasure proper to it. It will differ in structure from historical compositions, which of necessity present not a single action, but a single period, and all that happened within that period to one person or to many, little connected together as the events may be. For as the sea-fight at Salamis and the battle with the Carthaginians in Sicily took place at the same time, but did not tend to any one result, so in the sequence of events, one thing some-times follows another, and yet no single result is thereby produced. Such is the practice, we may say, of most poets. Here again, then, as has

---

[37] *Diphron mochtheron katatheis mikran te trapezan.* He set a shabby stool and a small table.

[38] *Eiones boóosin, eiones krazousin.* The seashore is roaring; the seashore is shrieking.

[39] *Domaton apo* instead of *apo domaton.* From the houses away *instead of* from the houses.

[40] *Sethen,* a rare form of the genitive, meaning "yours."

[41] *Ego de nin.* *Nin* is a rarer form for *auton.* Both mean "him."

[42] *Achilleos peri* instead of *peri Achilleos.* Round about Achilles *instead of* around Achilles.

been already observed, the transcendent excellence of Homer is manifest. He never attempts to make the whole war of Troy the subject of his poem, through that war had a beginning and an end. It would have been too vast a theme, and not easily embraced in a single view. If, again, he had kept it within moderate limits, it must have been over-complicated by the variety of the incidents. As it is, he detaches a single portion, and admits as episodes many events from the general story of the war—such as the Catalogue of the ships and others—thus diversifying the poem. All other poets take a single hero, a single period, or an action single indeed, but with a multiplicity of parts. Thus did the author of the Cypria and of the Little Iliad. For this reason the Iliad and the Odyssey each furnish the subject of one tragedy, or, at most, of two; while the Cypria supplies materials for many, and the Little Iliad for eight—the Award of the Arms, the Philoctetes, the Neoptolemus, the Eurypylus, the Mendicant Odysseus, the Laconian Women, the Fall of Ilium, the Departure of the Fleet.

## XXIV

Again, Epic poetry must have as many kinds as Tragedy: it must be simple, or complex, or 'ethical,' or 'pathetic.' The parts also, with the exception of song and spectacle, are the same; for it requires Reversals of the Situation, Recognitions, and Scenes of Suffering. Moreover, the thoughts and the diction must be artistic. In all these respects Homer is our earliest and sufficient model. Indeed each of his poems has a twofold character. The Iliad is at once simple and 'pathetic,' and the Odyssey complex (for Recognition scenes run through it), and at the same time 'ethical.' Moreover, in diction and thought they are supreme.

Epic poetry differs from Tragedy in the scale on which it is constructed, and in its metre. As regards scale or length, we have already laid down an adequate limit:—the beginning and the end must be capable of being brought within a single view. This condition will be satisfied by poems on a smaller scale than the old epics, and answering in length to the group of tragedies presented at a single sitting.

Epic poetry has, however, a great—a special— capacity for enlarging its dimensions, and we can see the reason. In Tragedy we cannot imitate several lines of actions carried on at one and the same time; we must confine ourselves to the action on the stage and the part taken by the players. But in Epic poetry, owing to the narrative form, many events simultaneously transacted can be presented; and these, if relevant to the subject, add mass and dignity to the poem. The Epic has here an advantage, and one that conduces to grandeur of effect, to diverting the mind of the hearer, and relieving the story with varying episodes. For sameness of incident soon produces satiety, and makes tragedies fail on the stage.

As for the metre, the heroic measure has proved its fitness by the test of experience.   If a narrative poem in any other metre or in many metres were now composed, it would be found incongruous.   For of all measures the heroic is the stateliest and the most massive; and hence it most readily admits rare words and metaphors, which is another point in which the narrative form of imitation stands alone.   On the other hand, the iambic and the trochaic tetrameter are stirring measures, the latter being akin to dancing, the former expressive of action.   Still more absurd would it be to mix together different metres, as was done by Chaeremon.   Hence no one has ever composed a poem on a great scale in any other than heroic verse. Nature herself, as we have said, teaches the choice of the proper measure.

Homer, admirable in all respects, has the special merit of being the only poet who rightly appreciates the part he should take himself.   The poet should speak as little as possible in his own person, for it is not this that makes him an imitator.   Other poets appear themselves upon the scene throughout, and imitate but little and rarely.   Homer, after a few prefatory words, at once brings in a man, or woman, or other personage; none of them wanting in characteristic qualities, but each with a character of his own.

The element of the wonderful is required in Tragedy.   The irrational, on which the wonderful depends for its chief effects, has wider scope in Epic poetry, because there the person acting is not seen.   Thus, the pursuit of Hector would be ludicrous if placed upon the stage—the Greeks standing still and not joining in the pursuit, and Achilles waving them back.   But in the Epic poem the absurdity passes unnoticed.   Now the wonderful is pleasing: as may be inferred from the fact that every one tells a story with some addition of his own, knowing that his hearers like it.   It is Homer who has chiefly taught other poets the art of telling lies skilfully. The secret of it lies in a fallacy.   For, assuming that if one thing is or becomes, a second is or becomes, men imagine that, if the second is, the first likewise is or becomes.   But this is a false inference.   Hence, where the first thing is untrue, it is quite unnecessary, provided the second be true, to add that the first is or has become.   For the mind, knowing the second to be true, falsely infers the truth of the first.   There is an example of this in the Bath Scene of the Odyssey.

Accordingly, the poet should prefer probable impossibilities to improbable possibilities.   The tragic plot must not be composed of irrational parts.   Everything irrational should, if possible, be excluded; or, at all events, it should lie outside the action of the play (as, in the Oedipus, the hero's ignorance as to the manner of Laius' death); not within the drama, —as in the Electra, the messenger's account of the Pythian games; or, as in the Mysians, the man who has come from Tegea to Mysia and is still speechless.  The plea that otherwise the plot would have been ruined, is ridiculous; such a plot should not in the first instance be constructed. But once the irrational has been introduced and an air of likelihood imparted to it, we must accept it in spite of the absurdity.  Take even the irrational incidents in the Odyssey, where Odysseus is left upon the shore of Ithaca.  How intolerable even these might have been would be apparent if an inferior poet were to treat the subject.  As it is, the absurdity is veiled by the poetic charm with which the poet invests it.

The diction should be elaborated in the pauses of the action, where there is no expression of character or thought.  For, conversely, character and thought are merely obscured by a diction that is over brilliant.

## XXV

With respect to critical difficulties and their solutions, the number and nature of the sources from which they may be drawn may be thus exhibited.

The poet being an imitator, like a painter or any other artist, must of necessity imitate one of three objects,—things as they were or are, things as they are said or thought to be, or things as they ought to be.  The vehicle of expression is language,—either current terms or, it may be, rare words or metaphors.  There are also many modifications of language, which we concede to the poets.  Add to this, that the standard of correctness is not the same in poetry and politics, any more than in poetry and any other art.  Within the art of poetry itself there are two kinds of faults, —those which touch its essence, and those which are accidental.  If a poet has chosen to imitate something, ⟨but has imitated it incorrectly⟩ through want of capacity, the error is inherent in the poetry.  But if the failure is due to a wrong choice—if he has represented a horse as throwing out both his off legs at once, or introduced technical inaccuracies in medicine, for example, or in any other art—the error is not essential to the poetry.  These are the points of view from which we should consider and answer the objections raised by the critics.

First as to matters which concern the poet's own art.  If he describes the impossible, he is guilty of an error; but the error may be justified, if the end of the art be thereby attained (the end being that already mentioned),—if, that is, the effect of this or any other part of the poem is thus rendered more striking.  A case in point is the pursuit of Hector.  If, however, the end might have been as well, or better, attained without violating the special rules of the poetic art, the error is not justified: for every kind of error should, if possible, be avoided.

Again, does the error touch the essentials of the poetic art, or some accident of it?  For example,—not to know that a hind has no horns is a less serious matter than to paint it inartistically.

Further, if it be objected that the description is not true to fact, the poet may perhaps reply,—'But the objects are as they ought to be': just as Sophocles said that he drew men as they ought to be; Euripides, as they are. In this way the objection may be met. If, however, the representation be of neither kind, the poet may answer,—'This is how men say the thing is.' This applies to tales about the gods. It may well be that these stories are not higher than fact nor yet true to fact: they are, very possibly, what Xenophanes says of them. But anyhow, 'this is what is said.' Again, a description may be no better than the fact: still, it was the fact; as in the passage about the arms: 'Upright upon their butt-ends stood the spears.' This was the custom then, as it now is among the Illyrians.

Again, in examining whether what has been said or done by some one is poetically right or not, we must not look merely to the particular act or saying, and ask whether it is poetically good or bad. We must also consider by whom it is said or done, to whom, when, by what means, or for what end; whether, for instance, it be to secure a greater good, or avert a greater evil.

Other difficulties may be resolved by due regard to the usage of language. We may note a rare word, as in οὐρῆας, μὲν πρῶτον,[43] where the poet perhaps employs οὐρῆας not in the sense of mules, but of sentinels. So, again, of Dolon: 'ill-favoured indeed he was to look upon.' It is not meant that his body was ill-shaped, but that his face was ugly; for the Cretans use the word εὐειδές,[44] 'well-favoured,' to denote a fair face. Again, ζωρότερον δὲ κέραιε,[45] 'mix the drink livelier,' does not mean 'mix it stronger' as for hard drinkers, but 'mix it quicker.'

Sometimes an expression is metaphorical, as 'Now all gods and men were sleeping through the night,'—while at the same time the poet says: 'Often indeed as he turned his gaze to the Trojan plain, he marvelled at the sound of flutes and pipes.' 'All' is here used metaphorically for 'many,' all being a species of many. So in the verse,—'alone she hath no part . . , οἴη,[46] 'alone,' is metaphorical; for the best known may be called the only one.

Again, the solution may depend upon accent or breathing. Thus Hippias of Thasos solved the difficulties in the lines,—δίδομεν (διδόμεν) δέ οἱ, and τὸ μὲν οὖ (οὐ) καταπύθεται ὄμβρῳ.[47]

Or again, the question may be solved by punctuation, as in Empedocles,

---

[43] *Oureas, men proton*, first the mules. By "mules" Homer may have meant "Sentinels."
[44] *Eueides.*
[45] *Zoroteron de keraie.*
[46] *Oie.*
[47] *Dídomen (didómen) de oi* and *to men oŭ (où) kataputhetai ombro.* "And we grant . . .," to the command form directed to the dream, "Grant to him . . ." A change of meaning from "rots not at all" to "part of it rots."

—'Of a sudden things became mortal that before had learnt to be immortal, and things unmixed before mixed'

Or again, by ambiguity of meaning,— as παρῴχηκεν δὲ πλέω νύξ,[48] where the word πλέω is ambiguous.

Or by the usage of language. Thus any mixed drink is called οἶνος,[49] 'wine.' Hence Ganymede is said 'to pour the wine to Zeus,' though the gods do not drink wine. So too workers in iron are called χαλκέας,[50] or workers in bronze. This, however, may also be taken as a metaphor.

Again, when a word seems to involve some inconsistency of meaning, we should consider how many senses it may bear in the particular passage. For example: 'there was stayed the spear of bronze'—we should ask in how many ways we may take 'being checked there.' The true mode of interpretation is the precise opposite of what Glaucon mentions. Critics, he says, jump at certain groundless conclusions; they pass adverse judgment and then proceed to reason on it; and, assuming that the poet has said whatever they happen to think, find fault if a thing is inconsistent with their own fancy. The question about Icarius has been treated in this fashion. The critics imagine he was a Lacedaemonian. They think it strange, therefore, that Telemachus should not have met him when he went to Lacedaemon. But the Cephallenian story may perhaps be the true one. They allege that Odysseus took a wife from among themselves, and that her father was Icadius not Icarius. It is merely a mistake, then, that gives plausibility to the objection.

In general, the impossible must be justified by reference to artistic requirements, or to the higher reality, or to received opinion. With respect to the requirements of art, a probable impossibility is to be preferred to a thing improbable and yet possible. Again, it may be impossible that there should be men such as Zeuxis painted. 'Yes,' we say, 'but the impossible is the higher thing; for the ideal type must surpass the reality.' To justify the irrational, we appeal to what is commonly said to be. In addition to which, we urge that the irrational sometimes does not violate reason; just as 'it is probable that a thing may happen contrary to probability.'

Things that sound contradictory should be examined by the same rules as in dialectical refutation—whether the same thing is meant, in the same relation, and in the same sense. We should therefore solve the question by reference to what the poet says himself, or to what is tacitly assumed by a person of intelligence.

[48] *Parocheken de pleo nux pleo*, and of the night more than two watches have past. *Pleo* does not mean "full" here, but "full two-thirds."

[49] *Oinos*.

[50] *Chalkeas*, brazen.

The element of the irrational, and, similarly, depravity of character, are justly censured when there is no inner necessity for introducing them. Such is the irrational element in the introduction of Aegeus by Euripides and the badness of Menelaus in the Orestes.

Thus, there are five sources from which critical objections are drawn. Things are censured either as impossible, or irrational, or morally hurtful, or contradictory, or contrary to artistic correctness. The answers should be sought under the twelve heads above mentioned.

## XXVI

The question may be raised whether the Epic or Tragic mode of imitation is the higher. If the more refined art is the higher, and the more refined in every case is that which appeals to the better sort of audience, the art which imitates anything and everything is manifestly most unrefined. The audience is supposed to be too dull to comprehend unless something of their own is thrown in by the performers, who therefore indulge in restless movements. Bad flute-players twist and twirl, if they have to represent 'the quoit-throw,' or hustle the coryphaeus when they perform the 'Scylla.' Tragedy, it is said, has this same defect. We may compare the opinion that the older actors entertained of their successors. Mynniscus used to call Callippides 'ape' on account of the extravagance of his action, and the same view was held of Pindarus. Tragic art, then, as a whole, stands to Epic in the same relation as the younger to the elder actors. So we are told that Epic poetry is addressed to a cultivated audience, who do not need gesture; Tragedy, to an inferior public. Being then unrefined, it is evidently the lower of the two.

Now, in the first place, this censure attaches not to the poetic but to the histrionic art; for gesticulation may be equally overdone in epic recitation, as by Sosistratus, or in lyrical competition, as by Mnasitheus the Opuntian. Next, all action is not to be condemned— any more than all dancing—but only that of bad performers. Such was the fault found in Callippides, as also in others of our own day, who are censured for representing degraded women. Again, Tragedy like Epic poetry produces its effect even without action; it reveals its power by mere reading. If, then, in all other respects it is superior, this fault, we say, is not inherent in it.

And superior it is, because it has all the epic elements—it may even use the epic metre—with the music and spectacular effects as important accessories; and these produce the most vivid of pleasures. Further, it has vividness of impression in reading as well as in representation. Moreover, the art attains its end within narrower limits; for the concentrated effect is more pleasurable than one which is spread over a long time and so diluted. What, for example, would be the effect of the Oedipus of Sophocles, if it were cast into a form as long as the Iliad? Once more, the Epic imitation has less unity; as is shown by this, that any Epic poem will furnish subjects for several tragedies. Thus if the story adopted by the poet has a strict unity, it must either be concisely told and appear truncated; or, if it conform to the Epic canon of length, it must seem weak and watery. ⟨Such length implies some loss of unity,⟩ if, I mean, the poem is constructed out of several actions, like the Iliad and the Odyssey, which have many such parts, each with a certain magnitude of its own. Yet these poems are as perfect as possible in structure; each is, in the highest degree attainable, an imitation of a single action.

If, then, Tragedy is superior to Epic poetry in all these respects, and, moreover, fulfils its specific function better as an art—for each art ought to produce, not any chance pleasure, but the pleasure proper to it, as already stated—it plainly follows that Tragedy is the higher art, as attaining its end more perfectly.

Thus much may suffice concerning Tragic and Epic poetry in general; their several kinds and parts, with the number of each and their differences; the causes that make a poem good or bad; the objections of the critics and the answers to these objections. * * *

# LONGINUS

# On the Sublime

## THIRD CENTURY [?]

*Whoever he was, "Longinus" defines his work as a "technical treatise"*
*as early as his second sentence. As such, it will be an examination of*
*the specific methods by which a subject under inquiry may be under-*
*stood; it will deal with the process by which a particular effect may*
*be achieved. This is certainly a brisk and businesslike attitude toward*
*a subject that might not at first appear to lend itself to such a no-*
*nonsense approach: the heightened emotional response that great*
*literature evokes in us, that ecstasy or transport that results from*
*"eminence and excellence in language" in oratory as well as in poetry.*
*Longinus intends to remove the mystery, confident that Nature "is no*
*creature of random impulse" and that every effect has its discoverable*
*causes. But, listing the five sources of the sublime, he assigns the first*
*two to natural gifts. And, although this is to be a technical treatise on*
*language, he declares, "Sublimity is the note which rings from a great*
*mind." If this is true, then how can the methods of achieving it be*
*taught?*

*The issue that is confronted is the nature vs. art controversy that*
*was to become the central question in the late seventeenth and eigh-*
*teenth centuries. One aspect of the classical tradition that is held in*
*great respect emphasizes the value of the rules, presumably as Aristotle*
*had laid them down; but Longinus here gives the warrant for the*
*doctrine of inspired (though not unlearned) creativity. Art as the*

From Longinus, *On the Sublime*, tr. A. O. Prickard; Oxford: The Clarendon Press,
1906. Reprinted by permission of Oxford University Press. Traditionally deemed
the work of Longinus and called *On the Sublime*, this treatise is often ascribed to
various other authors and may have been written around 40 A.D. Its various trans-
lators have suggested other titles: *A Treatise on Sublimity, Impressiveness of Style,
On Great Writing* are among them.

*product of knowledge and training or art as self-expression? The analysis of the Sapphic ode in Chapter X shows Longinus as a practical critic, but exactly what is he analyzing? Is he a psychological or a linguistic critic?*

*In categorizing the other three sources of the sublime, Longinus provides a handbook of rhetorical and grammatical devices that constitute what every writer aspiring to sublimity should know. It is all technique and shop talk, reflecting an attitude similar to that expressed in our own time by Thornton Wilder:*

> *I am always uncomfortable, when in "studio" conversation, I hear young artists talking about "truth" and "humanity" and "what is art," and most happy when I hear them talking about pigments and the timbre of the flute in its lower range or the spelling of dialects or James's "center of consciousness."*

*Finally, in what might appear to be an irrelevant conclusion, Longinus surveys the contemporary literary situation and states some melancholy facts—the literary technician turns moralist and bemoans the prevalence of hack or formula writers. Is this last chapter irrelevant? Is there a connection, given Longinus' basic position, between the growth of materialism and the decline in literary achievement?*

I

THE TREATISE written by Caecilius 'concerning Sublimity' appeared to us, as you will remember, dear Postumius Terentianus, when we looked into it together, to fall below the level of the general subject, failing especially in grasp of vital points; and to give his readers but little of that assistance which should be the first aim of every writer. In any technical treatise two points are essential; the first, that the writer should show what the thing proposed for inquiry is; the second, but in effect the more important, that he should tell us by what specific methods that thing may be made our own. Now Caecilius endeavours to show us by a vast number of instances what the sublime is, as though we did not know; the process by which we may raise our natural powers to a required advance in scale he unaccountably passed over as unnecessary. So far as he is concerned, perhaps we ought to praise the man for his ingenuity and pains, not to blame him for the omissions. Since, however, you lay your commands upon me, that I should take up the subject in my turn, and without fail put something on paper about Sublimity as a favour to yourself, give me your company; let us see whether there is anything in the views which I have formed really serviceable to men in public life. You, comrade, will help me by passing judgement, with perfect frankness, upon all particulars you can and you ought. It was well answered by one who wished to show wherein we resemble gods: 'in doing good,' said he, 'and in speaking truth.'

Writing to you, my dear friend, with your perfect knowledge of all liberal study, I am almost relieved at the outset from the necessity of showing at any length that Sublimity is always an eminence and excellence in language; and that from this, and this alone, the greatest poets and writers of prose have attained the first place and have clothed their fame with immortality. For it is not to persuasion but to ecstasy that passages of extraordinary genius carry the hearer: now the marvellous, with its power to amaze, is always and necessarily stronger than that which seeks to persuade and to please: to be persuaded rests usually with ourselves, genius brings force sovereign and irresistible to bear upon every hearer, and takes its stand high above him. Again, skill in invention and power of orderly arrangement are not seen from one passage nor from two, but emerge with effort out of the whole context; Sublimity, we know, brought out at the happy moment, parts all the matter this way and that, and like a lightning flash, reveals, at a stroke and in its entirety, the power of the orator. These and suchlike considerations I think, my dear Terentianus, that your own experience might supply.

## II

We, however, must at once raise this further question; is there any art of sublimity or of its opposite? For some go so far as to think all who would bring such terms under technical rules to be entirely mistaken. 'Genius,' says one, 'is inbred, not taught; there is one art for the things of genius, to be born with them.' All natural effects are spoilt, they think, by technical rules, and become miserable skeletons. I assert that the reverse will prove true on examination, if we consider that Nature, a law to herself as she mostly is in all that is passionate and lofty, yet is no creature of random impulse delighting in mere absence of method; that she is indeed herself the first and originating principle which underlies all things, yet rules of degree, of fitting occasion, of unerring practice, and of application can be determined by method and are its contribution; in a sense all greatness is exposed to a danger of its own, if left to itself without science to control, 'unsteadied, unballasted,' abandoned to mere velocity and uninstructed venture; greatness needs the spur often, it also needs the bit. What Demosthenes shows to be true of the common life of men—that of all good things the greatest is good fortune, but a second, not inferior to the first, is good counsel, and that where the latter is wanting the former is at once cancelled— we may properly apply to literature; here Nature fills the place of good fortune, Art of good counsel.   Also, and this is most important, it is only from Art that we can learn the very fact that certain effects in literature rest on Nature and on her alone.   If, as I said, the critic who finds fault with earnest students, would take all these things into his account, he would in my opinion no longer deem inquiry upon the subjects before us to be unnecessary or unfruitful.

[*Here a portion of the essay has been lost.*]

### III

> Stay they the furnace! quench the far-flung blaze!
> For if I spy one crouching habitant,
> I'll twist a lock, one lock of storm-borne flame,
> And fire the roof, and char the halls to ash:
> Not yet, not now my noble strain is raised.

All this is tragic no longer, but burlesque of tragic; 'locks,' 'to vomit up to heaven,' 'Boreas turned flute player,' and the rest.   It is turbid in expression, and confused in imagery, not forcible; and if you examine each detail in clear light, you see a gradual sinking from the terrible to the contemptible.   Now when in tragedy, which by its nature is pompous and admits bombast, tasteless rant is found to be unpardonable, I should be slow to allow that it could be in place in true history.   Thus we laugh at Gorgias of Leontini for writing 'Xerxes the Zeus of the Persians' and 'vultures, those living tombs,' and at some passages in Callisthenes as being stilted, not sublime, and even more at some in Cleitarchus; he is a mere fantastic, he 'puffs,' to apply the words of Sophocles, 'on puny pipes, *but* with no mellowing gag.'   So with Amphicrates, Hegesias, and Matris; they often appear to themselves to be possessed, really they are no inspired revellers but children at play.   We may take it that turgidity is of all faults perhaps the most difficult to avoid.   It is a fact of Nature that all men who aim at grandeur, in avoiding the reproach of being weak and dry, are, we know not how, borne off into turgidity, caught by the adage:—'To lapse from greatness were a generous fault.'   As in bodies, so in writings, all swellings which are hollow and unreal are bad, and very possibly work round to the opposite condition, for 'nothing,' they say, 'so dry as a man with dropsy.'

While tumidity thus tends to overshoot the sublime, puerility is the direct opposite of all that is great; it is in every sense low and small spirited, and essentially a most ignoble fault.   What then is puerility?   Clearly it is a pedantic conceit, which overdoes itself and becomes frigid at the last.   Authors glide into this when they make for what is

unusual, artificial, above all, agreeable, and so run on the reefs of nonsense and affectation.   By the side of these is a third kind of vice, found
in passages of strong feeling, and called by Theodorus 'Parenthyrsus.'
This is passion out of place and unmeaning, where there is no call for
passion, or unrestrained where restraint is needed.   Men are carried
aside, as if under strong drink, into expressions of feeling which have
nothing to do with the subject, but are personal to themselves and academic: then they play clumsy antics before an audience which has never
been moved; it cannot be otherwise, when the speakers are in an ecstasy,
and the hearers are not.   But we reserve room to speak of the passions
elsewhere.

## IV

Of the second fault which we mentioned, frigidity, Timaeus is full; an
able author in other respects, and not always wanting in greatness of
style; learned, acute, but extremely critical of the faults of others, while
insensible to his own; often sinking into mere childishness from an
incessant desire to start new notions.   I will set down one or two instances only from this author, since Caecilius has been before me with
most of them.   Praising Alexander the Great, he writes: 'who annexed
all Asia in fewer years than Isocrates took to write his *Panegyricus* in
support of war against the Persians.'   Truly a wonderful comparison
between the Macedonian and the Sophist: yes, Timaeus, clearly the
Lacedaemonians were far out-matched by Isocrates in valour, for they
took Messene in thirty years, he composed his *Panegyricus* in ten! Then
how he turns upon the Athenians captured in Sicily: 'Because they
committed impiety against Hermes, and defaced his images, they suffered
punishment for it, largely on account of one man, a descendant, on the
father's side, of the injured god, Hermocrates, son of Hermon.'   This
makes me wonder, dear Terentianus, that he does not also write of the
tyrant Dionysius: 'He had shown impiety towards Zeus and Heracles;
therefore he was deprived of his kingdom by Dion and Heraclides.'
What need to speak of Timaeus, when those heroes Xenophon and Plato,
although they were of Socrates' own school, sometimes forgot themselves
in such paltry attempts to please.   Thus Xenophon writes in the *Constitution of the Lacedaemonians*: 'I mean to say that you can no more hear their
voices than if they were made of stone, no more draw their eyes aside
than if they were made of brass; you might think them more modest than
the maiden-pupils in their eyes.'   It was worthy of Amphicrates, not of
Xenophon, to call the pupils in our eyes 'modest maidens': but what
a notion, to believe that the eyes of a whole row were modest, whereas
they say that immodesty in particular persons is expressed by nothing

so much as by the eyes.   Addressing a forward person, 'Wine laden, dog-eyed!' says Homer.   Timaeus, however, as if clutching at stolen goods, has not left to Xenophon even this point of frigidity.   He says, speaking of Agathocles, that he even carried off his cousin, who had been given in marriage to another man, from the solemnity of Unveiling; 'Now who would have done this, who had maidens, not harlots, in his eyes?'   Nay, Plato, the divine, as at other times he is, wishing to mention tablets, says: 'they will write and store in the temples memorials of cypress wood,' and again 'concerning walls, O Megillus, I would take the Spartan view, to allow our walls to sleep on the ground where they lie, and not be raised again.'   And Herodotus is hardly clear of this fault, when he calls beautiful women 'pains to the eyes'; though he has some excuse, for the speakers in Herodotus are barbarians and in drink: still, not even through the mouths of such characters is it well, out of sheer pettiness, to cut a clumsy figure before all time.

## V

All these undignified faults spring up in literature from a single cause, the craving for intellectual novelties, on which, above all else, our own generation goes wild.   It would almost be true to say that the sources of all the good in us are also the sources of all the bad.   Thus beauties of expression, and all which is sublime, I will add, all which is agreeable, contribute to success in our writing; and yet every one of these becomes a principle and a foundation, as of success, so of its opposite.   Much the same is to be said of changes of construction, hyperboles, plurals for sin-gulars; we will show in the sequel the danger which seems to attend each. Therefore it is necessary at once to raise the question directly, and to show how it is possible for us to escape the vices thus intimately mingled with the sublime.

## VI

It is possible, my friend, to do this, if we could first of all arrive at a clear and discriminating knowledge of what true sublimity is.   Yet this is hard to grasp: judgement of style is the last and ripest fruit of much experience.   Still, if I am to speak in the language of precept, it is perhaps not impossible, from some such remarks as follow, to attain to a right decision upon the matter.

## VII

We must, dear friend, know this truth.   As in our ordinary life nothing is great which it is a mark of greatness to despise; as fortunes, offices, honours, kingdoms, and such like, things which are praised so pompously from without, could never appear, at least to a sensible man, to be surpassingly good, since actual contempt for them is a good of no mean kind (certainly men admire, more than those who have them, those who might have them, but in greatness of soul let them pass); even so it is with all that is elevated in poetry and prose writings; we have to ask whether it may be that they have that image of greatness to which so much careless praise is attached, but on a close scrutiny would be found vain and hollow, things which it is nobler to despise than to admire. For it is a fact of Nature that the soul is raised by true sublimity, it gains a proud step upwards, it is filled with joy and exultation, as though itself had produced what it hears. Whenever therefore anything is heard frequently by a man of sense and literary experience, but does not dispose his mind to high thoughts, nor leave in it material for fresh reflection, beyond what is actually said; while it sinks, if you look carefully at the whole context, and dwindles away, this can never be true sublimity, being preserved so long only as it is heard. That is really great, which gives much food for fresh reflection; which it is hard, nay impossible, to resist; of which the memory is strong and indelible. You may take it that those are beautiful and genuine effects of sublimity which please always, and please all. For when men of different habits, lives, ambitions, ages, all take one and the same view about the same writings, the verdict and pronouncement of such dissimilar individuals give a powerful assurance, beyond all.gainsaying, in favour of that which they admire.

## VIII

Now there are five different sources, so to call them, of lofty style, which are the most productive; power of expression being presupposed as a foundation common to all five types, and inseparable from any. First and most potent is the faculty of grasping great conceptions, as I have defined it in my work on Xenophon. Second comes passion, strong and impetuous. These two constituents of sublimity are in most cases native-born, those which now follow come through art: the proper handling of figures, which again seem to fall under two heads, figures of thought, and figures of diction; then noble phraseology, with its subdivisions, choice of words, and use of tropes and of elaboration; and fifthly, that cause of greatness which includes in itself all that preceded it, dignified and spirited composition. Let us now look together at what is included under each of these heads, premising that Caecilius has passed over some of the five, for instance, passion. If he did so under the idea that sublimity and feeling are one and the same thing, coexistent and of common origin, he is entirely wrong. For some passions may be found which are distinct from sublimity and are humble, as those of pity, grief, fear; and again, in many cases, there is sublimity without passion; take, besides countless other instances, the poet's own venturesome lines on the Aloadae:

> Upon Olympus Ossa, leafy Pelion
> On Ossa would they pile, a stair to heaven;

and the yet grander words which follow:

> Now had they worked their will.

In the Orators, again, speeches of panegyric, pomp, display, exhibit on every hand majesty and the sublime, but commonly lack passion: hence Orators of much passion succeed least in panegyric, and again the panegyrists are not strong in passion. Or if, on the other hand, Caecilius did not think that passion ever contributes to sublimity, and, therefore, held it undeserving of mention, he is quite in error. I should feel confidence in maintaining that nothing reaches great eloquence so surely as genuine passion in the right place; it breathes the vehemence of frenzy and divine possession, and makes the very words inspired.

## IX

After all, however, the first element, great natural genius, covers far more ground than the others: therefore, as to this also, even if it be a gift rather than a thing acquired, yet so far as is possible we must nurture our souls to all that is great, and make them, as it were, teem with noble endowment. How? you will ask. I have myself written in another place to this effect:—'Sublimity is the note which rings from a great mind.' Thus it is that, without any utterance, a notion, unclothed and unsupported, often moves our wonder, because the very thought is great; the silence of Ajax in the book of the Lower World is great, and more sublime than any words. First, then, it is quite necessary to presuppose the principle from which this springs: the true Orator must have no low ungenerous spirit, for it is not possible that they who think small thoughts, fit for slaves, and practise them in all their daily life, should put out anything to deserve wonder and immortality. Great words issue, and it cannot be otherwise, from those whose thoughts are weighty. So it is on the lips of men of the highest spirit that words of rare greatness are found. Take the answer of Alexander to Parmenio, who had said 'I were content . . .'

[*Here several pages have been lost.*]

. . . the distance from earth to heaven, a measure one may call it of the stature as well of Homer as of Strife. Unlike this is the passage of

Hesiod about Gloom (if *The Shield* is really to be assigned to Hesiod),
'From out her nostrils rheum in streams was poured': he has made the
picture hateful, not terrible.   But how does Homer make great all that
belongs to gods?

> Far as the region of blank air in sight
> Of one who sitting on some beacon height
> Views the long wine-dark barrens of the deep,
> Such space the horses of the realm of light
> Urged by the gods, as on they strain and sweep,
> While their hoofs thunder aloft, bound over at one leap.

He measures their leap by the interval of the boundaries of the world.
Who might not justly exclaim, when he marked this extravagance in
greatness, that, if the horses of the gods make two leaps, leap after leap,
they will no longer find room within the world.   Passing great too are
the appearances in the Battle of the Gods:—

> Heaven sent its clarion forth: Olympus too:
>
> .    .    .    .    .    .    .    .    .
>
> Trembled too Hades in his gloomy reign,
> And leapt up with a scream, lest o'er his head
> Poseidon cleave the solid earth in twain,
> And open the pale kingdom of the dead
> Horrible, foul with blight, which e'en Immortals dread.

You see, comrade, how, when earth is torn up from its foundations,
and Tartarus itself laid bare, and the Universe suffers overthrow and
dissolution, all things at once, heaven and hell, things mortal and immortal, mingle in the war and the peril of that fight.   Yet all this is
terrible indeed, though, unless taken as allegory, thoroughly impious and
out of proportion.   For when Homer presents to us woundings of the
gods, their factions, revenges, tears, bonds, sufferings, all massed together,
it seems to me that, as he has done his uttermost to make the men of the
Trojan war gods, so he has made the gods men.   Only for us, when we
are miserable, a harbour from our ills is reserved in death; the gods, as
he draws them, are everlasting, not in their nature, but in their unhap-
piness.   Far better than the 'Battle of the Gods' are the passages which
show us divinity as something undefiled and truly great, with no admixture; for instance, to take a passage which has been worked out by
many before us, the lines on Poseidon:

> Tall mountains and wild woods, from height to height,
> The city and the vessels by the main . . .
> Rocked to the immortal feet that, hurrying, bare
> Poseidon in his wrath . . .

> ... the light wheels along the sea-plain rolled;
> From cave and lair the creatures of the deep
> Flocked to sport round him, and the crystal heap
> Of waters in wild joy disparting know
> Their lord, and as the fleet pair onward sweep ...

Thus too the lawgiver of the Jews, no common man, when he had duly conceived the power of the Deity, showed it forth as duly. At the very beginning of his Laws, 'God said,' he writes—What? 'Let there be light, and there was light, let there be earth, and there was earth.' Perhaps I shall not seem wearisome, comrade, if I quote to you one other passage from the poet, this time on a human theme, that you may learn how he accustoms his readers to enter with him into majesties which are more than human. Gloom and impenetrable night suddenly cover the battle of the Greeks before him: then Ajax, in his helplessness, says:—

> Zeus, sire, do thou the veil of darkness rend,
> And make clear daylight, that our eyes may see:
> Then in the light e'en slay us—.

Here is the very truth of the passion of Ajax: he does not pray to live—such a petition were too humble for the hero—but when in impracticable darkness he could dispose his valour to no good purpose, chafing that he stands idle for the battle, he prays for light at the speediest, sure of finding therein at the worst a burial worthy of his valour, even if Zeus be arrayed against him. Truly the spirit of Homer goes along with every struggle, in full and carrying gale; he feels the very thing himself, he 'rages;—

> Not fire in densest mountain glade,
> Nor spear-armed Ares e'er raged dreadfuller:
> Foam started from his lips, ...'

Yet he shows throughout the *Odyssey* (for there are many reasons why we must look closely into passages from that poem also), that, when a great genius begins to decline, the love of story-telling is a mark of its old age. It is clear from many other indications that this work was the second; but more particularly from the fact that he introduces throughout the *Odyssey* remnants of the sufferings before Ilium, as so many additional episodes of the Trojan war; aye, and renders to its heroes fresh lamentations and words of pity, as though awarded in some far distant time. Yes, the *Odyssey* is nothing but an epilogue of the *Iliad*:—

> There the brave Aias and Achilleus lie;
> Patroclus there, whose wisdom matched the gods on high;
> There too Antilochus my son ...

From the same cause, I think, writing the *Iliad* in the heyday of his spirit, he made the whole structure dramatic and combative; that of the *Odyssey* is in the main narrative, which is the special mark of age.   So it is that in the *Odyssey* one might liken Homer to a setting sun; the intensity is gone, but there remains the greatness.   Here the tone of those great lays of Ilium is no longer maintained—the passages on one level of sublimity with no sinking anywhere, the same stream of passion poured upon passion, the readiness of turn, the closeness to life, the throng of images all drawn from the truth: as when Ocean retires into himself, and is left lonely around his proper bounds, only the ebbings of his greatness are left to our view, and a wandering among the shallows of the fabulous and the incredible.   While I say this, I have not forgotten the storms in the *Odyssey*, nor the story of the Cyclops, nor certain other passages; I am describing an old age, but the old age of Homer.   Still in all these, as they follow one another, fable prevails over action.   I entered upon this digression, as I said, in order to show how very easily great genius, when the prime is passed, is turned aside to trifling: there are the stories of the wine-skin, of the companions turned by Circe to swine (whom Zoilus called 'porkers in tears'), of Zeus fed by doves like a young bird, of Ulysses ten days without food on the wreck, there are the incredible details of the slaying of the Suitors.   What can we call these but in very truth 'dreams of Zeus'?   A second reason why the incidents of the *Odyssey* also should be discussed is this; that you may recognize how the decline of passion in great writers and poets passes away into character-drawing; the sketches of the life in the household of Ulysses much resemble a comedy of character.

## X

I will now ask you to consider with me whether we may possibly arrive at anything further, which has power to make our writings sublime. Since with all things are associated certain elements, constituents which are essentially inherent in the substance of each, one factor of sublimity must necessarily be the power of choosing the most vital of the included elements, and of making these, by mutual superposition, form as it were a single body.   On one side the hearer is attracted by the choice of ideas, on another by the accumulation of those which have been chosen. Thus Sappho, in all cases, takes the emotions incident to the frenzy of love from the attendant symptoms and from actual truth.   But wherein does she show her great excellence?   In her power of first selecting and   then   closely   combining   those   which   are   conspicuous   and intense:—

Blest as the immortal gods is he
The youth whose eyes may look on thee,
Whose ears thy tongue's sweet melody
          May still devour.

Thou smilest too!—sweet smile, whose charm
Has struck my soul with wild alarm,
And, when I see thee, bids disarm
          Each vital power.

Speechless I gaze: the flame within
Runs swift o'er all my quivering skin;
My eyeballs swim; with dizzy din
          My brain reels round;

And cold drops fall; and tremblings frail
Seize every limb; and grassy pale
I grow; and then—together fail
          Both sight and sound.[1]

Do you not marvel how she seeks to gather soul and body into one, hearing and tongue, eyes and complexion; all dispersed and strangers before: now, by a series of contradictions, she is cold at once and burns, is irrational, is sensible (for she is either in terror or at the point of death), so that it may not appear to be a single passion which is upon her, but an assemblage of passions? All the symptoms are found severally in lovers; to the choice of those which are conspicuous, and to their concentration into one, is due the pre-eminent merit here. So is it, I think, with the Poet and his storms; he picks out the grimmest of the attendant circumstances. The author of the *Arimaspeia* thinks these lines terrible:—

Here too is mighty marvel for our thought:
Mid seas men dwell, on water, far from land:
Wretches they are, for sorry toil is theirs;
Eyes on the stars, heart on the deep they fix.
Oft to the gods, I ween, their hands are raised,
Their inward parts in evil case upheaved.

Any one, I think, will see that there is more embroidery than terror in it all. Now for Homer; take one instance out of many:—

---

[1] This ode of Sappho, the great woman-poet of Lesbos (about 600 B.C.), written in the metre which bears her name, has only been preserved to us in this treatise. It has been partly translated by Catullus into Latin, in the same metre. The version in the text is by J. Herman Merivale (1833).

> As when a wave swoln by the wild wind's blore[2]
> Down from the clouds upon a ship doth light,
> And the whole hulk with scattering foam is white,
> And through the sails all tattered and forlorn
> Roars the fell blast: the seamen with affright
> Shake, out from death a hand-breadth they are borne.

Aratus has attempted to transfer this very notion:—

> Tiny the plank which thrusts grim death away.

Only the result is petty and smooth, not terrible.   Moreover, he makes the danger limited, by the words 'the plank thrusts death away': and so it does!   Again our Poet does not limit the terror to one occurrence; he gives us the picture of men meeting destruction continually, wellnigh in every wave.   Yet again, by forcing together prepositions naturally inconsistent, and compelling them to combine (I refer to the words 'out from death'), he has so strained the verse as to match the trouble which fell upon them; has so pressed it together as to give the very presentment of that trouble; has stamped, I had almost said, upon the language the form and features of the peril: 'out from death a handbreadth they are borne.'   Just so Archilochus in describing the shipwreck, and Demosthenes, when the news of Elateia comes: 'For it was evening,' he says.   They chose the expressions of real eminence, looking only to merit (if one may use the word), took them out clean, and placed them one upon another, introducing between them nothing trivial, or undignified, or low.   For such things mar the whole effect, much as, in building, massive blocks, intended to cohere and hold together in one, are spoilt by stop-gaps and rubble.

## XI

Closely connected with the excellencies which I have named is that called Amplification; in which, when the facts and issues admit of several fresh beginnings and fresh halting-places, in periodic arrangement, great phrases come rolling upon others which have gone before, in a continuously ascending order.   Whether this be done by way of enlarging upon commonplace topics, or of exaggeration, or of intensifying facts or reasoning, or of handling deeds done or suffering endured (for there are numberless varieties of amplification), the orator must in any case know that none of these can possibly stand by itself without sublimity as a perfect structure.   The only exceptions are where pity or depreciation are required; in all other processes of amplification, take away the

---

[2] Blore, i.e. blast.

sublime, and you will take soul out of body; they are effective no longer, and become nerveless and hollow unless braced by passages of sublimity. But, for clearness' sake, I must shortly lay down wherein the difference lies between my present precepts, and what I said above (there I spoke of a sketch embracing the principal ideas and arranging them into one); and the broad difference between Amplification and Sublimity.

XII

I am not satisfied with the definition given by the technical writers. Amplification is, they say, language which invests the subject with greatness.   Of course this definition may serve in common for sublimity, and passion, and tropes, since they, too, invest the language with greatness of a particular kind.   To me it seems that they differ from one another in this, that Sublimity lies in intensity, Amplification also in multitude; consequently sublimity often exists in a single idea, amplification necessarily implies quantity and abundance.   Amplification is—to define it in outline—an accumulation of all the parts and topics inherent in a subject, strengthening the fabric of the argument by insistence; and differs in this from rhetorical proof that the latter seeks to demonstrate the point required. . . .

[*Here several pages have been lost.*]

In richest abundance, like a very sea, Plato often pours into an open expanse of grandeur.   Hence it is, I think, that, if we look to style, the Orator, appealing more strongly to passions, has a large element of fire and of spirit aglow; Plato, calm in his stately and dignified magnificence, I will not say, is cold, but is not so intense.   It is on these and no other points, as it seems to me, dear Terentianus (that is, if we as Greeks are allowed to form an opinion), that Cicero and Demosthenes differ in their grand passages.   Demosthenes' strength is in sheer height of sublimity, that of Cicero in its diffusion.   Our countryman, because he burns and ravages all in his violence, swift, strong, terrible, may be compared to a lightning flash or a thunderbolt.   Cicero, like a spreading conflagration, ranges and rolls over the whole field; the fire which burns is within him, plentiful and constant, distributed at his will now in one part, now in another, and fed with fuel in relays.   These are points on which you can best judge: certainly the moment for the sublimity and tension of Demosthenes is where accumulated invective and strong passion are in play, and generally where the hearer is to be hard struck: the moment for diffusion is where he is to be flooded with detail, as it is always appropriate in enlargement upon commonplaces, in perorations and digressions, and in all passages written for the style and for display, in scientific and physical exposition, and in several other branches of literature.

## XIII

That Plato (to return to him) flowing 'in some such noiseless stream', none the less reaches greatness, you will not fail to recognize, since you have read the *Republic*, and know this typical passage:— 'Those who are unversed in wisdom and virtue,' it runs, 'and spend all their days in feastings and the like, are borne downwards, and wander so through life. They never yet raised their eyes to the true world above them, nor were lifted up, nor tasted of solid or pure pleasure; but, like cattle, looking down, and bowed to earth and to the table, they feed and fill themselves and gender; and in the greediness of these desires they kick and butt one another with horns and hoofs of iron, and kill because they cannot be satisfied.'

This author shows us, if we would choose not to neglect the lesson, that there is also another road, besides all that we have mentioned, which leads to the sublime. What, and what manner of road as that? Imitation and emulation of great writers and poets who have been before us. Here is our mark, my friend, let us hold closely to it: for many are borne along inspired by a breath which comes from another; even as the story is that the Pythian prophetess, approaching the tripod, where is a cleft in the ground, inhales, so they say, vapour sent by a god; and then and there, impregnated by the divine power, sings her inspired chants; even so from the great genius of the men of old do streams pass off to the souls of those who emulate them, as though from holy caves; inspired by which, even those not too highly susceptible to the god are possessed by the greatness which was in others.

Was Herodotus alone 'most Homeric'? There was Stesichorus before him, and Archilochus; but more than any, Plato drew into himself from that Homeric fountain countless runlets and channels of water. (Perhaps we ought to have given examples, had not Ammonius drawn up a selection under headings.) Here is no theft, but such a rendering as is made from beautiful spectacles or from carvings or other works of art. I do not think that there would be such a bloom as we find on some of his philosophical dogmas, or that he could have entered so often into poetical matter and expressions, unless he had entered for the first place against Homer, aye, with all his soul, a young champion against one long approved; and striven for the mastery, too emulously perhaps and in the spirit of the lists, yet not without his reward; for 'good,' says Hesiod, 'is this strife for mortals.' Yes, that contest for fame is fair, and its crown worthy of the winning, wherein even to be defeated by our forerunners is not inglorious.

## XIV

Therefore even we, when we are working out a theme which requires lofty speech and greatness of thought, do well to imagine within ourselves how, if need were, Homer would have said this same thing, how Plato or Demosthenes, or, in history, Thucydides would have made it sublime. The figures of those great men will meet us on the way while we vie with them, they will stand out before our eyes, and lead our souls upwards towards the measure of the ideal which we have conjured up. Still more so if we add to our mental picture this; how would Homer, were he here, have listened to this phrase of mine? or Demosthenes? how would they have felt at this? Truly great is this competition, where we assume for our own words such a jury, such an audience, and pretend that before judges and witnesses of that heroic build we undergo a scrutiny of what we write. Yet more stimulating than all will it be if you add: 'If I write this, in what spirit will all future ages hear me?' If any man fear this consequence, that he may say something which shall pass beyond his own day and his own life, then needs must all which such a soul can grasp be barren, blunted, dull; for it posthumous fame can bring no fulfilment.

## XV

Weight, grandeur, and energy of speaking are further produced in a very high degree, young friend, by appeals to Imagination, called by some 'image making.' Imagination is no doubt a name given generally to anything which suggests, no matter how, a thought which engenders speech; but the word has in our time come to be applied specially to those cases, where, moved by enthusiasm and passion, you seem to see the things of which you speak, and place them under the eyes of your hearers. Imagination means one thing in rhetoric, another with the poets; and you cannot fail to observe that the object of the latter is to amaze, of the former to give distinctness; both, however, seek to stir the mind strongly.

> My mother, never hound these maids on me,
> Of bloody visages and snaky locks:
> Here! here! upon me, nearer yet they leap!

and

> Alas! she'll slay me: whither may I flee?

There the poet saw the Furies with his own eyes, and what his imagination presented he almost compelled his hearers to behold. Now Euripides is most painstaking in employing for the purposes of Tragedy the two passions of madness and love, and is more successful with these than, so far as I know, with any others; not that he lacks boldness in essaying other efforts of imagination. Though his own natural genius was far from being great, he yet forced it in many instances to become tragic: in every detail of his great passages, as the poet has it,

> Sides and loins he lashes to and fro
> With his swift tail, and stirs up battle's thirst.

Thus Helios, handing over the reins to Phaethon, says:—

> But drive thou not within the Libyan clime,
> Th' unmoistened burning air will split thy car.

Then he goes on:—

> Right for the seven Pleiads shape thy course:
> So spake the sire; the son now grasped the reins.
> And lashed the flanks of those winged coursers. They,
> Set free, sped onwards through th' expanse of air:
> The sire, astride great Sirius in the rear,
> Rode, and the boy instructed:—thither drive!
> Here wheel thy car, yea here!

Would you not say that the soul of the writer treads the car with the driver, and shares the peril, and wears wings, as the horses do; such details could never have been imagined by it, if it had not moved in that heavenly display, and kept even pace. So in his Cassandra, 'Ho, ye horse loving Trojans . . .'

Now, whereas Aeschylus hazards the most heroic flights of imagination, as where the Seven chieftains against Thebes, in the play of that name:—

> Seven impetuous warriors, captains bold,
> Slaying the sacred bull o'er black-rimm'd shields
> And touching with their hands the victim's gore,
> Ares, Enyo, and blood-thirsting Fear
> Invoked, and swear . . .

swearing to one another oaths of death, each man of his own, with 'no word of ruth'; yet sometimes produces thoughts which are not wrought out, but left in the rough, and harsh; Euripides in emulation forces himself upon the same perils. Thus in Aeschylus the palace of Lycurgus is troubled by the Gods in a manner passing strange when Dionysus is made manifest:—

> See how the palace is possessed, its halls
> Are all a revel . . .

Euripides has smoothed this over and worded it differently:—

And all the mountain joined their revelry.

Sophocles has used imagination finely about the dying Oedipus, when he passes to his own burial amidst elemental portents; and again where Achilles, as the Greeks are sailing away, appears to them above his tomb, just when they were standing out to sea, an appearance which no one has expressed with more vivid imagery than Simonides; but it is impossible to put down all instances.   We may, however, say generally, that those found in poets admit an excess which passes into the mythical and goes beyond all that is credible; in rhetorical imagination that which has in it reality and truth is always best.   Deviations from this rule become strange and exotic when the texture of the speech is poetic and mythical, and passes into impossibility of every sort; surely we need look no further than to our own clever orators, who, like tragedians, see Furies, and cannot, honest gentlemen, learn so much as this, that when Orestes says:—

Unhand me; one of my own Furies thou;
Dost grasp my waist, to thrust me down to hell?

he imagines all this because he is mad.   What then can imagination in rhetoric do?   It can probably contribute much else to our speeches in energy and passion; but certainly in passages dealing with facts an admixture of it not only persuades a listener, but makes him its slave. 'Now mark me,' says Demosthenes, 'if at this very moment a cry should be heard in front of our courts, and then one said that the prison has been opened, and the prisoners are escaping, there is no one, be he old or young, so careless but will help all he can.   But if one were to come forward and say, that the man who released them is now before you, that man would have no hearing, and would instantly die.'   So Hyperides when put on his trial, because he had proposed, after our defeat, to make the slaves free; 'This proposal,' he said, 'was moved not by the Orator, but by the battle at Chaeroneia'; here, while he deals with the facts, he at the same time has used imagination, the audacity of the conception has borne him outside and beyond persuasion.   In all such instances it is a fact of nature that we listen to that which is strongest.   We are therefore drawn away from mere demonstration to that which has in it imagination and surprise, the element of fact being wrapped and lost amid the light which shines around it.   This process is only what we might expect; when two forces are combined in one, the stronger always attracts into itself the potency of the other.

What I have now written about the sublime effects which belong to high thoughts, and which are produced by the greatness of man's soul, and secondarily by imitation, or by imagination, will suffice.

## XVI

Here comes the place reserved for Figures, our next topic; for these, if handled as they ought to be, should, as I said, form no minor element in greatness. As however it would be a laborious, or rather an unlimited task to give an accurate enumeration of all, we will go through a few of those productive of greatness of speech, in order to make good my assertion, and will begin thus. Demosthenes is offering a demonstration in defending his public acts. Now what was the natural way to deal with it? 'You made no mistake, men of Athens, when you took upon yourselves the struggle for the freedom of the Greeks: you have examples of this near home. For they also made no mistake who fought at Marathon, at Salamis, at Plataea.' But when, as one suddenly inspired and possessed, he breaks out with that oath by the bravest men of Greece: 'It cannot be that you made a mistake; no, by those who bore the brunt at Marathon,' he appears by use of a single figure, that of adjuration (which here I call apostrophe), to have deified those ancestors; suggesting the thought that we ought to swear, as by gods, by men who died so; and implanting in the judges the spirit of the men who there hazarded their lives of old; changing the very nature of demonstration into sublimity and passion of the highest order, and the assured conviction of new and more than natural oaths; and, withal, infusing into the souls of his hearers a plea of sovereign and specific virtue; that so, relieved by the medicine of his words of praise, they should be brought to pride themselves no less on the battle against Philip than on the triumphs won at Marathon and at Salamis. Doing all this, he caught his hearers up and bore them with him, by his use of a figure.

It is said, I know, that the germ of this oath is found in Eupolis:—

I swear by Marathon, the fight, my fight,
No man of them unscathed shall vex my heart.

But then it is not the mere swearing by a name which is great; place, manner, occasion, purpose are all essential. In these lines there is an oath, and that is all; it is addressed to Athenians when prosperous and needing no comfort; besides the poet has not made immortals of the men, and sworn by them, that so he may implant within the hearts of his hearers a worthy record of their valour; he has passed away from the men who bore the brunt to the inanimate thing, the battle. In Demosthenes the oath has been framed to suit beaten men, that so Chaeroneia might appear a failure no longer; it is, as I said, at once a demonstration that they made no mistake, an example, an assurance resting on oaths, a word of praise, an exhortation.   And whereas the orator was liable to be met by this objection: 'You are speaking of a defeat under your administration, and yet you swear by victories,' in the next words he squares his phrase by rule, and makes his very words safe, giving us a lesson that 'even in Bacchic transports we must yet be sober.'   'By those who bore the brunt,' are his words, 'at Marathon, by those who fought on sea by Salamis and off Artemisium, by those who stood in the ranks at Plataea!'

Nowhere does he say 'who conquered,' but throughout he has furtively kept back the word which should give the result, because that result was a happy one, the contrary to that of Chaeroneia.   Therefore he gives his hearer no time, and at once adds:—'To all of whom the city gave public burial, Aeschines, not to those only who succeeded.'

## XVII

At this point I must not omit, my dear friend, to state one of my own conclusions.   It shall be given quite concisely, and is this.   As though by nature, the figures ally themselves with sublimity, and in turn are marvellously supported by the alliance.   Where and how this is so, I will explain.   There is a peculiar prejudice against a promiscuous use of the figures: it suggests a suspicion of ambuscade, plot, sophistry; and the more so when the speech is addressed to a judge with absolute powers, above all to tyrants, kings, magistrates of the highest rank: any of these at once becomes indignant, if he feels that there is an attempt to outwit him, like a silly child, by the paltry figure of a skilled orator; he takes the fallacy to be used in contempt for himself, and either rages like a wild beast, or, if he master his wrath, yet is wholly disinclined to be convinced by the arguments.   Accordingly a figure is best, when the very fact that it is a figure passes unnoticed.   Therefore sublimity and passion are a help against the suspicion attaching to the use of figures, and a resource of marvellous power; because the treacherous art, being once associated with what is beautiful and great, enters and remains, without exciting the least suspicion.   This is sufficiently proved in the words quoted above, 'By the men who fought at Marathon!'   By what device has the orator concealed the figure?   Clearly, by its very light.   Much as duller lights are extinguished in the encircling beams of the sun, so the artifices of rhetoric are obscured by the grandeur poured about them.   An effect not far removed from this occurs in painting.   When colours are used, and the light and the shadow lie upon the same surface beside one another, the light meets the eye before the shadow, and seems not only more prominent, but also much nearer.   So it is in speeches; sublimity and passion, lying closer to our souls, always come into view sooner than the figures, because of what I may call natural kinship, and also of brilliance; the artfulness of the figures is thrown into shadow, and, as it were, veiled.

## XVIII

What are we to say of the Questions and Interrogations, which come next? Is it not true that, by the very form which this figure takes, our orator gives intensity to his language and makes it much more effective and vehement? 'Or do ye wish (answer me, sir!) to go round and inquire one of another: "is there any news?" What can be greater news than this, that a man of Macedonia is subduing Greece? Is Philip dead? Not dead, Heaven knows, but sick. What matter to you? if anything happen to him, you will quickly make you another Philip.' Again, 'Let us sail to Macedonia. "What harbour shall we ever find to put into?" asked some one. War will discover for itself the weak points in Philip's resources.' The thing put simply would be quite inadequate: as it is, the rush and swift return of question and answer, and the meeting of his own difficulty as if it came from another, make the words not only more sublime by his use of the figure, but actually more convincing. For passionate language is more attractive when it seems to be born of the occasion, rather than deliberately adopted by the speaker: question and answer carried on with a man's self reproduce the spontaneity of passion. Much as those who are questioned by others, when spurred by the sudden appeal, meet the point vigorously and with the plain truth, so it is with the figure of question and answer; it draws the hearer off till he thinks that each point in the inquiry has been raised and put into words without preparation, and so imposes upon him. Again (for the instance from Herodotus has passed for one of the most sublime), if it be this . . .

[*Here several pages have been lost.*]

## XIX

The words drop unconnected, and are, so to say, poured forth, almost too fast for the speaker himself. 'Locking their shields,' says Xenophon, 'they pushed, fought, slew, died.' Or take the words of Eurylochus in Homer:—

> E'en as thou bad'st, we ranged the thickets through,
> We found a house fair fashioned in a glade.

Phrases cut off from one another, yet spoken rapidly, carry the impression of a struggle, where the meaning is at once checked and hurried on. Such an effect Homer has produced by his Asyndeta.

## XX

An excellent and stirring effect is often given by the concurrence of figures, when two or three mingled in one company throw into a common fund their force, cogency, beauty.    Thus in the speech against Midias we have Asyndeta interwoven with repetitions and vivid presentation. 'There are many things which the striker might do, yet some of which the person struck could never tell another, by gesture, by look, by voice.' Then, in order that the passage may not continue travelling in the same track (for rest shows calm, disarrangement passion, which is a rush and a stirring of the mind), he passes with a bound to fresh Asyndeta and to repetitions: 'by gesture, by look, by voice; when in insult, when in enmity, when with fists, when as slave.'    In these phrases the orator does what the striker did, he belabours the intellect of the judges by the speed of blow following blow.    Then he goes back from this point, and makes a fresh onset, as gusts of wind do; 'when with fists, when on the face,' he goes on, 'these things stir, these make men frantic, to whom insult is not familiar.    No one by telling of these things could possibly represent their atrocity.'

Thus he keeps up in essence throughout the passage his repetitions and Asyndeta, while he continually varies them; so that his order is disorderly, and again his violation of order has in it order of a kind.

## XXI

Now insert, if you will, conjunctions, as the school of Isocrates does: 'Again we must not omit this point either, that there are many things which the striker might do, first by gesture, and then by look, and yet further by his very voice': if you rewrite the passage in full sequence, you will recognize how the press and rough effectiveness of passion, when smoothed to one level by conjunctions, fails to pierce the ear, and its fire at once goes out.    For as, if one should tie up the limbs of runners, their speed is gone, so passion chafes to be shackled by conjunctions and other additions.    The freedom of running is destroyed, and the momentum as of bolt from catapult.

## XXII

Under the same head we must set cases of Hyperbaton.    This is a disturbance of the proper sequence of phrases or thoughts, and is the surest impress of vehement passion.    For as those who are really angry, or in fear, or indignant, or who fall under the influence of jealousy or any other passion (for passions are many, nay countless, past the power of man to reckon), are seen to put forward one set of ideas, then spring aside to another, thrusting in a parenthesis out of all logic, then wheel round to the first, and in their excitement, like a ship before an unsteady gale, drag phrases and thoughts sharply across, now this way, now that, and so divert the natural order into turnings innumerable; so is it in the best writers: imitation of nature leads them by way of Hyperbata to the effects of nature. For art is perfect just when it seems to be nature, and nature successful when the art underlies it unnoticed. Take the speech of Dionysius of Phocaea in Herodotus:—'Our fortunes rest on the edge of a razor, O Ionians, whether we are to be free or slaves, aye runaway slaves. Now, therefore, if you choose to take up hardships, there is toil for you in the present, but you will be able to overcome your enemies.' The natural order was, 'O Ionians, now is the time for you to accept toils, for our fortunes rest on the edge of a razor.' He has transported the words 'Men of Ionia', starting at once with the mention of the fear, and entirely omitting, in view of the pressing terror, to find time to name his audience. Then he has inverted the order of the thoughts. Before saying that they must endure toil (which is the point of his exhortation) he first assigns the cause why they should do so: 'our fortunes', he says, 'rest on the edge of a razor': so that his words seem not to have been prepared, but to be forced out of him. Even more marvellous is Thucydides in the skill with which he separates, by the use of Hyperbata, things which nature has made one and inseparable. Demosthenes is not so arbitrary as he; yet he is never tired of the use of this figure in all its applications; the effect of vehemence which he produces by transposition is great, and also that of speaking on the call of the moment; besides all this he draws his hearers with him to face the hazards of his long Hyperbata. For he often leaves suspended the thought with which he began, and interposes, as though he struck into a train of reasoning foreign to it and dissimilar, matter which he rolls upon other matter, all drawn from some source outside, till he strikes his hearer with fear that an entire collapse of the sentence will follow, and forces him by mere vehemence to share the risk with the speaker: then, when you least expect, after a long interval, he makes good the thought which has so long been owing, and works in his own way to a happy conclusion: making the whole a great deal more impressive by the very hazard and imminence of failure which goes with his Hyperbata. Let us spare more instances: there are so many.

## XXIII

Next come the figures of many cases, so-called; groupings, changes, gradations, which are very effective, as you know, and work in with ornament, sublimity of every kind, and passion. Only look at variations of case, tense, person, number, gender: how they embroider and enliven

our expressions! Of those which are concerned with number, I assert
that not only are those instances ornamental where the form is singular,
and the meaning, when you look into them, is found to be plural:—

> At once the people in its multitude
> Break man from man, shout 'tunny!' o'er the beach;

but the other class deserves even more attention, because there are cases
where plurals fall on the ear with grander effect, and catch our applause
by the effect of multitude which the number gives. Take an instance
from Sophocles in the *Oedipus*:—

> O marriage rites
> That gave me birth, and having borne me, gave
> To me in turn an offspring, and ye showed
> Fathers and sons, and brothers, all in one,
> Mothers and wives, and daughters, hateful names,
> All foulest deeds that men have ever done.

All these express one name, Oedipus, and on the other side Jocasta;
but for all that, the number, spread out into plurals, has made the misfortunes plural also; or in another case of many for one: 'Forth Hectors
issued and Sarpedons.' And there is the passage of Plato, which I have
quoted also in another place, about the Athenians:—

'No Pelopses, nor Cadmuses, nor Aegyptuses, nor Danai, nor other of
the natural-born barbarian dwell here with us; pure Greeks with no
cross of barbarian blood are we that dwell in the land,' and so forth.
For things strike on the ear with more sonorous effect when the names
are thus piled upon one another in groups. Yet this should be done in
those cases alone where the subject admits of enlargement, or multiplication, or hyperbole, or passion, either one of these, or several: for we
know that to go everywhere 'hung about with bells' is a sophist's trick
indeed.

## XXIV

Yet, on the other hand, contraction from plural to singular sometimes produces an effect conspicuously sublime. 'Then all Peloponnesus
was ranged on different sides,' says the Orator. And look at this, 'when
Phrynichus exhibited his drama, the *Taking of Miletus*, the whole theatre
fell into tears.' Where separate individuals are compressed into unity
the notion of a single body is produced. In both cases the cause of the
ornamental effect is the same: where terms are properly singular, to turn
them into plurals shows emotion into which the speaker is surprised;
where plural, to bring several individuals under one sonorous head is a
change in the opposite direction, and equally unexpected.

## XXV

Again, where you introduce things past and done as happening in the actual present, you will make your account no longer a narrative but a living action. 'A man who has fallen under the horse of Cyrus,' says Xenophon, 'and is being trampled, strikes his sword into the belly of the horse: the horse plunges and unseats Cyrus, and he falls.' So Thucydides in most instances.

## XXVI

Effective also in the same way is the transposition of persons, which often makes a hearer think that he is moving in the midst of the dangers described:—

> Of toughest kind
> Thou wouldst have called those hosts, so manfully
> Each fought with each.

And Aratus has:—

> Not in that month may seas about thee surge!

In much the same way Herodotus: 'You will sail up stream from the city Elephantina, and then you will come to a level plain. Passing through this tract, you will again embark on another and sail for two days; then you will reach a great city, whose name is Meroe.' You see, comrade, how he takes your spirit with him through the place, and turns hearing into seeing. All such passages, being addressed to the reader in his own person, make him take his place at the very centre of the action. Again, when you speak as though to a single individual, not to all:—

> Nor of the son of Tydeus couldst thou know
> If he with Trojans or Achaians were;

you will render him more moved by the passions and also more attentive; he is filled full of the combat, because he is roused by being himself addressed.

## XXVII

Then there are other cases where the writer is giving a narrative about a person, and by a sudden transition himself passes into that person; in this class there is an outburst of passion:—

> But Hector warned the Trojans with loud cry,
> To rush upon the ships, and pass the plunder by:
> 'But whom elsewhere than at the ships I sight,
> Death shall be his that moment.'

Here the poet has assigned the narrative part to himself, as is fitting: the sharp threat he has suddenly, without previous explanation, attached to the angry chieftain: it would have been cold had he inserted 'Hector then said so and so,' whereas now the change of construction has anticipated the poet's change of speaker.

Hence the proper use of the figure is where the occasion is short and sharp, and does not allow the writer to stop, but forces him to hurry from person to person, as in Hecataeus: 'Ceyx, indignant at this, at once commanded the Heraclidae of the later generation to leave the country: "for I have no power to help you; therefore, that you may not perish yourselves, and inflict a wound on me, depart to another people." ' Demosthenes, in his Aristogeiton speech, has found a different method to throw passion and swiftness into this change of persons: 'And will none of you be found,' he says, 'to entertain wrath or indignation at the violence of this shameless miscreant; who, thou foulest of mankind, when thy effrontery is stopped, not by barriers nor by gates, such as man might open ——' He has not finished what he intended, but passing quickly aside, and, I had almost said, splitting a single sentence between two persons, because he is so angry—'Who, thou foulest of mankind,' he says; with the result that, having turned his speech away from Aristogeiton, and having done with him, you think, he directs it upon him again with far more intensity through the passion.

Much in the same way Penelope:—

> What brings thee, herald, thee, the pioneer
> Of these imperious suitors?  Do they send
> To bid the servants of my husband dear
> Of their appointed task-work to make end,
> And on their lordly revelries attend?
> Never elsewhere may they survive to meet!
> Here in these halls, while our estates they rend,
> May they their latest and their last now eat,
> Who thus with outrage foul Telemachus entreat.
> Ye to your parents heedful ear lend none,
> Nor hearken how Odysseus lived of yore.

## XXVIII

No one I think would be in doubt as to Periphrasis being a factor of sublimity.  For as in music Paraphones make the principal melody sweeter, so Periphrasis often chimes in with the plain expression, and the concurrence adds to the beauty, more especially if it have not any windy, unmusical effect, but be pleasantly compounded.  In proof of this it will be sufficient to quote Plato at the beginning of the Funeral Speech:—

'Of all that we can give, these have now what is rightly theirs, and, having received it, they pass on their appointed journey, escorted publicly by the city, personally each man by those of his kin.'   Here he has called death an 'appointed journey,' and the bestowal of the usual rites 'a public escort given by their country.'   Is the dignity added to the thought by these turns but a small matter?   Or has he rather taken language plain and unadorned, and made it melodious by pouring around it the harmonies which came of periphrasis?  Xenophon again:—'Ye reckon toil to be the guide to happy life, and have received it into your souls as the fairest and the most gallant of all possessions: for ye take more delight in being praised than in any other thing.'   By calling toil 'the guide to happy life,' and giving a like expansion to the other points, he has attached to his words of praise a great and definite thought.   And that inimitable phrase of Herodotus:—'On those of the Scythians who plundered the temple the goddess sent a plague which made them women.'

## XXIX

Yet Periphrasis is exposed to special risks, more special than any of the figures, if used by a writer without sense of proportion: for it falls feebly on the ear, and savours of trifling and of rank stupidity.   So when Plato, (for he always employs the figure with great force, occasionally out of season,) says in the *Laws*: 'we must not allow wealth, either of silver or of gold, to be established in the city and settle there,' mocking critics say that, if he had wanted to forbid them to possess sheep, he would clearly have talked of 'wealth of sheep and wealth of cattle.'

Enough however of this disquisition (which came in by way of parenthesis) on the use of figures in producing sublime effects, all those which we have mentioned make speeches more passionate and stirring; and passion is as large an ingredient in sublimity as sense of character in an agreeable style.

## XXX

Next, since the thought and the diction of a speech are in most cases mutually interlaced, I will ask you to consider with me whether any particulars of what concerns expression still remain.   That a choice of the right words and of grand words wonderfully attracts and charms hearers—that this stands very high as a point of practice with all orators and all writers, because, of its own inherent virtue, it brings greatness, beauty, raciness, weight, strength, mastery, and an exultation all its own, to grace our words, as though they were the fairest statues—that it imparts to mere facts a soul which has speech—it may perhaps be super-

fluous to set out at length, for my readers know it.   For beautiful words
are, in a real and special sense, the light of thought.   Yet their majesty
is not of service in all places: to apply to trifling details grand and solemn
words would appear much the same as if one were to fasten a large mask
upon a little child.   Yet in poetry . . .

[*Here several pages have been lost.*]


## XXXI

. . . very rich and pithy; and this of Anacreon:—

The Thracian filly has no more my care.

So too the novel phrase of Theopompus has merit, from the closeness
of the correspondence it appears to me most expressive, yet Caecilius has
strangely found fault with it.   'Philip,' he says, 'has a rare power of
swallowing down facts perforce.'   So vulgar idiom is sometimes much
more expressive than ornamental language; it is recognized at once as a
touch of common life; and what is familiar is on the way to be credible.
Therefore, when applied to a man who patiently puts up with and enjoys
what is mean and repulsive in order to better himself, the phrase adopted,
'to swallow down perforce,' is very telling.   So in Herodotus:—'Then
Cleomenes went mad, and cut his own flesh with the knife into little
strips, until he had made collops of himself and so died'.   And 'Pythes
held on to his ship and fought until he was chopped to pieces.'   These
scrape the corner of vulgar idiom, but they are not vulgar because they
are so expressive.


## XXXII

As to number of Metaphors, Caecilius appears to agree with those who
lay down a rule allowing two, or at the most three, applied to the same
object.   About such figures again Demosthenes is the true standard,
and the time for their use is, when passions are driven onwards like a
torrent, and draw with themselves, as necessary to the passage, the
multiplication of metaphors.

'Men foul and flatterers,' he says, 'having mutilated their fatherlands,
every one of them, having pledged away their freedom in wine, first to
Philip, now to Alexander, measuring happiness by their belly and by
the appetites which are most shameful, having thrown to the ground
that freedom and that life without a master, wherein the Greeks of old
found their very standard and definition of good.'   Here the orator's
wrath against the traitors screens the number of the metaphors used.
Accordingly Aristotle and Theophrastus say that bold metaphors are

softened by such devices as the insertion of 'as though,' and 'as it were,' and
'if I may speak thus,' and 'if I am right in using somewhat venturesome
phrase'; for 'censure,' they say, 'cures bold expression.' For myself, I
accept all these; yet I affirm, as I said in speaking of figures, that bursts
of passion, being seasonable and vehement, and sublimity when genuine,
are sure specifics for numerous and daring metaphors; because as they
surge and sweep, they naturally draw everything their own way, and force
it onwards, rather, I would say, they require and exact bold metaphors,
and do not allow the hearer leisure to go into questions of their number,
because the speaker's excitement is his. Yet further, in speeches about
commonplaces and in set descriptions, nothing is so expressive as continued and successive tropes. It is by means of these that in Xenophon
the anatomy of man's bodily tabernacle is painted with so much magnificence, and still more admirably in Plato. The head he calls the citadel;
between this and the chest an isthmus has been constructed, the neck,
to which vertebrae have been attached like hinges; pleasure is a bait
tempting men to their hurt, and the tongue supplies the test of taste;
the heart is the knot of the veins, and the fountain of the blood which
courses violently around, is appointed to be the guard-house. The
passages or pores he calls lanes. 'For the beating of the heart, in the
expectation of danger or on the summons of wrath, because it is a fiery
organ, they devised a resource, introducing the structure of the lungs,
which are soft and bloodless, and perforated with cavities like a sponge,
in order that, when wrath boils up within it, the heart may beat upon a
yielding substance, and so receive no hurt.' The chamber where the
appetites dwell he styled the women's chamber, that where the passions,
the men's chamber. The spleen is a napkin for the parts within; filled
with their purgings it grows large and unsound. 'After this,' he goes
on, 'they enshrouded all with fleshy parts, placing the flesh in front, to
be a protection from matter outside, like layers of felt.' He called blood
the food of the fleshy parts. 'And for the sake of nourishment they made
water-courses through the body, like water-courses cut in gardens, that
the currents of the veins might run as from an inflowing stream, the body
being a narrow canal.' But when the end is at hand, he says that the
cables of the souls are loosed, as though of a ship, and it is let go free.
Countless similar details follow: those which we have set down suffice to
show how grand in their nature tropical expressions are, and how metaphors produce sublimity, and that impassioned and descriptive passages
admit them most readily. Yet that the use of tropes, like all other
beauties of style, leads writers on to neglect proportion, is clear without
my saying it. For it is upon these especially that critics pull Plato to
pieces, he is so often led on, as though his style were possessed, into

untempered and harsh metaphors and portentous allegory. 'For it is
not easy to realize,' he says, 'that a city ought to be mixed like a cup,
whereinto wine is poured and boils; yet, when chastened by another
and a temperate god, in that fair partnership forms an honest and a
sober draught.' For to call water 'a temperate god,' they say, and
admixture 'chastening,' is the mark of a poet who is anything but sober.
Caecilius however, taking up such weak points as this in his pamphlets
in praise of Lysias, actually dared to make out Lysias better all round
than Plato, mixing up two different feelings: for loving Lysias more than
he loved himself, he yet hates Plato more thoroughly than he loves
Lysias. Only he is carried away by combativeness, nor are his premisses
admitted as he thought them to be. For he puts forward his orator as
without a fault and clear in his record, as against Plato who had
made many mistakes. The fact is not so, nor anything like it.

## XXXIII

Come now: let us find some writer who is really clear and beyond
criticism. Upon this point, is it not worth while to raise the question in
a general form, whether in poems and prose writings a greatness with some
failings is the better, or a genius which is limited in its successes, but is
always sound and never drops? Aye, and this further question; whether
the first prize should be carried off by the most numerous excellences
in literature or by the greatest? These questions are germane to the
subject of Sublimity, and absolutely require a decision. I know, for my
own part, that genius of surpassing greatness has always the least clear
record. Precision in every detail comes perilously near littleness; in
great natures, as in great fortunes, there ought to be something which may
even be neglected. Further, this may perhaps be a necessary law, that
humble or modest genius, which never runs a risk, and never aims at
excellence, remains in most cases without a failure and in comparative
safety; but that what is great is hazardous by very reason of the greatness.
Not that I fail to recognize this second law, that all human things are
more easily recognized on their worse side; that the memory of failures
remains indelible, while that of the good points passes quickly away. I
have myself brought forward not a few failures in Homer and in others of
the very greatest, yet never take pleasure in their slips, which I do not call
voluntary mistakes, but rather oversights caused by the random, haphazard carelessness of great genius, and passed unmarked by it; and I
remain unshaken in my opinion, that in all cases great excellence, although
not kept up to one level throughout, should always bear off first award,
if for nothing else, yet for the sake of simple intellectual greatness. To
take an instance, Apollonius in the *Argonautae* is a poet who never drops,

and Theocritus in his *Pastorals* is most successful, except as to a few
extraneous matters: now this being so, would you not rather be Homer
than Apollonius? Take again Eratosthenes in the *Erigone*, a little poem
with nothing in it to blame; is he a greater poet than Archilochus, who
drags much ill-arranged matter along in that outpouring of divine inspiration which it is difficult to range under a law? In lyrics again,
would you choose to be Bacchylides rather than Pindar, in Tragedy
Ion of Chios than Sophocles himself? These poets no doubt never drop,
their language is always smooth and the writing beautiful, whereas
Pindar and Sophocles at one time set all ablaze in their rush, but the
fire is quenched when you least expect it, and they fail most unhappily.
Am I not right in saying that no man in his senses, if he put the works of
Ion together in a row, would value them against a single play, the
*Oedipus*?

## XXXIV

If successful passages were to be numbered, not weighed, Hyperides
would, on this reckoning, far surpass Demosthenes. He sounds more
notes, and has more points of excellence; he wins a second place in pretty
well every competition, like the hero of the Pentathlon, being beaten for
the first prize by some trained competitor in each, but standing first of
the non-professionals. Hyperides certainly, besides matching the successful points in Demosthenes, always excepting composition, has included,
over and above these, the virtues and graces of Lysias. He talks with
simplicity, when it is required, not in a sustained monotonous manner
like Demosthenes, and he shows sense of character, a flavouring added
with a light hand; he has indescribable graces, the wit of a man who
knows life, good breeding, irony with readiness of fence, jokes not vulgar
nor ill-bred as in those great Attic orators, but appropriate, clever raillery,
comic power in plenty, the sting which goes with well-aimed fun, and with
all this what I may call inimitable charm. He has a strong natural
gift for compassion, and also for telling a story fluently, running through
a description before a flowing breeze with admirable ease in tacking:
for instance, the story of Latona he has treated rather as a poet, the
Funeral Speech as a set, perhaps an unmatched, effort of the oratory of
display. Demosthenes has no touches of character, no flowing style;
certainly he is not supple, and cannot speak for display: he lacks the whole
list of qualities mentioned above: when he is forced to be witty and
smart, he raises a laugh against, rather than with himself; when he wants
to approach charm of manner he passes farthest from it. We may be
sure that if he had attempted to write the little speech on *Phryne* or that
on *Athenogenes*, he would have established even more firmly the fame of

Hyperides. As I see it, the case stands thus:—The beauties of the latter though they be many, are devoid of greatness, dull 'to a sober man's heart', and allow the hearer to rest unmoved (who feels fear when he reads Hyperides?); Demosthenes 'taking up the tale,' adds excellences of the highest genius and of consummate perfection, sublimity of tone, passions in living embodiment, copiousness, versatility, speed; also, which is his own prerogative, ability and force beyond approach. Now whereas, I say, he has drawn to himself in one all those marvellous and heaven-sent gifts, for human we may not call them, therefore by the beauties which he has he surpasses all other men and outmatches those which he has not. With his thunder, with his lightning, he bears down the orators of all time; sooner might one open one's eyes in the face of thunderbolts as they rush, than gaze full upon the passions which follow upon passions in Demosthenes.

## XXXV

When we come to Plato, there is, as I said, another kind of pre-eminence. For Lysias, who is far below him in the number, as well as in the magnitude of his good points, is yet more in excess of him in faults than in defect as to good points. What then did those immortals see, the writers who aimed at all which is greatest, and scorned the accuracy which lies in every detail? They saw many other things, and they also saw this, that Nature determined man to be no low or ignoble animal; but introducing us into life and this entire universe as into some vast assemblage, to be spectators, in a sort, of her contests, and most ardent competitors therein, did then implant in our souls an invincible and eternal love of that which is great and, by our own standard, more divine. Therefore it is, that for the speculation and thought which are within the scope of human endeavour not all the universe together is sufficient, our conceptions often pass beyond the bounds which limit it; and if one were to look upon life all round, and see how in all things the extraordinary, the great, the beautiful stand supreme, he will at once know for what ends we have been born. So it is that, as by some physical law, we admire, not surely the little streams, transparent though they be, and useful too, but Nile, or Tiber, or Rhine, and far more than all, Ocean; nor are we awed by this little flame of our kindling, because it keeps its light clear, more than by those heavenly bodies, often obscured though they be, nor think it more marvellous than the craters of Etna, whose eruptions bear up stones and entire masses, and sometimes pour forth rivers of that Titanic and unalloyed fire. Regarding all such things we may say this, that what is serviceable or perhaps necessary to man, man can procure; what passes his thought wins wonder.

## XXXVI

Hence, when we speak of men of great genius in literature, where the greatness does not necessarily fall outside the needs and service of man, we must at once arrive at the conclusion, that men of this stature, though far removed from flawless perfection, yet all rise above the mortal: other qualities prove those who possess them to be men, sublimity raises them almost to the intellectual greatness of God.   No failure, no blame; but greatness has our very wonder.   What need still to add, that each of these great men is often seen to redeem all his failures by a single sublimity, a single success; and further, which is most convincing, that if we were to pick out all the failures of Homer, Demosthenes, Plato, and the other greatest writers, and to mass them together, the result would be a small, an insignificant fraction of the successes which men of that heroic build everywhere exhibit.   Therefore every age and all time, which envy itself can never prove to be in its dotage, has bestowed upon them the assured prizes of victory; it guards and keeps them to this day safe and inalienable, and will as it seems, keep them

As long as waters flow and poplars bloom.

To the writer, however, who objects that the faulty Colossus is not better work than the Spearman of Polycleitus I might say much, but I say this. In Art the most accurate work is admired, in the works of Nature greatness.   Now it is by Nature that man is a being endowed with speech; therefore in statues we seek what is like man, in speech what surpasses, as I said, human standards.   Yet it is right (for our precept returns to the early words of this treatise), because the success of never failing is in most cases due to Art, the success of high although not uniform excellence, to Genius; that, therefore, Art should ever be brought in to aid Nature; where they are reciprocal the result should be perfection. It was necessary to go thus far towards a decision upon the points raised: let every one take the view which pleases him, and enjoy it.

## XXXVII

In close neighbourhood to Metaphors, for we must go back to them, come Illustrations and Similes, which differ from them in this respect . . .
[*Here several pages have been lost.*]

## XXXVIII

Such Hyperboles as this are also ludicrous, 'unless you wear your brains in your heels to be trampled down'.   Hence we ought to know exactly how far each should go, for sometimes to advance beyond these limits destroys the hyperbole; in such cases extreme tension brings relaxation, and even works right round to its opposite. Thus Isocrates fell into a strange puerility owing to his ambition to amplify at all points. The Argument of his *Panegyricus* is that the state of the Athenians surpasses that of the Lacedaemonians in services to the Greeks; but at the very beginning he has this;—'Moreover words are so potent, that it is possible thereby to make what is great lowly, and to throw greatness about what is small, and to treat old things in a new fashion, and those which have recently happened in an old fashion.' 'What, Isocrates,' some one will say, 'do you mean then to change the parts of the Lacedaemonians and Athenians?' For this set praise of speech goes near to an open warning at the outset not to believe him. Possibly then the best hyperboles, as we said above in speaking of figures, are those which are not noticed as hyperboles at all. This result is obtained when they are uttered in an outburst of strong feeling, and in harmony with a certain grandeur in the crisis described, as where Thucydides is speaking of the men slaughtered in Sicily. 'For the Syracusans', he says, 'also came down and butchered them, but especially those in the water, which was thus immediately spoiled, but which they went on drinking just the same, mud and all, bloody as it was, even fighting to have it.' That blood and mud were drunk together, and yet were things fought over passes for credible in the intensity of the feeling and in the crisis. The passage in Herodotus about the men of Thermopylae is similar: 'On this spot,' he says, 'while defending themselves with daggers, that is, those who still had them left, and also with hands and with teeth, they were buried alive under the missiles of the Barbarians.' Here 'What sort of thing is it,' you will say, 'to fight with very teeth against armed men,' or what to be 'buried alive under missiles'? But it passes for true like the other; for the fact does not appear to be introduced for the sake of the hyperbole, but the hyperbole to pass because fathered by the fact. For, as I am never tired of saying, every bold experiment in language finds a solvent and a specific in deeds and passions which approach frenzy. So, in Comedy, utterances which approach the incredible pass for true because of the ludicrous:—

> He had a field no bigger than the sheet
> Which holds a Spartan letter.

For laughter too is a passion, a passion which lies in pleasure. There is an hyperbole on the side of excess, and also one on the side of defect: the common point is a straining of the truth. And, in a manner of speaking, satire is an exaggeration, namely of pettiness.

## XXXIX

The fifth of the factors which we mentioned at the outset, as contributing to Sublimity, still remains to be considered, my excellent friend; composition in words, or the precise manner of arranging them. I have already published two treatises on this subject, in which I have rendered full account of such theoretical views as I could form; and need, therefore, only add, as necessary for our present purpose, that melody is not only an instrument natural to man, which produces persuasion and pleasure; it is a marvellous instrument, which produces passion, yet leaves him free. Does not the flute implant within the hearers certain passions, and place them out of their senses, full of wild revelry? Does it not set a certain rhythmical step, and force them to keep step with it, and to conform themselves to the air, though a man have 'no music in him'? Do not the notes of the harp, which in themselves signify nothing, yet by the interchange of sounds, the mutual accompaniment, the mingled harmony, cast upon us a spell, which is, you well know, often marvellous; although these are but images and bastard copies of persuasion, not genuine forces operative upon human nature? And then are we not to think that composition—being as it is, a special melody of words, words which are in man by nature and which reach his very soul, and not his ears alone; stirring, as it does, manifold ideas of words, thoughts, actions, beauty, tunefulness, all of them things born and bred within us; carrying moreover, by the very commixture and multiplicity of its own sounds, the passion which is present to the speaker into the souls of the bystanders, and bringing them into partnership with himself; building phrase on phrase and so shaping whole passages of greatness—that Composition, I say, must by all these means at once soothe us as we hear and also dispose to stateliness, and high mood, and sublimity, and everything which it contains with itself, in each and every direction gaining the mastery over minds? Although it is mere folly to raise problems about things which are so fully admitted, for experience is proof sufficient, I am sure that you will think that a sublime thought, and marvellous indeed it is, which Demosthenes applied to his decree:—'This decree made the danger, which then encompassed the city, to pass away like a vapour.' But the harmony of the thought, no less than the thought itself, has given it voice. For the whole expression rests upon the dactylic rhythms, the most noble and productive of grandeur, which make the structure of heroic metre the noblest known to us. Take any word out of its own place, and transfer it where you will:—'This proposal, like a vapour, made the danger of that day to pass away'; or, again, cut off one syllable only:—'made it to pass like vapour'; and you will learn how closely the rhythm echoes

the sublimity.   For the actual phrase 'like a vapour' moves with the
first rhythm long, if measured by four times.   Cut out the one syllable,
you have 'as vapour', the curtailment mutilates the grandeur; as, on
the other hand, if you lengthen it out, 'made to pass away like to a vapour', the sense is the same, but not the effect on the ear, because by the
length of the times at the end of the phrase, its sheer sublimity is broken
up and unstrung.

## XL

Language is made grand in the highest degree by that which corresponds to the collocation of limbs in the body, of which no one, if cut off
from another, has anything noticeable in itself, yet all in combination
produce a perfect structure.   So great passages, when separate and scattered in different parts, scatter also the sublimity; but if they are formed
by partnership into a body, and also enclosed by the bond of rhythm,
the limits which encircle them give them new voice; one might put it
that grand effects within a period contribute to a common fund of grandeur.   However it has been already shown that many prose writers and
poets of no natural sublimity, possibly themselves altogether wanting in
grandeur, and using in general common and popular words, such as
contribute nothing remarkable, have yet, by mere arrangement and
adjustment, attained a real dignity and distinction of style, in which
no pettiness is apparent; so, amongst many others, Philistus, Aristophanes in certain passages, Euripides in most.   After the murder of his
children Hercules cries:—

I am full fraught with ills—no stowing more.

The phrase is quite popular, but has become  sublime because the
handling of the words conforms to the subject.   If you place the words
in other combinations, you will see clearly that Euripides is a poet of
composition rather than of intellect.—  When Dirce is being dragged
away by the bull:—

Where'er it chanced,
Rolling around he with him ever drew
Wife, oak-tree, rock, in constant interchange.

The conception in itself is a noble one, but has become more forcible
from the rhythm not being hurried, nor borne along as on rollers; the
words are solidly attached to one another, and checks caused by the
syllabic quantities, which result in stability and grandeur.

## XLI

There is nothing which introduces pettiness into sublime passages
so much as a broken and excited rhythm, as pyrrhics, trochees, and
dichorees, which fall into a thorough dancing measure.   For in prose
complete rhythm appears dainty and trivial, and entirely lacks passion,
because the sameness makes it superficial.   The worst point of all about this
is, that, as ballad-music draws away the hearers perforce from the subject
to itself, so prose which is made over-rhythmical does not give the hearers
the effect of the prose but that of the rhythm; so that in some cases,
knowing beforehand the endings as they become due, people actually
beat time with the speakers, and get before them, and render the movement too soon, as though in a dance.   Equally devoid of grandeur are
passages which lie too close, cut up into scraps and minute syllables, and
bound together by clamps between piece and piece in the way of socket
and insertion.

## XLII

Another means of lowering sublimity is excessive conciseness of expression; a grand phrase is maimed when it is gathered into too short a
compass.   I must be understood to refer not to mere undue compression,
but to what is absolutely small and comminuted: contraction stunts the
sense, a short cut goes straight.   In the other direction it is clear that
what is spun out is lifeless, all 'which conjures up unseasonable length.'

## XLIII

Pettiness of words, again, is strangely potent in making fine passages
mean.   Thus in Herodotus the storm has been finely described with
great spirit, so far as the ideas go, but certain words are included which
are surely too ignoble for the subject; this in particular, 'when the sea
boiled', the word 'boiled' greatly spoils the sublimity, being so poor in
sound; then he has 'the wind flagged,' and again 'Those who were about
the wreck and clutching it met an unwelcome end,' 'flagged' is an
undignified vulgarism, and 'unwelcome' is an inadequate word for such a
disaster.   So also Theopompus, in a brilliant and elaborate account of
the descent of the Persian army upon Egypt, by a few paltry words has
spoilt the whole passage:—'For what city of Asia, or what tribe, did not
send envoys to the King?   What beautiful or costly thing which earth
grows, or art produces, was not brought as a gift to him? Were there
not many and costly coverlets and cloaks, purple, and variegated, and
white pieces, and many tents of gold, furnished with all things
serviceable; many costly robes and couches?   There were also vessels of

wrought gold and silver, drinking cups and bowls, of which you might have seen some crusted with precious stones, others worked with elaborate and costly art: besides these were untold quantities of arms, some Greek, some barbarian, beasts of burden in exceedingly great numbers, and victims fatted for slaughter, many bushels of spices, many sacks and bags and sheets of papyrus and all other commodities; and so many pickled carcases of all sorts of animals, that the size of the heaps made those who approached from a distance think that they were mounds and hillocks as they jostled one another.' He runs off from the loftier to the more humble details, whereas he ought to have made his description rise in the other direction. With his marvellous account of the whole provision he has mixed up his bags and spices, and has drawn to the imagination—a cook-shop! Suppose one had really placed among those things of show, in the middle of the gold and the gem-crusted cups and the silver vessels, common bags and sacks, the effects to the eye would have been unseemly; so in a description each of such words placed there out of season is an ugliness and, so to say, a blot where it stands. It was open to him to go through all in broad outline: as he has told us of heaps taken to be hillocks, so he might have given us all the rest of the pageant, camels, a multitude of beasts of burden carrying all supplies for luxury and the enjoyment of the table, or he might have specified heaps of every sort of grain of all that is best for confectionery and daintiness; or, if he meant, at all costs, to put the whole down in an inclusive list, he might have said 'all the dainties known to victuallers and confectioners.' For we ought not in sublime passages to stoop to mean and discredited terms unless we are compelled by some strong necessity; but it would be proper even in words to keep to those which sound worthy of the subject, and to copy Nature who fashioned man; for she did not place our less honourable parts in front, nor the purgings of all gross matter, but hid them away so far as she could, and, as Xenophon tells us, removed the channels of such things to as great a distance as possible, nowhere disfiguring the beauty of the whole animal. But there is no present need to enumerate by their kinds the means of producing pettiness; when we have once shown what things make writings noble and sublime, it is clear that their opposites will make them in most cases low and uncouth.

## XLIV

One point remains, which in view of your diligence in learning, I shall not hesitate to add. This is to give a clear answer to a question lately put to me by one of our philosophers: 'I wonder,' he said, 'as assuredly do many others, how it is that in our age we have men whose genius is persuasive and statesman-like in the extreme, keen and versatile; but minds of a high order of sublimity and greatness are no longer produced, or quite exceptionally, such is the world-wide barrenness of literature that now pervades our life. Are we indeed,' he went on, 'to believe the common voice, that democracy is a good nurse of all that is great; that with free government nearly all powerful orators attained their prime, and died with it? For Freedom, they say, has the power of breeding noble spirits; it gives them hopes, and passes hand in hand with them through their eager mutual strife and their ambition to reach the first prizes. Further, because of the prizes offered to competition in common-wealths, the intellectual gifts of orators are kept in exercise and whetted by use; the rub of politics, if I may use the word, kindles them to fire; they shine, as shine they must, with the light of public freedom. But we in our day,' he went on, 'seem to be from our childhood scholars of a dutiful slavery; in its customs and practices we are enwrapped and swathed from the very infancy of our thoughts, never tasting that fairest and most abundant fount of eloquence, I mean Freedom; wherefore we turn out nothing but flatterers of portentous growth.' Other faculties, he asserted, might be the portion of mere household servants, but no slave becomes an orator; for instantly there surges up the helplessness to speak out, there is the guard on the lips enforced by the cudgel of habitude. As Homer has it:—

'Half that man's virtue doth Zeus take away,
Whom he surrenders to the servile day.'

'As then,' he went on, 'if what I hear is to be believed, the cages in which the Pygmies, also called dwarfs, are reared, not only hinder the growth of those who are shut up in them, but actually shrivel them because of the bonds lying about their bodies, so one might show that all slavery, though it be never so dutiful, is a cage of the soul and a public prison'. Here I rejoined: 'Sir,' I said, 'it is easy, and it is man's special habit, always to find fault with things present: but consider whether it may not be that what spoils noble natures is, not the peace of the universal world, but much rather this war which masters our desires, and to which no bounds are set, aye, and more than that, these passions which keep our life a prisoner and make spoil of it altogether? The love of money, which cannot be satisfied and is a disease with us all, and the love of pleasure both lead us into slavery, or rather, as one might put it, thrust our lives and ourselves down into the depths: the love of money, a disease which makes us little, the love of pleasure, which is utterly ignoble. I try to reckon it up, but I cannot discover how it is possible that we who so greatly honour boundless wealth, who, to speak more truly, make it a god, can fail to receive into our souls the kindred evils which enter it.   There follows on unmeasured and unchecked wealth, bound to it and keeping step for step, as they say, costliness of living; which, when wealth opens the way into cities and houses, enters and settles therein. When these evils have passed much time in our lives, they build nests, the wise tell us, and soon proceed to breed and engender boasting, and vapouring, and luxury; no spurious brood, but all too truly their own. For this must perforce be so; men will no longer look up, nor otherwise take any account of good reputation; little by little the ruin of their whole life is effected; all greatness of soul dwindles and withers, and ceases to be emulated, while men admire their own mortal parts, and neglect to improve the immortal.   A judge bribed for his verdict could never be a free and sound judge of things just and good, for to the corrupted judge the side which he is to take must needs appear good and just.   Even so, where bribes already rule our whole lives, and the hunt for other men's deaths, and the lying in wait for their wills, and where we purchase with our soul gain from wherever it comes, led captive each by his own luxury, do we really expect, amidst this ruin and undoing of our life, that any is yet left a free and uncorrupted judge of great things and things which reads to eternity; and that we are not downright bribed by our desire to better ourselves?   For such men as we are, it may possibly be better to be governed than to be free; since greed and grasping, if let loose together against our neighbours, as beasts out of den, would soon deluge the world evils.'   I gave the general explanation that what eats up our modern characters is the indolence in which, with few exceptions, we all now live, never working or undertaking work save for the sake of praise or of pleasure, instead of that assistance to others which is a thing worthy of emulation and of honour.

'Best leave such things to take their chance,' and pass we to the next topic; this was to be the passions, about which I promised beforehand to write in a separate paper, inasmuch as they cover a side of the general subject of speech, and of sublimity in particular.

# Epistle to the Pisones
# *(The Art of Poetry)*

### ABOUT 20 B.C.

*At the time he wrote this letter to the wealthy Piso family, Quintus Horatius Flaccus was regarded as the greatest living man of letters, a renowned and mature professional author. Assume that you are an aspiring young poet, and that you are the recipient of this epistle. What would your reactions be? And do you think that Horace wants you to react in that way? For the tone of this letter is almost as important as the substance: some have characterized it as slick or cool, and Alexander Pope described it as follows:*

> *Horace still charms with graceful negligence,*
> *And without method talks us into sense;*
> *Will, like a friend, familiarly convey*
> *The truest notions in the easiest way.*

*Whether Horace wrote without method is debatable, for, despite an apparent lack of organization, the work starts with the sketch of a mad painter and ends with one of a mad poet. His views on poetic inspiration as opposed to painstaking labor are crystal clear. He is full of professional wisdom and practical strategy; he knows the ropes. But is he cynical about literature, and does he regard poetry as merely a marketable commodity? His remarks about some of the types that*

---

Translated by Norman J. DeWitt and copyright © 1961 by Norman J. DeWitt; used by permission of Mrs. Norman J. DeWitt. First published in *Drama Survey* I, 2 (October, 1961). The numbers inserted in the translation give the approximate location of every tenth line in the Latin text; the original translation was made from Bennett and Rolfe's annotated text; the revision presented here has been checked against F. Klingner's Teubner text of 1950. (Translator's note) *people the world of literature—the arrogant amateurs, the insincere critics—should be noted.*

*As a professional, for Horace the nature of the audience is a primary source of value. Compare, for example, the bases for his discussion of character with those of Aristotle. Likewise, while Aristotle gives a history of tragedy in terms of the growth of its respective elements, Horace writes another kind of history, one based on the changing nature of the audiences. Three centuries after Aristotle, Horace passes along the Aristotelian observations regarding plot, but they are now rules: Aristotle's discussion of unity and of magnitude becomes Horace's explanation in terms of audience response and the conventions of the time. Another important change to be noted is in the concept of imitation. For Horace, as for other Romans conscious of tradition, imitation means imitation of the Greek models. This interpretation, as you will see later, is to play an important part in future critical debate, and form part of the Horatian tradition in English literary criticism.*

*If Horace has a theory of literature, it does not have the profundity of Plato's or Aristotle's, but he certainly has a theory of the literary life. What, after all, is the subject matter of approximately the last third of this epistle?*

Suppose a painter meant to attach a horse's neck to the head of a man, and to put fancy-work of many-colored feathers on limbs of creatures picked at random; the kind of thing where the torso of a shapely maiden merges into the dark rear half of a fish; would you smother your amusement, my friends, if you were let in to see the result?

Believe me, Pisones, a book will be very much like that painting if the meaningless images are put together like the dreams of a man in a fever, to the end that the head and the foot do not match the one body.

"Poets and painters have always enjoyed this fair privilege, of experimenting however they will." (10)

I know it; and I claim that privilege as a poet and, as a poet, I grant it to the painter; but not to the extent that vicious creatures mate with gentle ones, that snakes are paired with birds, lambs with tigers.

When a poem has a pretentious introduction, promising great themes, a bright red patch or two is usually stitched on, to achieve an expansive, colorful effect, as when a sacred grove and an altar of Diana are described, or a hurrying rivulet of water wandering through the lovely meadows, or the river Rhine, or a rainbow. All very well; but there was no place for these scenes at this point in the poem.

And perhaps you know how to represent a cypress tree: what good is this when the client who has paid your fee in advance is swimming for his life in the picture from the wreckage of his ship? (20)   I have started to mould a two-handled jar to hold wine: why does a pitcher come off the potter's turning wheel?   What I am getting at is this: let the work of art be whatever you want, as long as it is simple and has unity.

To you, Piso senior, and to you sons worthy of your father, I admit that the majority of us poets are tricked by our own standards.   I work hard to be brief; I turn out to be obscure.   When I try to achieve smoothness and polish, I lose punch, the work lacks life; the poet who proposes grandeur is merely pompous; the poet who tries to be too conservative creeps on the ground, afraid of gusts of wind; if he is anxious to lend marvellous variety to a single subject, he paints a dolphin in the forest, a boar in the breakers. (30) The avoidance of mistakes leads to serious defects if one is lacking in artistic sense.   The sculptor in the last studio around the [gladiatorial] school of Aemilius will mould fingernails and imitate wavy hair in bronze, but the net effect of the work will be unfortunate because he will not know how to represent the whole. If I wanted to make a comparison, I would not care to be like him any more than to go through life with an ugly nose but good-looking otherwise, with dark eyes and dark hair.

If you plan to write, adopt material to match your talents, and think over carefully what burdens your shoulders will not carry and how strong they really are.   When a writer's chosen material matches his powers, the flow of words will not fail nor will clarity and orderly arrangement. (40)   This is the virtue and charm of such arrangement, unless I am mistaken: that one says now what ought to be said and puts off for later and leaves out a great deal for the present.   The author of a poem that has been [asked for and] promised likes one thing and rejects another, is sensitive and careful in putting words together.

Again, you will have expressed yourself with distinction if a clever association gives an old word new meaning.   If it turns out to be necessary to explain recent discoveries with new terms, you will be allowed to invent words never heard by the Cethegi in their loin-cloths; (50) and licence will be given if you exercise it with due restraint; and new words, recently invented, will win acceptance if they spring from a Greek source with a minor twist in meaning.   For that matter, what will a Roman grant to Caecilius and Plautus that he takes away from Vergil and Varius?   As for me, why should I be criticized if I add a few words to my vocabulary, when the language of Cato and Ennius enriched the speech of our fathers and produced new names for things?   It has always been permissible, and always will be, to mint words stamped with the mark of contemporary coinage. (60)

As the forests change their foliage in the headlong flight of years, as the first leaves fall, so does the old crop of words pass away, and the newly born, like men in the bloom of their youth, come then to the prime of their vigor. We and our works are mortgaged to die. It may be that the land embraces Neptune and diverts the north wind from our navy, the engineering of a king; or a swamp, long unproductive, and good only for boating, now feeds nearby towns and feels the heavy burden of the plow; or it may be that a river, a ravager of fruitful fields, has changed its course, has been taught to follow a better channel: no matter, human accomplishments will pass away, much less does the status of speech endure and popular favor persist. Many things are resurrected which once had passed away, and expressions which are now respected in turn will pass, (70) if usage so decrees—the usage over which the authority and norm of daily speech have final jurisdiction.

The careers of kings and leaders, and sorrow-bringing battles: the meter in which to compose these, Homer has shown us. Laments were first expressed in couplets of unequal lines; later, sentiments of vows fulfilled were included [in this verse] as well. However, what author first published dainty elegiacs, the philologists are arguing, and up to now the dispute rests unresolved. A nasty temper armed Archilochus with his specialty, iambic lines; the sock of comedy and the elevated boot of tragedy took on this meter, (80) just the thing for on-stage conversation, to rise above the noisy audience and quite natural for relations of events. The Muse gave men of wealth and sons of gods, and the victor in the boxing ring and the horse first in the contest, and the heartaches of youth and relaxing wine, to lyric poetry to sing about.

The standard distinctions and overtones of poetic forms: why should I be addressed as a poet if I cannot observe and know nothing about them? Why should I, with a feeble sense of shame, prefer to be ignorant rather than learn them? A comic situation does not want to be treated in tragic verse forms; in the same way, the banquet of Thyestes repudiates a telling in the lines of everyday affairs, close to the level of comedy. (90) Let each form of poetry occupy the proper place allotted to it.

There are times, however, when comedy raises its voice and an angry Chremes scolds in fury with his swollen cheeks; and, in tragedy, Telephus and Peleus very often express their pain in prose, when the penniless hero and the exile both project inflated lines and complicated compound words, if they are anxious to touch the hearts of the audience with their complaints of deep distress.

It is not enough for poems to be pretty; they must have charm and they must take the heart of the hearer wheresoever they will. (100) Just as the faces of men smile back at those who smile at them, so they join with those who weep. If you want me to weep, you must first feel sorrows yourself; then your misfortunes, Telephus or Peleus, hurt me, too.  If you speak your lines badly, I'll go to sleep—or laugh out loud.  Sad words fit a mournful face, words full of threats an angry face, playful words a face in fun, words seriously expressed, a sober face.  I mean that Nature has already shaped us inwardly for every phase of fortune: fortune makes us happy, or drives us into anger or  brings us down to earth with a burden of grief and then torments us. (110)  Afterwards it brings out our emotions and our tongue acts as interpreter.  If the lines do not correspond to the emotional state of the speaker, the members of the Roman audience will  burst out laughing, regardless of their income bracket.

It will make a great deal of difference whether a comedy slave or a tragic hero is speaking, or a man of ripe old age, or a hothead in the flower of youth, or a great lady, or a worrying nursemaid, or a traveling merchant or the farmer of a few flourishing acres, a character from Colchis or an Assyrian, a native of Thebes or of Argos.

You have two choices: either follow the conventions of the stage or invent materials that are self-consistent.

If, as a writer, you happen to bring back on the stage an Achilles (120) whose honor has been satisfied, energetic, hotheaded, ruthless, eager, let him claim that laws were not made for him, that there is nothing not subject to possession by force.  Let Medea be wild and untamed, Ino an object of pity and tears, Ixion treacherous, Io a wanderer, Orestes depressed.

If you risk anything new and original on the stage and have the courage to invent a new character, let it maintain to the very end the qualities with which it first appeared—and let it be self-consistent.

It is difficult to develop everyday themes in an original way, and you would do better to present the *Iliad* in dramatic form than if you were the first to produce unknown materials never used before on stage. Material in the public domain will become your private property if you do not waste your time going around in worn-out circles, and do not be a literal translator, faithfully rendering word for word from Greek, and do not be merely an imitator, thereby getting yourself into a hole from which either good conscience, or the laws of the work itself, will forbid you to climb out.

And do not start off like this, the way a cyclic poet once did: "I shall sing of the fate of Priam and a war of renown."  What did this promise produce to match such a wide open mouth?  The mountains will go into labor and deliver a silly mouse!  How much more properly this poet began who undertook nothing in poor taste: (140) "Sing to me, Muse, of the man who, after the time of the capture of Troy, saw the ways of numbers of men and their cities." He gives thought to producing a light from the smoke, not smoke from the gleam of the firelight, so that he may bring forth beauty thereafter, and wonder, Antiphates and Scylla and with the Cyclops, Charybdis; nor does he in detail relate the return of Diomedes after the passing of Meleager, or the story of the Trojan War, starting with the twin eggs. He speeds always on to the outcome, and rushes his hearer into the midst of the action just as if the setting were known, and the events that he cannot hope to treat with brilliance, he omits. (150) And then, too, his inventions are such that fiction is mingled with fact to the end that the middle may match with the start and the end with the middle.

Listen to me: here is what I look for in a play, and with me, the public.

If you want a fan in the audience who waits for the final curtain and stays in his seat to the very end, when the singer says, "Give us a hand," you must observe the habits and manners of each period in men's lives, and the proper treatment must be given to their quickly changing characters and their years. The little boy who already knows how to talk plants his feet firmly on the ground, and is eager to play with boys of his own age, and loses his temper and for no good reason gets it back, and changes his disposition every hour. (160)

The adolescent boy with no beard as yet, when [to his relief] he at last is on his own, has fun with hounds and horses and the turf of the sunny Campus, soft as wax to be moulded to folly, resentful of advice, slow to anticipate what is good for him, throwing his money around, high-spirited and eager, quick to change his interests.

The age of maturity brings a change of interests, and the manly character seeks influence and friends, becomes a slave to ambition and is wary of commitments that he will soon have to break off with great difficulty.

Many disagreeable circumstances surround the old man; for example, he still seeks for wealth, and poor fellow, shrinks from spending it, (170) or, again, his management of everything is over-cautious and without any fire, he is indecisive, hopeful without reason, slow to act, grasping for time, hard to get along with, always complaining, always praising the way things were when he was a boy, scolding and correcting the young generation. The years as they come bring with them many advantages, and as they go, take many things away.

Do not by any chance let the character of the elderly be assigned to a younger man, or a man to a boy; we shall always insist upon the qualities of character joined and fitted to the proper age of man.

An event is either acted on the stage or is reported as happening elsewhere. (180) Events arouse our thoughts more slowly when transmitted
through the ears than when presented to the accuracy of the eye and reported to the spectator by himself.   On the other hand, do not bring out
on stage actions that should properly take place inside, and remove from
view the many events which the descriptive powers of an actor present
on the stage will soon relate.   Do not have Medea butcher her sons before
the audience, or have the ghoulish Atreus cook up human organs out in
public, or Procne turn into a bird, Cadmus into a snake.   If you show
me anything of this kind, I will not be fooled and I shall resent it.

Do not let a play consist of less than five acts or be dragged out to more
than this length, if you want it to enjoy popular demand and have a
repeat performance.

Do not have a god intervene unless the complication of the plot turns
out to be appropriate to divine solution; and do not have a fourth leading
character working hard to get in with his lines.

Have the chorus carry the part of an actor and take a manly role in the
play, and do not let them sing anything between the acts which does not
contribute to the plot and fit properly into it.   The chorus should side
with the good and give friendly advice, curb those who are angry and
befriend those who fear to do wrong; the chorus should praise a dinner
which has but few courses, healthy legal processes and law, and the conditions of peace when the gates of the city stand open; the chorus will
keep secrets, entreat the gods and pray that good fortune will come
back to the afflicted and desert the overconfident. (200)

The pipes (not, as now, displaced by the brass and their rival the
trumpet, but slender in tone and simple, with only a few stops) used to
be helpful in accompanying and supporting the chorus and in filling the
auditorium (which was not, in those days, overcrowded) with its music—
the audience in which the entire community gathered was then such
as one could count, what with its small size; it was thrifty, moral and
proper.

After the community began to win wars and extend its domain, and
the walls of the city enclosed a wider area, and one's guardian spirit was
appeased on holidays without reproach with wine in the daytime, (210)
greater license in meters and modes came to the theater.   This is to say:
what critical sense could an ignorant community have when freed from
work, the farmer mingling with the townsman, the commoner with the
gentleman?   And so the flute player added movement and display to
the old-fashioned art and trailed his costume about on the platform.
And so, again, they invented special notes for the once sober lyre, and the
unrestrained speech of the chorus gave rise to a new kind of eloquence,

wise in advice on matters of state, and its divine utterances of things to come were quite in the oracular manner of Delphic ambiguities.

The writer who entered the contest for a common goat (220) in tragic verse soon added rustic satyrs with scanty clothing, and crudely tried his hand at humor without loss of tragic dignity, for the reason that the member of the audience had to be kept in his seat by the enticements of novelties, because after taking part in the Bacchic rituals, he was drunk and rowdy. But it is expedient, nonetheless, to sanction the merry, impudent satyrs, to turn solemnity into jest, so that whatever god, whatever hero, may have been but now presented on the stage in gold and royal purple, shall not move into the slums; use vulgar speech, or, while avoiding the ground, grasp at verbal clouds and empty words. (230)

Tragedy is above spouting frivolous lines, like a modest matron told to dance on festive days; the [tragedy] will have little to do, as a respectable woman, with the boisterous satyrs.

As a writer of satyr-plays, my Pisones, I for one will not favor the commonplace and current nouns and verbs, and I shall not try to differ in vocabulary, from the speech that gives tragedy its color; it will make a difference whether Davus is speaking and the saucy Pythias who has swindled a talent out of Simo, or Silenus, the guardian and attendant of a divine foster child.

I shall follow a poetic style from well-known material, just the same as anyone may expect to do himself; (240) and just the same, if he tries it, he will perspire freely and make little progress: that's how difficult the order and connections of words are: that's how much distinction is attached to our everyday vocabulary.

Fauns imported from the woodlands, in my opinion, should be careful not to carouse around in polished lines, like boys reared at the four corners and practically brought up in the Forum, nor shout out dirty words, make scandalous remarks. I mean, they will offend members of the audience who have a house, a distinguished father, and wealth, who will not accept calmly and give the prize to entertainment that pleases the purchaser of dried peas and nuts. (250)

A long syllable following a short is called "iambic," a rapid foot; for this reason, it had the name "three-measure iambic" [trimeter] applied to itself although the beat, the same from first to last, adds up to six per line. Not so very long ago, so that the line might come to the ear more slowly and with a little more weight, the iambic shared its traditional privileges with the steady spondee, accommodating and tolerant, with the reservation that the iambic foot would not, as a partner, move out of its first and fourth position. The spondee, I may add, rarely appears in

Accius' "noble" trimeters; and it burdens Ennius' verses, sent ponderously
out on the stage, (260) with the charge of overhasty work and the lack
of care and attention, or shameful neglect of the principles of art.

No critic whom you may name in Rome can see that a poem is unmusical; and Roman poets have been given unwarranted freedom.
Because of that, am I to wander around and write free verse? Or am
I to assume that everyone will see my mistakes and play it safe and stay
cautiously within the limits of the license I may be granted? No;
what I have been saying simply amounts to this: I have merely managed
to escape criticism; I have not earned praise.

You—turn our Greek models in your hands at night, turn them
in the daytime. But, you say, your forefathers praised the lives and
jokes of Plautus; (270) they were much too tolerant of both; they admired him, if I may so, stupidly, assuming that you and I know how to
tell the difference between expressions in poor and good taste, and
have had enough experience to tell, on our fingers and by ear, when a
sound has been produced according to the rules of meter.

Thespis is said to have discovered the form of tragic poetry and to
have hauled his plays around on carts: plays sung and acted by those
who had smeared their faces with sediment from wine jars.

After Thespis: the discoverer of the mask and colorful costume, Aeschylus, also constructed the stage on a limited scale, and taught how to speak
in lofty style and to walk in the high boots of tragedy. (280)

After these came old comedy, not without considerable popular
approval; but its freedom of speech fell off into license and a violence
that deserved restraint by law: law was acknowledged and the chorus
was disgraced into silence when its right to libel was removed.

Our Roman poets have not failed to try all forms of drama; they
deserve no honor whatsoever for venturing to desert the trail blazed by
the Greeks and attempting to give fame to Roman events—those who
presented serious history or comedies of daily life. Nor would the land
of the Latins be more mighty in valor and glory in war than in words,
if the toil of time and polish did not discourage our poets, every one of
them. (290) As for you, who represent the bloodline of Pompilius, see
that you are severe in your censure of a poem that many a day and many
an erasure has not trimmed down, and not corrected ten times by the
test of a newly-cut fingernail.

Because Democritus believed natural talent to contribute more to
success than pitiful technical competence, he barred from Helicon all
poets who were mentally well-balanced; most poets do not bother to
trim their nails, their beards, they look for out-of-the-way places, steer
clear of the baths. I mean, one will acquire the title of poet and the

reputation, if he never entrusts his head—too crazy to be cured by medicine even from three Anticyras—to Licinus the barber. (300)

Oh, how inept I am! I have myself purged of bile as the spring season comes on! Otherwise no man could write a better poem. But it isn't worth the trouble. I'll play the role of whetstone, which is good enough to put an edge on iron but is out of luck when it comes to cutting. While I write nothing myself, I'll teach the gift, the business of the poet, where he gets his material, what nourishes and forms the poet, what is appropriate, the way of right and wrong.

The origin and source of poetry is the wisdom to write according to moral principles: the Socratic dialogues will be able to clarify your philosophy, (310) and the words themselves will freely follow the philosophy, once it has been seen before you write. The man who has learned what he owes to his country, what he owes to his friends, what love is due a father, how a brother and a family friend are loved, what the duties of a senator are, what the duties of a judge, what roles a leader sent to war should play: he knows, as a matter of course, how to assign to each character what is appropriate for it.

I shall tell you to respect the examples of life and of good character—you who have learned the art of imitation—and from this source bring forth lines that live. Quite often a play which is impressive in spots and portrays good character, but with no particular charm, without real content and really good writing (320) will give the public more pleasure and hold them better than lines without ideas and with resounding platitudes.

To the Greeks, genius, the gift of speaking in well-rounded phrases—these the Muse presented. The Greeks are greedy for nothing save acclaim. The Roman boys learn to calculate percentages of money by long divison. "Let the son of Albinus tell me: if one-twelfth is taken from five-twelfths, what's the remainder? You should have been able to tell us by this time." "One-third." "*Très bien!* You'll make a good businessman. Add a twelfth, what happens?" "One-half." (330) When this smut, this worrying about business arithmetic, has permeated our minds, do you think we can expect to put together poems to be treated with oil of cedar and kept in cypress-wood cases?

Poets aim either to help or to amuse the reader, or to say what is pleasant and at the same time what is suitable. Whatever you have in the way of a lesson, make it short, so that impressionable minds can quickly grasp your words and hold them faithfully: every unnecessary word spills over and is lost to a heart that is already filled up to the brim.

Whatever you invent to please, see that it is close to truth, so your play does not require belief in anything it wants; do not have it pull a living child from Lamia's insides just after she has eaten lunch. (340)

The centuries of elders in the audience cannot stand a play that has no moral; the noble young gentlemen ignore an austere composition; but the writer who has combined the pleasant with the useful [*miscuit utile dulci*] wins on all points, by delighting the reader while he gives advice. This kind of book makes money for the Sosii [publishers], this kind of book is sold across the sea and prolongs the famous writer's age.

There are, however, faults which I should like to overlook: I mean that the string, when plucked, does not give forth the sound that heart and hand desire; it very often gives back a high note when one calls for a low; and the arrow does not always hit precisely the mark at which it aimed and threatened.   (350) So, when most of the passages are brilliant, I am personally not bothered by blots, which are spattered here and there by oversight or those which human nature failed to guard against enough.

Well, what's the point?

If a library copyist keeps on making the same mistake, even though he has been warned about it, there is no excuse for him, and a lyre player who always strikes the same sour note is laughed at; so a writer who is consistently sloppy is in a class with Choerilus—you know who I mean— whom I regard with amused admiration if he happens to write two or three good passages.   Similarly, I think it's too bad whenever good old Homer dozes off, as he does from time to time, but when all is said and done, it is natural enough for drowsiness to creep up on a long job of writing.   (360) A poem is like a painting: you will find a picture which will attract you more if you stand up close, another if you stand farther back.   This picture favors shadow, another likes to be viewed in the light—neither has apprehensions about the keen perceptions of the good critic.   Here's one that pleases you only once; here's another that you'll like if you come back to it ten times.

And now to address the older of the two of you: ah, even though your tastes have been formed to appreciate the right things by your father (as well as by others), and you have much good sense of your own, acknowledge what I am going to say and remember it: perfectly proper concessions are made to second-raters in certain fields.   A second-rate legal authority and member of the bar (370) can be far from having the qualities of Messala, a very able speaker, and not be as learned as Cascellius Aulus, but still he has a certain value—*a second-rate poet gets no advertising posters from either men, gods, or booksellers.*

You know how music off-key grates on your nerves at an otherwise pleasant banquet, and greasy ointment for your hair, and bitter honey from Sardinia mixed with poppy seeds, because the banquet could be carried on without them.   That is how it is with poetry: created and developed to give joy to human hearts; but if it takes one step down from the very highest point of merit, it slides all the way back to the bottom.

The lad who does not know how to take part in sports keeps out of the cavalry exercises in the Campus; and if he has not learned how to work with the ball, the disc or the hoop (380)—he sits where he is because he is afraid that the spectators, jammed together, will laugh at his expense—there will be nothing he can do about it. For all of that, the man who has no notion of how to compose poetry has the nerve to go ahead anyhow. Why shouldn't he? After all, he's a free man and born free and what's more to the point, his income is in the top brackets—which puts him beyond criticism.

As for you, my boy, don't do or say anything that Minerva would not approve: that's your standard of judgment, that's your philosophy. However, if you ever do write something, see that it comes into court—to the ears of Maecius as critic, or your father's, or mine, and also see that it is weighted down in storage, put away between the leaves of parchment for revision in the ninth year; you can always edit what you haven't published: the word that is uttered knows no return. (390)

Orpheus, a holy man and spokesman for the gods, forced the wild men of the woods to give up human killing and gruesome feasting; he is said, because of these powers, to soothe tigers and the raging of the lion; yes and Amphion, the builder of the city of Thebes, is said to move rocks with his lyre and with the softness of song to lead them where he will.

I will tell you what was once the poet's wisdom: to decide what were public and what were private suits at law, to say what was sacred and what was not, to enjoin from sexual license, provide a code of conduct for marriage, to build up towns, and carve the laws on wooden tablets. This was the way honor and renown came to god-like poet-preachers and their songs. (400)

After these, Homer gained renown, and Tyrtaeus with his verses whetted the spirits of males for Mars and war; oracles were given in the form of poems and the way of life was shown; the favor of kings was sought in Pierian strains; and dramatic festivals were invented and thus the end of a long task [of development]—in case the Muse in her lyric artistry and Apollo with his song embarrass you.

The question has been asked: is good poetry created by nature or by training?

Personally, I cannot see what good enthusiasm is or uncultivated talent without a rich vein of genius; (410) each requires the help of the other and forms a friendly compact. The would-be poet whose passion is to reach the hoped-for goal in this race for fame, has worked hard in boyhood and endured a great deal, has sweated and shivered, abstained from women and wine; the artist who plays the pipe at the Pythian games has first learned his art and lived in terror of a teacher. Nowadays it's enough to have said, "I beat out wonderful poems; the hell with the rest of the mob; it's a dirty deal for me to be left at the starting line and admit that I obviously don't know what I never learned."

Like a huckster who collects a crowd to buy his wares, the poet with his wealth in land, with wealth resting on coin put out at interest, tells yes-men to come to his readings for gain. (420) Yes, indeed; if there is a man who can set out a really fat banquet, and co-sign notes for irresponsible paupers, and save the neck of the client tangled in a murder trial, I'll be surprised if, for all his wealth, he can tell the difference between a liar and an honest friend! Whether you have already given someone a present or only expect to do so, don't let him near your verses when he's full of joy: I mean, he'll gush "Lovely! Great! Swell!" On top of this, he'll turn pale, he'll even squeeze drops of dew from sympathetic eyes, leap to his feet and stamp on the ground. (430)

The way hired mourners wail at a funeral and—so they say—carry on more painfully than those who sorrow quite sincerely, thus the critic with his tongue in cheek is more deeply moved than the ordinary flatterer. Rich men are said to keep pushing glasses of wine at, and to torment with wine poured straight, the man whom they are trying hard to see through—to see if he is worthy of friendship. If you will put together poems, motives disguised with a foxy expression will never deceive you.

If you were to read anything to Quintilius, "Change this, please," he kept saying, "and this." If you said you couldn't do better, you'd tried twice, three times, with no success, (440) Quintilius used to say to rub it out and put back on the anvil the lines that were spoiled on the lathe. If you preferred to defend your mistake, not revise it, he would not waste another word or go to more useless trouble to keep you from being your only friend, with no competitors.

A true critic and a wise one will scold you for weak lines, blame you for rough ones, he'll indicate unpolished lines with a black cross-mark made with his pen, he'll cut out pretentious embellishments, make you clarify obscure phrases, remove ambiguities, mark things to be changed, he'll turn into an Aristarchus, and he will not say, "Why should I hurt the feelings of a friend over these trifles?" (450) Well, these trifles will get you into serious trouble once you have been laughed down and given a poor reception.

As in the case of a man with a bad attack of the itch or inflammation of the liver or one who's offended Diana—he's moon-struck—everyone with any sense is afraid to touch the madman and keeps out of the way of the poet; small boys pester him and don't know any better than to follow him around. If, while burping out his lines and thinking they're sublime, he goes off the roadway, falls into an excavation or a well, like a hunter intent on his blackbirds—he can yell so you can hear him a mile away, "Help! Hey, neighbors!"—no one would be worried about fishing him out. (460) If someone should get excited about rescuing him and let down a rope, I'll say, "How do you know that he didn't do it on purpose when he threw himself down there, and doesn't want to be rescued?" And I'll tell the story about the death of the Sicilian poet.

While he had a yearning to be regarded as an immortal god, Empedocles was cool enough to jump down into the red-hot crater of Aetna. Let poets have the right to perish; issue them a license! When you rescue a man against his will, you do the same as kill him. This isn't the first time he's done it, either; and if he's hauled out, he still won't behave like a human and give up his love of dying for publicity. And it isn't very clear, either, why he keeps on grinding out his verses, (470) whether he's used his father's funeral urn as a pisspot or whether he's tampered with the boundary markers of a holy plot of ground—an act of sacrilege. He's crazy, that's sure; and like a bear that's powerful enough to break the bars at the front of his cage, this dedicated elocutionist puts to flight the scholar and the layman without discrimination. Yes, and when he catches one, he'll hold on to him and recite him to death. You can be sure he won't let go of the hide of his victim until he's as full of blood as a leech.

# An Apology for Poetry

## 1595

*Sidney slips into his defense of poetry casually, almost apologetically (but contrast it to the vigorous eloquence of the conclusion): an anecdote, a story that makes its point indirectly. That is how stories work, by conveying their moral truths artistically, much as a cherry-flavored medicine works its good upon us. That poetry delights us even Plato had granted—the pleasure it provides is, in fact, one source of its danger—but Sidney's purpose is to show that it is a better teacher than moral philosophy or history; he will prove that poetry is the very best agent for leading men to act virtuously. But why must men be taught to act virtuously? Sidney's psychological model is the Christian concept of fallen man, possessed of an "erected wit" and an "infected will." In one sense the essay may be regarded as a treatise on educational psychology, for to "move men to virtuous action" is to motivate them to be better than they are. In Sidney's curriculum, neither philosophy nor history can do what poetry does, since poetry combines the precepts of one with the examples of the other, and in addition uses all the pleasurable devices of art to make instruction palatable.*

From *Criticism: The Major Texts*, edited by Walter Jackson Bate; copyright, 1952, by Harcourt Brace Jovanovich, Inc. and reprinted with their permission. Written probably in 1583, and first published in 1595 in two slightly different versions: the *Defense of Poesie* (printed by Ponsonby) and the *Apologie for Poetrie* (printed by Olney). The latter text is used here, and the spelling has been modernized.

*Primarily a moral critic, Sidney ranges widely over all history for evidence to support his case. In so doing he expands his definition of poetry beyond mere "rhyming and versing," although these too are justified on the grounds of their educational benefits; finally among the ranks of poets he welcomes the historian Herodotus and Plato, the enemy of poets. What Sidney means by poetry, eventually, is a concept worth examining. It is also instructive to note how Sidney responds to Plato's argument that poetry injures man's moral character. Does he answer Plato's charges or does he shift the terms of the argument?*

*Like other Renaissance critics, Sidney draws heavily from classical sources; thus, for example, his formal definition of poetry as a speaking picture echoes Horace. (Incidentally, you might wonder why this definition is withheld until well into the essay.) In this same definition, Sidney also cites Aristotle, but in a way that might make Aristotle question the legitimacy of the allusion. Is Sidney primarily an Aristotelian or a Horatian critic? In this connection, also, why does Sidney not rank tragedy as the highest form of poetry?*

WHEN THE right virtuous Edward Wotton and I were at the Emperor's Court together, we gave ourselves to learn horsemanship of John Pietro Pugliano, one that with great commendation had the place of an esquire in his stable. And he, according to the fertileness of the Italian wit, did not only afford us the demonstration of his practice, but sought to enrich our minds with the contemplations therein which he thought most precious. But with none I remember mine ears were at any time more loaden, than when (either angered with slow payment, or moved with our learner-like admiration) he exercised his speech in the praise of his faculty. He said, soldiers were the noblest estate of mankind, and horsemen the noblest of soldiers. He said they were the masters of war and ornaments of peace; speedy goers and strong abiders; triumphers both in camps and courts. Nay, to so unbelieved a point he proceeded, as that no earthly thing bred such wonder to a prince as to be a good horseman. Skill of government was but a *pedanteria*[1] in comparison. Then would he add certain praises, by telling what a peerless beast a horse was, the only serviceable courtier without flattery, the beast of most beauty, faithfulness, courage, and such more, that, if I had not been a piece of a logician before I came to him, I think he would have persuaded me to have wished myself a horse.

[1] That is, mere pedantry, or schoolbook knowledge, in comparison.

But thus much at least with his no few words he drove into me, that self-love is better than any gilding to make that seem gorgeous wherein ourselves are parties.   Wherein, if Pugliano's strong affection and weak arguments will not satisfy you, I will give you a nearer example of myself, who (I know not by what mischance) in these my not old years and idlest times having slipped into the title of a poet, am provoked to say something unto you in the defence of that my unelected vocation, which if I handle with more good will than good reasons, bear with me, since the scholar is to be pardoned that followeth the steps of his master.   And yet I must say that, as I have just cause to make a pitiful defence of poor Poetry, which from almost the highest estimation of learning is fallen to be the laughing-stock of children, so have I need to bring some more available proofs, since the former is by no man barred of his deserved credit, the silly latter hath had even the names of philosophers used to the defacing of it, with great danger of civil war among the Muses.

And first, truly, to all them that professing learning inveigh against Poetry may justly be objected, that they go very near to ungratefulness, to seek to deface that which, in the noblest nations and languages that are known, hath been the first light-giver to ignorance, and first nurse, whose milk by little and little enabled them to feed afterwards of tougher knowledges.   And will they now play the hedgehog that, being received into the den, drove out his host, or rather the vipers, that with their birth kill their parents?   Let learned Greece in any of her manifold sciences be able to show me one book before Musaeus, Homer, and Hesiod, all three nothing else but poets.   Nay, let any history be brought that can say any writers were there before them, if they were not men of the same skill, as Orpheus, Linus, and some other are named, who, having been the first of that country that made pens deliverers of their knowledge to their posterity, may justly challenge to be called their fathers in learning, for not only in time they had this priority (although in itself antiquity be venerable) but went before them, as causes to draw with their charming sweetness the wild untamed wits to an admiration of knowledge, so, as Amphion was said to move stones with his poetry to build Thebes, and Orpheus to be listened to by beasts—indeed stony and beastly people.   So among the Romans were Livius Andronicus, and Ennius.   So in the Italian language the first that made it aspire to be a treasure-house of Science were the poets Dante, Boccaccio, and Petrarch.   So in our English were Gower and Chaucer.

After whom, encouraged and delighted with their excellent fore-going, others have followed, to beautify our mother tongue, as well in the same kind as in other arts.   This did so notably show itself, that the philosophers of Greece durst not a long time appear to the world but under the masks of poets.  So Thales, Empedocles, and Parmenides sang their natural philosophy in verses; so did Pythagoras and Phocylides their moral counsels; so did Tyrtaeus in war matters, and Solon in matters of policy: or rather, they, being poets, did exercise their delightful vein in those points of highest knowledge, which before them lay hid to the world. For that wise Solon was directly a poet it is manifest, having written in verse the notable fable of the Atlantic Island, which was continued by Plato.

And truly, even Plato, whosoever well considereth shall find that in the body of his work, though the inside and strength were Philosophy, the skin as it were and beauty depended most of Poetry: for all standeth upon dialogues, wherein he feigneth many honest burgesses of Athens to speak of such matters, that, if they had been set on the rack, they would never have confessed them, besides his poetical describing the circumstances of their meetings, as the well ordering of a banquet, the delicacy of a walk, with interlacing mere tales, as Gyges' Ring, and others, which who knoweth not to be flowers of poetry did never walk into Apollo's garden.

And even historiographers (although their lips sound of things done, and verity be written in their foreheads) have been glad to borrow both fashion and perchance weight of poets.  So Herodotus entitled his history by the name of the nine Muses; and both he and all the rest that followed him either stole or usurped of Poetry their passionate describing of passions, the many particularities of battles, which no man could affirm, or, if that be denied me, long orations put in the mouths of great kings and captains, which it is certain they never pronounced.  So that, truly, neither philosopher nor historiographer could at the first have entered into the gates of popular judgements, if they had not taken a great passport of Poetry, which in all nations at this day, where learning flourisheth not, is plain to be seen, in all which they have some feeling of poetry.  In Turkey, besides their law-giving divines, they have no other writers but poets.  In our neighbour country Ireland, where truly learning goeth very bare, yet are their poets held in a devout reverence. Even among the most barbarous and simple Indians where no writing is, yet have they their poets, who make and sing songs, which they call *Areytos*, both of their ancestors' deeds and praises of their gods—a sufficient probability that, if ever learning come among them, it must be by having their hard dull wits softened and sharpened with the sweet delights of Poetry.  For until they find a pleasure in the exercises of the mind, great promises of much knowledge will little persuade them that know not the fruits of knowledge.  In Wales, the true remnant of the ancient Britons, as there are good authorities to show the long time they had poets, which they called bards, so through all the conquests of Romans, Saxons, Danes, and Normans, some of whom did seek to ruin all memory of learning from among them, yet do their poets, even to this day, last; so as it is not more notable in soon beginning than in long continuing. But since the authors of most of our sciences were the Romans, and before them the Greeks, let us a little stand upon their authorities, but even so far as to see what names they have given unto this now scorned skill.

Among the Romans a poet was called *Vates*, which is as much as a diviner, foreseer, or prophet, as by his conjoined words *vaticinium* and *vaticinari* is manifest: so heavenly a title did that excellent people bestow upon this heart-ravishing knowledge.   And so far were they carried into the admiration thereof, that they thought in the chanceable hitting upon any such verses great foretokens of their following fortunes were placed. Whereupon grew the word of *Sortes Virgilianae,* when, by sudden opening Virgil's book, they lighted upon any verse of his making: whereof the histories of the emperors' lives are full, as of Albinus, the governor of our island, who in his childhood met with this verse,

*Arma amens capio nec sat rationis in armis:*[2]

and in his age performed it: which, although it were a very vain and god-less superstition, as also it was to think that spirits were commanded by such verses—whereupon this word charms, derived of *carmina,* cometh—so yet serveth it to show the great reverence those wits were held in. And altogether not without ground, since both the Oracles of Delphos and Sybilla's prophecies were wholly delivered in verses.   For that same exquisite observing of number and measure in words, and that high flying liberty of conceit proper to the poet, did seem to have some divine force in it.

And may not I presume a little further, to show the reasonableness of this word *Vates,* and say that the holy David's Psalms are a divine poem? If I do, I shall not do it without the testimony of great learned men, both ancient and modern.   But even the name Psalms will speak for me, which, being interpreted, is nothing but Songs; then that it is fully written in metre, as all learned Hebricians agree, although the rules be not yet fully found; lastly and principally, his handling his prophecy, which is merely poetical.   For what else is the awaking his musical instruments, the often and free changing of persons, his notable *prosopopeias,*[3] when he maketh you, as it were, see God coming in His majesty, his telling of the beasts' joyfulness, and hills' leaping, but a heavenly poesy, wherein almost he showeth himself a passionate lover of that unspeakable and

---

[2] I seize upon arms, while frenzied; nor is there enough reason for arms (*Aeneid,* II, 314).
[3] Use of personification.

everlasting beauty to be seen by the eyes of the mind, only cleared by faith? But truly now having named him, I fear me I seem to profane that holy name, applying it to Poetry, which is among us thrown down to so ridiculous an estimation. But they that with quiet judgements will look a little deeper into it, shall find the end and working of it such, as, being rightly applied, deserveth not to be scourged out of the Church of God.

But now, let us see how the Greeks named it, and how they deemed of it. The Greeks called him "a poet," which name hath, as the most excellent, gone through other languages. It cometh of this word *Poiein*, which is "to make": wherein, I know not whether by luck or wisdom, we Englishmen have met with the Greeks in calling him "a maker": which name, how high and incomparable a title it is, I had rather were known by marking the scope of other sciences than by my partial allegation.

There is no art delivered to mankind that hath not the works of Nature for his principal object, without which they could not consist, and on which they so depend, as they become actors and players, as it were, of what Nature will have set forth. So doth the astronomer look upon the stars, and, by that he seeth, setteth down what order Nature hath taken therein. So do the geometrician and arithmetician in their diverse sorts of quantities. So doth the musician in times tell you which by nature agree, which not. The natural philosopher thereon hath his name, and the moral philosopher standeth upon the natural virtues, vices, and passions of man; and "follow Nature" (saith he) "therein, and thou shalt not err." The lawyer saith what men have determined; the historian what men have done. The grammarian speaketh only of the rules of speech; and the rhetorician and logician, considering what in Nature will soonest prove and persuade, thereon give artificial rules, which still are compassed within the circle of a question according to the proposed matter. The physician weigheth the nature of a man's body, and the nature of things helpful or hurtful unto it. And the metaphysic, though it be in the second and abstract notions, and therefore be counted supernatural, yet doth he indeed build upon the depth of Nature. Only the poet, disdaining to be tied to any such subjection, lifted up with the vigour of his own invention, doth grow in effect another nature, in making things either better than Nature bringeth forth, or, quite anew, forms such as never were in Nature, as the Heroes, Demigods, Cyclopes, Chimeras, Furies, and such like: so as he goeth hand in hand with Nature, not enclosed within the narrow warrant of her gifts, but freely ranging only within the zodiac of his own wit.

Nature never set forth the earth in so rich tapestry as divers poets have done—neither with pleasant rivers, fruitful trees, sweet-smelling flowers, nor whatsoever else may make the too much loved earth more lovely. Her world is brazen, the poets only deliver a golden. But let those things alone, and go to man—for whom as the other things are, so it seemeth in him her uttermost cunning is employed—and know whether she have brought forth so true a lover as Theagenes, so constant a friend as Pylades, so valiant a man as Orlando, so right a prince as Xenophon's Cyrus, so excellent a man every way as Virgil's Aeneas. Neither let this be jestingly conceived, because the works of the one be essential, the other in imitation or fiction; for any understanding knoweth the skill of the artificer standeth in that idea or foreconceit of the work, and not in the work itself. And that the poet hath that idea is manifest, by delivering them forth in such excellency as he hath imagined them. Which delivering forth also is not wholly imaginative as, we are wont to say by them that build castles in the air: but so far substantially it worketh, not only to make a Cyrus, which had been but a particular excellency, as Nature might have done, but to bestow a Cyrus upon the world, to make many Cyruses, if they will learn aright why and how that maker made him.

Neither let it be deemed too saucy a comparison to balance the highest point of man's wit with the efficacy of Nature; but rather give right honour to the heavenly Maker of that maker, who, having made man to His own likeness, set him beyond and over all the works of that second nature: which in nothing he showeth so much as in Poetry, when with the force of a divine breath he bringeth things forth far surpassing her doings, with no small argument to the incredulous of that first accursed fall of Adam, since our erected wit maketh us know what perfection is, and yet our infected will keepeth us from reaching unto it. But these arguments will by few be understood, and by fewer granted. Thus much (I hope) will be given me, that the Greeks with some probability of reason gave him the name above all names of learning. Now let us go to a more ordinary opening of him, that the truth may be more palpable: and so I hope, though we get not so unmatched a praise as the etymology of his names will grant, yet his very description, which no man will deny, shall not justly be barred from a principal commendation.

Poesy therefore is an art of imitation, for so Aristotle termeth it in his word *Mimesis*, that is to say, a representing, counterfeiting, or figuring forth—to speak metaphorically, a speaking picture; with this end, to teach and delight. Of this have been three several kinds. The chief, both in antiquity and excellency, were they that did imitate the inconceivable excellencies of God. Such were David in his Psalms; Solomon in his Song of Songs, in his Ecclesiastes, and Proverbs; Moses and Deborah in their Hymns; and the writer of Job, which, beside other, the learned

Emanuel Tremellius and Franciscus Junius do entitle the poetical part of the Scripture. Against these none will speak that hath the Holy Ghost in due holy reverence.

In this kind, though in a full wrong divinity, were Orpheus, Amphion, Homer in his Hymns, and many other, both Greeks and Romans, and this poesy must be used by whosoever will follow St. James's counsel in singing psalms when they are merry, and I know is used with the fruit of comfort by some, when, in sorrowful pangs of their death-bringing sins, they find the consolation of the never-leaving goodness.

The second kind is of them that deal with matters philosophical: either moral, as Tyrtaeus, Phocylides, and Cato; or natural, as Lucretius and Virgil's Georgics; or astronomical, as Manilius and Pontanus; or historical, as Lucan; which who mislike, the fault is in their judgements quite out of taste, and not in the sweet food of sweetly uttered knowledge. But because this second sort is wrapped within the fold of the proposed subject, and takes not the course of his own invention, whether they properly be poets or no let grammarians dispute; and go to the third, indeed right poets, of whom chiefly this question ariseth, betwixt whom and these second is such a kind of difference as betwixt the meaner sort of painters, who counterfeit only such faces as are set before them, and the more excellent, who, having no law but wit, bestow that in colours upon you which is fittest for the eye to see, as the constant though lamenting look of Lucretia, when she punished in herself another's fault.

Wherein he painteth not Lucretia whom he never saw, but painteth the outward beauty of such a virtue. For these third be they which most properly do imitate to teach and delight, and to imitate borrow nothing of what is, hath been, or shall be; but range, only reined with learned discretion, into the divine consideration of what may be, and should be. These be they that, as the first and most noble sort may justly be termed *Vates*, so there are waited on in the excellentest languages and best understandings, with the foredescribed name of Poets; for these indeed do merely make to imitate, and imitate both to delight and teach, and delight to move men to take that goodness in hand, which without delight they would fly as from a stranger, and teach, to make them know that goodness whereunto they are moved: which being the noblest scope to which ever any learning was directed, yet want there not idle tongues to bark at them. These be subdivided into sundry more special denom-inations. The most notable be the Heroic, Lyric, Tragic, Comic, Satiric, Iambic, Elegiac, Pastoral, and certain others, some of these being termed according to the matter they deal with, some by the sorts of verses they liked best to write in; for indeed the greatest part of poets have apparelled their poetical inventions in that numbrous kind of writing which is called verse—indeed but apparelled, verse being but an ornament and no cause to Poetry, since there have been many most excellent poets that never versified, and now swarm many versifiers that need never answer to the name of poets. For Xenophon, who did imitate so excellently as to give us *effigiem iusti imperii*, "the portraiture of a just Empire," under name of Cyrus (as Cicero saith of him), made therein an absolute heroical poem.

So did Heliodorus in his sugared invention of that picture of love in Theagenes and Chariclea; and yet both these writ in prose: which I speak to show that it is not rhyming and versing that maketh a poet—no more than a long gown maketh an advocate, who though he pleaded in armour should be an advocate and no soldier. But it is that feigning notable images of virtues, vices, or what else, with that delightful teaching, which must be the right describing note to know a poet by, although indeed the Senate of Poets hath chosen verse as their fittest raiment, meaning, as in matter they passed all in all, so in manner to go beyond them—not speaking (table talk fashion or like men in a dream) words as they chanceably fall from the mouth, but prizing each syllable of each word by just proportion according to the dignity of the subject.

Now therefore it shall not be amiss first to weigh this latter sort of Poetry by his works, and then by his parts, and, if in neither of these anatomies he be condemnable, I hope we shall obtain a more favourable sentence. This purifying of wit, this enriching of memory, enabling of judgement, and enlarging of conceit, which commonly we call learning, under what name soever it come forth, or to what immediate end soever it be directed, the final end is to lead and draw us to as high a perfection as our degenerate souls, made worse by their clayey lodgings, can be capable of. This, according to the inclination of the man, bred many formed impressions. For some that thought this felicity principally to be gotten by knowledge and no knowledge to be so high and heavenly as acquaintance with the stars, gave themselves to Astronomy; others, persuading themselves to be demigods if they knew the causes of things, became natural and super-natural philosophers; some an admirable delight drew to Music; and some the certainty of demonstration to the Mathematics. But all, one and other, having this scope—to know, and by knowledge to lift up the mind from the dungeon of the body to the enjoying his own divine essence. But when by the balance of experience it was found that the astronomer looking to the stars might fall into a ditch, that the inquiring philosopher might be blind in himself, and the mathematician might draw forth a straight line with a crooked heart, then, lo, did proof, the overruler of opinions, make manifest that all these are but serving sciences, which, as they have each a private end in themselves, so yet are they all directed to the highest end of the mistress-knowledge, by the Greeks called *Architectonike*, which stands (as I think) in the knowledge of a man's self, in the ethic and politic consideration, with the end of well doing and not of well knowing only:—even as the saddler's next end is to make a good saddle, but his farther end to serve a nobler faculty, which is horseman-ship; so the horseman's to soldiery, and the soldier not only to have the skill, but to perform the practice of a soldier. So that, the ending end of all earthly learning being virtuous action, those skills, that most serve to bring forth that, have a most just title to be princes over all the rest. Wherein we can show the poet's nobleness, by setting him before his other competitors, among whom as principal challengers step forth the moral philosophers, whom, me thinketh, I see coming towards me with a sullen gravity, as though they could not abide vice by daylight, rudely clothed for to witness outwardly their contempt of outward things, with books in their hands against glory, whereto they set their names, sophistically speaking against sublety, and angry with any man in whom they see the foul fault of anger. These men casting largesse as they go of definitions, divisions, and distinctions, with a scornful interrogative do soberly ask whether it be possible to find any path so ready to lead a man to virtue as that which teacheth what virtue is—and teacheth it not only by delivering forth his very being, his causes, and effects, but also by making known his enemy, Vice (which must be destroyed), and his cumbersome servant, Passion (which must be mastered), by showing the generalities that containeth it, and the specialities that are derived from it; lastly, by plain setting down, how it extendeth itself out of the limits of a man's own little world to the government of families, and maintaining of public societies.

The historian scarcely giveth leisure to the moralist to say so much, but that he, laden with old mouse-eaten records, authorizing himself (for the most part) upon other histories, whose greatest authorities are built upon the notable foundation of hearsay; having much ado to accord differing writers and to pick truth out of partiality; better acquainted with a thousand years ago than with the present age, and yet better knowing how this world goeth than how his own wit runneth; curious for antiquities and inquisitive of novelties; a wonder to young folks and a tyrant in table talk, denieth, in a great chafe, that any man for teaching of virtue, and virtuous actions, is comparable to him. "I am *Lux vitae, Temporum magistra, Vita memoriae, Nuncia vetustatis,*" &c.[4]

[4] The light of life, the master of the times, the life of memory, the messenger of antiquity (Cicero, *De Oratore*, II, 9, 36).

The philosopher (saith he) "teacheth a disputative virtue, but I do an active. His virtue is excellent in the dangerless Academy of Plato, but mine showeth forth her honourable face in the battles of Marathon, Pharsalia, Poitiers, and Agincourt. He teacheth virtue by certain abstract considerations, but I only bid you follow the footing of them that have gone before you. Old-aged experience goeth beyond the fine-witted philosopher, but I give the experience of many ages. Lastly, if he make the song-book, I put the learner's hand to the lute; and if he be the guide, I am the light."

Then would he allege you innumerable examples, conferring story by story, how much the wisest senators and princes have been directed by the credit of history, as Brutus, Alphonsus of Aragon, and who not, if need be? At length the long line of their disputation maketh a point in this, that the one giveth the precept, and the other the example.

Now, whom shall we find (since the question standeth for the highest form in the School of Learning) to be Moderator? Truly, as me seemeth, the poet; and if not a Moderator, even the man that ought to carry the title from them both, and much more from all other serving sciences. Therefore compare we the poet with the historian, and with the moral philosopher; and, if he go beyond them both, no other human skill can match him. For as for the Divine, with all reverence it is ever to be excepted, not only for having his scope as far beyond any of these as eternity exceedeth a moment, but even for passing each of these in themselves.

And for the lawyer, though Jus be the daughter of Justice, and Justice the chief of virtues, yet because he seeketh to make men good rather *formidine poenae* than *virtutis amore,*[5] or, to say righter, doth not endeavour to make men good, but that their evil hurt not others, having no care, so he be a good citizen, how bad a man he be: therefore, as our wickedness maketh him necessary, and necessity maketh him honourable, so is he not in the deepest truth to stand in rank with these who all endeavour to take naughtiness away, and plant goodness even in the secretest cabinet of our souls. And these four are all that any way deal in that consideration of men's manners, which being the supreme knowledge, they that best breed it deserve the best commendation.

The philosopher therefore and the historian are they which would win the goal, the one by precept, the other by example. But both, not having both, do both halt. For the philosopher, setting down with thorny argument the bare rule, is so hard of utterance, and so misty to be conceived, that one that hath no other guide but him shall wade in him till he be old before he shall find sufficient cause to be honest. For his

---

[5] By fear of punishment rather than love of virtue.

knowledge standeth so upon the abstract and general, that happy is that man who may understand him, and more happy that can apply what he doth understand.

On the other side, the historian, wanting the precept, is so tied, not to what should be but to what is, to the particular truth of things and not to the general reason of things, that his example draweth no necessary consequence, and therefore a less fruitful doctrine.

Now doth the peerless poet perform both: for whatsoever the philosopher saith should be done, he giveth a perfect picture of it in some one by whom he presupposeth it was done; so as he coupleth the general notion with the particular example. A perfect picture I say, for he yieldeth to the powers of the mind an image of that whereof the philosopher bestoweth but a wordish description: which doth neither strike, pierce, nor possess the sight of the soul so much as that other doth.

For as in outward things, to a man that had never seen an elephant or a rhinoceros, who should tell him most exquisitely all their shapes, colour, bigness, and particular marks, or of a gorgeous palace the architecture, with declaring the full beauties might well make the hearer able to repeat, as it were by rote, all he had heard, yet should never satisfy his inward conceits with being witness to itself of a true lively knowledge: but the same man, as soon as he might see those beasts well painted, or the house well in model, should straightways grow, without need of any description, to a judicial comprehending of them: so no doubt the philosopher with his learned definition—be it of virtue, vices, matters of public policy or private government—replenisheth the memory with many infallible grounds of wisdom, which notwithstanding, lie dark before the imaginative and judging power, if they be not illuminated or figured forth by the speaking picture of Poesy.

Tully taketh much pains, and many times not without poetical helps, to make us know the force love of our country hath in us. Let us but hear old Anchises speaking in the midst of Troy's flames, or see Ulysses in the fullness of all Calypso's delights bewail his absence from barren and beggarly Ithaca. Anger, the Stoics say, was a short madness: let but Sophocles bring you Ajax on a stage, killing and whipping sheep and oxen, thinking them the army of Greeks, with their chieftains Agamemnon and Menelaus, and tell me if you have not a more familiar insight into anger than finding in the Schoolmen his genus and difference. See whether wisdom and temperance in Ulysses and Diomedes, valour in Achilles, friendship in Nisus and Euryalus, even to an ignorant man carry not an apparent shining, and, contrarily, the remorse of conscience in Oedipus, the soon repenting pride of Agamemnon, the self-devouring cruelty in his father Atreus, the violence of ambition in the two Theban brothers, the sour-sweetness of revenge in Medea, and, to fall lower, the Terentian Gnatho and our Chaucer's Pandar so expressed that we now use their names to signify their trades; and finally, all virtues, vices, and passions so in their own natural seats laid to the view, that we seem not to hear of them, but clearly to see through them.  But even in the most excellent determination of goodness, what philosopher's counsel can so readily direct a prince, as the feigned Cyrus in Xenophon; or a virtuous man in all fortunes, as Aeneas in Virgil; or a whole Common-wealth, as the way of Sir Thomas More's *Utopia*?  I say the way, because where Sir Thomas More erred, it was the fault of the man and not of the poet, for that way of patterning a Commonwealth was most absolute, though he perchance hath not so absolutely performed it.  For the question is, whether the feigned image of Poesy or the regular instruction of Philosophy hath the more force in teaching: wherein if the philosophers have more rightly showed themselves philosophers than the poets have attained to the high top of their profession, as in truth,

> *Mediocribus esse poetis,*
> *Non Dii, non homines, non concessere Columnae:* [6]

it is, I say again, not the fault of the art, but that by few men that art can be accomplished.

Certainly, even our Saviour Christ could as well have given the moral commonplaces of uncharitableness and humbleness as the divine nar-ration of Dives and Lazarus; or of disobedience and mercy, as that heavenly discourse of the lost child and the gracious father; but that His through-searching wisdom knew the estate of Dives burning in hell, and of Lazarus being in Abraham's bosom, would more constantly (as it were) inhabit both the memory and judgement.  Truly, for myself, meseems I see before my eyes the lost child's disdainful prodigality, turned to envy a swine's dinner: which by the learned Divines are thought not historical acts, but instructing parables.  For conclusion, I say the Philosopher teacheth, but he teacheth obscurely, so as the learned only can understand him; that is to say, he teacheth them that are al-ready taught.  But the poet is the food for the tenderest stomachs, the poet is indeed the right popular philosopher, whereof Aesop's tales give good proof: whose pretty allegories, stealing under the formal tales of beasts, make many, more beastly than beasts, begin to hear the sound of virtue from these dumb speakers.

But now may it be alleged that, if this imagining of matters be so fit for the imagination, then must the historian needs surpass, who bringeth

---

[6] Mediocre poets are not endured by gods, men, or booksellers (Horace, *Art of Poetry*, ll. 372-373).

you images of true matters, such as indeed were done, and not such as fantastically or falsely may be suggested to have been done. Truly, Aristotle himself, in his discourse of Poesy, plainly determineth this question, saying that Poetry is *Philosophoteron* and *Spoudaioteron*, that is to say, it is more philosophical and more studiously serious than history. His reason is, because Poesy dealeth with *Katholon*, that is to say, with the universal consideration, and the history with *Kathekaston*, the particular "now," saith he, "the universal weighs what is fit to be said or done, either in likelihood or necessity (which the Poesy considereth in his imposed names), and the particular only marks whether Alcibiades did, or suffered, this or that." Thus far Aristotle: which reason of his (as all his) is most full of reason. For indeed, if the question were whether it were better to have a particular act truly or falsely set down, there is no doubt which is to be chosen, no more than whether you had rather have Vespasian's picture right as he was, or at the painter's pleasure nothing resembling. But if the question be for your own use and learning, whether it be better to have it set down as it should be, or as it was, then certainly is more doctrinable the feigned Cyrus in Xenophon than the true Cyrus in Justin, and the feigned Aeneas in Virgil than the right Aeneas in Dares Phrygius.

As to a lady that desired to fashion her countenance to the best grace, a painter should more benefit her to portrait a most sweet face, writing Canidia upon it, than to paint Canidia as she was, who, Horace sweareth, was foul and ill favoured.

If the poet do his part aright, he will show you in Tantalus, Atreus, and such like, nothing that is not to be shunned; in Cyrus, Aeneas, Ulysses, each thing to be followed; where the historian, bound to tell things as things were, cannot be liberal (without he will be poetical) of a perfect pattern, but, as in Alexander or Scipio himself, show doings, some to be liked, some to be misliked. And then how will you discern what to follow but by your own discretion, which you had without reading Quintus Curtius? And whereas a man may say, though in universal consideration of doctrine the poet prevaileth, yet that the history, in his saying such a thing was done, doth warrant a man more in that he shall follow.

The answer is manifest: that if he stand upon that *was*—as if he should argue, because it rained yesterday, therefore it should rain to-day—then indeed it hath some advantage to a gross conceit; but if he know an example only informs a conjectured likelihood, and so go by reason, the poet doth so far exceed him, as he is to frame his example to that which is most reasonable, be it in warlike, politic, or private matters; where the historian in his bare *was* hath many times that which we call fortune to overrule the best wisdom.    Many times he must tell events whereof he can yield no cause: or, if he do, it must be poetical.    For that a feigned example hath as much force to teach as a true example (for as for to move, it is clear, since the feigned may be tuned to the highest key of passion), let us take one example wherein a poet and a historian do concur.

Herodotus and Justin do both testify that Zopyrus, King Darius's faithful servant, seeing his master long resisted by the rebellious Babylonians, feigned himself in extreme disgrace of his king: for verifying of which, he caused his own nose and ears to be cut off, and so flying to the Babylonians, was received, and for his known valour so far credited, that he did find means to deliver them over to Darius.    Much like matter doth Livy record of Tarquinius and his son.    Xenophon excellently feigneth such another stratagem performed by Abradates in Cyrus's behalf.    Now would I fain know, if occasion be presented unto you to serve your prince by such an honest dissimulation, why you do not as well learn it of Xenophon's fiction as of the other's verity—and truly so much the better, as you shall save your nose by the bargain; for Abradates did not counterfeit so far.    So then the best of the historian is subject to the poet; for whatsoever action, or faction, whatsoever counsel, policy, or war stratagem the historian is bound to recite, that may the poet (if he list) with his imitation make his own, beautifying it both for further teaching, and more delighting, as it pleaseth him, having all, from Dante's heaven to his hell, under the authority of his pen. Which if I be asked what poets have done so, as I might well name some, yet say I, and say again, I speak of the art, and not of the artificer.

Now, to that which commonly is attributed to the praise of histories, in respect of the notable learning is gotten by marking the success, as though therein a man should see virtue exalted and vice punished— truly that commendation is peculiar to Poetry, and far off from History. For indeed Poetry ever setteth virtue so out in her best colours, making Fortune her well-waiting handmaid, that one must needs be enamoured of her.    Well may you see Ulysses in a storm, and in other hard plights; but they are but exercises of patience and magnanimity, to make them shine the more in the near-following prosperity.    And of the contrary part, if evil men come to the stage, they ever go out (as the tragedy writer answered to one that misliked the show of such persons) so manacled as they little animate folks to follow them.    But the historian, being captived to the truth of a foolish world, is many times a terror from well doing, and an encouragement to unbridled wickedness.

For see we not valiant Miltiades rot in his fetters: the just Phocion and the accomplished Socrates put to death like traitors; the cruel Severus live prosperously; the excellent Severus miserably murdered; Sylla and Marius dying in their beds; Pompey and Cicero slain then when they would have thought exile a happiness?

See we not virtuous Cato driven to kill himself, and rebel Caesar so advanced that his name yet, after 1,600 years, lasteth in the highest honour? And mark but even Caesar's own words of the forenamed Sylla (who in that only did honestly, to put down his dishonest tyranny), *Literas nescivit*,[7] as if want of learning caused him to do well. He meant it not by Poetry, which, not content with earthly plagues, deviseth new punishments in hell for tyrants, nor yet by Philosophy, which teacheth *Occidendos esse;*[8] but no doubt by skill in History, for that indeed can afford your Cypselus, Periander, Phalaris, Dionysius, and I know not how many more of the same kennel, that speed well enough in their abominable injustice or usurpation. I conclude, therefore, that he excelleth History, not only in furnishing the mind with knowledge, but in setting it forward to that which deserveth to be called and accounted good: which setting forward, and moving to well doing, indeed setteth the laurel crown upon the poet as victorious, not only of the historian, but over the philosopher, howsoever in teaching it may be questionable.

For suppose it be granted (that which I suppose with great reason may be denied) that the philosopher, in respect of his methodical proceeding, doth teach more perfectly than the poet, yet do I think that no man is so much *Philophilosophos*[9] as to compare the philosopher, in moving, with the poet.

And that moving is of a higher degree than teaching, it may by this appear, that it is wellnigh the cause and the effect of teaching. For who will be taught, if he be not moved with desire to be taught, and what so much good doth that teaching bring forth (I speak still of moral doctrine) as that it moveth one to do that which it doth teach? For, as Aristotle saith, it is not *Gnosis* but *Praxis*[10] must be the fruit. And how *Praxis* cannot be, without being moved to practise, it is no hard matter to consider.

The philosopher showeth you the way, he informeth you of the particularities, as well of the tediousness of the way, as of the pleasant lodging you shall have when your journey is ended, as of the many by-turnings that may divert you from your way. But this is to no man but to him that will read him, and read him with attentive studious painfulness; which constant desire whosoever hath in him, hath already passed half the

---

[7] He did not know literature.
[8] They are to be killed.
[9] A lover of the philosopher.
[10] Not mere abstract *knowledge*, that is, but *action*.

hardness of the way, and therefore is beholding to the philosopher but for the other half.  Nay truly, learned men have learnedly thought that where once reason hath so much overmastered passion, as that the mind hath a free desire to do well: the inward light each mind hath in itself is as good as a philosopher's book; seeing in nature we know it is well to do well, and what is well and what is evil, although not in the words of art which philosophers bestow upon us.  For out of natural conceit the philosophers drew it; but to be moved to do that which we know, or to be moved with desire to know, *Hoc opus, hic labor est.*[11]

Now therein of all sciences (I speak still of human, and according to the humane conceits) is our poet the monarch.  For  he doth not only show the way, but giveth so sweet a prospect into the way, as will entice any man to enter into it.  Nay, he doth, as if your journey should lie through a fair vineyard, at the first give you a cluster of grapes, that, full of that taste, you may long to pass further.  He beginneth not with obscure definitions, which must blur the margent with interpretations, and load the memory with doubtfulness; but he cometh to you with words set in delightful proportion, either accompanied with, or prepared for, the well enchanting skill of music; and with a tale forsooth he cometh unto you, with a tale which holdeth children from play, and old men from the chimney corner.  And, pretending no more, doth intend the winning of the mind from wickedness to virtue: even as the child is often brought to take most wholesome things by hiding them in such other as have a pleasant taste: which, if one should begin to tell them the nature of aloes or rhubarb they should receive, would sooner take their physic at their ears than at their mouth.  So is it in men (most of which are childish in the best things, till they be cradled in their graves): glad they will be to hear the tales of Hercules, Achilles, Cyrus, and Aeneas; and, hearing them, must needs hear the right description of wisdom, valour, and justice; which, if they had been barely, that is to say philosophically, set out, they would swear they be brought to school again.

That imitation whereof Poetry is, hath the most conveniency to Nature of all other, insomuch that, as Aristotle saith, those things which in themselves are horrible, as cruel battles, unnatural monsters, are made in poetical imitation delightful.  Truly, I have known men, that even with reading *Amadis de Gaule* (which God knoweth wanteth much of a perfect poesy) have found their hearts moved to the exercise of courtesy, liberality, and especially courage.

Who readeth Aeneas carrying old Anchises on his back, that wisheth not it were his fortune to perform so excellent an act?  Whom do not the

---

[11] This is the work, this the labor (*Aeneid*, VI, 129).

words of Turnus move, the tale of Turnus having planted his image in the imagination?—

*Fugientem haec terra videbit?*
*Usque adeone mori miserum est?*[12]

Where the philosophers, as they scorn to delight, so must they be content little to move, saving wrangling whether Virtue be the chief or the only good, whether the contemplative or the active life do excel: which Plato and Boethius well knew, and therefore made Mistress Philosophy very often borrow the masking raiment of Poesy. For even those hard-hearted evil men who think virtue a school name, and know no other good but *indulgere genio*,[13] and therefore despise the austere admonitions of the philosopher, and feel not the inward reason they stand upon, yet will be content to be delighted—which is all the good fellow poet seemeth to promise—and so steal to see the form of goodness, which seen they cannot but love ere themselves be aware, as if they took a medicine of cherries. Infinite proofs of the strange effects of this poetical invention might be alleged; only two shall serve, which are so often remembered as I think all men know them.

The one of Menenius Agrippa, who, when the whole people of Rome had resolutely divided themselves from the Senate, with apparent show of utter ruin, though he were (for that time) an excellent orator, came not among them upon trust of figurative speeches or cunning insinuations, and much less with farfetched maxims of Philosophy, which (especially if they were Platonic) they must have learned geometry before they could well have conceived; but forsooth he behaves himself like a homely and familiar poet. He telleth them a tale, that there was a time when all the parts of the body made a mutinous conspiracy against the belly, which they thought devoured the fruits of each other's labour: they concluded they would let so unprofitable a spender starve. In the end, to be short (for the tale is notorious, and as notorious that it was a tale), with punishing the belly they plagued themselves. This applied by him wrought such effect in the people, as I never read that ever words brought forth but then so sudden and so good an alteration; for upon reasonable conditions a perfect reconcilement ensued. The other is of Nathan the Prophet, who, when the holy David had so far forsaken God as to confirm adultery with murder, when he was to do the tenderest office of a friend, in laying his own shame before his eyes, sent by God to call again so chosen a servant, how doth he it but by telling of a man

[12] Shall this land see [Turnus] fleeing away? Is it so wretched a thing to die as that? (*Aeneid*, XII, 645-646).
[13] To indulge one's nature.

whose beloved lamb was ungratefully taken from his bosom?—the application most divinely true, but the discourse itself feigned. Which made David (I speak of the second and instrumental cause) as in a glass to see his own filthiness, as that heavenly Psalm of Mercy well testifieth.

By these, therefore, examples and reasons, I think it may be manifest that the Poet, with that same hand of delight, doth draw the mind more effectually than any other art doth: and so a conclusion not unfitly ensueth, that, as Virtue is the most excellent resting place for all worldly learning to make his end of, so Poetry, being the most familiar to teach it, and most princely to move towards it, in the most excellent work is the most excellent workman. But I am content not only to decipher him by his works (although works in commendation or dispraise must ever hold an high authority), but more narrowly will examine his parts: so that, as in a man, though all together may carry a presence full of majesty and beauty, perchance in some one defectious piece we may find a blemish. Now in his parts, kinds, or species (as you list to term them), it is to be noted that some poesies have coupled together two or three kinds, as tragical and comical, whereupon is risen the tragi-comical. Some, in the like manner, have mingled prose and verse, as Sannazzaro and Boethius. Some have mingled matters heroical and pastoral. But that cometh all to one in this question, for, if severed they be good, the conjunction cannot be hurtful. Therefore, perchance forgetting some, and leaving some as needless to be remembered, it shall not be amiss in a word to cite the special kinds, to see what faults may be found in the right use of them.

Is it then the Pastoral Poem which is misliked? For perchance where the hedge is lowest they will soonest leap over. Is the poor pipe disdained, which sometime out of Melibaeus' mouth can show the misery of people under hard lords or ravening soldiers, and again, by Tityrus, what blessedness is derived to them that lie lowest from the goodness of them that sit highest? sometimes, under the pretty tales of wolves and sheep, can include the whole considerations of wrongdoing and patience; sometimes show that contention for trifles can get but a trifling victory; where perchance a man may see that even Alexander and Darius, when they strave who should be cock of this world's dunghill, the benefit they got was that the afterlivers may say,

> *Haec memini et victum frustra contendere Thirsin;*
> *Ex illo Coridon, Coridon est tempore nobis.*[14]

[14] I recall those things, and that the conquered Thyrsis strove in vain: From that time, Corydon for us is Corydon (Virgil, *Eclogue*, VII, 69-70).

Or is it the lamenting Elegiac, which in a kind heart would move rather pity than blame, who bewails with the great philosopher Heraclitus the weakness of mankind and the wretchedness of the world; who surely is to be praised, either for compassionate accompanying just causes of lamentation, or for rightly pointing out how weak be the passions of woefulness? Is it the bitter but wholesome Iambic, which rubs the galled mind, in making shame the trumpet of villainy with bold and open crying out against naughtiness? Or the Satiric, who

*Omne vafer vitium ridenti tangit amico:*[15]

who sportingly never leaveth until he make a man laugh at folly, and, at length ashamed, to laugh at himself, which he cannot avoid, without avoiding the folly; who, while

*circum praecordia ludit,*[16]

giveth us to feel how many headaches a passionate life bringeth us to; how, when all is done,

*Est Ulubris animus si nos non deficit aequus?*[17]

No, perchance it is the Comic, whom naughty play-makers and stage-keepers have justly made odious. To the argument of abuse I will answer after. Only thus much now is to be said, that the Comedy is an imitation of the common errors of our life, which he representeth in the most ridiculous and scornful sort that may be, so as it is impossible that any beholder can be content to be such a one.

Now, as in Geometry the oblique must be known as well as the right, and in Arithmetic the odd as well as the even, so in the actions of our life who seeth not the filthiness of evil wanteth a great foil to perceive the beauty of virtue. This doth the Comedy handle so in our private and domestical matters, as with hearing it we get as it were an experience, what is to be looked for of a niggardly Demea, of a crafty Davus, of a flattering Gnatho, of a vainglorious Thraso; and not only to know what effects are to be expected, but to know who be such, by the signifying badge given them by the comedian. And little reason hath any man to say that men learn evil by seeing it so set out; since, as I said before, there is no man living but, by the force truth hath in nature, no sooner seeth these men play their parts, but wisheth them in *pistrinum;*[18]

[15] The rogue touches every vice while causing his friend to laugh (Persius, *Satires*, I, 116-117).

[16] He plays around the heart-strings (same passage).

[17] Happiness is found in Ulabrae [an extinct or dead city] if we have a sane mind (Horace, *Epistles*, I, 11, 30).

[18] A Roman mill to which slaves were often condemned as punishment.

although perchance the sack of his own faults lie so behind his back that he seeth not himself dance the same measure; whereto yet nothing can more open his eyes than to find his own actions contemptibly set forth. So that the right use of Comedy will (I think) by nobody be blamed, and much less of the high and excellent Tragedy, that openeth the greatest wounds, and showeth forth the ulcers that are covered with tissue; that maketh kings fear to be tyrants, and tyrants manifest their tyrannical humours; that, with stirring the affects of admiration and commiseration, teacheth the uncertainty of this world, and upon how weak foundations gilden roofs are builded; that maketh us know,

*Qui sceptra saevus duro imperio regit,*
*Timet timentes, metus in auctorem redit.*[19]

But how much it can move, Plutarch yieldeth a notable testimony of the abominable tyrant Alexander Pheraeus, from whose eyes a tragedy, well made and represented, drew abundance of tears, who, without all pity, had murdered infinite numbers, and some of his own blood, so as he, that was not ashamed to make matters for tragedies, yet could not resist the sweet violence of a tragedy.

And if it wrought no further good in him, it was that he, in despite of himself, withdrew himself from hearkening to that which might mollify his hardened heart. But it is not the Tragedy they do mislike; for it were too absurd to cast out so excellent a representation of whatsoever is most worthy to be learned. Is it the Lyric that most displeaseth, who with his tuned lyre, and well-accorded voice, giveth praise, the reward of virtue, to virtuous acts, who gives moral precepts, and natural problems, who sometimes raiseth up his voice to the height of the heavens, in singing the lauds of the immortal God? Certainly, I must confess my own barbarousness, I never heard the old song of Percy and Douglas that I found not my heart moved more than with a trumpet; and yet is it sung but by some blind crowder, with no rougher voice than rude style; which, being so evil apparelled in the dust and cobwebs of that uncivil age, what would it work, trimmed in the gorgeous eloquence of Pindar? In Hungary I have seen it the manner at all feasts, and other such meetings, to have songs of their ancestors' valour; which that right soldier-like nation think the chiefest kindlers of brave courage. The incomparable Lacedemonians did not only carry that kind of music ever with them to the field, but even at home, as such songs were made, so were they all content to be the singers of them, when the lusty men were to tell what they did, the old men what they had done, and the young men what

[19] The savage ruler who wields the sceptre with a hard hand fears his frightened subjects, and fear thus returns to the author of it (Seneca, *Oedipus,* 705-706).

they would do. And where a man may say that Pindar many times praiseth highly victories of small moment, matters rather of sport than virtue; as it may be answered, it was the fault of the poet, and not of the poetry, so indeed the chief fault was in the time and custom of the Greeks, who set those toys at so high a price that Philip of Macedon reckoned a horse-race won at Olympus among his three fearful felicities. But as the inimitable Pindar often did, so is that kind most capable and most fit to awake the thoughts from the sleep of idleness, to embrace honourable enterprises.

There rests the Heroical, whose very name (I think) should daunt all backbiters; for by what conceit can a tongue be directed to speak evil of that which draweth with it no less champions than Achilles, Cyrus, Aeneas, Turnus, Tydeus, and Rinaldo? who doth not only teach and move to a truth, but teacheth and moveth to the most high and excellent truth; who maketh magnanimity and justice shine throughout all misty fearfulness and foggy desires; who, if the saying of Plato and Tully be true, that who could see Virtue would be wonderfully ravished with the love of her beauty—this man sets her out to make her more lovely in her holiday apparel, to the eye of any that will deign not to disdain until they understand. But if anything be already said in the defence of sweet Poetry, all concurreth to the maintaining the Heroical, which is not only a kind, but the best and most accomplished kind of Poetry. For as the image of each action stirreth and instructeth the mind, so the lofty image of such worthies most inflameth the mind with desire to be worthy, and informs with counsel how to be worthy. Only let Aeneas be worn in the tablet of your memory, how he governeth himself in the ruin of his country, in the preserving his old father, and carrying away his religious ceremonies, in obeying the god's commandment to leave Dido, though not only all passionate kindness, but even the human consideration of virtuous gratefulness, would have craved other of him; how in storms, how in sports, how in war, how in peace, how a fugitive, how victorious, how besieged, how besieging, how to strangers, how to allies, how to enemies, how to his own; lastly, how in his inward self, and how in his outward government, and I think, in a mind not prejudiced with a prejudicating humour, he will be found in excellency fruitful, yea, even as Horace saith,

*Melius Chrysippo et Crantore.*[20]

But truly I imagine it falleth out with these poet-whippers, as with some good women, who often are sick, but in faith they cannot tell where.

[20] Better than do Chrysippus and Crantor (*Epistles*, I, 2, 4). Horace is stating that the knowledge of the good is better learned from Homer than from the above two philosophers.

So the name of Poetry is odious to them, but neither his cause nor effects, neither the sum that contains him nor the particularities descending from him, give any fast handle to their carping dispraise.

Since then Poetry is of all human learning the most ancient and of most fatherly antiquity, as from whence other learnings have taken their beginnings; since it is so universal that no learned nation doth despise it, nor no barbarous nation is without it; since both Roman and Greek gave divine names unto it, the one of "prophesying," the other of "making," and that indeed that name of "making" is fit for him, considering that whereas other Arts retain themselves within their subject, and receive, as it were, their being from it, the poet only bringeth his own stuff, and doth not learn a conceit out of a matter, but maketh matter for a conceit; since neither his description nor his end containeth any evil, the thing described cannot be evil; since his effects be so good as to teach goodness and to delight the learners; since therein (namely in moral doctrine, the chief of all knowledges) he doth not only far pass the historian, but, for instructing, is wellnigh comparable to the philosopher, and, for moving, leaves him behind him; since the Holy Scripture (wherein there is no uncleanness) hath whole parts in it poetical, and that even our Saviour Christ vouchsafed to use the flowers of it; since all his kinds are not only in their united forms but in their severed dissections fully commendable; I think (and think I think rightly) the laurel crown appointed for triumphing captains doth worthily (of all other learnings) honour the poet's triumph.  But because we have ears as well as tongues, and that the lightest reasons that may be will seem to weigh greatly, if nothing be put in the counterbalance, let us hear, and, as well as we can, ponder, what objections may be made against this art, which may be worthy either of yielding or answering.

First, truly I note not only in these *Mysomousoi*, poet-haters, but in all that kind of people who seek a praise by dispraising others, that they do prodigally spend a great many wandering words in quips and scoffs, carping and taunting at each thing, which, by stirring the spleen, may stay the brain from a thorough beholding the worthiness of the subject.

Those kind of objections, as they are full of very idle easiness, since there is nothing of so sacred a majesty but that an itching tongue may rub itself upon it, so deserve they no other answer, but, instead of laughing at the jest, to laugh at the jester.  We know a playing wit can praise the discretion of an ass, the comfortableness of being in debt, and the jolly commodity of being sick of the plague.  So of the contrary side, if we will turn Ovid's verse,

*Ut lateat virtus proximitate mali,*

that "good lie hid in nearness of the evil," Agrippa will be as merry in showing the vanity of Science as Erasmus was in commending of folly. Neither shall any man or matter escape some touch of these smiling railers. But for Erasmus and Agrippa, they had another foundation than the superficial part would promise. Marry, these other pleasant faultfinders, who will correct the verb before they understand the noun, and confute others' knowledge before they confirm their own, I would have them only remember that scoffing cometh not of wisdom; so as the best title in true English they get with their merriments is to be called good fools, for so have our grave forefathers ever termed that humorous kind of jesters. But that which giveth greatest scope to their scorning humours is rhyming and versing. It is already said (and, as I think, truly said) it is not rhyming and versing that maketh Poesy. One may be a poet without versing, and a versifier without poetry. But yet presuppose it were inseparable (as indeed it seemeth Scaliger judgeth) truly it were an inseparable commendation. For if *Oratio* next to *Ratio*, Speech next to Reason, be the greatest gift bestowed upon mortality, that cannot be praiseless which doth most polish that blessing of speech; which considers each word, not only (as a man may say) by his forcible quality, but by his best measured quantity, carrying even in themselves a harmony (without, perchance, number, measure, order, proportion be in our time grown odious). But lay aside the just praise it hath, by being the only fit speech for Music (Music, I say, the most divine striker of the senses), thus much is undoubtedly true, that if reading be foolish without remembering, memory being the only treasurer of knowledge, those words which are fittest for memory are likewise most convenient for knowledge.

Now, that verse far exceedeth prose in the knitting up of the memory, the reason is manifest,—the words (besides their delight, which hath a great affinity to memory) being so set as one word cannot be lost but the whole work fails; which accuseth itself, calleth the remembrance back to itself, and so most strongly confirmeth it. Besides, one word so, as it were, begetting another, as, be it in rhyme or measured verse, by the former a man shall have a near guess to the follower: lastly, even they that have taught the art of memory have showed nothing so apt for it as a certain room divided into many places well and thoroughly known. Now, that hath the verse in effect perfectly, every word having his natural seat, which seat must needs make the words remembered. But what needeth more in a thing so known to all men? Who is it that ever was a scholar that doth not carry away some verses of Virgil, Horace, or Cato, which in his youth he learned, and even to his old age serve him for hourly lessons? But the fitness it hath for memory is notably proved by all delivery of Arts: wherein for the most part, from Grammar to Logic,

Mathematic, Physic, and the rest, the rules chiefly necessary to be borne away are compiled in verses. So that, verse being in itself sweet and orderly, and being best for memory, the only handle of knowledge, it must be in jest that any man can speak against it. Now then go we to the most important imputations laid to the poor poets. For aught I can yet learn, they are these. First, that there being many other more fruitful knowledges, a man might better spend his time in them than in this. Secondly, that it is the mother of lies. Thirdly, that it is the nurse of abuse, infecting us with many pestilent desires, with a siren's sweetness drawing the mind to the serpent's tale of sinful fancy,—and herein, especially, comedies give the largest field to ear (as Chaucer saith),—how both in other nations and in ours, before poets did soften us, we were full of courage, given to martial exercises, the pillars of manlike liberty, and not lulled asleep in shady idleness with poets' pastimes. And lastly, and chiefly, they cry out with an open mouth, as if they outshot Robin Hood, that Plato banished them out of his Commonwealth. Truly, this is much, if there be much truth in it. First, to the first, that a man might better spend his time is a reason indeed: but it doth (as they say) but *petere principium*:[21] for if it be, as I affirm, that no learning is so good as that which teacheth and moveth to virtue, and that none can both teach and move thereto so much as Poetry, then is the conclusion manifest that ink and paper cannot be to a more profitable purpose employed. And certainly, though a man should grant their first assumption, it should follow (methinks) very unwillingly, that good is not good because better is better. But I still and utterly deny that there is sprung out of earth a more fruitful knowledge. To the second therefore, that they should be the principal liars, I answer paradoxically, but truly, I think truly, that of all writers under the sun the poet is the least liar, and, though he would, as a poet can scarcely be a liar. The astronomer, with his cousin the geometrician, can hardly escape, when they take upon them to measure the height of the stars.

How often, think you, do the physicians lie, when they aver things good for sicknesses, which afterwards send Charon a great number of souls drowned in a potion before they come to his ferry? And no less of the rest, which take upon them to affirm. Now, for the poet, he nothing affirms, and therefore never lieth. For, as I take it, to lie is to affirm that to be true which is false; so as the other artists, and especially the historian, affirming many things, can, in the cloudy knowledge of mankind, hardly escape from many lies. But the poet (as I said before) never affirmeth. The poet never maketh any circles about your imagination, to conjure you to believe for true what he writes. He citeth not author-

[21] Beg the question.

ities of other histories, but even for his entry calleth the sweet Muses to inspire into him a good invention; in truth, not labouring to tell you what is, or is not, but what should or should not be. And therefore, though he recount things not true, yet because he telleth them not for true, he lieth not,—without we will say that Nathan lied in his speech, before alleged, to David; which as a wicked man durst scarce say, so think I none so simple would say that Aesop lied in the tales of his beasts: for who thinks that Aesop writ it for actually true were well worthy to have his name chronicled among the beasts he writeth of.

What child is there that, coming to a play, and seeing *Thebes* written in great letters upon an old door, doth believe that it is Thebes? If then a man can arrive, at that child's age, to know that the poets' persons and doings are but pictures what should be, and not stories what have been, they will never give the lie to things not affirmatively but allegorically and figuratively written. And therefore, as in History, looking for truth, they go away full fraught with falsehood, so in Poesy, looking for fiction, they shall use the narration but as an imaginative ground-plot of a profitable invention.

But hereto is replied, that the poets give names to men they write of, which argueth a conceit of an actual truth, and so, not being true, proves a falsehood. And doth the lawyer lie then, when under the names of "John a Stile" and "John a Noakes" he puts his case? But that is easily answered. Their naming of men is but to make their picture the more lively, and not to build any history; painting men, they cannot leave men nameless. We see we cannot play at chess but that we must give names to our chessmen; and yet, methinks, he were a very partial champion of truth that would say we lied for giving a piece of wood the reverend title of a bishop. The poet nameth Cyrus or Aeneas no other way than to show what men of their fames, fortunes, and estates should do.

Their third is, how much it abuseth men's wit, training it to wanton sinfulness and lustful love: for indeed that is the principal, if not the only, abuse I can hear alleged. They say the Comedies rather teach than reprehend amorous conceits. They say the Lyric is larded with passionate sonnets, the Elegiac weeps the want of his mistress, and that even to the Heroical Cupid hath ambitiously climbed. Alas, Love, I would thou couldst as well defend thyself as thou canst offend others. I would those on whom thou dost attend could either put thee away, or yield good reason why they keep thee. But grant love of beauty to be a beastly fault (although it be very hard, since only man, and no beast, hath that gift to discern beauty); grant that lovely name of Love to deserve all hateful reproaches (although even some of my masters the philosophers spent a good deal of their lamp-oil in setting forth the excellency of it);

grant, I say, whatsoever they will have granted; that not only love, but lust, but vanity, but (if they list) scurrility, possesseth many leaves of the poets' books: yet think I, when this is granted, they will find their sentence may with good manners put the last words foremost, and not say that Poetry abuseth man's wit, but that man's wit abuseth Poetry.

For I will not deny but that man's wit may make Poesy, which should be *Eikastike*, which some learned have defined, "figuring forth good things," to be *Phantastike*, which doth, contrariwise, infect the fancy with unworthy objects, as the painter, that should give to the eye either some excellent perspective, or some fine picture, fit for building or fortification, or containing in it some notable example, as Abraham sacrificing his son Isaac, Judith killing Holofernes, David fighting with Goliath, may leave those, and please an ill-pleased eye with wanton shows of better hidden matters.    But what, shall the abuse of a thing make the right use odious? Nay truly, though I yield that Poesy may not only be abused, but that being abused, by the reason of his sweet charming force, it can do more hurt than any other army of words, yet shall it be so far from concluding that the abuse should give reproach to the abused, that contrariwise it is a good reason, that whatsoever, being abused, doth most harm, being rightly used (and upon the right use each thing conceiveth his title), doth most good.

Do we not see the skill of Physic (the best rampire to our often-assaulted bodies), being abused, teach poison, the most violent destroyer?    Doth not knowledge of Law, whose end is to even and right all things, being abused, grow the crooked fosterer of horrible injuries?    Doth not (to go to the highest) God's word abused breed heresy, and His Name abused become blasphemy?    Truly, a needle cannot do much hurt, and as truly (with leave of ladies be it spoken) it cannot do much good.    With a sword thou mayest kill thy father, and with a sword thou mayest defend thy prince and country.    So that, as in their calling poets the fathers of lies they say nothing, so in this their argument of abuse they prove the commendation.

They allege herewith, that before poets began to be in price our nation hath set their heart's delight upon action, and not upon imagination, rather doing things worthy to be written, than writing things fit to be done.    What that beforetime was, I think scarcely Sphinx can tell, since no memory is so ancient that hath the precedence of Poetry.    And certain it is that, in our plainest homeliness, yet never was the Albion nation without Poetry.    Marry, this argument, though it be levelled against Poetry, yet is it indeed a chain-shot against all learning, or bookishness, as they commonly term it.    Of such mind were certain Goths, of whom it is written that, having in the spoil of a famous city taken a fair library, one hangman, belike, fit to execute the fruits of their wits, who had murdered a great number of bodies, would have set fire on it. "No," said another very gravely, "take heed what you do, for while they are busy about these toys, we shall with more leisure conquer their countries."

This indeed is the ordinary doctrine of ignorance, and many words sometimes I have heard spent in it: but because this reason is generally against all learning, as well as Poetry, or rather, all learning but Poetry; because it were too large a digression to handle, or at least too superfluous (since it is manifest that all government of action is to be gotten by knowledge, and knowledge best by gathering many knowledges, which is reading), I only, with Horace, to him that is of that opinion,

*Iubeo stultum esse libenter:*[22]

for as for Poetry itself, it is the freest from this objection. For poetry is the companion of the camps.

I dare undertake, Orlando Furioso, or honest King Arthur, will never displease a soldier: but the quiddity of *Ens* and *Prima materia* will hardly agree with a corslet. And therefore, as I said in the beginning, even Turks and Tartars are delighted with poets. Homer, a Greek, flourished before Greece flourished. And if to a slight conjecture a conjecture may be opposed, truly it may seem, that, as by him their learned men took almost their first light of knowledge, so their active men received their first motions of courage. Only Alexander's example may serve, who by Plutarch is accounted of such virtue, that Fortune was not his guide but his footstool; whose acts speak for him, though Plutarch did not,—indeed the Phoenix of warlike princes. This Alexander left his schoolmaster, living Aristotle, behind him, but took dead Homer with him. He put the philosopher Callisthenes to death for his seeming philosophical, indeed mutinous, stubbornness, but the chief thing he ever was heard to wish for was that Homer had been alive. He well found he received more bravery of mind by the pattern of Achilles than by hearing the definition of fortitude: and therefore, if Cato misliked Fulvius for carrying Ennius with him to the field, it may be answered that, if Cato misliked it, the noble Fulvius liked it, or else he had not done it: for it was not the excellent Cato Uticensis (whose authority I would much more have reverenced), but it was the former, in truth a bitter punisher of faults, but else a man that had never well sacrificed to the Graces. He misliked and cried out upon all Greek learning, and yet, being 80 years old, began to learn it, belike fearing that Pluto understood

---

[22] I ask him to be as much of a fool as he wishes (*Satires*, I, 1, 63).

not Latin. Indeed, the Roman laws allowed no person to be carried to the wars but he that was in the soldier's roll, and therefore, though Cato misliked his unmustered person, he misliked not his work. And if he had, Scipio Nasica, judged by common consent the best Roman, loved him. Both the other Scipio brothers, who had by their virtues no less surnames than of Asia and Afric, so loved him that they caused his body to be buried in their sepulchre. So as Cato's authority being but against his person, and that answered with so far greater than himself, is herein of no validity. But now indeed my burden is great; now Plato's name is laid upon me, whom, I must confess, of all philosophers I have ever esteemed most worthy of reverence, and with great reason, since of all philosophers he is the most poetical. Yet if he will defile the fountain out of which his flowing streams have proceeded, let us boldly examine with what reasons he did it. First truly, a man might maliciously object that Plato, being a philosopher, was a natural enemy of poets. For indeed, after the philosophers had picked out of the sweet mysteries of Poetry the right discerning true points of knowledge, they forthwith, putting it in method, and making a school art of that which the poets did only teach by a divine delightfulness, beginning to spurn at their guides, like ungrateful prentices, were not content to set up shops for themselves, but sought by all means to discredit their masters; which by the force of delight being barred them, the less they could overthrow them, the more they hated them. For indeed, they found for Homer seven cities strove who should have him for their citizen; where many cities banished philosophers as not fit members to live among them. For only repeating certain of Euripides' verses, many Athenians had their lives saved of the Syracusians, when the Athenians themselves thought many philosophers unworthy to live.

Certain poets, as Simonides and Pindarus, had so prevailed with Hiero the First, that of a tyrant they made him a just king; where Plato could do so little with Dionysius, that he himself of a philosopher was made a slave. But who should do thus, I confess, should requite the objections made against poets with like cavillation against philosophers; as likewise one should do that should bid one read Phaedrus or Symposium in Plato, or the discourse of love in Plutarch, and see whether any poet do authorize abominable filthiness, as they do. Again, a man might ask out of what Commonwealth Plato did banish them. In sooth, thence where he himself alloweth community of women. So as belike this banishment grew not for effeminate wantonness, since little should poetical sonnets be hurtful when a man might have what woman he listed. But I honour philosophical instructions, and bless the wits which bred them: so as they be not abused, which is likewise stretched to Poetry.

St. Paul himself, who yet, for the credit of poets, allegeth twice two poets, and one of them by the name of a prophet, setteth a watchword upon Philosophy,—indeed upon the abuse. So doth Plato upon the abuse, not upon Poetry. Plato found fault that the poets of his time filled the world with wrong opinions of the gods, making light tales of that unspotted essence, and therefore would not have the youth depraved with such opinions. Herein may much be said; let this suffice: the poets did not induce such opinions, but did imitate those opinions already induced. For all the Greek stories can well testify that the very religion of that time stood upon many and many-fashioned gods, not taught so by the poets, but followed according to their nature of imitation. Who list may read in Plutarch the discourses of Isis and Osiris, of the cause why oracles ceased, of the divine providence, and see whether the theology of that nation stood not upon such dreams which the poets indeed super-stitiously observed, and truly (since they had not the light of Christ) did much better in it than the philosophers, who, shaking off superstition, brought in atheism. Plato therefore (whose authority I had much rather justly construe than unjustly resist) meant not in general of poets, in those words of which Julius Scaliger saith, *Qua authoritate barbari quidam atque hispidi abuti velint ad poetas e republica exigendos;*[23] but only meant to drive out those wrong opinions of the Deity (whereof now, without further law, Christianity hath taken away all the hurtful belief), perchance (as he thought) nourished by the then esteemed poets. And a man need go no further than to Plato himself to know his meaning: who, in his Dialogue called *Ion*, giveth high and rightly divine commendation to Poetry. So as Plato, banishing the abuse, not the thing, not banishing it, but giving due honour unto it, shall be our patron and not our adversary. For indeed I had much rather (since truly I may do it) show their mis-taking of Plato (under whose lion's skin they would make an ass-like braying against Poesy) than go about to overthrow his authority; whom, the wiser a man is, the more just cause he shall find to have in admiration; especially since he attributeth unto Poesy more than myself do, namely, to be a very inspiring of a divine force, far above man's wit, as in the aforenamed Dialogue is apparent.

Of the other side, who would show the honours have been by the best sort of judgements granted them, a whole sea of examples would present themselves: Alexanders, Caesars, Scipios, all favourers of poets; Laelius, called the Roman Socrates, himself a poet, so as part of *Heaut-ontimorumenos* in Terence was supposed to be made by him, and even the Greek Socrates, whom Apollo confirmed to be the only wise man, is

---

[23] The rude and barbarous would abuse such an authority in order to drive the poets out of the state (*Poetice*, 1, 2).

said to have spent part of his old time in putting Aesop's fables into verses. And therefore, full evil should it become his scholar Plato to put such words in his master's mouth against poets. But what need more? Aristotle writes the Art of Poesy: and why, if it should not be written? Plutarch teacheth the use to be gathered of them, and how, if they should not be read? And who reads Plutarch's either history or philosophy, shall find he trimmeth both their garments with guards of Poesy. But I list not to defend Poesy with the help of her underling Historiography. Let it suffice that it is a fit soil for praise to dwell upon; and what dispraise may set upon it, is either easily overcome, or transformed into just commendation. So that, since the excellencies of it may be so easily and so justly confirmed, and the low-creeping objections so soon trodden down; it not being an art of lies, but of true doctrine; not of effeminateness, but of notable stirring of courage; not of abusing man's wit, but of strengthening man's wit; not banished, but honoured by Plato; let us rather plant more laurels for to engarland our poets' heads (which honour of being laureate, as besides them only triumphant captains wear, is a sufficient authority to show the price they ought to be had in) than suffer the ill-favouring breath of such wrong-speakers once to blow upon the clear springs of Poesy.

But since I have so long a career in this matter, methinks, before I give my pen a full stop, it shall be but a little more lost time to inquire why England (the mother of excellent minds) should be grown so hard a stepmother to poets, who certainly in wit ought to pass all other, since all only proceedeth from their wit, being indeed makers of themselves, not takers of others. How can I but exclaim,

*Musa, mihi causas memora, quo numine laeso!*[24]

Sweet Poesy, that hath anciently had kings, emperors, senators, great captains, such as, besides a thousand others, David, Adrian, Sophocles, Germanicus, not only to favour poets, but to be poets; and of our nearer times can present for her patrons a Robert, king of Sicily, the great King Francis of France, King James of Scotland; such cardinals as Bembus and Bibbiena: such famous preachers and teachers as Beza and Melancthon; so learned philosophers as Fracastorius and Scaliger; so great orators as Pontanus and Muretus; so piercing wits as George Buchanan; so grave counsellors as, besides many, but before all, that Hospital of France, than whom (I think) that realm never brought forth a more accomplished judgement, more firmly builded upon virtue—I say these, with numbers of others, not only to read others' poesies, but to poetize

---

[24] Tell me, O Muse, in what way was her divinity injured (*Aeneid*, I, 8).

for others' reading—that Poesy, thus embraced in all other places, should only find in our time a hard welcome in England, I think the very earth lamenteth it, and therefore decketh our soil with fewer laurels than it was accustomed. For heretofore poets have in England also flourished, and, which is to be noted, even in those times when the trumpet of Mars did sound loudest. And now that an overfaint quietness should seem to strew the house for poets, they are almost in as good reputation as the mountebanks at Venice. Truly even that, as of the one side it giveth great praise to Poesy, which like Venus (but to better purpose) hath rather be troubled in the net with Mars than enjoy the homely quiet of Vulcan; so serves it for a piece of a reason why they are less grateful to idle England, which now can scarce endure the pain of a pen. Upon this necessarily followeth, that base men with servile wits undertake it, who think it enough if they can be rewarded of the printer. And so as Epaminondas is said, with the honour of his virtue, to have made an office, by his exercising it, which before was contemptible, to become highly respected, so these, no more but setting their names to it, by their own disgracefulness disgrace the most graceful Poesy. For now, as if all the Muses were got with child, to bring forth bastard poets, without any commission they do post over the banks of Helicon, till they make the readers more weary than posthorses, while, in the meantime, they,

*Queis meliore luto finxit praecordia Titan,*[25]

are better content to suppress the outflowing of their wit, than, by publishing them, to be accounted knights of the same order. But I that, before ever I durst aspire unto the dignity, am admitted into the company of the paper-blurrers, do find the very true cause of our wanting estimation is want of desert, taking upon us to be poets in despite of Pallas. Now, wherein we want desert were a thankworthy labour to express: but if I knew, I should have mended myself. But I, as I never desired the title, so have I neglected the means to come by it. Only, overmastered by some thoughts, I yielded an inky tribute unto them. Marry, they that delight in Poesy itself should seek to know what they do, and how they do, and, especially, look themselves in an unflattering glass of reason, if they be inclinable unto it. For Poesy must not be drawn by the ears; it must be gently led, or rather it must lead; which was partly the cause that made the ancient-learned affirm it was a divine gift, and no human skill; since all other knowledges lie ready for any that hath strength of wit; a poet no industry can make, if his own genius be not carried unto it; and therefore is it an old proverb, *Orator fit, Poeta nascitur.*[26] Yet confesse

[25] Whose hearts Titan has fashioned of finer clay (Juvenal, *Satires*, XIV, 35).
[26] The orator is made, the poet is born.

I always that as the fertilest ground must be manured, so must the highest-flying wit have a Daedalus to guide him. That Daedalus, they say, both in this and in other, hath three wings to bear itself up into the air of due commendation: that is, Art, Imitation, and Exercise. But these, neither artificial rules nor imitative patterns, we much cumber ourselves withal. Exercise indeed we do, but that very fore-backwardly: for where we should exercise to know, we exercise as having known: and so is our brain delivered of much matter which never was begotten by knowledge. For, there being two principal parts—matter to be expressed by words and words to express the matter—in neither we use Art or Imitation rightly. Our matter is *Quodlibet* indeed, though wrongly performing Ovid's verse,

*Quicquid conabar dicere, versus erat;*[27]

never marshalling it into an assured rank, that almost the readers cannot tell where to find themselves. Chaucer, undoubtedly, did excellently in his *Troilus and Cressida*; of whom, truly, I know not whether to marvel more, either that he in that misty time could see so clearly, or that we in this clear age walk so stumblingly after him. Yet had he great wants, fit to be forgiven in so reverent antiquity. I account the *Mirrour of Magistrates* meetly furnished of beautiful parts, and in the Earl of Surrey's *Lyrics* many things tasting of a noble birth, and worthy of a noble mind. The *Shepheard's Calender* hath much poetry in his Eclogues, indeed worthy the reading, if I be not deceived. That same framing of his style to an old rustic language I dare not allow, since neither Theocritus in Greek, Virgil in Latin, nor Sannazzaro in Italian did affect it. Besides these, do I not remember to have seen but few (to speak boldly) printed, that have poetical sinews in them: for proof whereof, let but most of the verses be put in prose, and then ask the meaning; and it will be found that one verse did but beget another, without ordering at the first what should be at the last; which becomes a confused mass of words, with a tingling sound of rhyme, barely accompanied with reason.

Our Tragedies and Comedies (not without cause cried out against), observing rules neither of honest civility nor of skilful Poetry, excepting *Gorboduc* (again, I say, of those that I have seen), which notwithstanding, as it is full of stately speeches and well-sounding phrases, climbing to the height of Seneca's style, and as full of notable morality, which it doth most delightfully teach, and so obtain the very end of Poesy, yet in truth it is very defectious in the circumstances, which grieveth me, because it might not remain as an exact model of all Tragedies. For it is faulty both in

---

[27] Whatever I shall try to say will be verse (*Tristia*, IV, 10, 26).

place and time, the two necessary companions of all corporal actions. For where the stage should always represent but one place, and the uttermost time presupposed in it should be, both by Aristotle's precept and common reason, but one day, there is both many days, and many places, inartificially imagined. But if it be so in *Gorboduc*, how much more in all the rest, where you shall have Asia of the one side, and Afric of the other, and so many other under-kingdoms, that the player, when he cometh in, must ever begin with telling where he is, or else the tale will not be conceived? Now ye shall have three ladies walk to gather flowers and then we must believe the stage to be a garden. By and by we hear news of shipwreck in the same place, and then we are to blame if we accept it not for a rock.

Upon the back of that comes out a hideous monster, with fire and smoke, and then the miserable beholders are bound to take it for a cave. While in the meantime two armies fly in, represented with four swords and bucklers, and then what hard heart will not receive it for a pitched field? Now, of time they are much more liberal, for ordinary it is that two young princes fall in love. After many traverses, she is got with child, delivered of a fair boy; he is lost, groweth a man, falls in love, and is ready to get another child; and all this in two hours' space: which, how absurd it is in sense, even sense may imagine, and Art hath taught, and all ancient examples justified, and, at this day, the ordinary players in Italy will not err in. Yet will some bring in an example of Eunuchus in Terence,[28] that containeth matter of two days, yet far short of twenty years. True it is, and so was it to be played in two days, and so fitted to the time it set forth. And though Plautus hath in one place done amiss, let us hit with him, and not miss with him. But they will say, How then shall we set forth a story, which containeth both many places and many times? And do they not know that a Tragedy is tied to the laws of Poesy, and not of History; not bound to follow the story, but, having liberty, either to feign a quite new matter, or to frame the history to the most tragical conveniency? Again, many things may be told which cannot be showed, if they know the difference betwixt reporting and representing. As, for example, I may speak (though I am here) of Peru, and in speech digress from that to the description of Calicut; but in action I cannot represent it without Pacolet's horse. And so was the manner the ancients took, by some Nuncius[29] to recount things done in former time or other place. Lastly, if they will represent an history, they must not (as Horace saith) begin *ab ovo*,[30] but they must come to the principal

---

[28] The *Heautontimorumenos* (or *Self-Punisher*) of Terence, not the *Eunuchus*.
[29] Messenger.
[30] From the egg (or beginning); *Art of Poetry*, 1, 147.

point of that one action which they will represent.  By example this will be best expressed.  I have a story of young Polydorus, delivered for safety's sake, with great riches, by his father Priam to Polymnestor, king of Thrace, in the Trojan war time.  He, after same years, hearing the overthrow of Priam, for to make the treasure his own, murdereth the child. The body of the child is taken up by Hecuba.  She, the same day, findeth a slight to be revenged most cruelly of the tyrant.  Where now would one of our tragedy writers begin, but with the delivery of the child? Then should he sail over into Thrace, and so spend I know not how many years, and travel numbers of places.  But where doth Euripides?  Even with the finding of the body, leaving the rest to be told by the spirit of Polydorus.  This need no further to be enlarged; the dullest wit may conceive it.  But besides these gross absurdities, how all their plays be neither right tragedies, nor right comedies, mingling kings and clowns, not because the matter so carrieth it, but thrust in clowns by head and shoulders, to play a part in majestical matters, with neither decency[31] nor discretion, so as neither the admiration and commiseration, nor the right sportfulness, is by their mongrel tragi-comedy obtained.  I know Apuleius did somewhat so, but that is a thing recounted with space of time, not represented in one moment: and I know the ancients have one or two examples of tragi-comedies, as Plautus hath *Amphitrio*.  But, if we mark them well, we shall find, that they never, or very daintily, match hornpipes and funerals. So falleth it out that, having indeed no right comedy, in that comical part of our tragedy we have nothing but scurrility, unworthy of any chaste ears, or some extreme show of doltishness, indeed fit to lift up a loud laughter, and nothing else: where the whole tract of a comedy should be full of delight, as the tragedy should be still maintained in a well-raised admiration.  But our comedians think there is no delight without laughter; which is very wrong, for though laughter may come with delight, yet cometh it not of delight, as though delight should be the cause of laughter; but well may one thing breed both together.  Nay, rather in themselves they have, as it were, a kind of contrariety: for delight we scarcely do but in things that have a conveniency to ourselves or to the general nature: laughter almost ever cometh of things most disproportioned to ourselves and nature.  Delight hath a joy in it, either permanent or present.  Laughter hath only a scornful tickling.

For example, we are ravished with delight to see a fair woman, and yet are far from being moved to laughter.  We laugh at deformed creatures, wherein certainly we cannot delight.  We delight in good chances, we laugh at mischances; we delight to hear the happiness of our friends,

[31] Decorum (what is suitable or fitting).

or country, at which he were worthy to be laughed at that would laugh. We shall, contrarily, laugh sometimes to find a matter quite mistaken and go down the hill against the bias, in the mouth of some such men, as for the respect of them one shall be heartily sorry, yet he cannot choose but laugh; and so is rather pained than delighted with laughter. Yet deny I not but that they may go well together. For as in Alexander's picture well set out we delight without laughter, and in twenty mad antics we laugh without delight, so in Hercules, painted with his great beard and furious countenance, in woman's attire, spinning at Omphale's command- ment, it breedeth both delight and laughter. For the representing of so strange a power in love procureth delight: and the scornfulness of the action stirreth laughter. But I speak to this purpose, that all the end of the comical part be not upon such scornful matters as stirreth laughter only, but, mixed with it, that delightful teaching which is the end of Poesy. And the great fault even in that point of laughter, and forbidden plainly by Aristotle, is that they stir laughter in sinful things, which are rather execrable than ridiculous; or in miserable, which are rather to be pitied than scorned. For what is it to make folks gape at a wretched beggar, or a beggarly clown; or, against law of hospitality, to jest at stran- gers, because they speak not English so well as we do? What do we learn, since it is certain

> *Nil habet infelix paupertas durius in se,*
> *Quam quod ridiculos homines facit?*[32]

But rather a busy loving courtier, a heartless threatening Thraso, a self- wise-seeming schoolmaster, an awry-transformed traveller—these if we saw walk in stage names, which we play naturally, therein were delightful laughter, and teaching delightfulness: as in the other, the tragedies of Buchanan do justly bring forth a divine admiration. But I have lavished out too many words of this play matter. I do it because, as they are excelling parts of Poesy, so is there none so much used in England, and none can be more pitifully abused; which, like an unmannerly daughter showing a bad education, causeth her mother Poesy's honesty to be called in question. Other sorts of Poetry almost have we none, but that lyrical kind of songs and sonnets: which, Lord, if He gave us so good minds, how well it might be employed, and with how heavenly fruit, both private and public, in singing the praises of the immortal beauty, the immortal goodness of that God who giveth us hands to write and wits to conceive; of which we might well want words, but never matter; of which we could turn our eyes to nothing, but we should ever have

[32] Unhappy poverty has nothing worse than that it makes men ridiculous (Juvenal, *Satires*, III, 152-153).

new budding occasions.  But truly many of such writings as come under the banner of unresistible love, if I were a mistress, would never persuade me they were in love; so coldly they apply fiery speeches, as men that had rather read lovers' writings and so caught up certain swelling phrases (which hang together like a man which once told me the wind was at north-west, and by south, because he would be sure to name winds enough), than that in truth they feel those passions, which easily (as I think) may be betrayed by that same forcibleness or *Energia* (as the Greeks call it) of the writer.  But let this be a sufficient though short note, that we miss the right use of the material point of Poesy.

Now, for the outside of it, which is words, or (as I may term it) Diction, it is even well worse.  So is that honey-flowing matron Eloquence apparelled, or rather disguised, in a courtesan-like painted affectation: one time with so far-fetched words, they may seem monsters, but must seem strangers, to any poor Englishman; another time, with coursing of a letter, as if they were bound to follow the method of a dictionary; another time, with figures and flowers, extremely winter-starved.  But I would this fault were only peculiar to versifiers, and had not as large possession among prose-printers, and (which is to be marvelled) among many scholars, and (which is to be pitied) among some preachers.  Truly I could wish, if at least I might be so bold to wish in a thing beyond the reach of my capacity, the diligent imitators of Tully and Demosthenes (most worthy to be imitated) did not so much keep Nizolian paper-books of their figures and phrases, as by attentive translation (as it were) devour them whole, and make them wholly theirs.  For now they cast sugar and spice upon every dish that is served to the table, like those Indians, not content to wear earrings at the fit and natural place of the ears, but they will thrust jewels through their nose and lips, because they will be sure to be fine.

Tully, when he was to drive out Catiline, as it were with a thunderbolt of eloquence, often used that figure of repetition, *Vivit. Vivit? Imo in Senatum venit*, &c.[33]  Indeed, inflamed with a well-grounded rage, he would have his words (as it were) double out of his mouth, and so do that artificially which we see men do in choler naturally.  And we, having noted the grace of those words, hale them in sometime to a familiar epistle, when it were too much choler to be choleric.  Now for similitudes in certain printed discourses, I think all Herberists, all stories of beasts, fowls, and fishes are rifled up, that they come in multitudes to wait upon any of our conceits; which certainly is as absurd a surfeit to the ears as is possible: for the force of a similitude not being to prove anything to a contrary disputer, but only to explain to a willing hearer; when that is

[33] He lives. Lives?—He even comes into the senate.

done, the rest is a most tedious prattling, rather over-swaying the memory from the purpose whereto they were applied, than any whit informing the judgment, already either satisfied, or by similitudes not to be satisfied. For my part, I do not doubt, when Antonius and Crassus, the great forefathers of Cicero in eloquence, the one (as Cicero testifieth of them) pretended not to know art, the other not to set by it, because with a plain sensibleness they might win credit of popular ears; which credit is the nearest step to persuasion; which persuasion is the chief mark of Oratory— I do not doubt (I say) that but they used these knacks very sparingly; which, who doth generally use, any man may see doth dance to his own music; and so be noted by the audience more careful to speak curiously than to speak truly.

Undoubtedly (at least to my opinion undoubtedly) I have found in divers small-learned courtiers a more sound style than in some professors of learning: of which I can guess no other cause, but that the courtier, following that which by practice he findeth fittest to nature, therein (though he know it not) doth according to Art, though not by Art: where the other, using Art to show Art, and not to hide Art (as in these cases he should do), flieth from nature, and indeed abuseth Art.

But what? Methinks I deserve to be pounded for straying from Poetry to Oratory: but both have such an affinity in this wordish consideration, that I think this digression will make my meaning receive the fuller understanding—which is not to take upon me to teach poets how they should do, but only, finding myself sick among the rest, to show some one or two spots of the common infection grown among the most part of writers: that, acknowledging ourselves somewhat awry, we may bend to the right use both of matter and manner; whereto our language giveth us great occasion, being indeed capable of any excellent exercising of it. I know some will say it is a mingled language. And why not so much the better, taking the best of both the other? Another will say it wanteth grammar. Nay truly, it hath that praise, that it wanteth grammar: for grammar it might have, but it needs it not; being so easy of itself, and so void of those cumbersome differences of cases, genders, moods, and tenses, which I think was a piece of the Tower of Babylon's curse, that a man should be put to school to learn his mother-tongue. But for the uttering sweetly and properly the conceits of the mind, which is the end of speech, that hath it equally with any other tongue in the world: and is particularly happy in compositions of two or three words together, near the Greek, far beyond the Latin: which is one of the greatest beauties can be in a language.

Now, of versifying there are two sorts, the one ancient, the other modern: the ancient marked the quantity of each syllable, and according to that framed his verse; the modern observing only number (with some regard of the accent), the chief life of it standeth in that like sounding of the words, which we call rhyme. Whether of these be the most excellent, would bear many speeches. The ancient (no doubt) more fit for music, both words and tune observing quantity, and more fit lively to express divers passions, by the low and lofty sound of the well-weighed syllable. The latter likewise, with his rhyme, striketh a certain music to the ear: and, in fine, since it doth delight, though by another way, it obtains the same purpose: there being in either sweetness, and wanting in neither majesty. Truly the English, before any other vulgar language I know, is fit for both sorts: for, for the ancient, the Italian is so full of vowels that it must ever be cumbered with elisions; the Dutch so, of the other side, with consonants, that they cannot yield the sweet sliding fit for a verse; the French, in his whole language, hath not one word that hath his accent in the last syllable saving two, called *Antepenultima;* and little more hath the Spanish: and, therefore, very gracelessly may they use dactyls. The English is subject to none of these defects.

Now, for the rhyme, though we do not observe quantity, yet we observe the accent very precisely: which other languages either cannot do, or will not do so absolutely. That *caesura,* or breathing place in the midst of the verse, neither Italian nor Spanish have, the French, and we, never almost fail of. Lastly, even the very rhyme itself the Italian cannot put in the last syllable, by the French named the "masculine rhyme," but still in the next to the last, which the French call the "female," or the next·before that, which the Italians term *sdrucciola.* The example of the former is *buono: suono,* of the *sdrucciola, femina: semina.* The French, of the other side, hath both the male, as *bon: son,* and the female, as *plaise: taise* but the *sdrucciola* he hath not: where the English hath all three, as *due: true, father:rather, motion: potion,* with much more which might be said, but that I find already the triflingness of this discourse is much too much enlarged. So that since the ever-praise-worthy Poesy is full of virtue-breeding delightfulness, and void of no gift that ought to be in the noble name of learning; since the blames laid against it are either false or feeble; since the cause why it is not esteemed in England is the fault of poet-apes, not poets; since, lastly, our tongue is most fit to honour Poesy, and to be honoured by Poesy; I conjure you all that have had the evil luck to read this ink-wasting toy of mine, even in the name of the Nine Muses, no more to scorn the sacred mysteries of Poesy, no more to laugh at the name of "poets," as though they were next inheritors to fools, no more to jest at the reverent title of a "rhymer"; but to believe, with Aristotle, that they were the ancient treasurers of the Grecians' Divinity; to believe, with Bembus, that they were first bringers-in of all civility; to believe, with Scaliger, that no philosopher's precepts can sooner make you an honest man than the reading of Virgil; to believe, with Clauserus, the translator of Cornutus, that it pleased the heavenly Deity, by Hesiod and Homer, under the veil of fables, to give us all knowledge, Logic, Rhetoric, Philosophy, natural and moral, and *Quid non?*,[34] to believe, with me, that there are many mysteries contained in Poetry, which of purpose were written darkly, lest by profane wits it should be abused; to believe, with Landino, that they are so beloved of the gods that whatsoever they write proceeds of a divine fury; lastly, to believe themselves, when they tell you they will make you immortal by their verses.

Thus doing, your name shall flourish in the printers' shops; thus doing, you shall be of kin to many a poetical preface; thus doing, you shall be most fair, most rich, most wise, most all; you shall dwell upon superlatives. Thus doing, though you be *libertino patre natus*, you shall suddenly grow *Herculea proles*,

*Si quid mea carmina possunt.*[35]

Thus doing, your soul shall be placed with Dante's Beatrix, or Virgil's Anchises. But if (fie of such a but) you be born so near the dull-making cataract of Nilus that you cannot hear the planet-like music of Poetry, if you have so earth-creeping a mind that it cannot lift itself up to look to the sky of Poetry, or rather, by a certain rustical disdain, will become such a Mome as to be a Momus of Poetry; then, though I will not wish unto you the ass's ears of Midas, nor to be driven by a poet's verses (as Bubonax was) to hang himself, nor to be rhymed to death, as is said to be done in Ireland; yet thus much curse I must send you, in the behalf of all poets, that while you live, you live in love, and never get favour for lacking skill of a Sonnet, and, when you die, your memory die from the earth for want of an Epitaph.

---

[34] What not?

[35] The whole sentence may be rendered, "Thus doing, though you be the son of a former slave, you shall suddenly grow Herculean offspring, if my poems are able to do anything." The Latin phrases are, in order, from Horace, Ovid, and Virgil.

# An Essay of Dramatic Poesy

## 1668

*Dryden's artistry calls attention to itself: The essay, which is really a dramatization of a debate, is set in a narrative framework. Why this day, of all days (it happens to be June 3, 1665), does he engage in an urbane literary argument on a barge floating in the Thames? Dryden's first sentence indicates his purpose, "to vindicate the honour of our English writers," including the redemption of the then somewhat tarnished reputation of Shakespeare; so the larger naval battle in which the English defeat the Dutch serves to prefigure the outcome of the debate aboard the barge. The form of the dialogue allows Dryden to present four critical perspectives on every major issue of the late seventeenth century: the value of the unities, the ancients vs. the moderns, the neoclassical French vs. the Elizabethans, narrative vs. action, Shakespeare vs. Jonson, rhyme vs. blank verse, and so forth. Throughout, the basic contraries are art vs. nature; although each speaker uses nature as an aesthetic norm and the basis of his argument, each attaches a different meaning to that term. During the course of the debate we see alliances formed, based on the assumptions each holds; we also hear practical as well as theoretical criticism, rebuttal as well as formulation of theory.*

*Despite this lively and varied argument the essay is not finally inconclusive. The dialectical form allows for the gradual development of*

---

From *Essays of John Dryden*, ed. W. P. Ker; Oxford: Clarendon Press, 1900, reprinted 1926.

*principles that will apply to all poetic drama, for Dryden is attempting to establish universal principles, not merely to defend his own age. As the concluding speaker in the first round, Neander ("the new man") introduces the new criterion of the imagination: the nature of the human mind, which includes the mind of the audience as well as that of the poet. This leads directly to the "entr'acte," the Shakespeare-Jonson comparison and the analysis of "The Silent Woman," in which art and nature are combined. Incidentally, Jonson plays an important symbolic role in this essay; note the various uses the speakers make of him.*

*The shorter debate on rhyme may be thought of as a separate issue; however, seen as a second act in this drama, it is logically coherent with what has gone before. It is worthwhile to consider why now only Crites and Neander speak, and how their arguments here relate to what they have said earlier. It should also be remembered that Dryden was a playwright, concerned with the question of where he himself would be placed among the ranks that already included Shakespeare, Jonson, and Corneille.*

## TO THE READER

THE DRIFT of the ensuing Discourse was chiefly to vindicate the honour of our English writers, from the censure of those who unjustly prefer the French before them. This I intimate, lest any should think me so exceeding vain, as to teach others an art which they understand much better than myself. But if this incorrect Essay, written in the country without the help of books, or advice of friends, shall find any acceptance in the world, I promise to myself a better success of the second part, wherein the virtues and faults of the English poets, who have written either in this, the epic, or the lyric way, will be more fully treated of, and their several styles impartially imitated.

It was that memorable day, in the first summer of the late war, when our navy engaged the Dutch; a day wherein the two most mighty and best appointed fleets which any age had ever seen, disputed the command of the greater half of the globe, the commerce of nations, and the riches of the universe. While these vast floating bodies, on either side, moved against each other in parallel lines, and our countrymen, under the happy conduct of his Royal Highness, went breaking, by little and little, into the line of the enemies; the noise of the cannon from both navies reached our ears about the City, so that all men being alarmed with it, and in a dreadful suspense of the event which we knew was then deciding, every one went following the sound as his fancy led him; and leaving the town almost empty, some took towards the park, some cross the river, others down it; all seeking the noise in the depth of silence.

Among the rest, it was the fortune of Eugenius, Crites, Lisideius, and Neander, to be in company together; three of them persons whom their wit and quality have made known to all the town; and whom I have chose to hide under these borrowed names, that they may not suffer by so ill a relation as I am going to make of their discourse.

Taking then a barge which a servant of Lisideius had provided for them, they made haste to shoot the bridge, and left behind them that great fall of waters which hindered them from hearing what they desired: after which, having disengaged themselves from many vessels which rode at anchor in the Thames, and almost blocked up the passage towards Greenwich, they ordered the watermen to let fall their oars more gently; and then, every one favouring his own curiosity with a strict silence, it was not long ere they perceived the air break about them like the noise of distant thunder, or of swallows in a chimney: those little undulations of sound, though almost vanishing before they reached them, yet still seeming to retain somewhat of their first horror, which they had betwixt the fleets. After they had attentively listened till such time as the sound by little and little went from them, Eugenius, lifting up his head, and taking notice of it, was the first who congratulated to the rest that happy omen of our Nation's victory: adding, we had but this to desire in confirmation of it, that we might hear no more of that noise, which was now leaving the English coast. When the rest had concurred in the same opinion, Crites, a person of a sharp judgment, and somewhat too delicate a taste in wit, which the world have mistaken in him for ill-nature, said, smiling to us, that if the concernment of this battle had not been so exceeding great, he could scarce have wished the victory at the price he knew he must pay for it, in being subject to the reading and hearing of so many ill verses as he was sure would be made upon it. Adding, that no argument could scape some of those eternal rhymers, who watch a battle with more diligence than the ravens and birds of prey; and the worst of them surest to be first in upon the quarry: while the better able either out of modesty writ not at all, or set that due value upon their poems, as to let them be often called for and long expected! 'There are some of those impertinent people you speak of,' answered Lisideius, 'who to my knowledge are already so provided, either way, that they can produce not only a Panegyric upon the victory, but, if need be, a Funeral Elegy on the Duke; and after they have crowned his valour with many laurels, at last deplore the odds under which he fell, concluding that his courage deserved a better destiny.' All the company smiled at the conceit of

Lisideius; but Crites, more eager than before, began to make particular exceptions against some writers, and said, the public magistrate ought to send betimes to forbid them; and that it concerned the peace and quiet of all honest people, that ill poets should be as well silenced as seditious preachers. 'In my opinion,' replied Eugenius, 'you pursue your point too far; for as to my own particular, I am so great a lover of poesy, that I could wish them all rewarded, who attempt but to do well; at least, I would not have them worse used than Sylla the Dictator did one of their brethren heretofore:—*Quem in concione vidimus* (says Tully) *cum ei libellum malus poeta de populo subjecisset, quod epigramma in eum fecisset tantummodo alternis versibus longiusculis, statim ex iis rebus quas tunc vendebat jubere ei præmium tribui, sub ea conditione ne quid postea scriberet.*[1] 'I could wish with all my heart,' replied Crites, 'that many whom we know were as bountifully thanked upon the same condition,—that they would never trouble us again. For amongst others, I have a mortal apprehension of two poets, whom this victory, with the help of both her wings, will never be able to escape.' ' 'Tis easy to guess whom you intend,' said Lisideius; 'and without naming them, I ask you, if one of them does not perpetually pay us with clenches upon words, and a certain clownish kind of raillery? if now and then he does not offer at a catachresis or Clevelandism, wresting and torturing a word into another meaning: in fine, if he be not one of those whom the French would call *un mauvais buffon;* one that is so much a well-willer to the satire, that he spares no man; and though he cannot strike a blow to hurt any, yet ought to be punished for the malice of the action, as our witches are justly hanged, because they think themselves so; and suffer deservedly for believing they did mischief, because they meant it.' 'You have described him,' said Crites, 'so exactly, that I am afraid to come after you with my other extremity of poetry. He is one of those who, having had some advantage of education and converse, knows better than the other what a poet should be, but puts it into practice more unluckily than any man; his style and matter are everywhere alike: he is the most calm, peaceable writer you ever read: he never disquiets your passions with the least concernment, but still leaves you in as even a temper as he found you; he is a very Leveller in poetry: he creeps along with ten little words in every line, and helps out his numbers with *For to,* and *Unto,* and all the pretty expletives he can find, till he drags them to the end of another line; while the sense is left tired half way behind it: he doubly starves all his verses, first for want of thought, and then

---

[1] When in the assembly we saw *(says Tully)* that a bad poet from the crowd offered him a complimentary poem in rough elegiacs, he immediately ordered that a reward from the goods he was now selling should be given to him on condition that he should never afterwards write.

of expression; his poetry neither has wit in it, nor seems to have it; like him in Martial:

*Pauper videri Cinna vult, et est pauper.*[2]

'He affects plainness, to cover his want of imagination: when he writes the serious way, the highest flight of his fancy is some miserable antithesis, or seeming contradiction; and in the comic he is still reaching at some thin conceit, the ghost of a jest, and that too flies before him, never to be caught; these swallows which we see before us on the Thames are the just resemblance of his wit: you may observe how near the water they stoop, how many proffers they make to dip, and yet how seldom they touch it; and when they do, 'tis but the surface: they skim over it but to catch a gnat, and then mount into the air and leave it.'

'Well, gentlemen,' said Eugenius, 'you may speak your pleasure of these authors; but though I and some few more about the town may give you a peaceable hearing, yet assure yourselves, there are multitudes who would think you malicious and them injured: especially him whom you first described; he is the very Withers of the city: they have bought more editions of his works than would serve to lay under all their pies at the Lord Mayor's Christmas.   When his famous poem first came out in the year 1660, I have seen them reading it in the midst of 'Change time; nay so vehement they were at it, that they lost their bargain by the candles' ends; but what will you say, if he has been received amongst the great ones?   I can assure you he is, this day, the envy of a great Person who is lord in the art of quibbling; and who does not take it well, that any man should intrude so far into his province.' 'All I would wish,' replied Crites, 'is that they who love his writings, may still admire him, and his fellow poet: *Qui Bavium non odit, &c.,*[3] is curse sufficient.' 'And farther,' added Lisideius, 'I believe there is no man who writes well, but would think himself very hardly dealt with, if their admirers should praise anything of his: *Nam quos contemnimus, eorum quoque laudes contemnimus.*'[4] 'There are so few who write well in this age,' says Crites, 'that methinks any praises should be welcome; they neither rise to the dignity of the last age, nor to any of the Ancients: and we may cry out of the writers of this time, with more reason than Petronius of his, *Pace vestra liceat dixisse, primi omnium eloquentiam perdidistis*[5]: you have debauched the true old poetry so far, that Nature, which is the soul of it, is not in any of your writings.'

[2] Cinna pretends to be poor—and, in fact, he is poor.
[3] Who does not hate Bavius.
[4] For we despise the praise of people whom we despise.
[5] With your permission, let me say that you were the first of all to lose your eloquence.

'If your quarrel,' said Eugenius, 'to those who now write, be grounded only on your reverence to antiquity, there is no man more ready to adore those great Greeks and Romans than I am: but on the other side, I cannot think so contemptibly of the age I live in, or so dishonourably of my own country, as not to judge we equal the Ancients in most kinds of poesy, and in some surpass them; neither know I any reason why I may not be as zealous for the reputation of our age, as we find the Ancients themselves in reference to those who lived before them.   For you hear your Horace saying,

> *Indignor quidquam reprehendi, non quia crasse*
> *Compositum, illepidève putetur, sed quia nuper.*[6]

And after:

> *Si meliora dies, ut vina, poemata reddit,*
> *Scire velim, pretium chartis quotus arroget annus?*[7]

'But I see I am engaging in a wide dispute, where the arguments are not like to reach close on either side; for Poesy is of so large an extent, and so many both of the Ancients and Moderns have done well in all kinds of it, that in citing one against the other, we shall take up more time this evening than each man's occasions will allow him: therefore I would ask Crites to what part of Poesy he would confine his arguments, and whether he would defend the general cause of the Ancients against the Moderns, or oppose any age of the Moderns against this of ours?'

Crites, a little while considering upon this demand, told Eugenius he approved his propositions, and if he pleased, he would limit their dispute to Dramatic Poesy; in which he thought it not difficult to prove, either that the Ancients were superior to the Moderns, or the last age to this of ours.

Eugenius was somewhat surprised, when he heard Crites make choice of that subject.   'For ought I see,' said he, 'I have undertaken a harder province than I imagined; for though I never judged the plays of the Greek or Roman poets comparable to ours, yet, on the other side, those we now see acted come short of many which were written in the last age: but my comfort is, if we are o'ercome, it will be only by our own countrymen: and if we yield to them in this one part of poesy, we more surpass them in all the other: for in the epic or lyric way, it will be hard for them to show us one such amongst them, as we have many now living, or who lately were so: they can produce nothing so courtly writ, or which ex-

---

[6] I resent anything's being condemned merely because it is new and not because it is considered to be crudely or coarsely written.

[7] If time improves poems, as it does wines, I should like to know how many years give value to literature.

presses so much the conversation of a gentleman, as Sir John Suckling; nothing so even, sweet, and flowing, as Mr. Waller; nothing so majestic, so correct, as Sir John Denham; nothing so elevated, so copious, and full of spirit, as Mr. Cowley; as for the Italian, French, and Spanish plays, I can make it evident, that those who now write surpass them; and that the Drama is wholly ours.'

All of them were thus far of Eugenius his opinion, that the sweetness of English verse was never understood or practised by our fathers; even Crites himself did not much oppose it: and every one was willing to acknowledge how much our poesy is improved by the happiness of some writers yet living; who first taught us to mould our thoughts into easy and significant words; to retrench the superfluities of expression, and to make our rhyme so properly a part of the verse, that it should never mislead the sense, but itself be led and governed by it.

Eugenius was going to continue this discourse, when Lisideius told him it was necessary, before they proceeded further, to take a standing measure of their controversy; for how was it possible to be decided who writ the best plays, before we know what a play should be?  But, this once agreed on by both parties, each might have recourse to it, either to prove his own advantages, or to discover the failings of his adversary.

He had no sooner said this, but all desired the favour of him to give the definition of a play; and they were the more importunate, because neither Aristotle, nor Horace, nor any other, who writ of that subject, had ever done it.

Lisideius, after some modest denials, at last confessed he had a rude notion of it; indeed, rather a description than a definition; but which served to guide him in his private thoughts, when he was to make a judgment of what others writ: that he conceived a play ought to be, *A just and lively image of human nature, representing its passions and humours, and the changes of fortune to which it is subject, for the delight and instruction of mankind.*

This definition, though Crites raised a logical objection against it; that it was only *a genere et fine*, and so not altogether perfect; was yet well received by the rest: and after they had given order to the watermen to turn their barge, and row softly, that they might take the cool of the evening in their return, Crites, being desired by the company to begin, spoke on behalf of the Ancients, in this manner:

'If confidence presage a victory, Eugenius, in his own opinion, has already triumphed over the Ancients: nothing seems more easy to him, than to overcome those whom it is our greatest praise to have imitated well; for we do not only build upon their foundation, but by their models. Dramatic Poesy had time enough, reckoning from Thespis (who first invented it) to Aristophanes, to be born, to grow up, and to flourish in maturity. It has been observed of arts and sciences, that in one and the same century they have arrived to a great perfection; and no wonder, since every age has a kind of universal genius, which inclines those that live in it to some particular studies: the work then being pushed on by many hands, must of necessity go forward.

'Is it not evident, in these last hundred years (when the study of philosophy has been the business of all the Virtuosi in Christendom), that almost a new Nature has been revealed to us?—that more errors of the school have been detected, more useful experiments in philosophy have been made, more noble secrets in optics, medicine, anatomy, astronomy, discovered, than in all those credulous and doting ages from Aristotle to us?—so true it is, that nothing spreads more fast than science, when rightly and generally cultivated.

'Add to this, the more than common emulation that was in those times of writing well; which though it be found in all ages and all persons that pretend to the same reputation, yet Poesy, being then in more esteem than now it is, had greater honours decreed to the professors of it, and consequently the rivalship was more high between them; they had judges ordained to decide their merit, and prizes to reward it; and historians have been diligent to record of Eschylus, Euripides, Sophocles, Lycophron, and the rest of them, both who they were that vanquished in these wars of the theatre, and how often they were crowned: while the Asian kings and Grecian commonwealths scarce afforded them a nobler subject than the unmanly luxuries of a debauched court, or giddy intrigues of a factious city. *Alit æmulatio ingenia*, (says Paterculus,) *et nunc invidia, nunc admiratio incitationem accendit:* Emulation is the spur of wit; and sometimes envy, sometimes admiration, quickens our endeavours.

'But now, since the rewards of honour are taken away, that virtuous emulation is turned into direct malice; yet so slothful, that it contents itself to condemn and cry down others, without attempting to do better: 'tis a reputation too unprofitable, to take the necessary pains for it; yet, wishing they had it is incitement enough to hinder others from it. And this, in short, Eugenius, is the reason why you have now so few good poets, and so many severe judges. Certainly, to imitate the Ancients well, much labour and long study is required; which pains, I have already shown, our poets would want encouragement to take, if yet they had ability to go through with it. Those Ancients have been faithful imitators and wise observers of that Nature which is so torn and ill represented in our plays; they have handed down to us a perfect resemblance of her; which we, like ill copiers, neglecting to look on, have rendered monstrous, and disfigured. But, that you may know how much you are indebted to those your masters, and be ashamed to have so ill requited them, I must remember you, that all the rules by which we practise the Drama at this day, (either such as relate to the justness and symmetry of the plot, or the episodical ornaments, such as descriptions, narrations and other beauties, which are not essential to the play,) were delivered to us from the observations which Aristotle made, of those poets, which either lived before him, or were his contemporaries: we have added nothing of our own, except we have the confidence to say our wit is better; of which none boast in this our age, but such as understand not theirs.    Of that book which Aristotle has left us, περὶ τῆς Ποιητικῆς,[8] Horace his *Art of Poetry* is an excellent comment, and, I believe, restores to us that Second Book of his concerning *Comedy*, which is wanting in him.

'Out of these two have been extracted the famous Rules, which the French call *Des Trois Unitez*, or, the Three Unities, which ought to be observed in every regular play; namely, of Time, Place, and Action.

'The Unity of Time they comprehend in twenty-four hours, the compass of a natural day, or as near as it can be contrived; and the reason of it is obvious to every one,—that the time of the feigned action, or fable of the play, should be proportioned as near as can be to the duration of that time in which it is represented: since therefore, all plays are acted on the theatre in a space of time much within the compass of twenty-four hours, that play is to be thought the nearest imitation of nature, whose plot or action is confined within that time; and, by the same rule which concludes this general proportion of time, it follows, that all the parts of it are to be equally subdivided; as namely, that one act take not up the supposed time of half a day, which is out of proportion to the rest; since the other four are then to be straitened within the compass of the remaining half: for it is unnatural that one act, which being spoke or written is not longer than the rest, should be supposed longer by the audience; 'tis therefore the poet's duty, to take care that no act should be imagined to exceed the time in which it is represented on the stage; and that the intervals and inequalities of time be supposed to fall out between the acts.

'This rule of time, how well it has been observed by the Ancients, most of their plays will witness; you see them in their tragedies, (wherein to follow this rule, is certainly most difficult,) from the very beginning of their plays, falling close into that part of the story which they intend for the action or principal object of it, leaving the former part to be delivered by narration: so that they set the audience, as it were, at the post where the race is to be concluded; and, saving them the tedious expectation of seeing the poet set out and ride the beginning of the course, you behold him not till he is in sight of the goal, and just upon you.

---

[8] *Peri tes Poietikes*, "The Poetics."

'For the second Unity, which is that of Place, the Ancients meant by it, that the scene ought to be continued through the play, in the same place where it was laid in the beginning: for the stage on which it is represented being but one and the same place, it is unnatural to conceive it many; and those far distant from one another.    I will not deny but, by the variation of painted scenes, the fancy, which in these cases will contribute to its own deceit, may sometimes imagine it several places, with some appearance of probability; yet it still carries the greater likelihood of truth, if those places be supposed so near each other, as in the same town or city; which may all be comprehended under the larger denomination of one place; for a greater distance will bear no proportion to the shortness of time which is allotted in the acting, to pass from one of them to another; for the observation of this, next to the Ancients, the French are to be most commended.    They tie themselves so strictly to the Unity of Place, that you never see in any of their plays, a scene changed in the middle of an act: if the act begins in a garden, a street, or chamber, 'tis ended in the same place; and that you may know it to be the same, the stage is so supplied with persons, that it is never empty all the time: he that enters the second, has business with him who was on before; and before the second quits the stage, a third appears who has business with him.    This Corneille calls *la liaison des scènes*, the continuity or joining of the scenes; and 'tis a good mark of a well-contrived play, when all the persons are known to each other, and every one of them has some affairs with all the rest.

'As for the third Unity, which is that of Action, the Ancients meant no other by it than what the logicians do by their *finis*, the end or scope of any action; that which is the first in intention, and last in execution: now the poet is to aim at one great and complete action, to the carrying on of which all things in his play, even the very obstacles, are to be subservient; and the reason of this is as evident as any of the former.

'For two actions, equally laboured and driven on by the writer, would destroy the unity of the poem; it would be no longer one play, but two: not but that there may be many actions in a play, as Ben Jonson has observed in his *Discoveries;* but they must be all subservient to the great one, which our language happily expresses in the name of *under-plots:* such as in Terence's *Eunuch* is the difference and reconcilement of Thais and Phædria, which is not the chief business of the play, but promotes the marriage of Chærea and Chremes's sister, principally intended by the poet. There ought to be but one action, says Corneille, that is, one complete action which leaves the mind of the audience in a full repose; but this cannot be brought to pass but by many other imperfect actions, which conduce to it, and hold the audience in a delightful suspense of what will be.

'If by these rules (to omit many other drawn from the precepts and practice of the Ancients) we should judge our modern plays, 'tis probable that few of them would endure the trial: that which should be the business of a day, takes up in some of them an age; instead of one action, they are the epitomes of a man's life; and for one spot of ground (which the stage should represent) we are sometimes in more countries than the map can show us.

'But if we will allow the Ancients to have contrived well, we must acknowledge them to have writ better; questionless we are deprived of a great stock of wit in the loss of Menander among the Greek poets, and of Cæcilius, Afranius, and Varius, among the Romans; we may guess at Menander's excellency by the plays of Terence, who translated some of his; and yet wanted so much of him, that he was called by C. Caesar the half-Menander; and may judge of Varius, by the testimonies of Horace, Martial, and Velleius Paterculus. 'Tis probable that these, could they be recovered, would decide the controversy; but so long as Aristophanes in the old Comedy, and Plautus in the new are extant, while the tragedies of Euripides, Sophocles, and Seneca, are to be had, I can never see one of those plays which are now written, but it increases my admiration of the Ancients. And yet I must acknowledge farther, that to admire them as we ought, we should understand them better than we do. Doubtless many things appear flat to us, whose wit depended on some custom or story, which never came to our knowledge; or perhaps on some criticism in their language, which being so long dead, and only remaining in their books, 'tis not possible they should make us know it perfectly. To read Macrobius, explaining the propriety and elegancy of many words in Virgil, which I had before passed over without consideration, as common things, is enough to assure me that I ought to think the same of Terence; and that in the purity of his style (which Tully so much valued that he ever carried his works about him) there is yet left in him great room for admiration, if I knew but where to place it. In the mean time I must desire you to take notice, that the greatest man of the last age (Ben Jonson) was willing to give place to them in all things: he was not only a professed imitator of Horace, but a learned plagiary of all the others; you track him every where in their snow: if Horace, Lucan, Petronius Arbiter, Seneca, and Juvenal, had their own from him, there are few serious thoughts which are new in him: you will pardon me, therefore, if I presume he loved their fashion, when he wore their clothes. But since I have otherwise a great veneration for him, and you, Eugenius, prefer him above all other poets, I will use no farther argument to you than his example: I will produce Father Ben to you, dressed in all the ornaments and colours of the Ancients; you will need no other guide to our party, if you follow him; and whether you consider the bad plays of our age, or regard the good ones of the last, both the best and worst of the modern poets will equally instruct you to esteem the Ancients.'

Crites had no sooner left speaking, but Eugenius, who had waited with some impatience for it, thus began:

'I have observed in your speech, that the former part of it is convincing as to what the Moderns have profited by the rules of the Ancients; but in the latter you are careful to conceal how much they have excelled them; we own all the helps we have from them, and want neither veneration nor gratitude while we acknowledge that to overcome them we must make use of the advantages we have received from them: but to these assistances we have joined our own industry; for, had we sat down with a dull imitation of them, we might then have lost somewhat of the old perfection, but never acquired any that was new. We draw not therefore after their lines, but those of Nature; and having the life before us, besides the experience of all they knew, it is wonder if we hit some airs and features which they have missed. I deny not what you urge of arts and sciences, that they have flourished in some ages more than others; but your instance in philosophy makes for me: for if natural causes be more known now than in the time of Aristotle, because more studied, it follows that poesy and other arts may, with the same pains, arrive still nearer to perfection; and, that granted, it will rest for you to prove that they wrought more perfect images of human life than we; which seeing in your discourse you have avoided to make good, it shall now be my task to show you some part of their defects, and some few excellencies of the Moderns. And I think there is none among us can imagine I do it enviously, or with purpose to detract from them; for what interest of fame or profit can the living lose by the reputation of the dead? On the other side, it is a great truth which Velleius Paterculus affirms: *Audita visis libentius laudamus; et præsentia invidia, præterita admiratione prosequimur; et his nos obrui, illis instrui credimus*[9]: that praise or censure is certainly the most sincere, which unbribed posterity shall give us.

'Be pleased then in the first place to take notice, that the Greek poesy, which Crites has affirmed to have arrived to perfection in the reign of the Old Comedy, was so far from it, that the distinction of it into acts was not known to them; or if it were, it is yet so darkly delivered to us that we cannot make it out.

'All we know of it is, from the singing of their Chorus; and that too is so uncertain, that in some of their plays we have reason to conjecture they

---

[9] What is heard we praise more willingly than what is seen, and we follow the present with envy, the past with admiration; and we believe ourselves harmed by the former but edified by the latter.

sung more than five times.   Aristotle indeed divides the integral parts of
play into four.   First, the *Protasis*, or entrance, which gives light only to
the characters of the persons, and proceeds very little into any part of the
action.   Secondly, the *Epitasis*, or working up of the plot; where the play
grows warmer, the design or action of it is drawing on, and you see something promising that it will come to pass.   Thirdly, the *Catastasis*, or
counterturn, which destroys that expectation, imbroils the action in new
difficulties, and leaves you far distant from that hope in which it found
you; as you may have observed in a violent stream resisted by a narrow
passage,—it runs round to an eddy, and carries back the waters with more
swiftness than it brought them on.   Lastly, the *Catastrophe*, which the
Grecians called λύσις [lysis], the French *le dénouement*, and we the discovery or unravelling of the plot: there you see all things settling again
upon their first foundations; and, the obstacles which hindered the design
or action of the play once removed, it ends with that resemblance of truth
and nature, that the audience are satisfied with the conduct of it.   Thus
this great man delivered to us the image of a play; and I must confess it is
so lively, that from thence much light has been derived to the forming it
more perfectly into acts and scenes: but what poet first limited to five the
number of the acts, I know not; only we see it so firmly established in the
time of Horace, that he gives it for a rule in comedy; *Neu brevior quinto, neu
sit productior actu.*[10]   So that you see the Grecians cannot be said to have
consummated this art; writing rather by entrances, than by acts, and
having rather a general indigested notion of a play, than knowing how
and where to bestow the particular graces of it.

'But since the Spaniards at this day allow but three acts, which they
call *Jornadas*, to a play, and the Italians in many of theirs follow them,
when I condemn the Ancients, I declare it is not altogether because they
have not five acts to every play, but because they have not confined themselves to one certain number: it is building an house without a model; and
when they succeeded in such undertakings, they ought to have sacrificed
to Fortune, not to the Muses.

'Next, for the plot, which Aristotle called τὸ μῦθος,[11] and often τῶν
πραγμάτων σύνθεσις,[12] and from him the Romans *Fabula*, it has already
been judiciously observed by a late writer, that in their tragedies it was
only some tale derived from Thebes or Troy, or at least something that
happened in those two ages; which was worn so threadbare by the pens of
all the epic poets, and even by tradition itself of the talkative Greeklings,
(as Ben Jonson calls them,) that before it came upon the stage, it was

[10] Let it be neither shorter than five acts, nor longer.
[11] *To mythos;* compare English *myth.*
[12] *Ton pragmaton synthesis,* the putting together of the action.

already known to all the audience: and the people, so soon as ever they heard the name of Œdipus, knew as well as the poet, that he had killed his father by a mistake, and committed incest with his mother, before the play; that they were now to hear of a great plague, an oracle, and the ghost of Laius: so that they sat with a yawning kind of expectation, till he was to come with his eyes pulled out, and speak a hundred or two of verses in a tragic tone, in complaint of his misfortunes.    But one Œdipus, Hercules, or Medea, had been tolerable: poor people, they scaped not so good cheap; they had still the *chapon bouillé*[13] set before them, till their appetites were cloyed with the same dish, and, the novelty being gone, the pleasure vanished; so that one main end of Dramatic Poesy in its definition, which was to cause delight, was of consequence destroyed.

'In their comedies, the Romans generally borrowed their plots from the Greek poets; and theirs was commonly a little girl stolen or wandered from her parents, brought back unknown to the same city, there got with child by some lewd young fellow, who, by the help of his servant, cheats his father; and when her time comes, to cry *Juno Lucina, fer opem*,[14] one or other sees a little box or cabinet which was carried away with her, and so discovers her to her friends, if some god do not prevent it, by coming down in a machine, and take the thanks of it to himself.

'By the plot you may guess much of the characters of the persons.    An old father, who would willingly, before he dies, see his son well married; his debauched son, kind in his nature to his wench, but miserably in want of money; a servant or slave, who has so much wit to strike in with him, and help to dupe his father; a braggadochio captain, a parasite, and a lady of pleasure.

'As for the poor honest maid, whom all the story is built upon, and who ought to be one of the principal actors in the play, she is commonly a mute in it: she has the breeding of the old Elizabeth way, for maids to be seen and not to be heard; and it is enough you know she is willing to be married, when the fifth act requires it.

'These are plots built after the Italian mode of houses; you see through them all at once: the characters are indeed the imitations of Nature, but so narrow, as if they had imitated only an eye or an hand, and did not dare to venture on the lines of a face, or the proportion of a body.

'But in how strait a compass soever they have bounded their plots and characters, we will pass it by, if they have regularly pursued them, and perfectly observed those three Unities of Time, Place, and Action; the knowledge of which you say is derived to us from them.    But in the first place give me leave to tell you, that the Unity of Place, however it might

---

[13] Boiled capon, *literally. Probably meaning* a luxury.
[14] Juno, goddess of childbirth, bring help.

be practised by them, was never any of their rules: we neither find it in
Aristotle, Horace, or any who have written of it, till in our age the French
poets first made it a precept of the stage.   The Unity of Time, even
Terence himself (who was the best and most regular of them) has neglected: his *Heautontimorumenos*, or *Self-Punisher*, takes up visibly two days;
therefore, says Scaliger, the two first acts concluding the first day were
acted overnight; the three last on the ensuing day; and Euripides, in tying
himself to one day, has committed an absurdity never to be forgiven him;
for in one of his tragedies he has made Theseus go from Athens to Thebes,
which was about forty English miles, under the walls of it to give battle,
and appear victorious in the next act; and yet, from the time of his
departure to the return of the Nuntius, who gives the relation of his victory,
Æthra and the Chorus have but thirty-six verses; that is not for every mile
a verse.

'The like error is as evident in Terence his *Eunuch*, when Laches, the old
man, enters in a mistake the house of Thais; where, betwixt his exit and
the entrance of Pythias, who comes to give an ample relation of the
garboyles he has raised within, Parmeno, who was left upon the stage, has
not above five lines to speak.   *C'est bien employer un temps si court*,[15] says the
French poet, who furnished me with one of the observations: and almost
all their tragedies will afford us examples of the like nature.

' 'Tis true, they have kept the continuity, or, as you called it, *liaison des
scènes*, somewhat better: two do not perpetually come in together, talk, and
go out together; and other two succeed them, and do the same throughout
the act, which the English call by the name of single scenes; but the reason
is, because they have seldom above two or three scenes, properly so called,
in every act; for it is to be accounted a new scene, not every time the stage
is empty; but every person who enters, though to others, makes it so;
because he introduces a new business.   Now the plots of their plays being
narrow, and the persons few, one of their acts was written in a less compass
than one of our well-wrought scenes; and yet they are often deficient even
in this.   To go no further than Terence; you find in the *Eunuch* Antipho
entering single in the midst of the third act, after Cremes and Pythias
were gone off; in the same play you have likewise Dorias beginning the
fourth act alone; and after she had made a relation of what was done at
the Soldier's entertainment (which by the way was very inartificial,
because she was presumed to speak directly to the audience, and to acquaint them with what was necessary to be known, but yet should have
been so contrived by the poet as to have been told by persons of the drama
to one another, and so by them to have come to the knowledge of the
people), she quits the stage, and Phædria enters next, alone likewise: he

---

[15] So short a time is well used.

also gives you an account of himself, and of his returning from the country, in monologue; to which unnatural way of narration Terence is subject in all his plays.    In his *Adelphi*, or Brothers, Syrus and Demea enter after the scene was broken by the departure of Sostrata, Geta, and Canthara; and indeed you can scarce look into any of his comedies, where you will not presently discover the same interruption.

'But as they have failed both in laying of their plots, and managing of them, swerving from the rules of their own art by misrepresenting Nature to us, in which they have ill satisfied one intention of a play, which was delight; so in the instructive part they have erred worse: instead of punishing vice and rewarding virtue, they have often shown a prosperous wickedness, and an unhappy piety: they have set before us a bloody image of revenge in Medea, and given her dragons to convey her safe from punishment; a Priam and Astyanax murdered, and Cassandra ravished, and the lust and murder ending in the victory of him who acted them: in short, there is no indecorum in any of our modern plays, which if I would excuse, I could not shadow with some authority from the Ancients.

'And one farther note of them let me leave you: tragedies and comedies were not writ then as they are now, promiscuously, by the same person; but he who found his genius bending to the one, never attempted the other way.    This is so plain, that I need not instance to you, that Aristophanes, Plautus, Terence, never any of them writ a tragedy; Æschylus, Euripides, Sophocles, and Seneca, never meddled with comedy: the sock and buskin were not worn by the same poet.    Having then so much care to excel in one kind, very little is to be pardoned them, if they miscarried in it; and this would lead me to the consideration of their wit, had not Crites given me sufficient warning not to be too bold in my judgment of it; because, the languages being dead, and many of the customs and little accidents on which it depended lost to us, we are not competent judges of it.    But though I grant that here and there we may miss the application of a proverb or a custom, yet a thing well said will be wit in all languages; and though it may lose something in the translation, yet to him who reads it in the original, 'tis still the same: he has an idea of its excellency, though it cannot pass from his mind into any other expression or words than those in which he finds it.    When Phædria, in the *Eunuch*, had a command from his mistress to be absent two days, and, encouraging himself to go through with it, said, *Tandem ego non illa caream, si sit opus, vel totum triduum?*[16]— Parmeno, to mock the softness of his master, lifting up his hands and eyes, cries out, as it were in admiration, *Hui! universum triduum!*[17] the elegancy of which *universum*, though it cannot be rendered in our language, yet

---

[16] Shall I not do without her for even three days if necessary?
[17] Alas, all of three days!

leaves an impression on our souls: but this happens seldom in him; in Plautus oftener, who is infinitely too bold in his metaphors and coining words, out of which many times his wit is nothing; which questionless was one reason why Horace falls upon him so severely in those verses:—

> Sed proavi nostri Plautinos et nummeros et
> Laudavere sales, nimium patienter utrumque,
> Ne dicam stolidè.[18]

For Horace himself was cautious to obtrude a new word on his readers, and makes custom and common use the best measure of receiving it into our writings:

> Multa renascentur quae nunc cecidere cadentque
> Quae nunc sunt honore vocabula, si volet usus,
> Quem penes arbitrium est, et jus, et norma loquendi.[19]

'The not observing this rule is that which the world has blamed in our satyrist, Cleveland: to express a thing hard and unnaturally, is his new way of elocution. 'Tis true, no poet but may sometimes use a cata-chresis: Virgil does it—

> Mistaque ridenti colocasia fundet acantho—[20]

in his eclogue of Pollio; and in his 7th Æneid,

> . . . mirantur et undae,
> Miratur nemus insuetum fulgentia longe
> Scuta virum fluvio pictasque innare carinas.[21]

And Ovid once so modestly, that he asks leave to do it:

> . . . quem, si verbo audacia detur,
> Haud metuam summi dixisse Palatia caeli;[22]

calling the court of Jupiter by the name of Augustus his palace; though in another place he is more bold, where he says,—et longas visent Capitolia pompas.[23]   But to do this always, and never be able to write a line without it, though it may be admired by some few pedants, will not pass upon those who know that wit is best conveyed to us in the most easy language; and is most to be admired when a great thought comes dressed in words so

---

[18] Our ancestors praised the meter and wit of Plautus all too tolerantly, if not stupidly.

[19] Many words now disused will revive, and many now esteemed will wither, if custom demands; for custom determines the right usage in language.

[20] And the colocasia shall flower, joined with the smiling acanthus.

[21] The woods and waters wonder at the gleam/Of shields, and painted ships, that stem the stream.   (Dryden)

[22] If I may be allowed a bold metaphor, I should not fear to call it the imperial palace.

[23] The capitol will see long processions.

commonly received, that it is understood by the meanest apprehensions, as the best meat is the most easily digested: but we cannot read a verse of Cleveland's without making a face at it, as if every word were a pill to swallow: he gives us many times a hard nut to break our teeth, without a kernel for our pains.   So that there is this difference betwixt his *Satires* and doctor Donne's; that the one gives us deep thoughts in common language, though rough cadence; the other gives us common thoughts in abstruse words: 'tis true, in some places his wit is independent of his words, as in that of the *Rebel Scot:*

> Had *Cain* been *Scot*, God would have chang'd his doom;
> Not forc'd him wander, but confin'd him home.

'*Si sic omnia dixisset!*[24] This is wit in all languages: 'tis like Mercury, never to be lost or killed:—and so that other—

> For beauty, like white powder, makes no noise,
> And yet the silent hypocrite destroys.

You see, the last line is highly metaphorical, but it is so soft and gentle, that it does not shock us as we read it.

'But, to return from whence I have digressed, to the consideration of the Ancients' writing, and their wit; of which by this time you will grant us in some measure to be fit judges.   Though I see many excellent thoughts in Seneca, yet he of them who had a genius most proper for the stage, was Ovid; he had a way of writing so fit to stir up a pleasing admiration and concernment, which are the objects of a tragedy, and to show the various movements of a soul combating betwixt two different passions, that, had he lived in our age, or in his own could have writ with our advantages, no man but must have yielded to him; and therefore I am confident the *Medea* is none of his: for, though I esteem it for the gravity and sententiousness of it, which he himself concludes to be suitable to a tragedy,—*Omne genus scripti gravitate tragaedia vincit*,[25]—yet it moves not my soul enough to judge that he, who in the epic way wrote things so near the drama as the story of Myrrha, of Caunus and Biblis, and the rest, should stir up no more concernment where he most endeavoured it.   The master-piece of Seneca I hold to be that scene in the *Troades*, where Ulysses is seeking for Astyanax to kill him; there you see the tenderness of a mother so represented in Andromache, that it raises compassion to a high degree in the reader, and bears the nearest resemblance of any thing in their tragedies to the excellent scenes of passion in Shakespeare, or in Fletcher: for love-scenes, you will find few among them; their tragic poets dealt not

---

[24] If only he had said everything thus.
[25] Tragedy exceeds every other kind of writing in gravity.

with that soft passion, but with lust, cruelty, revenge, ambition, and those bloody actions they produced; which were more capable of raising horror than compassion in an audience: leaving love untouched, whose gentleness would have tempered them, which is the most frequent of all the passions, and which, being the private concernment of every person, is soothed by viewing its own image in a public entertainment.

'Among their comedies, we find a scene or two of tenderness, and that where you would least expect it, in Plautus; but to speak generally, their lovers say little, when they see each other, but *anima mea, vita mea; ζωη καὶ ψυχη*,[26] as the women in Juvenal's time used to cry out in the fury of their kindness: then indeed to speak sense were an offence. Any sudden gust of passion (as an extasy of love in an unexpected meeting) cannot better be expressed than in a word and a sigh, breaking one another. Nature is dumb on such occasions; and to make her speak, would be to represent her unlike herself. But there are a thousand other concernments of lovers, as jealousies, complaints, contrivances, and the like, where not to open their minds at large to each other, were to be wanting to their own love, and to the expectation of the audience; who watch the movements of their minds, as much as the changes of their fortunes. For the imaging of the first is properly the work of a poet; the latter he borrows of the historian.'

Eugenius was proceeding in that part of his discourse, when Crites interrupted him. 'I see,' said he, 'Eugenius and I are never like to have this question decided betwixt us; for he maintains the Moderns have acquired a new perfection in writing; I can only grant they have altered the mode of it. Homer described his heroes men of great appetites, lovers of beef broiled upon the coals, and good fellows; contrary to the practice of the French Romances, whose heroes neither eat, nor drink, nor sleep, for love. Virgil makes Æneas a bold avower of his own virtues:

*Sum pius Æneas, fama super aethera notus:*[27]

which in the civility of our poets is the character of a fanfaron or Hector: for with us the knight takes occasion to walk out, or sleep, to avoid the vanity of telling his own story, which the trusty squire is ever to perform for him. So in their love-scenes, of which Eugenius spoke last, the Ancients were more hearty, we more talkative: they writ love as it was then the mode to make it; and I will grant thus much to Eugenius, that perhaps one of their poets, had he lived in our age, *si foret hoc nostrum fato delapsus in œvum*[28] (as Horace says of Lucilius), he had altered many things; not that

---

[26] *Zoe kai psyche*, my soul, my life.
[27] I am pious Aeneas, whose fame is known above the heavens.
[28] If he had been dropped into our age by fate.

they were not as natural before, but that he might accommodate himself to the age he lived in.     Yet in the mean time, we are not to conclude any thing rashly against those great men, but preserve to them the dignity of masters, and give that honour to their memories, *quos Libitina sacravit,*[29] part of which we expect may be paid to us in future times.'

This moderation of Crites, as it was pleasing to all the company, so it put an end to that dispute; which Eugenius, who seemed to have the better of the argument, would urge no farther: but Lisideius, after he had acknowledged himself of Eugenius his opinion concerning the Ancients, yet told him, he had forborne, till his discourse were ended, to ask him why he preferred the English plays above those of other nations? and whether we ought not to submit our stage to the exactness of our neighbours?

'Though,' said Eugenius, 'I am at all times ready to defend the honour of my country against the French, and to maintain, we are as well able to vanquish them with our pens, as our ancestors have been with their swords; yet, if you please,' added he, looking upon Neander, 'I will commit this cause to my friend's management; his opinion of our plays is the same with mine: and besides, there is no reason, that Crites and I, who have now left the stage, should re-enter so suddenly upon it; which is against the laws of comedy.'

'If the question had been stated,' replied Lisideius, 'who had writ best, the French or English, forty years ago, I should have been of your opinion, and adjudged the honour to our own nation; but since that time' (said he, turning towards Neander) 'we have been so long together bad Englishmen, that we had not leisure to be good poets. Beaumont, Fletcher, and Jonson (who were only capable of bringing us to that degree of perfection which we have) were just then leaving the world; as if (in an age of so much horror) wit, and those milder studies of humanity, had no farther business among us.     But the Muses, who ever follow peace, went to plant in another country: it was then that the great Cardinal of Richelieu began to take them into his protection; and that, by his encouragement, Corneille, and some other Frenchmen, reformed their theatre, which before was as much below ours, as it now surpasses it and the rest of Europe.     But because Crites in his discourse for the Ancients has prevented me, by touching upon many rules of the stage which the Moderns have borrowed from them, I shall only, in short, demand of you, whether you are not convinced that of all nations the French have best observed them?     In the Unity of Time you find them so scrupulous, that it yet remains a dispute among their poets, whether the artificial day of twelve hours, more or less, be not meant by Aristotle, rather than the natural one of twenty-four; and consequently, whether all plays ought not to be

---

[29] Which Libitina has consecrated.

reduced into that compass. This I can testify, that in all their dramas writ within these last twenty years and upwards, I have not observed any that have extended the time to thirty hours: in the Unity of Place they are full as scrupulous; for many of their critics limit it to that very spot of ground where the play is supposed to begin; none of them exceed the compass of the same town or city. The Unity of Action in all plays is yet more conspicuous; for they do not burden them with underplots, as the English do: which is the reason why many scenes of our tragi-comedies carry on a design that is nothing of kin to the main plot; and that we see two distinct webs in a play, like those in ill-wrought stuffs; and two actions, that is, two plays, carried on together, to the confounding of the audience; who, before they are warm in their concernments for one part, are diverted to another; and by that means espouse the interest of neither. From hence likewise it arises, that the one half of our actors are not known to the other. They keep their distances, as if they were Montagues and Capulets, and seldom begin an acquaintance till the last scene of the fifth act, when they are all to meet upon the stage. There is no theatre in the world has any thing so absurd as the English tragi-comedy; 'tis a drama of our own invention, and the fashion of it is enough to proclaim it so; here a course of mirth, there another of sadness and passion, a third of honour, and fourth a duel: thus, in two hours and a half, we run through all the fits of Bedlam. The French affords you as much variety on the same day, but they do it not so unseasonably, or *mal à propos*, as we: our poets present you the play and the farce together; and our stages still retain somewhat of the original civility of the *Red Bull:*

*Atque ursum et pugiles media inter carmina poscunt.*[30]

The end of tragedies or serious plays, says Aristotle, is to beget admiration, compassion, or concernment; but are not mirth and compassion things incompatible? and is it not evident that the poet must of necessity destroy the former by intermingling of the latter? that is, he must ruin the sole end and object of his tragedy, to introduce somewhat that is forced in, and is not of the body of it. Would you not think that physician mad, who, having prescribed a purge, should immediately order you to take re-stringents upon it?

'But to leave our plays, and return to theirs. I have noted one great advantage they have had in the plotting of their tragedies; that is, they are always grounded upon some known history: according to that of Horace, *Ex noto fictum carmen sequar*[31]; and in that they have so imitated the Ancients, that they have surpassed them. For the Ancients, as was

---

[30] In the middle of plays they ask for a bear and boxers.
[31] From a well-known story, I should bring a poem.

observed before, took for the foundation of their plays some poetical fiction, such as under that consideration could move but little concernment in the audience, because they already knew the event of it. But the French goes farther:

*Atque ita mentitur, sic veris falsa remiscet,*
*Primo ne medium, medio ne discrepet imum.*[32]

He so interweaves truth with probable fiction, that he puts a pleasing fallacy upon us; mends the intrigues of fate, and dispenses with the severity of history, to reward that virtue which has been rendered to us there unfortunate. Sometimes the story has left the success so doubtful, that the writer is free, by the privilege of a poet, to take that which of two or more relations will best suit with his design: as for example, the death of Cyrus, whom Justin and some others report to have perished in the Scythian war, but Xenophon affirms to have died in his bed of extreme old age. Nay more, when the event is past dispute, even then we are willing to be deceived, and the poet, if he contrives it with appearance of truth, has all the audience of his party; at least during the time his play is acting: so naturally we are kind to virtue, when our own interest is not in question, that we take it up as the general concernment of mankind. On the other side, if you consider the historical plays of Shakespeare, they are rather so many chronicles of kings, or the business many times of thirty or forty years, cramped into a representation of two hours and an half; which is not to imitate or paint Nature, but rather to draw her in miniature, to take her in little; to look upon her through the wrong end of a perspective, and receive her images not only much less, but infinitely more imperfect than the life: this, instead of making a play delightful, renders it ridiculous:—

*Quodcunque ostendis mihi sic, incredulus odi.*[33]

For the spirit of man cannot be satisfied but with truth, or at least verisimility; and a poem is to contain, if not τὰ ἔτυμα, yet ἐτύμοισιν ὁμοῖα,[34] as one of the Greek poets has expressed it.

'Another thing in which the French differ from us and from the Spaniards, is, that they do not embarrass, or cumber themselves with too much plot; they only represent so much of a story as will constitute one whole and great action sufficient for a play; we, who undertake more, do but multiply adventures; which, not being produced from one another,

---

[32] He so lies, and mixes the false with the true, that you cannot tell apart the beginning, middle, or end.

[33] Whatever you show me in this way I find unbelievable and disgusting.

[34] *Ta etuma; etumoisin omoia.* True things; things like the truth.

as effects from causes, but barely following, constitute many actions in the drama, and consequently make it many plays.

'But by pursuing close one argument, which is not cloyed with many turns, the French have gained more liberty for verse, in which they write; they have leisure to dwell on a subject which deserves it; and to represent the passions (which we have acknowledged to be the poet's work), without being hurried from one thing to another, as we are in the plays of Calderon, which we have seen lately upon our theatres, under the name of Spanish plots. I have taken notice but of one tragedy of ours, whose plot has that uniformity and unity of design in it, which I have commended in the French; and that is *Rollo*, or rather, under the name of Rollo, the story of Bassianus and Geta in Herodian: there indeed the plot is neither large nor intricate, but just enough to fill the minds of the audience, not to cloy them. Besides, you see it founded upon the truth of history, only the time of the action is not reduceable to the strictness of the rules; and you see in some places a little farce mingled, which is below the dignity of the other parts; and in this all our poets are extremely peccant: even Ben Jonson himself, in *Sejanus* and *Catiline*, has given us this oleo of a play, this unnatural mixture of comedy and tragedy; which to me sounds just as ridiculously as the history of David with the merry humours of Golias. In *Sejanus* you may take notice of the scene betwixt Livia and the physician, which is a pleasant satire upon the artificial helps of beauty: in *Catiline* you may see the parliament of women; the little envies of them to one another; and all that passes betwixt Curio and Fulvia: scenes admirable in their kind, but of an ill mingle with the rest.

'But I return again to the French writers, who, as I have said, do not burden themselves too much with plot, which has been reproached to them by an *ingenious person* of our nation as a fault; for, he says, they commonly make but one person considerable in a play; they dwell on him, and his concernments, while the rest of the persons are only subservient to set him off. If he intends this by it, that there is one person in the play who is of greater dignity than the rest, he must tax, not only theirs, but those of the Ancients, and which he would be loth to do, the best of ours; for it is impossible but that one person must be more conspicuous in it than any other, and consequently the greatest share in the action must devolve on him. We see it so in the management of all affairs; even in the most equal aristocracy, the balance cannot be so justly poised, but some one will be superior to the rest, either in parts, fortune, interest, or the consideration of some glorious exploit; which will reduce the greatest part of business into his hands.

'But, if he would have us to imagine, that in exalting one character the rest of them are neglected, and that all of them have not some share or other in the action of the play, I desire him to produce any of Corneille's tragedies, wherein every person, like so many servants in a well-governed family, has not some employment, and who is not necessary to the carrying on of the plot, or at least to your understanding it.

'There are indeed some protatick persons in the Ancients, whom they make use of in their plays, either to hear or give the relation: but the French avoid this with great address, making their narrations only to, or by such, who are some way interested in the main design. And now I am speaking of relations, I cannot take a fitter opportunity to add this in favour of the French, that they often use them with better judgment and more à propos than the English do. Not that I commend narrations in general,—but there are two sorts of them. One, of those things which are antecedent to the play, and are related to make the conduct of it more clear to us. But 'tis a fault to choose such subjects for the stage as will force us on that rock, because we see they are seldom listened to by the audience, and that is many times the ruin of the play; for, being once let pass without attention, the audience can never recover themselves to understand the plot: and indeed it is somewhat unreasonable that they should be put to so much trouble, as that, to comprehend what passes in their sight, they must have recourse to what was done, perhaps, ten or twenty years ago.

'But there is another sort of relations, that is, of things happening in the action of the play, and supposed to be done behind the scenes; and this is many times both convenient and beautiful; for by it the French avoid the tumult which we are subject to in England, by representing duels, battles, and the like; which renders our stage too like the theatres where they fight prizes. For what is more ridiculous than to represent an army with a drum and five men behind it; all which the hero of the other side is to drive in before him; or to see a duel fought, and one slain with two or three thrusts of the foils, which we know are so blunted, that we might give a man an hour to kill another in good earnest with them.

'I have observed that in all our tragedies, the audience cannot forbear laughing when the actors are to die; it is the most comic part of the whole play. All *passions* may be lively represented on the stage, if to the well-writing of them the actor supplies a good commanded voice, and limbs that move easily, and without stiffness; but there are many *actions* which can never be imitated to a just height: dying especially is a thing which none but a Roman gladiator could naturally perform on the stage, when he did not imitate or represent, but naturally do it; and therefore it is better to omit the representation of it.

'The words of a good writer, which describe it lively, will make a deeper impression of belief in us than all the actor can persuade us to, when he seems to fall dead before us; as a poet in the description of a beautiful garden, or a meadow, will please our imagination more than the place itself can please our sight. When we see death represented, we are convinced it is but fiction; but when we hear it related, our eyes, the strongest witnesses, are wanting, which might have undeceived us; and we are all willing to favour the sleight, when the poet does not too grossly impose on us. They therefore who imagine these relations would make no concernment in the audience, are deceived, by confounding them with the other, which are of things antecedent to the play: those are made often in cold blood, as I may say, to the audience; but these are warmed with our concernments, which were before awakened in the play. What the philosophers say of motion, that, when it is once begun, it continues of itself, and will do so to eternity, without some stop put to it, is clearly true on this occasion: the soul, being already moved with the characters and fortunes of those imaginary persons, continues going of its own accord; and we are no more weary to hear what becomes of them when they are not on the stage, than we are to listen to the news of an absent mistress. But it is objected, that if one part of the play may be related, then why not all? I answer, some parts of the action are more fit to be represented, some to be related. Corneille says judiciously, that the poet is not obliged to expose to view all particular actions which conduce to the principal: he ought to select such of them to be seen, which will appear with the greatest beauty, either by the magnificence of the show, or the vehemence of passions which they produce, or some other charm which they have in them; and let the rest arrive to the audience by narration. 'Tis a great mistake in us to believe the French present no part of the action on the stage; every alteration or crossing of a design, every new-sprung passion, and turn of it, is a part of the action, and much the noblest, except we conceive nothing to be action till they come to blows; as if the painting of the hero's mind were not more properly the poet's work than the strength of his body. Nor does this anything contradict the opinion of Horace, where he tells us,

> Segnius irritant animos demissa per aurem,
> Quam quae sunt oculis subjecta fidelibus.[35]

For he says immediately after,

> . . . . . Non tamen intus
> Digna geri promes in scenam; multaque tolles
> Ex oculis, quae mox narret facundia praesens.[36]

[35] What we hear through our ears stirs us less strongly than what we see through our eyes.

[36] You should not bring on stage what should be done off it: many things should be kept out of sight, and instead told with a vivid eloquence.

Among which many he recounts some:

*Nec pueros coram populo Medea trucidet,*
*Aut in avem Procne mutetur, Cadmus in anguem: &c.*[37]

That is, those actions which by reason of their cruelty will cause aversion in us, or by reason of their impossibility, unbelief, ought either wholly to be avoided by a poet, or only delivered by narration.   To which we may have leave to add such as to avoid tumult (as was before hinted), or to reduce the plot into a more reasonable compass of time, or for defect of beauty in them, are rather to be related than presented to the eye. Examples of all these kinds are frequent, not only among all the Ancients, but in the best received of our English poets.   We find Ben Jonson using them in his *Magnetick Lady*, where one comes out from dinner, and relates the quarrels and disorders of it, to save the undecent appearance of them on the stage, and to abbreviate the story; and this in express imitation of Terence, who had done the same before him in his *Eunuch*, where Pythias makes the like relation of what had happened within at the Soldier's entertainment.   The relations likewise of Sejanus's death, and the prodigies before it, are remarkable; the one of which was hid from sight, to avoid the horror and tumult of the representation; the other, to shun the introducing of things impossible to be believed.   In that excellent play, *The King and no King*, Fletcher goes yet farther; for the whole unravelling of the plot is done by narration in the fifth act, after the manner of the Ancients; and it moves great concernment in the audience, though it be only a relation of what was done many years before the play.   I could multiply other instances, but these are sufficient to prove that there is no error in choosing a subject which requires this sort of narrations; in the ill managing of them, there may.

'But I find I have been too long in this discourse, since the French have many other excellencies not common to us; as that you never see any of their plays end with a conversion, or simple change of will, which is the ordinary way which our poets use to end theirs.   It shows little art in the conclusion of a dramatic poem, when they who have hindered the felicity during the four acts, desist from it in the fifth, without some powerful cause to take them off; and though I deny not but such reasons may be found, yet it is a path that is cautiously to be trod, and the poet is to be sure he convinces the audience that the motive is strong enough.   As for example, the conversion of the Usurer in *The Scornful Lady*, seems to me a little forced; for, being an Usurer, which implies a lover of money to the highest degree of covetousness (and such the poet has represented him),

---

[37] Medea should not cut up her children in front of the audience, Procne should not be changed into a bird there, nor Cadmus into a snake, etc.

the account he gives for the sudden change is, that he has been duped by the wild young fellow; which in reason might render him more wary another time, and make him punish himself with harder fare and coarser clothes, to get it up again: but that he should look on it as a judgment, and so repent, we may expect to hear of in a sermon, but I should never endure it in a play.

'I pass by this; neither will I insist on the care they take, that no person after his first entrance shall ever appear, but the business which brings him upon the stage shall be evident; which, if observed, must needs render all the events in the play more natural; for there you see the probability of every accident, in the cause that produced it; and that which appears chance in the play, will seem so reasonable to you, that you will there find it almost necessary: so that in the exits of the actors you have a clear account of their purpose and design in the next entrance (though, if the scene be well wrought, the event will commonly deceive you), for there is nothing so absurd, says Corneille, as for an actor to leave the stage, only because he has no more to say.

'I should now speak of the beauty of their rhyme, and the just reason I have to prefer that way of writing in tragedies before ours in blank verse; but because it is partly received by us, and therefore not altogether peculiar to them, I will say no more of it in relation to their plays.   For our own, I doubt not but it will exceedingly beautify them; and I can see but one reason why it should not generally obtain, that is, because our poets write so ill in it.   This indeed may prove a more prevailing argument than all others which are used to destroy it, and therefore I am only troubled when great and judicious poets, and those who are acknowledged such, have writ or spoke against it: as for others, they are to be answered by that one sentence of an ancient author:—*Sed ut primo ad consequendos eos quos priores ducimus, accendimur, ita ubi aut præteriri, aut æquari eos posse desperavimus, studium cum spe senescit: quod, scilicet, assequi non potest, sequi desinit; . . . præteritoque eo in quo eminere non possumus, aliquid in quo nitamur, conquirimus.*'[38]

Lisideius concluded in this manner; and Neander, after a little pause, thus answered him:

'I shall grant Lisideius, without much dispute, a great part of what he has urged against us; for I acknowledge that the French contrive their plots more regularly, and observe the laws of comedy, and decorum of the stage (to speak generally), with more exactness than the English.

---

[38] Just as we are inspired to follow those we consider most worthy, so—when we despair of excelling or equaling them—our enthusiasm and hope diminish.   For what it cannot attain, it ceases to follow; . . . after we have abandoned what we are unable to excel in, we look for something else for which to strive. (Velleius Paterculus, I, 17)

Farther, I deny not but he has taxed us justly in some irregularities of ours, which he has mentioned; yet, after all, I am of opinion that neither our faults nor their virtues are considerable enough to place them above us.

'For the lively imitation of Nature being in the definition of a play, those which best fulfil that law ought to be esteemed superior to the others. 'Tis true, those beauties of the French poesy are such as will raise perfection higher where it is, but are not sufficient to give it where it is not: they are indeed the beauties of a statue, but not of a man, because not animated with the soul of Poesy, which is imitation of humour and passions: and this Lisideius himself, or any other, however biassed to their party, cannot but acknowledge, if he will either compare the humours of our comedies, or the characters of our serious plays, with theirs. He that will look upon theirs which have been written till these last ten years, or thereabouts, will find it an hard matter to pick out two or three passable humours amongst them. Corneille himself, their arch-poet, what has he produced except *The Liar*, and you know how it was cried up in France; but when it came upon the English stage, though well translated, and that part of Dorant acted to so much advantage by Mr. Hart as I am confident it never received in its own country, the most favourable to it would not put it in competition with many of Fletcher's or Ben Jonson's. In the rest of Corneille's comedies you have little humour; he tells you himself, his way is, first to show two lovers in good intelligence with each other; in the working up of the play to embroil them by some mistake, and in the latter end to clear it, and reconcile them.

'But of late years Molière, the younger Corneille, Quinault, and some others, have been imitating afar off the quick turns and graces of the English stage. They have mixed their serious plays with mirth, like our tragi-comedies, since the death of Cardinal Richelieu; which Lisideius and many others not observing, have commended that in them for a virtue which they themselves no longer practice. Most of their new plays are, like some of ours, derived from the Spanish novels. There is scarce one of them without a veil, and a trusty Diego, who drolls much after the rate of the *Adventures*. But their humours, if I may grace them with that name, are so thin-sown, that never above one of them comes up in any play. I dare take upon me to find more variety of them in some one play of Ben Jonson's, than in all theirs together; as he who has seen *The Alchemist*, *The Silent Woman*, or *Bartholomew-Fair*, cannot but acknowledge with me.

'I grant the French have performed what was possible on the groundwork of the Spanish plays; what was pleasant before, they have made regular: but there is not above one good play to be writ on all those plots;

they are too much alike to please often; which we need not the experience of our own stage to justify. As for their new way of mingling mirth with serious plot, I do not, with Lisideius, condemn the thing, though I cannot approve their manner of doing it. He tells us, we cannot so speedily recollect ourselves after a scene of great passion and concernment, as to pass to another of mirth and humour, and to enjoy it with any relish: but why should he imagine the soul of man more heavy than his senses? Does not the eye pass from an unpleasant object to a pleasant in a much shorter time than is required to this? and does not the unpleasantness of the first commend the beauty of the latter? The old rule of logic might have convinced him, that contraries, when placed near, set off each other. A continued gravity keeps the spirit too much bent; we must refresh it sometimes, as we bait in a journey, that we may go on with greater ease. A scene of mirth, mixed with tragedy, has the same effect upon us which our music has betwixt the acts; and that we find a relief to us from the best plots and language of the stage, if the discourses have been long. I must therefore have stronger arguments, ere I am convinced that compassion and mirth in the same subject destroy each other; and in the mean time cannot but conclude, to the honour of our nation, that we have invented, increased, and perfected a more pleasant way of writing for the stage, than was ever known to the ancients or moderns of any nation, which is tragi-comedy.

'And this leads me to wonder why Lisideius and many others should cry up the barrenness of the French plots, above the variety and copiousness of the English. Their plots are single; they carry on one design, which is pushed forward by all the actors, every scene in the play contributing and moving towards it. Our plays, besides the main design, have underplots or by-concernments, of less considerable persons and intrigues, which are carried on with the motion of the main plot: just as they say the orb of the fixed stars, and those of the planets, though they have motions of their own, are whirled about by the motion of the *Primum Mobile*, in which they are contained. That similitude expresses much of the English stage; for if contrary motions may be found in nature to agree; if a planet can go east and west at the same time, one way by virtue of his own motion, the other by the force of the First Mover, it will not be difficult to imagine how the under-plot, which is only different, not contrary to the great design, may naturally be conducted along with it.

'Eugenius has already shown us, from the confession of the French poets, that the Unity of Action is sufficiently preserved, if all the imperfect actions of the play are conducing to the main design; but when those petty intrigues of a play are so ill ordered, that they have no coherence with the other, I must grant that Lisideius has reason to tax that want of due connexion; for co-ordination in a play is as dangerous and unnatural as in a state. In the mean time he must acknowledge, our variety, if well ordered, will afford a greater pleasure to the audience.

'As for his other argument, that by pursuing one single theme they gain an advantage to express and work up the passions, I wish any example he could bring from them would make it good; for I confess their verses are to me the coldest I have ever read. Neither, indeed, is it possible for them, in the way they take, so to express passion, as that the effects of it should appear in the concernment of an audience, their speeches being so many declamations, which tire us with the length; so that instead of persuading us to grieve for their imaginary heroes, we are concerned for our own trouble, as we are in the tedious visits of bad company; we are in pain till they are gone. When the French stage came to be reformed by Cardinal Richelieu, those long harangues were introduced, to comply with the gravity of a churchman. Look upon the *Cinna* and the *Pompey;* they are not so properly to be called plays, as long discourses of reason of state; and *Poliéucte* in matters of religion is as solemn as the long stops upon our organs. Since that time it is grown into a custom, and their actors speak by the hour-glass, as our parsons do; nay, they account it the grace of their parts, and think themselves disparaged by the poet, if they may not twice or thrice in a play entertain the audience with a speech of an hundred or two hundred lines. ·I deny not but this may suit well enough with the French; for as we, who are a more sullen people, come to be diverted at our plays, so they, who are of an airy and gay temper, come thither to make themselves more serious: and this I conceive to be one reason why comedy is more pleasing to us, and tragedies to them. But to speak generally: it cannot be denied that short speeches and replies are more apt to move the passions and beget concernment in us, than the other; for it is unnatural for any one in a gust of passion to speak long together, or for another in the same condition to suffer him, without interruption. Grief and passion are like floods raised in little brooks by a sudden rain; they are quickly up; and if the concernment be poured unexpectedly in upon us, it overflows us: but a long sober shower gives them leisure to run out as they came in, without troubling the ordinary current. As for Comedy, repartee is one of its chiefest graces; the greatest pleasure of the audience is a chace of wit, kept up on both sides, and swiftly managed. And this our forefathers, if not we, have had in Fletcher's plays, to a much higher degree of perfection than the French poets can arrive at.

'There is another part of Lisideius his discourse, in which he has rather excused our neighbours, than commended them; that is, for aiming only to make one person considerable in their plays. 'Tis very true what he has urged, that one character in all plays, even without the poet's care, will have advantage of all the others; and that the design of the whole drama will chiefly depend on it. But this hinders not that there may be more shining characters in the play: many persons of a second magnitude, nay, some so very near, so almost equal to the first, that greatness may be opposed to greatness, and all the persons be made considerable, not only by their quality, but their action. 'Tis evident that the more the persons are, the greater will be the variety of the plot. If then the parts are managed so regularly, that the beauty of the whole be kept entire, and that the variety become not a perplexed and confused mass of accidents, you will find it infinitely pleasing to be led in a labyrinth of design, where you see some of your way before you, yet discern not the end till you arrive at it. And that all this is practicable, I can produce for examples many of our English plays: as *The Maid's Tragedy, The Alchemist, The Silent Woman:* I was going to have named *The Fox*, but that the unity of design seems not exactly observed in it; for there appear two actions in the play; the first naturally ending with the fourth act; the second forced from it in the fifth: which yet is the less to be condemned in him, because the disguise of Volpone, though it suited not with his character as a crafty or covetous person, agreed well enough with that of a voluptuary; and by it the poet gained the end he aimed at, the punishment of vice, and the reward of virtue, which that disguise produced. So that to judge equally of it, it was an excellent fifth act, but not so naturally proceeding from the former.

'But to leave this, and pass to the latter part of Lisideius his discourse, which concerns relations: I must acknowledge with him, that the French have reason when they hide that part of the action which would occasion too much tumult on the stage, and choose rather to have it made known by narration to the audience. Farther, I think it very convenient, for the reasons he has given, that all incredible actions were removed; but, whether custom has so insinuated itself into our countrymen, or nature has so formed them to fierceness, I know not; but they will scarcely suffer combats and other objects of horror to be taken from them. And indeed, the indecency of tumults is all which can be objected against fighting: for why may not our imagination as well suffer itself to be deluded with the probability of it, as with any other thing in the play? For my part, I can with as great ease persuade myself that the blows which are struck, are given in good earnest, as I can, that they who strike them are kings or princes, or those persons which they represent. For objects of incredibility, I would be satisfied from Lisideius, whether we have any so removed from all appearance of truth, as are those of Corneille's *Andromède;* a play which has been frequented the most of any he has writ. If the Perseus, or the son of an heathen god, the Pegasus, and the Monster, were not capable to choke a strong belief, let him blame any representation of ours hereafter. Those indeed were objects of delight; yet the reason is the same as to the probability: for he makes it not a Ballet or masque, but a play, which is to resemble truth. But for death, that it ought not to be represented, I have, besides the arguments alleged by Lisideius, the authority of Ben Jonson, who has forborn it in his tragedies; for both the death of Sejanus and Catiline are related: though in the latter I cannot but observe one irregularity of that great poet; he has removed the scene in the same act from Rome to Catiline's army, and from thence again to Rome; and besides, has allowed a very inconsiderable time, after Catiline's speech, for the striking of the battle, and the return of Petreius, who is to relate the event of it to the senate: which I should not animadvert on him, who was otherwise a painful observer of τὸ πρέπον,[39] or the *decorum* of the stage, if he had not used extreme severity in his judgment on the incomparable Shakespeare for the same fault.—To conclude on this subject of relations; if we are to be blamed for showing too much of the action, the French are as faulty for discovering too little of it: a mean betwixt both should be observed by every judicious writer, so as the audience may neither be left unsatisfied by not seeing what is beautiful, or shocked by beholding what is either incredible or undecent.

'I hope I have already proved in this discourse, that though we are not altogether so punctual as the French, in observing the laws of Comedy, yet our errors are so few, and little, and those things wherein we excel them so considerable, that we ought of right to be preferred before them. But what will Lisideius say, if they themselves acknowledge they are too strictly tied up by those laws, for breaking which he has blamed the English? I will allege Corneille's words, as I find them in the end of his Discourse of the Three Unities:—*Il est facile aux spéculatifs d'estre sévères, etc.* " 'Tis easy for speculative persons to judge severely; but if they would produce to public view ten or twelve pieces of this nature, they would perhaps give more latitude to the rules than I have done, when, by experience, they had known how much we are bound up and constrained by them, and how many beauties of the stage they banished from it." To illustrate a little what he has said: by their servile observations of the Unities of Time and Place, and integrity of scenes, they have brought on themselves that dearth of plot, and narrowness of imagination, which may be observed in all their plays. How many beautiful accidents might naturally happen in two or three days, which cannot arrive with any probability in the compass of twenty-four hours? There is time to be allowed also for maturity of design, which, amongst great and prudent

[39] *To prepon.*

persons, such as are often represented in Tragedy, cannot, with any likelihood of truth, be brought to pass at so short a warning.  Farther; by tying themselves strictly to the Unity of Place, and unbroken scenes, they are forced many times to omit some beauties which cannot be shown where the act began; but might, if the scene were interrupted, and the stage cleared for the persons to enter in another place; and therefore the French poets are often forced upon absurdities; for if the act begins in a chamber, all the persons in the play must have some business or other to come thither, or else they are not to be shown that act; and sometimes their characters are very unfitting to appear there.  As, suppose it were the king's bed-chamber; yet the meanest man in the tragedy must come and dispatch his business there, rather than in the lobby or courtyard (which is fitter for him), for fear the stage should be cleared, and the scenes broken.  Many times they fall by it in a greater inconvenience; for they keep their scenes unbroken, and yet change the place; as in one of their newest plays, where the act begins in the street.  There a gentleman is to meet his friend; he sees him with his man, coming out from his father's house; they talk together, and the first goes out: the second, who is a lover, has made an appointment with his mistress; she appears at the window, and then we are to imagine the scene lies under it.  This gentleman is called away, and leaves his servant with his mistress; presently her father is heard from within; the young lady is afraid the servingman should be discovered, and thrusts him in through a door, which is supposed to be her closet.  After this, the father enters to the daughter, and now the scene is in a house; for he is seeking from one room to another for this poor Philipin, or French Diego, who is heard from within, drolling and breaking many a miserable conceit upon his sad condition.  In this ridiculous manner the play goes on, the stage being never empty all the while: so that the street, the window, the houses, and the closet, are made to walk about, and the persons to stand still.  Now what, I beseech you, is more easy than to write a regular French play, or more difficult than to write an irregular English one, like those of Fletcher, or of Shakespeare?

'If they content themselves, as Corneille did, with some flat design, which, like an ill riddle, is found out ere it be half proposed, such plots we can make every way regular, as easily as they; but whene'er they endeavour to rise to any quick turns and counterturns of plot, as some of them have attempted, since Corneille's plays have been less in vogue, you see they write as irregularly as we, though they cover it more speciously. Hence the reason is perspicuous, why no French plays, when translated, have, or ever can succeed on the English stage.  For, if you consider the plots, our own are fuller of variety; if the writing, ours are more quick and fuller of spirit; and therefore 'tis a strange mistake in those who decry the way of writing plays in verse, as if the English therein imitated the French. We have borrowed nothing from them; our plots are weaved in English looms: we endeavour therein to follow the variety and greatness of characters which are derived to us from Shakespeare and Fletcher; the copiousness and well-knitting of the intrigues we have from Jonson; and for the verse itself we have English precedents of elder date than any of Corneille's plays. Not to name our old comedies before Shakespeare, which were all writ in verse of six feet, or Alexandrines, such as the French now use, I can show in Shakespeare, many scenes of rhyme together, and the like in Ben Jonson's tragedies: in *Catiline* and *Sejanus* sometimes thirty or forty lines, I mean besides the Chorus, or the monologues; which, by the way, showed Ben no enemy to this way of writing, especially if you look upon his *Sad Shepherd*, which goes sometimes on rhyme, sometimes on blank verse, like an horse who eases himself on trot and amble. You find him likewise commending Fletcher's pastoral of *The Faithful Shepherdess*, which is for the most part rhyme, though not refined to that purity to which it hath since been brought. And these examples are enough to clear us from a servile imitation of the French.

'But to return from whence I have digressed: I dare boldly affirm these two things of the English drama;—First, that we have many plays of ours as regular as any of theirs, and which, besides, have more variety of plot and characters; and secondly, that in most of the irregular plays of Shakespeare or Fletcher (for Ben Jonson's are for the most part regular) there is a more masculine fancy and greater spirit in the writing, than there is in any of the French. I could produce, even in Shakespeare's and Fletcher's works, some plays which are almost exactly formed; as *The Merry Wives of Windsor*, and *The Scornful Lady:* but because (generally speaking) Shakespeare, who writ first, did not perfectly observe the laws of Comedy, and Fletcher, who came nearer to perfection, yet through carelessness made many faults; I will take the pattern of a perfect play from Ben Jonson, who was a careful and learned observer of the dramatic laws, and from all his comedies I shall select *The Silent Woman*; of which I will make a short examen, according to those rules which the French observe.'

As Neander was beginning to examine *The Silent Woman*, Eugenius, looking earnestly upon him; 'I beseech you, Neander,' said he, 'gratify the company, and me in particular, so far, as before you speak of the play, to give us a character of the author; and tell us frankly your opinion, whether you do not think all writers, both French and English, ought to give place to him.'

'I fear,' replied Neander, 'that in obeying your commands I shall draw a little envy on myself. Besides, in performing them, it will be first necessary to speak somewhat of Shakespeare and Fletcher, his rivals in poesy; and one of them, in my opinion, at least his equal, perhaps his superior.

'To begin, then, with Shakespeare. He was the man who of all modern, and perhaps ancient poets, had the largest and most comprehensive soul. All the images of Nature were still present to him, and he drew them, not laboriously, but luckily; when he describes any thing, you more than see it, you feel it too. Those who accuse him to have wanted learning, give him the greater commendation: he was naturally learned; he needed not the spectacles of books to read Nature; he looked inwards, and found her there. I cannot say he is everywhere alike; were he so, I should do him injury to compare him with the greatest of mankind. He is many times flat, insipid; his comic wit degenerating into clenches, his serious swelling into bombast. But he is always great, when some great occasion is presented to him; no man can say he ever had a fit subject for his wit, and did not then raise himself as high above the rest of poets,

*Quantum lenta solent inter viburna cupressi.*[40]

The consideration of this made Mr. Hales of Eaton say, that there was no subject of which any poet ever writ, but he would produce it much better treated of in Shakespeare; and however others are now generally preferred before him, yet the age wherein he lived, which had contemporaries with him Fletcher and Jonson, never equalled them to him in their esteem: and in the last King's court, when Ben's reputation was at highest, Sir John Suckling, and with him the greater part of the courtiers, set our Shakespeare far above him.

'Beaumont and Fletcher, of whom I am next to speak, had, with the advantage of Shakespeare's wit, which was their precedent, great natural gifts, improved by study: Beaumont especially being so accurate a judge of plays, that Ben Jonson, while he lived, submitted all his writings to his censure, and, 'tis thought, used his judgment in correcting, if not contriving, all his plots. What value he had for him, appears by the verses he writ to him; and therefore I need speak no farther of it. The first play that brought Fletcher and him in esteem was their *Philaster:* for before that, they had written two or three very unsuccessfully, as the like is reported of Ben Jonson, before he writ *Every Man in his Humour.* Their plots were generally more regular than Shakespeare's, especially those which were made before Beaumont's death; and they understood and imitated the conversation of gentlemen much better; whose wild debaucheries, and quickness of wit in repartees, no poet can ever paint as

[40] As cypresses raise themselves above scraggly shrubs.

they have done.   Humour, which Ben Jonson derived from particular persons, they made it not their business to describe: they represented all the passions very lively, but above all, love.   I am apt to believe the English language in them arrived to its highest perfection: what words have since been taken in, are rather superfluous than ornamental.   Their plays are now the most pleasant and frequent entertainments of the stage; two of theirs being acted through the year for one of Shakespeare's or Jonson's: the reason is, because there is a certain gaiety in their comedies, and pathos in their more serious plays, which suits generally with all men's humours.   Shakespeare's language is likewise a little obsolete, and Ben Jonson's wit comes short of theirs.

'As for Jonson, to whose character I am now arrived, if we look upon him while he was himself (for his last plays were but his dotages), I think him the most learned and judicious writer which any theatre ever had. He was a most severe judge of himself, as well as others.   One cannot say he wanted wit, but rather that he was frugal of it.   In his works you find little to retrench or alter.   Wit, and language, and humour also in some measure, we had before him; but something of art was wanting to the Drama, till he came.   He managed his strength to more advantage than any who preceded him.   You seldom find him making love in any of his scenes, or endeavouring to move the passions; his genius was too sullen and saturnine to do it gracefully, especially when he knew he came after those who had performed both to such an height.   Humour was his proper sphere; and in that he delighted most to represent mechanic people.   He was deeply conversant in the Ancients, both Greek and Latin, and he borrowed boldly from them: there is scarce a poet or historian among the Roman authors of those times whom he has not translated in *Sejanus* and *Catiline*.   But he has done his robberies so openly, that one may see he fears not to be taxed by any law.   He invades authors like a monarch; and what would be theft in other poets, is only victory in him.   With the spoils of these writers he so represents old Rome to us, in its rites, ceremonies, and customs, that if one of their poets had written either of his tragedies, we had seen less of it than in him.   If there was any fault in his language, 'twas that he weaved it too closely and laboriously, in his serious plays: perhaps too, he did a little too much Romanize our tongue, leaving the words which he translated almost as. much Latin as he found them: wherein, though he learnedly followed the idiom of their language, he did not enough comply with the idiom of ours. If I would compare him with Shakespeare, I must acknowledge him the more correct poet, but Shakespeare the greater wit.   Shakespeare was the Homer, or father of our dramatic poets; Jonson was the Virgil, the pattern of elaborate writing; I admire him, but I love Shakespeare.   To conclude of him; as he has given us the most correct plays, so in the precepts which he has laid down in his *Discoveries*, we have as many and profitable rules for perfecting the stage, as any wherewith the French can furnish us.

'Having thus spoken of the author, I proceed to the examination of his comedy, *The Silent Woman*.

## '*EXAMEN OF* THE SILENT WOMAN

'To begin first with the length of the action; it is so far from exceeding the compass of a natural day, that it takes not up an artificial one. 'Tis all included in the limits of three hours and an half, which is no more than is required for the presentment on the stage. A beauty perhaps not much observed; if it had, we should not have looked on the Spanish translation of *Five Hours* with so much wonder. The scene of it is laid in London; the latitude of place is almost as little as you can imagine; for it lies all within the compass of two houses, and after the first act, in one. The continuity of scenes is observed more than in any of our plays, except his own *Fox* and *Alchemist*. They are not broken above twice or thrice at most in the whole comedy; and in the two best of Corneille's plays, the *Cid* and *Cinna*, they are interrupted once apiece. The action of the play is entirely one; the end or aim of which is the settling Morose's estate on Dauphine. The intrigue of it is the greatest and most noble of any pure unmixed comedy in any language; you see in it many persons of various characters and humours, and all delightful: as first, Morose, or an old man, to whom all noise but his own talking is offensive. Some who would be thought critics, say this humour of his is forced: but to remove that objection, we may consider him first to be naturally of a delicate hearing, as many are, to whom all sharp sounds are unpleasant; and secondly, we may attribute much of it to the peevishness of his age, or the wayward authority of an old man in his own house, where he may make himself obeyed; and this the poet seems to allude to in his name Morose. Besides this, I am assured from divers persons, that Ben Jonson was actually acquainted with such a man, one altogether as ridiculous as he is here represented. Others say, it is not enough to find one man of such an humour; it must be common to more, and the more common the more natural. To prove this, they instance in the best of comical characters, Falstaff: there are many men resembling him; old, fat, merry, cowardly, drunken, amorous, vain, and lying. But to convince these people, I need but tell them, that humour is the ridiculous extravagance of conversation, wherein one man differs from all others. If then it be common, or com-municated to many, how differs it from other men's? or what indeed causes it to be ridiculous so much as the singularity of it? As for Falstaff, he is not properly one humour, but a miscellany of humours or images, drawn from so many several men: that wherein he is singular is his wit, or those things he says *præter expectatum*, unexpected by the audience; his quick evasions, when you imagine him surprised, which, as they are extremely diverting of themselves, so receive a great addition from his person; for the very sight of such an unwieldy old debauched fellow is a comedy alone. And here, having a place so proper for it, I cannot but enlarge somewhat upon this subject of humour into which I am fallen. The ancients had little of it in their comedies; for the τὸ γελοῖον[41] of the Old Comedy, of which Aristophanes was chief, was not so much to imitate a man, as to make the people laugh at some odd conceit, which had commonly somewhat of unnatural or obscene in it. Thus, when you see Socrates brought upon the stage, you are not to imagine him made ridiculous by the imitation of his actions, but rather by making him perform something very unlike himself; something so childish and absurd, as by comparing it with the gravity of the true Socrates, makes a ridiculous object for the spectators. In their New Comedy which succeeded, the poets sought indeed to express the ἦθος,[42] as in their tragedies the πάθος[43] of mankind. But this ἦθος contained only the general characters of men and manners; as old men, lovers, serving-men, courtezans, parasites, and such other persons as we see in their comedies; all which they made alike: that is, one old man or father, one lover, one courtezan, so like another, as if the first of them had begot the rest of every sort: *Ex homine hunc natum dicas.*[44] The same custom they observed likewise in their tragedies. As for the French, though they have the word *humeur* among them, yet they have small use of it in their comedies or farces; they being but ill imitations of the *ridiculum*, or that which stirred up laughter in the Old Comedy. But among the English 'tis otherwise: where by humour is meant some extravagant habit, passion, or affection, particular (as I said before) to some one person, by the oddness of which, he is immediately distinguished from the rest of men; which being lively and naturally represented, most frequently begets that malicious pleasure in the audience which is testified by laughter; as all things which are deviations from common customs are ever the aptest to produce it: though by the way this laughter is only accidental, as the person represented is fantastic or bizarre; but pleasure is essential to it, as the imitation of what is natural. The description of these humours, drawn from the knowledge and observation of

[41] *To geloion*, the laughable.
[42] *Ethos*, character.
[43] *Pathos*, emotion.
[44] You would say that one was born from another.

particular persons, was the peculiar genius and talent of Ben Jonson; to whose play I now return.

'Besides Morose, there are at least nine or ten different characters and humours in *The Silent Woman;* all which persons have several concernments of their own, yet are all used by the poet, to the conducting of the main design to perfection.    I shall not waste time in commending the writing of this play; but I will give you my opinion, that there is more wit and acuteness of fancy in it than in any of Ben Jonson's.    Besides, that he has here described the conversation of gentlemen in the persons of True-Wit, and his friends, with more gaiety, air, and freedom, than in the rest of his comedies.    For the contrivance of the plot, 'tis extreme elaborate, and yet withal easy; for the λύσις,[45] or untying of it, 'tis so admirable, that when it is done, no one of the audience would think the poet could have missed it; and yet it was concealed so much before the last scene, that any other way would sooner have entered into your thoughts.    But I dare not take upon me to commend the fabric of it, because it is altogether so full of art, that I must unravel every scene in it to commend it as I ought.    And this excellent contrivance is still the more to be admired, because 'tis comedy, where the persons are only of common rank, and their business private, not elevated by passions or high concernments, as in serious plays. Here every one is a proper judge of all he sees, nothing is represented but that with which he daily converses: so that by consequence all faults lie open to discovery, and few are pardonable.    'Tis this which Horace has judiciously observed:

> *Creditur, ex medio quia res arcessit, habere*
> *Sudoris minimum: sed habet Comedia tanto*
> *Plus oneris, quanto veniæ minus.*[46]

But our poet who was not ignorant of these difficulties, had prevailed himself of all advantages; as he who designs a large leap takes his rise from the highest ground.    One of these advantages is that which Corneille has laid down as the greatest which can arrive to any poem, and which he himself could never compass above thrice in all his plays; viz. the making choice of some signal and long-expected day, whereon the action of the play is to depend.    This day was that designed by Dauphine for the settling of his uncle's estate upon him; which to compass, he contrives to marry him.    That the marriage had been plotted by him long beforehand, is made evident by what he tells True-Wit in the second act, that in one moment he had destroyed what he had been raising many months.

---

[45] *Lysis.*
[46] Comedy is thought to demand the least work; for it draws its subjects from ordinary life.    But the less indulgence it has, the more work it requires.

'There is another artifice of the poet, which I cannot here omit, because by the frequent practice of it in his comedies he has left it to us almost as a rule; that is, when he has any character or humour wherein he would show a *coup de Maistre*, or his highest skill, he recommends it to your observation by a pleasant description of it before the person first appears. Thus, in *Bartholomew-Fair* he gives you the pictures of Numps and Cokes, and in this those of Daw, Lafoole, Morose, and the Collegiate Ladies; all which you hear described before you see them. So that before they come upon the stage, you have a longing expectation of them, which prepares you to receive them favourably; and when they are there, even from their first appearance you are so far acquainted with them, that nothing of their humour is lost to you.

'I will observe yet one thing further of this admirable plot; the business of it rises in every act. The second is greater than the first; the third than the second; and so forward to the fifth. There too you see, till the very last scene, new difficulties arising to obstruct the action of the play; and when the audience is brought into despair that the business can naturally be effected, then, and not before, the discovery is made. But that the poet might entertain you with more variety all this while, he reserves some new characters to show you, which he opens not till the second and third act. In the second Morose, Daw, the Barber, and Otter; in the third the Collegiate Ladies: all which he moves afterwards in by-walks, or under-plots, as diversions to the main design, lest it should grow tedious, though they are still naturally joined with it, and somewhere or other subservient to it. Thus, like a skilful chess-player, by little and little he draws out his men, and makes his pawns of use to his greater persons.

'If this comedy and some others of his were translated into French prose (which would now be no wonder to them, since Moliere has lately given them plays out of verse, which have not displeased them), I believe the controversy would soon be decided betwixt the two nations, even making them the judges. But we need not call our heroes to our aid; be it spoken to the honour of the English, our nation can never want in any age such who are able to dispute the empire of wit with any people in the universe. And though the fury of a civil war, and power for twenty years together abandoned to a barbarous race of men, enemies of all good learning, had buried the Muses under the ruins of monarchy; yet, with the restoration of our happiness, we see revived Poesy lifting up its head, and already shaking off the rubbish which lay so heavy on it. We have seen since his Majesty's return, many dramatic poems which yield not to those of any foreign nation, and which deserve all laurels but the English. I will set aside flattery and envy: it cannot be denied but we have had some little blemish either in the plot or writing of all those plays which have been made within these seven years (and perhaps there is no nation in the world so quick to discern them, or so difficult to pardon them, as ours): yet if we can persuade ourselves to use the candour of that poet, who, though the most severe of critics, has left us this caution by which to moderate our censures—

> . . . *ubi plura nitent in carmine, non ego paucis*
> *Offendar maculis:*—[47]

if, in consideration of their many and great beauties, we can wink at some slight and little imperfections, if we, I say, can be thus equal to ourselves, I ask no favour from the French. And if I do not venture upon any particular judgment of our late plays, 'tis out of the consideration which an ancient writer gives me: *vivorum, ut magna admiratio, ita censura difficilis:*[48] betwixt the extremes of admiration and malice, 'tis hard to judge uprightly of the living. Only I think it may be permitted me to say, that as it is no lessening to us to yield to some plays, and those not many, of our own nation in the last age, so can it be no addition to pronounce of our present poets, that they have far surpassed all the Ancients, and the modern writers of other countries.'

This, my Lord, was the substance of what was then spoke on that occasion; and Lisideius, I think, was going to reply, when he was prevented thus by Crites: 'I am confident,' said he, 'that the most material things that can be said have been already urged on either side; if they have not, I must beg of Lisideius that he will defer his answer till another time: for I confess I have a joint quarrel to you both, because you have concluded, without any reason given for it, that rhyme is proper for the stage. I will not dispute how ancient it hath been among us to write this way; perhaps our ancestors knew no better till Shakespeare's time. I will grant it was not altogether left by him, and that Fletcher and Ben Jonson used it frequently in their Pastorals, and sometimes in other plays. Farther, I will not argue whether we received it originally from our own countrymen, or from the French; for that is an inquiry of as little benefit, as theirs who, in the midst of the great Plague, were not so solicitous to provide against it as to know whether we had it from the malignity of our own air, or by transportation from Holland. I have therefore only to affirm, that it is not allowable in serious plays; for comedies, I find you already concluding with me. To prove this, I might satisfy myself to tell you, how much in vain it is for you to strive against the stream of the people's inclination; the greatest part of which are prepossessed so much

---

[47] When many beauties shine out in a poem, I shall not be offended at small faults.
[48] Just as admiration for the living is great, it is difficult to criticize them.

with those excellent plays of Shakespeare, Fletcher, and Ben Jonson, which
have been written out of rhyme, that except you could bring them such as
were written better in it, and those too by persons of equal reputation with
them, it will be impossible for you to gain your cause with them, who will
still be judges.    This it is to which, in fine, all your reasons must submit.
The unanimous consent of an audience is so powerful, that even Julius
Cæsar (as Macrobius reports of him), when he was perpetual dictator,
was not able to balance it on the other side.    But when Laberius, a
Roman Knight, at his request contended in the Mime with another poet,
he was forced to cry out, *Etiam favente me victus es, Laberi.*[49]    But I will not
on this occasion take the advantage of the greater number, but only urge
such reasons against rhyme, as I find in the writings of those who have
argued for the other way.    First then, I am of opinion, that rhyme is unnatural in a play, because dialogue there is presented as the effect of
sudden thought: for a play is the imitation of Nature; and since no man
without premeditation speaks in rhyme, neither ought he to do it on the
stage.    This hinders not but the fancy may be there elevated to an higher
pitch of thought than it is in ordinary discourse; for there is a probability
that men of excellent and quick parts may speak noble things *ex tempore:*
but those thoughts are never fettered with the numbers or sound of
verse without study, and therefore it cannot be but unnatural to present
the most free way of speaking in that which is the most constrained.    For
this reason, says Aristotle, 'tis best to write tragedy in that kind of verse
which is the least such, or which is nearest prose: and this amongst the
Ancients was the iambic, and with us is blank verse, or the measure of
verse kept exactly without rhyme.    These numbers therefore are fittest
for a play; the others for a paper of verses, or a poem; blank verse being
as much below them, as rhyme is improper for the Drama.    And if it
be objected that neither are blank verses made *ex tempore*, yet, as nearest
nature, they are still to be preferred.—But there are two particular exceptions, which many besides myself have had to verse; by which it
will appear yet more plainly how improper it is in plays.    And the first of
them is grounded on that very reason for which some have commended
rhyme; they say, the quickness of repartees in argumentative scenes
receives an ornament from verse.    Now what is more unreasonable than
to imagine that a man should not only light upon the wit, but the rhyme
too, upon the sudden?    This nicking of him who spoke before both
in sound and measure, is so great an happiness, that you must at least
suppose the persons of your play to be born poets: *Arcades omnes, et cantare
pares, et respondere parati*[50]*:* they must have arrived to the degree of *quicquid*

49 You are defeated even with me on your side, Laberius.
50 All Arcadians, prepared to sing on equal terms and reply.

*conabar dicere*[51];—to make verses almost whether they will or no. If they are any thing below this, it will look rather like the design of two, than the answer of one: it will appear that your actors hold intelligence together; that they perform their tricks like fortune-tellers, by confederacy. The hand of art will be too visible in it, against that maxim of all professions, *Ars est celare artem*,[52] that it is the greatest perfection of art to keep itself undiscovered. Nor will it serve you to object, that however you manage it, 'tis still known to be a play; and, consequently, the dialogue of two persons understood to be the labour of one poet. For a play is still an imitation of Nature; we know we are to be deceived, and we desire to be so; but no man ever was deceived but with a probability of truth; for who will suffer a gross lie to be fastened on him? Thus we sufficiently understand, that the scenes which represent cities and countries to us are not really such, but only painted on boards and canvas; but shall that excuse the ill painture or designment of them? Nay, rather ought they not to be laboured with so much the more diligence and exactness, to help the imagination? since the mind of man does naturally tend to, and seek after truth; and therefore the nearer any thing comes to the imitation of it, the more it pleases.

'Thus, you see, your rhyme is uncapable of expressing the greatest thoughts naturally, and the lowest it cannot with any grace: for what is more unbefitting the majesty of verse, than to call a servant, or bid a door be shut in rhyme? And yet this miserable necessity you are forced upon. But verse, you say, circumscribes a quick and luxuriant fancy, which would extend itself too far on every subject, did not the labour which is required to well-turned and polished rhyme, set bounds to it. Yet this argument, if granted, would only prove that we may write better in verse, but not more naturally. Neither is it able to evince that; for he who wants judgment to confine his fancy in blank verse, may want it as much in rhyme: and he who has it will avoid errors in both kinds. Latin verse was as great a confinement to the imagination of those poets, as rhyme to ours; and yet you find Ovid saying too much on every subject. *Nescivit* (says Seneca) *quod bene cessit relinquere*[53]: of which he gives you one famous instance in his description of the deluge:

> *Omnia pontus erat, deerant quoque litora ponto.*
> Now all was sea, nor had that sea a shore.

Thus Ovid's fancy was not limited by verse, and Virgil needed not verse to have bounded his.

[51] Of singing whatever they attempted.
[52] It is an art to conceal art.
[53] He did not know how to end when he should have.

'In our own language we see Ben Jonson confining himself to what ought to be said, even in the liberty of blank verse; and yet Corneille, the most judicious of the French poets, is still varying the same sense an hundred ways, and dwelling eternally on the same subject, though confined by rhyme. Some other exceptions I have to verse; but being these I have named are for the most part already public, I conceive it reasonable they should first be answered.'

'It concerns me less than any,' said Neander (seeing he had ended), 'to reply to this discourse; because when I should have proved that verse may be natural in plays, yet I should always be ready to confess, that those which I have written in this kind come short of that perfection which is required. Yet since you are pleased I should undertake this province, I will do it, though with all imaginable respect and deference, both to that person from whom you have borrowed your strongest arguments, and to whose judgment, when I have said all, I finally submit. But before I proceed to answer your objections, I must first remember you, that I exclude all Comedy from my defence; and next that I deny not but blank verse may be also used; and content myself only to assert, that in serious plays where the subject and characters are great, and the plot unmixed with mirth, which might allay or divert these concernments which are produced, rhyme is there as natural and more effectual than blank verse.

'And now having laid down this as a foundation,— to begin with Crites, I must crave leave to tell him, that some of his arguments against rhyme reach no farther than, from the faults or defects of ill rhyme, to conclude against the use of it in general. May not I conclude against blank verse by the same reason? If the words of some poets who write in it, are either ill chosen, or ill placed, which makes not only rhyme, but all kind of verse in any language unnatural, shall I, for their vicious affectation, condemn those excellent lines of Fletcher, which are written in that kind? Is there any thing in rhyme more constrained than this line in blank verse, *I heaven invoke, and strong resistance make?* where you see both the clauses are placed unnaturally, that is, contrary to the common way of speaking, and that without the excuse of a rhyme to cause it: yet you would think me very ridiculous, if I should accuse the stubbornness of blank verse for this, and not rather the stiffness of the poet. Therefore, Crites, you must either prove that words, though well chosen, and duly placed, yet render not rhyme natural in itself; or that, however natural and easy the rhyme may be, yet it is not proper for a play. If you insist on the former part, I would ask you, what other conditions are required to make rhyme natural in itself, besides an election of apt words, and a right disposing of them? For the due choice of your words expresses your sense naturally, and the due placing them adapts the rhyme to it.    If you object that one verse may be made for the sake of another, though both the words and rhyme be apt, I answer, it cannot possibly so fall out; for either there is a dependance of sense betwixt the first line and the second, or there is none: if there be that connection, then in the natural position of the words the latter line must of necessity flow from the former; if there be no dependance, yet still the due ordering of words makes the last line as natural in itself as the other: so that the necessity of a rhyme never forces any but bad or lazy writers to say what they would not otherwise.    'Tis true, there is both care and art required to write in verse.    A good poet never concludes upon the first line, till he has sought out such a rhyme as may fit the sense, already prepared to heighten the second: many times the close of the sense falls into the middle of the next verse, or farther off, and he may often prevail himself of the same advantages in English which Virgil had in Latin; he may break off in the hemistich, and begin another line.    Indeed, the not observing these two last things, makes plays which are writ in verse so tedious: for though, most commonly, the sense is to be confined to the couplet, yet nothing that does *perpetuo tenore fluere*, run in the same channel, can please always.    'Tis like the murmuring of a stream, which not varying in the fall, causes at first attention, at last drowsiness.    Variety of cadences is the best rule; the greatest help to the actors, and refreshment to the audience.

'If then verse may be made natural in itself, how becomes it improper to a play?    You say the stage is the representation of Nature, and no man in ordinary conversation speaks in rhyme.    But you foresaw when you said this, that it might be answered—neither does any man speak in blank verse, or in measure without rhyme. Therefore you concluded, that which is nearest Nature is still to be preferred.    But you took no notice that rhyme might be made as natural as blank verse, by the well placing of the words, &c.    All the difference between them, when they are both correct, is, the sound in one, which the other wants; and if so, the sweetness of it, and all the advantage resulting from it, which are handled in the Preface to *The Rival Ladies*, will yet stand good.    As for that place of Aristotle, where he says, plays should be writ in that kind of verse which is nearest prose, it makes little for you; blank verse being properly but measured prose.    Now measure alone, in any modern language, does not constitute verse; those of the Ancients in Greek and Latin consisted in quantity of words, and a determinate number of feet.    But when, by the inundation of the Goths and Vandals into Italy, new languages were brought in, and barbarously mingled with the Latin, of which the Italian, Spanish, French, and ours (made out of them and the Teutonic) are dialects, a new way of poesy was practised; new, I say, in those countries, for in all probability it was that of the conquerors in their own nations.

This new way consisted in measure or number of feet, and rhyme; the sweetness of rhyme, and observation of accent, supplying the place of quantity in words, which could neither exactly be observed by those Barbarians, who knew not the rules of it, neither was it suitable to their tongues, as it had been to the Greek and Latin.    No man is tied in modern poesy to observe any farther rule in the feet of his verse, but that they be dissyllables; whether spondee, trochee, or iambic, it matters not; only he is obliged to rhyme.    Neither do the Spanish, French, Italian, or Germans, acknowledge at all, or very rarely, any such kind of poesy as blank verse amongst them.    Therefore, at most 'tis but a poetic prose, a *sermo pedestris;* and as such, most fit for comedies, where I acknowledge rhyme to be improper.    Farther; as to that quotation of Aristotle, our couplet verses may be rendered as near prose as blank verse itself, by using those advantages I lately named, as breaks in a hemistich, or running the sense into another line, thereby making art and order appear as loose and free as nature: or not tying ourselves to couplets strictly, we may use the benefit of the Pindaric way practised in *The Siege of Rhodes;* where the numbers vary, and the rhyme is disposed carelessly, and far from often chiming.    Neither is that other advantage of the Ancients to be despised, of changing the kind of verse when they please, with the change of the scene, or some new entrance; for they confine not themselves always to iambics, but extend their liberty to all lyric numbers, and sometimes even to hexameter.    But I need not go so far to prove that rhyme, as it succeeds to all other offices of Greek and Latin verse, so especially to this of plays, since the custom of all nations at this day confirms it, all the French, Italian, and Spanish tragedies are generally writ in it; and sure the universal consent of the most civilized parts of the world ought in this, as it doth in other customs, to include the rest.

'But perhaps you may tell me, I have proposed such a way to make rhyme natural, and consequently proper to plays, as is unpracticable; and that I shall scarce find six or eight lines together in any play, where the words are so placed and chosen as is required to make it natural.    I answer, no poet need constrain himself at all times to it.    It is enough he makes it his general rule; for I deny not but sometimes there may be a greatness in placing the words otherwise; and sometimes they may sound better, sometimes also the variety itself is excuse enough.    But if, for the most part, the words be placed as they are in the negligence of prose, it is sufficient to denominate the way practicable; for we esteem that to be such, which in the trial oftener succeeds than misses.    And thus far you may find the practice made good in many plays: where you do not, remember still, that if you cannot find six natural rhymes together, it will be as hard for you to produce as many lines in blank verse, even among the greatest of our poets, against which I cannot make some reasonable exception.

'And this, Sir, calls to my remembrance the beginning of your discourse, where you told us we should never find the audience favourable to this kind of writing, till we could produce as good plays in rhyme, as Ben Jonson, Fletcher, and Shakespeare, had writ out of it. But it is to raise envy to the living, to compare them with the dead. They are honoured, and almost adored by us, as they deserve; neither do I know any so presumptuous of themselves as to contend with them. Yet give me leave to say thus much, without injury to their ashes; that not only we shall never equal them, but they could never equal themselves, were they to rise and write again. We acknowledge them our fathers in wit; but they have ruined their estates themselves, before they came to their children's hands. There is scarce an humour, a character, or any kind of plot, which they have not blown upon. All comes sullied or wasted to us: and were they to entertain this age, they could not make so plenteous treatments out of such decayed fortunes. This therefore will be a good argument to us, either not to write at all, or to attempt some other way. There is no bays to be expected in their walks: *tentanda via est, qua me quoque possum tollere humo.*[54]

'This way of writing in verse they have only left free to us; our age is arrived to a perfection in it, which they never knew; and which (if we may guess by what of theirs we have seen in verse, as *The Faithful Shepherdess*, and *Sad Shepherd*) 'tis probable they never could have reached. For the genius of every age is different; and though ours excel in this, I deny not but that to imitate Nature in that perfection which they did in prose, is a greater commendation than to write in verse exactly. As for what you have added, that the people are not generally inclined to like this way; if it were true, it would be no wonder, that betwixt the shaking off an old habit, and the introducing of a new, there should be difficulty. Do we not see them stick to Hopkins' and Sternhold's psalms, and forsake those of David, I mean Sandys his translation of them? If by the people you understand the multitude, ὃι πολλοί,[55] 'tis no matter what they think; they are sometimes in the right, sometimes in the wrong: their judgment is a mere lottery. *Est ubi plebs recte putat, est ubi peccat.*[56] Horace says it of the vulgar, judging poesy. But if you mean the mixed audience of the populace and the noblesse, I dare confidently affirm that a great part of the latter sort are already favourable to verse; and that no serious plays written since the King's return have been more kindly

---

[54] I must explore new ways in which to raise my name aloft.
[55] *Hoi polloi*, the many, the masses.
[56] Sometimes the people think rightly, sometimes not.

received by them, than *The Siege of Rhodes*, the *Mustapha*, *The Indian Queen*, and *Indian Emperor*.

'But I come now to the inference of your first argument.  You said the dialogue of plays is presented as the effect of sudden thought, but no man speaks suddenly, or *ex tempore*, in rhyme; and you inferred from thence, that rhyme, which you acknowledge to be proper to epic poesy, cannot equally be proper to dramatic, unless we could suppose all men born so much more than poets, that verses should be made in them, not by them.

'It has been formerly urged by you, and confessed by me, that since no man spoke any kind of verse *ex tempore*, that which was nearest Nature was to be preferred.  I answer you, therefore, by distinguishing betwixt what is nearest to the nature of Comedy, which is the imitation of common persons and ordinary speaking, and what is nearest the nature of a serious play: this last is indeed the representation of Nature, but 'tis Nature wrought up to an higher pitch.  The plot, the characters, the wit, the passions, the descriptions, are all exalted above the level of common converse, as high as the imagination of the poet can carry them, with proportion to verisimility.  Tragedy, we know, is wont to image to us the minds and fortunes of noble persons, and to portray these exactly; heroic rhyme is nearest Nature, as being the noblest kind of modern verse.

> *Indignatur enim privatis et prope socco*
> *Dignis carminibus narrari cæna Thyestæ*,[57]

says Horace: and in another place,

> *Effutire leves indigna tragædia versus.*[58]

Blank verse is acknowledged to be too low for a poem, nay more, for a paper of verses; but if too low for an ordinary sonnet, how much more for Tragedy, which is by Aristotle, in the dispute betwixt the epic poesy and the dramatic, for many reasons he there alleges, ranked above it?

'But setting this defence aside, your argument is almost as strong against the use of rhyme in poems as in plays; for the epic way is every where interlaced with dialogue, or discoursive scenes; and therefore you must either grant rhyme to be improper there, which is contrary to your assertion, or admit it into plays by the same title which you have given it to poems.  For though Tragedy be justly preferred above the other, yet there is a great affinity between them, as may easily be discovered in that definition of a play which Lisideius gave us.  The *genus* of them is the

---

[57] The banquet of Thyestes should not be told in the familiar verses appropriate to comedy.

[58] It is not proper for tragedy to babble forth light verse.

same, a just and lively image of human nature, in its actions, passions, and traverses of fortune: so is the end, namely, for the delight and benefit of mankind. The characters and persons are still the same, viz. the greatest of both sorts; only the manner of acquainting us with those actions, passions, and fortunes, is different. Tragedy performs it *viva voce*, or by action, in dialogue; wherein it excels the Epic Poem, which does it chiefly by narration, and therefore is not so lively an image of human nature. However, the agreement betwixt them is such, that if rhyme be proper for one, it must be for the other. Verse, 'tis true, is not the effect of sudden thought; but this hinders not that sudden thought may be represented in verse, since those thoughts are such as must be higher than Nature can raise them without premeditation, especially to a continuance of them, even out of verse; and consequently you cannot imagine them to have been sudden either in the poet or in the actors. A play, as I have said, to be like Nature, is to be set above it; as statues which are placed on high are made greater than the life, that they may descend to the sight in their just proportion.

'Perhaps I have insisted too long on this objection; but the clearing of it will make my stay shorter on the rest. You tell us, Crites, that rhyme appears most unnatural in repartees, or short replies: when he who answers, it being presumed he knew not what the other would say, yet makes up that part of the verse which was left incomplete, and supplies both the sound and measure of it. This, you say, looks rather like the confederacy of two, than the answer of one.

'This, I confess, is an objection which is in every one's mouth, who loves not rhyme: but suppose, I beseech you, the repartee were made only in blank verse, might not part of the same argument be turned against you? for the measure is as often supplied there, as it is in rhyme; the latter half of the hemistich as commonly made up, or a second line subjoined as a reply to the former; which any one leaf in Jonson's plays will sufficiently clear to you. You will often find in the Greek tragedians, and in Seneca, that when a scene grows up into the warmth of repartees, which is the close fighting of it, the latter part of the trimeter is supplied by him who answers; and yet it was never observed as a fault in them by any of the ancient or modern critics. The case is the same in our verse, as it was in theirs; rhyme to us being in lieu of quantity to them. But if no latitude is to be allowed a poet, you take from him not only his licence of *quidlibet audendi*,[59] but you tie him up in a straiter compass than you would a philosopher. This is indeed *Musas colere severiores*.[60] You would have him follow Nature, but he must follow her on foot: you have dismounted

[59] Of taking any liberty he wishes.
[60] To cultivate the more serious Muses.

him from his Pegasus.  But you tell us, this supplying the last half of a verse, or adjoining a whole second to the former, looks more like the design of two, than the answer of one.  Supposing we acknowledge it: how comes this confederacy to be more displeasing to you, than in a dance which is well contrived?  You see there the united design of many persons to make up one figure: after they have separated themselves in many petty divisions, they rejoin one by one into a gross: the confederacy is plain amongst them, for chance could never produce any thing so beautiful; and yet there is nothing in it, that shocks your sight.  I acknowledge the hand of art appears in repartee, as of necessity it must in all kinds of verse. But there is also the quick and poynant brevity of it (which is an high imitation of Nature in those sudden gusts of passion) to mingle with it; and this, joined with the cadency and sweetness of the rhyme, leaves nothing in the soul of the hearer to desire.   'Tis an art which appears; but it appears only like the shadowings of painture, which being to cause the rounding of it, cannot be absent; but while that is considered, they are lost: so while we attend to the other beauties of the matter, the care and labour of the rhyme is carried from us, or at least drowned in its own sweetness, as bees are sometimes buried in their honey.   When a poet has found the repartee, the last perfection he can add to it, is to put it into verse.   However good the thought may be, however apt the words in which 'tis couched, yet he finds himself at a little unrest, while rhyme is wanting: he cannot leave it till that comes naturally, and then is at ease, and sits down contented.

'From replies, which are the most elevated thoughts of verse, you pass to the most mean ones, those which are common with the lowest of household conversation.  In these, you say, the majesty of verse suffers. You instance in the calling of a servant, or commanding a door to be shut, in rhyme.  This, Crites, is a good observation of yours, but no argument: for it proves no more but that such thoughts should be waved, as often as may be, by the address of the poet.  But suppose they are necessary in the places where he uses them, yet there is no need to put them into rhyme. He may place them in the beginning of a verse, and break it off, as unfit, when so debased, for any other use; or granting the worst,—that they require more room than the hemistich will allow, yet still there is a choice to be made of the best words, and least vulgar (provided they be apt) to express such thoughts.  Many have blamed rhyme in general, for this fault, when the poet with a little care might have redressed it.  But they do it with no more justice, than if English Poesy should be made ridiculous for the sake of the Water Poet's rhymes.  Our language is noble, full, and significant; and I know not why he who is master of it may not clothe ordinary things in it as decently as the Latin, if he use the same diligence in his choice of words.  *Delectus verborum origo est eloquentiae.*[61]  It was the saying of Julius Cæsar, one so curious in his, that none of them can be changed but for a worse.  One would think, *unlock the door*, was a thing as vulgar as could be spoken; and yet Seneca could make it sound high and lofty in his Latin:

> *Reserate clusos regii postes laris.*
> Set wide the palace gates.

'But I turn from this exception, both because it happens not above twice or thrice in any play that those vulgar thoughts are used; and then too, were there no other apology to be made, yet the necessity of them which is alike in all kind of writing, may excuse them.  Besides that the great eagerness and precipitation with which they are spoken makes us rather mind the substance than the dress; that for which they are spoken, rather than what is spoken.  For they are always the effect of some hasty concernment, and something of consequence depends on them.

'Thus, Crites, I have endeavoured to answer your objections; it remains only that I should vindicate an argument for verse, which you have gone about to overthrow.  It had formerly been said, that the easiness of blank verse renders the poet too luxuriant, but that the labour of rhyme bounds and circumscribes an overfruitful fancy; the sense there being commonly confined to the couplet, and the words so ordered that the rhyme naturally follows them, not they the rhyme.  To this you answered, that it was no argument to the question in hand; for the dispute was not which way a man may write best, but which is most proper for the subject on which he writes.

'First, give me leave, Sir, to remember you, that the argument against which you raised this objection, was only secondary: it was built on this hypothesis, that to write in verse was proper for serious plays.  Which supposition being granted (as it was briefly made out in that discourse, by showing how verse might be made natural), it asserted, that this way of writing was an help to the poet's judgment, by putting bounds to a wild overflowing fancy.  I think, therefore, it will not be hard for me to make good what it was to prove.  But you add, that were this let pass, yet he who wants judgment in the liberty of his fancy, may as well show the defect of it when he is confined to verse; for he who has judgment will avoid errors, and he who has it not, will commit them in all kinds of writing.

'This argument, as you have taken it from a most acute person, so I confess it carries much weight in it: but by using the word judgment here indefinitely, you seem to have put a fallacy upon us.  I grant, he who has

[61] The origin of eloquence is the proper choice of words.

judgment, that is, so profound, so strong, so infallible a judgment, that he needs no helps to keep it always poised and upright, will commit no faults either in rhyme or out of it.    And on the other extreme, he who has a judgment so weak and crazed that no helps can correct or amend it, shall write scurvily out of rhyme, and worse in it.    But the first of these judgments is no where to be found, and the latter is not fit to write at all. To speak therefore of judgment as it is in the best poets; they who have the greatest proportion of it, want other helps than from it, within.    As for example, you would be loth to say, that he who was endued with a sound judgment had no need of History, Geography, or Moral Philosophy, to write correctly.    Judgment is indeed the master-workman in a play; but he requires many subordinate hands, many tools to his assistance.    And verse I affirm to be one of these; 'tis a rule and line by which he keeps his building compact and even, which otherwise lawless imagination would raise either irregularly or loosely.    At least, if the poet commits errors with this help, he would make greater and more without it: 'tis, in short, a slow and painful, but the surest kind of working.    Ovid, whom you accuse for luxuriancy in verse, had perhaps been farther guilty of it, had he writ in prose.    And for your instance of Ben Jonson, who, you say, writ exactly without the help of rhyme; you are to remember, 'tis only an aid to a luxuriant fancy, which his was not: as he did not want imagination, so none ever said he had much to spare.    Neither was verse then refined so much to be an help to that age, as it is to ours.    Thus then the second thoughts being usually the best, as receiving the maturest digestion from judgment, and the last and most mature product of those thoughts being artful and laboured verse, it may well be inferred, that verse is a great help to a luxuriant fancy; and this is what that argument which you opposed was to evince.'

Neander was pursuing this discourse so eagerly, that Eugenius had called to him twice or thrice, ere he took notice that the barge stood still, and that they were at the foot of Somerset Stairs, where they had appointed it to land.    The company were all sorry to separate so soon, though a great part of the evening was already spent; and stood a while looking back on the water, which the moon-beams played upon, and made it appear like floating quick-silver: at last they went up through a crowd of French people, who were merrily dancing in the open air, and nothing concerned for the noise of guns which had alarmed the town that afternoon.    Walking thence together to the Piazze, they parted there; Eugenius and Lisideius to some pleasant appointment they had made, and Crites and Neander to their several lodgings.

# An Essay on Criticism

## 1711

*In writing an essay in the form of a poem, young Alexander Pope (he was twenty-three when the work was published, and he may have written it at nineteen) was not being deliberately perverse but conscientiously traditional. The poem is in a genre that had the sanction of both classical precedent (Horace's "Art of Poetry" being only one instance) and many seventeenth-century examples; thus his poem is an imitation of a classical model. But Pope's subject matter is not poetry; it is criticism itself, a shift in emphasis that reflects the period's self-consciousness about literary standards. Again, however, Pope's originality is limited: The substance of his verse essay consists of familiar neoclassical critical values and doctrines. Taking the doctrines for granted, he codified and condensed them into witty and memorable language so that many of his lines have become aphorisms with the weight of proverbial wisdom. To use his own words, the essay is "what oft was thought but ne'er so well expressed." And for an example of his virtuoso versification, study lines 137–173 in Part II, which illustrate the doctrine of "representative meter."*

*At the heart of the essay is the same nature vs. art controversy found in Dryden's "Essay of Dramatic Poesy." Which of the four critics in that debate most nearly states the views that Pope expounds? To*

From *Complete Poetical Works;* Cambridge Edition, Boston and New York, Houghton Mifflin Company, 1903.

*answer this question is to establish one distinction between Dryden and Pope. Pope, too, has to allow for the "Great Wits," those who deviate from the rules and yet achieve greatness; but can you imagine that he would say with Neander, "I admire Jonson but I love Shakespeare"? In connection with this perplexing problem, two of Pope's statements on nature should be studied: "The rules of old are Nature methodiz'd" and also "True Wit is Nature to advantage dress'd." What, then, is the relationship between the rules and true wit? How can tradition and natural gifts be reconciled? Watch for the recurrence of this question, even though it may be stated in different terms by future critics.*

*The three-part organization of the poem is also worth studying for its internal structure, both for the subject matter in each part and the sequence in which these topics are presented. In Part III, Pope's history of criticism consists of a gallery of great critics; are his criteria for greatness spelled out explicitly?*

## PART I

'T is hard to say if greater want of skill
Appear in writing or in judging ill;
But of the two less dangerous is th' offence
To tire our patience than mislead our sense:
Some few in that, but numbers err in this;
Ten censure wrong for one who writes amiss;
A fool might once himself alone expose;
Now one in verse makes many more in prose.
    'T is with our judgments as our watches, none
Go just alike, yet each believes his own.                        10
In Poets as true Genius is but rare,
True Taste as seldom is the Critic's share;
Both must alike from Heav'n derive their light,
These born to judge, as well as those to write.
Let such teach others who themselves excel,
And censure freely who have written well;
Authors are partial to their wit, 'tis true,
But are not Critics to their judgment too?
    Yet if we look more closely, we shall find
Most have the seeds of judgment in their mind:                   20
Nature affords at least a glimm'ring light;

The lines, tho' touch'd but faintly, are drawn right:
But as the slightest sketch, if justly traced,
Is by ill col'ring but the more disgraced,
So by false learning is good sense defaced:
Some are bewilder'd in the maze of schools,
And some made coxcombs Nature meant but fools:
In search of wit these lose their common sense,
And then turn Critics in their own defence:
Each burns alike, who can or cannot write,　　　　30
Or with a rival's or an eunuch's spite.
All fools have still an itching to deride,
And fain would be upon the laughing side.
If Mævius scribble in Apollo's spite,
There are who judge still worse than he can write.
　　Some have at first for Wits, then Poets pass'd;
Turn'd Critics next, and prov'd plain Fools at last.
Some neither can for Wits nor Critics pass,
As heavy mules are neither horse nor ass.
Those half-learn'd witlings, numerous in our isle,　　40
As half-form'd insects on the banks of Nile;
Unfinish'd things, one knows not what to call,
Their generation 's so equivocal;
To tell them would a hundred tongues require,
Or one vain Wit's, that might a hundred tire.
　　But you who seek to give and merit fame,
And justly bear a Critic's noble name,
Be sure yourself and your own reach to know,
How far your Genius, Taste, and Learning go,
Launch not beyond your depth, but be discreet,　　50
And mark that point where Sense and Dulness meet.
　　Nature to all things fix'd the limits fit,
And wisely curb'd proud man's pretending wit.
As on the land while here the ocean gains,
In other parts it leaves wide sandy plains;
Thus in the soul while Memory prevails,
The solid power of Understanding fails;
Where beams of warm Imagination play,
The Memory's soft figures melt away.
One Science only will one genius fit;　　　　　60
So vast is Art, so narrow human wit:
Not only bounded to peculiar arts,
But oft in those confin'd to single parts.

Like Kings we lose the conquests gain'd before,
By vain ambition still to make them more:
Each might his sev'ral province well command,
Would all but stoop to what they understand.
    First follow Nature, and your judgment frame
By her just standard, which is still the same;
Unerring Nature, still divinely bright,                    70
One clear, unchanged, and universal light,
Life, force, and beauty must to all impart,
At once the source, and end, and test of Art.
Art from that fund each just supply provides,
Works without show, and without pomp presides.
In some fair body thus th' informing soul
With spirits feeds, with vigour fills the whole;
Each motion guides, and every nerve sustains,
Itself unseen, but in th' effects remains.
Some, to whom Heav'n in wit has been profuse,              80
Want as much more to turn it to its use;
For Wit and Judgment often are at strife,
Tho' meant each other's aid, like man and wife.
'T is more to guide than spur the Muse's steed,
Restrain his fury than provoke his speed:
The winged courser, like a gen'rous horse,
Shows most true mettle when you check his course.
    Those rules of old, discover'd, not devised,
Are Nature still, but Nature methodized;
Nature, like Liberty, is but restrain'd                    90
By the same laws which first herself ordain'd.
    Hear how learn'd Greece her useful rules indites
When to repress and when indulge our flights:
High on Parnassus' top her sons she show'd,
And pointed out those arduous paths they trod;
Held from afar, aloft, th' immortal prize,
And urged the rest by equal steps to rise.
Just precepts thus from great examples giv'n,
She drew from them what they derived from Heav'n.
The gen'rous Critic fann'd the poet's fire,                100
And taught the world with reason to admire.
Then Criticism the Muse's handmaid prov'd,
To dress her charms, and make her more belov'd:
But following Wits from that intention stray'd:
Who could not win the mistress woo'd the maid;

Against the Poets their own arms they turn'd,
Sure to hate most the men from whom they learn'd.
So modern 'pothecaries, taught the art
By doctors' bills to play the doctor's part,
Bold in the practice of mistaken rules,                    110
Prescribe, apply, and call their masters fools.
Some on the leaves of ancient authors prey;
Nor time nor moths e'er spoil'd so much as they;
Some drily plain, without invention's aid,
Write dull receipts how poems may be made;
These leave the sense their learning to display,
And those explain the meaning quite away.
  You then whose judgment the right course would steer,
Know well each ancient's proper character;
His fable, subject, scope in every page;                    120
Religion, country, genius of his age:
Without all these at once before your eyes,
Cavil you may, but never criticise.
Be Homer's works your study and delight,
Read them by day, and meditate by night;
Thence form your judgment, thence your maxims bring,
And trace the Muses upward to their spring.
Still with itself compared, his text peruse;
And let your comment be the Mantuan Muse.
  When first young Maro in his boundless mind        130
A work t' outlast immortal Rome design'd,
Perhaps he seem'd above the critic's law,
And but from Nature's fountains scorn'd to draw;
But when t' examine ev'ry part he came,
Nature and Homer were, he found, the same.
Convinced, amazed, he checks the bold design,
And rules as strict his labour'd work confine
As if the Stagyrite o'erlook'd each line.
Learn hence for ancient rules a just esteem;
To copy Nature is to copy them.                              140
  Some beauties yet no precepts can declare,
For there 's a happiness as well as care.
Music resembles poetry; in each
Are nameless graces which no methods teach,
And which a master-hand alone can reach.
If, where the rules not far enough extend,
(Since rules were made but to promote their end)

Some lucky license answer to the full
Th' intent proposed, that license is a rule.
Thus Pegasus, a nearer way to take,                    150
May boldly deviate from the common track.
Great Wits sometimes may gloriously offend,
And rise to faults true Critics dare not mend;
From vulgar bounds with brave disorder part,
And snatch a grace beyond the reach of Art,
Which, without passing thro' the judgment, gains
The heart, and all its end at once attains.
In prospects thus some objects please our eyes,
Which out of Nature's common order rise,
The shapeless rock, or hanging precipice.              160
But tho' the ancients thus their rules invade,
(As Kings dispense with laws themselves have made)
Moderns, beware! or if you must offend
Against the precept, ne'er transgress its end;
Let it be seldom, and compell'd by need;
And have at least their precedent to plead;
The Critic else proceeds without remorse,
Seizes your fame, and puts his laws in force.
    I know there are to whose presumptuous thoughts
Those freer beauties, ev'n in them, seem faults.       170
Some figures monstrous and misshaped appear,
Consider'd singly, or beheld too near,
Which, but proportion'd to their light or place,
Due distance reconciles to form and grace.
A prudent chief not always must display
His powers in equal ranks and fair array,
But with th' occasion and the place comply,
Conceal his force, nay, seem sometimes to fly.
Those oft are stratagems which errors seem,
Nor is it Homer nods, but we that dream.               180
    Still green with bays each ancient altar stands
Above the reach of sacrilegious hands,
Secure from flames, from Envy's fiercer rage,
Destructive war, and all-involving Age.
See from each clime the learn'd their incense bring!
Hear in all tongues consenting pæans ring!
In praise so just let ev'ry voice be join'd,
And fill the gen'ral chorus of mankind.
Hail, Bards triumphant! born in happier days,

Immortal heirs of universal praise!                              190
Whose honours with increase of ages grow,
As streams roll down, enlarging as they flow;
Nations unborn your mighty names shall sound,
And worlds applaud that must not yet be found!
O may some spark of your celestial fire
The last, the meanest of your sons inspire,
(That on weak wings, from far, pursues your flights,
Glows while he reads, but trembles as he writes)
To teach vain Wits a science little known,
T' admire superior sense, and doubt their own.                  200

## PART II

Of all the causes which conspire to blind
Man's erring judgment, and misguide the mind,
What the weak head with strongest bias rules,
Is Pride, the never failing vice of fools.
Whatever Nature has in worth denied
She gives in large recruits of needful Pride:
For as in bodies, thus in souls, we find
What wants in blood and spirits swell'd with wind:
Pride, where Wit fails, steps in to our defence,
And fills up all the mighty void of Sense:                      10
If once right Reason drives that cloud away,
Truth breaks upon us with resistless day.
Trust not yourself; but your defects to know,
Make use of ev'ry friend—and ev'ry foe.
   A little learning is a dangerous thing;
Drink deep, or taste not the Pierian spring:
There shallow draughts intoxicate the brain,
And drinking largely sobers us again.
Fired at first sight with what the Muse imparts,
In fearless youth we tempt the heights of arts,                 20
While from the bounded level of our mind
Short views we take, nor see the lengths behind:
But more advanc'd, behold with strange surprise
New distant scenes of endless science rise!
So pleas'd at first the tow'ring Alps we try,
Mount o'er the vales, and seem to tread the sky;
Th' eternal snows appear already past,
And the first clouds and mountains seem the last:

But those attain'd, we tremble to survey
The growing labours of the lengthen'd way;                    30
Th' increasing prospect tires our wand'ring eyes,
Hills peep o'er hills, and Alps on Alps arise!
  A perfect judge will read each work of wit
With the same spirit that its author writ;
Survey the whole, nor seek slight faults to find
Where Nature moves, and Rapture warms the mind:
Nor lose, for that malignant dull delight,
The gen'rous pleasure to be charm'd with wit.
But in such lays as neither ebb nor flow,
Correctly cold, and regularly low,                            40
That shunning faults one quiet tenor keep,
We cannot blame indeed—but we may sleep.
In Wit, as Nature, what affects our hearts
Is not th' exactness of peculiar parts;
'T is not a lip or eye we beauty call,
But the joint force and full result of all.
Thus when we view some well proportion'd dome,
(The world's just wonder, and ev'n thine, O Rome!)
No single parts unequally surprise,
All comes united to th' admiring eyes;                        50
No monstrous height, or breadth, or length, appear;
The whole at once is bold and regular.
  Whoever thinks a faultless piece to see,
Thinks what ne'er was, nor is, nor e'er shall be.
In every work regard the writer's end,
Since none can compass more than they intend;
And if the means be just, the conduct true,
Applause, in spite of trivial faults, is due.
As men of breeding, sometimes men of wit,
T' avoid great errors must the less commit;                   60
Neglect the rules each verbal critic lays,
For not to know some trifles is a praise.
Most critics, fond of some subservient art,
Still make the whole depend upon a part:
They talk of Principles, but Notions prize,
And all to one lov'd folly sacrifice.
  Once on a time La Mancha's Knight, they say,
A certain bard encount'ring on the way,
Discours'd in terms as just, with looks as sage,
As e'er could Dennis, of the Grecian Stage;                   70

Concluding all were desperate sots and fools
Who durst depart from Aristotle's rules.
Our author, happy in a judge so nice,
Produced his play, and begg'd the knight's advice;
Made him observe the Subject and the Plot,
The Manners, Passions, Unities; what not?
All which exact to rule were brought about,
Were but a combat in the lists left out.
'What! leave the combat out?' exclaims the knight.
'Yes, or we must renounce the Stagyrite.'                    80
'Not so, by Heaven! (he answers in a rage)
Knights, squires, and steeds must enter on the stage.'
'So vast a throng the stage can ne'er contain.'
'Then build a new, or act it in a plain.'
   Thus critics of less judgment than caprice,
Curious, not knowing, not exact, but nice,
Form short ideas, and offend in Arts
(As most in Manners), by a love to parts.
   Some to Conceit alone their taste confine,
And glitt'ring thoughts struck out at every line;          90
Pleas'd with a work where nothing 's just or fit,
One glaring chaos and wild heap of wit.
Poets, like painters, thus unskill'd to trace
The naked 'nature and the living grace,
With gold and jewels cover every part,
And hide with ornaments their want of Art.
True Wit is Nature to advantage dress'd,
What oft was thought, but ne'er so well express'd;
Something whose truth convinced at sight we find,
That gives us back the image of our mind.                   100
As shades more sweetly recommend the light,
So modest plainness sets off sprightly wit:
For works may have more wit than does them good,
As bodies perish thro' excess of blood.
   Others for language all their care express,
And value books, as women men, for dress:
Their praise is still—the Style is excellent;
The Sense they humbly take upon content.
Words are like leaves; and where they most abound,
Much fruit of sense beneath is rarely found.               110
False eloquence, like the prismatic glass,
Its gaudy colours spreads on every place;

The face of Nature we no more survey,
All glares alike, without distinction gay;
But true expression, like th' unchanging sun,
Clears and improves whate'er it shines upon;
It gilds all objects, but it alters none.
Expression is the dress of thought, and still
Appears more decent as more suitable.
A vile Conceit in pompous words express'd                120
Is like a clown in regal purple dress'd.
For diff'rent styles with diff'rent subjects sort,
As sev'ral garbs with country, town, and court.
Some by old words to fame have made pretence,
Ancients in phrase, mere moderns in their sense;
Such labour'd nothings, in so strange a style,
Amaze th' unlearn'd, and make the learned smile;
Unlucky as Fungoso in the play,
These sparks with awkward vanity display
What the fine gentleman wore yesterday;                  130
And but so mimic ancient wits at best,
As apes our grandsires in their doublets drest.
In words as fashions the same rule will hold,
Alike fantastic if too new or old:
Be not the first by whom the new are tried,
Nor yet the last to lay the old aside.
   But most by Numbers judge a poet's song,
And smooth or rough with them is right or wrong.
In the bright Muse tho' thousand charms conspire,
Her voice is all these tuneful fools admire;             140
Who haunt Parnassus but to please their ear,
Not mend their minds; as some to church repair,
Not for the doctrine, but the music there.
These equal syllables alone require,
Tho' oft the ear the open vowels tire,
While expletives their feeble aid do join,
And ten low words oft creep in one dull line:
While they ring round the same unvaried chimes,
With sure returns of still expected rhymes;
Where'er you find 'the cooling western breeze,'          150
In the next line, it 'whispers thro' the trees;'
If crystal streams 'with pleasing murmurs creep,'
The reader's threaten'd (not in vain) with 'sleep;'
Then, at the last and only couplet, fraught

With some unmeaning thing they call a thought,
A needless Alexandrine ends the song,
That, like a wounded snake, drags its slow length along.
Leave such to tune their own dull rhymes, and know
What 's roundly smooth, or languishingly slow;
And praise the easy vigour of a line                      160
Where Denham's strength and Waller's sweetness join.
True ease in writing comes from Art, not Chance,
As those move easiest who have learn'd to dance.
'T is not enough no harshness gives offence;
The sound must seem an echo to the sense.
Soft is the strain when zephyr gently blows,
And the smooth stream in smoother numbers flows;
But when loud surges lash the sounding shore,
The hoarse rough verse should like the torrent roar.
When Ajax strives some rock's vast weight to throw,       170
The line, too, labours, and the words move slow:
Not so when swift Camilla scours the plain,
Flies o'er th' unbending corn, and skims along the main.
Hear how Timotheus' varied lays surprise,
And bid alternate passions fall and rise!
While at each change the son of Libyan Jove
Now burns with glory, and then melts with love;
Now his fierce eyes with sparkling fury glow,
Now sighs steal out, and tears begin to flow:
Persians and Greeks like turns of nature found,          180
And the world's Victor stood subdued by sound!
The power of music all our hearts allow
And what Timotheus was is Dryden now.
    Avoid extremes, and shun the fault of such
Who still are pleas'd too little or too much.
At ev'ry trifle scorn to take offence;
That always shows great pride or little sense:
Those heads, as stomachs, are not sure the best
Which nauseate all, and nothing can digest.
Yet let not each gay turn thy rapture move;              190
For fools admire, but men of sense approve:
As things seem large which we thro' mist descry,
Dulness is ever apt to magnify.
    Some foreign writers, some our own despise;
The ancients only, or the moderns prize.
Thus Wit, like Faith, by each man is applied

To one small sect, and all are damn'd beside.
Meanly they seek the blessing to confine,
And force that sun but on a part to shine,
Which not alone the southern wit sublimes,                    200
But ripens spirits in cold northern climes;
Which from the first has shone on ages past,
Enlights the present, and shall warm the last;
Tho' each may feel increases and decays,
And see now clearer and now darker days.
Regard not then if wit be old or new,
But blame the False and value still the True.
    Some ne'er advance a judgment of their own,
But catch the spreading notion of the town;
They reason and conclude by precedent,                    210
And own stale nonsense which they ne'er invent.
Some judge of authors' names, not works, and then
Nor praise nor blame the writings, but the men.
Of all this servile herd, the worst is he
That in proud dulness joins with quality;
A constant critic at the great man's board,
To fetch and carry nonsense for my lord.
What woful stuff this madrigal would be
In some starv'd hackney sonneteer or me!
But let a lord once own the happy lines,                    220
How the Wit brightens! how the Style refines!
Before his sacred name flies every fault,
And each exalted stanza teems with thought!
    The vulgar thus thro' imitation err,
As oft the learn'd by being singular;
So much they scorn the crowd, that if the throng
By chance go right, they purposely go wrong.
So schismatics the plain believers quit,
And are but damn'd for having too much wit.
Some praise at morning what they blame at night,                    230
But always think the last opinion right.
A Muse by these is like a mistress used,
This hour she 's idolized, the next abused;
While their weak heads, like towns unfortified,
'Twixt sense and nonsense daily change their side.
Ask them the cause; they 're wiser still they say;
And still to-morrow 's wiser than to-day.
We think our fathers fools, so wise we grow;

Our wiser sons no doubt will think us so.
Once school-divines this zealous isle o'erspread;                240
Who knew most sentences was deepest read.
Faith, Gospel, all seem'd made to be disputed,
And none had sense enough to be confuted.
Scotists and Thomists now in peace remain
Amidst their kindred cobwebs in Duck-lane.
If Faith itself has diff'rent dresses worn,
What wonder modes in Wit should take their turn?
Oft, leaving what is natural and fit,
The current Folly proves the ready Wit;
And authors think their reputation safe,                        250
Which lives as long as fools are pleas'd to laugh.
    Some, valuing those of their own side or mind,
Still make themselves the measure of mankind:
Fondly we think we honour merit then,
When we but praise ourselves in other men.
Parties in wit attend on those of state,
And public faction doubles private hate.
Pride, Malice, Folly, against Dryden rose,
In various shapes of parsons, critics, beaux:
But sense survived when merry jests were past;                  260
For rising merit will buoy up at last.
Might he return and bless once more our eyes,
New Blackmores and new Milbournes must arise.
Nay, should great Homer lift his awful head,
Zoilus again would start up from the dead.
Envy will Merit as its shade pursue,
But like a shadow proves the substance true;
For envied Wit, like Sol eclips'd, makes known
Th' opposing body's grossness, not its own.
When first that sun too powerful beams displays,               270
It draws up vapours which obscure its rays;
But ev'n those clouds at last adorn its way,
Reflect new glories, and augment the day.
    Be thou the first true merit to befriend;
His praise is lost who stays till all commend.
Short is the date, alas! of modern rhymes,
And 't is but just to let them live betimes.
No longer now that Golden Age appears,
When patriarch wits survived a thousand years:
Now length of fame (our second life) is lost,                   280

And bare threescore is all ev'n that can boast:
Our sons their fathers' failing language see,
And such as Chaucer is shall Dryden be.
So when the faithful pencil has design'd
Some bright idea of the master's mind,
Where a new world leaps out at his command,
And ready Nature waits upon his hand;
When the ripe colours soften and unite,
And sweetly melt into just shade and light;
When mellowing years their full perfection give,                    290
And each bold figure just begins to live,
The treach'rous colours the fair art betray,
And all the bright creation fades away!
      Unhappy Wit, like most mistaken things,
Atones not for that envy which it brings:
In youth alone its empty praise we boast,
But soon the short-lived vanity is lost;
Like some fair flower the early Spring supplies,
That gaily blooms, but ev'n in blooming dies.
What is this Wit, which must our cares employ?                    300
The owner's wife that other men enjoy;
Then most our trouble still when most admired,
And still the more we give, the more required;
Whose fame with pains we guard, but lose with ease,
Sure some to vex, but never all to please,
'T is what the vicious fear, the virtuous shun;
By fools 't is hated, and by knaves undone!
      If Wit so much from Ignorance undergo,
Ah, let not Learning too commence its foe!
Of old those met rewards who could excel,                    310
And such were prais'd who but endeavour'd well;
Tho' triumphs were to gen'rals only due,
Crowns were reserv'd to grace the soldiers too.
Now they who reach Parnassus' lofty crown
Employ their pains to spurn some others down;
And while self-love each jealous writer rules,
Contending wits become the sport of fools;
But still the worst with most regret commend,
For each ill author is as bad a friend.
To what base ends, and by what abject ways,                    320
Are mortals urged thro' sacred lust of praise!
Ah, ne'er so dire a thirst of glory boast,

Nor in the critic let the man be lost!
Good nature and good sense must ever join;
To err is human, to forgive divine.
　　But if in noble minds some dregs remain,
Not yet purged off, of spleen and sour disdain,
Discharge that rage on more provoking crimes,
Nor fear a dearth in these flagitious times.
No pardon vile obscenity should find,　　　　　　　　330
Tho' Wit and Art conspire to move your mind;
But dulness with obscenity must prove
As shameful sure as impotence in love.
In the fat age of pleasure, wealth, and ease
Sprung the rank weed, and thrived with large increase:
When love was all an easy monarch's care,
Seldom at council, never in a war;
Jilts ruled the state, and statesmen farces writ;
Nay wits had pensions, and young lords had wit;　　340
The Fair sat panting at a courtier's play,
And not a mask went unimprov'd away;
The modest fan was lifted up no more,
And virgins smil'd at what they blush'd before.
The following license of a foreign reign
Did all the dregs of bold Socinus drain;
Then unbelieving priests reform'd the nation,
And taught more pleasant methods of salvation;
Where Heav'n's free subjects might their rights dispute,
Lest God himself should seem too absolute;
Pulpits their sacred satire learn'd to spare,　　　　350
And vice admired to find a flatt'rer there!
Encouraged thus, Wit's Titans braved the skies,
And the press groan'd with licens'd blasphemies.
These monsters, Critics! with your darts engage,
Here point your thunder, and exhaust your rage!
Yet shun their fault, who, scandalously nice,
Will needs mistake an author into vice:
All seems infected that th' infected spy,
As all looks yellow to the jaundic'd eye.

## PART III

Learn then what morals Critics ought to show,
For 't is but half a judge's task to know.

'T is not enough Taste, Judgment, Learning join;
In all you speak let Truth and Candour shine;
That not alone what to your Sense is due
All may allow, but seek your friendship too.
  Be silent always when you doubt your Sense,
And speak, tho' sure, with seeming diffidence.
Some positive persisting fops we know,
Who if once wrong will needs be always so;                    10
But you with pleasure own your errors past,
And make each day a critique on the last.
  'T is not enough your counsel still be true;
Blunt truths more mischief than nice falsehoods do.
Men must be taught as if you taught them not,
And things unknown proposed as things forgot.
Without good breeding truth is disapprov'd;
That only makes superior Sense belov'd.
  Be niggards of advice on no pretence,
For the worst avarice is that of Sense.                    20
With mean complacence ne'er betray your trust,
Nor be so civil as to prove unjust.
Fear not the anger of the wise to raise;
Those best can bear reproof who merit praise.
  'T were well might critics still this freedom take,
But Appius reddens at each word you speak,
And stares tremendous, with a threat'ning eye,
Like some fierce tyrant in old tapestry.
Fear most to tax an honourable fool,
Whose right it is, uncensured to be dull:                    30
Such without Wit, are poets when they please,
As without Learning they can take degrees.
Leave dangerous truths to unsuccessful satires,
And flattery to fulsome dedicators;
Whom, when they praise, the world believes no more
Than when they promise to give scribbling o'er.
'T is best sometimes your censure to restrain,
And charitably let the dull be vain;
Your silence there is better than your spite,
For who can rail so long as they can write?                    40
Still humming on their drowsy course they keep,
And lash'd so long, like tops, are lash'd asleep.
False steps but help them to renew the race,
As, after stumbling, jades will mend their pace.

What crowds of these, impenitently bold,
In sounds and jingling syllables grown old,
Still run on poets, in a raging vein,
Ev'n to the dregs and squeezings of the brain,
Strain out the last dull dropping of their sense,
And rhyme with all the rage of impotence!                    50
    Such shameless bards we have; and yet 't is true
There are as mad abandon'd critics too.
The bookful blockhead ignorantly read,
With loads of learned lumber in his head,
With his own tongue still edifies his ears,
And always list'ning to himself appears.
All books he reads, and all he reads assails,
From Dryden's Fables down to Durfey's Tales.
With him most authors steal their works, or buy;
Garth did not write his own Dispensary.                    60
Name a new play, and he 's the poet's friend;
Nay, show'd his faults—but when would poets mend?
No place so sacred from such fops is barr'd,
Nor is Paul's church more safe than Paul's churchyard:
Nay, fly to altars, there they 'll talk you dead;
For fools rush in where angels fear to tread.
Distrustful sense with modest caution speaks,
It still looks home, and short excursions makes;
But rattling nonsense in full volleys breaks
And never shock'd, and never turn'd aside,                    70
Bursts out, resistless, with a thund'ring tide.
    But where's the man who counsel can bestow,
Still pleas'd to teach, and yet not proud to know?
Unbiass'd or by favour or by spite;
Not dully prepossess'd nor blindly right;
Tho' learn'd, well bred, and tho' well bred sincere;
Modestly bold, and humanly severe;
Who to a friend his faults can freely show,
And gladly praise the merit of a foe;
Bless'd with a taste exact, yet unconfin'd,                    80
A knowledge both of books and humankind;
Gen'rous converse; a soul exempt from pride;
And love to praise, with reason on his side?
Such once were critics; such the happy few
Athens and Rome in better ages knew.
The mighty Stagyrite first left the shore,
Spread all his sails, and durst the deeps explore;

He steer'd securely, and discover'd far,
Led by the light of the Mæonian star.
Poets, a race long unconfin'd and free,                    90
Still fond and proud of savage liberty,
Receiv'd his laws, and stood convinc'd 't was fit
Who conquer'd Nature should preside o'er Wit.
    Horace still charms with graceful negligence,
And without method talks us into sense;
Will, like a friend, familiarly convey
The truest notions in the easiest way.
He who, supreme in judgment as in wit,
Might boldly censure as he boldly writ,
Yet judg'd with coolness, though he sung with fire;        100
His precepts teach but what his works inspire.
Our critics take a contrary extreme,
They judge with fury, but they write with phlegm;
Nor suffers Horace more in wrong translations
By Wits, than Critics in as wrong quotations.
See Dionysius Homer's thoughts refine,
And call new beauties forth from ev'ry line!
Fancy and art in gay Petronius please,
The Scholar's learning with the courtier's ease.
    In grave Quintilian's copious work we find            110
The justest rules and clearest method join'd.
Thus useful arms in magazines we place,
All ranged in order, and disposed with grace;
But less to please the eye then arm the hand,
Still fit for use, and ready at command.
    Thee, bold Longinus! all the Nine inspire,
And bless their critic with a poet's fire:
An ardent judge, who, zealous in his trust,
With warmth gives sentence , yet is always just;
Whose own example strengthens all his laws,               120
And is himself that great sublime he draws.
    Thus long succeeding critics justly reign'd,
License repress'd, and useful laws ordain'd:
Learning and Rome alike in empire grew,
And arts still follow'd where her eagles flew;
From the same foes at last both felt their doom,
And the same age saw learning fall and Rome.
With tyranny then superstition join'd,
As that the body, this enslaved the mind;
Much was believ'd, but little understood,                 130

And to be dull was construed to be good;
A second deluge learning thus o'errun,
And the monks finish'd what the Goths begun.
　　At length Erasmus, that great injur'd name,
(The glory of the priesthood and the shame!)
Stemm'd the wild torrent of a barb'rous age,
And drove those holy Vandals off the stage.
　　But see! each Muse in Leo's golden days
Starts from her trance, and trims her wither'd bays.
Rome's ancient genius, o'er its ruins spread,　　　　140
Shakes off the dust, and rears his rev'rend head.
Then sculpture and her sister arts revive;
Stones leap'd to form, and rocks began to live;
With sweeter notes each rising temple rung;
A Raphael painted and a Vida sung:
Immortal Vida! on whose honour'd brow
The poet's bays and critic's ivy grow:
Cremona now shall ever boast thy name,
As next in place to Mantua, next in fame!
　　But soon by impious arms from Latium chased,　　150
Their ancient bounds the banish'd Muses pass'd;
Thence arts o'er all the northern world advance,
But critic learning flourish'd most in France;
The rules a nation born to serve obeys,
And Boileau still in right of Horace sways.
But we, brave Britons, foreign laws despised,
And kept unconquer'd and uncivilized;
Fierce for the liberties of wit, and bold,
We still defied the Romans, as of old.
Yet some there were, among the sounder few　　　　160
Of those who less presumed and better knew,
Who durst assert the juster ancient cause,
And here restor'd Wit's fundamental laws.
Such was the Muse whose rules and practice tell
'Nature's chief masterpiece is writing well.'
Such was Roscommon, not more learn'd than good,
With manners gen'rous as his noble blood;
To him the wit of Greece and Rome was known,
And every author's merit but his own.
Such late was Walsh—the Muse's judge and friend,　　170
Who justly knew to blame or to commend;

To failings mild but zealous for desert,
The clearest head, and the sincerest heart.
This humble praise, lamented Shade! receive;
This praise at least a grateful Muse may give:
The Muse whose early voice you taught to sing,
Prescribed her heights, and pruned her tender wing,
(Her guide now lost), no more attempts to rise,
But in low numbers short excursions tries;
Content if hence th' unlearn'd their wants may view,        180
The learn'd reflect on what before they knew;
Careless of censure, nor too fond of fame;
Still pleas'd to praise, yet not afraid to blame;
Averse alike to flatter or offend;
Not free from faults, nor yet too vain to mend.

SAMUEL JOHNSON

# Preface to Shakespeare

## 1765

*The sonorous diction and the sculptured syntax of Dr. Johnson's first paragraph may tend to confirm one's fearful impression of him as the magisterial defender of the classical rules, the classicist par excellence. But that picture of him surely vanishes when we later read, "That this is a practice contrary to the rules of criticism will be readily allowed; but there is always an appeal open from criticism to nature." (Or, elsewhere, in his essay on Dryden: "Reason wants not Horace to support it.") Whatever his classicism, he is not a mere formalist following or issuing arbitrary edicts about literature, so it comes as no surprise that in the conflict between the "three unities" and the "irregularities" of Shakespeare, it is the validity of the rules that loses out. (In 1822, when Stendhal was attacking French neoclassicism, he cited Johnson as the authority for his argument.) Examining the concepts of time, place, and action, Johnson works his way back by common sense to the same conclusion that Aristotle reached as to the only essential unity in the drama.*

*The long-sustained experience of mankind, not an antiquarian worship of the past, is Johnson's test for older writers, and Shakespeare is preeminent because he is the poet of "general nature." Opposed to the general—for which we may read universal and therefore truthful—is the particular, the special, the individual. Shakespeare's appeal rests upon his ability to portray human nature, not kings or Romans; this is Shakespeare's "mirrour of life" that has stood the test of time,*

From *Johnson on Shakespeare*, ed. Walter Raleigh; London: Henry Frowde, Oxford University Press, 1908.

*and that narrower critics have misunderstood. Johnson is likewise indifferent to the objection that Shakespeare mixed comedy and tragedy; again, Johnson regards the differentiation of Shakespeare's plays into formal genres as merely a critical convenience, useful neither to the audience nor to Shakespeare, "who never fails to attain his purpose." It is the end and not the means that Johnson values.*

*About that end he is unambiguous: It is "to instruct by pleasing." The moral criterion is another measurement for evaluating Shakespeare, and Johnson's discussion of how the plays instruct, as well as when and why they do not, should be studied as an example of a firm critical mind drawing distinctions and making judgments based on a clearly defined system of values.*

THAT PRAISES are without reason lavished on the dead, and that the honours due only to excellence are paid to antiquity, is a complaint likely to be always continued by those, who, being able to add nothing to truth, hope for eminence from the heresies of paradox; or those, who, being forced by disappointment upon consolatory expedients, are willing to hope from posterity what the present age refuses, and flatter themselves that the regard which is yet denied by envy, will be at last bestowed by time.

Antiquity, like every other quality that attracts the notice of mankind, has undoubtedly votaries that reverence it, not from reason, but from prejudice. Some seem to admire indiscriminately whatever has been long preserved, without considering that time has sometimes co-operated with chance; all perhaps are more willing to honour past than present excellence; and the mind contemplates genius through the shades of age, as the eye surveys the sun through artificial opacity. The great contention of criticism is to find the faults of the moderns, and the beauties of the ancients. While an author is yet living we estimate his powers by his worst performance, and when he is dead, we rate them by his best.

To works, however, of which the excellence is not absolute and definite, but gradual and comparative; to works not raised upon principles demonstrative and scientific, but appealing wholly to observation and experience, no other test can be applied than length of duration and continuance of esteem. What mankind have long possessed they have often examined and compared; and if they persist to value the possession, it is because frequent comparisons have confirmed opinion in its favour. As among the works of nature no man can properly call a river deep, or a mountain high, without the knowledge of many mountains, and many rivers; so in the productions of genius, nothing can be stiled excellent till it has been compared with other works of the same kind. Demonstration immediately displays its power, and has nothing to hope or fear from the flux of years; but works tentative and experimental must be estimated by their proportion to the general and collective ability of man, as it is discovered in a long succession of endeavours.  Of the first building that was raised, it might be with certainty determined that it was round or square; but whether it was spacious or lofty must have been referred to time.  The Pythagorean scale of numbers was at once discovered to be perfect; but the poems of Homer we yet know not to transcend the common limits of human intelligence, but by remarking, that nation after nation, and century after century, has been able to do little more than transpose his incidents, new-name his characters, and paraphrase his sentiments.

The reverence due to writings that have long subsisted arises therefore not from any credulous confidence in the superior wisdom of past ages, or gloomy persuasion of the degeneracy of mankind, but is the consequence of acknowledged and indubitable positions, that what has been longest known has been most considered, and what is most considered is best understood.

The Poet, of whose works I have undertaken the revision, may now begin to assume the dignity of an ancient, and claim the privilege of established fame and prescriptive veneration.  He has long outlived his century, the term commonly fixed as the test of literary merit.  Whatever advantages he might once derive from personal allusions, local customs, or temporary opinions, have for many years been lost; and every topick of merriment, or motive of sorrow, which the modes of artificial life afforded him, now only obscure the scenes which they once illuminated. The effects of favour and competition are at an end; the tradition of his friendships and his enmities has perished; his works support no opinion with arguments, nor supply any faction with invectives; they can neither indulge vanity nor gratify malignity; but are read without any other reason than the desire of pleasure, and are therefore praised only as pleasure is obtained; yet, thus unassisted by interest or passion, they have past through variations of taste and changes of manners, and, as they devolved from one generation to another, have received new honours at every transmission.

But because human judgment, though it be gradually gaining upon certainty, never becomes infallible; and approbation, though long continued, may yet be only the approbation of prejudice or fashion; it is proper to inquire, by what peculiarities of excellence Shakespeare has gained and kept the favour of his countrymen.

Nothing can please many, and please long, but just representations of general nature.  Particular manners can be known to few, and therefore few only can judge how nearly they are copied.  The irregular combinations of fanciful invention may delight a-while, by that novelty of which the common satiety of life sends us all in quest; but the pleasures of sudden wonder are soon exhausted, and the mind can only repose on the stability of truth.

Shakespeare is above all writers, at least above all modern writers, the poet of nature; the poet that holds up to his readers a faithful mirrour of manners and of life. His characters are not modified by the customs of particular places, unpractised by the rest of the world; by the peculiarities of studies or professions, which can operate but upon small numbers; or by the accidents of transient fashions or temporary opinions: they are the genuine progeny of common humanity, such as the world will always supply, and observation will always find. His persons act and speak by the influence of those general passions and principles by which all minds are agitated, and the whole system of life is continued in motion. In the writings of other poets a character is too often an individual; in those of Shakespeare is commonly a species.

It is from this wide extension of design that so much instruction is derived. It is this which fills the plays of Shakespeare with practical axioms and domestick wisdom. It was said of Euripides, that every verse was a precept; and it may be said of Shakespeare, that from his works may be collected a system of civil and oeconomical prudence. Yet his real power is not shewn in the splendour of particular passages, but by the progress of his fable, and the tenour of his dialogue; and he that tries to recommend him by select quotations, will succeed like the pedant in Hierocles, who, when he offered his house to sale, carried a brick in his pocket as a specimen.

It will not easily be imagined how much Shakespeare excells in accommodating his sentiments to real life, but by comparing him with other authours. It was observed of the ancient schools of declamation, that the more diligently they were frequented, the more was the student disqualified for the world, because he found nothing there which he should ever meet in any other place. The same remark may be applied to every stage but that of Shakespeare. The theatre, when it is under any other direction, is peopled by such characters as were never seen, conversing in a language which was never heard, upon topicks which will never arise in the commerce of mankind. But the dialogue of this authour is often so evidently determined by the incident which produces it, and is pursued with so much ease and simplicity, that it seems scarcely to claim the merit of fiction, but to have been gleaned by diligent selection out of common conversation, and common occurrences.

Upon every other stage the universal agent is love, by whose power all good and evil is distributed, and every action quickened or retarded. To bring a lover, a lady and a rival into the fable; to entangle them in contradictory obligations, perplex them with oppositions of interest, and harass them with violence of desires inconsistent with each other; to make them meet in rapture and part in agony; to fill their mouths with hyperbolical joy and outrageous sorrow; to distress them as nothing human ever was distressed; to deliver them as nothing human ever was delivered; is the business of a modern dramatist. For this probability is violated, life is misrepresented, and language is depraved. But love is only one of many passions; and as it has no great influence upon the sum of life, it has little operation in the dramas of a poet, who caught his ideas from the living world, and exhibited only what he saw before him. He knew, that any other passion, as it was regular or exorbitant, was a cause of happiness or calamity.

Characters thus ample and general were not easily discriminated and preserved, yet perhaps no poet ever kept his personages more distinct from each other. I will not say with Pope, that every speech may be assigned to the proper speaker, because many speeches there are which have nothing characteristical; but perhaps, though some may be equally adapted to every person, it will be difficult to find, any that can be properly transferred from the present possessor to another claimant. The choice is right, when there is reason for choice.

Other dramatics can only gain attention by hyperbolical or aggravated characters, by fabulous and unexampled excellence or depravity, as the writers of barbarous romances invigorated the reader by a giant and a dwarf; and he that should form his expectations of human affairs from the play, or from the tale, would be equally deceived. Shakespeare has no heroes; his scenes are occupied only by men, who act and speak as the reader thinks that he should himself have spoken or acted on the same occasion: Even where the agency is supernatural the dialogue is level with life. Other writers disguise the most natural passions and most frequent incidents; so that he who contemplates them in the book will not know them in the world: Shakespeare approximates the remote, and familiarizes the wonderful; the event which he represents will not happen, but if it were possible, its effects would probably be such as he has assigned; and it may be said, that he has not only shewn human nature as it acts in real exigencies, but as it would be found in trials, to which it cannot be exposed.

This therefore is the praise of Shakespeare, that his drama is the mirrour of life; that he who has mazed his imagination, in following the phantoms which other writers raise up before him, may here be cured of his delirious extasies, by reading human sentiments in human language, by scenes from which a hermit may estimate the transactions of the world, and a confessor predict the progress of the passions.

His adherence to general nature has exposed him to the censure of criticks, who form their judgments upon narrower principles. Dennis and Rhymer think his Romans not sufficiently Roman; and Voltaire censures his kings as not completely royal.  Dennis is offended, that Menenius, a senator of Rome, should play the buffoon; and Voltaire perhaps thinks decency violated when the Danish Usurper is represented as a drunkard.  But Shakespeare always makes nature predominate over accident; and if he preserves the essential character, is not very careful of distinctions superinduced and adventitious.  His story requires Romans or kings, but he thinks only on men.  He knew that Rome, like every other city, had men of all dispositions; and wanting a buffoon, he went into the senate-house for that which the senate-house would certainly have afforded him.  He was inclined to shew an usurper and a murderer not only odious but despicable, he therefore added drunkenness to his other qualities, knowing that kings love wine like other men, and that wine exerts its natural power upon kings.  These are the petty cavils of petty minds; a poet overlooks the casual distinction of country and condition, as a painter, satisfied with the figure, neglects the drapery.

The censure which he has incurred by mixing comick and tragick scenes, as it extends to all his works, deserves more consideration.  Let the fact be first stated, and then examined.

Shakespeare's plays are not in the rigorous and critical sense either tragedies or comedies, but compositions of a distinct kind; exhibiting the real state of sublunary nature, which partakes of good and evil, joy and sorrow, mingled with endless variety of proportion and innumerable modes of combination; and expressing the course of the world, in which the loss of one is the gain of another; in which, at the same time, the reveller is hasting to his wine, and the mourner burying his friend; in which the malignity of one is sometimes defeated by the frolick of another; and many mischiefs and many benefits are done and hindered without design.

Out of this chaos of mingled purposes and casualties the ancient poets, according to the laws which custom had prescribed, selected some the crimes of men, and some their absurdities; some the momentous vicissitudes of life, and some the lighter occurrences; some the terrours of distress, and some the gayeties of prosperity.  Thus rose the two modes of imitation, known by the names of tragedy and comedy, compositions intended to promote different ends by contrary means, and considered as so little allied, that I do not recollect among the Greeks or Romans a single writer who attempted both.

Shakespeare has united the powers of exciting laughter and sorrow not only in one mind, but in one composition.  Almost all his plays are divided between serious and ludicrous characters, and, in the successive evolutions of the design, sometimes produce seriousness and sorrow, and sometimes levity and laughter.

That this is a practice contrary to the rules of criticism will be readily allowed; but there is always an appeal open from criticism to nature.

The end of writing is to instruct; the end of poetry is to instruct by pleasing. That the mingled drama may convey all the instruction of tragedy or comedy cannot be denied, because it includes both in its alternations of exhibition and approaches nearer than either to the appearance of life, by shewing how great machinations and slender designs may promote or obviate one another, and the high and the low co-operate in the general system by unavoidable concatenation.

It is objected, that by this change of scenes the passions are interrupted in their progression, and that the principal event, being not advanced by a due gradation of preparatory incidents, wants at last the power to move, which constitutes the perfection of dramatick poetry. This reasoning is so specious, that it is received as true even by those who in daily experience feel it to be false. The interchanges of mingled scenes seldom fail to produce the intended vicissitudes of passion. Fiction cannot move so much, but that the attention may be easily transferred; and though it must be allowed that pleasing melancholy be sometimes interrupted by unwelcome levity, yet let it be considered likewise, that melancholy is often not pleasing, and that the disturbance of one man may be the relief of another; that different auditors have different habitudes; and that, upon the whole, all pleasure consists in variety.

The players, who in their edition divided our authour's works into comedies, histories, and tragedies, seem not to have distinguished the three kinds by any very exact or definite ideas.

An action which ended happily to the principal persons, however serious or distressful through its intermediate incidents, in their opinion, constituted a comedy. This idea of a comedy continued long amongst us; and plays were written, which, by changing the catastrophe, were tragedies to-day, and comedies to-morrow.

Tragedy was not in those times a poem of more general dignity or elevation than comedy; it required only a calamitous conclusion, with which the common criticism of that age was satisfied, whatever lighter pleasure it afforded in its progress.

History was a series of actions, with no other than chronological succession, independent on each other, and without any tendency to introduce or regulate the conclusion. It is not always very nicely distinguished from tragedy. There is not much nearer approach to unity of action in the tragedy of *Antony and Cleopatra*, than in the history of *Richard the Second*. But a history might be continued through many plays; as it had no plan, it had no limits.

Through all these denominations of the drama, Shakespeare's mode of composition is the same; an interchange of seriousness and merriment, by which the mind is softened at one time, and exhilarated at another. But whatever be his purpose, whether to gladden or depress, or to conduct the story, without vehemence or emotion, through tracts of easy and familiar dialogue, he never fails to attain his purpose; as he commands us, we laugh or mourn, or sit silent with quiet expectation, in tranquillity without indifference.

When Shakespeare's plan is understood, most of the criticisms of Rhymer and Voltaire vanish away. The play of *Hamlet* is opened, without impropriety, by two sentinels; Iago bellows at Brabantio's window, without injury to the scheme of the play, though in terms which a modern audience would not easily endure; the character of Polonius is seasonable and useful; and the Grave-diggers themselves may be heard with applause.

Shakespeare engaged in dramatick poetry with the world open before him; the rules of the ancients were yet known to few; the publick judgment was unformed; he had no example of such fame as might force him upon imitation, nor criticks of such authority as might restrain his extravagance: He therefore indulged his natural disposition, and his disposition, as Rhymer has remarked, led him to comedy. In tragedy he often writes, with great appearance of toil and study, what is written at last with little felicity; but in his comick scenes, he seems to produce without labour, what no labour can improve. In tragedy he is always struggling after some occasion to be comick; but in comedy he seems to repose, or to luxuriate, as in a mode of thinking congenial to his nature. In his tragick scenes there is always something wanting, but his comedy often surpasses expectation or desire. His comedy pleases by the thoughts and the language, and his tragedy for the greater part by incident and action. His tragedy seems to be skill, his comedy to be instinct.

The force of his comick scenes has suffered little diminution from the changes made by a century and a half, in manners or in words. As his personages act upon principles arising from genuine passion, very little modified by particular forms, their pleasures and vexations are communicable to all times and to all places; they are natural, and therefore durable; the adventitious peculiarities of personal habits, are only superficial dies, bright and pleasing for a little while, yet soon fading to a dim tinct, without any remains of former lustre; but the discriminations of true passion are the colours of nature; they pervade the whole mass, and can only perish with the body that exhibits them. The accidental compositions of heterogeneous modes are dissolved by the chance which combined them; but the uniform simplicity of primitive qualities neither admits increase, nor suffers decay. The sand heaped by one flood is scattered by another, but the rock always continues in its place. The stream of time, which is continually washing the dissoluble fabricks of other poets, passes without injury by the adamant of Shakespeare.

If there be, what I believe there is, in every nation, a stile which never becomes obsolete, a certain mode of phraseology so consonant and congenial to the analogy and principles of its respective language as to remain settled and unaltered; this style is probably to be sought in the common intercourse of life, among those who speak only to be understood, without ambition of elegance. The polite are always catching modish innovations, and the learned depart from established forms of speech, in hope of finding or making better; those who wish for distinction forsake the vulgar, when the vulgar is right; but there is a conversation above grossness and below refinement, where propriety resides, and where this poet seems to have gathered his comick dialogue. He is therefore more agreeable to the ears of the present age than any other authour equally remote, and among his other excellencies deserves to be studied as one of the original masters of our language.

These observations are to be considered not as unexceptionably constant, but as containing general and predominant truth. Shakespeare's familiar dialogue is affirmed to be smooth and clear, yet not wholly without ruggedness or difficulty; as a country may be eminently fruitful, though it has spots unfit for cultivation: His characters are praised as natural, though their sentiments are sometimes forced, and their actions improbable; as the earth upon the whole is spherical, though its surface is varied with protuberances and cavities.

Shakespeare with his excellencies has likewise faults, and faults sufficient to obscure and overwhelm any other merit. I shall shew them in the proportion in which they appear to me, without envious malignity or superstitious veneration. No question can be more innocently discussed than a dead poet's pretensions to renown; and little regard is due to that bigotry which sets candour higher than truth.

His first defect is that to which may be imputed most of the evil in books or in men. He sacrifices virtue to convenience, and is so much more careful to please than to instruct, that he seems to write without any moral purpose. From his writings indeed a system of social duty may be selected, for he that thinks reasonably must think morally; but his precepts and axioms drop casually from him; he makes no just distribution of good or evil, nor is always careful to shew in the virtuous a disapprobation of the wicked; he carries his persons indifferently through right and wrong, and at the close dismisses them without further care, and leaves their examples to operate by chance. This fault the barbarity of his age cannot extenuate; for it is always a writer's duty to make the world better, and justice is a virtue independant on time or place.

The plots are often so loosely formed, that a very slight consideration may improve them, and so carelessly pursued, that he seems not always fully to comprehend his own design. He omits opportunities of instructing or delighting which the train of his story seems to force upon him, and apparently rejects those exhibitions which would be more affecting, for the sake of those which are more easy.

It may be observed, that in many of his plays the latter part is evidently neglected.   When he found himself near the end of his work, and, in view of his reward, he shortened the labour to snatch the profit.   He therefore remits his efforts where he should most vigorously exert them, and his catastrophe is improbably produced or imperfectly represented.

He had no regard to distinction of time or place, but gives to one age or nation, without scruple, the customs, institutions, and opinions of another, at the expence not only of likelihood, but of possibility. These faults Pope has endeavoured, with more zeal than judgment, to transfer to his imagined interpolators.   We need not wonder to find Hector quoting Aristotle, when we see the loves of Theseus and Hippolyta combined with the Gothick mythology of fairies.   Shakespeare, indeed, was not the only violator of chronology, for in the same age Sidney, who wanted not the advantages of learning, has, in his *Arcadia*, confounded the pastoral with the feudal times, the days of innocence, quiet and security, with those of turbulence, violence, and adventure.

In his comick scenes he is seldom very successful, when he engages his characters in reciprocations of smartness and contests of sarcasm; their jests are commonly gross, and their pleasantry licentious; neither his gentlemen nor his ladies have much delicacy, nor are sufficiently distinguished from his clowns by any appearance of refined manners. Whether he represented the real conversation of his time is not easy to determine; the reign of Elizabeth is commonly supposed to have been a time of stateliness, formality and reserve; yet perhaps the relaxations of that severity were not very elegant.   There must, however, have been always some modes of gayety preferable to others, and a writer ought to chuse the best.

In tragedy his performance seems constantly to be worse, as his labour is more.   The effusions of passion which exigence forces out are for the most part striking and energetick; but whenever he solicits his invention, or strains his faculties, the offspring of his throes is tumour, meanness, tediousness, and obscurity.

In narration he affects a disproportionate pomp of diction, and a wearisome train of circumlocution, and tells the incident imperfectly in many words, which might have been more plainly delivered in few. Narration in dramatick poetry is naturally tedious, as it is unanimated and inactive, and obstructs the progress of the action; it should therefore always be rapid, and enlivened by frequent interruption.   Shakespeare found it an encumbrance, and instead of lightening it by brevity, endeavoured to recommend it by dignity and splendour.

His declamations or set speeches are commonly cold and weak, for his power was the power of nature; when he endeavoured, like other tragick writers, to catch opportunities of amplification, and instead of inquiring what the occasion demanded, to show how much his stores of knowledge could supply, he seldom escapes without the pity or resentment of his reader.

It is incident to him to be now and then entangled with an unwieldy sentiment, which he cannot well express, and will not reject; he struggles with it a while, and if it continues stubborn, comprises it in words such as occur, and leaves it to be disentangled and evolved by those who have more leisure to bestow upon it.

Not that always where the language is intricate the thought is subtle, or the image always great where the line is bulky; the equality of words to things is very often neglected, and trivial sentiments and vulgar ideas disappoint the attention, to which they are recommended by sonorous epithets and swelling figures.

But the admirers of this great poet have never less reason to indulge their hopes of supreme excellence, than when he seems fully resolved to sink them in dejection, and mollify them with tender emotions by the fall of greatness, the danger of innocence, or the crosses of love. He is not long soft and pathetick without some idle conceit, or contemptible equivocation. He no sooner begins to move, than he counteracts himself; and terrour and pity, as they are rising in the mind, are checked and blasted by sudden frigidity.

A quibble is to Shakespeare, what luminous vapours are to the traveller; he follows it at all adventures; it is sure to lead him out of his way, and sure to engulf him in the mire. It has some malignant power over his mind, and its fascinations are irresistible. Whatever be the dignity or profundity of his disquisition, whether he be enlarging knowledge or exalting affection, whether he be amusing attention with incidents, or enchaining it in suspense, let but a quibble spring up before him, and he leaves his work unfinished. A quibble is the golden apple for which he will always turn aside from his career, or stoop from his elevation. A quibble, poor and barren as it is, gave him such delight, that he was content to purchase it, by the sacrifice of reason, propriety and truth. A quibble was to him the fatal Cleopatra for which he lost the world, and was content to lose it.

It will be thought strange, that, in enumerating the defects of this writer, I have not yet mentioned his neglect of the unities; his violation of those laws which have been instituted and established by the joint authority of poets and of criticks.

For his other deviations from the art of writing I resign him to critical justice, without making any other demand in his favour, than that which must be indulged to all human excellence: that his virtues be rated with his failings: But, from the censure which this irregularity may bring upon him, I shall, with due reverence to that learning which I must oppose, adventure to try how I can defend him.

His histories, being neither tragedies nor comedies are not subject to any of their laws; nothing more is necessary to all the praise which they expect, than that the changes of action be so prepared as to be understood, that the incidents be various and affecting, and the characters consistent, natural, and distinct.   No other unity is intended, and therefore none is to be sought.

In his other works he has well enough preserved the unity of action. He has not, indeed, an intrigue regularly perplexed and regularly unravelled: he does not endeavour to hide his design only to discover it, for this is seldom the order of real events, and Shakespeare is the poet of nature: But his plan has commonly what Aristotle requires, a beginning, a middle, and an end; one event is concatenated with another, and the conclusion follows by easy consequence.   There are perhaps some incidents that might be spared, as in other poets there is much talk that only fills up time upon the stage; but the general system makes gradual advances, and the end of the play is the end of expectation.

To the unities of time and place he has shewn no regard; and perhaps a nearer view of the principles on which they stand will diminish their value, and withdraw from them the veneration which, from the time of Corneille, they have very generally received, by discovering that they have given more trouble to the poet, than pleasure to the auditor.

The necessity of observing the unities of time and place arises from the supposed necessity of making the drama credible.   The criticks hold it impossible, that an action of months or years can be possibly believed to pass in three hours; or that the spectator can suppose himself to sit in the theatre, while ambassadors go and return between distant kings, while armies are levied and towns besieged, while an exile wanders and returns, or till he whom they saw courting his mistress, shall lament the untimely fall of his son.   The mind revolts from evident falsehood, and fiction loses its force when it departs from the resemblance of reality.

From the narrow limitation of time necessarily arises the contraction of place.   The spectator, who knows that he saw the first act at Alexandria, cannot suppose that he sees the next at Rome, at a distance to which not the dragons of Medea could, in so short a time, have transported him; he knows with certainty that he has not changed his place, and he knows that place cannot change itself; that what was a house cannot become a plain; that what was Thebes can never be Persepolis.

Such is the triumphant language with which a critick exults over the misery of an irregular poet, and exults commonly without resistance or reply.   It is time therefore to tell him by the authority of Shakespeare, that he assumes, as an unquestionable principle, a position, which, while his breath is forming it into words, his understanding pronounces to be false. It is false, that any representation is mistaken for reality; that any dramatick fable in its materiality was ever credible, or, for a single moment, was ever credited.

The objection arising from the impossibility of passing the first hour at Alexandria, and the next at Rome, supposes, that when the play opens, the spectator really imagines himself at Alexandria, and believes that his walk to the theatre has been a voyage to Egypt, and that he lives in the days of Antony and Cleopatra. Surely he that imagines this may imagine more. He that can take the stage at one time for the palace of the Ptolemies, may take it in half an hour for the promontory of Actium. Delusion, if delusion be admitted, has no certain limitation; if the spectator can be once persuaded, that his old acquaintance are Alexander and Cæsar, that a room illuminated with candles is the plain of Pharsalia, or the bank of Granicus, he is in a state of elevation above the reach of reason, or of truth, and from the heights of empyrean poetry, may despise the circumscriptions of terrestrial nature. There is no reason why a mind thus wandering in extasy should count the clock, or why an hour should not be a century in that calenture of the brains that can make the stage a field.

The truth is, that the spectators are always in their senses, and know, from the first act to the last, that the stage is only a stage, and that the players are only players. They came to hear a certain number of lines recited with just gesture and elegant modulation. The lines relate to some action, and an action must be in some place; but the different actions that compleat a story may be in places very remote from each other; and where is the absurdity of allowing that space to represent first Athens, and then Sicily, which was always known to be neither Sicily nor Athens, but a modern theatre?

By supposition, as place is introduced, time may be extended; the time required by the fable elapses for the most part between the acts; for, of so much of the action as is represented, the real and poetical duration is the same. If, in the first act, preparations for war against Mithridates are represented to be made in Rome, the event of the war may, without absurdity, be represented, in the catastrophe, as happening in Pontus; we know that there is neither war, nor preparation for war; we know that we are neither in Rome nor Pontus; that neither Mithridates nor Lucullus are before us. The drama exhibits successive imitations of successive actions; and why may not the second imitation represent an action that happened years after the first, if it be so connected with it, that nothing but time can be supposed to intervene? Time is, of all modes of existence, most obsequious to the imagination; a lapse of years is as easily conceived as a passage of hours. In contemplation we easily contract the time of real actions, and therefore willingly permit it to be contracted when we only see their imitation.

It will be asked, how the drama moves, if it is not credited. It is credited with all the credit due to a drama. It is credited, whenever it moves, as a just picture of a real original; as representing to the auditor what he would himself feel, if he were to do or suffer what is there feigned to be suffered or to be done. The reflection that strikes the heart is not, that the evils before us are real evils, but that they are evils to which we ourselves may be exposed. If there be any fallacy, it is not that we fancy the players, but that we fancy ourselves unhappy for a moment; but we rather lament the possibility than suppose the presence of misery, as a mother weeps over her babe, when she remembers that death may take it from her. The delight of tragedy proceeds from our consciousness of fiction; if we thought murders and treasons real, they would please no more.

Imitations produce pain or pleasure, not because they are mistaken for realities, but because they bring realities to mind. When the imagination is recreated by a painted landscape, the trees are not supposed capable to give us shade, or the fountains coolness; but we consider, how we should be pleased with such fountains playing beside us, and such woods waving over us. We are agitated in reading the history of *Henry the Fifth*, yet no man takes his book for the field of Agencourt. A dramatick exhibition is a book recited with concomitants that encrease or diminish its effect. Familiar comedy is often more powerful on the theatre, than in the page; imperial tragedy is always less. The humour of Petruchio may be heightened by grimace; but what voice or what gesture can hope to add dignity or force to the soliloquy of Cato.

A play read, affects the mind like a play acted. It is therefore evident, that the action is not supposed to be real; and it follows, that between the acts a longer or shorter time may be allowed to pass, and that no more account of space or duration is to be taken by the auditor of a drama, than by the reader of a narrative, before whom may pass in an hour the life of a hero, or the revolution of an empire.

Whether Shakespeare knew the unities, and rejected them by design, or deviated from them by happy ignorance, it is, I think, impossible to decide, and useless to enquire. We may reasonably suppose, that, when he rose to notice, he did not want the counsels and admonitions of scholars and criticks, and that he at last deliberately persisted in a practice, which he might have begun by chance. As nothing is essential to the fable, but unity of action, and as the unities of time and place arise evidently from false assumptions, and, by circumscribing the extent of the drama, lessen its variety, I cannot think it much to be lamented, that they were not known by him, or not observed: Nor, if such another poet could arise, should I very vehemently reproach him, that his first act passed at Venice, and his next in Cyprus. Such violations of rules merely positive, become the comprehensive genius of Shakespeare, and such censures are suitable to the minute and slender criticism of Voltaire:

*Non usque adea permiscuit imis*
*Longus summa dies, ut non, si voce Metelli*
*Serventur leges, malint a Cæsare tolli.*[1]

Yet when I speak thus slightly of dramatick rules, I cannot but recollect how much wit and learning may be produced against me; before such authorities I am afraid to stand, not that I think the present question one of those that are to be decided by mere authority, but because it is to be suspected, that these precepts have not been so easily received but for better reasons than I have yet been able to find. The result of my enquiries, in which it would be ludicrous to boast of impartiality, is, that the unities of time and place are not essential to a just drama, that though they may sometimes conduce to pleasure, they are always to be sacrificed to the nobler beauties of variety and instruction; and that a play, written with nice observation of critical rules, is to be contemplated as an elaborate curiosity, as the product of superfluous and ostentatious art, by which is shewn, rather what is possible, than what is necessary.

He that, without diminution of any other excellence, shall preserve all the unities unbroken, deserves the like applause with the architect, who shall display all the orders of architecture in a citadel, without any deduction from its strength; but the principal beauty of a citadel is to exclude the enemy; and the greatest graces of a play, are to copy nature and instruct life.

Perhaps, what I have here not dogmatically but deliberately written, may recall the principles of the drama to a new examination. I am almost frighted at my own temerity; and when I estimate the fame and the strength of those that maintain the contrary opinion, am ready to sink down in reverential silence; as Æneas withdrew from the defence of Troy, when he saw Neptune shaking the wall, and Juno heading the besiegers.

Those whom my arguments cannot persuade to give their approbation to the judgment of Shakespeare, will easily, if they consider the condition of his life, make some allowance for his ignorance.

Every man's performances, to be rightly estimated, must be compared with the state of the age in which he lived, and with his own particular opportunities; and though to the reader a book be not worse or better for the circumstances of the authour, yet as there is always a silent reference

[1] A long period of time does not bring such confusion that the laws made by Metellus should need to be abolished by Caesar.

of human works to human abilities, and as the enquiry, how far man may extend his designs, or how high he may rate his native force, is of far greater dignity than in what rank we shall place any particular perform- ance, curiosity is always busy to discover the instruments, as well as to survey the workmanship, to know how much is to be ascribed to original powers, and how much to casual and adventitious help.  The palaces of Peru or Mexico were certainly mean and incommodious habitations, if compared to the houses of European monarchs; yet who could forbear to view them with astonishment, who remembered that they were built without the use of iron?

The English nation, in the time of Shakespeare, was yet struggling to emerge from barbarity.  The philology of Italy had been transplanted hither in the reign of Henry the Eighth; and the learned languages had been successfully cultivated by Lilly, Linacer, and More; by Pole, Cheke, and Gardiner; and afterwards by Smith, Clerk, Haddon, and Ascham. Greek was now taught to boys in the principal schools; and those who united elegance with learning, read, with great diligence, the Italian and Spanish poets.  But literature was yet confined to professed scholars, or to men and women of high rank.  The publick was gross and dark; and to be able to read and write, was an accomplishment still valued for its rarity.

Nations, like individuals, have their infancy.  A people newly awak- ened to literary curiosity, being yet unacquainted with the true state of things, knows not how to judge of that which is proposed as its resem- blance.  Whatever is remote from common appearances is always welcome to vulgar as to childish credulity; and of a country unenlightened by learning, the whole people is the vulgar.  The study of those who then aspired to plebeian learning was laid out upon adventures, giants, dragons, and enchantments.  *The Death of Arthur* was the favourite volume.

The mind, which has feasted on the luxurious wonders of fiction, has no taste of the insipidity of truth.  A play which imitated only the common occurrences of the world, would, upon the admirers of *Palmerin* and *Guy of Warwick*, have made little impression; he that wrote for such an audience was under the necessity of looking round for strange events and fabulous transactions, and that incredibility, by which maturer knowledge is offended, was the chief recommendation of writings, to unskilful curiosity.

Our authour's plots are generally borrowed from novels, and it is reasonable to suppose, that he chose the most popular, such as were read by many, and related by more; for his audience could not have followed him through the intricacies of the drama, had they not held the thread of the story in their hands.

The stories, which we now find only in remoter authours, were in his time accessible and familiar.    The fable of *As you like it*, which is supposed to be copied from Chaucer's *Gamelyn*, was a little pamphlet of those times; and old Mr. Cibber remembered the tale of *Hamlet* in plain English prose, which the criticks have now to seek in Saxo Grammaticus.

His English histories he took from English chronicles and English ballads; and as the ancient writers were made known to his countrymen by versions, they supplied him with new subjects; he dilated some of Plutarch's lives into plays, when they had been translated by North.

His plots, whether historical or fabulous, are always crouded with incidents, by which the attention of a rude people was more easily caught than by sentiment or argumentation; and such is the power of the marvellous even over those who despise it, that every man finds his mind more strongly seized by the tragedies of Shakespeare than of any other writer; others please us by particular speeches, but he always makes us anxious for the event, and has perhaps excelled all but Homer in securing the first purpose of a writer, by exciting restless and unquenchable curiosity and compelling him that reads his work to read it through.

The shows and bustle with which his plays abound have the same original.    As knowledge advances, pleasure passes from the eye to the ear, but returns, as it declines, from the ear to the eye.    Those to whom our authour's labours were exhibited had more skill in pomps or processions than in poetical language, and perhaps wanted some visible and discriminated events, as comments on the dialogue.    He knew how he should most please; and whether his practice is more agreeable to nature, or whether his example has prejudiced the nation, we still find that on our stage something must be done as well as said, and inactive declamation is very coldly heard, however musical or elegant, passionate or sublime.

Voltaire expresses his wonder, that our authour's extravagances are endured by a nation, which has seen the tragedy of *Cato*.    Let him be answered, that Addison speaks the language of poets, and Shakespeare, of men.    We find in *Cato* innumerable beauties which enamour us of its authour, but we see nothing that acquaints us with human sentiments or human actions; we place it with the fairest and the noblest progeny which judgment propagates by conjunction with learning, but *Othello* is the vigorous and vivacious offspring of observation impregnated by genius. *Cato* affords a splendid exhibition of artificial and fictitious manners, and delivers just and noble sentiments, in diction easy, elevated and harmonious, but its hopes and fears communicate no vibration to the heart; the composition refers us only to the writer; we pronounce the name of *Cato*, but we think on Addison.

The work of a correct and regular writer is a garden accurately formed and diligently planted, varied with shades, and scented with flowers; the composition of Shakespeare is a forest, in which oaks extend their branches, and pines tower in the air, interspersed sometimes with weeds and brambles, and sometimes giving shelter to myrtles and to roses; filling the eye with awful pomp, and gratifying the mind with endless diversity. Other poets display cabinets of precious rarities, minutely finished, wrought into shape, and polished unto brightness. Shakespeare opens a mine which contains gold and diamonds in unexhaustible plenty, though clouded by incrustations, debased by impurities, and mingled with a mass of meaner minerals.

It has been much disputed, whether Shakespeare owed his excellence to his own native force, or whether he had the common helps of scholastick education, the precepts of critical science, and the examples of ancient authours.

There has always prevailed a tradition, that Shakespeare wanted learning, that he had no regular education, nor much skill in the dead languages. Jonson, his friend, affirms, that *he had small Latin, and no Greek;* who, besides that he had. no imaginable temptation to falsehood, wrote at a time when the character and acquisitions of Shakespeare were known to multitudes. His evidence ought therefore to decide the controversy, unless some testimony of equal force could be opposed.

Some have imagined, that they have discovered deep learning in many imitations of old writers; but the examples which I have known urged, were drawn from books translated in his time; or were such easy co-incidencies of thought, as will happen to all who consider the same subjects; or such remarks on life or axioms of morality as float in conversation, and are transmitted through the world in proverbial sentences.

I have found it remarked, that, in this important sentence, *Go before, I'll follow*, we read a translation of, *I prae, sequar.* I have been told, that when *Caliban*, after a pleasing dream, says, *I cry'd to sleep again*, the authour imitates Anacreon, who had, like every other man, the same wish on the same occasion.

There are a few passages which may pass for imitations, but so few, that the exception only confirms the rule; he obtained them from accidental quotations, or by oral communication, and as he used what he had, would have used more if he had obtained it.

The *Comedy of Errors* is confessedly taken from the *Menæchmi* of Plautus; from the only play of Plautus which was then in English. What can be more probable, than that he who copied that, would have copied more; but that those which were not translated were inaccessible?

Whether he knew the modern languages is uncertain. That his plays have some French scenes proves but little; he might easily procure them to be written, and probably, even though he had known the language in the common degree, he could not have written it without assistance. In the story of *Romeo and Juliet* he is observed to have followed the English translation, where it deviates from the Italian; but this on the other part proves nothing against his knowledge of the original.   He was to copy, not what he knew himself, but what was known to his audience.

It is most likely that he had learned Latin sufficiently to make him acquainted with construction, but that he never advanced to an easy perusal of the Roman authours.   Concerning his skill in modern languages, I can find no sufficient ground of determination; but as no imitations of French or Italian authours have been discovered, though the Italian poetry was then high in esteem, I am inclined to believe, that he read little more than English, and chose for his fables only such tales as he found translated.

That much knowledge is scattered over his works is very justly observed by Pope, but it is often such knowledge as books did not supply.   He that will understand Shakespeare, must not be content to study him in the closet, he must look for his meaning sometimes among the sports of the field, and sometimes among the manufactures of the shop.

There is however proof enough that he was a very diligent reader, nor was our language then so indigent of books, but that he might very liberally indulge his curiosity without excursion into foreign literature. Many of the Roman authours were translated, and some of the Greek; the reformation had filled the kingdom with theological learning; most of the topicks of human disquisition had found English writers; and poetry had been cultivated, not only with diligence, but success.   This was a stock of knowledge sufficient for a mind so capable of appropriating and improving it.

But the greater part of his excellence was the product of his own genius.   He found the English stage in a state of the utmost rudeness; no essays either in tragedy or comedy had appeared, from which it could be discovered to what degree of delight either one or other might be carried. Neither character nor dialogue were yet understood.   Shakespeare may be truly said to have introduced them both amongst us, and in some of his happier scenes to have carried them both to the utmost height.

By what gradations of improvement he proceeded, is not easily known; for the chronology of his works is yet unsettled.   Rowe is of opinion, that *perhaps we are not to look for his beginning, like those of other writers, in his least perfect works; art had so little, and nature so large a share in what he did, that for ought I know,* says he, *the performances of his youth, as they were the most vigorous, were the best.*   But the power of nature is only the power of using to any certain purpose the materials which diligence procures, or opportunity supplies.   Nature gives no man knowledge, and when images are collected by study and experience, can only assist in combining or applying them. Shakespeare, however favoured by nature, could impart only what he had learned; and as he must increase his ideas, like other mortals, by gradual acquisition, he, like them, grew wiser as he grew older, could display life better, as he knew it more, and instruct with more efficacy, as he was himself more amply instructed.

There is a vigilance of observation and accuracy of distinction which books and precepts cannot confer; from this almost all original and native excellence proceeds. Shakespeare must have looked upon mankind with perspicacity, in the highest degree curious and attentive. Other writers borrow their characters from preceding writers, and diversify them only by the accidental appendages of present manners; the dress is a little varied, but the body is the same. Our authour had both matter and form to provide; for except the characters of Chaucer, to whom I think he is not much indebted, there were no writers in English, and perhaps not many in other modern languages, which shewed life in its native colours.

The contest about the original benevolence or malignity of man had not yet commenced. Speculation had not yet attempted to analyse the mind, to trace the passions to their sources, to unfold the seminal principles of vice and virtue, or sound the depths of the heart for the motives of action. All those enquiries, which from that time that human nature became the fashionable study, have been made sometimes with nice discernment, but often with idle subtilty, were yet unattempted. The tales, with which the infancy of learning was satisfied, exhibited only the superficial appearances of action, related the events but omitted the causes, and were formed for such as delighted in wonders rather than in truth. Mankind was not then to be studied in the closet; he that would know the world, was under the necessity of gleaning his own remarks, by mingling as he could in its business and amusements.

Boyle congratulated himself upon his high birth, because it favoured his curiosity, by facilitating his access. Shakespeare had no such advantage; he came to London a needy adventurer, and lived for a time by very mean employments. Many works of genius and learning have been performed in states of life, that appear very little favourable to thought or to enquiry; so many, that he who considers them is inclined to think that he sees enterprise and perseverance predominating over all external agency, and bidding help and hindrance vanish before them. The genius of Shakespeare was not to be depressed by the weight of poverty, nor limited by the narrow conversation to which men in want are inevitably condemned; the incumbrances of his fortune were shaken from his mind, *as dewdrops from a lion's mane.*

Though he had so many difficulties to encounter, and so little assistance to surmount them, he has been able to obtain an exact knowledge of many modes of life, and many casts of native dispositions; to vary them with great multiplicity; to mark them by nice distinctions; and to shew

them in full view by proper combinations.   In this part of his performances he had none to imitate, but has himself been imitated by all
succeeding writers; and it may be doubted, whether from all his successors
more maxims of theoretical knowledge, or more rules of practical prudence, can be collected, than he alone has given to his country.

Nor was his attention confined to the actions of men; he was an exact
surveyor of the inanimate world; his descriptions have always some
peculiarities, gathered by contemplating things as they really exist.   It
may be observed, that the oldest poets of many nations preserve their
reputation, and that the following generations of wit, after a short
celebrity, sink into oblivion.   The first, whoever they be, must take their
sentiments and descriptions immediately from knowledge; the resemblance is therefore just, their descriptions are verified by every eye, and
their sentiments acknowledged by every breast.   Those whom their fame
invites to the same studies, copy partly them, and partly nature, till the
books of one age gain such authority, as to stand in the place of nature to
another, and imitation, always deviating a little, becomes at last capricious
and casual.   Shakespeare, whether life or nature be his subject, shews
plainly, that he has seen with his own eyes; he gives the image which he
receives, not weakened or distorted by the intervention of any other
mind; the ignorant feel his representations to be just, and the learned see
that they are compleat.

Perhaps it would not be easy to find any authour, except Homer, who
invented so much as Shakespeare, who so much advanced the studies
which he cultivated, or effused so much novelty upon his age or country.
The form, the characters, the language, and the shows of the English
drama are his.   *He seems,* says Dennis, *to have been the very original of our
English tragical harmony, that is, the harmony of blank verse, diversified often by
dissyllable and trissyllable terminations.   For the diversity distinguishes it from
heroick harmony, and by bringing it nearer to common use makes it more proper to
gain attention, and more fit for action and dialogue.   Such verse we make when we
are writing prose; we make such verse in common conversation.*

I know not whether this praise is rigorously just.   The dissyllable
termination, which the critick rightly appropriates to the drama, is to be
found, though, I think, not in *Gorboduc* which is confessedly before our
authour; yet in *Hieronnymo,* of which the date is not certain, but which
there is reason to believe at least as old as his earliest plays.   This however
is certain, that he is the first who taught either tragedy or comedy to
please, there being no theatrical piece of any older writer, of which the
name is known, except to antiquaries and collectors of books, which are
sought because they are scarce, and would not have been scarce, had they
been much esteemed.

To him we must ascribe the praise, unless Spenser may divide it with him, of having first discovered to how much smoothness and harmony the English language could be softened. He has speeches, perhaps sometimes scenes, which have all the delicacy of Rowe, without his effeminacy. He endeavours indeed commonly to strike by the force and vigour of his dialogue, but he never executes his purpose better, than when he tries to sooth by softness.

Yet it must be at last confessed, that as we owe every thing to him, he owes something to us; that, if much of his praise is paid by perception and judgement, much is likewise given by custom and veneration. We fix our eyes upon his graces, and turn them from his deformities, and endure in him what we should in another loath or despise. If we endured without praising, respect for the father of our drama might excuse us; but I have seen, in the book of some modern critick, a collection of anomalies, which shew that he has corrupted language by every mode of depravation, but which his admirer has accumulated as a monument of honour.

He has scenes of undoubted and perpetual excellence, but perhaps not one play, which, if it were now exhibited as the work of a contemporary writer, would be heard to the conclusion. I am indeed far from thinking, that his works were wrought to his own ideas of perfection; when they were such as would satisfy the audience, they satisfied the writer. It is seldom that authours, though more studious of fame than Shakespeare, rise much above the standard of their own age; to add a little of what is best will always be sufficient for present praise, and those who find themselves exalted into fame, are willing to credit their encomiasts, and to spare the labour of contending with themselves.

It does not appear, that Shakespeare thought his works worthy of posterity, that he levied any ideal tribute upon future times, or had any further prospect, than of present popularity and present profit. When his plays had been acted, his hope was at an end; he solicited no addition of honour from the reader. He therefore made no scruple to repeat the same jests in many dialogues, or to entangle different plots by the same knot of perplexity, which may be at least forgiven him, by those who recollect, that of Congreve's four comedies, two are concluded by a marriage in a mask, by a deception, which perhaps never happened, and which, whether likely or not, he did not invent.

So careless was this great poet of future fame, that, though he retired to ease and plenty, while he was yet little *declined into the vale of years*, before he could be disgusted with fatigue, or disabled by infirmity, he made no collection of his works, nor desired to rescue those that had been already published from the depravations that obscured them, or secure to the rest a better destiny, by giving them to the world in their genuine state.

Of the plays which bear the name of Shakespeare in the late editions, the greater part were not published till about seven years after his death, and the few which appeared in his life are apparently thrust into the world without the care of the authour, and therefore probably without his knowledge.

Of all the publishers, clandestine or professed, their negligence and unskilfulness has by the late revisers been sufficiently shown. The faults of all are indeed numerous and gross, and have not only corrupted many passages perhaps beyond recovery, but have brought others into suspicion, which are only obscured by obsolete phraseology, or by the writer's unskilfulness and affectation. To alter is more easy than to explain, and temerity is a more common quality than diligence. Those who saw that they must employ conjecture to a certain degree, were willing to indulge it a little further. Had the authour published his own works, we should have sat quietly down to disentangle his intricacies, and clear his obscurities; but now we tear what we cannot loose, and eject what we happen not to understand.

The faults are more than could have happened without the concurrence of many causes. The stile of Shakespeare was in itself ungrammatical, perplexed and obscure; his works were transcribed for the players by those who may be supposed to have seldom understood them; they were transmitted by copiers equally unskilful, who still multiplied errours; they were perhaps sometimes mutilated by the actors, for the sake of shortening the speeches; and were at last printed without correction of the press.

In this state they remained, not as Dr. Warburton supposes, because they were unregarded, but because the editor's art was not yet applied to modern languages, and our ancestors were accustomed to so much negligence of English printers, that they could very patiently endure it. At last an edition was undertaken by Rowe; not because a poet was to be published by a poet, for Rowe seems to have thought very little on correction or explanation, but that our authour's works might appear like those of his fraternity, with the appendages of a life and recommendatory preface. Rowe has been clamorously blamed for not performing what he did not undertake, and it is time that justice be done him, by confessing, that though he seems to have had no thought of corruption beyond the printer's errours, yet he has made many emendations, if they were not made before, which his successors have received without acknowledgement, and which, if they had produced them, would have filled pages and pages with censures of the stupidity by which the faults were committed, with displays of the absurdities which they involved, with ostentatious expositions of the new reading, and self congratulations on the happiness of discovering it.

Of Rowe, as of all the editors, I have preserved the preface, and have likewise retained the authour's life, though not written with much elegance or spirit; it relates however what is now to be known, and therefore deserves to pass through all succeeding publications.

The nation had been for many years content enough with Mr. Rowe's performance, when Mr. Pope made them acquainted with the true state of Shakespeare's text, shewed that it was extremely corrupt, and gave reason to hope that there were means of reforming it. He collated the old copies, which none had thought to examine before, and restored many lines to their integrity; but, by a very compendious criticism, he rejected whatever he disliked, and thought more of amputation than of cure.

I know not why he is commended by Dr. Warburton for distinguishing the genuine from the spurious plays. In this choice he exerted no judgement of his own; the plays which he received, were given by Hemings and Condel, the first editors; and those which he rejected, though, according to the licentiousness of the press in those times, they were printed during Shakespeare's life, with his name, had been omitted by his friends, and were never added to his works before the edition of 1664, from which they were copied by the later printers.

This was a work which Pope seems to have thought unworthy of his abilities, being not able to suppress his contempt of *the dull duty of an editor*. He understood but half his undertaking. The duty of a collator is indeed dull, yet, like other tedious tasks, is very necessary; but an emendatory critick would ill discharge his duty, without qualities very different from dullness. In perusing a corrupted piece, he must have before him all possibilities of meaning, with all possibilities of expression. Such must be his comprehension of thought, and such his copiousness of language. Out of many readings possible, he must be able to select that which best suits with the state of opinions, and modes of language prevailing in every age, and with his authour's particular cast of thought, and turn of expression. Such must be his knowledge, and such his taste. Conjectural criticism demands more than humanity possesses, and he that exercises it with most praise has very frequent need of indulgence. Let us now be told no more of the dull duty of an editor.

Confidence is the common consequence of success. They whose excellence of any kind has been loudly celebrated, are ready to conclude, that their powers are universal. Pope's edition fell below his own expectations, and he was so much offended, when he was found to have left any thing for others to do, that he past the latter part of his life in a state of hostility with verbal criticism.

I have retained all his notes, that no fragment of so great a writer may be lost; his preface, valuable alike for elegance of composition and justness of remark, and containing a general criticism on his authour, so extensive that little can be added, and so exact, that little can be disputed, every editor has an interest to suppress, but that every reader would demand its insertion.

Pope was succeeded by Theobald, a man of narrow comprehension and small acquisitions, with no native and intrinsick splendour of genius, with little of the artificial light of learning, but zealous for minute accuracy, and not negligent in pursuing it.   He collated the ancient copies, and rectified many errors.   A man so anxiously scrupulous might have been expected to do more, but what little he did was commonly right.

In his report of copies and editions he is not to be trusted, without examination.   He speaks sometimes indefinitely of copies, when he has only one.   In his enumeration of editions, he mentions the two first folios as of high, and the third folio as of middle authority; but the truth is, that the first is equivalent to all others, and that the rest only deviate from it by the printer's negligence.   Whoever has any of the folios has all, excepting those diversities which mere reiteration of editions will produce.   I collated them all at the beginning, but afterwards used only the first.

Of his notes I have generally retained those which he retained himself in his second edition, except when they were confuted by subsequent annotators, or were too minute to merit preservation.   I have sometimes adopted his restoration of a comma, without inserting the panegyrick in which he celebrated himself for his atchievement.   The exuberant excrescence of his diction I have often lopped, his triumphant exultations over Pope and Rowe I have sometimes suppressed, and his contemptible ostentation I have frequently concealed; but I have in some places shewn him, as he would have shewn himself, for the reader's diversion, that the inflated emptiness of some notes may justify or excuse the contraction of the rest.

Theobald, thus weak and ignorant, thus mean and faithless, thus petulant and ostentatious, by the good luck of having Pope for his enemy, has escaped, and escaped alone, with reputation, from this undertaking. So willingly does the world support those who solicite favour, against those who command reverence; and so easily is he praised, whom no man can envy.

Our authour fell then into the hands of Sir Thomas Hanmer, the Oxford editor, a man, in my opinion, eminently qualified by nature for such studies.   He had, what is the first requisite to emendatory criticism, that intuition by which the poet's intention is immediately discovered, and that dexterity of intellect which despatches its work by the easiest means. He had undoubtedly read much; his acquaintance with customs, opinions, and traditions, seems to have been large; and he is often learned without shew.  He seldom passes what he does not understand, without an attempt to find or to make a meaning, and sometimes hastily makes what a little more attention would have found.  He is solicitous to reduce to grammar, what he could not be sure that his authour intended to be grammatical.  Shakespeare regarded more the series of ideas, than of words; and his language, not being designed for the reader's desk, was all that he desired it to be, if it conveyed his meaning to the audience.

Hanmer's care of the metre has been too violently censured.  He found the measures reformed in so many passages, by the silent labours of some editors, with the silent acquiescence of the rest, that he thought himself allowed to extend a little further the license, which had already been carried so far without reprehension; and of his corrections in general, it must be confessed, that they are often just, and made commonly with the least possible violation of the text.

But, by inserting his emendations, whether invented or borrowed, into the page, without any notice of varying copies, he has appropriated the labour of his predecessors, and made his own edition of little authority.  His confidence indeed, both in himself and others, was too great; he supposes all to be right that was done by Pope and Theobald; he seems not to suspect a critick of fallibility, and it was but reasonable that he should claim what he so liberally granted.

As he never writes without careful enquiry and diligent consideration, I have received all his notes, and believe that every reader will wish for more.

Of the last editor it is more difficult to speak.  Respect is due to high place, tenderness to living reputation, and veneration to genius and learning; but he cannot be justly offended at that liberty of which he has himself so frequently given an example, nor very solicitous what is thought of notes, which he ought never to have considered as part of his serious employments, and which, I suppose, since the ardour of composition is remitted, he no longer numbers among his happy effusions.

The original and predominant errour of his commentary, is acquiescence in his first thoughts; that precipitation which is produced by consciousness of quick discernment; and that confidence which pre- sumes to do, by surveying the surface, what labour only can perform, by penetrating the bottom.  His notes exhibit sometimes perverse inter- pretations, and sometimes improbable conjectures; he at one time gives the authour more profundity of meaning, than the sentence admits, and at another discovers absurdities, where the sense is plain to every other reader.  But his emendations are likewise often happy and just; and his interpretation of obscure passages learned and sagacious.

Of his notes, I have commonly rejected those, against which the general voice of the publick has exclaimed, or which their own incongruity immediately condemns, and which, I suppose, the authour himself would desire to be forgotten. Of the rest, to part I have given the highest approbation, by inserting the offered reading in the text; part I have left to the judgment of the reader, as doubtful, though specious; and part I have censured without reserve, but I am sure without bitterness of malice, and, I hope, without wantonness of insult.

It is no pleasure to me, in revising my volumes, to observe how much paper is wasted in confutation. Whoever considers the revolutions of learning, and the various questions of greater or less importance, upon which wit and reason have exercised their powers, must lament the unsuccessfulness of enquiry, and the slow advances of truth, when he reflects, that great part of the labour of every writer is only the destruction of those that went before him. The first care of the builder of a new system, is to demolish the fabricks which are standing. The chief desire of him that comments an authour, is to shew how much other commentators have corrupted and obscured him. The opinions prevalent in one age, as truths above the reach of controversy, are confuted and rejected in another, and rise again to reception in remoter times. Thus the human mind is kept in motion without progress. Thus sometimes truth and errour, and sometimes contrarieties of errour, take each other's place by reciprocal invasion. The tide of seeming knowledge which is poured over one generation, retires and leaves another naked and barren; the sudden meteors of intelligence which for a while appear to shoot their beams into the regions of obscurity, on a sudden withdraw their lustre, and leave mortals again to grope their way.

These elevations and depressions of renown, and the contradictions to which all improvers of knowledge must for ever be exposed, since they are not escaped by the highest and brightest of mankind, may surely be endured with patience by criticks and annotators, who can rank themselves but as the satellites of their authours. How canst thou beg for life, says Achilles to his captive, when thou knowest that thou art now to suffer only what must another day be suffered by Achilles?

Dr. Warburton had a name sufficient to confer celebrity on those who could exalt themselves into antagonists, and his notes have raised a clamour too loud to be distinct. His chief assailants are the authours of the Canons of criticism and of the Review of Shakespeare's text; of whom one ridicules his errours with airy petulance, suitable enough to the levity of the controversy; the other attacks them with gloomy malignity, as if he were dragging to justice an assassin or incendiary. The one stings like a fly, sucks a little blood, takes a gay flutter, and returns for more; the other bites like a viper, and would be glad to leave inflammations and gangrene behind him. When I think on one, with his confederates, I remember the danger of Coriolanus, who was afraid that *girls with spits, and boys with stones, should slay him in puny battle;* when the other crosses my imagination, I remember the prodigy in *Macbeth,*

> *An eagle tow'ring in his pride of place,*
> *Was by a mousing owl hawk'd at and kill'd.*

Let me however do them justice. One is a wit, and one a scholar. They have both shown acuteness sufficient in the discovery of faults, and have both advanced some probable interpretations of obscure passages; but when they aspire to conjecture and emendation, it appears how falsely we all estimate our own abilities, and the little which they have been able to perform might have taught them more candour to the endeavours of others.

Before Dr. Warburton's edition, *Critical observations on Shakespeare* had been published by Mr. Upton, a man skilled in languages, and acquainted with books, but who seems to have had no great vigour of genius or nicety of taste. Many of his explanations are curious and useful, but he likewise, though he professed to oppose the licentious confidence of editors, and adhere to the old copies, is unable to restrain the rage of emendation, though his ardour is ill seconded by his skill. Every cold empirick, when his heart is expanded by a successful experiment, swells into a theorist, and the laborious collator at some unlucky moment frolicks in conjecture.

Critical, historical and explanatory notes have been likewise published upon Shakespeare by Dr. Grey, whose diligent perusal of the old English writers has enabled him to make some useful observations. What he undertook he has well enough performed, but as he neither attempts judicial nor emendatory criticism, he employs rather his memory than his sagacity. It were to be wished that all would endeavour to imitate his modesty who have not been able to surpass his knowledge.

I can say with great sincerity of all my predecessors, what I hope will hereafter be said of me, that not one has left Shakespeare without improvement, nor is there one to whom I have not been indebted for assistance and information. Whatever I have taken from them it was my intention to refer to its original authour, and it is certain, that what I have not given to another, I believed when I wrote it to be my own. In some perhaps I have been anticipated; but if I am ever found to encroach upon the remarks of any other commentator, I am willing that the honour, be it more or less, should be transferred to the first claimant, for his right, and his alone, stands above dispute; the second can prove his pretensions only to himself, nor can himself always distinguish invention, with sufficient certainty, from recollection.

They have all been treated by me with candour, which they have not been careful of observing to one another.   It is not easy to discover from what cause the acrimony of a scholiast can naturally proceed.   The subjects to be discussed by him are of very small importance; they involve neither property nor liberty; nor favour the interest of sect or party.   The various readings of copies, and different interpretations of a passage, seem to be questions that might exercise the wit, without engaging the passions. But, whether it be, that *small things make mean men proud*, and vanity catches small occasions; or that all contrariety of opinion, even in those that can defend it no longer, makes proud men angry; there is often found in commentaries a spontaneous strain of invective and contempt, more eager and venomous than is vented by the most furious controvertist in politicks against those whom he is hired to defame.

Perhaps the lightness of the matter may conduce to the vehemence of the agency; when the truth to be investigated is so near to inexistence, as to escape attention, its bulk is to be enlarged by rage and exclamation: That to which all would be indifferent in its original state, may attract notice when the fate of a name is appended to it.   A commentator has indeed great temptations to supply by turbulence what he wants of dignity, to beat his little gold to a spacious surface, to work that to foam which no art or diligence can exalt to spirit.

The notes which I have borrowed or written are either illustrative, by which difficulties are explained; or judicial, by which faults and beauties are remarked; or emendatory, by which depravations are corrected.

The explanations transcribed from others, if I do not subjoin any other interpretation, I suppose commonly to be right, at least I intend by acquiescence to confess, that I have nothing better to propose.

After the labours of all the editors, I found many passages which appeared to me likely to obstruct the greater number of readers, and thought it my duty to facilitate their passage.   It is impossible for an expositor not to write too little for some, and too much for others.   He can only judge what is necessary by his own experience; and how long soever he may deliberate, will at last explain many lines which the learned will think impossible to be mistaken, and omit many for which the ignorant will want his help.   These are censures merely relative, and must be quietly endured.   I have endeavoured to be neither superfluously copious, nor scrupulously reserved, and hope that I have made my authour's meaning accessible to many who before were frighted from perusing him, and contributed something to the publick, by diffusing innocent and rational pleasure.

The compleat explanation of an authour not systematick and consequential, but desultory and vagrant, abounding in casual allusions and light hints, is not to be expected from any single scholiast.   All personal reflections, when names are suppressed, must be in a few years irrecoverably obliterated; and customs, too minute to attract the notice of law, such as modes of dress, formalities of conversation, rules of visits, disposition of furniture, and practices of ceremony, which naturally find places in familiar dialogue, are so fugitive and unsubstantial, that they are not easily retained or recovered. What can be known, will be collected by chance, from the recesses of obscure and obsolete papers, perused commonly with some other view. Of this knowledge every man has some, and none has much; but when an authour has engaged the publick attention, those who can add any thing to his illustration, communicate their discoveries, and time produces what had eluded diligence.

To time I have been obliged to resign many passages, which, though I did not understand them, will perhaps hereafter be explained, having, I hope, illustrated some, which others have neglected or mistaken, sometimes by short remarks, or marginal directions, such as every editor has added at his will, and often by comments more laborious than the matter will seem to deserve; but that which is most difficult is not always most important, and to an editor nothing is a trifle by which his authour is obscured.

The poetical beauties or defects I have not been very diligent to observe. Some plays have more, and some fewer judicial observations, not in proportion to their difference of merit, but because I gave this part of my design to chance and to caprice. The reader, I believe, is seldom pleased to find his opinion anticipated; it is natural to delight more in what we find or make, than in what we receive. Judgement, like other faculties, is improved by practice, and its advancement is hindered by submission to dictatorial decisions, as the memory grows torpid by the use of a table book. Some initiation is however necessary; of all skill, part is infused by precept, and part is obtained by habit; I have therefore shewn so much as may enable the candidate of criticism to discover the rest.

To the end of most plays, I have added short strictures, containing a general censure of faults, or praise of excellence; in which I know not how much I have concurred with the current opinion; but I have not, by any affectation of singularity, deviated from it. Nothing is minutely and particularly examined, and therefore it is to be supposed, that in the plays which are condemned there is much to be praised, and in those which are praised much to be condemned.

The part of criticism in which the whole succession of editors has laboured with the greatest diligence, which has occasioned the most arrogant ostentation, and excited the keenest acrimony, is the emendation, of corrupted passages, to which the publick attention having been first drawn by the violence of contention between Pope and Theobald, has been continued by the persecution, which, with a kind of conspiracy, has been since raised against all the publishers of Shakespeare.

That many passages have passed in a state of depravation through all the editions is indubitably certain; of these the restoration is only to be attempted by collation of copies or sagacity of conjecture. The collator's province is safe and easy, the conjecturer's perilous and difficult. Yet as the greater part of the plays are extant only in one copy, the peril must not be avoided, nor the difficulty refused.

Of the readings which this emulation of amendment has hitherto produced, some from the labours of every publisher I have advanced into the text; those are to be considered as in my opinion sufficiently supported; some I have rejected without mention, as evidently erroneous; some I have left in the notes without censure or approbation, as resting in equipoise between objection and defence; and some, which seemed specious but not right, I have inserted with a subsequent animadversion.

Having classed the observations of others, I was at last to try what I could substitute for their mistakes, and how I could supply their omissions. I collated such copies as I could procure, and wished for more, but have not found the collectors of these rarities very communicative. Of the editions which chance or kindness put into my hands I have given an enumeration, that I may not be blamed for neglecting what I had not the power to do.

By examining the old copies, I soon found that the later publishers, with all their boasts of diligence, suffered many passages to stand unauthorised, and contented themselves with Rowe's regulation of the text, even where they knew it to be arbitrary, and with a little consideration might have found it to be wrong. Some of these alterations are only the ejection of a word for one that appeared to him more elegant or more intelligible. These corruptions I have often silently rectified; for the history of our language, and the true force of our words, can only be preserved, by keeping the text of authours free from adulteration. Others, and those very frequent, smoothed the cadence, or regulated the measure; on these I have not exercised the same rigour; if only a word was transposed, or a particle inserted or omitted, I have sometimes suffered the line to stand; for the inconstancy of the copies is such, as that some liberties may be easily permitted. But this practice I have not suffered to proceed far, having restored the primitive diction wherever it could for any reason be preferred.

The emendations, which comparison of copies supplied, I have inserted in the text; sometimes where the improvement was slight, without notice, and sometimes with an account of the reasons of the change.

Conjecture, though it be sometimes unavoidable, I have not wantonly nor licentiously indulged.   It has been my settled principle, that the reading of the ancient books is probably true, and therefore is not to be disturbed for the sake of elegance, perspicuity, or mere improvement of the sense.   For though much credit is not due to the fidelity, nor any to the judgement of the first publishers, yet they who had the copy before their eyes were more likely to read it right, than we who read it only by imagination.   But it is evident that they have often made strange mistakes by ignorance or negligence, and that therefore something may be properly attempted by criticism, keeping the middle way between presumption and timidity.

Such criticism I have attempted to practise, and where any passage appeared inextricably perplexed, have endeavoured to discover how it may be recalled to sense, with least violence.   But my first labour is, always to turn the old text on every side, and try if there be any interstice, through which light can find its way; nor would Huetius himself condemn me, as refusing the trouble of research, for the ambition of alteration.   In this modest industry I have not been unsuccessful.   I have rescued many lines from the violations of temerity, and secured many scenes from the inroads of correction.   I have adopted the Roman sentiment, that it is more honourable to save a citizen, than to kill an enemy, and have been more careful to protect than to attack.

I have preserved the common distribution of the plays into acts, though I believe it to be in almost all the plays void of authority.   Some of those which are divided in the later editions have no division in the first folio, and some that are divided in the folio have no division in the preceding copies.   The settled mode of the theatre requires four intervals in the play, but few, if any, of our authour's compositions can be properly distributed in that manner.   An act is so much of the drama as passes without intervention of time or change of place.   A pause makes a new act.   In every real, and therefore in every imitative action, the intervals may be more or fewer, the restriction of five acts being accidental and arbitrary.   This Shakespeare knew, and this he practised; his plays were written, and at first printed in one unbroken continuity, and ought now to be exhibited with short pauses, interposed as often as the scene is changed, or any considerable time is required to pass.   This method would at once quell a thousand absurdities.

In restoring the authour's works to their integrity, I have considered the punctuation as wholly in my power; for what could be their care of colons and commas, who corrupted words and sentences.   Whatever could be done by adjusting points is therefore silently performed, in some plays with much diligence, in others with less; it is hard to keep a busy eye steadily fixed upon evanescent atoms, or a discursive mind upon evanescent truth.

The same liberty has been taken with a few particles, or other words of slight effect. I have sometimes inserted or omitted them without notice. I have done that sometimes, which indeed the state of the text may sufficiently justify.

The greater part of readers, instead of blaming us for passing trifles, will wonder that on mere trifles so much labour is expended, with such importance of debate, and such solemnity of diction. To these I answer with confidence, that they are judging of an art which they do not understand; yet cannot much reproach them with their ignorance, nor promise that they would become in general, by learning criticism, more useful, happier or wiser.

As I practised conjecture more, I learned to trust it less; and after I had printed a few plays, resolved to insert none of my own readings in the text. Upon this caution I now congratulate myself, for every day encreases my doubt of my emendations.

Since I have confined my imagination to the margin, it must not be considered as very reprehensible, if I have suffered it to play some freaks in its own dominion. There is no danger in conjecture, if it be proposed as conjecture; and while the text remains uninjured, those changes may be safely offered, which are not considered even by him that offers them as necessary or safe.

If my readings are of little value, they have not been ostentatiously displayed or importunately obtruded. I could have written longer notes, for the art of writing notes is not of difficult attainment. The work is performed, first by railing at the stupidity, negligence, ignorance, and asinine tastelessness of the former editors, and shewing, from all that goes before and all that follows, the inelegance and absurdity of the old reading; then by proposing something, which to superficial readers would seem specious, but which the editor rejects with indignation; then by producing the true reading, with a long paraphrase, and concluding with loud acclamations on the discovery, and a sober wish for the advancement and prosperity of genuine criticism.

All this may be done, and perhaps done sometimes without impropriety. But I have always suspected that the reading is right, which requires many words to prove it wrong; and the emendation wrong, that cannot without so much labour appear to be right. The justness of a happy restoration strikes at once, and the moral precept may be well applied to criticism, *quod dubitas ne feceris.*[2]

To dread the shore which he sees spread with wrecks, is natural to the sailor. I had before my eye, so many critical adventures ended in mis-

---

[2] When in doubt, refrain.

carriage, that caution was forced upon me.    I encountered in every page Wit struggling with its own sophistry, and Learning confused by the multiplicity of its views.    I was forced to censure those whom I admired, and could not but reflect, while I was dispossessing their emendations, how soon the same fate might happen to my own, and how many of the readings which I have corrected may be by some other editor defended and established.

> *Criticks, I saw, that other's names efface,*
> *And fix their own, with labour, in the place;*
> *Their own, like others, soon their place resign'd,*
> *Or disappear'd, and left the first behind.*—POPE.

That a conjectural critick should often be mistaken, cannot be wonderful, either to others or himself, if it be considered, that in his art there is no system, no principal and axiomatical truth that regulates subordinate positions.    His chance of errour is renewed at every attempt; an oblique view of the passage, a slight misapprehension of a phrase, a casual inattention to the parts connected, is sufficient to make him not only fail, but fail ridiculously; and when he succeeds best, he produces perhaps but one reading of many probable, and he that suggests another will always be able to dispute his claims.

It is an unhappy state, in which danger is hid under pleasure.    The allurements of emendation are scarcely resistible.    Conjecture has all the joy and all the pride of invention, and he that has once started a happy change, is too much delighted to consider what objections may rise against it.

Yet conjectural criticism has been of great use in the learned world; nor is it my intention to depreciate a study, that has exercised so many mighty minds, from the revival of learning to our own age, from the Bishop of Aleria to English Bentley.    The criticks on ancient authours have, in the exercise of their sagacity, many assistances, which the editor of Shakespeare is condemned to want.    They are employed upon grammatical and settled languages, whose construction contributes so much to perspicuity, that Homer has fewer passages unintelligible than Chaucer. The words have not only a known regimen, but invariable quantities, which direct and confine the choice.    There are commonly more manuscripts than one; and they do not often conspire in the same mistakes.    Yet Scaliger could confess to Salmasius how little satisfaction his emendations gave him.    *Illudunt nobis conjecturæ nostræ, quarum nos pudet, posteaquam in meliores codices incidimus.*[3]    And Lipsius could complain, that

---

[3] Our conjectures make fools of us, putting us to shame, when we later discover better manuscripts.

criticks were making faults, by trying to remove them, *Ut olim vitiis, ita nunc remediis laboratur.*[4]   And indeed, where mere conjecture is to be used, the emendations of Scaliger and Lipsius, notwithstanding their wonderful sagacity and erudition, are often vague and disputable, like mine or Theobald's.

Perhaps I may not be more censured for doing wrong, than for doing little; for raising in the publick expectations, which at last I have not answered.   The expectation of ignorance is indefinite, and that of knowledge is often tyrannical.   It is hard to satisfy those who know not what to demand, or those who demand by design what they think impossible to be done.   I have indeed disappointed no opinion more than my own; yet I have endeavoured to perform my task with no slight solicitude.   Not a single passage in the whole work has appeared to me corrupt, which I have not attempted to restore; or obscure, which I have not endeavoured to illustrate.   In many I have failed like others; and from many, after all my efforts, I have retreated, and confessed the repulse.   I have not passed over, with affected superiority, what is equally difficult to the reader and to myself, but where I could not instruct him, have owned my ignorance.   I might easily have accumulated a mass of seeming learning upon easy scenes; but it ought not to be imputed to negligence, that, where nothing was necessary, nothing has been done, or that, where others have said enough, I have said no more.

Notes are often necessary, but they are necessary evils.   Let him, that is yet unacquainted with the powers of Shakespeare, and who desires to feel the highest pleasure that the drama can give, read every play from the first scene to the last, with utter negligence of all his commentators. When his fancy is once on the wing, let it not stoop at correction or explanation.   When his attention is strongly engaged, let it disdain alike to turn aside to the name of Theobald and of Pope.   Let him read on through brightness and obscurity, through integrity and corruption; let him preserve his comprehension of the dialogue and his interest in the fable.   And when the pleasures of novelty have ceased, let him attempt exactness, and read the commentators.

Particular passages are cleared by notes, but the general effect of the work is weakened.   The mind is refrigerated by interruption; the thoughts are diverted from the principal subject; the reader is weary, he suspects not why; and at last throws away the book, which he has too diligently studied.

Parts are not to be examined till the whole has been surveyed; there is a kind of intellectual remoteness necessary for the comprehension of any

---

[4] As before we toiled over corruptions, now we struggle with corrections.

great work in its full design and its true proportions; a close approach shews the smaller niceties, but the beauty of the whole is discerned no longer.

It is not very grateful to consider how little the succession of editors has added to this authour's power of pleasing. He was read, admired, studied, and imitated, while he was yet deformed with all the improprieties which ignorance and neglect could accumulate upon him; while the reading was yet not rectified, nor his allusions understood; yet then did Dryden pronounce "that Shakespeare was the man, who, of all modern and perhaps ancient poets, had the largest and most comprehensive soul. All the images of nature were still present to him, and he drew them not laboriously, but luckily: When he describes any thing, you more than see it, you feel it too. Those who accuse him to have wanted learning, give him the greater commendation: he was naturally learned: he needed not the spectacles of books to read nature; he looked inwards, and found her there. I cannot say he is every where alike; were he so, I should do him injury to compare him with the greatest of mankind. He is many times flat and insipid; his comick wit degenerating into clenches, his serious swelling into bombast. But he is always great, when some great occasion is presented to him: No man can say, he ever had a fit subject for his wit, and did not then raise himself as high above the rest of poets,

*Quantum lenta solent inter viburna cupressi.*"[5]

It is to be lamented, that such a writer should want a commentary; that his language should become obsolete, or his sentiments obscure. But it is vain to carry wishes beyond the condition of human things; that which must happen to all, has happened to Shakespeare, by accident and time; and more than has been suffered by any other writer since the use of types, has been suffered by him through his own negligence of fame, or perhaps by that superiority of mind, which despised its own performances, when it compared them with its powers, and judged those works unworthy to be preserved, which the criticks of following ages were to contend for the fame of restoring and explaining.

Among these candidates of inferiour fame, I am now to stand the judgment of the publick; and wish that I could confidently produce my commentary as equal to the encouragement which I have had the honour of receiving. Every work of this kind is by its nature deficient, and I should feel little solicitude about the sentence, were it to be pronounced only by the skilful and the learned.

[5] As cypresses raise themselves above scraggly shrubs.

# Preface to *Lyrical Ballads*

## 1800

*The most immediately striking aspect of Wordsworth's essay is the disappearance of the critical terminology of the eighteenth century. The older issues have not been finally settled; Wordsworth is simply not interested in the struggle between the ancients and the moderns, or the relative claims of genius as against learning.*

*Wordsworth's attack on both the subject matter and the "poetic diction" of the preceding age has psychological, sociological, and moral frames of reference. The aim of poetry, which is the communication of pleasure, is not to be achieved by inducing stereotyped reactions and stock responses; modern man, already suffering from the psychosocial pressures imposed upon him by urban life, is prevented from realizing himself and his relation to nature by this "artificial" literature. What Wordsworth is proposing is nothing less than revivifying the human mind through poetry by insisting on the primacy of the imagination as a moral agent. The key words repeated throughout are "relationship" and "association": By portraying and exemplifying the psychological laws that govern human nature, even in the most humble, commonplace persons, the poet "binds together by passion and knowledge the vast empire of human society." This is the "moral purpose" of his poems twice referred to. The poet, "a man speaking to men" in*

---

From *Wordsworth's Literary Criticism*, ed. Nowell C. Smith; London: Henry Frowde, Oxford University Press, 1905. Reprinted by permission of Oxford University Press.

*"the language of men," records his own sensations, observations, re-
flections, and conclusions, creating a pleasurable imaginative response
that is inseparable from the highest kind of knowledge. The scientist
provides information, but the poet provides insight.*

*The conjunction of the terms "knowledge" and "pleasure" should
remind you of the Platonic challenge that poetry must teach and delight. Does Wordsworth mean the same thing by "knowledge" that
Plato does? Also note, in this connection, Wordsworth's discussion of
the relationship between poetry and prose (unfortunately relegated
to a footnote). The distinctions he makes here lead him later in the
essay to some conclusions about the function of metrical language—
conclusions to be challenged, as you will see next, by his erstwhile
collaborator on the* Lyrical Ballads.

THE FIRST volume of these Poems has already been submitted to general
perusal.   It was published, as an experiment, which, I hoped, might be
of some use to ascertain, how far, by fitting to metrical arrangement a
selection of the real language of men in a state of vivid sensation, that sort
of pleasure and that quantity of pleasure may be imparted, which a Poet
may rationally endeavour to impart.

I had formed no very inaccurate estimate of the probable effect of those
Poems: I flattered myself that they who should be pleased with them
would read them with more than common pleasure: and, on the other
hand, I was well aware, that by those who should dislike them, they would
be read with more than common dislike.   The result has differed from
my expectation in this only, that a greater number have been pleased than
I ventured to hope I should please.

.    .    .    .    .    .    .    .    .    .

Several of my Friends are anxious for the success of these Poems, from
a belief, that if the views with which they were composed were indeed
realized, a class of Poetry would be produced, well adapted to interest
mankind permanently, and not unimportant in the quality, and in the
multiplicity of its moral relations: and on this account they have advised
me to prefix a systematic defence of the theory upon which the Poems
were written.   But I was unwilling to undertake the task, knowing that
on this occasion the Reader would look coldly upon my arguments, since

I might be suspected of having been principally influenced by the selfish
and foolish hope of *reasoning* him into an approbation of these particular
Poems: and I was still more unwilling to undertake the task, because,
adequately to display the opinions, and fully to enforce the arguments,
would require a space wholly disproportionate to a preface. For, to treat
the subject with the clearness and coherence of which it is susceptible, it
would be necessary to give a full account of the present state of the public
taste in this country, and to determine how far this taste is healthy or
depraved; which, again, could not be determined, without pointing out
in what manner language and the human mind act and re-act on each
other, and without retracing the revolutions, not of literature alone, but
likewise of society itself. I have therefore altogether declined to enter
regularly upon this defence; yet I am sensible, that there would be something like impropriety in abruptly obtruding upon the Public, without a
few words of introduction, Poems so materially different from those upon
which general approbation is at present bestowed.

It is supposed, that by the act of writing in verse an Author makes a
formal engagement that he will gratify certain known habits of association;
that he not only thus apprises the Reader that certain classes of ideas and
expressions will be found in his book, but that others will be carefully
excluded. This exponent or symbol held forth by metrical language
must in different eras of literature have excited very different expectations:
for example, in the age of Catullus, Terence, and Lucretius, and that of
Statius or Claudian; and in our own country, in the age of Shakespeare
and Beaumont and Fletcher, and that of Donne and Cowley, or Dryden,
or Pope. I will not take upon me to determine the exact import of the
promise which, by the act of writing in verse, an Author in the present day
makes to his reader: but it will undoubtedly appear to many persons that
I have not fulfilled the terms of an engagement thus voluntarily contracted.
They who have been accustomed to the gaudiness and inane phraseology
of many modern writers, if they persist in reading this book to its conclusion, will, no doubt, frequently have to struggle with feelings of
strangeness and awkwardness: they will look round for poetry, and will
be induced to inquire by what species of courtesy these attempts can be
permitted to assume that title. I hope therefore the reader will not
censure me for attempting to state what I have proposed to myself to
perform; and also (as far as the limits of a preface will permit) to explain
some of the chief reasons which have determined me in the choice of my
purpose: that at least he may be spared any unpleasant feeling of disappointment, and that I myself may be protected from one of the most
dishonourable accusations which can be brought against an Author;
namely, that of an indolence which prevents him from endeavouring to

ascertain what is his duty, or, when his duty is ascertained, prevents him from performing it.

The principal object, then, proposed in these Poems was to choose incidents and situations from common life, and to relate or describe them, throughout, as far as was possible in a selection of language really used by men, and, at the same time, to throw over them a certain colouring of imagination, whereby ordinary things should be presented to the mind in an unusual aspect; and, further, and above all, to make these incidents and situations interesting by tracing in them, truly though not ostentatiously, the primary laws of our nature: chiefly, as far as regards the manner in which we associate ideas in a state of excitement. Humble and rustic life was generally chosen, because, in that condition, the essential passions of the heart find a better soil in which they can attain their maturity, are less under restraint, and speak a plainer and more emphatic language; because in that condition of life our elementary feelings coexist in a state of greater simplicity, and, consequently, may be more accurately contemplated, and more forcibly communicated; because the manners of rural life germinate from those elementary feelings, and, from the necessary character of rural occupations, are more easily comprehended, and are more durable; and, lastly, because in that condition the passions of men are incorporated with the beautiful and permanent forms of nature. The language, too, of these men has been adopted (purified indeed from what appear to be its real defects, from all lasting and rational causes of dislike or disgust) because such men hourly communicate with the best objects from which the best part of language is originally derived; and because, from their rank in society and the sameness and narrow circle of their intercourse, being less under the influence of social vanity, they convey their feelings and notions in simple and unelaborated expressions. Accordingly, such a language, arising out of repeated experience and regular feelings, is a more permanent, and a far more philosophical language, than that which is frequently substituted for it by Poets, who think that they are conferring honour upon themselves and their art, in proportion as they separate themselves from the sympathies of men, and indulge in arbitrary and capricious habits of expression, in order to furnish food for fickle tastes, and fickle appetites, of their own creation.[1]

I cannot, however, be insensible to the present outcry against the triviality and meanness, both of thought and language, which some of my contemporaries have occasionally introduced into their metrical compositions; and I acknowledge that this defect, where it exists, is more

---

[1] It is worth while here to observe, that the affecting parts of Chaucer are almost always expressed in language pure and universally intelligible even to this day.

dishonourable to the Writer's own character than false refinement or arbitrary innovation, though I should contend at the same time, that it is far less pernicious in the sum of its consequences. From such verses the Poems in these volumes will be found distinguished at least by one mark of difference, that each of them has a worthy *purpose*. Not that I always began to write with a distinct purpose formally conceived; but habits of meditation have, I trust, so prompted and regulated my feelings, that my descriptions of such objects as strongly excite those feelings, will be found to carry along with them a *purpose*. If this opinion be erroneous, I can have little right to the name of a Poet. For all good poetry is the spontaneous overflow of powerful feelings: and though this be true, Poems to which any value can be attached were never produced on any variety of subjects but by a man who, being possessed of more than usual organic sensibility, had also thought long and deeply. For our continued influxes of feeling are modified and directed by our thoughts, which are indeed the representatives of all our past feelings; and, as by contemplating the relation of these general representatives to each other, we discover what is really important to men, so, by the repetition and continuance of this act, our feelings will be connected with important subjects, till at length, if we be originally possessed of much sensibility, such habits of mind will be produced, that, by obeying blindly and mechanically the impulses of those habits, we shall describe objects, and utter sentiments, of such a nature, and in such connexion with each other, that the understanding of the Reader must necessarily be in some degree enlightened, and his affections strengthened and purified.

It has been said that each of these poems has a purpose. Another circumstance must be mentioned which distinguishes these Poems from the popular Poetry of the day; it is this, that the feeling therein developed gives importance to the action and situation, and not the action and situation to the feeling.

A sense of false modesty shall not prevent me from asserting, that the Reader's attention is pointed to this mark of distinction, far less for the sake of these particular Poems than from the general importance of the subject. The subject is indeed important! For the human mind is capable of being excited without the application of gross and violent stimulants; and he must have a very faint perception of its beauty and dignity who does not know this, and who does not further know, that one being is elevated above another, in proportion as he possesses this capability. It has therefore appeared to me, that to endeavour to produce or enlarge this capability is one of the best services in which, at any period, a Writer can be engaged; but this service, excellent at all times, is especially so at the present day. For a multitude of causes, unknown to former times, are now acting with a combined force to blunt the discriminating powers of the mind, and, unfitting it for all voluntary exertion, to reduce it to a state of almost savage torpor. The most effective of these causes are the great national events which are daily taking place, and the increasing accumulation of men in cities, where the uniformity of their occupations produces a craving for extraordinary incident, which the rapid communication of intelligence hourly gratifies. To this tendency of life and manners the literature and theatrical exhibitions of the country have conformed themselves. The invaluable works of our elder writers, I had almost said the works of Shakespeare and Milton, are driven into neglect by frantic novels, sickly and stupid German Tragedies, and deluges of idle and extravagant stories in verse.— When I think upon this degrading thirst after outrageous stimulation, I am almost ashamed to have spoken of the feeble endeavour made in these volumes to counteract it; and, reflecting upon the magnitude of the general evil, I should be oppressed with no dishonourable melancholy, had I not a deep impression of certain inherent and indestructible qualities of the human mind, and likewise of certain powers in the great and permanent objects that act upon it, which are equally inherent and indestructible; and were there not added to this impression a belief, that the time is approaching when the evil will be systematically opposed, by men of greater powers, and with far more distinguished success.

Having dwelt thus long on the subjects and aim of these Poems, I shall request the Reader's permission to apprise him of a few circumstances relating to their *style*, in order, among other reasons, that he may not censure me for not having performed what I never attempted. The Reader will find that personifications of abstract ideas rarely occur in these volumes; and are utterly rejected, as an ordinary device to elevate the style, and raise it above prose. My purpose was to imitate, and, as far as possible, to adopt the very language of men; and assuredly such personifications do not make any natural or regular part of that language. They are, indeed, a figure of speech occasionally prompted by passion, and I have made use of them as such; but have endeavoured utterly to reject them as a mechanical device of style, or as a family language which Writers in metre seem to lay claim to by prescription. I have wished to keep the Reader in the company of flesh and blood, persuaded that by so doing I shall interest him. Others who pursue a different track will interest him likewise; I do not interfere with their claim, but wish to prefer a claim of my own. There will also be found in these volumes little of what is usually called poetic diction; as much pains has been taken to avoid it as is ordinarily taken to produce it; this has been done for the reason already alleged, to bring my language near to the language of men; and further, because the pleasure which I have proposed to myself to impart, is of a kind very different from that which is supposed by many persons to be the proper object of poetry. Without being culpably particular, I do not know how to give my Reader a more exact notion of the style in which it was my wish and intention to write, than by informing him that I have at all times endeavoured to look steadily at my subject; consequently, there is I hope in these Poems little falsehood of description, and my ideas are expressed in language fitted to their respective importance. Something must have been gained by this practice, as it is friendly to one property of all good poetry, namely, good sense: but it has necessarily cut me off from a large portion of phrases and figures of speech which from father to son have long been regarded as the common inheritance of Poets. I have also thought it expedient to restrict myself still further, having abstained from the use of many expressions, in themselves proper and beautiful, but which have been foolishly repeated by bad Poets, till such feelings of disgust are connected with them as it is scarcely possible by any art of association to overpower.

If in a poem there should be found a series of lines, or even a single line, in which the language, though naturally arranged, and according to the strict laws of metre, does not differ from that of prose, there is a numerous class of critics, who, when they stumble upon these prosaisms, as they call them, imagine that they have made a notable discovery, and exult over the Poet as over a man ignorant of his own profession. Now these men would establish a canon of criticism which the Reader will conclude he must utterly reject, if he wishes to be pleased with these volumes. And it would be a most easy task to prove to him, that not only the language of a large portion of every good poem, even of the most elevated character, must necessarily, except with reference to the metre, in no respect differ from that of good prose, but likewise that some of the most interesting parts of the best poems will be found to be strictly the language of prose when prose is well written. The truth of this assertion might be demonstrated by innumerable passages from almost all the poetical writings, even of Milton himself. To illustrate the subject in a general manner, I will here adduce a short composition of Gray, who was at the head of those who, by their reasonings, have attempted to widen the space of separation betwixt Prose and Metrical composition, and was more than any other man curiously elaborate in the structure of his own poetic diction.

> In vain to me the smiling mornings shine,
> And reddening Phœbus lifts his golden fire:
> The birds in vain their amorous descant join,
> Or cheerful fields resume their green attire.

These ears, alas! for other notes repine;
*A different object do these eyes require:*
*My lonely anguish melts no heart but mine:*
*And in my breast the imperfect joys expire:*
Yet morning smiles the busy race to cheer,
And new-born pleasure brings to happier men;
The fields to all their wonted tribute bear;
To warm their little loves the birds complain.
*I fruitless mourn to him that cannot hear,*
*And weep the more because I weep in vain.*

It will easily be perceived, that the only part of this Sonnet which is of any value is the lines printed in Italics; it is equally obvious, that, except in the rhyme, and in the use of the single word 'fruitless' for fruitlessly, which is so far a defect, the language of these lines does in no respect differ from that of prose.

By the foregoing quotation it has been shown that the language of Prose may yet be well adapted to Poetry; and it was previously asserted, that a large portion of the language of every good poem can in no respect differ from that of good Prose. We will go further. It may be safely affirmed, that there neither is, nor can be, any *essential* difference between the language of prose and metrical composition. We are fond of tracing the resemblance between Poetry and Painting, and, accordingly, we call them Sisters: but where shall we find bonds of connexion sufficiently strict to typify the affinity betwixt metrical and prose composition? They both speak by and to the same organs; the bodies in which both of them are clothed may be said to be of the same substance, their affections are kindred, and almost identical, not necessarily differing even in degree; Poetry[2] sheds no tears 'such as Angels weep,' but natural and human tears; she can boast of no celestial ichor that distinguishes her vital juices from those of prose; the same human blood circulates through the veins of them both.

If it be affirmed that rhyme and metrical arrangement of themselves constitute a distinction which overturns what has just been said on the strict affinity of metrical language with that of prose, and paves the way for other artificial distinctions which the mind voluntarily admits, I answer that the language of such Poetry as is here recommended is, as far as is

---

[2] I here use the word 'Poetry' (though against my own judgement) as opposed to the word Prose, and synonymous with metrical composition. But much confusion has been introduced into criticism by this contradistinction of Poetry and Prose, instead of the more philosophical one of Poetry and Matter of Fact, or Science. The only strict antithesis to Prose is Metre; nor is this, in truth, a *strict* antithesis, because lines and passages of metre so naturally occur in writing prose, that it would be scarcely possible to avoid them, even were it desirable.

possible, a selection of the language really spoken by men; that this selection, wherever it is made with true taste and feeling, will of itself form a distinction far greater than would at first be imagined, and will entirely separate the composition from the vulgarity and meanness of ordinary life; and, if metre be superadded thereto, I believe that a dissimilitude will be produced altogether sufficient for the gratification of a rational mind. What other distinction would we have? Whence is it to come? And where is it to exist? Not, surely, where the Poet speaks through the mouths of his characters: it cannot be necessary here, either for elevation of style, or any of its supposed ornaments: for, if the Poet's subject be judiciously chosen, it will naturally, and upon fit occasion, lead him to passions the language of which, if selected truly and judiciously, must necessarily be dignified and variegated, and alive with metaphors and figures. I forbear to speak of an incongruity which would shock the intelligent Reader, should the Poet interweave any foreign splendour of his own with that which the passion naturally suggests: it is sufficient to say that such addition is unnecessary. And, surely, it is more probable that those passages, which with propriety abound with metaphors and figures, will have their due effect, if, upon other occasions where the passions are of a milder character, the style also be subdued and temperate.

But, as the pleasure which I hope to give by the Poems now presented to the Reader must depend entirely on just notions upon this subject, and, as it is in itself of high importance to our taste and moral feelings, I cannot content myself with these detached remarks. And if, in what I am about to say, it shall appear to some that my labour is unnecessary, and that I am like a man fighting a battle without enemies, such persons may be reminded, that, whatever be the language outwardly holden by men, a practical faith in the opinions which I am wishing to establish is almost unknown. If my conclusions are admitted, and carried as far as they must be carried if admitted at all, our judgements concerning the works of the greatest Poets both ancient and modern will be far different from what they are at present, both when we praise, and when we censure: and our moral feelings influencing and influenced by these judgements will, I believe, be corrected and purified.

Taking up the subject, then, upon general grounds, let me ask, what is meant by the word Poet? What is a Poet? To whom does he address himself? And what language is to be expected from him?—He is a man speaking to men: a man, it is true, endowed with more lively sensibility, more enthusiasm and tenderness, who has a greater knowledge of human nature, and a more comprehensive soul, than are supposed to be common among mankind; a man pleased with his own passions and volitions, and who rejoices more than other men in the spirit of life that is in him;

delighting to contemplate similar volitions and passions as manifested in
the goings-on of the Universe, and habitually impelled to create them
where he does not find them.    To these qualities he has added a disposition to be affected more than other men by absent things as if they were
present; an ability of conjuring up in himself passions, which are indeed
far from being the same as those produced by real events, yet (especially
in those parts of the general sympathy which are pleasing and delightful)
do more nearly resemble the passions produced by real events, than anything which, from the motions of their own minds merely, other men are
accustomed to feel in themselves:—whence, and from practice, he has
acquired a greater readiness and power in expressing what he thinks and
feels, and especially those thoughts and feelings which, by his own choice,
or from the structure of his own mind, arise in him without immediate
external excitement.

But whatever portion of this faculty we may suppose even the greatest
Poet to possess, there cannot be a doubt that the language which it will
suggest to him, must often, in liveliness and truth, fall short of that which
is uttered by men in real life, under the actual pressure of those passions,
certain shadows of which the Poet thus produces, or feels to be produced,
in himself.

However exalted a notion we would wish to cherish of the character of
a Poet, it is obvious, that while he describes and imitates passions, his
employment is in some degree mechanical, compared with the freedom
and power of real and substantial action and suffering.    So that it will be
the wish of the Poet to bring his feelings near to those of the persons whose
feelings he describes, nay, for short spaces of time, perhaps, to let himself
slip into an entire delusion, and even confound and identify his own
feelings with theirs; modifying only the language which is thus suggested
to him by a consideration that he describes for a particular purpose, that
of giving pleasure.    Here, then, he will apply the principle of selection
which has been already insisted upon.    He will depend upon this for
removing what would otherwise be painful or disgusting in the passion;
he will feel that there is no necessity to trick out or to elevate nature: and,
the more industriously he applies this principle, the deeper will be his
faith that no words, which *his* fancy or imagination can suggest, will be to
be compared with those which are the emanations of reality and truth.

But it may be said by those who do not object to the general spirit of
these remarks, that, as it is impossible for the Poet to produce upon all
occasions language as exquisitely fitted for the passion as that which the
real passion itself suggests, it is proper that he should consider himself as
in the situation of a translator, who does not scruple to substitute excellencies of another kind for those which are unattainable by him; and

endeavours occasionally to surpass his original, in order to make some amends for the general inferiority to which he feels that he must submit. But this would be to encourage idleness and unmanly despair. Further, it is the language of men who speak of what they do not understand; who talk of Poetry as of a matter of amusement and idle pleasure; who will converse with us as gravely about a *taste* for Poetry, as they express it, as if it were a thing as indifferent as a taste for rope-dancing, or Frontiniac or Sherry. Aristotle, I have been told, has said, that Poetry is the most philosophic of all writing: it is so: its object is truth, not individual and local, but general, and operative; not standing upon external testimony, but carried alive into the heart by passion; truth which is its own testimony, which gives competence and confidence to the tribunal to which it appeals, and receives them from the same tribunal. Poetry is the image of man and nature. The obstacles which stand in the way of the fidelity of the Biographer and Historian, and of their consequent utility, are incalculably greater than those which are to be encountered by the Poet who comprehends the dignity of his art. The Poet writes under one restriction only, namely, the necessity of giving immediate pleasure to a human Being possessed of that information which may be expected from him, not as a lawyer, a physician, a mariner, an astronomer, or a natural philosopher, but as a Man. Except this one restriction, there is no object standing between the Poet and the image of things; between this, and the Biographer and Historian, there are a thousand.

Nor let this necessity of producing immediate pleasure be considered as a degradation of the Poet's art. It is far otherwise. It is an acknowledgement of the beauty of the universe, an acknowledgement the more sincere, because not formal, but indirect; it is a task light and easy to him who looks at the world in the spirit of love: further, it is a homage paid to the native and naked dignity of man, to the grand elementary principle of pleasure, by which he knows, and feels, and lives, and moves. We have no sympathy but what is propagated by pleasure: I would not be misunderstood; but wherever we sympathize with pain, it will be found that the sympathy is produced and carried on by subtle combinations with pleasure. We have no knowledge, that is, no general principles drawn from the contemplation of particular facts, but what has been built up by pleasure, and exists in us by pleasure alone. The Man of science, the Chemist and Mathematician, whatever difficulties and disgusts they may have had to struggle with, know and feel this. However painful may be the objects with which the Anatomist's knowledge is connected, he feels that his knowledge is pleasure; and where he has no pleasure he has no knowledge. What then does the Poet? He considers man and the objects that surround him as acting and re-acting upon each other, so as to produce an infinite complexity of pain and pleasure; he considers man in his own nature and in his ordinary life as contemplating this with a certain quantity of immediate knowledge, with certain convictions, intuitions, and deductions, which from habit acquire the quality of intuitions; he considers him as looking upon this complex scene of ideas and sensations, and finding everywhere objects that immediately excite in him sympathies which, from the necessities of his nature, are accompanied by an overbalance of enjoyment.

To this knowledge which all men carry about with them, and to these sympathies in which, without any other discipline than that of our daily life, we are fitted to take delight, the Poet principally directs his attention. He considers man and nature as essentially adapted to each other, and the mind of man as naturally the mirror of the fairest and most interesting properties of nature. And thus the Poet, prompted by this feeling of pleasure, which accompanies him through the whole course of his studies, converses with general nature, with affections akin to those, which, through labour and length of time, the Man of science has raised up in himself, by conversing with those particular parts of nature which are the objects of his studies. The knowledge both of the Poet and the Man of science is pleasure; but the knowledge of the one cleaves to us as a necessary part of our existence, our natural and unalienable inheritance; the other is a personal and individual acquisition, slow to come to us, and by no habitual and direct sympathy connecting us with our fellow-beings. The Man of science seeks truth as a remote and unknown benefactor; he cherishes and loves it in his solitude: the Poet, singing a song in which all human beings join with him, rejoices in the presence of truth as our visible and hourly companion. Poetry is the breath and finer spirit of all knowledge; it is the impassioned expression which is in the countenance of all Science. Emphatically may it be said of the Poet, as.Shakespeare hath said of man, 'that he looks before and after.' He is the rock of defence for human nature; an upholder and preserver, carrying everywhere with him relationship and love. In spite of difference of soil and climate, of language and manners, of laws and customs: in spite of things silently gone out of mind, and things violently destroyed; the Poet binds together by passion and knowledge the vast empire of human society, as it is spread over the whole earth, and over all time. The objects of the Poet's thoughts are everywhere; though the eyes and senses of man are, it is true, his favourite guides, yet he will follow wheresoever he can find an atmosphere of sensation in which to move his wings. Poetry is the first and last of all knowledge—it is as immortal as the heart of man. If the labours of Men of science should ever create any material revolution, direct or indirect, in our condition, and in the impressions which we habitually receive, the Poet will sleep then no more than at present; he will be ready to follow the steps of the Man of science, not only in those general indirect effects, but he will be at his side, carrying sensation into the midst of the objects of the science itself. The remotest discoveries of the Chemist, the Botanist, or Mineralogist, will be as proper objects of the Poet's art as any upon which it can be employed, if the time should ever come when these things shall be familiar to us, and the relations under which they are contemplated by the followers of these respective sciences shall be manifestly and palpably material to us as enjoying and suffering beings. If the time should ever come when what is now called science, thus familiarized to men, shall be ready to put on, as it were, a form of flesh and blood, the Poet will lend his divine spirit to aid the trans-figuration, and will welcome the Being thus produced, as a dear and genuine inmate of the household of man.—It is not, then, to be supposed that any one, who holds that sublime notion of Poetry which I have attempted to convey, will break in upon the sanctity and truth of his pictures by transitory and accidental ornaments, and endeavour to excite admiration of himself by arts, the necessity of which must manifestly depend upon the assumed meanness of his subject.

What has been thus far said applies to Poetry in general; but especially to those parts of composition where the Poet speaks through the mouths of his characters; and upon this point it appears to authorize the con-clusion that there are few persons of good sense, who would not allow that the dramatic parts of composition are defective, in proportion as they deviate from the real language of nature, and are coloured by a diction of the Poet's own, either peculiar to him as an individual Poet or belonging simply to Poets in general; to a body of men who, from the circumstance of their compositions being in metre, it is expected will employ a particular language.

It is not, then, in the dramatic parts of composition that we look for this distinction of language; but still it may be proper and necessary where the Poets speaks to us in his own person and character. To this I answer by referring the Reader to the description before given of a Poet. Among the qualities there enumerated as principally conducing to form a Poet, is implied nothing differing in kind from other men, but only in degree. The sum of what was said is, that the Poet is chiefly distinguished from other men by a greater promptness to think and feel without immediate external excitement, and a greater power in expressing such thoughts and feelings as are produced in him in that manner. But these passions and thoughts and feelings are the general passions and thoughts and feelings of men. And with what are they connected? Undoubtedly with our moral sentiments and animal sensations, and with the causes which excite these; with the operations of the elements, and the appearances of the visible universe; with storm and sunshine, with the revolutions of the seasons, with cold and heat, with loss of friends and kindred, with injuries and resentments, gratitude and hope, with fear and sorrow. These, and the like, are the sensations and objects which the Poet describes, as they are the sensations of other men, and the objects which interest them. The Poet thinks and feels in the spirit of human passions. How, then, can his language differ in any material degree from that of all other men who feel vividly and see clearly? It might be *proved* that it is impossible. But supposing that this were not the case, the Poet might then be allowed to use a peculiar language when expressing his feelings for his own gratification, or that of men like himself. But Poets do not write for Poets alone, but for men. Unless therefore we are advocates for that admiration which subsists upon ignorance, and that pleasure which arises from hearing what we do not understand, the Poet must descend from this supposed height; and, in order to excite rational sympathy, he must express himself as other men express themselves. To this it may be added, that while he is only selecting from the real language of men, or, which amounts to the same thing, composing accurately in the spirit of such selection, he is treading upon safe ground, and we know what we are to expect from him. Our feelings are the same with respect to metre; for, as it may be proper to remind the Reader, the distinction of metre is regular and uniform, and not, like that which is produced by what is usually called POETIC DICTION, arbitrary, and subject to infinite caprices upon which no calculation whatever can be made. In the one case, the Reader is utterly at the mercy of the Poet, respecting what imagery or diction he may choose to connect with the passion; whereas, in the other, the metre obeys certain laws, to which the Poet and Reader both willingly submit because they are certain, and because no interference is made by them with the passion, but such as the concurring testimony of ages has shown to heighten and improve the pleasure which co-exists with it.

It will now be proper to answer an obvious question, namely, Why, professing these opinions, have I written in verse? To this, in addition to such answer as is included in what has been already said, I reply, in the first place, Because, however I may have restricted myself, there is still left open to me what confessedly constitutes the most valuable object of all writing, whether in prose or verse; the great and universal passions of men, the most general and interesting of their occupations, and the entire world of nature before me—to supply endless combinations of forms and imagery. Now, supposing for a moment that whatever is interesting in these objects may be as vividly described in prose, why should I be condemned for attempting to superadd to such description the charm which, by the consent of all nations, is acknowledged to exist in metrical language?   To this, by such as are yet unconvinced, it may be answered that a very small part of the pleasure given by Poetry depends upon the metre, and that it is injudicious to write in metre, unless it be accompanied with the other artificial distinctions of style with which metre is usually accompanied, and that, by such deviation, more will be lost from the shock which will thereby be given to the Reader's associations than will be counterbalanced by any pleasure which he can derive from the general power of numbers.   In answer to those who still contend for the necessity of accompanying metre with certain appropriate colours of style in order to the accomplishment of its appropriate end, and who also, in my opinion, greatly underrate the power of metre in itself, it might, perhaps, as far as relates to these Volumes, have been almost sufficient to observe, that poems are extant, written upon more humble subjects, and in a still more naked and simple style, which have continued to give pleasure from generation to generation.   Now, if nakedness and simplicity be a defect, the fact here mentioned affords a strong presumption that poems some-what less naked and simple are capable of affording pleasure at the present day; and, what I wished *chiefly* to attempt, at present, was to justify myself for having written under the impression of this belief.

But various causes might be pointed out why, when the style is manly, and the subject of some importance, words metrically arranged will long continue to impart such a pleasure to mankind as he who proves the extent of that pleasure will be desirous to impart.   The end of Poetry is to produce excitement in co-existence with an overbalance of pleasure; but, by the supposition, excitement is an unusual and irregular state of the mind; ideas and feelings do not, in that state, succeed each other in accustomed order.   If the words, however, by which this excitement is produced be in themselves powerful, or the images and feelings have an undue proportion of pain connected with them, there is some danger that the excitement may be carried beyond its proper bounds.   Now the co-presence of something regular, something to which the mind has been accustomed in various moods and in a less excited state, cannot but have great efficacy in tempering and restraining the passion by an intertexture of ordinary feeling, and of feeling not strictly and necessarily connected with the passion.   This is unquestionably true; and hence, though the opinion will at first appear paradoxical, from the tendency of metre to divest language, in a certain degree, of its reality, and thus to throw a sort of half-consciousness of unsubstantial existence over the whole com-position, there can be little doubt but that more pathetic situations and sentiments, that is, those which have a greater proportion of pain con-nected with them, may be endured in metrical composition, especially in rhyme, than in prose. The metre of the old ballads is very artless; yet they contain many passages which would illustrate this opinion; and, I hope, if the following Poems be attentively perused, similar instances will be found in them. This opinion may be further illustrated by appealing to the Reader's own experience of the reluctance with which he comes to the re-perusal of the distressful parts of *Clarissa Harlowe,* or *The Gamester;* while Shakespeare's writings, in the most pathetic scenes, never act upon us, as pathetic, beyond the bounds of pleasure—an effect which, in a much greater degree than might at first be imagined, is to be ascribed to small, but continual and regular impulses of pleasurable surprise from the metrical arrangement.—On the other hand (what it must be allowed will much more frequently happen) if the Poet's words should be incommensurate with the passion, and inadequate to raise the Reader to a height of desirable excitement, then (unless the Poet's choice of his metre has been grossly injudicious), in the feelings of pleasure which the Reader has been accustomed to connect with metre in general, and in the feeling, whether cheerful or melancholy, which he has been accustomed to connect with that particular movement of metre, there will be found something which will greatly contribute to impart passion to the words, and to effect the complex end which the Poet proposes to himself.

If I had undertaken a SYSTEMATIC defence of the theory here maintained, it would have been my duty to develop the various causes upon which the pleasure received from metrical language depends. Among the chief of these causes is to be reckoned a principle which must be well known to those who have made any of the Arts the object of accurate reflection; namely, the pleasure which the mind derives from the perception of similitude in dissimilitude. This principle is the great spring of the activity of our minds, and their chief feeder. From this principle the direction of the sexual appetite, and all the passions connected with it, take their origin: it is the life of our ordinary conversation; and upon the accuracy with which similitude in dissimilitude, and dissimilitude in similitude are perceived, depend our taste and our moral feelings. It would not be a useless employment to apply this principle to the consideration of metre, and to show that metre is hence enabled to afford much pleasure, and to point out in what manner that pleasure is produced. But my limits will not permit me to enter upon this subject, and I must content myself with a general summary.

I have said that poetry is the spontaneous overflow of powerful feelings: it takes its origin from emotion recollected in tranquillity: the emotion is contemplated till, by a species of reaction, the tranquillity gradually disappears, and an emotion, kindred to that which was before the subject of contemplation, is gradually produced, and does itself actually exist in the mind. In this mood successful composition generally begins, and in a mood similar to this it is carried on; but the emotion, of whatever kind, and in whatever degree, from various causes, is qualified by various pleasures, so that in describing any passions whatsoever, which are voluntarily described, the mind will, upon the whole, be in a state of enjoyment. If Nature be thus cautious to preserve in a state of enjoyment a being so employed, the Poet ought to profit by the lesson held forth to him, and ought especially to take care, that, whatever passions he communicates to his Reader, those passions, if his Reader's mind be sound and vigorous, should always be accompanied with an overbalance of pleasure. Now the music of harmonious metrical language, the sense of difficulty overcome, and the blind association of pleasure which has been previously received from works of rhyme or metre of the same or similar construction, an indistinct perception perpetually renewed of language closely resembling that of real life, and yet, in the circumstance of metre, differing from it so widely—all these imperceptibly make up a complex feeling of delight, which is of the most important use in tempering the painful feeling always found intermingled with powerful descriptions of the deeper passions. This effect is always produced in pathetic and impassioned poetry; while, in lighter compositions, the ease and gracefulness with which the Poet manages his numbers are themselves confessedly a principal source of the gratification of the Reader. All that it is *necessary* to say, however, upon this subject, may be effected by affirming, what few persons will deny, that, of two descriptions, either of passions, manners, or characters, each of them equally well executed, the one in prose and the other in verse, the verse will be read a hundred times where the prose is read once.

Having thus explained a few of my reasons for writing in verse, and why I have chosen subjects from common life, and endeavoured to bring my language near to the real language of men, if I have been too minute in pleading my own cause, I have at the same time been treating a subject of general interest; and for this reason a few words shall be added with reference solely to these particular poems, and to some defects which will probably be found in them. I am sensible that my associations must have sometimes been particular instead of general, and that, consequently, giving to things a false importance, I may have sometimes written upon unworthy subjects; but I am less apprehensive on this account, than that my language may frequently have suffered from those arbitrary connexions of feelings and ideas with particular words and phrases, from which no man can altogether protect himself. Hence I have no doubt, that, in some instances, feelings, even of the ludicrous, may be given to my Readers by expressions which appeared to me tender and pathetic. Such faulty expressions, were I convinced they were faulty at present, and that they must necessarily continue to be so, I would willingly take all reasonable pains to correct. But it is dangerous to make these alterations on the simple authority of a few individuals, or even of certain classes of men; for where the understanding of an Author is not convinced, or his feelings altered, this cannot be done without great injury to himself: for his own feelings are his stay and support; and, if he set them aside in one instance, he may be induced to repeat this act till his mind shall lose all confidence in itself, and become utterly debilitated. To this it may be added, that the critic ought never to forget that he is himself exposed to the same errors as the Poet, and, perhaps, in a much greater degree: for there can be no presumption in saying of most readers, that it is not probable they will be so well acquainted with the various stages of meaning through which words have passed, or with the fickleness or stability of the relations of particular ideas to each other; and, above all, since they are so much less interested in the subject, they may decide lightly and carelessly.

Long as the Reader has been detained, I hope he will permit me to caution him against a mode of false criticism which has been applied to Poetry, in which the language closely resembles that of life and nature. Such verses have been triumphed over in parodies, of which Dr. Johnson's stanza is a fair specimen:—

> I put my hat upon my head
> And walked into the Strand,
> And there I met another man
> Whose hat was in his hand.

Immediately under these lines let us place one of the most justly admired stanzas of the 'Babes in the Wood.'

> These pretty Babes with hand in hand
> Went wandering up and down;
> But never more they saw the Man
> Approaching from the Town.

In both these stanzas the words, and the order of the words, in no respect differ from the most unimpassioned conversation. There are words in both, for example, 'the Strand,' and 'the Town,' connected with none but the most familiar ideas; yet the one stanza we admit as admirable, and the other as a fair example of the superlatively contemptible. Whence arises this difference? Not from the metre, not from the language, not from the order of the words; but the *matter* expressed in Dr. Johnson's stanza is contemptible. The proper method of treating trivial and simple verses, to which Dr. Johnson's stanza would be a fair parallelism, is not to say, this is a bad kind of poetry, or, this is not poetry; but, this wants sense; it is neither interesting in itself, nor can *lead* to anything interesting; the images neither originate in that sane state of feeling which arises out of thought, nor can excite thought or feeling in the Reader.    This is the only sensible manner of dealing with such verses. Why trouble yourself about the species till you have previously decided upon the genus?    Why take pains to prove that an ape is not a Newton, when it is self-evident that he is not a man?

One request I must make of my reader, which is, that in judging these Poems he would decide by his own feelings genuinely, and not by reflection upon what will probably be the judgement of others.    How common is it to hear a person say, I myself do not object to this style of composition, or this or that expression, but, to such and such classes of people it will appear mean or ludicrous!    This mode of criticism, so destructive of all sound unadulterated judgement, is almost universal: let the Reader then abide, independently, by his own feelings, and, if he finds himself affected, let him not suffer such conjectures to interfere with his pleasure.

If an Author, by any single composition, has impressed us with respect for his talents, it is useful to consider this as affording a presumption, that on other occasions where we have been displeased, he, nevertheless, may not have written ill or absurdly; and further, to give him so much credit for this one composition as may induce us to review what has displeased us, with more care than we should otherwise have bestowed upon it. This is not only an act of justice, but, in our decisions upon poetry especially, may conduce, in a high degree, to the improvement of our own taste; for an *accurate* taste in poetry, and in all the other arts, as Sir Joshua Reynolds has observed, is an *acquired* talent, which can only be produced by thought and a long continued intercourse with the best models of composition.    This is mentioned, not with so ridiculous a purpose as to prevent the most inexperienced Reader from judging for himself (I have already said that I wish him to judge for himself), but merely to temper the rashness of decision, and to suggest, that, if Poetry be a subject on which much time has not been bestowed, the judgement may be erroneous; and that, in many cases, it necessarily will be so.

Nothing would, I know, have so effectually contributed to further the end which I have in view, as to have shown of what kind the pleasure is, and how that pleasure is produced, which is confessedly produced by metrical composition essentially different from that which I have here endeavoured to recommend: for the Reader will say that he has been pleased by such composition; and what more can be done for him?    The power of any art is limited; and he will suspect, that, if it be proposed to furnish him with new friends, that can be only upon condition of his abandoning his old friends.    Besides, as I have said, the Reader is himself conscious of the pleasure which he has received from such composition, composition to which he has peculiarly attached the endearing name of Poetry; and all men feel an habitual gratitude, and something of an honourable bigotry, for the objects which have long continued to please them: we not only wish to be pleased, but to be pleased in that particular way in which we have been accustomed to be pleased.    There is in these feelings enough to resist a host of arguments; and I should be the less able to combat them successfully, as I am willing to allow, that, in order entirely to enjoy the Poetry which I am recommending, it would be necessary to give up much of what is ordinarily enjoyed.    But, would my limits have permitted me to point out how this pleasure is produced, many obstacles might have been removed, and the Reader assisted in perceiving that the powers of language are not so limited as he may suppose; and that it is possible for poetry to give other enjoyments, of a purer, more lasting, and more exquisite nature.    This part of the subject has not been altogether neglected, but it has not been so much my present aim to prove, that the interest excited by some other kinds of poetry is less vivid, and less worthy of the nobler powers of the mind, as to offer reasons for presuming, that if my purpose were fulfilled, a species of poetry would be produced, which is genuine poetry; in its nature well adapted to interest mankind permanently, and likewise important in the multiplicity and quality of its moral relations.

From what has been said, and from a perusal of the Poems, the Reader will be able clearly to perceive the object which I had in view: he will determine how far it has been attained; and, what is a much more important question, whether it be worth attaining: and upon the decision of these two questions will rest my claim to the approbation of the Public.

# Selections from
# *Biographia Literaria*

## 1817

*Coleridge's definition of "a legitimate poem" in Chapter XIV stresses the idea of its organic unity, harkening back to Aristotle. In his "Shakespeare Lectures," Coleridge distinguishes "organic" from "mechanic" form: "The form is mechanic, when on any given material we impress a pre-determined form, not necessarily arising out of the properties of the material;—as when to a mass of wet clay we give whatever shape we wish it to retain when hardened. The organic form, on the other hand, is innate; it shapes, as it develops, itself from within, and the fulness of its development is one and the same with the perfection of its outward form. Such as the life is, such is the form."*

*Given this theory, Coleridge's objection to Wordsworth's statement that meter is a "superadded" element is clearly understood. Concerned with questions of form, Coleridge also takes issue with Wordsworth's blurring of the distinction between poetry and prose, for what makes a poem is the immediate pleasure that it communicates, not its ultimate truth. (He raises a further objection, to Wordsworth's theories about diction, in Chapter XVII.) Thus far, Coleridge is the formal critic, defining and differentiating the particular qualities of a poem.*

*But when he equates the questions, "What is poetry?" and "What is a poet?", he moves into the realm of psychological criticism. The discussion of Fancy and Imagination in Chapter XIII is his attempt to distinguish and define those "faculties" which are the source of all mental activity, including the creative. It should be said here that*

From *Biographia Literaria*, ed. John Shawcross; Oxford: The Clarendon Press, 1907. A selection from Chapter XIII has been placed between Chapters XIV and XV in an attempt at greater clarity.

*Coleridge scholars and critics are still not in unanimous agreement over the interpretation of some of the knottier passages. However, these terms and others, such as "the poetic genius" and "the whole soul of man," imply a psychological model in which various faculties are arranged in a hierarchy of value, all in their totality, represented and subordinated, comprising the whole soul of man. Ideally, a legitimate poem is thus the externalization of the poetic genius; the poet's soul is expressed in his poem. "Such as the life is, such is the form."*

*Coleridge as the practical critic is seen at work in Chapter XV, and the obvious question to be considered is the extent to which the specific comments on Shakespeare derive from his theories. But even here Coleridge introduces some new theoretical considerations, such as the necessary "aloofness" of the poet from his subject matter (a concept developed further by later critics). Despite the rather disordered and rambling sequence of the* Biographia Literaria, *Coleridge clearly exemplifies the shift in critical focus that is taking place, from the poem to the character of the poet, from the rules and the conventions of poetry to the activity of poem-making.*

## XIV

*Occasion of the Lyrical Ballads, and the objects originally proposed—Preface to the second edition—The ensuing controversy, its causes and acrimony—Philosophic definitions of a poem and poetry with scholia.*

DURING THE first year that Mr. Wordsworth and I were neighbours, our conversations turned frequently on the two cardinal points of poetry, the power of exciting the sympathy of the reader by a faithful adherence to the truth of nature, and the power of giving the interest of novelty by the modifying colors of imagination. The sudden charm, which accidents of light and shade, which moon-light or sun-set diffused over a known and familiar landscape, appeared to represent the practicability of combining both. These are the poetry of nature. The thought suggested itself (to which of us I do not recollect) that a series of poems might be composed of two sorts. In the one, the incidents and agents were to be, in part at least, supernatural; and the excellence aimed at was to consist in the interesting of the affections by the dramatic truth of such emotions, as would naturally accompany such situations, supposing them real. And real in *this* sense they have been to every human being who, from whatever source of delusion, has at any time believed himself under supernatural agency. For the second class, subjects were to be chosen from ordinary life; the characters and incidents were to be such, as will be found in every village and its vicinity, where there is a meditative and feeling mind to seek after them, or to notice them, when they present themselves.

In this idea originated the plan of the "Lyrical Ballads"; in which it was agreed, that my endeavours should be directed to persons and characters supernatural, or at least romantic; yet so as to transfer from our inward nature a human interest and a semblance of truth sufficient to procure for these shadows of imagination that willing suspension of disbelief for the moment, which constitutes poetic faith. Mr. Wordsworth, on the other hand, was to propose to himself as his object, to give the charm of novelty to things of every day, and to excite a feeling analogous to the supernatural, by awakening the mind's attention from the lethargy of custom, and directing it to the loveliness and the wonders of the world before us; an inexhaustible treasure, but for which, in consequence of the film of familiarity and selfish solicitude we have eyes, yet see not, ears that hear not, and hearts that neither feel nor understand.

With this view I wrote "The Ancient Mariner," and was preparing among other poems, "The Dark Ladie," and the "Christabel," in which I should have more nearly realized my ideal, than I had done in my first attempt. But Mr. Wordsworth's industry had proved so much more successful, and the number of his poems so much greater, that my compositions, instead of forming a balance, appeared rather an interpolation of heterogeneous matter. Mr. Wordsworth added two or three poems written in his own character, in the impassioned, lofty, and sustained diction, which is characteristic of his genius. In this form the "Lyrical Ballads" were published; and were presented by him, as an *experiment*, whether subjects, which from their nature rejected the usual ornaments and extra-colloquial style of poems in general, might not be so managed in the language of ordinary life as to produce the pleasureable interest, which it is the peculiar business of poetry to impart. To the second edition he added a preface of considerable length; in which, notwithstanding some passages of apparently a contrary import, he was understood to contend for the extension of this style to poetry of all kinds, and to reject as vicious and indefensible all phrases and forms of style that were not included in what he (unfortunately, I think, adopting an equivocal expression) called the language of *real* life. From this preface, prefixed to poems in which it was impossible to deny the presence of original genius, however mistaken its direction might be deemed, arose the whole long-continued controversy. For from the conjunction of perceived power with supposed heresy I explain the inveteracy and in some instances, I grieve to say, the acrimonious passions, with which the controversy has been conducted by the assailants.

Had Mr. Wordsworth's poems been the silly, the childish things, which they were for a long time described as being; had they been really distinguished from the compositions of other poets merely by meanness of language and inanity of thought; had they indeed contained nothing more than what is found in the parodies and pretended imitations of them; they must have sunk at once, a dead weight, into the slough of oblivion, and have dragged the preface along with them. But year after year increased the number of Mr. Wordsworth's admirers. They were found too not in the lower classes of the reading public, but chiefly among young men of strong sensibility and meditative minds; and their admiration (inflamed perhaps in some degree by opposition) was distinguished by its intensity, I might almost say, by its *religious* fervor. These facts, and the intellectual energy of the author, which was more or less consciously felt, where it was outwardly and even boisterously denied, meeting with sentiments of aversion to his opinions, and of alarm at their consequences, produced an eddy of criticism, which would of itself have borne up the poems by the violence, with which it whirled them round and round. With many parts of this preface, in the sense attributed to them, and which the words undoubtedly seem to authorize, I never concurred; but on the contrary objected to them as erroneous in principle, and as contradictory (in appearance at least) both to other parts of the same preface, and to the author's own practice in the greater number of the poems themselves. Mr. Wordsworth in his recent collection has, I find, degraded this prefatory disquisition to the end of his second volume, to be read or not at the reader's choice. But he has not, as far as I can discover, announced any change in his poetic creed. At all events, considering it as the source of a controversy, in which I have been honored more than I deserve by the frequent conjunction of my name with his, I think it expedient to declare once for all, in what points I coincide with his opinions, and in what points I altogether differ. But in order to render myself intelligible I must previously, in as few words as possible, explain my ideas, first, of a POEM; and secondly, of POETRY itself, in *kind*, and in *essence*.

The office of philosophical *disquisition* consists in just *distinction;* while it is the priviledge of the philosopher to preserve himself constantly aware, that distinction is not division. In order to obtain adequate notions of any truth, we must intellectually separate its distinguishable parts; and this is the technical *process* of philosophy. But having so done, we must then restore them in our conceptions to the unity, in which they actually co-exist; and this is the *result* of philosophy. A poem contains the same elements as a prose composition; the difference there-fore must consist in a different combination of them, in consequence of a different object being proposed.   According to the difference of the object will be the difference of the combination.   It is possible, that the object may be merely to facilitate the recollection of any given facts or observations by artificial arrangement; and the composition will be a poem, merely because it is distinguished from prose by metre, or by rhyme, or by both conjointly.   In this, the lowest sense, a man might attribute the name of a poem to the well known enumeration of the days in the several months;

> "Thirty days hath September,
> April, June, and November," &c.

and others of the same class and purpose.   And as a particular pleasure is found in anticipating the recurrence of sounds and quantities, all compositions that have this charm super-added, whatever be their contents, *may* be entitled poems.

So much for the superficial *form*.   A difference of object and contents supplies an additional ground of distinction.   The immediate purpose may be the communication of truths; either of truth absolute and demonstrable, as in works of science; or of facts experienced and recorded, as in history.   Pleasure, and that of the highest and most permanent kind, may *result* from the *attainment* of the end; but it is not itself the immediate end.   In other works the communication of pleasure may be the immediate purpose; and though truth, either moral or intellectual, ought to be the *ultimate* end, yet this will distinguish the character of the author, not the class to which the work belongs.   Blest indeed is that state of society, in which the immediate purpose would be baffled by the perversion of the proper ultimate end; in which no charm of diction or imagery could exempt the Bathyllus even of an Anacreon, or the Alexis of Virgil, from disgust and aversion!

But the communication of pleasure may be the immediate object of a work not metrically composed; and that object may have been in a high degree attained, as in novels and romances.   Would then the mere superaddition of metre, with or without rhyme, entitle *these* to the name of poems?   The answer is, that nothing can permanently please, which does not contain in itself the reason why it is so, and not otherwise.   If metre be superadded, all other parts must be made consonant with it. They must be such, as to justify the perpetual and distinct attention to each part, which an exact correspondent recurrence of accent and sound are calculated to excite.   The final definition then, so deduced, may be thus worded.   A poem is that species of composition, which is opposed to works of science by proposing for its *immediate* object pleasure, not truth; and from all other species (having *this* object in common with it) it is discriminated by proposing to itself such delight from the *whole,* as is compatible with a distinct gratification from each component *part.*

Controversy is not seldom excited in consequence of the disputants attaching each a different meaning to the same word; and in few instances has this been more striking, than in disputes concerning the present subject. If a man chooses to call every composition a poem, which is in rhyme, or measure, or both, I must leave his opinion uncontroverted. The distinction is at least competent to characterize the writer's intention. If it were subjoined, that the whole is likewise entertaining or affecting, as a tale, or as a series of interesting reflections, I of course admit this as another fit ingredient of a poem, and an additional merit. But if the definition sought for be that of a *legitimate* poem, I answer, it must be one, the parts of which mutually support and explain each other; all in their proportion harmonizing with, and supporting the purpose and known influences of metrical arrangement. The philosophic critics of all ages coincide with the ultimate judgement of all countries, in equally denying the praises of a just poem, on the one hand, to a series of striking lines or distiches, each of which, absorbing the whole attention of the reader to itself, disjoins it from its context, and makes it a separate whole, instead of an harmonizing part; and on the other hand, to an unsustained composition, from which the reader collects rapidly the general result, unattracted by the component parts. The reader should be carried forward, not merely or chiefly by the mechanical impulse of curiosity, or by a restless desire to arrive at the final solution; but by the pleasureable activity of mind excited by the attractions of the journey itself. Like the motion of a serpent, which the Egyptians made the emblem of intellectual power; or like the path of sound through the air; at every step he pauses and half recedes, and from the retrogressive movement collects the force which again carries him onward. "Praecipitandus est *liber* spiritus,"[1] says Petronius Arbiter most happily. The epithet, *liber,* here balances the preceding verb; and it is not easy to conceive more meaning condensed in fewer words.

But if this should be admitted as a satisfactory character of a poem, we have still to seek for a definition of poetry. The writings of PLATO, and Bishop TAYLOR, and the "Theoria Sacra" of BURNET, furnish undeniable proofs that poetry of the highest kind may exist without metre, and even without the contra-distinguishing objects of a poem. The first chapter of Isaiah (indeed a very large portion of the whole book) is poetry in the most emphatic sense; yet it would be not less irrational than strange to assert, that pleasure, and not truth, was the immediate object of the prophet. In short, whatever *specific* import we attach to the word, poetry, there will be found involved in it, as a necessary consequence,

---

[1] "A free spirit should be cast down headlong."

that a poem of any length neither can be, or ought to be, all poetry.  Yet if an harmonious whole is to be produced, the remaining parts must be preserved *in keeping* with the poetry; and this can be no otherwise effected than by such a studied selection and artificial arrangement, as will partake of *one*, though not a *peculiar* property of poetry.  And this again can be no other than the property of exciting a more continuous and equal attention than the language of prose aims at, whether colloquial or written.

My own conclusions on the nature of poetry, in the strictest use of the word, have been in part anticipated in the preceding disquisition on the fancy and imagination.[2]  What is poetry? is so nearly the same question with, what is a poet? that the answer to the one is involved in the solution of the other.  For it is a distinction resulting from the poetic genius itself, which sustains and modifies the images, thoughts, and emotions of the poet's own mind.

The poet, described in *ideal* perfection, brings the whole soul of man into activity, with the subordination of its faculties to each other, according to their relative worth and dignity.  He diffuses a tone and spirit of unity, that blends, and (as it were) *fuses*, each into each, by that synthetic and magical power, to which we have exclusively appropriated the name of imagination.  This power, first put in action by the will and understanding, and retained under their irremissive, though gentle and unnoticed, control (*laxis effertur habenis*) reveals itself in the balance or reconciliation of opposite or discordant qualities: of sameness, with difference; of the general, with the concrete; the idea, with the image; the individual, with the representative; the sense of novelty and freshness, with old and familiar objects; a more than usual state of emotion, with more than usual order; judgement ever awake and steady self-possession, with enthusiasm and feeling profound or vehement; and while it blends and harmonizes the natural and the artificial, still subordinates art to nature; the manner to the matter; and our admiration of the poet to our sympathy with the poetry.  "Doubtless," as Sir John Davies observes of the soul (and his words may with slight alteration be applied, and even more appropriately, to the poetic IMAGINATION)

> "Doubtless this could not be, but that she turns
>   Bodies to spirit by sublimation strange,
> As fire converts to fire the things it burns,
>   As we our food into our nature change.
>
> From their gross matter she abstracts their forms,
>   And draws a kind of quintessence from things;
> Which to her proper nature she transforms,
>   To bear them light on her celestial wings.

[2] See the selection from Chapter XIII, following.

Thus does she, when from individual states
She doth abstract the universal kinds;
Which then re-clothed in divers names and fates
Steal access through our senses to our minds."

Finally, GOOD SENSE is the BODY of poetic genius, FANCY its DRAPERY, MOTION its LIFE, and IMAGINATION the SOUL that is everywhere, and in each: and forms all into one graceful and intelligent whole.

## From XIII

The IMAGINATION then, I consider either as primary, or secondary. The primary IMAGINATION I hold to be the living Power and prime Agent of all human Perception, and as a repetition in the finite mind of the eternal act of creation in the infinite I AM. The secondary Imagination I consider as an echo of the former, co-existing with the conscious will, yet still as identical with the primary in the *kind* of its agency, and differing only in *degree*, and in the *mode* of its operation. It dissolves, diffuses, dissipates, in order to recreate; or where this process is rendered impossible, yet still at all events it struggles to idealize and to unify. It is essentially *vital*, even as all objects (*as* objects) are essentially fixed and dead.

FANCY, on the contrary, has no other counters to play with, but fixities and definites. The Fancy is indeed no other than a mode of Memory emancipated from the order of time and space; while it is blended with, and modified by that empirical phenomenon of the will, which we express by the word CHOICE. But equally with the ordinary memory the Fancy must receive all its materials ready made from the law of association.

Whatever more than this, I shall think it fit to declare concerning the powers and privileges of the imagination in the present work, will be found in the critical essay on the uses of the Supernatural in poetry, and the principles that regulate its introduction: which the reader will find prefixed to the poem of The Ancient Mariner.

## XV

*The specific symptoms of poetic power elucidated in a critical analysis of Shakespeare's Venus and Adonis, and Lucrece.*

In the application of these principles to purposes of practical criticism as employed in the appraisal of works more or less imperfect, I have endeavoured to discover what the qualities in a poem are, which may be deemed promises and specific symptoms of poetic power, as distinguished from general talent determined to poetic composition by accidental motives, by an act of the will, rather than by the inspiration of a genial and productive nature. In this investigation, I could not, I thought, do better, than keep before me the earliest work of the greatest genius, that perhaps human nature has yet produced, our *myriad-minded* Shakespeare. I mean the "Venus and Adonis," and the "Lucrece"; works which give at once strong promises of the strength, and yet obvious proofs of the immaturity, of his genius. From these I abstracted the following marks, as characteristics of original poetic genius in general.

1. In the "Venus and Adonis," the first and most obvious excellence is the perfect sweetness of the versification; its adaptation to the subject; and the power displayed in varying the march of the words without passing into a loftier and more majestic rhythm than was demanded by the thoughts, or permitted by the propriety of preserving a sense of melody predominant. The delight in richness and sweetness of sound, even to a faulty excess, if it be evidently original, and not the result of an easily imitable mechanism, I regard as a highly favourable promise in the compositions of a young man. "The man that hath not music in his soul" can indeed never be a genuine poet. Imagery (even taken from nature, much more when transplanted from books, as travels, voyages, and works of natural history); affecting incidents; just thoughts; interesting personal or domestic feelings; and with these the art of their combination or intertexture in the form of a poem; may all by incessant effort be acquired as a trade, by a man of talents and much reading, who, as I once before observed, has mistaken an intense desire of poetic reputation for a natural poetic genius; the love of the arbitrary end for a possession of the peculiar means. But the sense of musical delight, with the power of producing it, is a gift of imagination; and this together with the power of reducing multitude into unity of effect, and modifying a series of thoughts by some one predominant thought or feeling, may be cultivated and improved, but can never be learned. It is in these that "poeta nascitur non fit."

2. A second promise of genius is the choice of subjects very remote from the private interests and circumstances of the writer himself. At least I have found, that where the subject is taken immediately from the author's personal sensations and experiences, the excellence of a particular poem is but an equivocal mark, and often a fallacious pledge, of genuine poetic power. We may perhaps remember the tale of the statuary, who had acquired considerable reputation for the legs of his goddesses, though the rest of the statue accorded but indifferently with ideal beauty; till his wife, elated by her husband's praises, modestly acknowledged

that she herself had been his constant model. In the "Venus and Adonis" this proof of poetic power exists even to excess. It is throughout as if a superior spirit more intuitive, more intimately conscious, even than the characters themselves, not only of very outward look and act, but of the flux and reflux of the mind in all its subtlest thoughts and feelings, were placing the whole before our view; himself meanwhile unparticipating in the passions, and actuated only by that pleasureable excitement, which had resulted from the energetic fervor of his own spirit in so vividly exhibiting, what it had so accurately and profoundly contemplated. I think, I should have conjectured from these poems, that even then the great instinct, which impelled the poet to the drama, was secretly working in him, prompting him by a series and never broken chain of imagery, always vivid and, because unbroken, often minute; by the highest effort of the picturesque in words, of which words are capable, higher perhaps than was ever realized by any other poet, even Dante not excepted; to provide a substitute for that visual language, that constant intervention and running comment by tone, look and gesture, which in his dramatic works he was entitled to expect from the players. His "Venus and Adonis" seem at once the characters themselves, and the whole representation of those characters by the most consummate actors. You seem to be told nothing, but to see and hear everything. Hence it is, that from the perpetual activity of attention required on the part of the reader; from the rapid flow, the quick change, and the playful nature of the thoughts and images; and above all from the alienation, and, if I may hazard such an expression, the utter *aloofness* of the poet's own feelings, from those of which he is at once the painter and the analyst; that though the very subject cannot but detract from the pleasure of a delicate mind, yet never was poem less dangerous on a moral account. Instead of doing as Ariosto, and as, still more offensively, Wieland has done, instead of degrading and deforming passion into appetite, the trials of love into the struggles of concupiscence; Shakespeare has here represented the animal impulse itself, so as to preclude all sympathy with it, by dissipating the reader's notice among the thousand outward images, and now beautiful, now fanciful circumstances, which form its dresses and its scenery; or by diverting our attention from the main subject by those frequent witty or profound reflections, which the poet's ever active mind has deduced from, or connected with, the imagery and the incidents. The reader is forced into too much action to sympathize with the merely passive of our nature. As little can a mind thus roused and awakened be brooded on by mean and distinct emotion, as the low, lazy mist can creep upon the surface of a lake, while a strong gale is driving it onward in waves and billows.

3.  It has been before observed that images, however beautiful, though faithfully copied from nature, and as accurately represented in words, do not of themselves characterize the poet.  They become proofs of original genius only as far as they are modified by a predominant passion; or by associated thoughts or images awakened by that passion; or when they have the effect of reducing multitude to unity, or succession to an instant; or lastly, when a human and intellectual life is transferred to them from the poet's own spirit,

"Which shoots its being through earth, sea, and air."

In the two following lines for instance, there is nothing objectionable, nothing which would preclude them from forming, in their proper place, part of a descriptive poem:

"Behold yon row of pines, that shorn and bow'd
Bend from the sea-blast, seen at twilight eve."

But with a small alteration of rhythm, the same words would be equally in their place in a book of topography, or in a descriptive tour.   The same image will rise into semblance of poetry if thus conveyed:

"Yon row of bleak and visionary pines,
By twilight glimpse discerned, mark! how they flee
From the fierce sea-blast, all their tresses wild
Streaming before them."

I have given this as an illustration, by no means as an instance, of that particular excellence which I had in view, and in which Shakespeare even in his earliest, as in his latest, works surpasses all other poets.  It is by this, that he still gives a dignity and a passion to the objects which he presents.  Unaided by any previous excitement, they burst upon us at once in life and in power.

"Full many a glorious morning have I seen
*Flatter* the mountain tops with sovereign eye."
Shakespeare, Sonnet 33rd.

"Not mine own fears, nor the prophetic soul
Of the wide world dreaming on things to come—
\*       \*       \*       \*       \*       \*       \*
\*       \*       \*       \*       \*       \*       \*
The mortal moon hath her eclipse endur'd,
And the sad augurs mock their own presage;
Incertainties now crown themselves assur'd,
And Peace proclaims olives of endless age.
Now with the drops of this most balmy time
My Love looks fresh, and DEATH to me subscribes!

Since spite of him, I'll live in this poor rhyme,
While he insults o'er dull and speechless tribes.
And thou in this shalt find thy monument,
When tyrants' crests, and tombs of brass are spent."

Sonnet 107.

As of higher worth, so doubtless still more characteristic of poetic genius does the imagery become, when it moulds and colors itself to the circumstances, passion, or character, present and foremost in the mind. For unrivalled instances of this excellence, the reader's own memory will refer him to the LEAR, OTHELLO, in short to which not of the *"great, ever living, dead man's"* dramatic works? "Inopem me copia fecit."[3] How true it is to nature, he has himself finely expressed in the instance of love in Sonnet 98.

"From you have I been absent in the spring,
When proud pied April drest in all its trim
Hath put a spirit of youth in every thing,
That heavy Saturn laugh'd and leap'd with him.
Yet nor the lays of birds, nor the sweet smell
Of different flowers in odour and in hue,
Could make me any summer's story tell,
Or from their proud lap pluck them, where they grew:
Nor did I wonder at the lilies white,
Nor praise the deep vermilion in the rose;
They were, tho' sweet, but figures of delight,
Drawn after you, you pattern of all those.
Yet seem'd it winter still, and, you away,
*As with your shadow I with these did play!"*

Scarcely less sure, or if a less valuable, not less indispensable mark

Γονίμου μὲν ποιητοῦ——
——ὅστις ῥῆμα γενναῖον λάκοι,[4]

will the imagery supply, when, with more than the power of the painter, the poet gives us the liveliest image of succession with the feeling of simultaneousness!

"With this, he breaketh from the sweet embrace
Of those fair arms, that held him to her heart,
And homeward through the dark lawns runs apace:
*Look! how a bright star shooteth from the sky,
So glides he in the night from Venus' eye."*

---

3 Wealth has rendered me poor.
4 *Gonimou men poietou—ostis rema gennaion lakoi.* A creative poet . . . who gives vent to a single noble thought.

4. The last character I shall mention, which would prove indeed but little, except as taken conjointly with the former; yet without which the former could scarce exist in a high degree, and (even if this were possible) would give promises only of transitory flashes and a meteoric power; is DEPTH, and ENERGY of THOUGHT. No man was ever yet a great poet, without being at the same time a profound philosopher. For poetry is the blossom and the fragrancy of all human knowledge, human thoughts, human passions, motions, language. In Shakespeare's *poems* the creative power and the intellectual energy wrestle as in a war embrace. Each in its excess of strength seems to threaten the extinction of the other. At length in the DRAMA they were reconciled, and fought each with its shield before the breast of the other. Or like two rapid streams, that, at their first meeting within narrow and rocky banks, mutually strive to repel each other and intermix reluctantly and in tumult; but soon finding a wider channel and more yielding shores blend, and dilate, and flow on in one current and with one voice. The "Venus and Adonis" did not perhaps allow the display of the deeper passions. But the story of Lucretia seems to favor and even demand their intensest workings. And yet we find in *Shakespeare's* management of the tale neither pathos, nor any other *dramatic* quality. There is the same minute and faithful imagery as in the former poem, in the same vivid colors, inspirited by the same impetuous vigor of thought, and diverging and contracting with the same activity of the assimilative and of the modifying faculties; and with a yet larger display, a yet wider range of knowledge and reflection; and lastly, with the same perfect dominion, often *domination*, over the whole world of language. What then shall we say? even this; that Shakespeare, no mere child of nature; no automaton of genius; no passive vehicle of inspiration possessed by the spirit, not possessing it; first studied patiently, meditated deeply, understood minutely, till knowledge, become habitual and intuitive, wedded itself to his habitual feelings, and at length gave birth to that stupendous power, by which he stands alone, with no equal or second in his own class; to that power which seated him on one of the two glory-smitten summits of the poetic mountain, with Milton as his compeer, not rival. While the former darts himself forth, and passes into all the forms of human character and passion, the one Proteus of the fire and the flood; the other attracts all forms and things to himself, into the unity of his own IDEAL. All things and modes of action shape themselves anew in the being of MILTON; while SHAKESPEARE becomes all things, yet for ever remaining himself. O what great men hast thou not produced, England! my country! truly indeed—

"Must *we* be free or die, who speak the tongue,

Which SHAKESPEARE spake; the faith and morals hold,
Which MILTON held.   In every thing we are sprung
Of earth's first blood, have titles manifold!"

WORDSWORTH.

## XVII

*Examination of the tenets peculiar to Mr. Wordsworth—Rustic life (above all, low and rustic life) especially unfavorable to the formation of a human diction— The best parts of language the product of philosophers, not of clowns or shepherds —Poetry essentially ideal and generic—The language of Milton as much the language of real life, yea, incomparably more so than that of the cottager.*

As far then as Mr. Wordsworth in his preface contended, and most ably contended, for a reformation in our poetic diction, as far as he has evinced the truth of passion, and the *dramatic* propriety of those figures and metaphors in the original poets, which, stripped of their justifying reasons, and converted into mere artifices of connection or ornament, constitute the characteristic falsity in the poetic style of the moderns; and as far as he has, with equal acuteness and clearness, pointed out the process by which this change was effected, and the resemblances between that state into which the reader's mind is thrown by the pleasureable confusion of thought from an unaccustomed train of words and images; and that state which is induced by the natural language of empassioned feeling; he undertook a useful task, and deserves all praise, both for the attempt and for the execution.   The provocations to this remonstrance in behalf of truth and nature were still of perpetual recurrence before and after the publication of this preface.   I cannot likewise but add, that the comparison of such poems of merit, as have been given to the public within the last ten or twelve years, with the majority of those produced previously to the appearance of that preface, leave no doubt on my mind, that Mr. Wordsworth is fully justified in believing his efforts to have been by no means ineffectual.   Not only in the verses of those who have professed their admiration of his genius, but even of those who have distinguished themselves by hostility to his theory, and depreciation of his writings, are the impressions of his principles plainly visible.   It is possible, that with these principles others may have been blended, which are not equally evident; and some which are unsteady and subvertible from the narrowness or imperfection of their basis.   But it is more than possible, that these errors of defect or exaggeration, by kindling and feeding the controversy, may have conduced not only to the wider propagation of the accompanying truths, but that, by their frequent presentation to the mind in an excited state, they may have won for them a more permanent and practical result.   A man will borrow a part from his opponent the more easily, if he feels himself justified in continuing to reject a part. While there remain important points in which he can still feel himself in the right, in which he still finds firm footing for continued resistance, he will gradually adopt those opinions, which were the least remote from his own convictions, as not less congruous with his own theory than with that which he reprobates. In like manner with a kind of instinctive prudence, he will abandon by little and little his weakest posts, till at length he seems to forget that they had ever belonged to him, or affects to consider them at most as accidental and "petty annexments," the removal of which leaves the citadel unhurt and unendangered.

My own differences from certain supposed parts of Mr. Wordsworth's theory ground themselves on the assumption that his words had been rightly interpreted, as purporting that the proper diction for poetry in general consists altogether in a language taken, with due exceptions, from the mouths of men in real life, a language which actually constitutes the natural conversation of men under the influence of natural feelings. My objection is, first, that in *any* sense this rule is applicable only to *certain* classes of poetry; secondly, that even to these classes it is not applicable, except in such a sense, as hath never by any one (as far as I know or have read) been denied or doubted; and lastly, that as far as, and in that degree in which it is *practicable*, yet as a *rule* it is useless if not injurious, and therefore either need not, or ought not to be practised. The poet informs his reader, that he had generally chosen *low and rustic* life; but not *as* low and rustic, or in order to repeat that pleasure of doubtful moral effect, which persons of elevated rank and of superior refinement oftentimes derive from a happy *imitation* of the rude unpolished manners and discourse of their inferiors. For the pleasure so derived may be traced to three exciting causes. The first is the naturalness, in *fact*, of the things represented. The second is the apparent naturalness of the *representation*, as raised and qualified by an imperceptible infusion of the author's own knowledge and talent, which infusion does, indeed, constitute it an *imitation* as distinguished from a mere *copy*. The third cause may be found in the reader's conscious feeling of his superiority awakened by the contrast presented to him; even as for the same purpose the kings and great barons of yore retained sometimes *actual* clowns and fools, but more frequently shrewd and witty fellows in that *character*. These, however, were not Mr. Wordsworth's objects. *He* chose low and rustic life, "because in that condition the essential passions of the heart find a better soil, in which they can attain their maturity, are less under restraint, and speak a plainer and more emphatic language; because in that condition of life our elementary feelings coexist in a state of greater simplicity, and consequently may be more accurately contemplated, and more forcibly communicated; because the manners of rural life germinate from those elementary feelings; and from the necessary character of rural occupations are more easily comprehended, and are more durable; and lastly, because in that condition the passions of men are incorporated with the beautiful and permanent forms of nature."

Now it is clear to me, that in the most interesting of the poems, in which the author is more or less dramatic, as "the Brothers," "Michael," "Ruth," "the Mad Mother," &c., the persons introduced are by no means taken *from low or rustic life* in the common acceptation of those words; and it is not less clear, that the sentiments and languages, as far as they can be conceived to have been really transferred from the minds and conversation of such persons, are attributable to causes and circumstances not necessarily connected with "their occupations and abode." The thoughts, feelings, language, and manners of the shepherd-farmers in the vales of Cumberland and Westmoreland, as far as they are actually adopted in those poems, may be accounted for from causes, which will and do produce the same results in *every* state of life, whether in town or country. As the two principal I rank that INDEPENDENCE, which raises a man above servitude, or daily toil for the profit of others, yet not above the necessity of industry and a frugal simplicity of domestic life; and the accompanying unambitious, but solid and religious, EDUCATION, which has rendered few books familiar, but the Bible, and the liturgy or hymn book. To this latter cause, indeed, which is so far *accidental*, that it is the blessing of particular countries and a particular age, not the product of particular places or employments, the poet owes the show of probability, that his personages might really feel, think, and talk with any tolerable resemblance to his representation. It is an excellent remark of Dr. Henry More's, (Enthusiasmus triumphatus, Sec. XXXV.), that "a man of confined education, but of good parts, by constant reading of the Bible will naturally form a more winning and commanding rhetoric than those that are learned; the intermixture of tongues and of artificial phrases debasing *their* style."

It is, moreover, to be considered that to the formation of healthy feelings, and a reflecting mind, *negations* involve impediments not less formidable than sophistication and vicious intermixture. I am convinced, that for the human soul to prosper in rustic life a certain vantage-ground is pre-requisite. It is not every man that is likely to be improved by a country life or by country labors. Education, or original sensibility, or both, must pre-exist, if the changes, forms, and incidents of nature are to prove a sufficient stimulant. And where these are not sufficient, the mind contracts and hardens by want of stimulants: and the man becomes

selfish, sensual, gross, and hard-hearted.   Let the management of the
Poor Laws in Liverpool, Manchester, or Bristol be compared with the
ordinary dispensation of the poor rates in agricultural villages, where the
*farmers* are the overseers and guardians of the poor.   If my own experience
have not been particularly unfortunate, as well as that of the many
respectable country clergymen with whom I have conversed on the subject, the result would engender more than scepticism concerning the
desireable influences of low and rustic life in and for itself.   Whatever
may be concluded on the other side, from the stronger local attachments
and enterprising spirit of the Swiss, and other mountaineers, applies to
a particular mode of pastoral life, under forms of property that permit
and beget manners truly republican, not to rustic life in general, or to
the absence of artificial cultivation.   On the contrary the mountaineers,
whose manners have been so often eulogized, are in general better
educated and greater readers than men of equal rank elsewhere.
But where this is not the case, as among the peasantry of North Wales,
the ancient mountains, with all their terrors and all their glories, are
pictures to the blind, and music to the deaf.

I should not have entered so much into detail upon this passage, but
here seems to be the point, to which all the lines of difference converge
as to their source and centre.   (I mean, as far as, and in whatever
respect, my poetic creed *does* differ from the doctrines promulged in this
preface.) I adopt with full faith the principle of Aristotle, that poetry as
poetry is essentially[5] *ideal*, that it avoids and excludes all *accident*; that

---

[5] Say not that I am recommending abstractions; for these class-characteristics which
constitute the instructiveness of a character, are so modified and particularized in
each person of the Shakespearean Drama, that life itself does not excite more
distinctly that sense of individuality which belongs to real existence. Paradoxical as
it may sound, one of the essential properties of Geometry is not less essential to
dramatic excellence; and Aristotle has accordingly required of the poet an involu-
tion of the universal in the individual. The chief differences are, that in Geometry
it is the universal truth, which is uppermost in the consciousness; in poetry the
individual form, in which the truth is clothed. With the ancients, and not less with
the elder dramatists of England and France, both comedy and tragedy were considered as kinds of poetry. They neither sought in comedy to make us laugh merely;
much less to make us laugh by wry faces, accidents of jargon, *slang* phrases for the
day, or the clothing of common-place morals drawn from the shops or mechanic
occupations of their characters. Nor did they condescend in tragedy to wheedle
away the applause of the spectators, by representing before them facsimiles of their
own mean selves in all their existing meanness, or to work on the sluggish sympathies
by a pathos not a whit more respectable than the maudlin tears of drunkenness.
Their tragic scenes were meant to *affect* us indeed; but yet within the bounds of
pleasure, and in union with the activity both of our understanding and imagination.
They wished to transport the mind to a sense of its possible greatness, and to implant the germs of that greatness, during the temporary oblivion of the worthless
"thing we are," and of the peculiar state in which each man *happens* to be, suspending our individual recollections and lulling them to sleep amid the music of nobler
thoughts.

its apparent individualities of rank, character, or occupation must be *representative* of a class; and that the *persons* of poetry must be clothed with *generic* attributes, with the *common* attributes of the class: not with such as one gifted individual might *possibly* possess, but such as from his situation it is most probable before-hand that he *would* possess. If my premises are right and my deductions legitimate, it follows that there can be no *poetic* medium between the swains of Theocritus and those of an imaginary golden age.

The characters of the vicar and the shepherd-mariner in the poem of "The Brothers," that of the shepherd of Greenhead Ghyll in the "MICHAEL," have all the verisimilitude and representative quality, that the purposes of poetry can require. They are persons of a known and abiding class, and their manners and sentiments the natural product of circumstances common to the class. Take "MICHAEL" for instance:

> "An old man stout of heart, and strong of limb:
> His bodily frame had been from youth to age
> Of an unusual strength: his mind was keen,
> Intense, and frugal, apt for all affairs,
> And in his shepherd's calling he was prompt
> And watchful more than ordinary men.
> Hence he had learnt the meaning of all winds,
> Of blasts of every tone; and oftentimes
> When others heeded not, he heard the South
> Make subterraneous music, like the noise
> Of bagpipers on distant Highland hills.
> The shepherd, at such warning, of his flock
> Bethought him, and he to himself would say,
> The winds are now devising work for me!
> And truly at all times the storm, that drives
> The traveller to a shelter, summon'd him
> Up to the mountains. He had been alone
> Amid the heart of many thousand mists,
> That came to him and left him on the heights.
> So liv'd he, till his eightieth year was pass'd.
> And grossly that man errs, who should suppose
> That the green vallies, and the streams and rocks,
> Were things indifferent to the shepherd's thoughts.
> Fields, where with chearful spirits he had breath'd
> The common air; the hills, which he so oft
> Had climb'd with vigorous steps; which had impress'd
> So many incidents upon his mind
> Of hardship, skill or courage, joy or fear;
> Which, like a book, preserved the memory
> Of the dumb animals, whom he had sav'd,

Had fed or shelter'd, linking to such acts,
So grateful in themselves, the certainty
Of honorable gain; these fields, these hills
Which were his living being, even more
Than his own blood—what could they less?    had laid
Strong hold on his affections, were to him
A pleasureable feeling of blind love,
The pleasure which there is in life itself."

On the other hand, in the poems which are pitched at a lower note, as the "HARRY GILL", "IDIOT BOY," the *feelings* are those of human nature in general; though the poet has judiciously laid the *scene* in the country, in order to place *himself* in the vicinity of interesting images, without the necessity of ascribing a sentimental perception of their beauty to the persons of his drama.   In the "Idiot Boy," indeed, the mother's character is not so much a real and native product of a "situation where the essential passions of the heart find a better soil, in which they can attain their maturity and speak a plainer and more emphatic language," as it is an impersonation of an instinct abandoned by judgement.   Hence the two following charges seem to me not wholly groundless: at least, they are the only plausible objections, which I have heard to that fine poem. The one is, that the author has not, in the poem itself, taken sufficient care to preclude from the reader's fancy the disgusting images of *ordinary morbid idiocy*, which yet it was by no means his intention to represent. He has even by the "burr, burr, burr," uncounteracted by any preceding description of the boy's beauty, assisted in recalling them.   The other is, that the idiocy of the *boy* is so evenly balanced by the folly of the *mother*, as to present to the general reader rather a laughable burlesque on the blindness of anile dotage, than an analytic display of maternal affection in its ordinary workings.

In the "Thorn" the poet himself acknowledges in a note the necessity of an introductory poem, in which he should have portrayed the character of the person from whom the words of the poem are supposed to proceed: a superstitious man moderately imaginative, of slow faculties and deep feelings, "a captain of a small trading vessel, for example, who, being past the middle age of life, had retired upon an annuity, or small independent income, to some village or country town of which he was not a native, or in which he had not been accustomed to live.   Such men having nothing to do become credulous and talkative from indolence." But in a poem, still more in a lyric poem (and the NURSE in Shakespeare's Romeo and Juliet alone prevents me from extending the remark even to dramatic *poetry*, if indeed the Nurse itself can be deemed altogether a case in point) it is not possible to imitate truly a dull and garrulous discourser, without repeating the effects of dullness and garrulity.   However this may be, I dare assert, that the parts (and these form the far larger portion of the whole) which might as well or still better have proceeded from the poet's own imagination, and have been spoken in his own character, are those which have given, and which will continue to give, universal delight; and that the passages exclusively appropriate to the supposed narrator, such as the last couplet of the third stanza;[6] the seven last lines of the tenth;[7] and the five following stanzas, with the exception

[6] I've measured it from side to side;
'Tis three feet long, and two feet wide.

[7] Nay, rack your brain—'tis all in vain,
I'll tell you every thing I know;
But to the Thorn, and to the Pond
Which is a little step beyond,
I wish that you would go:
Perhaps when you are at the place,
You something of her tale may trace.
I'll give you the best help I can:
Before you up the mountain go,
Up to the dreary mountain-top,
I'll tell you all I know.
'Tis now some two-and-twenty years
Since she (her name is Martha Ray)
Gave, with a maiden's true good will,
Her company to Stephen Hill;
And she was blithe and gay,
And she was happy, happy still
Whene'er she thought of Stephen Hill.

And they had fix'd the wedding-day,
The morning that must wed them both;
But Stephen to another maid
Had sworn another oath;
And, with this other maid, to church
Unthinking Stephen went—
Poor Martha! on that woeful day
A pang of pitiless dismay
Into her soul was sent;
A fire was kindled in her breast,

Which might not burn itself to rest.
They say, full six months after this,
While yet the summer leaves were green,
She to the mountain-top would go,
And there was often seen.
'Tis said a child was in her womb,
As now to any eye was plain;
She was with child, and she was mad;
Yet often she was sober sad
From her exceeding pain.
Oh me! ten thousand times I'd rather
That he had died, that cruel father!
*     *     *     *     *     *

of the four admirable lines at the commencement of the fourteenth, are felt by many unprejudiced and unsophisticated hearts, as sudden and unpleasant sinkings from the height to which the poet had previously lifted them, and to which he again re-elevates both himself and his reader.

If then I am compelled to doubt the theory, by which the choice of *characters* was to be directed, not only *a priori*, from grounds of reason, but both from the few instances in which the poet himself *need* be supposed to have been governed by it, and from the comparative inferiority of those instances; still more must I hesitate in my assent to the sentence which immediately follows the former citation; and which I can neither admit as particular fact, or as general rule. "The language too of these men is adopted (purified indeed from what appear to be its real defects, from all lasting and rational causes of dislike or disgust) because such men hourly communicate with the best objects from which the best part of language is originally derived; and because, from their rank in society and the sameness and narrow circle of their intercourse, being less under the action of social vanity, they convey their feelings and notions in simple and unelaborated expressions." To this I reply; that a rustic's language, purified from all provincialism and grossness, and so far reconstructed as to be made consistent with the rules of grammar (which are in essence no other than the laws of universal logic, applied to psychological materials) will not differ from the language of any other man of common-sense, however learned or refined he may be, except as far as the notions, which the rustic has to convey, are fewer and more indiscriminate. This will become still clearer, if we add the consideration (equally important

---

\*　　\*　　\*　　\*　　\*　　\*
\*　　\*　　\*　　\*　　\*　　\*
\*　　\*　　\*　　\*　　\*　　\*

Last Christmas when we talked of this,
Old farmer Simpson did maintain,
That in her womb the infant wrought
About its mother's heart, and brought
Her senses back again:
And, when at last her time drew near,
Her looks were calm, her senses clear.
No more I know, I wish I did,
And I would tell it all to you:
For what became of this poor child
There's none that ever knew:
And if a child was born or no,
There's no one that could ever tell;
And if 'twas born alive or dead,
There's no one knows, as I have said:
But some remember well,
That Martha Ray about this time
Would up the mountain often climb.

though less obvious) that the rustic, from the more imperfect development of his faculties, and from the lower state of their cultivation, aims almost solely to convey *insulated facts*, either those of his scanty experience or his traditional belief; while the educated man chiefly seeks to discover and express those *connections* of things, or those relative *bearings* of fact to fact, from which some more or less general law is deducible. For *facts* are valuable to a wise man, chiefly as they lead to the discovery of the indwelling *law*, which is the true *being* of things, the sole solution of their modes of existence, and in the knowledge of which consists our dignity and our power.

As little can I agree with the assertion, that from the objects with which the rustic hourly communicates the best part of language is formed. For first, if to communicate with an object implies such an acquaintance with it, as renders it capable of being discriminately reflected on; the distinct knowledge of an uneducated rustic would furnish a very scanty vocabulary. The few things, and modes of action, requisite for his bodily conveniences, would alone be individualized; while all the rest of nature would be expressed by a small number of confused general terms. Secondly, I deny that the words and combinations of words derived from the objects, with which the rustic is familiar, whether with distinct or confused knowledge, can be justly said to form the *best* part of language. It is more than probable, that many classes of the brute creation possess discriminating sounds, by which they can convey to each other notices of such objects as concern their food, shelter, or safety. Yet we hesitate to call the aggregate of such sounds a language, otherwise than metaphorically. The best part of human language, properly so called, is derived from reflection on the acts of the mind itself. It is formed by a voluntary appropriation of fixed symbols to internal acts, to processes and results of imagination, the greater part of which have no place in the consciousness of uneducated man; though in civilized society, by imitation and passive remembrance of what they hear from their religious instructors and other superiors, the most uneducated share in the harvest which they neither sowed or reaped. If the history of the phrases in hourly currency among our peasants were traced, a person not previously aware of the fact would be surprised at finding so large a number, which three or four centuries ago were the exclusive property of the universities and the schools; and, at the commencement of the Reformation, had been transferred from the school to the pulpit, and thus gradually passed into common life. The extreme difficulty, and often the impossibility, of finding words for the simplest moral and intellectual processes of the languages of uncivilized tribes has proved perhaps the weightiest obstacle to the progress of our most zealous and adroit missionaries. Yet these tribes are surrounded by the same nature as our peasants are; but in still more impressive forms; and they are, moreover, obliged to *particularize* many more of them. When, therefore, Mr. Wordsworth adds, "accordingly, such a language" (meaning, as before, the langauge of rustic life purified from provincialism) "arising out of repeated experience and regular feelings, is a more permanent, and a far more philosophical language, than that which is frequently substituted for it by poets, who think they are conferring honor upon themselves and their art in proportion as they indulge in arbitrary and capricious habits of expression:" it may be answered, that the language, which he has in view, can be attributed to rustics with no greater right, than the style of Hooker or Bacon to Tom Brown or Sir Roger L'Estrange. Doubtless, if what is peculiar to each were omitted in each, the result must needs be the same. Further, that the poet, who uses an illogical diction, or a style fitted to excite only the low and changeable pleasure of wonder by means of groundless novelty, substitutes a language of *folly* and *vanity*, not for that of the *rustic*, but for that of *good sense* and *natural feeling*.

Here let me be permitted to remind the reader, that the positions, which I controvert, are contained in the sentences—"*a selection of the* REAL *language of men;*"—"*the language of these men*" (i.e. men in low and rustic life) "*I propose to myself to imitate, and, as far as is possible, to adopt the very language of men.*" "*Between the language of prose and that of metrical composition, there neither is, nor can be any essential difference.*" It is against these exclusively that my opposition is directed.

I object, in the very first instance, to an equivocation in the use of the word "real." Every man's language varies, according to the extent of his knowledge, the activity of his faculties, and the depth or quickness of his feelings. Every man's language has, first, its *individualities*; secondly, the common properties of the *class* to which he belongs; and thirdly, words and phrases of *universal* use. The language of Hooker, Bacon, Bishop Taylor, and Burke differs from the common language of the learned class only by the superior number and novelty of the thoughts and relations which they had to convey. The language of Algernon Sidney differs not at all from that, which every well-educated gentleman would wish to write, and (with due allowances for the undeliberateness, and less connected train, of thinking natural and proper to conversation) such as he would wish to talk. Neither one nor the other differ half so much from the general language of cultivated society, as the language of Mr. Wordsworth's homeliest composition differs from that of a common peasant. For "real" therefore, we must substitute *ordinary*, or *lingua communis*. And this, we have proved, is no more to be found in the phraseology of low and rustic life than in that of any other class. Omit the peculiarities of each, and the result of course must be common to all. And assuredly the omissions and changes to be made in the language of rustics, before it could be transferred to any species of poem, except the drama or other professed imitation, are at least as numerous and weighty, as would be required in adapting to the same purpose the ordinary language of tradesmen and manufactures. Not to mention, that the language so highly extolled by Mr. Wordsworth varies in every county, nay in every village, according to the accidental character of the clergy-man, the existence or non-existence of schools; or even, perhaps, as the exciseman, publican, or barber, happen to be, or not to be, zealous politicians, and readers of the weekly newspaper *pro bono publico*. Anterior to cultivation, the lingua communis of every country, as Dante has well observed, exists every where in parts, and no where as a whole.

Neither is the case rendered at all more tenable by the addition of the words, *in a state of excitement*. For the nature of a man's words, where he is strongly affected by joy, grief, or anger, must necessarily depend on the number and quality of the general truths, conceptions and images, and of the words expressing them, with which his mind had been previously stored. For the property of passion is not to *create*; but to set in increased activity. At least, whatever new connections of thoughts or images, or (which is equally, if not more than equally, the appropriate effect of strong excitement) whatever generalizations of truth or ex-perience, the heat of passion may produce; yet the terms of their convey-ance must have pre-existed in his former conversations, and are only collected and crowded together by the unusual stimulation. It is indeed very possible to adopt in a poem the unmeaning repetitions, habitual phrases, and other blank counters, which an unfurnished or confused understanding interposes at short intervals, in order to keep hold of his subject which is still slipping from him, and to give him time for recollec-tion; or in mere aid of vacancy, as in the scanty companies of a country stage the same player pops backwards and forwards, in order to prevent the appearance of empty spaces, in the procession of Macbeth, or Henry VIIIth. But what assistance to the poet, or ornament to the poem, these can supply, I am at a loss to conjecture. Nothing assuredly can differ either in origin or in mode more widely from the *apparent* tautologies of intense and turbulent feeling, in which the passion is greater and of longer endurance than to be exhausted or satisfied by a single representation of the image or incident exciting it. Such repetitions I admit to be a beauty of the highest kind; as illustrated by Mr. Wordsworth himself from the song of Deborah. "*At her feet he bowed, he fell, he lay down; at her feet he bowed, he fell; where he bowed, there he fell down dead.*"

## JOHN KEATS

# Four Letters

## 1817-1818

*What is the poetical "self"? How does the poet differ from other men? Is his poetry only the expression of that self? The twenty-two-year-old John Keats, at the threshold of his most productive poetic year, has a head full of ideas about the poetic character, the creative process, the nature of the imagination, the meaning of beauty, and so forth—ideas that come tumbling out in a disorganized fashion in a series of personal letters to friends and family. These are not essayistic letters written with a larger audience in mind (as in Young, for example); reading Keats, we sense the pressure and the feverishness of an excited young poet scribbling about personal matters and gossip but unable to keep his ideas on poetry from forcing their way through. We see Keats observing himself in the process of forming his own conclusions, the most notable instance in Letter 45. Notice how his various activities, culminating in a fashionable dinner party, make things "dovetail" in his mind.*

*The true poet has no identity and no nature; "he is certainly the most unpoetical of all God's creatures," Keats declares. The poetical character "is every thing and nothing." Seeing the sparrow picking at the gravel, he feels himself becoming that sparrow through an empathetic identification; he delights "in conceiving an Iago as an Imogen." But to achieve these feats of the imagination he must pos-*

*sess Negative Capability, which is the central concept in Keats' defini-*
*tion of the poet: the faculty of not having to force his observations*
*into doctrinaire systems, philosophies, or opinions. Nor must he allow*
*his ego to interfere with his sensations; Keats everywhere rejects the*
*ego in art, as in the "wordsworthian or egotistical sublime." (Else-*
*where, he objects to being "bullied into a certain Philosophy en-*
*gendered in the whims of an Egotist"—Wordsworth again.) Truth is*
*attained not by thought or logic but by the "silent working" of the*
*imagination; what it "seizes as Beauty must be truth." Keats uses the*
*paradoxical phrase "diligent indolence" to refer to the necessary*
*receptivity and openness to experience that marks a great writer like*
*Shakespeare, whose own ego is nowhere to be found in his works.*

*We speak today of cognitive and affective ways of learning, a dis-*
*tinction that Keats seems to be making when he exclaims (Letter 43),*
*"O for a Life of Sensations rather than of Thoughts!" It is worthwhile*
*to raise the issue of whether Keats' position is, fundamentally, an*
*anti-intellectual one.*

## LETTER 43.    TO BENJAMIN BAILEY.    22 NOVEMBER 1817

My dear Bailey,

I will get over the first part of this (*un*said)[1] Letter as soon as possible for
it relates to the affair of poor Crips—To a Man of your nature, such a
Letter as Haydon's must have been extremely cutting—What occasions
the greater part of the World's Quarrels? simply this, two Minds meet and
do not understand each other time enough to p[r]aevent any shock or
surprise at the conduct of either party—As soon as I had known Haydon
three days I had got enough of his character not to have been surp[r]ised
at such a Letter as he has hurt you with. Nor when I knew it was it a
principle with me to drop his acquaintance although with you it would
have been an imperious feeling. I wish you knew all that I think about
Genius and the Heart—and yet I think you are thoroughly acquainted
with my innermost breast in that respect or you could not have known me
even thus long and still hold me worthy to be your dear friend. In passing however I must say of one thing that has pressed upon me lately and
encreased my Humility and capability of submission and that is this truth
— Men of Genius are great as certain ethereal Chemicals operating on
the Mass of neutral intellect—by[2] they have not any individuality, any

---

[1] A pun on the legal use of "said": " 'This said letter' ... would be Haydon's to
Bailey: 'this *un*said letter' " the present one.
[2] *For* but.

determined Character.   I would call the top and head of those who have a proper self Men of Power—

But I am running my head into a Subject[3] which I am certain I could not do justice to under five years s[t] udy and 3 vols octavo—and moreover long to be talking about the Imagination—so my dear Bailey do not think of this unpleasant affair if possible—do not—I defy any ha[r]m to come of it—I defy—I'll shall write to Crips this Week and reque[s]t him to tell me all his goings on from time to time by Letter whererever I may be—it will all go on well—so dont because you have suddenly discover'd a Coldness in Haydon suffer yourself to be teased.   Do not my dear fellow. O I wish I was as certain of the end of all your troubles as that of your momentary start about the authenticity of the Imagination.   I am certain of nothing but of the holiness of the Heart's affections and the truth of Imagination—What the imagination seizes as Beauty must be truth—whether it existed before or not—for I have the same Idea of all our Passions as of Love they are all in their sublime, creative of essential Beauty—In a Word, you may know my favorite Speculation by my first Book and the little song I sent in my last—which is a representation from the fancy of the probable mode of operating in these Matters—The Imagination may be compared to Adam's dream—he awoke and found it truth.   I am the more zealous in this affair, because I have never yet been able to perceive how any thing can be known for truth by consequitive reasoning—and yet it must be —Can it be that even the greatest Philosopher ever ⟨when⟩ arrived at his goal without putting aside numerous objections—However it may be, O for a Life of Sensations rather than of Thoughts!   It is 'a Vision in the form of Youth' a Shadow of reality to come—and this consideration has further conv[i]nced me for it has come as auxiliary to another favorite Speculation of mine, that we shall enjoy ourselves here after by having what we called happiness on Earth repeated in a finer tone and so repeated—And yet such a fate can only befall those who delight in sensation rather than hunger as you do after Truth—Adam's dream will do here and seems to be a conviction that Imagination and its empyreal reflection is the same as human Life and its spiritual repetition.   But as I was saying—the simple imaginative Mind may have its rewards in the repeti[ti]on of its own silent Working coming continually on the spirit with a fine suddenness—to compare great things with small—have you never by being surprised with an old Melody—in a delicious place—by a delicious voice, fe[l]t over again your very speculations and surmises at the time it first operated on your soul—do you not remember forming to youself the singer's face more beautiful that[4] it was possible and yet with

[3] See Letter 118.
[4] For than.

the elevation of the Moment you did not think so—even then you were mounted on the Wings of Imagination so high—that the Prototype must be here after—that delicious face you will see—What a time! I am continually running away from the subject—sure this cannot be exactly the case with a complex Mind—one that is imaginative and at the same time careful of its fruits—who would exist partly on sensation partly on thought—to whom it is necessary that years should bring the philosophic Mind—such an one I consider your's and therefore it is necessary to your

drink

eternal Happiness that you not only ⟨have⟩ this old Wine of Heaven which I shall call the redigestion of our most ethereal Musings on Earth; but also increase in knowledge and know all things.    I am glad to hear you are in a fair Way for Easter—you will soon get through your unpleasant reading and then!—but the world is full of troubles and I have not much reason to think myself pesterd with many—I think Jane or Marianne has a better opinion of me than I deserve—for really and truly I do not think my Brothers illness connected with mine—you know more of the real Cause than they do—nor have I any chance of being rack'd as you have been—you perhaps at one time thought there was such a thing as Worldly Happiness to be arrived at, at certain periods of time marked out—you have of necessity from your disposition been thus led away—I scarcely remember counting upon any Happiness—I look not for it if it be not in the present hour—nothing startles me beyond the Moment.    The setting sun will always set me to rights—or if a Sparrow come before my Window I take part in its existence and pick about the Gravel.    The first thing that strikes me on hea[r]ing a Misfortune having befalled another is this 'Well it cannot be helped.—he will have the pleasure of trying the re- sourses of his spirit, and I beg now my dear Bailey that hereafter should you observe any thing cold in me not to but[5] it to the account of heartless- ness but abstraction—for I assure you I sometimes feel not the influence of a Passion or Affection during a whole week—and so long this sometimes continues I begin to suspect myself and the genuiness of my feelings at other times—thinking them a few barren Tragedy-tears—My Brother Tom is much improved—he is going to Devonshire —whither I shall follow him—at present I am just arrived at Dorking to change the Scene— change the Air and give me a spur to wind up my Poem, of which there are wanting 500 Lines.    I should have been here a day sooner but the Reynoldses persuaded me to spop[6] in Town to meet your friend Christie— There were Rice and Martin—we talked about Ghosts—I will have some talk with Taylor and let you know—when please God I come down a[t]

⁵ *For* put.
⁶ *For* stop.

Christmas—I will find that Examiner if possible.   My best regards to
Gleig—My Brothers to you and M^{rs} Bentley

Your affectionate friend

JOHN KEATS—

I want to say much more to you—a few hints will set me going
Direct Burford Bridge near dorking


LETTER 45.   TO GEORGE AND TOM KEATS.   21, 27 [?]
DECEMBER 1817

*Hampstead Sunday*

*22 December 1817*

MY DEAR BROTHERS

I must crave your pardon for not having written ere this & & I saw
Kean return to the public in Richard III, & finely he did it, & at the
request of Reynolds I went to criticise his Luke in Riches—the critique is
in todays champion, which I send you with the Examiner in which you
will find very proper lamentation on the obsoletion of christmas Gambols
& pastimes: but it was mixed up with so much egotism of that drivelling
nature that pleasure is entirely lost.   Hone the publisher's trial, you
must find very amusing; & as Englishmen very ⟨amusing⟩ encouraging—
his *Not Guilty* is a thing, which not to have been, would have dulled still
more Liberty's Emblazoning—Lord Ellenborough has been paid in his
own coin—Wooler & Hone have done us an essential service—I have had
two very pleasant evenings with Dilke yesterday & today; & am at this
moment just come from him & feel in the humour to go on with this,
began in the morning, & from which he came to fetch me.   I spent
Friday evening with Wells & went the next morning to see *Death on the
Pale horse*.   It is a wonderful picture, when West's age is considered; But
there is nothing to be intense upon; no women one feels mad to kiss; no
face swelling into reality. the excellence of every Art is its intensity,
capable of making all disagreeables evaporate, from their being in close
relationship with Beauty & Truth—Examine King Lear & you will find
this examplified throughout; but in this picture we have unpleasantness
without any momentous depth of speculation excited, in which to bury its
repulsiveness—The picture is larger than Christ rejected—I dined with
Haydon the sunday after you left, & had a very pleasant day, I dined too
(for I have been out too much lately) with Horace Smith & met his two
Brothers with Hill & Kingston & one Du Bois, they only served to convince me, how superior humour is to wit in respect to enjoyment—These
men say things which make one start, without making one feel, they are
all alike; their manners are alike; they all know fashionables; they have

a mannerism in their very eating & drinking, in their mere handling a Decanter—They talked of Kean & his low company—Would I were with that company instead of yours said I to myself! I know such like acquaintance will never do for me & yet I am going to Reynolds, on wednesday—Brown & Dilke walked with me & back from the Christmas pantomime. I had not a dispute but a disquisition with Dilke, on various subjects; several things dovetailed in my mind, & at once it struck me, what quality went to form a Man of Achievement especially in Literature & which Shakespeare posessed so enormously—I mean *Negative Capability*, that is when man is capable of being in uncertainties, Mysteries, doubts, without any irritable reaching after fact & reason—Coleridge, for instance, would let go by a fine isolated verisimilitude caught from the Penetralium of mystery, from being incapable of remaining content with half knowledge. This pursued through Volumes would perhaps take us no further than this, that with a great poet the sense of Beauty overcomes every other consideration, or rather obliterates all consideration.

Shelley's poem is out & there are words about its being objected too, as much as Queen Mab was. Poor Shelley I think he has his Quota of good qualities, in sooth la!! Write soon to your most sincere friend & affectionate Brother

(Signed) JOHN

Mess<sup>rs</sup> Keats
Teignmouth Devonshire

## LETTER 62.  TO J. H. REYNOLDS.  19 FEBRUARY 1818

MY DEAR REYNOLDS,

I have an idea that a Man might pass a very pleasant life in this manner —let him on any certain day read a certain Page of full Poesy or distilled Prose and let him wander with it, and muse upon it, and reflect from it, and bring home to it, and prophesy upon it, and dream upon it—untill it becomes stale—but when will it do so? Never—When Man has arrived at a certain ripeness in intellect any one grand and spiritual passage serves him as a starting post towards all "the two-and thirty Pallaces" How happy is such a "voyage of conception," what delicious diligent Indolence! A doze upon a Sofa does not hinder it, and a nap upon Clover engenders ethereal finger-pointings—the prattle of a child gives it wings, and the converse of middle age a strength to beat them—a strain of musick conducts to 'an odd angle of the Isle' and when the leaves whisper it puts a 'girdle round the earth. Nor will this sparing touch of noble Books be any irreverance to their Writers—for perhaps the honors paid by Man to Man are trifles in comparison to the Benefit done by great

Works to the 'Spirit and pulse of good' by their mere passive existence. Memory should not be called knowledge—Many have original Minds who do not think it— they are led away by Custom—Now it appears to me that almost any Man may like the Spider spin from his own inwards his own airy Citadel— the points of leaves and twigs on which the Spider begins her work are few and she fills the Air with a beautiful circuiting: man should be content with as few points to tip with the fine Webb of his Soul and weave a tapestry empyrean—full of Symbols for his spiritual eye, of softness for his spiritual touch, of space for his wandering of distinctness for his Luxury—But the Minds of Mortals are so different and bent on such diverse Journeys that it may at first appear impossible for any common taste and fellowship to exist ⟨bettween⟩ between two or three under these suppositions—It is however quite the contrary—Minds would leave each other in contrary directions, traverse each other in Numberless points, and all[7] last greet each other at the Journeys end—A old Man and a child would talk together and the old Man be led on his Path, and the child left thinking—Man should not dispute or assert but whisper results to his neighbour, and thus by every germ of Spirit sucking the Sap from mould ethereal every human might become great, and Humanity instead of being a wide heath of Furse and Briars with here and there a remote Oak or Pine, would become a grand democracy of Forest Trees.   It has been an old Comparison for our urging on—the Bee hive—however it seems to me that we should rather be the flower than the Bee—for it is a false notion that more is gained by receiving than giving—no the receiver and the giver are equal in their benefits—The f[l]ower I doubt not receives a fair guerdon from the Bee—its leaves blush deeper in the next spring—and who shall say between Man and Woman which is the most delighted?   Now it is more noble to sit like Jove that[8] to fly like Mercury —let us not therefore go hurrying about and collecting honey-bee like, buzzing here and there impatiently from a knowledge of what is to be arrived at: but let us open our leaves like a flower and be passive and receptive—budding patiently under the eye of Apollo and taking hints from evey noble insect that favors us with a visit—sap will be given us for Meat and dew for drink—I was led into these thoughts, my dear Reynolds, by the beauty of the morning operating on a sense of Idleness—I have not read any Books—the Morning said I was right—I had no Idea but of the Morning and the Thrush said I was right—seeming to say—

'O thou whose face hath felt the Winter's wind;
    Whose eye has seen the Snow clouds hung in Mist

[7] *For* at.
[8] *For* than.

And the black-elm tops 'mong the freezing Stars
To thee the Spring will be a harvest-time—
O thou whose only book has been the light
Of supreme darkness which thou feddest on
Night after night, when Phœbus was away
To thee the Spring shall be a tripple morn—
O fret not after knowledge—I have none
And yet my song comes native with the warmth
O fret not after knowledge—I have none
And yet the Evening listens—He who saddens
At thought of Idleness cannot be idle,
And he's awake who thinks himself asleep.'

Now I am sensible all this is a mere sophistication, however it may neighbour to any truths, to excuse my own indolence—so I will not deceive
myself that Man should be equal with jove—but think himself very well
off as a sort of scullion-Mercury or even a humble Bee—It is not[9] matter
whether I am right or wrong either one way or another, if there is sufficient
to lift a little time from your Shoulders.          Your affectionate friend
JOHN KEATS—

## LETTER 118.  TO RICHARD WOODHOUSE.  27 OCTOBER 1818

MY DEAR WOODHOUSE,

Your Letter gave me a great satisfaction; more on account of its
friendliness, than any relish of that matter in it which is accounted so
acceptable in the 'genus irritabile.'  The best answer I can give you is in a
clerklike manner to make some observations on two principle points, which
seem to point like indices into the midst of the whole pro and con, about
genius, and views and atchievements and ambition and cœtera.  1st As to
the poetical Character itself, (I mean that sort of which, if I am any thing,
I am a Member; that sort distinguished from the wordsworthian or
egotistical sublime; which is a thing per se and stands alone) it is not itself
—it has no self—it is every thing and nothing—It has no character—it
enjoys light and shade; it lives in gusto, be it foul or fair, high or low, rich
or poor, mean or elevated—It has as much delight in conceiving an Iago
as an Imogen.  What shocks the virtuous philosop[h]er, delights the
camelion Poet.  It does no harm from its relish of the dark side of things
any more than from its taste for the bright one; because they both end in
speculation.  A Poet is the most unpoetical of any thing in existence;
because he has no Identity—he is continually in for—and filling some
other Body—The Sun, the Moon, the Sea and Men and Women who are

[9] *For* no.

creatures of impulse are poetical and have about them an unchangeable attribute—the poet has none; no identity—he is certainly the most unpoetical of all God's Creatures.    If then he has no self, and if I am a Poet,

write

where is the Wonder that I should say I would ⟨right⟩ no more?    Might I not at that very instant [have] been cogitating on the Characters of saturn and Ops?    It is a wretched thing to confess; but is a very fact that not one word I ever utter can be taken for granted as an opinion growing out of my identical nature—how can it, when I have no nature?    When I am in a room with People if I ever am free from speculating on creations of my own brain, then not myself goes home to myself: but the identity of every one in the room begins [to] to press upon me that, I am in a very little time annihilated—not only among Men; it would be the same in a Nursery of children: I know not whether I make myself wholly understood: I hope enough so to let you see that no dependence is to be placed on what I said that day.

In the second place I will speak of my views, and of the life I purpose to myself—I am ambitious of doing the world some good: if I should be spared that may be the work of maturer years—in the interval I will assay to reach to as high a summit in Poetry as the nerve bestowed upon me will suffer.    The faint conceptions I have of Poems to come brings the blood frequently into my forehead—All I hope is that I may not lose all interest in human affairs—that the solitary indifference I feel for applause even from the finest Spirits, will not blunt any acuteness of vision I may have. I do not think it will—I feel assured I should write from the mere yearning and fondness I have for the Beautiful even if my night's labours should be burnt every morning and no eye ever shine upon them.    But even now I am perhaps not speaking from myself; but from some character in whose soul I now live.    I am sure however that this next sentence is from myself. I feel your anxiety, good opinion and friendliness in the highest degree, and am

Your's most sincerely<br>JOHN KEATS

PERCY BYSSHE SHELLEY

# A Defence of Poetry

1821; published 1840

*Shelley's impassioned and at times rhapsodic defense should bring to mind Sidney's apology for poetry; and, like Sidney, he too vindicates poetry on moral grounds. But he goes far beyond Sidney in his conception of who the poets are, what they do, and how their creations effect improvements in men and in society. Shelley arrives at the often-quoted climactic metaphor, "Poets are the unacknowledged legislators of the world," by assuming a Platonic conception of the universe. But although he accepts Plato's idealistic premises, and his psychological model as well, he completely reverses Plato's conclusion about the place of poets in society. Not through reason (analysis) but through the imagination (synthesis) do we perceive the "indestructible order" and harmony of the universe. The poets perceive the existing but unrecognized relationships and either express their perceptions in language or embody them in ideal social, legal, or religious orders. To reveal the ideal is to reveal the good, the true, and the beautiful as a harmonious One. (Note how metrical language is justified on these grounds.) Thus the imaginative mind is creative and unifying; the "reasoners," who analyze and dissect, can never inspire the human mind as poets do. Plato had said that poets were useless; but, redefining utility, Shelley tells us, sounding strikingly modern, that we have accumulated more facts than we can digest, and that what we need are the large unifying views that the great imaginative thinkers (or "poets") can provide, and that enable us to find meaning in our lives. Which is more truly useful then?*

From *Shelley's Literary and Philosophical Criticism*, ed. John Shawcross; Oxford University Press, 1909.

*But how does poetry teach? It is important to distinguish between Sidney's conception of poetry as teaching specific moral doctrines and Shelley's view in which the imagination itself is made the teaching agent; in fact, Shelley praises Milton for boldly neglecting "a direct moral purpose" in his portrayal of Satan. Poetry works indirectly by awakening man's ability to identify and empathize. Shelley calls this "a going out of our own nature," and even implies that the difference between good and bad men is the degree to which they have active imaginations. Poetry creates a broadened range of sympathy and an enlargement of the circumference of the mind; therefore the poetic effect is associated with a beneficial awakening and change in ideas and institutions.*

*Shelley devotes about two-thirds of the essay to a history which is rather more polemical than factual. He was, in fact, replying to Thomas Love Peacock's charge in* The Four Ages of Poetry *that poetry was and always had been useless and irrelevant; in rebutting Peacock, Shelley employs a theory of history that should be analyzed in relation to the ideas in the first part of his essay.*

## PART I

ACCORDING TO one mode of regarding those two classes of mental action, which are called reason and imagination, the former may be considered as mind contemplating the relations borne by one thought to another, however produced; and the latter, as mind acting upon those thoughts so as to colour them with its own light, and composing from them, as from elements, other thoughts, each containing within itself the principle of its own integrity.   The one is the τὸ ποιεῖν,[1] or the principle of synthesis, and has for its objects those forms which are common to universal nature and existence itself; the other is the τὸ λογίζειν,[2] or principle of analysis, and its action regards the relations of things, simply as relations; considering thoughts, not in their integral unity, but as the algebraical representations which conduct to certain general results.   Reason is the enumeration of quantities already known; imagination is the perception of the value of those quantities, both separately and as a whole.   Reason respects the differences, and imagination the similitudes of things.   Reason is to the imagination as the instrument to the agent, as the body to the spirit, as the shadow to the substance.

Poetry, in a general sense, may be defined to be 'the expression of the imagination': and poetry is connate with the origin of man.   Man is an instrument over which a series of external and internal impressions are

[1] *To poiein.*
[2] *To logizein.*

driven, like the alternations of an ever-changing wind over an Aeolian lyre, which move it by their motion to ever-changing melody. But there is a principle within the human being, and perhaps within all sentient beings, which acts otherwise than in the lyre, and produces not melody alone, but harmony, by an internal adjustment of the sounds or motions thus excited to the impressions which excite them. It is as if the lyre could accommodate its chords to the motions of that which strikes them, in a determined proportion of sound; even as the musician can accommodate his voice to the sound of the lyre. A child at play by itself will express its delight by its voice and motions; and every inflexion of tone and every gesture will bear exact relation to a corresponding antitype in the pleasurable impressions which awakened it; it will be the reflected image of that impression; and as the lyre trembles and sounds after the wind has died away, so the child seeks, by prolonging in its voice and motions the duration of the effect, to prolong also a consciousness of the cause. In relation to the objects which delight a child, these expressions are, what poetry is to higher objects. The savage (for the savage is to ages what the child is to years) expresses the emotions produced in him by surrounding objects in a similar manner; and language and gesture, together with plastic or pictorial imitation, become the image of the combined effect of those objects, and of his apprehension of them. Man in society, with all his passions and his pleasures, next becomes the object of the passions and pleasures of man; an additional class of emotions produces an augmented treasure of expressions; and language, gesture, and the imitative arts, become at once the representation and the medium, the pencil and the picture, the chisel and the statue, the chord and the harmony. The social sympathies, or those laws from which, as from its elements, society results, begin to develop themselves from the moment that two human beings coexist; the future is contained within the present, as the plant within the seed; and equality, diversity, unity, contrast, mutual dependence, become the principles alone capable of affording the motives according to which the will of a social being is determined to action, inasmuch as he is social; and constitute pleasure in sensation, virtue in sentiment, beauty in art, truth in reasoning, and love in the intercourse of kind. Hence men, even in the infancy of society, observe a certain order in their words and actions, distinct from that of the objects and the impressions represented by them, all expression being subject to the laws of that from which it proceeds. But let us dismiss those more general considerations which might involve an inquiry into the principles of society itself, and restrict our view to the manner in which the imagination is expressed upon its forms.

In the youth of the world, men dance and sing and imitate natural objects, observing in these actions, as in all others, a certain rhythm or order. And, although all men observe a similar, they observe not the same order, in the motions of the dance, in the melody of the song, in the combinations of language, in the series of their imitations of natural objects. For there is a certain order or rhythm belonging to each of these classes of mimetic representation, from which the hearer and the spectator receive an intenser and purer pleasure than from any other; the sense of an approximation to this order has been called taste by modern writers. Every man in the infancy of art observes an order which approximates more or less closely to that from which this highest delight results: but the diversity is not sufficiently marked, as that its gradations should be sensible, except in those instances where the predominance of this faculty of approximation to the beautiful (for so we may be permitted to name the relation between this highest pleasure and its cause) is very great. Those in whom it exists in excess are poets, in the most universal sense of the word; and the pleasure resulting from the manner in which they express the influence of society or nature upon their own minds, communicates itself to others, and gathers a sort of reduplication from that community. Their language is vitally metaphorical; that is, it marks the before unapprehended relations of things and perpetuates their apprehension, until the words which represent them become, through time, signs for portions or classes of thoughts instead of pictures of integral thoughts; and then if no new poets should arise to create afresh the associations which have been thus disorganized, language will be dead to all the nobler purposes of human intercourse. These similitudes or relations are finely said by Lord Bacon to be 'the same footsteps of nature impressed upon the various subjects of the world'; and he considers the faculty which perceives them as the storehouse of axioms common to all knowledge. In the infancy of society every author is necessarily a poet, because language itself is poetry; and to be a poet is to apprehend the true and the beautiful, in a word, the good which exists in the relation, subsisting, first between existence and perception, and secondly between perception and expression. Every original language near to its source is in itself the chaos of a cyclic poem: the copiousness of lexicography and the distinctions of grammar are the works of a later age, and are merely the catalogue and the form of the creations of poetry.

But poets, or those who imagine and express this indestructible order, are not only the authors of language and of music, of the dance, and architecture, and statuary, and painting; they are the institutors of laws, and the founders of civil society, and the inventors of the arts of life, and the teachers, who draw into a certain propinquity with the beautiful and the true, that partial apprehension of the agencies of the invisible world which is called religion.   Hence all original religions are allegorical, or susceptible of allegory, and, like Janus, have a double face of false and true.   Poets, according to the circumstances of the age and nation in which they appeared, were called, in the earlier epochs of the world, legislators, or prophets: a poet essentially comprises and unites both these characters.   For he not only beholds intensely the present as it is, and discovers those laws according to which present things ought to be ordered, but he beholds the future in the present, and his thoughts are the germs of the flower and the fruit of latest time.   Not that I assert poets to be prophets in the gross sense of the word, or that they can foretell the form as surely as they foreknow the spirit of events: such is the pretence of superstition, which would make poetry an attribute of prophecy, rather than prophecy an attribute of poetry.   A poet participates in the eternal, the infinite, and the one; as far as relates to his conceptions, time and place and number are not.   The grammatical forms which express the moods of time, and the difference of persons, and the distinction of place, are convertible with respect to the highest poetry without injuring it as poetry; and the choruses of Aeschylus, and the book of *Job*, and Dante's *Paradise*, would afford, more than any other writings, examples of this fact, if the limits of this essay did not forbid citation.   The creations of sculpture, painting, and music, are illustrations still more decisive.

Language, colour, form, and religious and civil habits of action, are all the instruments and materials of poetry; they may be called poetry by that figure of speech which considers the effect as a synonym of the cause. But poetry in a more restricted sense expresses those arrangements of language, and especially metrical language, which are created by that imperial faculty, whose throne is curtained within the invisible nature of man.   And this springs from the nature itself of language, which is a more direct representation of the actions and passions of our internal being, and is susceptible of more various and delicate combinations, than colour, form, or motion, and is more plastic and obedient to the control of that faculty of which it is the creation.   For language is arbitrarily produced by the imagination, and has relation to thoughts alone; but all other materials, instruments, and conditions of art, have relations among each other, which limit and interpose between conception and expression. The former is as a mirror which reflects, the latter as a cloud which enfeebles, the light of which both are mediums of communication. Hence the fame of sculptors, painters, and musicians, although the intrinsic powers of the great masters of these arts may yield in no degree to that of those who have employed language as the hieroglyphic of their thoughts, has never equalled that of poets in the restricted sense of the term; as two performers of equal skill will produce unequal effects from a guitar and a harp.   The fame of legislators and founders of religions, so long as their institutions last, alone seems to exceed that of poets in the restricted sense; but it can scarcely be a question, whether, if we deduct the celebrity which their flattery of the gross opinions of the vulgar usually conciliates, together with that which belonged to them in their higher character of poets, any excess will remain.

We have thus circumscribed the word poetry within the limits of that art which is the most familiar and the most perfect expression of the faculty itself.   It is necessary, however, to make the circle still narrower, and to determine the distinction between measured and unmeasured language; for the popular division into prose and verse is inadmissible in accurate philosophy.

Sounds as well as thoughts have relation both between each other and towards that which they represent, and a perception of the order of those relations has always been found connected with a perception of the order of the relations of thoughts.   Hence the language of poets has ever affected a certain uniform and harmonious recurrence of sound, without which it were not poetry, and which is scarcely less indispensable to the communication of its influence, than the words themselves, without reference to that peculiar order.   Hence the vanity of translation; it were as wise to cast a violet into a crucible that you might discover the formal principle of its colour and odour, as seek to transfuse from one language into another the creations of a poet.   The plant must spring again from its seed, or it will bear no flower—and this is the burthen of the curse of Babel.

An observation of the regular mode of the recurrence of harmony in the language of poetical minds, together with its relation to music, produced metre, or a certain system of traditional forms of harmony and language.   Yet it is by no means essential that a poet should accommodate his language to this traditional form, so that the harmony, which is its spirit, be observed.   The practice is indeed convenient and popular, and to be preferred, especially in such composition as includes much action: but every great poet must inevitably innovate upon the example of his predecessors in the exact structure of his peculiar versification.   The distinction between poets and prose writers is a vulgar error.   The distinction between philosophers and poets has been anticipated.   Plato was essentially a poet—the truth and splendour of his imagery, and the melody of his language, are the most intense that it is possible to conceive. He rejected the measure of the epic, dramatic, and lyrical forms, because he sought to kindle a harmony in thoughts divested of shape and action, and he forbore to invent any regular plan of rhythm which would include, under determinate forms, the varied pauses of his style.   Cicero sought to imitate the cadence of his periods, but with little success. Lord Bacon was a poet. His language has a sweet and majestic rhythm, which satisfies the sense, no less than the almost superhuman wisdom of his philosophy satisfies the intellect; it is a strain which distends, and then bursts the circumference of the reader's mind, and pours itself forth together with it into the universal element with which it has perpetual sympathy. All the authors of revolutions in opinion are not only necessarily poets as they are inventors, nor even as their words unveil the permanent analogy of things by images which participate in the life of truth; but as their periods are harmonious and rhythmical, and contain in themselves the elements of verse; being the echo of the eternal music. Nor are those supreme poets, who have employed traditional forms of rhythm on account of the form and action of their subjects, less capable of perceiving and teaching the truth of things, than those who have omitted that form. Shakespeare, Dante, and Milton (to confine ourselves to modern writers) are philosophers of the very loftiest power.

A poem is the very image of life expressed in its eternal truth. There is this difference between a story and a poem, that a story is a catalogue of detached facts, which have no other connexion than time, place, circumstance, cause and effect; the other is the creation of actions according to the unchangeable forms of human nature, as existing in the mind of the Creator, which is itself the image of all other minds. The one is partial, and applies only to a definite period of time; and a certain combination of events which can never again recur; the other is universal, and contains within itself the germ of a relation to whatever motives or actions have place in the possible varieties of human nature. Time, which destroys the beauty and the use of the story of particular facts, stripped of the poetry which should invest them, augments that of poetry, and for ever develops new and wonderful applications of the eternal truth which it contains. Hence epitomes have been called the moths of just history; they eat out the poetry of it. A story of particular facts is as a mirror which obscures and distorts that which should be beautiful: poetry is a mirror which makes beautiful that which is distorted.

The parts of a composition may be poetical, without the composition as a whole being a poem. A single sentence may be considered as a whole, though it may be found in the midst of a series of unassimilated portions: a single word even may be a spark of inextinguishable thought. And thus all the great historians, Herodotus, Plutarch, Livy, were poets; and although the plan of these writers, especially that of Livy, restrained them from developing this faculty in its highest degree, they made copious and ample amends for their subjection, by filling all the interstices of their subjects with living images.

Having determined what is poetry, and who are poets, let us proceed to estimate its effects upon society.

Poetry is ever accompanied with pleasure: all spirits on which it falls open themselves to receive the wisdom which is mingled with its delight. In the infancy of the world, neither poets themselves nor their auditors are fully aware of the excellence of poetry: for it acts in a divine and un-apprehended manner, beyond and above consciousness; and it is reserved for future generations to contemplate and measure the mighty cause and effect in all the strength and splendour of their union. Even in modern times, no living poet ever arrived at the fullness of his fame; the jury which sits in judgement upon a poet, belonging as he does to all time, must be composed of his peers: it must be impanelled by Time from the selectest of the wise of many generations. A poet is a nightingale, who sits in darkness and sings to cheer its own solitude with sweet sounds; his auditors are as men entranced by the melody of an unseen musician, who feel that they are moved and softened, yet know not whence or why. The poems of Homer and his contemporaries were the delight of infant Greece; they were the elements of that social system which is the column upon which all succeeding civilization has reposed. Homer embodied the ideal perfection of his age in human character; nor can we doubt that those who read his verses were awakened to an ambition of becoming like to Achilles, Hector, and Ulysses: the truth and beauty of friendship, patriotism, and persevering devotion to an object, were unveiled to the depths in these immortal creations: the sentiments of the auditors must have been refined and enlarged by a sympathy with such great and lovely impersonations, until from admiring they imitated, and from imitation they identified themselves with the objects of their admiration. Nor let it be objected, that these characters are remote from moral perfection, and that they can by no means be considered as edifying patterns for general imitation. Every epoch, under names more or less specious, has deified its peculiar errors; Revenge is the naked idol of the worship of a semi-barbarous age; and Self-deceit is the veiled image of unknown evil, before which luxury and satiety lie prostrate. But a poet considers the vices of his contemporaries as a temporary dress in which his creations must be arrayed, and which cover without concealing the eternal proportions of their beauty. An epic or dramatic personage is understood to wear them around his soul, as he may the ancient armour or the modern uniform around his body; whilst it is easy to conceive a dress more graceful than either. The beauty of the internal nature cannot be so far concealed by its accidental vesture, but that the spirit of its form shall communicate itself to the very disguise, and indicate the shape it hides from the manner in which it is worn. A majestic form and graceful motions will express themselves through the most barbarous and tasteless costume. Few poets of the highest class have chosen to exhibit the beauty of their conceptions in its naked truth and splendour; and it is doubtful whether the alloy of costume, habit, &c., be not necessary to temper this planetary music for mortal ears.

The whole objection, however, of the immorality of poetry rests upon a misconception of the manner in which poetry acts to produce the moral improvement of man. Ethical science arranges the elements which poetry has created, and propounds schemes and proposes examples of civil and domestic life: nor is it for want of admirable doctrines that men hate, and despise, and censure, and deceive, and subjugate one another. But poetry acts in another and diviner manner. It awakens and enlarges the mind itself by rendering it the receptacle of a thousand unapprehended combinations of thought. Poetry lifts the veil from the hidden beauty of the world, and makes familiar objects be as if they were not familiar; it reproduces all that it represents, and the impersonations clothed in its Elysian light stand thenceforward in the minds of those who have once contemplated them, as memorials of that gentle and exalted content which extends itself over all thoughts and actions with which it coexists. The great secret of morals is love; or a going out of our own nature, and an identification of ourselves with the beautiful which exists in thought, action, or person, not our own. A man, to be greatly good, must imagine intensely and comprehensively; he must put himself in the place of another and of many others; the pains and pleasures of his species must become his own. The great instrument of moral good is the imagination; and poetry administers to the effect by acting upon the cause. Poetry enlarges the circumference of the imagination by replenishing it with thoughts of ever new delight, which have the power of attracting and assimilating to their own nature all other thoughts, and which form new intervals and interstices whose void for ever craves fresh food. Poetry strengthens the faculty which is the organ of the moral nature of man, in the same manner as exercise strengthens a limb. A poet therefore would do ill to embody his own conceptions of right and wrong, which are usually those of his place and time, in his poetical creations which participate in neither. By this assumption of the inferior office of interpreting the effect, in which perhaps after all he might acquit himself but imperfectly, he would resign a glory in a participation in the cause. There was little danger that Homer, or any of the eternal poets, should have so far misunderstood themselves as to have abdicated this throne of their widest dominion. Those in whom the poetical faculty, though great, is less intense, as Euripides, Lucan, Tasso, Spenser, have frequently affected a moral aim, and the effect of their poetry is diminished in exact proportion to the degree in which they compel us to advert to this purpose.

Homer and the cyclic poets were followed at a certain interval by the dramatic and lyrical poets of Athens, who flourished contemporaneously with all that is most perfect in the kindred expressions of the poetical faculty; architecture, painting, music, the dance, sculpture, philosophy, and, we may add, the forms of civil life. For although the scheme of Athenian society was deformed by many imperfections which the poetry existing in chivalry and Christianity has erased from the habits and institutions of modern Europe; yet never at any other period has so much energy, beauty, and virtue, been developed; never was blind strength and stubborn form so disciplined and rendered subject to the will of man, or that will less repugnant to the dictates of the beautiful and the true, as during the century which preceded the death of Socrates. Of no other epoch in the history of our species have we records and fragments stamped so visibly with the image of the divinity in man. But it is poetry alone, in form, in action, or in language, which has rendered this epoch memorable above all others, and the storehouse of examples to everlasting time. For written poetry existed at that epoch simultaneously with the other arts, and it is an idle inquiry to demand which gave and which received the light, which all, as from a common focus, have scattered over the darkest periods of succeeding time. We know no more of cause and effect than a constant conjunction of events: poetry is ever found to co-exist with whatever other arts contribute to the happiness and perfection of man. I appeal to what has already been established to distinguish between the cause and the effect.

It was at the period here adverted to, that the drama had its birth; and however a succeeding writer may have equalled or surpassed those few great specimens of the Athenian drama which have been preserved to us, it is indisputable that the art itself never was understood or practised according to the true philosophy of it, as at Athens. For the Athenians employed language, action, music, painting, the dance, and religious institutions, to produce a common effect in the representation of the highest idealisms of passion and of power; each division in the art was made perfect in its kind by artists of the most consummate skill, and was disciplined into a beautiful proportion and unity one towards the other. On the modern stage a few only of the elements capable of expressing the image of the poet's conception are employed at once. We have tragedy without music and dancing; and music and dancing without the highest impersonations of which they are the fit accompaniment, and both without religion and solemnity. Religious institution has indeed been usually banished from the stage. Our system of divesting the actor's face of a mask, on which the many expressions appropriated to his dramatic character might be moulded into one permanent and unchanging expression, is favourable only to a partial and inharmonious effect; it is fit for nothing but a monologue, where all the attention may be directed to some great master of ideal mimicry. The modern practice of blending comedy with tragedy, though liable to great abuse in point of practice, is undoubtedly an extension of the dramatic circle; but the comedy should be as in *King Lear*, universal, ideal, and sublime. It is perhaps the intervention of this principle which determines the balance in favour of *King Lear* against the *Oedipus Tyrannus* or the *Agamemnon*, or, if you will, the trilogies with which they are connected; unless the intense power of the choral poetry, especially that of the latter, should be considered as restoring the equilibrium. *King Lear*, if it can sustain this comparison, may be judged to be the most perfect specimen of the dramatic art existing in the world; in spite of the narrow conditions to which the poet was subjected by the ignorance of the philosophy of the drama which has prevailed in modern Europe. Calderon, in his religious *Autos*, has attempted to fulfil some of the high conditions of dramatic representation neglected by Shakespeare; such as the establishing a relation between the drama and religion, and the accommodating them to music and dancing; but he omits the observation of conditions still more important, and more is lost than gained by the substitution of the rigidly-defined and ever-repeated idealisms of a distorted superstition for the living impersonations of the truth of human passion.

But I digress.—The connexion of scenic exhibitions with the improvement or corruption of the manners of men, has been universally recognized: in other words, the presence or absence of poetry in its most perfect and universal form, has been found to be connected with good and evil in conduct or habit. The corruption which has been imputed to the drama as an effect, begins, when the poetry employed in its constitution ends: I appeal to the history of manners whether the periods of the growth of the one and the decline of the other have not corresponded with an exactness equal to any example of moral cause and effect.

The drama at Athens, or wheresoever else it may have approached to its perfection, ever co-existed with the moral and intellectual greatness of the age. The tragedies of the Athenian poets are as mirrors in which the spectator beholds himself, under a thin disguise of circumstance, stript of all but that ideal perfection and energy which every one feels to be the internal type of all that he loves, admires, and would become. The imagination is enlarged by a sympathy with pains and passions so mighty, that they distend in their conception the capacity of that by which they are conceived; the good affections are strengthened by pity, indignation, terror, and sorrow; and an exalted calm is prolonged from the satiety of this high exercise of them into the tumult of familiar life: even crime is disarmed of half its horror and all its contagion by being represented as the fatal consequence of the unfathomable agencies of nature; error is thus divested of its wilfulness; men can no longer cherish it as the creation of their choice.  In a drama of the highest order there is little food for censure or hatred; it teaches rather self-knowledge and self-respect. Neither the eye nor the mind can see itself, unless reflected upon that which it resembles.  The drama, so long as it continues to express poetry, is as a prismatic and many-sided mirror, which collects the brightest rays of human nature and divides and reproduces them from the simplicity of these elementary forms, and touches them with majesty and beauty, and multiplies all that it reflects, and endows it with the power of propagating its like wherever it may fall.

But in periods of the decay of social life, the drama sympathizes with that decay.  Tragedy becomes a cold imitation of the form of the great masterpieces of antiquity, divested of all harmonious accompaniment of the kindred arts; and often the very form misunderstood, or a weak attempt to teach certain doctrines, which the writer considers as moral truths; and which are usually no more than specious flatteries of some gross vice or weakness, with which the author, in common with his auditors, are infected.  Hence what has been called the classical and domestic drama.  Addison's *Cato* is a specimen of the one; and would it were not superfluous to cite examples of the other!  To such purposes poetry cannot be made subservient.  Poetry is a sword of lightning, ever unsheathed, which consumes the scabbard that would contain it.  And thus we observe that all dramatic writings of this nature are unimaginative in a singular degree; they affect sentiment and passion, which, divested of imagination, are other names for caprice and appetite.  The period in our own history of the grossest degradation of the drama is the reign of Charles II, when all forms in which poetry had been accustomed to be expressed became hymns to the triumph of kingly power over liberty and virtue.  Milton stood alone illuminating an age unworthy of him.  At such periods the calculating principle pervades all the forms of dramatic exhibition, and poetry ceases to be expressed upon them.  Comedy loses its ideal universality: wit succeeds to humour; we laugh from self-complacency and triumph, instead of pleasure; malignity, sarcasm, and contempt, succeed to sympathetic merriment; we hardly laugh, but we smile.  Obscenity, which is ever blasphemy against the divine beauty in life, becomes, from the very veil which it assumes, more active if less disgusting: it is a monster for which the corruption of society for ever brings forth new food, which it devours in secret.

The drama being that form under which a greater number of modes of expression of poetry are susceptible of being combined than any other, the connexion of poetry and social good is more observable in the drama than in whatever other form. And it is indisputable that the highest perfection of human society has ever corresponded with the highest dramatic excellence; and that the corruption or the extinction of the drama in a nation where it has once flourished, is a mark of a corruption of manners, and an extinction of the energies which sustain the soul of social life. But, as Machiavelli says of political institutions, that life may be preserved and renewed, if men should arise capable of bringing back the drama to its principles. And this is true with respect to poetry in its most extended sense: all language, institution and form require not only to be produced but to be sustained: the office and character of a poet participates in the divine nature as regards providence, no less than as regards creation.

Civil war, the spoils of Asia, and the fatal predominance first of the Macedonian, and then of the Roman arms, were so many symbols of the extinction or suspension of the creative faculty in Greece. The bucolic writers, who found patronage under the lettered tyrants of Sicily and Egypt, were the latest representatives of its most glorious reign. Their poetry is intensely melodious; like the odour of the tuberose, it overcomes and sickens the spirit with excess of sweetness; whilst the poetry of the preceding age was as a meadow-gale of June, which mingles the fragrance of all the flowers of the field, and adds a quickening and harmonizing spirit of its own, which endows the sense with a power of sustaining its extreme delight. The bucolic and erotic delicacy in written poetry is correlative with that softness in statuary, music, and the kindred arts, and even in manners and institutions, which distinguished the epoch to which I now refer. Nor is it the poetical faculty itself, or any misapplication of it, to which this want of harmony is to be imputed. An equal sensibility to the influence of the senses and the affections is to be found in the writings of Homer and Sophocles: the former, especially, has clothed sensual and pathetic images with irresistible attractions. Their superiority over these succeeding writers consists in the presence of those thoughts which belong to the inner faculties of our nature, not in the absence of those which are connected with the external: their incomparable perfection consists in a harmony of the union of all. It is not what the erotic poets have, but what they have not, in which their imperfection consists. It is not inasmuch as they were poets, but inasmuch as they were not poets, that they can be considered with any plausibility as connected with the corruption of their age. Had that corruption availed so as to extinguish in them the sensibility to pleasure, passion, and natural scenery, which is imputed to them as an imperfection, the last triumph of evil would have been achieved. For the end of social corruption is to destroy all sensibility to pleasure; and, therefore, it is corruption. It begins at the imagination and the intellect as at the core, and distributes itself thence as a paralysing venom, through the affections into the very appetites, until all become a torpid mass in which hardly sense survives.   At the approach of such a period, poetry ever addresses itself to those faculties which are the last to be destroyed, and its voice is heard, like the footsteps of Astraea, departing from the world.   Poetry ever communicates all the pleasure which men are capable of receiving: it is ever still the light of life; the source of whatever of beautiful or generous or true can have place in an evil time. It will readily be confessed that those among the luxurious citizens of Syracuse and Alexandria, who were delighted with the poems of Theo-critus, were less cold, cruel, and sensual than the remnant of their tribe. But corruption must utterly have destroyed the fabric of human society before poetry can ever cease.   The sacred links of that chain have never been entirely disjoined, which descending through the minds of many men is attached to those great minds, whence as from a magnet the invisible effluence is sent forth, which at once connects, animates, and sustains the life of all.   It is the faculty which contains within itself the seeds at once of its own and of social renovation.   And let us not circum-scribe the effects of the bucolic and erotic poetry within the limits of the sensibility of those to whom it was addressed.   They may have perceived the beauty of those immortal compositions, simply as fragments and isolated portions: those who are more finely organized, or born in a happier age, may recognize them as episodes to that great poem, which all poets, like the co-operating thoughts of one great mind, have built up since the beginning of the world.

The same revolutions within a narrower sphere had place in ancient Rome; but the actions and forms of its social life never seem to have been perfectly saturated with the poetical element.   The Romans appear to have considered the Greeks as the selectest treasuries of the selectest forms of manners and of nature, and to have abstained from creating in measured language, sculpture, music, or architecture, anything which might bear a particular relation to their own condition, whilst it should bear a general one to the universal constitution of the world.   But we judge from partial evidence, and we judge perhaps partially.   Ennius, Varro, Pacuvius, and Accius, all great poets, have been lost.   Lucretius is in the highest, and Virgil in a very high sense, a creator.   The chosen delicacy of expressions of the latter, are as a mist of light which conceal from us the intense and exceeding truth of his conceptions of nature.   Livy is instinct with poetry. Yet Horace, Catullus, Ovid, and generally the other great writers of the Virgilian age, saw man and nature in the mirror of Greece.   The institutions also, and the religion of Rome were less poetical than those of Greece, as the shadow is less vivid than the substance.   Hence poetry in

Rome, seemed to follow, rather than accompany, the perfection of political and domestic society. The true poetry of Rome lived in its institutions; for whatever of beautiful, true, and majestic, they contained, could have sprung only from the faculty which creates the order in which they consist. The life of Camillus, the death of Regulus; the expectation of the senators, in their godlike state, of the victorious Gauls: the refusal of the republic to make peace with Hannibal, after the battle of Cannae, were not the consequences of a refined calculation of the probable personal advantage to result from such a rhythm and order in the shows of life, to those who were at once the poets and the actors of these immortal dramas. The imagination beholding the beauty of this order, created it out of itself according to its own idea; the consequence was empire, and the reward everliving fame. These things are not the less poetry *quia carent vate sacro*.[3] They are the episodes of that cyclic poem written by Time upon the memories of men. The Past, like an inspired rhapsodist, fills the theatre of everlasting generations with their harmony.

At length the ancient system of religion and manners had fulfilled the circle of its revolutions. And the world would have fallen into utter anarchy and darkness, but that there were found poets among the authors of the Christian and chivalric systems of manners and religion, who created forms of opinion and action never before conceived; which, copied into the imaginations of men, become as generals to the bewildered armies of their thoughts. It is foreign to the present purpose to touch upon the evil produced by these systems: except that we protest, on the ground of the principles already established, that no portion of it can be attributed to the poetry they contain.

It is probable that the poetry of Moses, Job, David, Solomon, and Isaiah, had produced a great effect upon the mind of Jesus and his disciples. The scattered fragments preserved to us by the biographers of this extraordinary person, are all instinct with the most vivid poetry. But his doctrines seem to have been quickly distorted. At a certain period after the prevalence of a system of opinions founded upon those promulgated by him, the three forms into which Plato had distributed the faculties of mind underwent a sort of apotheosis, and became the object of the worship of the civilized world. Here it is to be confessed that 'Light seems to thicken', and

> The crow makes wing to the rooky wood,
> Good things of day begin to droop and drowse,
> And night's black agents to their preys do rouze.

---

[3] "Because they lack the divine bard" (Horace).

But mark how beautiful an order has sprung from the dust and blood of this fierce chaos! how the world, as from a resurrection, balancing itself on the golden wings of knowledge and of hope, has reassumed its yet unwearied flight into the heaven of time. Listen to the music, unheard by outward ears, which is as a ceaseless and invisible wind, nourishing its everlasting course with strength and swiftness.

The poetry in the doctrines of Jesus Christ, and the mythology and institutions of the Celtic conquerors of the Roman empire, outlived the darkness and the convulsions connected with their growth and victory, and blended themselves in a new fabric of manners and opinion. It is an error to impute the ignorance of the dark ages to the Christian doctrines or the predominance of the Celtic nations. Whatever of evil their agencies may have contained sprang from the extinction of the poetical principle, connected with the progress of despotism and superstition. Men, from causes too intricate to be here discussed, had become insensible and selfish: their own will had become feeble, and yet they were its slaves, and thence the slaves of the will of others: lust, fear, avarice, cruelty, and fraud, characterized a race amongst whom no one was to be found capable of *creating* in form, language, or institution. The moral anomalies of such a state of society are not justly to be charged upon any class of events immediately connected with them, and those events are most entitled to our approbation which could dissolve it most expeditiously. It is unfortunate for those who cannot distinguish words from thoughts, that many of these anomalies have been incorporated into our popular religion.

It was not until the eleventh century that the effects of the poetry of the Christian and chivalric systems began to manifest themselves. The principle of equality had been discovered and applied by Plato in his *Republic,* as the theoretical rule of the mode in which the materials of pleasure and of power, produced by the common skill and labour of human beings, ought to be distributed among them. The limitations of this rule were asserted by him to be determined only by the sensibility of each, or the utility to result to all. Plato, following the doctrines of Timaeus and Pythagoras, taught also a moral and intellectual system of doctrine, comprehending at once the past, the present, and the future condition of man. Jesus Christ divulged the sacred and eternal truths contained in these views to mankind, and Christianity, in its abstract purity, became the exoteric expression of the esoteric doctrines of the poetry and wisdom of antiquity. The incorporation of the Celtic nations with the exhausted population of the south, impressed upon it the figure of the poetry existing in their mythology and institutions. The result was a sum of the action and reaction of all the causes included in it; for it may be assumed as a maxim that no nation or religion can supersede any other without incorporating into itself a portion of that which it supersedes. The abolition of personal and domestic slavery, and the emancipation of women from a great part of the degrading restraints of antiquity, were among the consequences of these events.

The abolition of personal slavery is the basis of the highest political hope that it can enter into the mind of man to conceive. The freedom of women produced the poetry of sexual love. Love became a religion, the idols of whose worship were ever present. It was as if the statues of Apollo and the Muses had been endowed with life and motion, and had walked forth among their worshippers; so that earth became peopled by the inhabitants of a diviner world. The familiar appearance and proceedings of life became wonderful and heavenly, and a paradise was created as out of the wrecks of Eden. And as this creation itself is poetry, so its creators were poets; and language was the instrument of their art: 'Galeotto fù il libro, e chi lo scrisse.'[4] The Provençal Trouveurs, or inventors, preceded Petrarch, whose verses are as spells, which unseal the inmost enchanted fountains of the delight which is in the grief of love. It is impossible to feel them without becoming a portion of that beauty which we contemplate: it were superfluous to explain how the gentleness and the elevation of mind connected with these sacred emotions can render men more amiable, more generous and wise, and lift them out of the dull vapours of the little word of self. Dante understood the secret things of love even more than Petrarch. His *Vita Nuova* is an inexhaustible fountain of purity of sentiment and language: it is the idealized history of that period, and those intervals of his life which were dedicated to love. His apotheosis of Beatrice in Paradise, and the gradations of his own love and her loveliness, by which as by steps he feigns himself to have ascended to the throne of the Supreme Cause, is the most glorious imagination of modern poetry. The acutest critics have justly reversed the judgement of the vulgar, and the order of the great acts of the 'Divine Drama', in the measure of the admiration which they accord to the Hell, Purgatory, and Paradise. The latter is a perpetual hymn of everlasting love. Love, which found a worthy poet in Plato alone of all the ancients, has been celebrated by a chorus of the greatest writers of the renovated words; and the music has penetrated the caverns of society, and its echoes still drown the dissonance of arms and superstition. At successive intervals, Ariosto, Tasso, Shakespeare, Spenser, Calderon, Rousseau, and the great writers of our own age, have celebrated the dominion of love, planting as it were trophies in the human mind of that sublimest victory over sensuality and

4 "Galeotto was the book and he that wrote it" (Dante).

force. The true relation borne to each other by the sexes into which human kind is distributed, has become less misunderstood; and if the error which confounded diversity with inequality of the powers of the two sexes has been partially recognized in the opinions and institutions of modern Europe, we owe this great benefit to the worship of which chivalry was the law, and poets the prophets.

The poetry of Dante may be considered as the bridge thrown over the stream of time, which unites the modern and ancient world. The distorted notions of invisible things which Dante and his rival Milton have idealized, are merely the mask and the mantle in which these great poets walk through eternity enveloped and disguised. It is a difficult question to determine how far they were conscious of the distinction which must have subsisted in their minds between their own creeds and that of the people. Dante at least appears to wish to mark the full extent of it by placing Riphaeus, whom Virgil calls *justissimus unus*, in Paradise, and observing a most heretical caprice in his distribution of rewards and punishments. And Milton's poem contains within itself a philosophical refutation of that system, of which, by a strange and natural antithesis, it has been a chief popular support. Nothing can exceed the energy and magnificence of the character of Satan as expressed in *Paradise Lost*. It is a mistake to suppose that he could ever have been intended for the popular personification of evil. Implacable hate, patient cunning, and a sleepless refinement of device to inflict the extremest anguish on an enemy, these things are evil; and, although venial in a slave, are not to be forgiven in a tyrant; although redeemed by much that ennobles his defeat in one subdued, are marked by all that dishonours his conquest in the victor. Milton's Devil as a moral being is as far superior to his God, as one who perseveres in some purpose which he has conceived to be excellent in spite of adversity and torture, is to one who in the cold security of undoubted triumph inflicts the most horrible revenge upon his enemy, not from any mistaken notion of inducing him to repent of a perseverance in enmity, but with the alleged design of exasperating him to deserve new torments. Milton has so far violated the popular creed (if this shall be judged to be a violation) as to have alleged no superiority of moral virtue to his God over his Devil. And this bold neglect of a direct moral purpose is the most decisive proof of the supremacy of Milton's genius. He mingled as it were the elements of human nature as colours upon a single pallet, and arranged them in the composition of his great picture according to the laws of epic truth; that is, according to the laws of that principle by which a series of actions of the external universe and of intelligent and ethical beings is calculated to excite the sympathy of succeeding generations of mankind. The *Divina Commedia* and *Paradise Lost* have conferred upon modern mythology a systematic form; and when change and time shall have added one more superstition to the mass of those which have arisen and decayed upon the earth, commentators will be learnedly employed in elucidating the religion of ancestral Europe, only not utterly forgotten because it will have been stamped with the eternity of genius.

Homer was the first and Dante the second epic poet: that is, the second poet, the series of whose creations bore a defined and intelligible relation to the knowledge and sentiment and religion of the age in which he lived, and of the ages which followed it: developing itself in correspondence with their development. For Lucretius had limed the wings of his swift spirit in the dregs of the sensible world; and Virgil, with a modesty that ill became his genius, had affected the fame of an imitator, even whilst he created anew all that he copied; and none among the flock of mock-birds, though their notes were sweet, Apollonius Rhodius, Quintus Calaber, Nonnus, Lucan, Statius, or Claudian, have sought even to fulfil a single condition of epic truth. Milton was the third epic poet. For if the title of epic in its highest sense be refused to the *Aeneid*, still less can it be conceded to the *Orlando Furioso*, the *Gerusalemme Liberata*, the *Lusiad*, or the *Fairy Queen*.

Dante and Milton were both deeply penetrated with the ancient religion of the civilized world; and its spirit exists in their poetry probably in the same proportion as its forms survived in the unreformed worship of modern Europe. The one preceded and the other followed the Reformation at almost equal intervals. Dante was the first religious reformer, and Luther surpassed him rather in the rudeness and acrimony than in the boldness of his censures of papal usurpation. Dante was the first awakener of entranced Europe; he created a language, in itself music and persuasion, out of a chaos of inharmonious barbarisms. He was the congregator of those great spirits who presided over the resurrection of learning; the Lucifer of that starry flock which in the thirteenth century shone forth from republican Italy, as from a heaven, into the darkness of the benighted world. His very words are instinct with spirit; each is as a spark, a burning atom of inextinguishable thought; and many yet lie covered in the ashes of their birth, and pregnant with a lightning which has yet found no conductor. All high poetry is infinite; it is as the first acorn, which contained all oaks potentially. Veil after veil may be undrawn, and the inmost naked beauty of the meaning never exposed. A great poem is a fountain for ever overflowing with the waters of wisdom and delight; and after one person and one age has exhausted all its divine effluence which their peculiar relations enable them to share, another and yet another succeeds, and new relations are ever developed, the source of an unforeseen and an unconceived delight.

The age immediately succeeding to that of Dante, Petrarch, and

Boccaccio, was characterized by a revival of painting, sculpture, and architecture. Chaucer caught the sacred inspiration, and the super-structure of English literature is based upon the materials of Italian invention.

But let us not be betrayed from a defence into a critical history of poetry and its influence on society. Be it enough to have pointed out the effects of poets, in the large and true sense of the word, upon their own and all succeeding times.

But poets have been challenged to resign the civic crown to reasoners and mechanists, on another plea. It is admitted that the exercise of the imagination is most delightful, but it is alleged that that of reason is more useful. Let us examine as the grounds of this distinction, what is here meant by utility. Pleasure or good, in a general sense, is that which the consciousness of a sensitive and intelligent being seeks, and in which, when found, it acquiesces. There are two kinds of pleasure, one durable, universal and permanent; the other transitory and particular. Utility may either express the means of producing the former or the latter. In the former sense, whatever strengthens and purifies the affections, enlarges the imagination, and adds spirit to sense, is useful. But a narrower meaning may be assigned to the word utility, confining it to express that which banishes the importunity of the wants of our animal nat the surrounding men with security of life, the dispersing the grosser delusions of superstition, and the conciliating such a degree of mutual forbearance among men as may consist with the motives of personal advantage.

Undoubtedly the promotors of utility, in this limited sense, have their appointed office in society. They follow the footsteps of poets, and copy the sketches of their creations into the book of common life. They make space, and give time. Their exertions are of the highest value, so long as they confine their administration of the concerns of the inferior powers of our nature within the limits due to the superior ones. But whilst the sceptic destroys gross superstitions, let him spare to deface, as some of the French writers have defaced, the eternal truths charactered upon the imaginations of men. Whilst the mechanist abridges, and the political economist combines labour, let them beware that their speculations, for want of correspondence with those first principles which belong to the imagination, do not tend, as they have in modern England, to exasperate at once the extremes of luxury and want. They have exemplified the saying, 'To him that hath, more shall be given; and from him that hath not, the little that he hath shall be taken away.' The rich have become richer, and the poor have become poorer; and the vessel of the state is driven between the Scylla and Charybdis of anarchy and despotism.

Such are the effects which must ever flow from an unmitigated exercise of the calculating faculty.

It is difficult to define pleasure in its highest sense; the definition involving a number of apparent paradoxes. For, from an inexplicable defect of harmony in the constitution of human nature, the pain of the inferior is frequently connected with the pleasures of the superior portions of our being. Sorrow, terror, anguish, despair itself, are often the chosen expressions of an approximation to the highest good. Our sympathy in tragic fiction depends on this principle; tragedy delights by affording a shadow of the pleasure which exists in pain. This is the source also of the melancholy which is inseparable from the sweetest melody. The pleasure that is in sorrow is sweeter than the pleasure of pleasure itself. And hence the saying, 'It is better to go to the house of mourning, than to the house of mirth.' Not that this highest species of pleasure is necessarily linked with pain. The delight of love and friendship, the ecstasy of the admiration of nature, the joy of the perception and still more of the creation of poetry, is often wholly unalloyed.

The production and assurance of pleasure in this highest sense is true utility. Those who produce and preserve this pleasure are poets or poetical philosophers.

The exertions of Locke, Hume, Gibbon, Voltaire, Rousseau,[5] and their disciples, in favour of oppressed and deluded humanity, are entitled to the gratitude of mankind. Yet it is easy to calculate the degree of moral and intellectual improvement which the world would have exhibited, had they never lived. A little more nonsense would have been talked for a century or two; and perhaps a few more men, women, and children, burnt as heretics. We might not at this moment have been congratulating each other on the abolition of the Inquisition in Spain. But it exceeds all imagination to conceive what would have been the moral condition of the world if neither Dante, Petrarch, Boccaccio, Chaucer, Shakespeare, Calderon, Lord Bacon, nor Milton, had ever existed; if Raphael and Michael Angelo had never been born; if the Hebrew poetry had never been translated; if a revival of the study of Greek literature had never taken place; if no monuments of ancient sculpture had been handed down to us; and if the poetry of the religion of the ancient world had been extinguished together with its belief. The human mind could never, except by the intervention of these excitements, have been awakened to the invention of the grosser sciences, and that application of analytical reasoning to the aberrations of society, which it is now attempted to exalt over the direct expression of the inventive and creative faculty itself.

[5] Although Rousseau has been thus classed, he was essentially a poet. The others, even Voltaire, were mere reasoners. [Shelley's note.]

We have more moral, political and historical wisdom, than we know how to reduce into practice; we have more scientific and economical knowledge than can be accommodated to the just distribution of the produce which it multiplies.   The poetry in these systems of thought, is concealed by the accumulation of facts and calculating processes.   There is no want of knowledge respecting what is wisest and best in morals, government, and political economy, or at least, what is wiser and better than what men now practice and endure.   But we let '*I dare not* wait upon *I would*, like the poor cat in the adage.'   We want the creative faculty to imagine that which we know; we want the generous impulse to act that which we imagine; we want the poetry of life: our calculations have outrun conception; we have eaten more than we can digest.   The cultivation of those sciences which have enlarged the limits of the empire of man over the external world, has, for want of the poetical faculty, proportionally circumscribed those of the internal world; and man, having enslaved the elements, remains himself a slave.   To what but a cultivation of the mechanical arts in a degree disproportioned to the presence of the creative faculty, which is the basis of all knowledge, is to be attributed the abuse of all invention for abridging and combining labour, to the exasperation of the inequality of mankind?   From what other cause has it arisen that the discoveries which should have lightened, have added a weight to the curse imposed on Adam?   Poetry, and the principle of Self, of which money is the visible incarnation, are the God and Mammon of the world.

The functions of the poetical faculty are two-fold; by one it creates new materials of knowledge and power and pleasure; by the other it engenders in the mind a desire to reproduce and arrange them according to a certain rhythm and order which may be called the beautiful and the good.   The cultivation of poetry is never more to be desired than at periods when, from an excess of the selfish and calculating principle, the accumulation of the materials of external life exceed the quantity of the power of assimilating them to the internal laws of human nature.   The body has then become too unwieldy for that which animates it.

Poetry is indeed something divine.   It is at once the centre and circumference of knowledge; it is that which comprehends all science, and that to which all science must be referred.   It is at the same time the root and blossom of all other systems of thought; it is that from which all spring, and that which adorns all; and that which, if blighted, denies the fruit and the seed, and withholds from the barren world the nourishment and the succession of the scions of the tree of life.   It is the perfect and consummate surface and bloom of all things; it is as the odour and the colour of the rose to the texture of the elements which compose it, as the form and splendour of unfaded beauty to the secrets of anatomy and corruption. What were virtue, love, patriotism, friendship—what were the scenery of this beautiful universe which we inhabit; what were our consolations on this side of the grave—and what were our aspirations beyond it, if poetry did not ascend to bring light and fire from those eternal regions where the owl-winged faculty of calculation dare not ever soar? Poetry is not like reasoning, a power to be exerted according to the determination of the will. A man cannot say, 'I will compose poetry.' The greatest poet even cannot say it; for the mind in creation is as a fading coal, which some invisible influence, like an inconstant wind, awakens to transitory brightness; this power arises from within, like the colour of a flower which fades and changes as it is developed, and the conscious portions of our natures are unprophetic either of its approach or its departure. Could this influence be durable in its original purity and force, it is impossible to predict the greatness of the results; but when composition begins, inspiration is already on the decline, and the most glorious poetry that has ever been communicated to the world is probably a feeble shadow of the original conceptions of the poet. I appeal to the greatest poets of the present day, whether it is not an error to assert that the finest passages of poetry are produced by labour and study. The toil and the delay recommended by critics, can be justly interpreted to mean no more than a careful observation of the inspired moments, and an artificial connexion of the spaces between their suggestions by the inter-texture of conventional expressions; a necessity only imposed by the limitedness of the poetical faculty itself; for Milton conceived the *Paradise Lost* as a whole before he executed it in portions. We have his own authority also for the muse having 'dictated' to him the 'unpremeditated song.' And let this be an answer to those who would allege the fifty-six various readings of the first line of the *Orlando Furioso*. Compositions so produced are to poetry what mosaic is to painting. This instinct and intuition of the poetical faculty is still more observable in the plastic and pictorial arts; a great statue or picture grows under the power of the artist as a child in the mother's womb; and the very mind which directs the hands in formation is incapable of accounting to itself for the origin, the gradations, or the media of the process.

Poetry is the record of the best and happiest moments of the happiest and best minds. We are aware of evanescent visitations of thought and feeling sometimes associated with place or person, sometimes regarding our own mind alone, and always arising unforeseen and departing un-bidden, but elevating and delightful beyond all expression: so that even in the desire and regret they leave, there cannot but be pleasure, parti-cipating as it does in the nature of its object. It is as it were the interpenetration of a diviner nature through our own; but its footsteps are like those of a wind over the sea, which the coming calm erases, and whose traces remain only, as on the wrinkled sand which paves it.    These and corresponding conditions of being are experienced principally by those of the most delicate sensibility and the most enlarged imagination; and the state of mind produced by them is at war with every base desire.    The enthusiasm of virtue, love, patriotism, and friendship, is essentially linked with such emotions; and whilst they last, self appears as what it is, an atom to a universe.    Poets are not only subject to these experiences as spirits of the most refined organization, but they can colour all that they combine with the evanescent hues of this ethereal world; a word, a trait in the representation of a scene or a passion, will touch the enchanted chord, and reanimate, in those who have ever experienced these emotions, the sleeping, the cold, the buried image of the past.    Poetry thus makes immortal all that is best and most beautiful in the world; it arrests the vanishing apparitions which haunt the interlunations of life, and veiling them, or in language or in form, sends them forth among mankind, bearing sweet news of kindred joy to those with whom their sisters abide— abide, because there is no portal of expression from the caverns of the spirit which they inhabit into the universe of things.    Poetry redeems from decay the visitations of the divinity in man.

Poetry turns all things to loveliness; it exalts the beauty of that which is most beautiful, and it adds beauty to that which is most deformed; it marries exultation and horror, grief and pleasure, eternity and change; it subdues to union under its light yoke, all irreconcilable things.    It transmutes all that it touches, and every form moving within the radiance of its presence is changed by wondrous sympathy to an incarnation of the spirit which it breathes: its secret alchemy turns to potable gold the poisonous waters which flow from death through life; it strips the veil of familiarity from the world, and lays bare the naked and sleeping beauty, which is the spirit of its forms.

All things exist as they are perceived; at least in relation to the per- cipient.    'The mind is its own place, and of itself can make a heaven of hell, a hell of heaven.'    But poetry defeats the curse which binds us to be subjected to the accident of surrounding impressions.    And whether it spreads its own figured curtain, or withdraws life's dark veil from before the scene of things, it equally creates for us a being within our being.    It makes us the inhabitants of a world to which the familiar world is a chaos. It reproduces the common universe of which we are portions and per- cipients, and it purges from our inward sight the film of familiarity which obscures from us the wonder of our being.    It compels us to feel that which we perceive, and to imagine that which we know.    It creates anew the universe, after it has been annihilated in our minds by the recurrence of impressions blunted by reiteration.     It justifies the bold and true words of Tasso: *Non merita nome di creatore, se non Iddio ed il Poeta.*[6]

A poet, as he is the author to others of the highest wisdom, pleasure, virtue and glory, so he ought personally to be the happiest, the best, the wisest, and the most illustrious of men.   As to his glory, let time be challenged to declare whether the fame of any other institutor of human life be comparable to that of a poet.    That he is the wisest, the happiest, and the best, inasmuch as he is a poet, is equally incontrovertible: the greatest poets have been men of the most spotless virtue, of the most consummate prudence, and, if we would look into the interior of their lives, the most fortunate of men: and the exceptions, as they regard those who possessed the poetic faculty in a high yet inferior degree, will be found on consideration to confine rather than destroy the rule.    Let us for a moment stoop to the arbitration of popular breath, and usurping and uniting in our own persons the incompatible characters of accuser, witness, judge, and executioner, let us decide without trial, testimony, or form, that certain motives of those who are 'there sitting where we dare not soar,' are reprehensible.    Let us assume that Homer was a drunkard, that Virgil was a flatterer, that Horace was a coward, that Tasso was a madman, that Lord Bacon was a peculator, that Raphael was a libertine, that Spenser was a poet laureate.    It is inconsistent with this division of our subject to cite living poets, but posterity has done ample justice to the great names now referred to.    Their errors have been weighed and found to have been dust in the balance; if their sins 'were as scarlet, they are now white as snow': they have been washed in the blood of the mediator and redeemer, Time.    Observe in what a ludicrous chaos the imputations of real or fictitious crime have been confused in the contemporary calumnies against poetry and poets; consider how little is, as it appears—or appears, as it is; look to your own motives, and judge not, lest ye be judged.

Poetry, as has been said, differs in this respect from logic, that it is not subject to the control of the active powers of the mind, and that its birth and recurrence have no necessary connexion with the consciousness or will.   It is presumptuous to determine that these are the necessary conditions of all mental causation, when mental effects are experienced unsusceptible of being referred to them.    The frequent recurrence of the poetical power, it is obvious to suppose, may produce in the mind a habit of order and harmony correlative with its own nature and with its effects upon other minds.    But in the intervals of inspiration, and they may be frequent without being durable, a poet becomes a man, and is abandoned to the sudden reflux of the influences under which others habitually live.

[6] None but God and the poet deserve the name of creator.

But as he is more delicately organized than other men, and sensible to pain and pleasure, both his own and that of others, in a degree unknown to them, he will avoid the one and pursue the other with an ardour proportioned to this difference. And he renders himself obnoxious to calumny, when he neglects to observe the circumstances under which these objects of universal pursuit and flight have disguised themselves in one another's garments.

But there is nothing necessarily evil in this error, and thus cruelty, envy, revenge, avarice, and the passions purely evil, have never formed any portion of the popular imputations on the lives of poets.

I have thought it most favourable to the cause of truth to set down these remarks according to the order in which they were suggested to my mind, by a consideration of the subject itself, instead of observing the formality of a polemical reply; but if the view which they contain be just, they will be found to involve a refutation of the arguers against poetry, so far at least as regards the first division of the subject. I can readily conjecture what should have moved the gall of some learned and intelligent writers who quarrel with certain versifiers; I confess myself, like them, unwilling to be stunned by the Theseids of the hoarse Codri of the day. Bavius and Maevius undoubtedly are, as they ever were, insufferable persons. But it belongs to a philosophical critic to distinguish rather than confound.

The first part of these remarks has related to poetry in its elements and principles; and it has been shown, as well as the narrow limits assigned them would permit, that what is called poetry, in a restricted sense, has a common source with all other forms of order and of beauty, according to which the materials of human life are susceptible of being arranged, and which is poetry in a universal sense.

The second part will have for its object an application of these principles to the present state of the cultivation of poetry, and a defence of the attempt to idealize the modern forms of manners and opinions, and compel them into a subordination to the imaginative and creative faculty. For the literature of England, an energetic development of which has ever preceded or accompanied a great and free development of the national will, has arisen as it were from a new birth. In spite of the low-thoughted envy which would undervalue contemporary merit, our own will be a memorable age in intellectual achievements, and we live among such philosophers and poets as surpass beyond comparison any who have appeared since the last national struggle for civil and religious liberty. The most unfailing herald, companion, and follower of the awakening of a great people to work a beneficial change in opinion or institution, is poetry. At such periods there is an accumulation of the power of communicating and receiving intense and impassioned conceptions respecting man and nature.   The persons in whom this power resides may often, as far as regards many portions of their nature, have little apparent correspondence with that spirit of good of which they are the ministers.   But even whilst they deny and abjure, they are yet compelled to serve, the power which is seated on the throne of their own soul.   It is impossible to read the compositions of the most celebrated writers of the present day without being startled with the electric life which burns within their words. They measure the circumference and sound the depths of human nature with a comprehensive and all-penetrating spirit, and they are themselves perhaps the most sincerely astonished at its manifestations; for it is less their spirit than the spirit of the age.   Poets are the hierophants of an unapprehended inspiration; the mirrors of the gigantic shadows which futurity casts upon the present; the words which express what they understand not; the trumpets which sing to battle, and feel not what they inspire; the influence which is moved not, but moves.   Poets are the unacknowledged legislators of the world.

# The Poetic Principle

## 1850

*The first important American literary critic, Poe enunciated standards of judgment that ran directly opposite to the prevailing theories and ideas of mid-nineteenth-century American thought. Whereas most criticism had simply assumed the instrumental nature of art, and debated the specific political, social, or ethical ideas expressed by writers, Poe takes the bold view that poetry has a terminal value only, and is therefore to be judged only by aesthetic criteria. In effect, he meets Plato's challenge by denying that poetry's function is to teach; it has merely to delight.*

*This basic position is found in all of Poe's critical essays, both theoretical and practical; in fact, much of the substance of this essay is quoted directly from his 1842 review of a volume of Longfellow poems, and then incorporated into a lecture that Poe delivered during 1848 and 1849. That this printed version was originally a public performance helps to explain its organization and some of its content, particularly the poems that Poe recites. It is even possible to infer the nature of the intended audience from the organization of his lecture, as well as the effects that Poe is aiming for. He challenges two popular views of poetry, characterized as "the epic mania" and "the heresy of the Didactic." First he declares that there is no such thing as a long poem, and later he firmly separates poetry from both moral and philosophical associations. These statements are intended to be shockers,*

From *Complete Works of Edgar Allan Poe*, ed. James A. Harrison; New York: Thomas Y. Crowell and Co., 1902.

*but they are not unsupported, for Poe undergirds them by several
theoretical references to human psychology (no matter if derived from
sources as eclectic as the pseudoscience of phrenology and the philosophy of Kant). The effect of poetry is Poe's focus of concern.*

*An interesting topic in studying this essay is Poe's debt to Shelley,
for a phrase like "the Human Aspiration for Supernal Beauty" reminds
one of Shelley's praise of the imagination that perceives ideal beauty.
But Poe's concept of the function of poetry in no way resembles
Shelley's. How intrinsic, then, is the Platonic vision of the universe
to Poe's theory of poetry? To induce a particular kind of emotional
response is all that Poe demands of poetry, and Poe himself, in this
lecture-essay, illustrates that kind of emotional manipulation of his
audience. What is the relationship between his critical theory and the
poems that he recites? What effect is he attempting to induce in the
penultimate paragraph, as well as in the final poem?*

IN SPEAKING of the Poetic Principle, I have no design to be either thorough
or profound.   While discussing, very much at random, the essentiality of
what we call Poetry, my principal purpose will be to cite for consideration,
some few of those minor English or American poems which best suit my
own taste, or which, upon my own fancy, have left the most definite
impression.   By "minor poems" I mean, of course, poems of little length.
And here, in the beginning, permit me to say a few words in regard to a
somewhat peculiar principle, which, whether rightfully or wrongfully,
has always had its influence in my own critical estimate of the poem.   I
hold that a long poem does not exist.   I maintain that the phrase, "a
long poem," is simply a flat contradiction in terms.

I need scarcely observe that a poem deserves its title only inasmuch as
it excites, by elevating the soul.   The value of the poem is in the ratio of
this elevating excitement.   But all excitements are, through a psychal
necessity, transient.   That degree of excitement which would entitle a
poem to be so called at all, cannot be sustained throughout a composition
of any great length.   After the lapse of half an hour, at the very utmost,
it flags—fails—a revulsion ensues—and then the poem is, in effect, and
in fact, no longer such.

There are, no doubt, many who have found difficulty in reconciling
the critical dictum that the "Paradise Lost" is to be devoutly admired
throughout, with the absolute impossibility of maintaining for it, during
perusal, the amount of enthusiasm which that critical dictum would
demand.   This great work, in fact, is to be regarded as poetical, only
when, losing sight of that vital requisite in all works of Art, Unity, we

view it merely as a series of minor poems.   If, to preserve its Unity—its totality of effect or impression—we read it (as would be necessary) at a single sitting, the result is but a constant alternation of excitement and depression.   After a passage of what we feel to be true poetry, there follows, inevitably, a passage of platitude which no critical pre-judgment can force us to admire; but if, upon completing the work, we read it again; omitting the first book—that is to say, commencing with the second —we shall be surprised at now finding that admirable which we before condemned—that damnable which we had previously so much admired. It follows from all this that the ultimate, aggregate, or absolute effect of even the best epic under the sun, is a nullity:—and this is precisely the fact.

In regard to the Iliad, we have, if not positive proof, at least very good reason, for believing it intended as a series of lyrics; but, granting the epic intention, I can say only that the work is based in an imperfect sense of art.   The modern epic is, of the supposititious ancient model, but an inconsiderate and blindfold imitation.   But the day of these artistic anomalies is over.   If, at any time, any very long poem *were* popular in reality, which I doubt, it is at least clear that no very long poem will ever be popular again.

That the extent of a poetical work is, *ceteris paribus*,[1] the measure of its merit, seems undoubtedly, when we thus state it, a proposition sufficiently absurd—yet we are indebted for it to the Quarterly Reviews.   Surely there can be nothing in mere *size*, abstractly considered—there can be nothing in mere *bulk*, so far as a volume is concerned, which has so continuously elicited admiration from these saturnine pamphlets!   A mountain, to be sure, by the mere sentiment of physical magnitude which it conveys, *does* impress us with a sense of the sublime—but no man is impressed after *this* fashion by the material grandeur of even "The Columbiad."   Even the Quarterlies have not instructed us to be so impressed by it.   As yet, they have not *insisted* on our estimating Lamartine by the cubic foot, or Pollok by the pound—but what else are we to *infer* from their continual prating about "sustained effort?"   If, by "sustained effort," any little gentleman has accomplished an epic, let us frankly commend him for the effort—if this indeed be a thing commendable— but let us forbear praising the epic on the effort's account.   It is to be hoped that common sense, in the time to come, will prefer deciding upon a work of art, rather by the impression it makes, by the effect it produces, than by the time it took to impress the effect or by the amount of "sustained effort" which had been found necessary in effecting the

---

[1] Other things being equal.

impression. The fact is, that perseverance is one thing, and genius quite another—nor can all the Quarterlies in Christendom confound them. By-and-by, this proposition, with many which I have been just urging, will be received as self-evident. In the meantime, by being generally condemned as falsities, they will not be essentially damaged as truths.

On the other hand, it is clear that a poem may be improperly brief. Undue brevity degenerates into mere epigrammatism. A *very* short poem, while now and then producing a brilliant or vivid, never produces a profound or enduring effect. There must be the steady pressing down of the stamp upon the wax. De Béranger has wrought innumerable things, pungent and spirit-stirring; but, in general, they have been too imponderous to stamp themselves deeply into the public attention; and thus, as so many feathers of fancy, have been blown aloft only to be whistled down the wind.

A remarkable instance of the effect of undue brevity in depressing a poem—in keeping it out of the popular view—is afforded by the following exquisite little Serenade:

> I arise from dreams of thee
>   In the first sweet sleep of night,
> When the winds are breathing low,
>   And the stars are shining bright;
> I arise from dreams of thee,
>   And a spirit in my feet
> Hath led me—who knows how?—
>   To thy chamber-window, sweet!
>
> The wandering airs, they faint
>   On the dark, the silent stream—
> The champak odours fail
>   Like sweet thoughts in a dream;
> The nightingale's complaint,
>   It dies upon her heart,
> As I must die on thine,
>   O, beloved as thou art!
>
> O, lift me from the grass!
>   I die, I faint, I fail!
> Let thy love in kisses rain
>   On my lips and eyelids pale.
> My cheek is cold and white, alas!
>   My heart beats loud and fast:
> Oh! press it close to thine again,
>   Where it will break at last!

Very few, perhaps, are familiar with these lines—yet no less a poet than Shelley is their author. Their warm, yet delicate and ethereal imagination will be appreciated by all—but by none so thoroughly as by him who has himself arisen from sweet dreams of one beloved to bathe in the aromatic air of a southern midsummer night.

One of the finest poems by Willis—the very best, in my opinion, which he has ever written—has, no doubt, through this same defect of undue brevity, been kept back from its proper position, not less in the critical than in the popular view.

> The shadows lay along Broadway,
>   'Twas near the twilight-tide—
> And slowly there a lady fair
>   Was walking in her pride.
> Alone walk'd she; but, viewlessly,
>   Walk'd spirits at her side.
>
> Peace charm'd the street beneath her feet,
>   And Honour charm'd the air;
> And all astir looked kind on her,
>   And call'd her good and fair—
> For all God ever gave to her
>   She kept with chary care.
>
> She kept with care her beauties rare
>   From lovers warm and true—
> For her heart was cold to all but gold,
>   And the rich came not to woo—
> But honour'd well are charms to sell,
>   If priests the selling do.
>
> Now walking there was one more fair—
>   A slight girl, lily-pale;
> And she had unseen company
>   To make the spirit quail—
> 'Twixt Want and Scorn she walk'd forlorn,
>   And nothing could avail.
>
> No mercy now can clear her brow
>   For this world's peace to pray;
> For, as love's wild prayer dissolved in air,
>   Her woman's heart gave way!—
> But the sin forgiven by Christ in Heaven
>   By man is cursed alway!

In this composition we find it difficult to recognise the Willis who has written so many mere "verses of society." The lines are not only richly ideal, but full of energy; while they breathe an earnestness—an evident sincerity of sentiment—for which we look in vain throughout all the other works of this author.

While the epic mania—while the idea that, to merit in poetry, prolixity is indispensable—has, for some years past, been gradually dying out of the public mind, by mere dint of its own absurdity—we find it succeeded by a heresy too palpably false to be long tolerated, but one which, in the brief period it has already endured, may be said to have accomplished more in the corruption of our Poetical Literature than all its other enemies combined. I allude to the heresy of *The Didactic*. It has been assumed, tacitly and avowedly, directly and indirectly, that the ultimate object of all Poetry is Truth. Every poem, it is said, should inculcate a moral; and by this moral is the poetical merit of the work to be adjudged. We Americans especially have patronised this happy idea; and we Bostonians, very especially, have developed it in full. We have taken it into our heads that to write a poem simply for the poem's sake, and to acknowledge such to have been our design, would be to confess ourselves radically wanting in the true Poetic dignity and force;—but the simple fact is, that, would we but permit ourselves to look into our own souls, we should immediately there discover that under the sun there neither exists nor *can* exist any work more thoroughly dignified—more supremely noble than this very poem—this poem *per se*—this poem which is a poem and nothing more—this poem written solely for the poem's sake.

With as deep a reverence for the True as ever inspired the bosom of man, I would, nevertheless, limit, in some measure, its modes of inculcation. I would limit to enforce them. I would not enfeeble them by dissipation. The demands of Truth are severe. She has no sympathy with the myrtles. All *that* which is so indispensable in Song, is precisely all *that* with which *she* has nothing whatever to do. It is but making her a flaunting paradox, to wreathe her in gems and flowers. In enforcing a truth, we need severity rather than efflorescence of language. We must be simple, precise, terse. We must be cool, calm, unimpassioned. In a word, we must be in that mood which, as nearly as possible, is the exact converse of the poetical. *He* must be blind, indeed, who does not perceive the radical and chasmal differences between the truthful and the poetical modes of inculcation. He must be theory-mad beyond redemption who, in spite of these differences, shall still persist in attempting to reconcile the obstinate oils and waters of Poetry and Truth.

Dividing the world of mind into its three most immediately obvious distinctions, we have the Pure Intellect, Taste, and the Moral Sense. I place Taste in the middle, because it is just this position which, in the mind, it occupies. It holds intimate relations with either extreme; but from the Moral Sense is separated by so faint a difference that Aristotle has not hesitated to place some of its operations among the virtues themselves. Nevertheless, we find the *offices* of the trio marked with a sufficient distinction. Just as the Intellect concerns itself with Truth, so Taste informs us of the Beautiful while the Moral Sense is regardful of Duty. Of this latter, while Conscience teaches the obligation, and Reason the expediency, Taste contents herself with displaying the charms—waging war upon Vice solely on the ground of her deformity—her disproportion —her animosity to the fitting, to the appropriate, to the harmonious—in a word, to Beauty.

An immortal instinct, deep within the spirit of man, is thus, plainly, a sense of the Beautiful. This it is which administers to his delight in the manifold forms, and sounds, and odours, and sentiments amid which he exists. And just as the lily is repeated in the lake, or the eyes of Amaryllis in the mirror, so is the mere oral or written repetition of these forms, and sounds, and colours, and odours, and sentiments, a duplicate source of delight. But this mere repetition is not poetry. He who shall simply sing, with however glowing enthusiasm, or with however vivid a truth of description, of the sights, and sounds, and odours, and colours, and sentiments, which greet *him* in common with all mankind—he, I say, has yet failed to prove his divine title. There is still a something in the distance which he has been unable to attain. We have still a thirst unquenchable, to allay which he has not shown us the crystal springs. This thirst belongs to the immortality of Man. It is at once a consequence and an indication of his perennial existence. It is the desire of the moth for the star. It is no mere appreciation of the Beauty before us—but a wild effort to reach the Beauty above. Inspired by an ecstatic prescience of the glories beyond the grave, we struggle, by multiform combinations among the things and thoughts of Time, to attain a portion of that Loveliness whose very elements, perhaps, appertain to eternity alone. And thus when by Poetry—or when by Music, the most entrancing of the Poetic moods—we find ourselves melted into tears—we weep then—not as the Abbate Gravina supposes—through excess of pleasure, but through a certain, petulant, impatient sorrow at our inability to grasp *now*, wholly, here on earth, at once and for ever, those divine and rapturous joys, of which *through* the poem, or *through* the music, we attain to but brief and indeterminate glimpses.

The struggle to apprehend the supernal Loveliness—this struggle, on the part of souls fittingly constituted—has given to the world all *that* which it (the world) has ever been enabled at once to understand and *to feel* as poetic.

The Poetic Sentiment, of course, may develope itself in various modes

—in Painting, in Sculpture, in Architecture, in the Dance—very especially in Music—and very peculiarly, and with a wide field, in the composition of the Landscape Garden.  Our present theme, however, has regard only to its manifestation in words.  And here let me speak briefly on the topic of rhythm.  Contenting myself with the certainty that Music, in its various modes of metre, rhythm, and rhyme, is of so vast a moment in Poetry as never to be wisely rejected—is so vitally important an adjunct, that he is simply silly who declines its assistance, I will not now pause to maintain its absolute essentiality.  It is in Music, perhaps, that the soul most nearly attains the great end for which, when inspired by the Poetic Sentiment, it struggles—the creation of supernal Beauty.  It *may* be, indeed, that here this sublime end is, now and then, attained *in fact*.  We are often made to feel, with a shivering delight, that from an earthly harp are stricken notes which *cannot* have been unfamiliar to the angels.  And thus there can be little doubt that in the union of Poetry with Music in its popular sense, we shall find the widest field for the Poetic development.  The old Bards and Minnesingers had advantages which we do not possess—and Thomas Moore, singing his own songs, was, in the most legitimate manner, perfecting them as poems.

To recapitulate, then:—I would define, in brief, the Poetry of words as *The Rhythmical Creation of Beauty*.  Its sole arbiter is Taste.  With the Intellect or with the Conscience, it has only collateral relations.  Unless incidentally, it has no concern whatever either with Duty or with Truth.

A few words, however, in explanation.  *That* pleasure which is at once the most pure, the most elevating, and the most intense, is derived, I maintain, from the contemplation of the Beautiful.  In the contemplation of Beauty we alone find it possible to attain that pleasurable elevation, or excitement, *of the soul*, which we recognise as the Poetic Sentiment, and which is so easily distinguished from Truth, which is the satisfaction of the Reason, or from Passion, which is the excitement of the heart.  I make Beauty, therefore—using the word as inclusive of the sublime—I make Beauty the province of the poem, simply because it is an obvious rule of Art that effects should be made to spring as directly as possible from their causes:—no one as yet having been weak enough to deny that the peculiar elevation in question is at least *most readily* attainable in the poem.  It by no means follows, however, that the incitements of Passion, or the precepts of Duty, or even the lessons of Truth, may not be introduced into a poem, and with advantage; for they may subserve, incidentally, in various ways, the general purposes of the work:—but the true artist will always contrive to tone them down in proper subjection to that *Beauty* which is the atmosphere and the real essence of the poem.

I cannot better introduce the few poems which I shall present for your consideration, than by the citation of the Proem to Mr. Longfellow's "Waif":

The day is done, and the darkness
　Falls from the wings of Night,
As a feather is wafted downward
　From an Eagle in his flight.

I see the lights of the village
　Gleam through the rain and the mist,
And a feeling of sadness comes o'er me,
　That my soul cannot resist;

A feeling of sadness and longing,
　That is not akin to pain,
And resembles sorrow only
　As the mist resembles the rain.

Come, read to me some poem,
　Some simple and heartfelt lay,
That shall soothe this restless feeling,
　And banish the thoughts of day.

Not from the grand old masters,
　Not from the bards sublime,
Whose distant footsteps echo
　Through the corridors of Time.

For, like strains of martial music,
　Their mighty thoughts suggest
Life's endless toil and endeavour;
　And to-night I long for rest.

Read from some humbler poet,
　Whose songs gushed from his heart,
As showers from the clouds of summer,
　Or tears from the eyelids start;

Who through long days of labour,
　And nights devoid of ease,
Still heard in his soul the music
　Of wonderful melodies.

Such songs have power to quiet
　The restless pulse of care,
And come like the benediction
　That follows after prayer.

> Then read from the treasured volume
>   The poem of thy choice,
> And lend to the rhyme of the poet
>   The beauty of thy voice.
>
> And the night shall be filled with music,
>   And the cares that infest the day,
> Shall fold their tents, like the Arabs,
>   And as silently steal away.

With no great range of imagination, these lines have been justly admired for their delicacy of expression. Some of the images are very effective. Nothing can be better than—

> ————The bards sublime,
> Whose distant footsteps echo
> Down the corridors of Time.[2]

The idea of the last quatrain is also very effective. The poem, on the whole, however, is chiefly to be admired for the graceful *insouciance* of its metre, so well in accordance with the character of the sentiments, and especially for the *ease* of the general manner. This "ease," or naturalness, in a literary style, it has long been the fashion to regard as ease in appearance alone—as a point of really difficult attainment. But not so:—a natural manner is difficult only to him who should never meddle with it— to the unnatural. It is but the result of writing with the understanding, or with the instinct, that *the tone*, in composition, should always be that which the mass of mankind would adopt—and must perpetually vary, of course, with the occasion. The author who, after the fashion of "The North American Review," should be, upon *all* occasions, merely "quiet," must necessarily upon *many* occasions, be simply silly, or stupid; and has no more right to be considered "easy," or "natural," than a Cockney exquisite, or than the sleeping Beauty in the wax-works.

Among the minor poems of Bryant, none has so much impressed me as the one which he entitles "June." I quote only a portion of it:

> There, through the long, long summer hours,
>   The golden light should lie,
> And thick young herbs and groups of flowers
>   Stand in their beauty by.
> The oriole should build and tell
> His love-tale, close beside my cell;
>   The idle butterfly
> Should rest him there, and there be heard
> The housewife-bee and humming-bird.

[2] So quoted; compare stanzas.

And what if cheerful shouts, at noon,
    Come, from the village sent,
Or songs of maids, beneath the moon,
    With fairy laughter blent?
And what, if in the evening light,
Betrothed lovers walk in sight
    Of my low monument?
I would the lovely scene around
Might know no sadder sight nor sound.

I know, I know I should not see[3]
    The season's glorious show,
Nor would its brightness shine for me,
    Nor its wild music flow;
But if, around my place of sleep,
The friends I love should come to weep,
    They might not haste to go.
Soft airs, and song, and light, and bloom
Should keep them lingering by my tomb.

These to their softened hearts should bear
    The thought of what has been,
And speak of one who cannot share
    The gladness of the scene;
Whose part, in all the pomp that fills
The circuit of the summer hills,
    Is—that his grave is green;
And deeply would their hearts rejoice
To hear again his living voice.

The rhythmical flow, here, is even voluptuous—nothing could be more melodious. The poem has always affected me in a remarkable manner. The intense melancholy which seems to well up, perforce, to the surface of all the poet's cheerful sayings about his grave, we find thrilling us to the soul—while there is the truest poetic elevation in the thrill. The impression left is one of a pleasurable sadness. And if, in the remaining compositions which I shall introduce to you, there be more or less of a similar tone always apparent, let me remind you that (how or why we know not) this certain taint of sadness is inseparably connected with all the higher manifestations of true Beauty. It is, nevertheless,

A feeling of sadness and longing
    That is not akin to pain,
And resembles sorrow only
    As the mist resembles the rain.

[3] So quoted.

The taint of which I speak is clearly perceptible even in a poem so full of brilliancy and spirit as the "Health" of Edward Coate Pinckney:

> I fill this cup to one made up
>     Of loveliness alone,
> A woman, of her gentle sex
>     The seeming paragon;
> To whom the better elements
>     And kindly stars have given
> A form so fair, that, like the air,
>     'Tis less of earth than heaven.
>
> Her every tone is music's own,
>     Like those of morning birds,
> And something more than melody
>     Dwells ever in her words;
> The coinage of her heart are they,
>     And from her lips each flows
> As one may see the burden'd bee
>     Forth issue from the rose.
>
> Affections are as thoughts to her,
>     The measures of her hours;
> Her feelings have the fragrancy,
>     The freshness of young flowers;
> And lovely passions, changing oft,
>     So fill her, she appears
> The image of themselves by turns,—
>     The idol of past years!
>
> Of her bright face one glance will trace
>     A picture on the brain,
> And of her voice in echoing hearts
>     A sound must long remain;
> But memory, such as mine of her,
>     So very much endears,
> When death is nigh, my latest sigh
>     Will not be life's but hers.
>
> I fill this cup to one made up
>     Of loveliness alone,
> A woman, of her gentle sex
>     The seeming paragon—
> Her health! and would on earth there stood,
>     Some more of such a frame,
> That life might be all poetry,
>     And weariness a name.

It was the misfortune of Mr. Pinckney to have been born too far south. Had he been a New Englander, it is probable that he would have been ranked as the first of American lyrists, by that magnanimous cabal which has so long controlled the destinies of American Letters, in conducting the thing called "The North American Review." The poem just cited is especially beautiful; but the poetic elevation which it induces, we must refer chiefly to our sympathy in the poet's enthusiasm. We pardon his hyperboles for the evident earnestness with which they are uttered.

It was by no means my design, however, to expatiate upon the *merits* of what I should read you. These will necessarily speak for themselves. Boccalini, in his "Advertisements from Parnassus," tells us that Zoilus once presented Apollo a very caustic criticism upon a very admirable book:—whereupon the god asked him for the beauties of the work. He replied that he only busied himself about the errors. On hearing this, Apollo, handing him a sack of unwinnowed wheat, bade him pick out *all the chaff* for his reward.

Now this fable answers very well as a hit at the critics—but I am by no means sure that the god was in the right. I am by no means certain that the true limits of the critical duty are not grossly misunderstood. Excellence, in a poem especially, may be considered in the light of an axiom, which need only be properly *put*, to become self-evident. It is *not* excellence if it require to be demonstrated as such:—and thus, to point out too particularly the merits of a work of Art, is to admit that they are *not* merits altogether.

Among the "Melodies" of Thomas Moore, is one whose distinguished character as a poem proper, seems to have been singularly left out of view. I allude to his lines beginning—"Come rest in this bosom." The intense energy of their expression is not surpassed by anything in Byron. There are two of the lines in which a sentiment is conveyed that embodies the *all in all* of the divine passion of love—a sentiment which, perhaps, has found its echo in more, and in more passionate, human hearts than any other single sentiment ever embodied in words:

> Come, rest in this bosom, my own stricken deer,
> Though the herd have fled from thee, thy home is still here;
> Here still is the smile, that no cloud can o'ercast,
> And a heart and a hand all thy own to the last.
>
> Oh! what was love made for, if 't is not the same
> Through joy and through torment, through glory and shame?
> I know not, I ask not, if guilt 's in that heart,
> I but know that I love thee, whatever thou art.

Thou hast call'd me thy Angel in moments of bliss,
And thy Angel I 'll be, 'mid the horrors of this,—
Through the furnace, unshrinking, thy steps to pursue,
And shield thee, and save thee,—or perish there too!

It has been the fashion, of late days, to deny Moore imagination, while granting him fancy—a distinction originating with Coleridge—than whom no man more fully comprehended the great powers of Moore. The fact is, that the fancy of this poet so far predominates over all his other faculties, and over the fancy of all other men, as to have induced, very naturally, the idea that he is fanciful *only*. But never was there a greater mistake. Never was a grosser wrong done the fame of a true poet. In the compass of the English language I can call to mind no poem more profoundly—more weirdly *imaginative*, in the best sense, than the lines commencing—"I would I were by that dim lake"—which are the composition of Thomas Moore. I regret that I am unable to remember them.

One of the noblest—and, speaking of fancy, one of the most singularly fanciful of modern poets, was Thomas Hood. His "Fair Ines" had always, for me, an inexpressible charm:

O saw ye not fair Ines!
    She's gone into the West,
To dazzle when the sun is down,
    And rob the world of rest:
She took our daylight with her,
    The smiles that we love best,
With morning blushes on her cheek,
    And pearls upon her breast.

O turn again, fair Ines,
    Before the fall of night,
For fear the moon should shine alone,
    And stars unrivall'd bright;
And blessed will the lover be
    That walks beneath their light,
And breathes the love against thy cheek
    I dare not even write!

Would I had been, fair Ines,
    That gallant cavalier,
Who rode so gaily by thy side,
    And whisper'd thee so near!
Were there no bonny dames at home,
    Or no true lovers here,
That he should cross the seas to win
    The dearest of the dear?

I saw thee, lovely Ines,
   Descend along the shore,
With bands of noble gentlemen,
   And banners wav'd before;
And gentle youth and maidens gay,
   And snowy plumes they wore;
It would have been a beauteous dream,
   If it had been no more!

Alas, alas, fair Ines,
   She went away with song,
With Music waiting on her steps,
   And shoutings of the throng;
But some were sad and felt no mirth,
   But only Music's wrong,
In sounds that sang farewell, farewell,
   To her you 've loved so long.

Farewell, farewell, fair Ines,
   That vessel never bore
So fair a lady on its deck,
   Nor danced so light before,—
Alas for pleasure on the sea,
   And sorrow on the shore!
The smile that blest one lover's heart
   Has broken many more!

"The Haunted House," by the same author, is one of the truest poems ever written—one of the *truest*—one of the most unexceptionable—one of the most thoroughly artistic, both in its theme and in its execution. It is, moreover, powerfully ideal—imaginative. I regret that its length renders it unsuitable for the purposes of this Lecture. In place of it, permit me to offer the universally appreciated "Bridge of Sighs."

One more Unfortunate,
Weary of breath,
Rashly importunate,
Gone to her death!

Take her up tenderly,
Lift her with care;—
Fashion'd so slenderly,
Young, and so fair!

Look at her garments
Clinging like cerements;
Whilst the wave constantly
Drips from her clothing;

Take her up instantly,
Loving, not loathing.—

Touch her not scornfully;
Think of her mournfully,
Gently and humanly;
Not of the stains of her,
All that remains of her
Now, is pure womanly.

Make no deep scrutiny
Into her mutiny
Rash and undutiful;
Past all dishonour,
Death has left on her
Only the beautiful.

Still, for all slips of hers,
One of Eve's family—
Wipe those poor lips of hers
Oozing so clammily,
Loop up her tresses
Escaped from the comb,
Her fair auburn tresses;
Whilst wonderment guesses
Where was her home?

Who was her father?
Who was her mother?
Had she a sister?
Had she a brother?
Or was there a dearer one
Still, and a nearer one
Yet, than all other?

Alas! for the rarity
Of Christian charity
Under the sun!
Oh! it was pitiful!
Near a whole city full,
Home she had none.

Sisterly, brotherly,
Fatherly, motherly
Feelings had changed:
Love, by harsh evidence,
Thrown from its eminence,
Even God's providence
Seeming estranged.

Where the lamps quiver
So far in the river,
With many a light
From window and casement
From garret to basement,
She stood, with amazement,
Houseless by night.

The bleak wind of March
Made her tremble and shiver;
But not the dark arch,
Or the black flowing river:
Mad from life's history,
Glad to death's mystery,
Swift to be hurl'd—
Anywhere, anywhere
Out of the world!

In she plunged boldly,
No matter how coldly
The rough river ran,—
Over the brink of it,
Picture it—think of it,
Dissolute Man!
Lave in it, drink of it
Then, if you can!

Take her up tenderly,
Lift her with care;
Fashion'd so slenderly,
Young, and so fair!

Ere her limbs frigidly
Stiffen too rigidly,
Decently,—kindly,—
Smooth, and compose them;
And her eyes, close them,
Staring so blindly!

Dreadfully staring
Through muddy impurity,
As when with the daring
Last look of despairing
Fixed on futurity.

Perishing gloomily,
Spurred by contumely,
Cold inhumanity,

Burning insanity,
Into her rest,—
Cross her hands humbly,
As if praying dumbly,
Over her breast!
Owning her weakness,
Her evil behaviour,
And leaving, with meekness,
Her sins to her Saviour!

The vigour of this poem is no less remarkable than its pathos. The versification, although carrying the fanciful to the very verge of the fantastic, is nevertheless admirably adapted to the wild insanity which is the thesis of the poem.

Among the minor poems of Lord Byron, is one which has never received from the critics the praise which it undoubtedly deserves:

Though the day of my destiny 's over,
    And the star of my fate hath declined,
Thy soft heart refused to discover
    The faults which so many could find;
Though thy soul with my grief was acquainted
    It shrunk not to share it with me,
And the love which my spirit hath painted
    It never hath found but in *thee*.

Then when nature around me is smiling,
    The last smile which answers to mine,
I do not believe it beguiling,
    Because it reminds me of thine;
And when winds are at war with the ocean,
    As the breasts I believed in with me,
If their billows excite an emotion,
    It is that they bear me from *thee*.

Though the rock of my last hope is shivered,
    And its fragments are sunk in the wave,
Though I feel that my soul is delivered
    To pain—it shall not be its slave.
There is many a pang to pursue me:
    They may crush, but they shall not contemn—
They may torture, but shall not subdue me—
    'T is of *thee* that I think—not of them.

Though human, thou didst not deceive me,
    Though woman, thou didst not forsake,
Though loved, thou forborest to grieve me,
    Though slandered, thou never couldst shake,—

Though trusted, thou didst not disclaim me,
   Though parted, it was not to fly,
Though watchful, 't was not to defame me,
   Nor mute, that the world might belie.

Yet I blame not the world, nor despise it,
   Nor the war of the many with one—
If my soul was not fitted to prize it,
   'T was folly not sooner to shun:
And if dearly that error hath cost me,
   And more than I once could foresee,
I have found that whatever it lost me,
   It could not deprive me of *thee*.

From the wreck of the past, which hath perished,
   Thus much I at least may recall,
It hath taught me that what I most cherished
   Deserved to be dearest of all:
In the desert a fountain is springing,
   In the wide waste there still is a tree,
And a bird in the solitude singing,
   Which speaks to my spirit of *thee*.

Although the rhythm here is one of the most difficult, the versification could scarcely be improved. No nobler *theme* ever engaged the pen of poet. It is the soul-elevating idea, that no man can consider himself entitled to complain of Fate while, in his adversity, he still retains the unwavering love of woman.

From Alfred Tennyson—although in perfect sincerity I regard him as the noblest poet that ever lived—I have left myself time to cite only a very brief specimen. I call him, and *think* him the noblest of poets—*not* because the impressions he produces are, at *all* times, the most profound —*not* because the poetical excitement which he induces is, at *all* times, the most intense—but because it *is*, at all times, the most ethereal—in other words, the most elevating and the most pure. No poet is so little of the earth, earthy. What I am about to read is from his last long poem, "The Princess":

   Tears, idle tears, I know not what they mean,
Tears from the depth of some divine despair
Rise in the heart, and gather to the eyes,
In looking on the happy Autumn-fields,
And thinking of the days that are no more.

   Fresh as the first beam glittering on a sail,
That brings our friends up from the underworld,
Sad as the last which reddens over one

That sinks with all we love below the verge;
So sad, so fresh, the days that are no more.

Ah, sad and strange as in dark summer dawns
The earliest pipe of half-awaken'd birds
To dying ears, when unto dying eyes
The casement slowly grows a glimmering square;
So sad, so strange, the days that are no more.

Dear as remember'd kisses after death,
And sweet as those by hopeless fancy feign'd
On lips that are for others; deep as love,
Deep as first love, and wild with all regret;
O Death in Life, the days that are no more.

Thus, although in a very cursory and imperfect manner, I have endeavoured to convey to you my conception of the Poetic Principle. It has been my purpose to suggest that, while this Principle itself is, strictly and simply, the Human Aspiration for Supernal Beauty, the manifestation of the Principle is always found in *an elevating excitement of the Soul*—quite independent of that passion which is the intoxication of the Heart—or of that Truth which is the satisfaction of the Reason. For, in regard to Passion, alas! its tendency is to degrade, rather than to elevate the Soul. Love, on the contrary—Love—the true, the divine Eros—the Uranian, as distinguished from the Dionæan Venus—is unquestionably the purest and truest of all poetical themes. And in regard to Truth—if, to be sure, through the attainment of a truth, we are led to perceive a harmony where none was apparent before, we experience, at once, the true poetical effect—but this effect is referable to the harmony alone, and not in the least degree to the truth which merely served to render the harmony manifest.

We shall reach, however, more immediately a distinct conception of what the true Poetry is, by mere reference to a few of the simple elements which induce in the Poet himself the true poetical effect. He recognises the ambrosia which nourishes his soul, in the bright orbs that shine in Heaven—in the volutes of the flower—in the clustering of low shrubberies —in the waving of the grain-fields—in the slanting of tall, Eastern trees— in the blue distance of mountains—in the grouping of clouds—in the twinkling of half-hidden brooks—in the gleaming of silver rivers—in the repose of sequestered lakes—in the star-mirroring depths of lonely wells. He perceives it in the songs of birds—in the harp of Æolus—in the sighing of the night-wind—in the repining voice of the forest—in the surf that complains to the shore—in the fresh breath of the woods—in the scent of the violet—in the voluptuous perfume of the hyacinth—in the suggestive odour that comes to him, at eventide, from far-distant, undiscovered islands, over dim oceans, illimitable and unexplored.  He owns it in all noble thoughts—in all unworldly motives—in all holy impulses—in all chivalrous, generous, and self-sacrificing deeds.  He feels it in the beauty of woman—in the grace of her step—in the lustre of her eye—in the melody of her voice—in her soft laughter—in her sigh—in the harmony of the rustling of her robes. He deeply feels it in her winning endearments—in her burning enthusiasms—in her gentle charities—in her meek and devotional endurances—but above all—ah, far above all—he kneels to it—he worships it in the faith, in the purity, in the strength, in the altogether divine majesty—of her *love*.

Let me conclude—by the recitation of yet another brief poem—one very different in character from any that I have before quoted.   It is by Motherwell, and is called "The Song of the Cavalier."   With our modern and altogether rational ideas of the absurdity and impiety of warfare, we are not precisely in that frame of mind best adapted to sympathise with the sentiments, and thus to appreciate the real excellence of the poem. To do this fully, we must identify ourselves, in fancy, with the soul of the old cavalier.

> Then mounte! then mounte, brave gallants, all,
>   And don your helmes amaine:
> Deathe's couriers, Fame and Honour, call
>   Us to the field againe.
> No shrewish teares shall fill our eye
>   When the sword-hilt 's in our hand,—
> Heart-whole we 'll part, and no whit sighe
>   For the fayrest of the land;
> Let piping swaine, and craven wight,
>   Thus weepe and puling crye,
> Our business is like men to fight,
>   And hero-like to die!

# The Study of Poetry

## 1880

*At a time when established beliefs are brought into question, when all creeds, dogmas, and traditions seem to be failing, where can one turn for consolation and support? Matthew Arnold's essay restates what he had been saying for a decade about the social, religious, and cultural questions of his day; like other writers during the Victorian era—which has become, in the popular myth of our times, the epitome of assurance, solidity, and permanence—Arnold saw the central issue of his own day as a crisis of faith. Writing a preface for an anthology called* The English Poets, *Arnold seizes the opportunity to offer what is, in effect, another defense of poetry. As such, it should be compared with the essays by Sidney and Shelley, both of whom justify poetry on moral grounds and claim for it an important role in shaping men's minds and values. Like Wordsworth, too, Arnold attempts to correct misconceptions about the relative importance of science and poetry in terms of the kind of knowledge that each provides. What this adds up to is Arnold's notion of poetry as "a criticism of life," an interpretation and evaluation of the meaning of human existence—a substitute for what religion can no longer do.*

*Because only the best poetry can perform this high function, Arnold deals not only with the question of "Why study poetry?" but also with the question of how to study poetry so as to be able to distinguish the very best. Therefore, most of the essay is a discussion of his criteria for making a judgment and of three possible approaches to poetry.*

From *Essays in Criticism: Second Series;* New York: The Macmillan Company, 1913.

*Here Arnold gives the theoretical bases and exemplifies his principles
in a series of specific thumbnail judgments which amount to a brief
survey of the English poets from Chaucer to Burns. Arnold rejects two
of the customary academic criteria by which poetry has commonly
been judged, the historical and the impressionistic, on grounds which
any student of literature today might still find valid. Arnold proposes
instead a technique for making objective evaluations and permanent
classifications: This is his "touchstone" theory by which the measure
of a poet's work may be had by comparing it to a few selected passages
from the tradition of the "classic" writers. It is not difficult to find the
logical fallacy in Arnold's distinction between the personal and the
real estimates, or to see how his own personal values keep cropping up
(as in his judgments about Chaucer and Burns); but the comparative
method as a way of developing one's taste and judgment should not
therefore be slighted—think about how your own literary preferences
and values have been formed.*

'THE FUTURE of poetry is immense, because in poetry, where it is worthy
of its high destinies, our race, as time goes on, will find an ever surer and
surer stay. There is not a creed which is not shaken, not an accredited
dogma which is not shown to be questionable, not a received tradition
which does not threaten to dissolve. Our religion has materialised
itself in the fact, in the supposed fact; it has attached its emotion to the
fact, and now the fact is failing it. But for poetry the idea is everything;
the rest is a world of illusion, of divine illusion. Poetry attaches its
emotion to the idea; the idea *is* the fact. The strongest part of our
religion to-day is its unconscious poetry.'

Let me be permitted to quote these words of my own, as uttering the
thought which should, in my opinion, go with us and govern us in all our
study of poetry. In the present work it is the course of one great con-
tributory stream to the world-river of poetry that we are invited to follow.
We are here invited to trace the stream of English poetry. But whether
we set ourselves, as here, to follow only one of the several streams that
make the mighty river of poetry, or whether we seek to know them all, our
governing thought should be the same. We should conceive of poetry
worthily, and more highly than it has been the custom to conceive of it.
We should conceive of it as capable of higher uses, and called to higher
destinies, than those which in general men have assigned to it hitherto.
More and more mankind will discover that we have to turn to poetry
to interpret life for us, to console us, to sustain us. Without poetry,
our science will appear incomplete; and most of what now passes with us

for religion and philosophy will be replaced by poetry. Science, I say, will appear incomplete without it. For finely and truly does Wordsworth call poetry 'the impassioned expression which is in the countenance of all science'; and what is a countenance without its expression? Again, Wordsworth finely and truly calls poetry ' the breath and finer spirit of all knowledge': our religion, parading evidences such as those on which the popular mind relies now; our philosophy, pluming itself on its reasonings about causation and finite and infinite being; what are they but the shadows and dreams and false shows of knowledge? The day will come when we shall wonder at ourselves for having trusted to them, for having taken them seriously; and the more we perceive their hollowness, the more we shall prize 'the breath and finer spirit of knowledge' offered to us by poetry.

But if we conceive thus highly of the destinies of poetry, we must also set our standard for poetry high, since poetry, to be capable of fulfilling such high destinies, must be poetry of a high order of excellence. We must accustom ourselves to a high standard and to a strict judgment. Sainte-Beuve relates that Napoleon one day said, when somebody was spoken of in his presence as a charlatan: 'Charlatan as much as you please; but where is there *not* charlatanism?'—'Yes,' answers Sainte-Beuve, 'in politics, in the art of governing mankind, that is perhaps true. But in the order of thought, in art, the glory, the eternal honour is that charlatanism shall find no entrance; herein lies the inviolableness of that noble portion of man's being.' It is admirably said, and let us hold fast to it. In poetry, which is thought and art in one, it is the glory, the eternal honour, that charlatanism shall find no entrance; that this noble sphere be kept inviolate and inviolable. Charlatanism is for confusing or obliterating the distinctions between excellent and inferior, sound and unsound or only half-sound, true and untrue or only half-true. It is charlatanism, conscious or unconscious, whenever we confuse or obliterate these. And in poetry, more than anywhere else, it is unpermissible to confuse or obliterate them. For in poetry the distinction between excellent and inferior, sound and unsound or only half-sound, true and untrue or only half-true, is of paramount importance. It is of paramount importance because of the high destinies of poetry. In poetry, as a criticism of life under the conditions fixed for such a criticism by the laws of poetic truth and poetic beauty, the spirit of our race will find, we have said, as time goes on and as other helps fail, its consolation and stay. But the consolation and stay will be of power in proportion to the power of the criticism of life. And the criticism of life will be of power in proportion as the poetry conveying it is excellent rather than inferior, sound rather than unsound or half-sound, true rather than untrue or half-true.

The best poetry is what we want; the best poetry will be found to have a power of forming, sustaining, and delighting us, as nothing else can. A clearer, deeper sense of the best in poetry, and of the strength and joy to be drawn from it, is the most precious benefit which we can gather from a poetical collection such as the present. And yet in the nature and conduct of such a collection there is inevitably something which tends to obscure in us the consciousness of what our benefit should be, and to distract us from the pursuit of it. We should therefore steadily set it before our minds at the outset, and should compel ourselves to revert constantly to the thought of it as we proceed.

Yes; constantly in reading poetry, a sense for the best, the really excellent, and of the strength and joy to be drawn from it, should be present in our minds and should govern our estimate of what we read. But this real estimate, the only true one, is liable to be superseded, if we are not watchful, by two other kinds of estimate, the historic estimate and the personal estimate, both of which are fallacious. A poet or a poem may count to us historically, they may count to us on grounds personal to ourselves, and they may count to us really. They may count to us historically. The course of development of a nation's language, thought, and poetry, is profoundly interesting; and by regarding a poet's work as a stage in this course of development we may easily bring ourselves to make it of more importance as poetry than in itself it really is, we may come to use a language of quite exaggerated praise in criticising it; in short, to over-rate it. So arises in our poetic judgments the fallacy caused by the estimate which we may call historic. Then, again, a poet or a poem may count to us on grounds personal to ourselves. Our personal affinities, likings, and circumstances, have great power to sway our estimate of this or that poet's work, and to make us attach more importance to it as poetry than in itself it really possesses, because to us it is, or has been, of high importance. Here also we over-rate the object of our interest, and apply to it a language of praise which is quite exaggerated. And thus we get the source of a second fallacy in our poetic judgments—the fallacy caused by an estimate which we may call personal.

Both fallacies are natural. It is evident how naturally the study of the history and development of a poetry may incline a man to pause over reputations and works once conspicuous but now obscure, and to quarrel with a careless public for skipping, in obedience to mere tradition and habit, from one famous name or work in its national poetry to another, ignorant of what it misses, and of the reason for keeping what it keeps, and of the whole process of growth in its poetry. The French have become diligent students of their own early poetry, which they long neglected; the study makes many of them dissatisfied with their so-called classical poetry, the court-tragedy of the seventeenth century, a poetry which Pellisson long ago reproached with its want of the true poetic stamp, with its *politesse stérile et rampante*,[1] but which nevertheless has reigned in France as absolutely as if it had been the perfection of classical poetry indeed. The dissatisfaction is natural; yet a lively and accomplished critic, M. Charles d'Héricault, the editor of Clément Marot, goes too far when he says that 'the cloud of glory playing round a classic is a mist as dangerous to the future of a literature as it is intolerable for the purposes of history.' 'It hinders,' he goes on, 'it hinders us from seeing more than one single point, the culminating and exceptional point; the summary, fictitious and arbitrary, of a thought and of a work. It substitutes a halo for a physiognomy, it puts a statue where there was once a man, and hiding from us all trace of the labour, the attempts, the weaknesses, the failures, it claims not study but veneration; it does not show us how the thing is done, it imposes upon us a model. Above all, for the historian this creation of classic personages is inadmissible; for it withdraws the poet from his time, from his proper life, it breaks historical relationships, it blinds criticism by conventional admiration, and renders the investigation of literary origins unacceptable. It gives us a human personage no longer, but a God seated immovable amidst His perfect work, like Jupiter on Olympus; and hardly will it be possible for the young student, to whom such work is exhibited at such a distance from him, to believe that it did not issue ready made from that divine head.'

All this is brilliantly and tellingly said, but we must plead for a distinction. Everything depends on the reality of a poet's classic character. If he is a dubious classic, let us sift him; if he is a false classic, let us explode him. But if he is a real classic, if his work belongs to the class of the very best (for this is the true and right meaning of the word *classic*, *classical*), then the great thing for us is to feel and enjoy his work as deeply as ever we can, and to appreciate the wide difference between it and all work which has not the same high character. This is what is salutary, this is what is formative; this is the great benefit to be got from the study of poetry. Everything which interferes with it, which hinders it, is injurious. True, we must read our classic with open eyes, and not with eyes blinded with superstition; we must perceive when his work comes short, when it drops out of the class of the very best, and we must rate it, in such cases, at its proper value. But the use of this negative criticism is not in itself, it is entirely in its enabling us to have a clearer sense and a deeper enjoyment of what is truly excellent. To trace the labour, the attempts, the weaknesses, the failures of a genuine classic, to acquaint oneself with his time and his life and his

---

[1] Sterile and overstriding polish.

historical relationships, is mere literary dilettantism unless it has that clear sense and deeper enjoyment for its end. It may be said that the more we know about a classic the better we shall enjoy him; and, if we lived as long as Methuselah and had all of us heads of perfect clearness and wills of perfect steadfastness, this might be true in fact as it is plausible in theory. But the case here is much the same as the case with the Greek and Latin studies of our schoolboys. The elaborate philological ground-work which we require them to lay is in theory an admirable preparation for appreciating the Greek and Latin authors worthily. The more thoroughly we lay the groundwork, the better we shall be able, it may be said, to enjoy the authors. True, if time were not so short, and school-boys' wits not so soon tired and their power of attention exhausted; only, as it is, the elaborate philological preparation goes on, but the authors are little known and less enjoyed. So with the investigator of 'historic origins' in poetry. He ought to enjoy the true classic all the better for his investigations; he often is distracted from the enjoyment of the best, and with the less good he overbusies himself, and is prone to over-rate it in proportion to the trouble which it has cost him.

The idea of tracing historic origins and historical relationships cannot be absent from a compilation like the present. And naturally the poets to be exhibited in it will be assigned to those persons for exhibition who are known to prize them highly, rather than to those who have no special inclination towards them. Moreover the very occupation with an author, and the business of exhibiting him, disposes us to affirm and amplify his importance. In the present work, therefore, we are sure of frequent temptation to adopt the historic estimate, or the personal estimate, and to forget the real estimate; which latter, nevertheless, we must employ if we are to make poetry yield us its full benefit. So high is that benefit, the benefit of clearly feeling and of deeply enjoying the really excellent, the truly classic in poetry, that we do well, I say, to set it fixedly before our minds as our object in studying poets and poetry, and to make the desire of attaining it the one principle to which, as the *Imitation* says, whatever we may read or come to know, we always return. *Cum multa legeris et cognoveris, ad unum semper oportet redire principium.*[2]

The historic estimate is likely in especial to affect our judgment and our language when we are dealing with ancient poets; the personal estimate when we are dealing with poets our contemporaries, or at any rate modern. The exaggerations due to the historic estimate are not in themselves, perhaps, of very much gravity. Their report hardly enters the general ear; probably they do not always impose even on the literary men

[2] Although you have read and are acquainted with much, you should return to the one principle.

who adopt them.  But they lead to a dangerous abuse of language.  So we hear Cædmon, amongst our own poets, compared to Milton.  I have already noticed the enthusiasm of one accomplished French critic for 'historic origins.'  Another eminent French critic, M. Vitet, comments upon that famous document of the early poetry of his nation, the *Chanson de Roland*.  It is indeed a most interesting document.  The *joculator* or *jongleur* Taillefer, who was with William the Conqueror's army at Hastings, marched before the Norman troops, so said the tradition, singing 'of Charlemagne and of Roland and of Oliver, and of the vassals who died at Roncevaux'; and it is suggested that in the *Chanson de Roland* by one Turoldis or Théroulde, a poem preserved in a manuscript of the twelfth century in the Bodleian Library at Oxford, we have certainly the matter, perhaps even some of the words, of the chant which Taillefer sang. The poem has vigour and freshness; it is not without pathos.  But M. Vitet is not satisfied with seeing in it a document of some poetic value, and of very high historic and linguistic value; he sees in it a grand and beautiful work, a monument of epic genius.  In its general design he finds the grandiose conception, in its details he finds the constant union of simplicity with greatness, which are the marks, he truly says, of the genuine epic, and distinguish it from the artificial epic of literary ages. One thinks of Homer; this is the sort of praise which is given to Homer, and justly given.  Higher praise there cannot well be, and it is the praise due to epic poetry of the highest order only, and to no other.  Let us try, then the *Chanson de Roland* at its best.  Roland, mortally wounded, lays himself down under a pine-tree, with his face turned towards Spain and the enemy—

> 'De plusurs choses à remembrer li prist,
> De tantes teres cume li bers cunquist,
> De dulce France, des humes de sun lign,
> De Carlemagne sun seignor ki l'nurrit.'[3]

That is primitive work, I repeat, with an undeniable poetic quality of its own.  It deserves such praise, and such praise is sufficient for it. But now turn to Homer—

> "Ὣς φάτο· τοὺς δ᾽ ἤδη κατέχεν φυσίζοος αἶα
> ἐν Λακεδαίμονι αὖθι, φίλῃ ἐν πατρίδι γαίῃ.[4]

[3] Then began he to call many things to remembrance,—all the lands which his valour conquered, and pleasant France, and the men of his lineage, and Charlemagne his liege lord who nourished him.—*Chanson de Roland*, iii. 939-942.

[4] *Os phato; tous d ede katechen physizoos aia en Lakedaimoni authi phile en patridi gaie.*

> So said she; they long since in Earth's soft arms were reposing,
> There, in their own dear land, their fatherland, Lacedæmon.
> *Iliad*, iii. 243, 244 (translated by Dr. Hawtrey).

We are here in another world, another order of poetry altogether; here is
rightly due such supreme praise as that which M. Vitet gives to the
*Chanson de Roland.* If our words are to have any meaning, if our judgments
are to have any solidity, we must not heap that supreme praise upon
poetry of an order immeasurably inferior.

Indeed there can be no more useful help for discovering what poetry
belongs to the class of the truly excellent, and can therefore do us most
good, than to have always in one's mind lines and expressions of the
great masters, and to apply them as a touchstone to other poetry. Of
course we are not to require this other poetry to resemble them; it may
be very dissimilar. But if we have any tact we shall find them, when we
have lodged them well in our minds, an infallible touchstone for detecting
the presence or absence of high poetic quality, and also the degree of
this quality, in all other poetry which we may place beside them. Short
passages, even single lines, will serve our turn quite sufficiently. Take
the two lines which I have just quoted from Homer, the poet's comment
on Helen's mention of her brothers;—or take his

> Ἄ δειλώ, τί σφῶϊ δόμεν Πηλῆϊ ἄνακτι
> θανητᾴ; ὑμεῖς δ᾽ ἐστὸν ἀγήρω τ᾽ ἀθανάτω τε.
> ἦ ἵνα δυστήνοισι μετ᾽ ἀνδράσιν ἄλγε᾽ ἔχητον;[5]

the address of Zeus to the horses of Peleus;—or take finally his

> Καὶ σέ, λέρον, τὸ πρὶν μὲν ἀκ‍ουομεν ὄλβιον εἶναι.[6]

the words of Achilles to Priam, a suppliant before him. Take that incomparable line and a half of Dante, Ugolino's tremendous words—

> 'Io no piangeva; sì dentro impietrai.
> Piangevan elli . . .'[7]

take the lovely words of Beatrice to Virgil—

> 'Io son fatta da Dio, sua mercè, tale,
> Che la vostra miseria non mi tange,
> Nè fiamma d'esto incendio non m'assale . . .'[8]

---

[5] *A deilo ti sphoi domen Pelei anakti
thaneta; umeis d eston agero t athanato te
e ina dystenoisi met andrasin alge echeton.*

Ah, unhappy pair, why gave we you to King Peleus, to a mortal? but ye are without
old age, and immortal. Was it that with men born to misery ye might have sorrow?—
*Iliad,* xvii. 443-445.

[6] *Kai se, geron, to prin men akouomen olbion einai.* Nay, and thou too, old man, in former
days wast, as we hear, happy.—*Iliad,* xxiv. 543.

[7] I wailed not, so of stone grew I within;—*they* wailed.—*Inferno,* xxxiii. 39, 40.

[8] Of such sort hath God, thanked be His mercy, made me, that your misery toucheth
me not, neither doth the flame of this fire strike me.—*Inferno,* ii. 91-93.

take the simple, but perfect, single line—

> 'In la sua volontade è nostra pace.'[9]

Take of Shakespeare a line or two of Henry the Fourth's expostulation with sleep—

> 'Wilt thou upon the high and giddy mast
> Seal up the ship-boy's eyes, and rock his brains
> In cradle of the rude imperious surge . . .'

and take, as well, Hamlet's dying request to Horatio—

> 'If thou didst ever hold me in thy heart,
> Absent thee from felicity awhile,
> And in this harsh world draw thy breath in pain
> To tell my story . . .'

Take of Milton that Miltonic passage—

> 'Darken'd so, yet shone
> Above them all the archangel; but his face
> Deep scars of thunder had intrench'd, and care
> Sat on his faded cheek . . .'

add two such lines as—

> 'And courage never to submit or yield
> And what is else not to be overcome . . .'

and finish with the exquisite close to the loss of Proserpine, the loss

> '. . . which cost Ceres all that pain
> To seek her through the world.'

These few lines, if we have tact and can use them, are enough even of themselves to keep clear and sound our judgments about poetry, to save us from fallacious estimates of it, to conduct us to a real estimate.

The specimens I have quoted differ widely from one another, but they have in common this: the possession of the very highest poetical quality. If we are thoroughly penetrated by their power, we shall find that we have acquired a sense enabling us, whatever poetry may be laid before us, to feel the degree in which a high poetical quality is present or wanting there. Critics give themselves great labour to draw out what in the abstract constitutes the characters of a high quality of poetry. It is much better simply to have recourse to concrete examples;—to take specimens of poetry of the high, the very highest quality, and to say: The characters of a high quality of poetry are what is expressed *there*. They are far

---

[9] In His will is our peace.—*Paradiso*, iii. 85.

better recognised by being felt in the verse of the master, than by being perused in the prose of the critic.   Nevertheless if we are urgently pressed to give some critical account of them, we may safely, perhaps, venture on laying down, not indeed how and why the characters arise, but where and in what they arise.   They are in the matter and substance of the poetry, and they are in its manner and style.   Both of these, the substance and matter on the one hand, the style and manner on the other, have a mark, an accent, of high beauty, worth, and power.   But if we are asked to define this mark and accent in the abstract, our answer must be: No, for we should thereby be darkening the question, not clearing it. The mark and accent are as given by the substance and matter of that poetry, by the style and manner of that poetry, and of all other poetry which is akin to it in quality.

Only one thing we may add as to the substance and matter of poetry, guiding ourselves by Aristotle's profound observation that the superiority of poetry over history consists in its possessing a higher truth and a higher seriousness ($\phi\iota\lambda\sigma\sigma\phi\acute{\omega}\tau\epsilon\rho\sigma\nu$ $\kappa\alpha\grave{\iota}$ $\sigma\pi\sigma\upsilon\delta\alpha\iota\acute{\sigma}\tau\epsilon\rho\sigma\nu$).[10]   Let us add, therefore, to what we have said, this: that the substance and matter of the best poetry acquire their special character from possessing, in an eminent degree, truth and seriousness.   We may add yet further, what is in itself evident, that to the style and manner of the best poetry their special character, their accent, is given by their diction, and, even yet more, by their movement.   And though we distinguish between the two characters, the two accents, of superiority, yet they are nevertheless vitally connected one with the other.   The superior character of truth and seriousness, in the matter and substance of the best poetry, is inseparable from the superiority of diction and movement marking its style and manner.   The two superiorities are closely related, and are in steadfast proportion one to the other.   So far as high poetic truth and seriousness are wanting to a poet's matter and substance, so far also, we may be sure, will a high poetic stamp of diction and movement be wanting to his style and manner. In proportion as this high stamp of diction and movement, again, is absent from a poet's style and manner, we shall find, also, that high poetic truth and seriousness are absent from his substance and matter.

So stated, these are but dry generalities; their whole force lies in their application.   And I could wish every student of poetry to make the application of them for himself.   Made by himself, the application would impress itself upon his mind far more deeply than made by me.   Neither will my limits allow me to make any full application of the generalities above propounded; but in the hope of bringing out, at any rate, some significance in them, and of establishing an important principle more

---

[10] *Philosophoteron kai spoudaioteron.*

firmly by their means, I will, in the space which remains to me, follow rapidly from the commencement the course of our English poetry with them in my view.

Once more I return to the early poetry of France, with which our own poetry, in its origins, is indissolubly connected. In the twelfth and thirteenth centuries, that seed-time of all modern language and literature, the poetry of France had a clear predominance in Europe. Of the two divisions of that poetry, its productions in the *langue d'oil* and its productions in the *langue d'oc*,[11] the poetry of the *langue d'oc*, of southern France, of the troubadours, is of importance because of its effect on Italian literature;—the first literature of modern Europe to strike the true and grand note, and to bring forth, as in Dante and Petrarch it brought forth, classics. But the predominance of French poetry in Europe, during the twelfth and thirteenth centuries, is due to its poetry of the *langue d'oil*, the poetry of northern France and of the tongue which is now the French language. In the twelfth century the bloom of this romance-poetry was earlier and stronger in England, at the court of our Anglo-Norman kings, than in France itself. But it was a bloom of French poetry; and as our native poetry formed itself, it formed itself out of this. The romance-poems which took possession of the heart and imagination of Europe in the twelfth and thirteenth centuries are French; 'they are,' as Southey justly says, 'the pride of French literature, nor have we anything which can be placed in competition with them.' Themes were supplied from all quarters; but the romance-setting which was common to them all, and which gained the ear of Europe, was French. This constituted for the French poetry, literature, and language, at the height of the Middle Age, an unchallenged predominance. The Italian Brunetto Latini, the master of Dante, wrote his *Treasure* in French because, he says, 'la parleure en est plus délitable et plus commune à toutes gens.'[12] In the same century, the thirteenth, the French romance-writer, Christian of Troyes, formulates the claims, in chivalry and letters, of France, his native country, as follows.—

> 'Or vous ert par ce livre apris,
> Que Gresse ot de chevalerie
> Le premier los et de clergie;
> Puis vint chevalerie à Rome,
> Et de la clergie la some,
> Qui ore est en France venue.
> Diex doinst qu'ele i soit retenue,

[11] The words *oc (hoc)* and *oil (oui)* mean *yes*. The phrases mean *the language of*—, the forms of *yes* identifying the dialects.

[12] The speaking of it is most delectable and most common to all peoples.

Et que li lius li abelisse
Tant que de France n'isse
L'onor qui s'i est arestée!'

'Now by this book you will learn that first Greece had the renown for chivalry and letters: then chivalry and the primacy in letters passed to Rome, and now it is come to France. God grant it may be kept there; and that the place may please it so well, that the honour which has come to make stay in France may never depart thence!'

Yet it is now all gone, this French romance-poetry, of which the weight of substance and the power of style are not unfairly represented by this extract from Christian of Troyes. Only by means of the historic estimate can we persuade ourselves now to think that any of it is of poetical importance.

But in the fourteenth century there comes an Englishman nourished on this poetry, taught his trade by this poetry, getting words, rhyme, metre from this poetry; for even of that stanza which the Italians used, and which Chaucer derived immediately from the Italians, the basis and suggestion was probably given in France. Chaucer (I have already named him) fascinated his contemporaries, but so too did Christian of Troyes and Wolfram of Eschenbach. Chaucer's power of fascination, however, is enduring; his poetical importance does not need the assistance of the historic estimate; it is real. He is a genuine source of joy and strength, which is flowing still for us and will flow always. He will be read, as time goes on, far more generally than he is read now. His language is a cause of difficulty for us; but so also, and I think in quite as great a degree, is the language of Burns. In Chaucer's case, as in that of Burns, it is a difficulty to be unhesitatingly accepted and overcome.

If we ask ourselves wherein consists the immense superiority of Chaucer's poetry over the romance-poetry—why it is that in passing from this to Chaucer we suddenly feel ourselves to be in another world, we shall find that his superiority is both in the substance of his poetry and in the style of his poetry. His superiority in substance is given by his large, free, simple, clear yet kindly view of human life,—so unlike the total want, in the romance-poets, of all intelligent command of it. Chaucer has not their helplessness; he has gained the power to survey the world from a central, a truly human point of view. We have only to call to mind the Prologue to *The Canterbury Tales*. The right comment upon it is Dryden's: 'It is sufficient to say, according to the proverb, that *here is God's plenty*.' And again: 'He is a perpetual fountain of good sense.' It is by a large, free, sound representation of things, that poetry, this high criticism of life, has truth of substance; and Chaucer's poetry has truth of substance.

Of his style and manner, if we think first of the romance-poetry and then of Chaucer's divine liquidness of diction, his divine fluidity of movement, it is difficult to speak temperately.   They are irresistible, and justify all the rapture with which his successors speak of his 'gold dew-drops of speech.'   Johnson misses the point entirely when he finds fault with Dryden for ascribing to Chaucer the first refinement of our numbers, and says that Gower also can show smooth numbers and easy rhymes.   The refinement of our numbers means something far more than this.   A nation may have versifiers with smooth numbers and easy rhymes, and yet may have no real poetry at all.   Chaucer is the father of our splendid English poetry; he is our 'well of English undefiled,' because by the lovely charm of his diction, the lovely charm of his movement, he makes an epoch and founds a tradition.   In Spenser, Shakespeare, Milton, Keats, we can follow the tradition of the liquid diction, the fluid movement, of Chaucer; at one time it is his liquid diction of which in these poets we feel the virtue, and at another time it is his fluid movement.   And the virtue is irresistible.

Bounded as is my space, I must yet find room for an example of Chaucer's virtue, as I have given examples to show the virtue of the great classics.   I feel disposed to say that a single line is enough to show the charm of Chaucer's verse; that merely one line like this—

'O martyr souded[13] in virginitee!'

has a virtue of manner and movement such as we shall not find in all the verse of romance-poetry; —but this is saying nothing.   The virtue is such as we shall not find, perhaps, in all English poetry, outside the poets whom I have named as the special inheritors of Chaucer's tradition. A single line, however, is too little if we have not the strain of Chaucer's verse well in our memory; let us take a stanza.   It is from *The Prioress's Tale*, the story of the Christian child murdered in a Jewry—

> 'My throte is cut unto my nekke-bone
> Saidè this child, and as by way of kinde
> I should have deyd, yea, longè time agone;
> But Jesu Christ, as ye in bookès finde,
> Will that his glory last and be in minde,
> And for the worship of his mother dere
> Yet may I sing *O Alma* loud and clere.'

Wordsworth has modernised this Tale, and to feel how delicate and evanescent is the charm of verse, we have only to read Wordsworth's first three lines of this stanza after Chaucer's—

[13] The French *soudé;* soldered, fixed fast.

'My throat is cut unto the bone, I trow,
Said this young child, and by the law of kind
I should have died, yea, many hours ago.'

The charm is departed.   It is often said that the power of liquidness and
fluidity in Chaucer's verse was dependent upon a free, a licentious dealing
with language, such as is now impossible; upon a liberty, such as Burns
too enjoyed, of making words like *neck, bird,* into a dissyllable by adding
to them, and words like *cause, rhyme,* into a dissyllable by sounding the
*e* mute.   It is true that Chaucer's fluidity is conjoined with this liberty,
and is admirably served by it; but we ought not to say that it was dependent upon it.   It was dependent upon his talent.   Other poets with a like
liberty do not attain to the fluidity of Chaucer; Burns himself does not
attain to it.   Poets, again, who have a talent akin to Chaucer's, such as
Shakespeare or Keats, have known how to attain to his fluidity without
the like liberty.

And yet Chaucer is not one of the great classics.   His poetry transcends and effaces, easily and without effort, all the romance-poetry of
Catholic Christendom; it transcends and effaces all the English poetry
contemporary with it, it transcends and effaces all the English poetry
subsequent to it down to the age of Elizabeth.   Of such avail is poetic
truth of substance, in its natural and necessary union with poetic truth
of style.   And yet, I say, Chaucer is not one of the great classics.   He has
not their accent.   What is wanting to him is suggested by the mere mention
of the name of the first great classic of Christendom, the immortal poet who
died eighty years before Chaucer,—Dante.   The accent of such verse as

'In la sua volontade è nostra pace . . .'

is altogether beyond Chaucer's reach; we praise him, but we feel that
this accent is out of the question for him.   It may be said that it was
necessarily out of the reach of any poet in the England of that stage of
growth.   Possibly; but we are to adopt a real, not a historic, estimate of
poetry.   However we may account for its absence, something is wanting,
then, to the poetry of Chaucer, which poetry must have before it can be
placed in the glorious class of the best.   And there is no doubt what that
something is.   It is the σπουδαιότης,[14] the high and excellent seriousness,
which Aristotle assigns as one of the grand virtues of poetry.   The substance of Chaucer's poetry, his view of things and his criticism of life,
has largeness, freedom, shrewdness, benignity; but it has not this high
seriousness.   Homer's criticism of life has it, Dante's has it, Shakespeare's has it.   It is this chiefly which gives to our spirits what they can

[14] *Spoudaiotes.*

rest upon; and with the increasing demands of our modern ages upon poetry, this virtue of giving us what we can rest upon will be more and more highly esteemed.    A voice from the slums of Paris, fifty or sixty years after Chaucer, the voice of poor Villon out of his life of riot and crime, has at its happy moments (as, for instance, in the last stanza of *La Belle Heaulmière*)[15] more of this important poetic virtue of seriousness than all the productions of Chaucer.    But its apparition in Villon, and in men like Villon, is fitful; the greatness of the great poets, the power of their criticism of life, is that their virtue is sustained.

To our praise, therefore, of Chaucer as a poet there must be this limitation; he lacks the high seriousness of the great classics, and therewith an important part of their virtue.    Still, the main fact for us to bear in mind about Chaucer is his sterling value according to that real estimate which we firmly adopt for all poets.    He has poetic truth of substance, though he has not high poetic seriousness, and corresponding to his truth of substance he has an exquisite virtue of style and manner.    With him is born our real poetry.

For my present purpose I need not dwell on our Elizabethan poetry, or on the continuation and close of this poetry in Milton.    We all of us profess to be agreed in the estimate of this poetry; we all of us recognise it as great poetry, our greatest, and Shakespeare and Milton as our poetical classics.    The real estimate, here, has universal currency.    With the next age of our poetry divergency and difficulty begin.    An historic estimate of that poetry has established itself; and the question is, whether it will be found to coincide with the real estimate.

The age of Dryden, together with our whole eighteenth century which followed it, sincerely believed itself to have produced poetical classics of its own, and even to have made advance, in poetry, beyond all its predecessors.    Dryden regards as not seriously disputable the opinion 'that the sweetness of English verse was never understood or practised by

---

[15] The name *Heaulmière* is said to be derived from a headdress (helm) worn as a mark by courtesans.    In Villon's ballad, a poor old creature of this class laments her days of youth and beauty.    The last stanza of the ballad runs thus—

> 'Ainsi le bon temps regretons
> Entre nous, pauvres vieilles sottes,
> Assises bas, à croppetons,
> Tout en ung tas comme pelottes:
> A petit feu de chenevottes
> Tost allumées, tost estainctes.
> Et jadis fusmes si mignottes!
> Ainsi en prend à maintz et maintes.'

'Thus amongst ourselves we regret the good time, poor silly old things, low-seated on our heels, all in a heap like so many balls; by a little fire of hemp-stalks, soon lighted, soon spent.    And once we were such darlings!    So fares it with many and many a one.'

our fathers.' Cowley could see nothing at all in Chaucer's poetry. Dryden heartily admired it, and, as we have seen, praised its matter admirably; but of its exquisite manner and movement all he can find to say is that 'there is the rude sweetness of a Scotch tune in it, which is natural and pleasing, though not perfect.' Addison, wishing to praise Chaucer's numbers, compares them with Dryden's own. And all through the eighteenth century, and down even into our own times, the stereotyped phrase of approbation for good verse found in our early poetry has been, that it even approached the verse of Dryden, Addison, Pope, and Johnson.

Are Dryden and Pope poetical classics? Is the historic estimate, which represents them as such, and which has been so long established that it cannot easily give way, the real estimate? Wordsworth and Coleridge, as is well known, denied it; but the authority of Wordsworth and Coleridge does not weigh much with the young generation, and there are many signs to show that the eighteenth century and its judgments are coming into favour again. Are the favourite poets of the eighteenth century classics?

It is impossible within my present limits to discuss the question fully. And what man of letters would not shrink from seeming to dispose dictatorially of the claims of two men who are, at any rate, such masters in letters as Dryden and Pope; two men of such admirable talent, both of them, and one of them, Dryden, a man, on all sides, of such energetic and genial power? And yet, if we are to gain the full benefit from poetry, we must have the real estimate of it. I cast about for some mode of arriving, in the present case, at such an estimate without offence. And perhaps the best way is to begin, as it is easy to begin, with cordial praise.

When we find Chapman, the Elizabethan translator of Homer, expressing himself in his preface thus: 'Though truth in her very nakedness sits in so deep a pit, that from Gades to Aurora and Ganges few eyes can sound her, I hope yet those few here will so discover and confirm that, the date being out of her darkness in this morning of our poet, he shall now gird his temples with the sun,'—we pronounce that such a prose is intolerable. When we find Milton writing: 'And long it was not after, when I was confirmed in this opinion, that he, who would not be frustrate of his hope to write well hereafter in laudable things, ought himself to be a true poem,'—we pronounce that such a prose has its own grandeur, but that it is obsolete and inconvenient. But when we find Dryden telling us: 'What Virgil wrote in the vigour of his age, in plenty and at ease, I have undertaken to translate in my declining years; struggling with wants, oppressed with sickness, curbed in my genius, liable to be misconstrued in all I write,'—then we exclaim that here at last we have the true English prose, a prose such as we would all gladly use if we only knew how.  Yet Dryden was Milton's contemporary.

But after the Restoration the time had come when our nation felt the imperious need of a fit prose.  So, too, the time had likewise come when our nation felt the imperious need of freeing itself from the absorbing preoccupation which religion in the Puritan age had exercised.  It was impossible that this freedom should be brought about without some negative excess, without some neglect and impairment of the religious life of the soul; and the spiritual history of the eighteenth century shows us that the freedom was not achieved without them.  Still, the freedom was achieved; the preoccupation, an undoubtedly baneful and retarding one if it had continued, was got rid of. And as with religion amongst us at that period, so it was also with letters. A fit prose was a necessity; but it was impossible that a fit prose should establish itself amongst us without some touch of frost to the imaginative life of the soul.  The needful qualities for a fit prose are regularity, uniformity, precision, balance.  The men of letters, whose destiny it may be to bring their nation to the attainment of a fit prose, must of necessity, whether they work in prose or in verse, give a predominating, an almost exclusive attention to the qualities of regularity, uniformity, precision, balance.  But an almost exclusive attention to these qualities involves some repression and silencing of poetry.

We are to regard Dryden as the puissant and glorious founder, Pope as the splendid high priest, of our age of prose and reason, of our excellent and indispensable eighteenth century.  For the purposes of their mission and destiny their poetry, like their prose, is admirable.  Do you ask me whether Dryden's verse, take it almost where you will, is not good?

> 'A milk-white Hind, immortal and unchanged,
>     Fed on the lawns and in the forest ranged.'

I answer: Admirable for the purposes of the inaugurator of an age of prose and reason.  Do you ask me whether Pope's verse, take it almost where you will, is not good?

> 'To Hounslow Heath I point, and Banstead Down;
>     Thence comes your mutton, and these chicks my own.'

I answer: Admirable for the purposes of the high priest of an age of prose and reason.  But do you ask me whether such verse proceeds from men with an adequate poetic criticism of life, from men whose criticism of life has a high seriousness, or even, without that high seriousness, has poetic largeness, freedom, insight, benignity?  Do you ask me whether the application of ideas to life in the verse of these men, often a powerful application, no doubt, is a powerful *poetic* application? Do you ask me whether the poetry of these men has either the matter or the inseparable manner of such an adequate poetic criticism; whether it has the accent of

> 'Absent thee from felicity awhile . . .'

or of

> 'And what is else not to be overcome . . .'

or of

> 'O martyr souded in virginitee!'

I answer: It has not and cannot have them; it is the poetry of the builders of an age of prose and reason.    Though they may write in verse, though they may in a certain sense be masters of the art of versification, Dryden and Pope are not classics of our poetry, they are classics of our prose.

Gray is our poetical classic of that literature and age; the position of Gray is singular, and demands a word of notice here.    He has not the volume or the power of poets who, coming in times more favourable, have attained to an independent criticism of life.    But he lived with the great poets, he lived, above all, with the Greeks, through perpetually studying and enjoying them; and he caught their poetic point of view for regarding life, caught their poetic manner.    The point of view and the manner are not self-sprung in him, he caught them of others; and he had not the free and abundant use of them.    But whereas Addison and Pope never had the use of them, Gray had the use of them at times.    He is the scantiest and frailest of classics in our poetry, but he is a classic.

And now, after Gray, we are met, as we draw towards the end of the eighteenth century, we are met by the great name of Burns.    We enter now on times where the personal estimate of poets begins to be rife, and where the real estimate of them is not reached without difficulty.    But in spite of the disturbing pressures of personal partiality, of national partiality, let us try to reach a real estimate of the poetry of Burns.

By his English poetry Burns in general belongs to the eighteenth century, and has little importance for us.

> 'Mark ruffian Violence, distain'd with crimes,
> Rousing elate in these degenerate times;
> View unsuspecting Innocence a prey,
> As guileful Fraud points out the erring way;
> While subtle Ligitation's pliant tongue
> The life-blood equal sucks of Right and Wrong!'

Evidently this is not the real Burns, or his name and fame would have disappeared long ago.    Nor is Clarinda's love-poet, Sylvander, the real

Burns either. But he tells us himself: 'These English songs gravel me to death. I have not the command of the language that I have of my native tongue. In fact, I think that my ideas are more barren in English than in Scotch. I have been at *Duncan Gray* to dress it in English, but all I can do is desperately stupid.' We English turn naturally, in Burns, to the poems in our own language, because we can read them easily; but in those poems we have not the real Burns.

The real Burns is of course in his Scotch poems. Let us boldly say that of much of his poetry, a poetry dealing perpetually with Scotch drink, Scotch religion, and Scotch manners, a Scotchman's estimate is apt to be personal. A Scotchman is used to this world of Scotch drink, Scotch religion, and Scotch manners; he has a tenderness for it; he meets its poets half way. In this tender mood he reads pieces like the *Holy Fair* or *Halloween*. But this world of Scotch drink, Scotch religion, and Scotch manners is against a poet, not for him, when it is not a partial countryman who reads him; for in itself it is not a beautiful world, and no one can deny that it is of advantage to a poet to deal with a beautiful world. Burns's world of Scotch drink, Scotch religion, and Scotch manners, is often a harsh, a sordid, a repulsive world: even the world of his *Cotter's Saturday Night* is not a beautiful world. No doubt a poet's criticism of life may have such truth and power that it triumphs over its world and delights us. Burns may triumph over his world, often he does triumph over his world, but let us observe how and where. Burns is the first case we have had where the bias of the personal estimate tends to mislead; let us look at him closely, he can bear it.

Many of his admirers will tell us that we have Burns, convivial, genuine, delightful, here—

> 'Leeze me on drink! it gies us mair
>    Than either school or college;
> It kindles wit, it waukens lair,
>    It pangs us fou o' knowledge.
> Be 't whisky gill or penny wheep
>    Or ony stronger potion,
> It never fails, on drinking deep,
>    To kittle up our notion
>                   By night or day.'

There is a great deal of that sort of thing in Burns, and it is unsatisfactory, not because it is bacchanalian poetry, but because it has not that accent of sincerity which bacchanalian poetry, to do it justice, very often has. There is something in it of bravado, something which makes us feel that we have not the man speaking to us with his real voice; something, therefore, poetically unsound.

With still more confidence will his admirers tell us that we have the genuine Burns, the great poet, when his strain asserts the independence, equality, dignity, of men, as in the famous song *For a' that and a' that*—

> 'A prince can mak' a belted knight,
>     A marquis, duke, and a' that;
> But an honest man's aboon his might,
>     Guid faith he mauna fa' that!
>         For a' that, and a' that,
>             Their dignities, and a' that,
>         The pith o' sense, and pride o' worth,
>             Are higher rank than a' that.'

Here they find his grand, genuine touches; and still more, when this puissant genius, who so often set morality at defiance, falls moralising—

> 'The sacred lowe o' weel-placed love
>     Luxuriantly indulge it;
> But never tempt th' illicit rove,
>     Tho' naething should divulge it.
>         I waive the quantum o' the sin,
>             The hazard o' concealing,
>         But och! it hardens a' within,
>             And petrifies the feeling.'

Or in a higher strain—

> 'Who made the heart, 'tis He alone
>     Decidedly can try us;
> He knows each chord, its various tone;
>     Each spring, its various bias.
>         Then at the balance let's be mute,
>             We never can adjust it;
>         What's *done* we partly may compute,
>             But know not what's resisted.'

Or in a better strain yet, a strain, his admirers will say, unsurpassable—

> 'To make a happy fire-side clime
>         To weans and wife,
> That's the true pathos and sublime
>         Of human life.'

There is criticism of life for you, the admirers of Burns will say to us; there is the application of ideas to life! There is, undoubtedly. The doctrine of the last-quoted lines coincides almost exactly with what was the aim and end, Xenophon tells us, of all the teaching of Socrates. And the application is a powerful one; made by a man of vigorous understanding, and (need I say?) a master of language.

But for supreme poetical success more is required than the powerful application of ideas to life; it must be an application under the conditions fixed by the laws of poetic truth and poetic beauty. Those laws fix as an essential condition, in the poet's treatment of such matters as are here in question, high seriousness;—the high seriousness which comes from absolute sincerity. The accent of high seriousness, born of absolute sincerity, is what gives to such verse as

> 'In la sua volontade è nostra pace ...'

to such criticism of life as Dante's, its power. Is this accent felt in the passages which I have been quoting from Burns? Surely not; surely, if our sense is quick, we must perceive that we have not in those passages a voice from the very inmost soul of the genuine Burns; he is not speaking to us from these depths, he is more or less preaching. And the compensation for admiring such passages less, from missing the perfect poetic accent in them, will be that we shall admire more the poetry where that accent is found.

No; Burns, like Chaucer, comes short of the high seriousness of the great classics, and the virtue of matter and manner which goes with that high seriousness is wanting to his work. At moments he touches it in a profound and passionate melancholy, as in those four immortal lines taken by Byron as a motto for *The Bride of Abydos*, but which have in them a depth of poetic quality such as resides in no verse of Byron's own—

> 'Had we never loved sae kindly,
> Had we never loved sae blindly,
> Never met, or never parted,
> We had ne'er been broken-hearted.'

But a whole poem of that quality Burns cannot make; the rest, in the *Farewell to Nancy*, is verbiage.

We arrive best at the real estimate of Burns, I think, by conceiving his work as having truth of matter and truth of manner, but not the accent or the poetic virtue of the highest masters. His genuine criticism of life, when the sheer poet in him speaks, is ironic; it is not—

> 'Thou Power Supreme, whose mighty scheme
> These woes of mine fulfil,
> Here firm I rest, they must be best
> Because they are Thy will!'

It is far rather: *Whistle owre the lave o't!* Yet we may say of him as of

Chaucer, that of life and the world, as they come before him, his view is large, free, shrewd, benignant,—truly poetic, therefore; and his manner of rendering what he sees is to match.   But we must note, at the same time, his great difference from Chaucer.   The freedom of Chaucer is heightened, in Burns, by a fiery, reckless energy; the benignity of Chaucer deepens, in Burns, into an overwhelming sense of the pathos of things;—of the pathos of human nature, the pathos, also, of non-human nature.   Instead of the fluidity of Chaucer's manner, the manner of Burns has spring, bounding swiftness.   Burns is by far the greater force, though he has perhaps less charm.   The world of Chaucer is fairer, richer, more significant than that of Burns; but when the largeness and freedom of Burns get full sweep, as in *Tam o' Shanter*, or still more in that puissant and splendid production, *The Jolly Beggars*, his world may be what it will, his poetic genius triumphs over it.   In the world of *The Jolly Beggars* there is more than hideousness and squalor, there is bestiality; yet the piece is a superb poetic success.   It has a breadth, truth, and power which make the famous scene in Auerbach's Cellar, of Goethe's *Faust*, seem artificial and tame beside it, and which are only matched by Shakespeare and Aristophanes.

Here, where his largeness and freedom serve him so admirably, and also in those poems and songs where to shrewdness he adds infinite archness and wit, and to benignity infinite pathos, where his manner is flawless, and a perfect poetic whole is the result,—in things like the address to the mouse whose home he had ruined, in things like *Duncan Gray*, *Tam Glen*, *Whistle and I'll come to you my Lad*, *Auld Lang Syne* (this list might be made much longer),—here we have the genuine Burns, of whom the real estimate must be high indeed.   Not a classic, nor with the excellent σπουδαιότης[16] of the great classics, nor with a verse rising to a criticism of life and virtue like theirs; but a poet with thorough truth of substance and an answering truth of style, giving us a poetry sound to the core. We all of us have a leaning towards the pathetic, and may be inclined perhaps to prize Burns most for his touches of piercing, sometimes almost intolerable, pathos; for verse like—

> 'We twa hae paidl't i' the burn
> From mornin' sun till dine;
> But seas between us braid hae roar'd
> Sin auld lang syne . . .'

where he is as lovely as he is sound.   But perhaps it is by the perfection of soundness of his lighter and archer masterpieces that he is poetically most wholesome for us.   For the votary misled by a personal estimate of

---

[16] *Spoudaiotes*, "high and excellent seriousness."

Shelley, as so many of us have been, are, and will be,—of that
beautiful spirit building his many-coloured haze of words and images

'Pinnacled dim in the intense inane'—

no contact can be wholesomer than the contact with Burns at his archest
and soundest. Side by side with the

'On the brink of the night and the morning
My coursers are wont to respire,
But the Earth has just whispered a warning
That their flight must be swifter than fire . . .

of *Prometheus Unbound,* how salutary, how very salutary, to place this from
*Tam Glen*—

'My minnie does constantly deave me
And bids me beware o' young men;
They flatter, she says, to deceive me;
But wha can think sae o' Tam Glen?'

But we enter on burning ground as we approach the poetry of times
so near to us—poetry like that of Byron, Shelley, and Wordsworth—of
which the estimates are so often not only personal, but personal with
passion. For my purpose, it is enough to have taken the single case of
Burns, the first poet we come to of whose work the estimate formed is
evidently apt to be personal, and to have suggested how we may proceed,
using the poetry of the great classics as a sort of touchstone, to correct this
estimate, as we had previously corrected by the same means the historic
estimate where we met with it. A collection like the present, with its
succession of celebrated names and celebrated poems, offers a good opportunity to us for resolutely endeavouring to make our estimates of poetry
real. I have sought to point out a method which will help us in making
them so, and to exhibit it in use so far as to put any one who likes in a
way of applying it for himself.

At any rate the end to which the method and the estimate are designed to lead and from leading to which, if they do lead to it, they
get their whole value,—the benefit of being able clearly to feel and deeply
to enjoy the best, the truly classic, in poetry,—is an end, let me say it once
more at parting, of supreme importance. We are often told that an
era is opening in which we are to see multitudes of a common sort of
readers, and masses of a common sort of literature; that such readers
do not want and could not relish anything better than such literature,
and that to provide it is becoming a vast and profitable industry. Even
if good literature entirely lost currency with the world, it would still be

abundantly worth while to continue to enjoy it by oneself. But it never will lose currency with the world, in spite of momentary appearances; it never will lose supremacy. Currency and supremacy are insured to it, not indeed by the world's deliberate and conscious choice, but by something far deeper,—by the instinct of self-preservation in humanity.

# WALTER PATER

# Conclusion from
# *Studies in the History*
# *of the Renaissance*

## 1888 (THIRD EDITION)

*Like other too-familiar expressions, the phrase "art for art's sake"
deserves a closer look. When we find it as the culmination of Pater's
essay, it carries the accumulated burden of everything that has preceded
it, and is far from being a flip comment about the limitations of art.
But this five-paragraph essay is not primarily about art (for its own
sake), let alone literature: Pater offers no literary theory, is not concerned with formal problems, and discusses neither authors nor works.
His purpose may be inferred from his use of the Greek epigraph and
the repetition of the words "impressions" and "we," "us," and "our":
Pater's focus is on us, on how we understand the world, and on how
we are to live in it. If, as science has taught us, this is a world of perpetual process and change, characterized by flux both within and without, the apparent solidity of external objects is merely an illusion;
what is real is the swarm of single, sharp, but fleeting impressions
registered on the mind of each solitary observer. All experience is
merely subjective, and our lives consist only of a limited number of
moments; how then is one to live successfully? For Pater, the answer
is to crowd as many impressions as possible into our lives—to make
each moment count, to experience directly and intensely, to "burn*

From *Studies in the History of the Renaissance*, 3rd edition, The Macmillan Company,
1888.

\* This brief "Conclusion" was omitted in the second edition of this book, as I conceived
it might possibly mislead some of those young men into whose hands it might fall.    On
the whole, I have thought it best to reprint it here, with some slight changes which bring
it closer to my original meaning.    I have dealt more fully in *Marius the Epicurean* with
the thoughts suggested by it.

*always with this hard, gemlike flame." First-hand experience, not ab-
stractions about experience, is what is needed.*

*As T. S. Eliot has said, Pater is fundamentally a moralist, despite
his association with the so-called aesthetic movement in England. In
urging us to wake up, to live intensely, moment by moment, Pater is
hardly concerned with art as a unique activity or creation; it is a means
of providing "the highest quality to [our] moments as they pass." In
the fourth paragraph, Pater lists various kinds of pleasures, apparently
indiscriminately. In seeming to imply that "a curious odour" is intrinsically as valuable as any work of art, is Pater urging a "do your
own thing" or "whatever turns you on" life style?*

*His frank impressionism may usefully be compared with Poe's recog-
nition of individual subjectivity in the first paragraph of "The Poetic
Principle." But it is also useful to contrast Pater with Arnold on this
issue: How do their conceptions of the function of poetry affect their
attitudes on what Arnold calls the "personal estimate"? Finally, what
does the subjective approach do to any possibility of establishing critical standards? Anatole France defined criticism as "the adventures of
a soul among masterpieces." Does the impressionistic approach make
for a useful way of talking about literature, or does it lead, ultimately,
to another familiar expression: "I don't know anything about art, but
I know what I like"?*

Λέγει που Ἡράκλειτος ὅτι πάντα χωρεῖ καὶ οὐδὲν μένει[1]

To REGARD all things and principles of things as inconstant modes or
fashions has more and more become the tendency of modern thought.
Let us begin with that which is without—our physical life. Fix upon
it in one of its more exquisite intervals, the moment, for instance of delicious recoil from the flood of water in summer heat. What is the whole
physical life in that moment but a combination of natural elements to
which science gives their names? But these elements, phosphorus and
lime and delicate fibres, are present not in the human body alone: we
detect them in places most remote from it. Our physical life is a
perpetual motion of them—the passage of the blood, the wasting
and repairing of the lenses of the eye, the modification of the tissues
of the brain by every ray of light and sound—processes which
science reduces to simpler and more elementary forces. Like the
elements of which we are composed, the action of these forces extends
beyond us; it rusts iron and ripens corn. Far out on every side of us

[1] *Legei pou Herakleitos oti panta chorei kai ouden menei.*   Heraclitus says that all things
move and nothing remains.

those elements are broadcast, driven by many forces; and birth and gesture and death and the springing of violets from the grave are but a few out of ten thousand resultant combinations. That clear, perpetual outline of face and limb is but an image of ours, under which we group them—a design in a web, the actual threads of which pass out beyond it. This at least of flamelike our life has, that it is but the concurrence, renewed from moment to moment, of forces parting sooner or later on their ways.

Or if we begin with the inward world of thought and feeling, the whirlpool is still more rapid, the flame more eager and devouring. There it is no longer the gradual darkening of the eye and fading of colour from the wall,—the movement of the shore-side, where the water flows down indeed, though in apparent rest,—but the race of the midstream, a drift of momentary acts of sight and passion and thought. At first sight experience seems to bury us under a flood of external objects, pressing upon us with a sharp and importunate reality, calling us out of ourselves in a thousand forms of action. But when reflexion begins to act upon those objects they are dissipated under its influence; the cohesive force seems suspended like a trick of magic; each object is loosed into a group of impressions—colour, odour, texture—in the mind of the observer. And if we continue to dwell in thought on this world, not of objects in the solidity with which language invests them, but of impressions unstable, flickering, inconsistent, which burn and are extinguished with our consciousness of them, it contracts still further; the whole scope of observation is dwarfed to the narrow chamber of the individual mind. Experience, already reduced to a swarm of impressions, is ringed round for each one of us by that thick wall of personality through which no real voice has ever pierced on its way to us, or from us to that which we can only conjecture to be without. Every one of those impressions is the impression of the individual in his isolation, each mind keeping as a solitary prisoner its own dream of a world. Analysis goes a step farther still, and assures us that those impressions of the individual mind to which, for each one of us, experience dwindles down, are in perpetual flight; that each of them is limited by time, and that as time is infinitely divisible, each of them is infinitely divisible also; all that is actual in it being a single moment, gone while we try to apprehend it, of which it may ever be more truly said that it has ceased to be than that it is. To such a tremulous wisp constantly reforming itself on the stream, to a single sharp impression, with a sense in it, a relic more or less fleeting, of such moments gone by, what is real in our life fines itself down. It is with this movement, with the passage and dissolution of impressions, images, sensations, that analysis leaves off—that continual vanishing away, that strange, perpetual weaving and unweaving of ourselves.

*Philosophiren,* says Novalis, *ist dephlegmatisiren, vivificiren.*[2]　The service of philosophy, of speculative culture, towards the human spirit is to rouse, to startle it into sharp and eager observation.　Every moment some form grows perfect in hand or face; some tone on the hills or the sea is choicer than the rest; some mood of passion or insight or intellectual excitement is irresistibly real and attractive for us,—for that moment only.　Not the fruit of experience, but experience itself, is the end.　A counted number of pulses only is given to us of a variegated, dramatic life.　How may we see in them all that is to be seen in them by the finest senses?　How shall we pass most swiftly from point to point, and be present always at the focus where the greatest number of vital forces unite in their purest energy?

To burn always with this hard, gemlike flame, to maintain this ecstasy, is success in life.　In a sense it might even be said that our failure is to form habits: for, after all, habit is relative to a stereotyped world, and meantime it is only the roughness of the eye that makes any two persons, things, situations, seem alike.　While all melts under our feet we may well catch at any exquisite passion, or any contribution to knowledge that seems by a lifted horizon to set the spirit free for a moment, or any stirring of the senses, strange dyes, strange colours, and curious odours, or work of the artist's hands, or the face of one's friend.　Not to discriminate every moment some passionate attitude in those about us, and in the brilliancy of their gifts some tragic dividing of forces on their ways, is, on this short day of frost and sun, to sleep before evening.　With this sense of the splendour of our experience and of its awful brevity, gathering all we are into one desperate effort to see and touch, we shall hardly have time to make theories about the things we see and touch.　What we have to do is to be for ever curiously testing new opinions and courting new impressions, never acquiescing in a facile orthodoxy of Comte, or of Hegel, or of our own.　Philosophical theories or ideas, as points of view, instruments of criticism, may help us to gather up what might otherwise pass unregarded by us.　"Philosophy is the microscope of thought."　The theory or idea or system which requires of us the sacrifice of any part of this experience, in consideration of some interest into which we cannot enter, or some abstract theory we have not identified with ourselves, or what is only conventional, has no real claim upon us.

One of the most beautiful passages in the writings of Rousseau is that in the sixth book of the *Confessions,* where he describes the awakening in him of the literary sense.　An undefinable taint of death had always clung about him, and now in early manhood he believed himself smitten

[2] To philosophize is to rouse from inertia, to come alive.

by mortal disease. He asked himself how he might make as much as possible of the interval that remained; and he was not biassed by anything in his previous life when he decided that it must be by intellectual excitement, which he found just then in the clear, fresh writings of Voltaire. Well! we are all *condamnés*, as Victor Hugo says: we are all under sentence of death but with a sort of indefinite reprieve—*les hommes sont tous condamnés à mort avec des sursis indéfinis:* we have an interval, and then our place knows us no more. Some spend this interval in listlessness, some in high passions, the wisest, at least among "the children of this world," in art and song. For our one chance lies in expanding that interval, in getting as many pulsations as possible into the given time. Great passions may give us this quickened sense of life, ecstasy and sorrow of love, the various forms of enthusiastic activity, disinterested or otherwise, which come naturally to many of us. Only be sure it is passion—that it does yield you this fruit of a quickened, multiplied consciousness. Of this wisdom, the poetic passion, the desire of beauty, the love of art for art's sake, has most; for art comes to you professing frankly to give nothing but the highest quality to your moments as they pass, and simply for those moments' sake.

# The Art of Fiction

## 1884

*Here is another "defense" of art, but this time it is the novel, a relatively new genre, that in James' view needs some serious discussion. Because Walter Besant's pamphlet on "the art of fiction" is both conventional and superficial, James here will "edge in a few words" on the subject, and in so doing destroy Besant's position point for point. This rebuttal, James' best-known essay on the theory of fiction, touches on various issues amplified and developed in his extensive critical writing: the relationship between fiction and life, the freedom and responsibilities of the novelist, the task of the critic, the relationship between plot and character, the importance of technique, the place of subject matter in fiction, the morality of fiction, and the character of the novelist. How James deals with these topics should be studied, for in his essays we find the beginnings of modern fictional theory. The basic assumption is that, like any other art form, fiction must be taken seriously by authors, readers, and critics alike.*

*The word "free" occurs so often in the essay that it directs our attention to a major theme. James rejects conventional critical labels and distinctions; he rejects a priori prescriptions and rules about how to write a novel; he rejects limitations on the artist's freedom of choice in respect to subject matter and technique; he rejects traditional concepts of plot; and, climactically, he rejects Besant's formulation concerning "the conscious moral purpose" of the novel. If "the province of art is all life, all feeling, all observation, all vision . . . all experience," the novelist cannot be handcuffed in his attempts to represent life. Throughout, James stresses the artist's necessary sensitivity to experi-*

From *Partial Portraits;* The Macmillan Company, 1888.

*ence and the transformation of that experience by his imagination; as
critics and readers, we can judge him only by the "execution," the
"treatment," the rendering of the raw multitudinous materials of life
into a unified work of art.*

*When James declares that the novel is "a living thing, all one and
continuous, like any other organism," the very simile reminds us of
Aristotle, and how his discussion of character merges back into a discussion of plot, the two being inseparable. James' theory of fictional
form is equally organic, but for him a flawed structure and a failure
of execution are symptomatic of either intellectual or moral failures
on the part of the novelist: The integrity of a work is a reflection of
the artist's integrity. In this view, James denies that the novel must
have a conscious moral purpose. On the contrary, what is commonly
thought of as morality he defines as timidity—that is, the avoidance of
certain "improper" but nevertheless real subjects; to insist that a novel
be morally didactic is to restrict the artist's freedom from another direction. The requisite "moral energy" liberates the novelist; thus James
connects total artistic freedom, the "search for form," and morality in
the interest of rendering life in fiction.*

I SHOULD not have affixed so comprehensive a title to these few remarks,
necessarily wanting in any completeness upon a subject the full consideration of which would carry us far, did I not seem to discover a pretext for
my temerity in the interesting pamphlet lately published under this name
by Mr. Walter Besant.   Mr. Besant's lecture at the Royal Institution—
the original form of his pamphlet—appears to indicate that many persons
are interested in the art of fiction, and are not indifferent to such remarks,
as those who practise it may attempt to make about it.   I am therefore
anxious not to lose the benefit of this favourable association, and to edge
in a few words under cover of the attention which Mr. Besant is sure to
have excited.   There is something very encouraging in his having put
into form certain of his ideas on the mystery of story-telling.

It is a proof of life and curiosity—curiosity on the part of the brotherhood of novelists as well as on the part of their readers.   Only a short time
ago it might have been supposed that the English novel was not what the
French call *discutable*.   It had no air of having a theory, a conviction, a
consciousness of itself behind it—of being the expression of an artistic
faith, the result of choice and comparison.   I do not say it was necessarily the worse for that: it would take much more courage than I possess
to intimate that the form of the novel as Dickens and Thackeray (for
instance) saw it had any taint of incompleteness.   It was, however, *naïf* (if
I may help myself out with another French word); and evidently if it be

destined to suffer in any way for having lost its *naïveté* it has now an idea of making sure of the corresponding advantages.   During the period I have alluded to there was a comfortable, good-humoured feeling abroad that a novel is a novel, as a pudding is a pudding, and that our only business with it could be to swallow it.   But within a year or two, for some reason or other, there have been signs of returning animation—the era of discussion would appear to have been to a certain extent opened.   Art lives upon discussion, upon experiment, upon curiosity, upon variety of attempt, upon the exchange of views and the comparison of standpoints; and there is a presumption that those times when no one has anything particular to say about it, and has no reason to give for practice or prefer- ence, though they may be times of honour, are not times of development— are times, possibly even, a little of dulness.   The successful application of any art is a delightful spectacle, but the theory too is interesting; and though there is a great deal of the latter without the former I suspect there has never been a genuine success that has not had a latent core of con- viction.   Discussion, suggestion, formulation, these things are fertilising when they are frank and sincere.   Mr. Besant has set an excellent example in saying what he thinks, for his part, about the way in which fiction should be written, as well as about the way in which it should be published; for his view of the "art," carried on into an appendix, covers that too. Other labourers in the same  field will doubtless take up the argument, they will give it the light of their experience, and the effect will surely be to make our interest in the novel a little more what it had for some time threatened to fail to be—a serious, active, inquiring interest, under pro- tection of which this delightful study may, in moments of confidence, venture to say a little more what it thinks of itself.

It must take itself seriously for the public to take it so.   The old supersti- tion about fiction being "wicked" has doubtless died out in England; but the spirit of it lingers in a certain oblique regard directed toward any story which does not more or less admit that it is only a joke.   Even the most jocular novel feels in some degree the weight of the proscription that was formerly directed against literary levity: the jocularity does not always succeed in passing for orthodoxy.   It is still expected, though perhaps people are ashamed to say it, that a production which is after all only a "make-believe" (for what else is a "story"?) shall be in some degree apologetic—shall renounce the pretension of attempting really to re- present life.   This, of course, any sensible, wide-awake story declines to do, for it quickly perceives that the tolerance granted to it on such a condition is only an attempt to stifle it disguised in the form of generosity. The old evangelical hostility to the novel, which was as explicit as it was narrow, and which regarded it as little less favourable to our immortal part than a stage-play, was in reality far less insulting.   The only reason for the existence of a novel is that it does attempt to represent life. When it relinquishes this attempt, the same attempt that we see on the canvas of the painter, it will have arrived at a very strange pass. It is not expected of the picture that it will make itself humble in order to be forgiven; and the analogy between the art of the painter and the art of the novelist is, so far as I am able to see, complete. Their inspiration is the same, their process (allowing for the different quality of the vehicle), is the same, their success is the same. They may learn from each other, they may explain and sustain each other. Their cause is the same, and the honour of one is the honour of another. The Mahometans think a picture an unholy thing, but it is a long time since any Christian did, and it is therefore the more odd that in the Christian mind the traces (dissimulated though they may be) of a suspicion of the sister art should linger to this day. The only effectual way to lay it to rest is to emphasise the analogy to which I just alluded—to insist on the fact that as the picture is reality, so the novel is history. That is the only general description (which does it justice) that we may give of the novel. But history also is allowed to represent life; it is not, any more than painting, expected to apologise. The subject-matter of fiction is stored up likewise in documents and records, and if it will not give itself away, as they say in California, it must speak with assurance, with the tone of the historian. Certain accomplished novelists have a habit of giving themselves away which must often bring tears to the eyes of people who take their fiction seriously. I was lately struck, in reading over many pages of Anthony Trollope, with his want of discretion in this particular. In a digression, a parenthesis or an aside, he concedes to the reader that he and this trusting friend are only "making believe." He admits that the events he narrates have not really happened, and that he can give his narrative any turn the reader may like best. Such a betrayal of a sacred office seems to me, I confess, a terrible crime; it is what I mean by the attitude of apology, and it shocks me every whit as much in Trollope as it would have shocked me in Gibbon or Macaulay. It implies that the novelist is less occupied in looking for the truth (the truth, of course I mean, that he assumes, the premises that we must grant him, whatever they may be), than the historian, and in doing so it deprives him at a stroke of all his standing-room. To represent and illustrate the past, the actions of men, is the task of either writer, and the only difference that I can see is, in proportion as he succeeds, to the honour of the novelist, consisting as it does in his having more difficulty in collecting his evidence, which is so far from being purely literary. It seems to me to give him a great character, the fact that he has at once so much in common with the philosopher and the painter; this double analogy is a magnificent heritage.

It is of all this evidently that Mr. Besant is full when he insists upon the fact that fiction is one of the *fine* arts, deserving in its turn of all the honours and emoluments that have hitherto been reserved for the successful profession of music, poetry, painting, architecture. It is impossible to insist too much on so important a truth, and the place that Mr. Besant demands for the work of the novelist may be represented, a trifle less abstractly, by saying that he demands not only that it shall be reputed artistic, but that it shall be reputed very artistic indeed. It is excellent that he should have struck this note, for his doing so indicates that there was need of it, that his proposition may be to many people a novelty. One rubs one's eyes at the thought; but the rest of Mr. Besant's essay confirms the revelation. I suspect in truth that it would be possible to confirm it still further, and that one would not be far wrong in saying that in addition to the people to whom it has never occurred that a novel ought to be artistic, there are a great many others who, if this principle were urged upon them, would be filled with an indefinable mistrust. They would find it difficult to explain their repugnance, but it would operate strongly to put them on their guard. "Art," in our Protestant communities, where so many things have got so strangely twisted about, is supposed in certain circles to have some vaguely injurious effect upon those who make it an important consideration, who let it weigh in the balance. It is assumed to be opposed in some mysterious manner to morality, to amusement, to instruction. When it is embodied in the work of the painter (the sculptor is another affair!) you know what it is: it stands there before you, in the honesty of pink and green and a gilt frame; you can see the worst of it at a glance, and you can be on your guard. But when it is introduced into literature it becomes more insidious— there is danger of its hurting you before you know it. Literature should be either instructive or amusing, and there is in many minds an impression that these artistic preoccupations, the search for form, contribute to neither end, interfere indeed with both. They are too frivolous to be edifying, and too serious to be diverting; and they are moreover priggish and paradoxical and superfluous. That, I think, represents the manner in which the latent thought of many people who read novels as an exercise in skipping would explain itself if it were to become articulate. They would argue, of course, that a novel ought to be "good," but they would interpret this term in a fashion of their own, which indeed would vary considerably from one critic to another. One would say that being good means representing virtuous and aspiring characters, placed in prominent positions; another would say that it depends on a "happy ending," on a distribution at the last of prizes, pensions, husbands, wives, babies, millions, appended paragraphs, and cheerful remarks. Another still would say that it means being full of incident and movement, so that we shall wish to jump ahead, to see who was the mysterious stranger, and if the stolen will was ever found, and shall not be distracted from this pleasure by any tiresome analysis or "description." But they would all agree that the "artistic" idea would spoil some of their fun. One would hold it accountable for all the description, another would see it revealed in the absence of sympathy. Its hostility to a happy ending would be evident, and it might even in some cases render any ending at all impossible. The "ending" of a novel is, for many persons, like that of a good dinner, a course of dessert and ices, and the artist in fiction is regarded as a sort of meddlesome doctor who forbids agreeable aftertastes. It is therefore true that this conception of Mr. Besant's of the novel as a superior form encounters not only a negative but a positive indifference. It matters little that as a work of art it should really be as little or as much of its essence to supply happy endings, sympathetic characters, and an objective tone, as if it were a work of mechanics: the association of ideas, however incongruous, might easily be too much for it if an eloquent voice were not sometimes raised to call attention to the fact that it is at once as free and as serious a branch of literature as any other.

Certainly this might sometimes be doubted in presence of the enormous number of works of fiction that appeal to the credulity of our generation, for it might easily seem that there could be no great character in a commodity so quickly and easily produced. It must be admitted that good novels are much compromised by bad ones, and that the field at large suffers discredit from overcrowding. I think, however, that this injury is only superficial, and that the superabundance of written fiction proves nothing against the principle itself. It has been vulgarised, like all other kinds of literature, like everything else to-day, and it has proved more than some kinds accessible to vulgarisation. But there is as much difference as there ever was between a good novel and a bad one: the bad is swept with all the daubed canvases and spoiled marble into some unvisited limbo, or infinite rubbish-yard beneath the back-windows of the world, and the good subsists and emits its light and stimulates our desire for perfection. As I shall take the liberty of making but a single criticism of Mr. Besant, whose tone is so full of the love of his art, I may as well have done with it at once. He seems to me to mistake in attempting to say so definitely beforehand what sort of an affair the good novel will be. To indicate the danger of such an error as that has been the purpose of these few pages; to suggest that certain traditions on the subject, applied *a priori*, have already had much to answer for, and that the good health of an art which undertakes so immediately to reproduce life must demand that it be perfectly free. It lives upon exercise, and the very meaning of exercise is freedom. The only obligation to which in advance we may hold a novel, without incurring the accusation of being arbitrary, is that it be interesting. That general responsibility rests upon it, but it is the only one I can think of. The ways in which it is at liberty to accomplish this result (of interesting us) strike me as innumerable, and such as can only suffer from being marked out or fenced in by prescription. They are as various as the temperament of man, and they are successful in proportion as they reveal a particular mind, different from others. A novel is in its broadest definition a personal, a direct impression of life: that, to begin with, constitutes its value, which is greater or less according to the intensity of the impression. But there will be no intensity at all, and therefore no value, unless there is freedom to feel and say. The tracing of a line to be followed, of a tone to be taken, of a form to be filled out, is a limitation of that freedom and a suppression of the very thing that we are most curious about. The form, it seems to me, is to be appreciated after the fact: then the author's choice has been made, his standard has been indicated; then we can follow lines and directions and compare tones and resemblances. Then in a word we can enjoy one of the most charming of pleasures, we can estimate quality, we can apply the test of execution. The execution belongs to the author alone; it is what is most personal to him, and we measure him by that. The advantage, the luxury, as well as the torment and responsibility of the novelist, is that there is no limit to what he may attempt as an executant—no limit to his possible experiments, efforts, discoveries, successes. Here it is especially that he works, step by step, like his brother of the brush, of whom we may always say that he has painted his picture in a manner best known to himself. His manner is his secret, not necessarily a jealous one. He cannot disclose it as a general thing if he would; he would be at a loss to teach it to others. I say this with a due recollection of having insisted on the community of method of the artist who paints a picture and the artist who writes a novel. The painter *is* able to teach the rudiments of his practice, and it is possible, from the study of good work (granted the aptitude), both to learn how to paint and to learn how to write. Yet it remains true, without injury to the *rapprochement*, that the literary artist would be obliged to say to his pupil much more than the other, "Ah, well, you must do it as you can!" It is a question of degree, a matter of delicacy. If there are exact sciences, there are also exact arts, and the grammar of painting is so much more definite that it makes the difference.

I ought to add, however, that if Mr. Besant says at the beginning of his essay that the "laws of fiction may be laid down and taught with as much precision and exactness as the laws of harmony, perspective, and proportion," he mitigates what might appear to be an extravagance by applying his remark to "general" laws, and by expressing most of these rules in a manner with which it would certainly be unaccommodating to disagree. That the novelist must write from his experience, that his "characters must be real and such as might be met with in actual life," that "a young lady brought up in a quiet country village should avoid descriptions of garrison life," and "a writer whose friends and personal experiences belong to the lower middle-class should carefully avoid introducing his characters into society;" that one should enter one's notes in a common-place book; that one's figures should be clear in outline; that making them clear by some trick of speech or of carriage is a bad method and "describing them at length" is a worse one; that English Fiction should have a "conscious moral purpose;" that "it is almost impossible to estimate too highly the value of careful workmanship—that is, of style;" that "the most important point of all is the story," that "the story is everything": these are principles with most of which it is surely impossible not to sympathise. That remark about the lower middle-class writer and his knowing his place is perhaps rather chilling; but for the rest I should find it difficult to dissent from any one of these recommendations. At the same time, I should find it difficult positively to assent to them, with the exception, perhaps, of the injunction as to entering one's notes in a common-place book. They scarcely seem to me to have the quality that Mr. Besant attributes to the rules of the novelist—the "precision and exactness" of "the laws of harmony, perspective, and proportion." They are suggestive, they are even inspiring, but they are not exact, though they are doubtless as much so as the case admits of: which is a proof of that liberty of interpretation for which I just contended. For the value of these different injunctions—so beautiful and so vague—is wholly in the meaning one attaches to them. The characters, the situation, which strike one as real will be those that touch and interest one most, but the measure of reality is very difficult to fix. The reality of Don Quixote or of Mr. Micawber is a very delicate shade; it is a reality so coloured by the author's vision that, vivid as it may be, one would hesitate to propose it as a model: one would expose one's self to some very embarrassing questions on the part of a pupil. It goes without saying that you will not write a good novel unless you possess the sense of reality; but it will be difficult to give you a recipe for calling that sense into being. Humanity is immense, and reality has a myriad forms; the most one can affirm is that some of the flowers of fiction have the odour of it, and others have not; as for telling you in advance how your nosegay should be composed, that is another affair. It is equally excellent and inconclusive to say that one must write from experience; to our suppositious aspirant such a declaration might savour of mockery. What kind of experience is intended, and where does it begin and end? Experience is never limited, and it is never complete;

it is an immense sensibility, a kind of huge spider-web of the finest silken threads suspended in the chamber of consciousness, and catching every airborne particle in its tissue.    It is the very atmosphere of the mind; and when the mind is imaginative—much more when it happens to be that of a man of genius—it takes to itself the faintest hints of life, it converts the very pulses of the air into revelations.    The young lady living in a village has only to be a damsel upon whom nothing is lost to make it quite unfair (as it seems to me) to declare to her that she shall have nothing to say about the military.    Greater miracles have been seen than that, imagination assisting, she should speak the truth about some of these gentlemen.    I remember an English novelist, a woman of genius, telling me that she was much commended for the impression she had managed to give in one of her tales of the nature and way of life of the French Protestant youth. She had been asked where she learned so much about this recondite being, she had been congratulated on her peculiar opportunities.    These opportunities consisted in her having once, in Paris, as she ascended a staircase, passed an open door where, in the household of a *pasteur*, some of the young Protestants were seated at table round a finished meal.    The glimpse made a picture; it lasted only a moment, but that moment was experience.    She had got her direct personal impression, and she turned out her type.    She knew what youth was, and what Protestantism; she also had the advantage of having seen what it was to be French, so that she converted these ideas into a concrete image and produced a reality. Above all, however, she was blessed with the faculty which when you give it an inch takes an ell, and which for the artist is a much greater source of strength than any accident of residence or of place in the social scale.    The power to guess the unseen from the seen, to trace the implication of things, to judge the whole piece by the pattern, the condition of feeling life in general so completely that you are well on your way to knowing any particular corner of it—this cluster of gifts may almost be said to constitute experience, and they occur in country and in town, and in the most differing stages of education.    If experience consists of impressions, it may be said that impressions *are* experience, just as (have we not seen it?) they are the very air we breathe.    Therefore, if I should certainly say to a novice, "Write from experience and experience only," I should feel that this was rather a tantalising monition if I were not careful immediately to add, "Try to be one of the people on whom nothing is lost!"

I am far from intending by this to minimise the importance of exactness —of truth of detail.    One can speak best from one's own taste, and I may therefore venture to say that the air of reality (solidity of specification) seems to me to be the supreme virtue of a novel—the merit on which all its other merits (including that conscious moral purpose of which Mr. Besant speaks) helplessly and submissively depend.   If it be not there they are all as nothing, and if these be there, they owe their effect to the success with which the author has produced the illusion of life.   The cultivation of this success, the study of this exquisite process, form, to my taste, the beginning and the end of the art of the novelist.   They are his inspiration, his despair, his reward, his torment, his delight.   It is here in very truth that he competes with life; it is here that he competes with his brother the painter in *his* attempt to render the look of things, the look that conveys their meaning, to catch the colour, the relief, the expression, the surface, the substance of the human spectacle.   It is in regard to this that Mr. Besant is well inspired when he bids him take notes.   He cannot possibly take too many, he cannot possibly take enough.   All life solicits him, and to "render" the simplest surface, to produce the most momentary illusion, is a very complicated business.   His case would be easier, and the rule would be more exact, if Mr. Besant had been able to tell him what notes to take.   But this, I fear, he can never learn in any manual; it is the business of his life.   He has to take a great many in order to select a few, he has to work them up as he can, and even the guides and philosophers who might have most to say to him must leave him alone when it comes to the application of precepts, as we leave the painter in communion with his palette.   That his characters "must be clear in outline," as Mr. Besant says—he feels that down to his boots; but how he shall make them so is a secret between his good angel and himself.   It would be absurdly simple if he could be taught that a great deal of "description" would make them so, or that on the contrary the absence of description and the cultivation of dialogue, or the absence of dialogue and the multiplication of "incident," would rescue him from his difficulties.   Nothing, for instance, is more possible than that he be of a turn of mind for which this odd, literal opposition of description and dialogue, incident and description, has little meaning and light.   People often talk of these things as if they had a kind of internecine distinctness, instead of melting into each other at every breath, and being intimately associated parts of one general effort of expression.   I cannot imagine composition existing in a series of blocks, nor conceive, in any novel worth discussing at all, of a passage of description that is not in its intention narrative, a passage of dialogue that is not in its intention descriptive, a touch of truth of any sort that does not partake of the nature of incident, or an incident that derives its interest from any other source than the general and only source of the success of a work of art—that of being illustrative.   A novel is a living thing, all one and continuous, like any other organism, and in proportion as it lives will it be found, I think, that in each of the parts there is something of each of the other parts. The critic who over the close texture of a finished work shall pretend to trace a geography of items will mark some frontiers as artificial, I fear, as any that have been known to history. There is an old-fashioned distinction between the novel of character and the novel of incident which must have cost many a smile to the intending fabulist who was keen about his work. It appears to me as little to the point as the equally celebrated distinction between the novel and the romance—to answer as little to any reality. There are bad novels and good novels, as there are bad pictures and good pictures; but that is the only distinction in which I see any meaning, and I can as little imagine speaking of a novel of character as I can imagine speaking of a picture of character. When one says picture one says of character, when one says novel one says of incident, and the terms may be transposed at will. What is character but the determination of incident? What is incident but the illustration of character? What is either a picture or a novel that is *not* of character? What else do we seek in it and find in it? It is an incident for a woman to stand up with her hand resting on a table and look out at you in a certain way; or if it be not an incident I think it will be hard to say what it is. At the same time it is an expression of character. If you say you don't see it (character in *that—allons donc!*[1]), this is exactly what the artist who has reasons of his own for thinking he *does* see it undertakes to show you. When a young man makes up his mind that he has not faith enough after all to enter the church as he intended, that is an incident, though you may not hurry to the end of the chapter to see whether perhaps he doesn't change once more. I do not say that these are extraordinary or startling incidents. I do not pretend to estimate the degree of interest proceeding from them, for this will depend upon the skill of the painter. It sounds almost puerile to say that some incidents are instrinsically much more important than others, and I need not take this precaution after having professed my sympathy for the major ones in remarking that the only classification of the novel that I can understand is into that which has life and that which has it not.

The novel and the romance, the novel of incident and that of character —these clumsy separations appear to me to have been made by critics and readers for their own convenience, and to help them out of some of their occasional queer predicaments, but to have little reality or interest for the producer, from whose point of view it is of course that we are attempting to consider the art of fiction. The case is the same with another shadowy category which Mr. Besant apparently is disposed to set up—that of the "modern English novel"; unless indeed it be that in this matter he has fallen into an accidental confusion of standpoints. It is not quite clear

[1] Oh, come now!

whether he intends the remarks in which he alludes to it to be didactic or historical. It is as difficult to suppose a person intending to write a modern English as to suppose him writing an ancient English novel: that is a label which begs the question. One writes the novel, one paints the picture, of one's language and of one's time, and calling it modern English will not, alas! make the difficult task any easier. No more, unfortunately, will calling this or that work of one's fellow-artist a romance—unless it be, of course, simply for the pleasantness of the thing, as for instance when Hawthorne gave this heading to his story of *Blithedale*. The French, who have brought the theory of fiction to remarkable completeness, have but one name for the novel, and have not attempted smaller things in it, that I can see, for that. I can think of no obligation to which the "romancer" would not be held equally with the novelist; the standard of execution is equally high for each. Of course it is of execution that we are talking— that being the only point of a novel that is open to contention. This is perhaps too often lost sight of, only to produce interminable confusions and cross-purposes. We must grant the artist his subject, his idea, his *donnée:* our criticism is applied only to what he makes of it. Naturally I do not mean that we are bound to like it or find it interesting: in case we do not our course is perfectly simple—to let it alone. We may believe that of a certain idea even the most sincere novelist can make nothing at all, and the event may perfectly justify our belief; but the failure will have been a failure to execute, and it is in the execution that the fatal weakness is recorded. If we pretend to respect the artist at all, we must allow him his freedom of choice, in the face, in particular cases, of in-numerable presumptions that the choice will not fructify. Art derives a considerable part of its beneficial exercise from flying in the face of presumptions, and some of the most interesting experiments of which it is capable are hidden in the bosom of common things. Gustave Flaubert has written a story about the devotion of a servant girl to a parrot, and the production, highly finished as it is, cannot on the whole be called a suc-cess. We are perfectly free to find it flat, but I think it might have been interesting; and I, for my part, am extremely glad he should have written it; it is a contribution to our knowledge of what can be done—or what cannot. Ivan Turgénieff has written a tale about a deaf and dumb serf and a lap-dog, and the thing is touching, loving, a little masterpiece. He struck the note of life where Gustave Flaubert missed it—he flew in the face of a presumption and achieved a victory.

Nothing, of course, will ever take the place of the good old fashion of "liking" a work of art or not liking it: the most improved criticism will not abolish that primitive, that ultimate test. I mention this to guard myself from the accusation of intimating that the idea, the subject, of a novel or a picture, does not matter. It matters, to my sense, in the highest degree, and if I might put up a prayer it would be that artists should select none but the richest. Some, as I have already hastened to admit, are much more remunerative than others, and it would be a world happily arranged in which persons intending to treat them should be exempt from confusions and mistakes. This fortunate condition will arrive only, I fear, on the same day that critics become purged from error. Meanwhile, I repeat, we do not judge the artist with fairness unless we say to him, "Oh, I grant you your starting-point, because if I did not I should seem to prescribe to you, and heaven forbid I should take that responsibility. If I pretend to tell you what you must not take, you will call upon me to tell you then what you must take; in which case I shall be prettily caught. Moreover, it isn't till I have accepted your data that I can begin to measure you. I have the standard, the pitch; I have no right to tamper with your flute and then criticise your music. Of course I may not care for your idea at all; I may think it silly, or stale, or unclean; in which case I wash my hands of you altogether. I may content myself with believing that you will not have succeeded in being interesting, but I shall, of course, not attempt to demonstrate it, and you will be as indifferent to me as I am to you. I needn't remind you that there are all sorts of tastes: who can know it better? Some people, for excellent reasons, don't like to read about carpenters; others, for reasons even better, don't like to read about courtesans. Many object to Americans. Others (I believe they are mainly editors and publishers) won't look at Italians. Some readers don't like quiet subjects; others don't like bustling ones. Some enjoy a complete illusion, others the consciousness of large concessions. They choose their novels accordingly, and if they don't care about your idea they won't, *a fortiori*, care about your treatment."

So that it comes back very quickly, as I have said, to the liking: in spite of M. Zola, who reasons less powerfully than he represents, and who will not reconcile himself to this absoluteness of taste, thinking that there are certain things that people ought to like, and that they can be made to like. I am quite at a loss to imagine anything (at any rate in this matter of fiction) that people *ought* to like or to dislike. Selection will be sure to take care of itself, for it has a constant motive behind it. That motive is simply experience. As people feel life, so they will feel the art that is most closely related to it. This closeness of relation is what we should never forget in talking of the effort of the novel. Many people speak of it as a factitious, artificial form, a product of ingenuity, the business of which is to alter and arrange the things that surround us, to translate them into conventional, traditional moulds. This, however, is a view of the matter which carries us but a very short way, condemns the art to an eternal repetition of a few familiar *clichés*, cuts short its development, and leads us straight up to a dead wall. Catching the very note and trick, the strange irregular rhythm of life, that is the attempt whose strenuous force keeps Fiction upon her feet. In proportion as in what she offers us we see life *without* rearrangement do we feel that we are touching the truth; in proportion as we see it *with* rearrangement do we feel that we are being put off with a substitute, a compromise and convention. It is not uncommon to hear an extraordinary assurance of remark in regard to this matter of rearranging, which is often spoken of as if it were the last word of art. Mr. Besant seems to me in danger of falling into the great error with his rather unguarded talk about "selection." Art is essentially selection, but it is a selection whose main care is to be typical, to be inclusive. For many people art means rose-coloured window-panes, and selection means picking a bouquet for Mrs. Grundy. They will tell you glibly that artistic considerations have nothing to do with the disagreeable, with the ugly; they will rattle off shallow commonplaces about the province of art and the limits of art till you are moved to some wonder in return as to the province and the limits of ignorance. It appears to me that no one can ever have made a seriously artistic attempt without becoming conscious of an immense increase—a kind of revelation—of freedom. One perceives in that case—by the light of a heavenly ray—that the province of art is all life, all feeling, all observation, all vision. As Mr. Besant so justly intimates, it is all experience. That is a sufficient answer to those who maintain that it must not touch the sad things of life, who stick into its divine unconscious bosom little prohibitory inscriptions on the end of sticks, such as we see in public gardens—"It is forbidden to walk on the grass; it is forbidden to touch the flowers; it is not allowed to introduce dogs or to remain after dark; it is requested to keep to the right." The young aspirant in the line of fiction whom we continue to imagine will do nothing without taste, for in that case his freedom would be of little use to him; but the first advantage of his taste will be to reveal to him the absurdity of the little sticks and tickets. If he have taste, I must add, of course he will have ingenuity, and my disrespectful reference to that quality just now was not meant to imply that it is useless in fiction. But it is only a secondary aid; the first is a capacity for receiving straight impressions.

Mr. Besant has some remarks on the question of "the story" which I shall not attempt to criticise, though they seem to me to contain a singular ambiguity, because I do not think I understand them. I cannot see what is meant by talking as if there were a part of a novel which is the story and part of it which for mystical reasons is not—unless indeed the distinction be made in a sense in which it is difficult to suppose that any one should attempt to convey anything. "The story," if it represents anything,

represents the subject, the idea, the *donnée* of the novel; and there is surely
no "school"—Mr. Besant speaks of a school—which urges that a novel
should be all treatment and no subject. There must assuredly be
something to treat; every school is intimately conscious of that. This
sense of the story being the idea, the starting-point, of the novel, is the only
one that I see in which it can be spoken of as something different from its
organic whole; and since in proportion as the work is successful the idea
permeates and penetrates it, informs and animates it, so that every word
and every punctuation-point contribute directly to the expression, in that
proportion do we lose our sense of the story being a blade which may be
drawn more or less out of its sheath. The story and the novel, the idea
and the form, are the needle and thread, and I never heard of a guild of
tailors who recommended the use of the thread without the needle, or the
needle without the thread. Mr. Besant is not the only critic who may be
observed to have spoken as if there were certain things in life which
constitute stories, and certain others which do not—I find the same odd
implication in an entertaining article in the *Pall Mall Gazette*, devoted, as
it happens, to Mr. Besant's lecture. "The story is the thing!" says this
graceful writer, as if with a tone of opposition to some other idea. I
should think it was, as every painter who, as the time for "sending in" his
picture looms in the distance, finds himself still in quest of a subject—as
every belated artist not fixed about his theme will heartily agree. There
are some subjects which speak to us and others which do not, but he
would be a clever man who should undertake to give a rule—an index
expurgatorius—by which the story and the no-story should be known
apart. It is impossible (to me at least) to imagine any such rule which
shall not be altogether arbitrary. The writer in the *Pall Mall* opposes the
delightful (as I suppose) novel of *Margot la Balafrée* to certain tales in
which "Bostonian nymphs" appear to have "rejected English dukes for
psychological reasons." I am not acquainted with the romance just
designated, and can scarcely forgive the *Pall Mall* critic for not mentioning
the name of the author, but the title appears to refer to a lady who may
have received a scar in some heroic adventure. I am inconsolable at not
being acquainted with this episode, but am utterly at a loss to see why
it is a story when the rejection (or acceptance) of a duke is not, and why a
reason, psychological or other, is not a subject when a cicatrix is. They
are all particles of the multitudinous life with which the novel deals, and
surely no dogma which pretends to make it lawful to touch the one and
unlawful to touch the other will stand for a moment on its feet. It is the
special picture that must stand or fall, according as it seem to possess truth
or to lack it. Mr. Besant does not, to my sense, light up the subject by
intimating that a story must, under penalty of not being a story, consist of

"adventures." Why of adventures more than of green spectacles? He mentions a category of impossible things, and among them he places "fiction without adventure." Why without adventure, more than without matrimony, or celibacy, or parturition, or cholera, or hydropathy, or Jansenism? This seems to me to bring the novel back to the hapless little *rôle* of being an artificial, ingenious thing—bring it down from its large, free character of an immense and exquisite correspondence with life. And what *is* adventure, when it comes to that, and by what sign is the listening pupil to recognise it? It is an adventure—an immense one— for me to write this little article; and for a Bostonian nymph to reject an English duke is an adventure only less stirring, I should say, than for an English duke to be rejected by a Bostonian nymph. I see dramas within dramas in that, and innumerable points of view. A psychological reason is, to my imagination, an object adorably pictorial; to catch the tint of its complexion—I feel as if that idea might inspire one to Titianesque efforts. There are few things more exciting to me, in short, than a psychological reason, and yet, I protest, the novel seems to me the most magnificent form of art. I have just been reading, at the same time, the delightful story of *Treasure Island*, by Mr. Robert Louis Stevenson and, in a manner less consecutive, the last tale from M. Edmond de Goncourt, which is entitled *Chérie*. One of these works treats of murders, mysteries, islands of dreadful renown, hairbreadth escapes, miraculous coincidences and buried doubloons. The other treats of a little French girl who lived in a fine house in Paris, and died of wounded sensibility because no one would marry her. I call *Treasure Island* delightful, because it appears to me to have succeeded wonderfully in what it attempts; and I venture to bestow no epithet upon *Chérie*, which strikes me as having failed deplorably in what it attempts—that is in tracing the development of the moral consciousness of a child. But one of these productions strikes me as exactly as much of a novel as the other, and as having a "story" quite as much. The moral consciousness of a child is as much a part of life as the islands of the Spanish Main, and the one sort of geography seems to me to have those "surprises" of which Mr. Besant speaks quite as much as the other. For myself (since it comes back in the last resort, as I say, to the preference of the individual), the picture of the child's experience has the advantage that I can at successive steps (an immense luxury, near to the "sensual pleasure" of which Mr. Besant's critic in the *Pall Mall* speaks) say Yes or No, as it may be, to what the artist puts before me. I have been a child in fact, but I have been on a quest for a buried treasure only in supposition, and it is a simple accident that with M. de Goncourt I should have for the most part to say No. With George Eliot, when she painted that country with a far other intelligence, I always said Yes.

The most interesting part of Mr. Besant's lecture is unfortunately the briefest passage—his very cursory allusion to the "conscious moral purpose" of the novel.   Here again it is not very clear whether he be recording a fact or laying down a principle; it is a great pity that in the latter case he should not have developed his idea.   This branch of the subject is of immense importance, and Mr. Besant's few words point to considerations of the widest reach, not to be lightly disposed of.   He will have treated the art of fiction but superficially who is not prepared to go every inch of the way that these considerations will carry him.   It is for this reason that at the beginning of these remarks I was careful to notify the reader that my reflections on so large a theme have no pretension to be exhaustive.   Like Mr. Besant, I have left the question of the morality of the novel till the last, and at the last I find I have used up my space.   It is a question surrounded with difficulties, as witness the very first that meets us, in the form of a definite question, on the threshold.   Vagueness, in such a discussion, is fatal, and what is the meaning of your morality and your conscious moral purpose?   Will you not define your terms and explain how (a novel being a picture) a picture can be either moral or immoral?   You wish to paint a moral picture or carve a moral statue: will you not tell us how you would set about it?   We are discussing the Art of Fiction; questions of art are questions (in the widest sense) of execution; questions of morality are quite another affair, and will you not let us see how it is that you find it so easy to mix them up?   These things are so clear to Mr. Besant that he has deduced from them a law which he sees embodied in English Fiction, and which is "a truly admirable thing and a great cause for congratulation."   It is a great cause for congratulation indeed when such thorny problems become as smooth as silk.   I may add that in so far as Mr. Besant perceives that in point of fact English Fiction has addressed itself preponderantly to these delicate questions he will appear to many people to have made a vain discovery.   They will have been positively struck, on the contrary, with the moral timidity of the usual English novelist; with his (or with her) aversion to face the difficulties with which on every side the treatment of reality bristles.   He is apt to be extremely shy (whereas the picture that Mr. Besant draws is a picture of boldness), and the sign of his work, for the most part, is a cautious silence on certain subjects.   In the English novel (by which of course I mean the American as well), more than in any other, there is a traditional difference between that which people know and that which they agree to admit that they know, that which they see and that which they speak of, that which they feel to be a part of life and that which they allow to enter into literature.   There is the great difference, in short, between what they talk of in conversation and what they talk of in print.

The essence of moral energy is to survey the whole field, and I should directly reverse Mr. Besant's remark and say not that the English novel has a purpose, but that it has a diffidence.    To what degree a purpose in a work of art is a source of corruption I shall not attempt to inquire; the one that seems to me least dangerous is the purpose of making a perfect work.    As for our novel, I may say lastly on this score that as we find it in England to-day it strikes me as addressed in a large degree to "young people," and that this in itself constitutes a presumption that it will be rather shy.    There are certain things which it is generally agreed not to discuss, not even to mention, before young people.    That is very well, but the absence of discussion is not a symptom of the moral passion.    The purpose of the English novel—"a truly admirable thing, and a great cause for congratulation"—strikes me therefore as rather negative.

There is one point at which the moral sense and the artistic sense lie very near together; that is in the light of the very obvious truth that the deepest quality of a work of art will always be the quality of the mind of the producer.    In proportion as that intelligence is fine will the novel, the picture, the statue partake of the substance of beauty and truth.    To be constituted of such elements is, to my vision, to have purpose enough.    No good novel will ever proceed from a superficial mind; that seems to me an axiom which, for the artist in fiction, will cover all needful moral ground: if the youthful aspirant take it to heart it will illuminate for him many of the mysteries of "purpose."    There are many other useful things that might be said to him, but I have come to the end of my article, and can only touch them as I pass.    The critic in the *Pall Mall Gazette*, whom I have already quoted, draws attention to the danger, in speaking of the art of fiction, of generalising.    The danger that he has in mind is rather, I imagine, that of particularising, for there are some comprehensive remarks which, in addition to those embodied in Mr. Besant's suggestive lecture, might without fear of misleading him be addressed to the ingenuous student.    I should remind him first of the magnificence of the form that is open to him, which offers to sight so few restrictions and such innumerable opportunities.    The other arts, in comparison, appear confined and hampered; the various conditions under which they are exercised are so rigid and definite.    But the only condition that I can think of attaching to the composition of the novel is, as I have already said, that it be sincere. This freedom is a splendid privilege, and the first lesson of the young novelist is to learn to be worthy of it.    "Enjoy it as it deserves," I should say to him; "take possession of it, explore it to its utmost extent, publish it, rejoice in it.    All life belongs to you, and do not listen either to those who would shut you up into corners of it and tell you that it is only here and there that art inhabits, or to those who would persuade you that this heavenly messenger wings her way outside of life altogether, breathing a superfine air, and turning away her head from the truth of things.   There is no impression of life, no manner of seeing it and feeling it, to which the plan of the novelist may not offer a place; you have only to remember that talents so dissimilar as those of Alexandre Dumas and Jane Austen, Charles Dickens and Gustave Flaubert have worked in this field with equal glory.   Do not think too much about optimism and pessimism; try and catch the colour of life itself.   In France to-day we see a prodigious effort (that of Emile Zola, to whose solid and serious work no explorer of the capacity of the novel can allude without respect), we see an extraordinary effort vitiated by a spirit of pessimism on a narrow basis.   M. Zola is magnificent, but he strikes an English reader as ignorant; he has an air of working in the dark; if he had as much light as energy, his results would be of the highest value.   As for the aberrations of a shallow optimism, the ground (of English fiction especially) is strewn with their brittle particles as with broken glass.   If you must indulge in conclusions, let them have the taste of a wide knowledge.   Remember that your first duty is to be as complete as possible—to make as perfect a work.   Be generous and delicate and pursue the prize."

# What Is Art?

## 1898

*Of the various critics encountered thus far, clearly none places a greater emphasis on the instrumental nature of art than Count Leo Tolstoy. The words "purpose" and "function" seem to echo throughout, and concerning that purpose Tolstoy is redundantly emphatic: The purpose of art is to promote the universal brotherhood of man. "Good" art promotes that unity; "bad" art serves to divide men from one another. Insisting that art is and always must be an instrument for reform and progress, Tolstoy stands at a 180° remove from James, as may be seen, for example, by contrasting their views on the issues of the morality of art and the importance of artistic technique. But even when compared with a critic like Shelley, with whom Tolstoy has many striking points of similarity, Tolstoy's views seem extreme. In Chapter 20, sounding very Arnoldian, Tolstoy declares, "The task of art is enormous." But would Arnold agree with Tolstoy's definition of the means by which this task is to be accomplished? We have to go all the way back to Plato, with his directive that the imagination be employed in the interests of shaping human values and directing human conduct, in order to find Tolstoy's parallel. It is instructive to discover the many ways in which their positions are alike, particularly their awareness of the powerful emotional responses that art can evoke, the importance each attaches to subject matter, and the value they place on artistic technique as such. It is also useful to compare Plato and Tolstoy on what the latter calls the "infectiousness" of art (are they talking about the same kinds of feelings to be transmitted?); and to set them*

From *What Is Art? and Other Essays*. Translated by Aylmer Maude, and originally published by Thomas Y. Crowell Co., 1899.

*both against the Aristotelian theory of the catharsis evoked by tragedy.*

*Although the basic frame of reference is moralistic, Tolstoy also specifies an aesthetic theory. His categorizing of works of art as either "universal" or "exclusive" distinguishes between art that has the greatest popular appeal and art that appeals to a limited or restricted audience. The consequence of this theory is illustrated in Tolstoy's references to particular works. What makes for the widest appeal is familiar subject matter and easy comprehensibility; thus bad art is marked by complexity, allusiveness, indirection, formalism, "artificiality": any quality that interferes with the immediate apprehension of the message. Two passages in particular should be noted: his discussions of the drawing by Kramskoy and of Beethoven's Ninth Symphony. Also, do not overlook the footnote in which Tolstoy ruthlessly examines his own works.*

*The democratic argument that what everybody understands and enjoys is therefore the best art has the paradoxical result of wiping out much of the world's great art; behind the spokesman for the universal brotherhood of man stands the hard-nosed censor. Seen in this context, what degree of acceptance do you think Tolstoy is accorded in the Soviet Union?*

## XVI

How IN the subject-matter of art are we to decide what is good and what is bad?

Art like speech is a means of communication and therefore of progress, that is, of the movement of humanity forward towards perfection. Speech renders accessible to men of the latest generations all the knowledge discovered by the experience and reflection both of preceding generations and of the best and foremost men of their own times; art renders accessible to men of the latest generations all the feelings experienced by their predecessors and also those felt by their best and foremost contemporaries. And as the evolution of knowledge proceeds by truer and more necessary knowledge dislodging and replacing what was mistaken and unnecessary, so the evolution of feeling proceeds by means of art—feelings less kind and less necessary for the well-being of mankind being replaced by others kinder and more needful for that end. That is the purpose of art. And speaking now of the feelings which are its subject-matter, the more art fulfils that purpose the better the art, and the less it fulfils it the worse the art.

The appraisement of feelings (that is, the recognition of one or other set of feelings as more or less good, more or less necessary for the well-being of mankind) is effected by the religious perception of the age.

In every period of history and in every human society there exists an understanding of the meaning of life, which represents the highest level to which men of that society have attained—an understanding indicating the highest good at which that society aims. This understanding is the religious perception of the given time and society. And this religious perception is always clearly expressed by a few advanced men and more or less vividly perceived by members of the society generally. Such a religious perception and its corresponding expression always exists in every society. If it appears to us that there is no religious perception in our society, this is not because there really is none, but only because we do not wish to see it. And we often wish not to see it because it exposes the fact that our life is inconsistent with that religious perception.

Religious perception in a society is like the direction of a flowing river. If the river flows at all it must have a direction. If a society lives, there must be a religious perception indicating the direction in which, more or less consciously, all its members tend.

And so there always has been, and is, a religious perception in every society. And it is by the standard of this religious perception that the feelings transmitted by art have always been appraised. It has always been only on the basis of this religious perception of their age, that men have chosen from amid the endlessly varied spheres of art that art which transmitted feelings making religious perception operative in actual life. And such art has always been highly valued and encouraged, while art transmitting feelings already outlived, flowing from the antiquated religious perceptions of a former age, has always been condemned and despised. All the rest of art transmitting those most diverse feelings by means of which people commune with one another was not condemned and was tolerated if only it did not transmit feelings contrary to religious perception. Thus for instance among the Greeks, art transmitting feelings of beauty, strength, and courage (Hesiod, Homer, Phidias) was chosen, approved, and encouraged, while art transmitting feelings of rude sensuality, despondency, and effeminacy, was condemned and despised. Among the Jews, art transmitting feelings of devotion and submission to the God of the Hebrews and to His will (the epic of Genesis, the prophets, the Psalms) was chosen and encouraged, while art transmitting feelings of idolatry (the Golden Calf) was condemned and despised. All the rest of art—stories, songs, dances, ornamentation of houses, of utensils, and of clothes—which was not contrary to religious perception, was neither distinguished nor discussed. Thus as regards its subject-matter has art always and everywhere been appraised and thus it should be appraised, for this attitude towards art proceeds from the fundamental characteristics of human nature, and those characteristics do not change.

I know that according to an opinion current in our times religion is a superstition humanity has outgrown, and it is therefore assumed that no such thing exists as a religious perception common to us all by which art in our time can be appraised. I know that this is the opinion current in the pseudo-cultured circles of today. People who do not acknowledge Christianity in its true meaning because it undermines their social privileges, and who therefore invent all kinds of philosophic and aesthetic theories to hide from themselves the meaninglessness and wrongfulness of their lives, cannot think otherwise. These people intentionally, or sometimes unintentionally, confuse the notion of a religious cult with the notion of religious perception, and think that by denying the cult they get rid of the perception. But even the very attacks on religion and the attempts to establish an idea of life contrary to the religious perception of our times, most clearly demonstrate the existence of a religious perception condemning the lives that are not in harmony with it.

If humanity progresses, that is, moves forward, there must inevitably be a guide to the direction of that movement. And religions have always furnished that guide. All history shows that the progress of humanity is accomplished no otherwise than under the guidance of religion. But if the race cannot progress without the guidance of religion,—and progress is always going on, and consequently goes on also in our own times,— then there must be a religion of our times. So that whether it pleases or displeases the so-called cultured people of to-day, they must admit the existence of religion—not of a religious cult, Catholic, Protestant, or another, but of religious perception—which even in our times is the guide always present where there is any progress. And if a religious perception exists amongst us, then the feelings dealt with by our art should be appraised on the basis of that religious perception; and as has been the case always and everywhere, art transmitting feelings flowing from the religious perception of our time should be chosen from amid all the indifferent art, should be acknowledged, highly valued, and encouraged, while art running counter to that perception should be condemned and despised, and all the remaining, indifferent, art should neither be distinguished nor encouraged.

The religious perception of our time in its widest and most practical application is the consciousness that our well-being, both material and spiritual, individual and collective, temporal and eternal, lies in the growth of brotherhood among men—in their loving harmony with one another. This perception is not only expressed by Christ and all the best men of past ages, it is not only repeated in most varied forms and from

most diverse sides by the best men of our times, but it already serves
as a clue to all the complex labour of humanity, consisting as this labour
does on the one hand in the destruction of physical and moral obstacles
to the union of men, and on the other hand in establishing the principles
common to all men which can and should unite them in one universal
brotherhood. And it is on the basis of this perception that we should
appraise all the phenomena of our life and among the rest our art also:
choosing from all its realms and highly prizing and encouraging whatever
transmits feelings flowing from this relegous perception, rejecting whatever is contrary to it, and not attributing to the rest of art an importance
that does not properly belong to it.

The chief mistake made by people of the upper classes at the time of
the so-called Renaissance,—a mistake we still perpetuate,—was not
that they ceased to value and attach importance to religious art (people
of that period could not attach importance to it because, like our own
upper classes, they could not believe in what the majority considered
to be religion), but their mistake was that they set up in place of the
religious art that was lacking, an insignificant art which aimed merely
at giving pleasure, that is, they began to choose, to value, and to encourage, in place of religious art, something which in any case did not
deserve such esteem and encouragement.

One of the Fathers of the Church said that the great evil is not that men
do not know God, but that they have set up instead of God, that which
is not God. So also with art. The great misfortune of the people of
the upper classes of our time is not so much that they are without a religious art as that, instead of a supreme religious art chosen from all the rest
as being specially important and valuable, they have chosen a most
insignificant and, usually, harmful art, which aims at pleasing certain
people and which therefore, if only by its exclusive nature, stands in
contradiction to that Christian principle of universal union which
forms the religious perception of our time. Instead of religious art, an
empty and often vicious art is set up, and this hides from men's notice
the need of that true religious art which should be present in life to improve it.

It is true that art which satisfies the demands of the religious perception
of our time is quite unlike former art, but notwithstanding this dissimilarity, to a man who does not intentionally hide the truth from himself,
what forms the religious art of our age is very clear and definite. In
former times when the highest religious perception united only some
people (who even if they formed a large society were yet but one society
among others—Jews, or Athenian or Roman citizens), the feelings
transmitted by the art of that time flowed from a desire for the might,
greatness, glory, and prosperity, of that society, and the heroes of art

might be people who contributed to that prosperity by strength, by craft, by fraud, or by cruelty (Ulysses, Jacob, David, Samson, Hercules, and all the heroes). But the religious perception of our times does not select any one society of men; on the contrary it demands the union of all—absolutely of all people without exception—and above every other virtue it sets brotherly love of all men. And therefore the feelings transmitted by the art of our time not only cannot coincide with the feelings transmitted by former art, but must run counter to them.

Christian, truly Christian, art has been so long in establishing itself, and has not yet established itself, just because the Christian religious perception was not one of those small steps by which humanity advances regularly, but was an enormous revolution which, if it has not already altered, must inevitably alter the entire conception of life of mankind, and consequently the whole internal organization of that life. It is true that the life of humanity, like that of an individual, moves regularly; but in that regular movement come, as it were, turning-points which sharply divide the preceding from the subsequent life. Christianity was such a turning-point; such at least it must appear to us who live by the Christian perception of life. Christian perception gave another, a new, direction to all human feelings, and therefore completely altered both the content and the significance of art. The Greeks could make use of Persian art and the Romans could use Greek art, or, similarly, the Jews could use Egyptian art—the fundamental ideals were one and the same. Now the ideal was the greatness and prosperity of the Greeks, now that of the Romans. The same art was transferred to other conditions and served new nations. But the Christian ideal changed and reversed everything, so that, as the Gospel puts it, 'That which was exalted among men has become an abomination in the sight of God.' The ideal is no longer the greatness of Pharaoh or of a Roman emperor, not the beauty of a Greek nor the wealth of Phœnicia, but humility, purity, compassion, love. The hero is no longer Dives, but Lazarus the beggar; not Mary Magdalene in the day of her beauty but in the day of her repentance; not those who acquire wealth but those who have abandoned it; not those who dwell in palaces but those who dwell in catacombs and huts; not those who rule over others, but those who acknowledge no authority but God's. And the greatest work of art is no longer a cathedral of victory with statues of conquerors, but the representation of a human soul so transformed by love that a man who is tormented and murdered, yet pities and loves his persecutors.

And the change is so great that men of the Christian world find it difficult to resist the inertia of the heathen art to which they have been accustomed all their lives. The subject-matter of Christian religious art is so new to them, so unlike the subject-matter of former art, that it seems to them as though Christian art were a denial of art, and they cling desperately to the old art. But this old art, having no longer in our day any source in religious perception, has lost its meaning, and we shall have to abandon it whether we wish to or not.

The essence of the Christian perception consists in the recognition by every man of his sonship to God and of the consequent union of men with God and with one another, as is said in the Gospel (John xvii. 21[1]). Therefore the subject-matter of Christian art is of a kind that feeling can unite men with God and with one another.

The expression *unite men with God and with one another* may seem obscure to people accustomed to the misuse of these words that is so customary, but the words have a perfectly clear meaning nevertheless. They indicate that the Christian union of man (in contradiction to the partial, exclusive, union of only certain men) is that which unites all without exception.

Art, all art, has this characteristic, that it unites people. Every art causes those to whom the artist's feeling is transmitted to unite in soul with the artist and also with all who receive the same impression. But non-Christian art while uniting some people, makes that very union a cause of separation between these united people and others; so that union of this kind is often a source not merely of division but even of enmity towards others. Such is all patriotic art, with its anthems, poems, and monuments; such is all Church art, that is, the art of certain cults, with their images, statues, processions, and other local ceremonies. Such art is belated and non-Christian, uniting the people of one cult only to separate them yet more sharply from the members of other cults, and even to place them in relations of hostility to one another. Christian art is such only as tends to unite all without exception, either by evoking in them the perception that each man and all men stand in a like relation towards God and towards their neighbour, or by evoking in them identical feelings, which may even be the very simplest, provided that they are not repugnant to Christianity and are natural to every one without exception.

Good Christian art of our time may be unintelligible to people because of imperfections in its form or because men are inattentive to it, but it must be such that all men can experience the feelings it transmits. It must be the art not of some one group of people, or of one class, or of one nationality, or of one religious cult; that is, it must not transmit feelings accessible only to a man educated in a certain way, or only to an aristocrat, or a merchant, or only to a Russian, or a native of Japan, or a Roman Catholic, or a Buddhist, and so on, but it must transmit feelings accessible

---

[1] 'That they may all be one; even as thou, Father, art in me, and I in Thee, that they also may be in us.'

to every one. Only art of this kind can in our time be acknowledged to be good art, worthy of being chosen out from all the rest of art and encouraged.

Christian art, that is, the art of our time, should be catholic in the original meaning of the word, that is, universal, and therefore it should unite all men. And only two kinds of feeling unite all men: first, feelings flowing from a perception of our sonship to God and of the brotherhood of man; and next, the simple feelings of common life accessible to every one without exception—such as feelings of merriment, of pity, of cheerfulness, of tranquillity, and so forth. Only these two kinds of feelings can now supply material for art good in its subject-matter.

And the action of these two kinds of art apparently so dissimilar, is one and the same. The feelings flowing from the perception of our sonship to God and the brotherhood of man—such as a feeling of sureness in truth, devotion to the will of God, self-sacrifice, respect for and love of man—evoked by Christian religious perception; and the simplest feelings, such as a softened or a merry mood caused by a song or an amusing jest intelligible to every one, or by a touching story, or a drawing, or a little doll: both alike produce one and the same effect—the loving union of man with man. Sometimes people who are together, if not hostile to one another, are at least estranged in mood and feeling, till perhaps a story, a performance, a picture, or even a building, but oftenest of all music, unites them all as by an electric flash, and in place of their former isolation or even enmity they are conscious of union and mutual love. Each is glad that another feels what he feels; glad of the communion established not only between him and all present, but also with all now living who will yet share the same impression; and more than that, he feels the mysterious gladness of a communion which, reaching beyond the grave, unites us with all men of the past who have been moved by the same feelings and with all men of the future who will yet be touched by them. And this effect is produced both by religious art which transmits feelings of love of God and one's neighbour, and by universal art transmitting the very simplest feelings common to all men.

The art of our time should be appraised differently from former art chiefly in this, that the art of our time, that is, Christian art (basing itself on a religious perception which demands the union of man), excludes from the domain of art good in its subject-matter, everything transmitting exclusive feelings which do not unite men but divide them. It relegates such work to the category of art that is bad in its subject-matter; while on the other hand it includes in the category of art that is good in subject-matter a section not formerly admitted as deserving of selection and respect, namely, universal art transmitting even the most trifling and simple feelings if only they are accessible to all men without exception, and therefore unite them.   Such art cannot but be esteemed good in our time, for it attains the end which Christianity the religious perception of our time, sets before humanity.

Christian art either evokes in men feelings which through love of God and of one's neighbour draw them to closer and ever closer union and make them ready for, and capable of, such union; or evokes in them feelings which show them that they are already united in the joys and sorrows of life.   And therefore the Christian art of our time can be and is of two kinds: first, art transmitting feelings flowing from a religious perception of man's position in the world in relation to God and to his neighbour—religious art in the limited meaning of the term; and secondly, art transmitting the simplest feelings of common life, but such always as are accessible to all men in the whole world—the art of common life—the art of the people—universal art.   Only these two kinds of art can be considered good art in our time.

The first, religious art—transmitting both positive feelings of love of God and one's neighbour, and negative feelings of indignation and horror at the violation of love—manifests itself chiefly in the form of words, and to some extent also in painting and sculpture: the second kind, universal art, transmitting feelings accessible to all, manifests itself in words, in painting, in sculpture, in dances, in architecture, and most of all in music.

If I were asked to give modern examples of each of these kinds of art, then as examples of the highest art flowing from love of God and man (both of the higher, positive, and of the lower, negative kind), in literature I should name *The Robbers* by Schiller; Victor Hugo's *Les Pauvres Gens* and *Les Misérables*; the novels and stories of Dickens—*The Tale of Two Cities*, *The Christmas Carol*, *The Chimes*, and others—*Uncle Tom's Cabin*; Dostoévski's works—especially his *Memoirs from the House of Death*—and *Adam Bede* by George Eliot.

In modern painting, strange to say, works of this kind, directly transmitting the Christian feeling of love of God and of one's neighbour, are hardly to be found, especially among the works of the celebrated painters.   There are plenty of pictures treating of the Gospel stories; these however, while depicting historical events with great wealth of detail, do not and cannot transmit religious feelings not possessed by their painters.   There are many pictures treating of the personal feelings of various people, but of pictures representing great deeds of self-sacrifice and Christian love there are very few, and what there are are principally by artists who are not celebrated, and they are for the most part not pictures but merely sketches.   Such for instance is the drawing by Kramskóy (worth many of his finished pictures), showing a drawing-room with a balcony past which troops are marching in triumph on their return from the war. On the balcony stands a wet-nurse holding a baby, and a boy. They are admiring the procession of the troops, but the mother, covering her face with a handkerchief, has fallen back on the sofa sobbing. Such also is the picture by Walter Langley to which I have already referred, and such again is a picture by the French artist Morlon, depicting a lifeboat hastening in a heavy storm to the relief of a steamer that is being wrecked. Approaching these in kind are pictures which represent the hard-working peasant with respect and love. Such are the pictures by Millet and particularly his drawing, 'The Man with the Hoe,' also pictures in this style by Jules Breton, Lhermitte, Defregger, and others. As examples of pictures evoking indignation and horor at the violation of love of God and man, Gay's picture 'Judgment' may serve, and also Leizen-Mayer's 'Signing the Death Warrant.' But there are very few of this kind also. Anxiety about the technique and the beauty of the picture for the most part obscures the feeling. For instance, Gérôme's 'Pollice Verso' expresses, not so much horror at what is being perpetrated as attraction by the beauty of the spectacle.[2]

To give examples from the modern art of our upper classes, of art of the second kind: good universal art, or even of the art of a whole people, is yet more difficult, especially in literature and music. If there are some works which by their inner contents might be assigned to this class (such as *Don Quixote*, Molière's comedies, *David Copperfield* and *The Pickwick Papers* by Dickens, Gógol's and Púshkin's tales, and some things of Maupassant's), these works for the most part—owing to the exceptional nature of the feelings they transmit, and the superfluity of special details of time and locality, and above all on account of the poverty of their subject-matter in comparison with examples of universal ancient art (such, for instance, as the story of Joseph)—are comprehensible only to people of their own circle. That Joseph's brethren, being jealous of his father's affection, sell him to the merchants; that Potiphar's wife wishes to tempt the youth; that having attained to highest station he takes pity on his brothers, including Benjamin the favourite—these and all the rest are feelings accessible alike to a Russian peasant, a Chinese, an African, a child, or an old man, educated or uneducated; and it is all written with such restraint, is so free from any superfluous detail, that the story may be told to any circle and will be equally comprehensible and touching to everyone. But not such are the feelings of Don Quixote or of Molière's heroes (though Molière is perhaps the most universal, and therefore the most excellent, artist of modern times), nor of Pickwick

[2] In this picture the spectators in the Roman Amphitheatre are turning down their thumbs to show that they wish the vanquished gladiator to be killed. (Translator's note).

and his friends. These feelings are not common to all men but very exceptional, and therefore to make them contagious the authors have surrounded them with abundant details of time and place. And this abundance of detail makes the stories difficult of comprehension to all who do not live within reach of the conditions described by the author.

The author of the novel of Joseph did not need to describe in detail, as would be done nowadays, the blood-stained coat of Joseph, the dwelling and dress of Jacob, the pose and attire of Potiphar's wife, and how adjusting the bracelet on her left arm she said, 'Come to me,' and so on, because the content of feeling in this novel is so strong that all details except the most essential—such as that Joseph went out into another room to weep—are superfluous and would only hinder the transmission of emotion. And therefore this novel is accessible to all men, touches people of all nations and classes young and old, and has lasted to our times and will yet last for thousands of years to come. But strip the best novels of our time of their details and what will remain?

It is therefore impossible in modern literature to indicate works fully satisfying the demands of universality. Such works as exist are to a great extent spoilt by what is usually called 'realism', but would be better termed 'provincialism', in art.

In music the same occurs as in verbal art, and for similar reasons. In consequence of the poorness of the feeling they contain, the melodies of the modern composers are amazingly empty and insignificant. And to strengthen the impression produced by these empty melodies the new musicians pile complex modulations on each trivial melody, not only in their own national manner, but also in the way characteristic of their own exclusive circle and particular musical school. Melody—every melody—is free and may be understood of all men; but as soon as it is bound up with a particular harmony, it ceases to be accessible except to people trained to such harmony, and it becomes strange, not only to common men of another nationality, but to all who do not belong to the circle whose members have accustomed themselves to certain forms of harmonization. So that music, like poetry, travels in a vicious circle. Trivial and exclusive melodies, in order to make them attractive, are laden with harmonic, rhythmic, and orchestral complications and thus become yet more exclusive, and far from being universal are not even national, that is, they are not comprehensible to the whole people, but only to some people.

In music, besides marches and dances by various composers which satisfy the demands of universal art, one can indicate very few works of this class: Bach's famous violin *aria*, Chopin's nocturne in E flat major, and perhaps a dozen bits (not whole pieces, but parts) selected from the works of Haydn, Mozart, Schubert, Beethoven, and Chopin.[3]

Although in painting the same thing is repeated as in poetry and in music—namely, that in order to make them more interesting, works weak in conception are surrounded by minutely studied accessories of time and place which give them a temporary and local interest but make them less universal—still in painting more than in other spheres of art may be found works satisfying the demands of universal Christian art; that is to say, there are more works expressing feelings in which all men may participate.

In the arts of painting and sculpture, all pictures and statues in so-called genre style, representations of animals, landscapes, and caricatures with subjects comprehensible to every one, and also all kinds of ornaments, are universal in subject-matter. Such productions in painting and sculpture are very numerous (for instance, china dolls), but for the most part such objects (for instance, ornaments of all kinds) are either not considered to be art or are considered to be art of low quality. In reality all such objects if only they transmit a true feeling experienced by the artist and comprehensible to every one (however insignificant it may seem to us to be), are works of real, good, Christian, art.

I fear it will here be urged against me that having denied that the conception of beauty can supply a standard for works of art, I contradict myself by acknowledging ornaments to be works of good art. The reproach is unjust, for the subject-matter of all kinds of ornamentation consists not in the beauty but in the feeling (of admiration at, and delight in, the combination of lines and colours) which the artist has experienced and with which he infects the spectator. Art remains what it was and what it must be: nothing but the infection by one man of another or of others with the feelings experienced by the artist. Among these feelings is the feeling of delight at what pleases the sight. Objects pleasing the sight may be such as please a small or a large number of people, or such as please all men—and ornaments for the most part are of the latter kind. A landscape representing a very unusual view, or a genre picture of a special subject, may not please every one, but ornaments, from Yakútsk

---

[3] While offering as examples of art those that seem to me best, I attach no special importance to my selection; for, besides being insufficiently informed in all branches of art, I belong to the class of people whose taste has been perverted by false training. And therefore my old, inured habits may cause me to err, and I may mistake for absolute merit the impression a work produced on me in my youth. My only purpose in mentioning examples of works of this or that class is to make my meaning clearer and to show how, with my present views, I understand excellence in art in relation to its subject-matter. I must moreover mention that I consign my own artistic productions to the category of bad art, excepting the story *God sees the Truth but Waits*, which seeks a place in the first class, and *A Prisoner of the Caucasus*, which belongs to the second.

ornaments to Greek ones, are intelligible to every one and evoke a similar feeling of admiration in all, and therefore this despised kind of art should in Christian society be esteemed far above exceptional, pretentious, pictures and sculptures.

So that in relation to feelings conveyed, there are only two kinds of good Christian art, all the rest of art not comprised in these two divisions should be acknowledged to be bad art, deserving not to be encouraged but to be driven out, denied, and despised, as being art not uniting but dividing people. Such in literary art are all novels and poems which transmit ecclesiastical or patriotic feelings, and also exclusive feelings pertaining only to the class of the idle rich: such as aristocratic honour, satiety, spleen, pessimism, and refined and vicious feelings flowing from sex-love—quite incomprehensible to the great majority of mankind.

In painting we must similarly place in the class of bad art all ecclesiastical, patriotic, and exclusive pictures; all pictures representing the amusements and allurements of a rich and idle life; all so-called symbolic pictures in which the very meaning of the symbol is comprehensible only to those of a certain circle; and above all pictures with voluptuous subjects—all that odious female nudity which fills all the exhibitions and galleries. And to this class belongs almost all the chamber and opera music of our times,—beginning especially with Beethoven (Schumann, Berlioz, Liszt, Wagner),—by its subject-matter devoted to the expression of feelings accessible only to people who have developed in themselves an unhealthy nervous irritation evoked by this exclusive, artificial, and complex music.

'What! the *Ninth Symphony* not a good work of art!' I hear exclaimed by indignant voices.

And I reply: Most certainly it is not. All that I have written I have written with the sole purpose of finding a clear and reasonable criterion by which to judge the merits of works of art. And this criterion, coinciding with the indications of plain and sane sense, indubitably shows me that that symphony of Beethoven's is not a good work of art. Of course to people educated in the worship of certain productions and of their authors, to people whose taste has been perverted just by being educated in such a worship, the acknowledgment that such a celebrated work is bad, is amazing and strange. But how are we to escape the indications of reason and common sense?

Beethoven's *Ninth Symphony* is considered a great work of art. To verify its claim to be such I must first ask myself whether this work transmits the highest religious feeling? I reply in the negative, since music in itself cannot transmit those feelings; and therefore I ask myself next: Since this work does not belong to the highest kind of religious art, has it the other characteristic of the good art of our time—the quality of uniting all men in one common feeling—does it rank as Christian universal art? And again I have no option but to reply in the negative; for not only do I not see how the feelings transmitted by this work could unite people not specially trained to submit themselves to its complex hypnotism, but I am unable to imagine to myself a crowd of normal people who could understand anything of this long, confused, and artificial production, except short snatches which are lost in a sea of what is incomprehensible. And therefore, whether I like it or not, I am compelled to conclude that this work belongs to the rank of bad art. It is curious to note in this connexion, that attached to the end of this very symphony is a poem of Schiller's which (though somewhat obscurely) expresses this very thought, namely that feeling (Schiller speaks only of the feeling of gladness) unites people and evokes love in them. But though this poem is sung at the end of the symphony, the music does not accord with the thought expressed in the verses; for the music is exclusive and does not unite all men, but unites only a few, dividing them off from the rest of mankind.

And just in this same way, in all branches of art, many and many works considered great by the upper classes of our society will have to be judged. By this one sure criterion we shall have to judge the celebrated *Divine Comedy* and *Jerusalem Delivered*; and a great part of Shakespeare's and Goethe's work, and in painting every representation of miracles, including Raphael's Transfiguration, etc.

Whatever the work may be and however it may have been extolled, we have first to ask whether this work is one of real art, or a counterfeit. Having acknowledged, on the basis of the indication of its infectiousness even to a small class of people, that a certain production belongs to the realm of art, it is necessary on this basis to decide the next question. Does this work belong to the category of bad exclusive art opposed to religious perception, or of Christian art uniting people? And having acknowledged a work to belong to real Christian art, we must then, according to whether it transmits feelings flowing from love of God and man, or merely the simple feelings uniting all men, assign it a place in the ranks of religious art, or in those of universal art.

Only on the basis of such verification shall we find it possible to select from the whole mass of what in our society claims to be art, those works which form real, important, necessary, spiritual food, and to separate them from all the harmful and useless art and from the counterfeits of art which surround us. Only on the basis of such verification shall we be able to rid ourselves of the pernicious results of harmful art and avail ourselves of that beneficent action which is the purpose of true and good art, and which is indispensable for the spiritual life of man and of humanity.

# Creative Writers
# and Day-Dreaming

## 1908

*Although the perennially fascinating question of how a work of art comes into being is less a purely literary topic than a psychological one, we have already seen attempts by various poets and philosophers —Plato (in* The Ion*), Young, Coleridge, Keats, Shelley, and Poe, among others—to define the literary imagination. It remained for Sigmund Freud, the father of psychoanalysis, to attempt an explanation of the mysterious process of artistic creation on scientific grounds. It is not necessary to study either Freudian theory in its entirety or Freud's terminology in order to understand this theoretical account of the origin and nature of literary works and the reasons why they affect us so strongly.*

*From childhood play to fantasies to dreams to works of art, Freud establishes a common element: the human desire to alter the existing and often unsatisfactory or unpleasant world of reality. Mental activity is directed toward inventing a situation in which unsatisfied wishes will be fulfilled. When this activity becomes too powerful (when the person, as we say, "loses touch with reality"), the individual is close to mental illness. Plato identifies the poet as a madman, but Freud*

Chapter IX, from *Collected Papers of Sigmund Freud*, Volume 4; edited by Ernest Jones, M.D.: translation under the supervision of Joan Riviere. Published by Basic Books, Inc., by arrangement with The Hogarth Press Ltd. and The Institute of Psycho-Analysis, London. This paper also appears in Volume 9 of *The Standard Edition of the Complete Psychological Works of Sigmund Freud*, revised and edited by James Strachey. Reprinted by permission of Sigmund Freud Copyrights Ltd., The Institute of Psycho-Analysis, The Hogarth Press Ltd., and Basic Books, Inc.

*significantly stops short of the boundary line of pathology. Artists are not mad, but they are unsatisfied. However, if the impulse to create fantasies is universally present, as Freud indicates, what distinguishes the creative writer from the rest of us? Is Freud's position, as has been charged, that the artist is merely a successful neurotic?*

*The writer's choice of subject matter then seems to be dictated by unfulfilled childhood wishes as well as by a "recent provoking occasion"; past and present are projected toward the future through the medium of art. The artist dreams aloud and in public. But what is it that makes for the special pleasure we derive from the artist's depiction of painful or unpleasant events? Despite Freud's emphasis on the content or inner meaning of a work of art, he does deal with what he calls "poetical effects": the source of our pleasure is the formal control that the writer exercises over his day-deams. Freud calls this aesthetic response a "bribe" which enables us to overcome our repulsion and which frees us from our own anxieties. Sidney likewise uses a metaphor (the cherry-flavored medicine) to describe the relationship between form and content. But compare this theory with other statements about the relationship between pleasure and pain as put forth by Aristotle, Dr. Johnson, and Keats (see Letter 45).*

*In constructing his theory, Freud chooses to discuss not the "most highly esteemed writers" but those with the greatest mass appeal. The basis for this choice should be studied in the light of what Freud says about the effect of literature upon the audience. What effect, if any, would the contrary choice have on his theory?*


WE LAYMEN have always been intensely curious to know—like the Cardinal who put a similar question to Ariosto [1]—from what sources that strange being, the creative writer, draws his material, and how he manages to make such an impression on us with it and to arouse in us emotions of which, perhaps, we had not even thought ourselves capable. Our interest is only heightened the more by the fact that, if we ask him, the writer himself gives us no explanation, or none that is satisfactory; and it is not at all weakened by our knowledge that not even the clearest insight into the determinants of his choice of material and into the nature of the art of creating imaginative form will ever help to make creative writers of *us*.

---

[1] Cardinal Ippolito d'Este was Ariosto's first patron, to whom he dedicated the *Orlando Furioso*. The poet's only reward was the question: "Where did you find so many stories, Lodovico?" [The footnotes for this essay were supplied by the translator, I. F. Grant Duff.]

If we could at least discover in ourselves or in people like ourselves an activity which was in some way akin to creative writing! An examination of it would then give us a hope of obtaining the beginnings of an explanation of the creative work of writers. And, indeed, there is some prospect of this being possible. After all, creative writers themselves like to lessen the distance between their kind and the common run of humanity; they so often assure us that every man is a poet at heart and that the last poet will not perish till the last man does.

Should we not look for the first traces of imaginative activity as early as in childhood? The child's best-loved and most intense occupation is with his play or games. Might we not say that every child at play behaves like a creative writer, in that he creates a world of his own, or rather, rearranges the things of his world in a new way which pleases him? It would be wrong to think he does not take that world seriously; on the contrary, he takes his play very seriously and he expends large amounts of emotion on it. The opposite of play is not what is serious but what is real. In spite of all the emotion with which he cathects his world of play, the child distinguishes it quite well from reality; and he likes to link his imagined objects and situations to the tangible and visible things in the real world. This linking is all that differentiates the child's "play" from "phantasying."

The creative writer does the same as the child at play. He creates a world of phantasy which he takes very seriously—that is, which he invests with large amounts of emotion—while separating it sharply from reality. Language has preserved this relationship between children's play and poetic creation. It gives [in German] the name of *"Spiel"* ["play"] to those forms of imaginative writing which require to be linked to tangible objects and which are capable of representation. It speaks of a *"Lustspiel"* or *"Trauerspiel"* ["comedy" or "tragedy": literally, "pleasure play" or "mourning play"] and describes those who carry out the representation as *"Schauspieler"* ["players": literally "show-players"]. The unreality of the writer's imaginative world, however, has very important consequences for the technique of his art; for many things which, if they were real, could give no enjoyment, can do so in the play of phantasy, and many excitements which, in themselves, are actually distressing, can become a source of pleasure for the hearers and spectators at the performance of a writer's work.

There is another consideration for the sake of which we will dwell a moment longer on this contrast between reality and play. When the child has grown up and has ceased to play, and after he has been labouring for decades to envisage the realities of life with proper seriousness, he may one day find himself in a mental situation which once more undoes the contrast between play and reality. As an adult he can look back on the intense seriousness with which he once carried on his games in childhood; and, by equating his ostensibly serious occupations of to-day with his childhood games, he can throw off the too heavy burden imposed on him by life and win the high yield of pleasure afforded by *humour*.

As people grow up, then, they cease to play, and they seem to give up the yield of pleasure which they gained from playing. But whoever understands the human mind knows that hardly anything is harder for a man than to give up a pleasure which he has once experienced. Actually, we can never give anything up; we only exchange one thing for another. What appears to be a renunciation is really the formation of a substitute or surrogate. In the same way, the growing child, when he stops playing, gives up nothing but the link with real objects; instead of *playing*, he now *phantasies*. He builds castles in the air and creates what are called *day-dreams*. I believe that most people construct phantasies at times in their lives. This is a fact which has long been overlooked and whose importance has therefore not been sufficiently appreciated.

People's phantasies are less easy to observe than the play of children. The child, it is true, plays by himself or forms a closed psychical system with other children for the purposes of a game; but even though he may not play his game in front of the grown-ups, he does not, on the other hand, conceal it from them. The adult, on the contrary, is ashamed of his phantasies and hides them from other people. He cherishes his phantasies as his most intimate possessions, and as a rule he would rather confess his misdeeds than tell anyone his phantasies. It may come about that for that reason he believes he is the only person who invents such phantasies and has no idea that creations of this kind are widespread among other people. This difference in the behaviour of a person who plays and a person who phantasies is accounted for by the motives of these two activities, which are nevertheless adjuncts to each other.

A child's play is determined by wishes: in point of fact by a single wish—one that helps in his upbringing—the wish to be big and grown up. He is always playing at being "grown up," and in his games he imitates what he knows about the lives of his elders. He has no reason to conceal this wish. With the adult, the case is different. On the one hand, he knows that he is expected not to go on playing or phantasying any longer, but to act in the real world; on the other hand, some of the wishes which give rise to his phantasies are of a kind which it is essential to conceal. Thus he is ashamed of his phantasies as being childish and as being unpermissible.

But, you will ask, if people make such a mystery of their phantasying, how is it that we know such a lot about it? Well, there is a class of human beings upon whom, not a god, indeed, but a stern goddess—Necessity—has allotted the task of telling what they suffer and what things give them happiness.[2] These are the victims of nervous illness, who are obliged to tell their phantasies, among other things, to the doctor by whom they expect to be cured by mental treatment. This is our best source of knowledge, and we have since found good reason to suppose that our patients tell us nothing that we might not also hear from healthy people.

Let us now make ourselves acquainted with a few of the characteristics of phantasying. We may lay it down that a happy person never phantasies, only an unsatisfied one. The motive forces of phantasies are unsatisfied wishes, and every single phantasy is the fulfillment of a wish, a correlation of unsatisfying reality. These motivating wishes vary according to the sex, character and circumstances of the person who is having the phantasy; but they fall naturally into two main groups. They are either ambitious wishes, which serve to elevate the subject's personality; or they are erotic ones. In young women the erotic wishes predominate almost exclusively, for their ambition is as a rule absorbed by erotic trends. In young men egoistic and ambitious wishes come to the fore clearly enough alongside of erotic ones. But we will not lay stress on the opposition between the two trends; we would rather emphasize the fact that they are often united. Just as, in many altarpieces, the portrait of the donor is to be seen in a corner of the picture, so, in the majority of ambitious phantasies, we can discover in some corner or other the lady for whom the creator of the phantasy performs all his heroic deeds and at whose feet all his triumphs are laid. Here, as you see, there are strong enough motives for concealment; the well-brought-up young woman is only allowed a minimum of erotic desire, and the young man has to learn to suppress the excess of self-regard which he brings with him from the spoilt days of his childhood, so that he may find his place in a society which is full of other individuals making equally strong demands.

We must not suppose that the products of this imaginative activity —the various phantasies, castles in the air and day-dreams—are stereotyped or unalterable. On the contrary, they fit themselves in to the subject's shifting impressions of life, change with every change in his

---

2 This is an allusion to some well-known lines spoken by the poet-hero in the final scene of Goethe's *Torquato Tasso:*

    Und wenn der Mensch in seiner Qual verstummt,
    Gab mir ein Gott, zu sagen, wie ich leide.

"And when mankind is dumb in its torment, a god granted me to tell how I suffer."

situation, and receive from every fresh active impression what might be called a "date-mark." The relation of a phantasy to time is in general very important. We may say that it hovers, as it were, between three times—the three moments of time which our ideation involves. Mental work is linked to some current impression, some provoking occasion in the present which has been able to arouse one of the subject's major wishes. From there it harks back to a memory of an earlier experience (usually an infantile one) in which this wish was fulfilled; and it now creates a situation relating to the future which represents a fulfillment of the wish. What it thus creates is a day-dream or phantasy, which carries about it traces of its origin from the occasion which provoked it and from the memory. Thus past, present and future are strung together, as it were, on the thread of the wish that runs through them.

A very ordinary example may serve to make what I have said clear. Let us take the case of a poor orphan boy to whom you have given the address of some employer where he may perhaps find a job. On his way there he may indulge in a day-dream appropriate to the situation from which it arises. The content of his phantasy will perhaps be something like this. He is given a job, finds favour with his new employer, makes himself indispensable in the business, is taken into his employer's family, marries the charming young daughter of the house, and then himself becomes a director of the business, first as his employer's partner and then as his successor. In this phantasy, the dreamer has regained what he possessed in his happy childhood—the protecting house, the loving parents and the first objects of his affectionate feelings. You will see from this example the way in which the wish makes use of an occasion in the present to construct, on the pattern of the past, a picture of the future.

There is a great deal more that could be said about phantasies; but I will only allude as briefly as possible to certain points. If phantasies become over-luxuriant and over-powerful, the conditions are laid for an onset of neurosis or psychosis. Phantasies, moreover, are the immediate mental precursors of the distressing symptoms complained of by our patients. Here a broad by-path branches off into pathology.

I cannot pass over the relation of phantasies to dreams. Our dreams at night are nothing else than phantasies like these, as we can demonstrate from the interpretation of dreams. Language, in its unrivalled wisdom, long ago decided the question of the essential nature of dreams by giving the name of "day-dreams" to the airy creations of phantasy. If the meaning of our dreams usually remains obscure to us in spite of this pointer, it is because of the circumstance that at night there also arise in us wishes of which we are ashamed; these we must conceal from ourselves, and they have consequently been repressed, pushed into the unconscious. Repressed wishes of this sort and their derivatives are only allowed to come to expression in a very distorted form. When scientific work had succeeded in elucidating this factor of *dream-distortion*, it was no longer difficult to recognize that night-dreams are wish-fulfilments in just the same way as day-dreams—the phantasies which we all know so well.

So much for phantasies. And now for the creative writer. May we really attempt to compare the imaginative writer with the "dreamer in broad daylight," and his creations with day-dreams? Here we must begin by making an initial distinction. We must separate writers who, like the ancient authors of epics and tragedies, take over their material ready-made, from writers who seem to originate their own material. We will keep to the latter kind, and, for the purposes of our comparison, we will choose not the writers most highly esteemed by the critics, but the less pretentious authors of novels, romances and short stories, who nevertheless have the widest and most eager circle of readers of both sexes. One feature above all cannot fail to strike us about the creations of these story-writers: each of them has a hero who is the centre of interest, for whom the writer tries to win our sympathy by every possible means and whom he seems to place under the protection of a special Providence. If, at the end of one chapter of my story, I leave the hero unconscious and bleeding from severe wounds, I am sure to find him at the beginning of the next being carefully nursed and on the way to recovery; and if the first volume closes with the ship he is in going down in a storm at sea, I am certain, at the opening of the second volume, to read of his miraculous rescue—a rescue without which the story could not proceed. The feeling of security with which I follow the hero through his perilous adventures is the same as the feeling with which a hero in real life throws himself into the water to save a drowning man or exposes himself to the enemy's fire in order to storm a battery. It is the true heroic feeling, which one of our best writers has expressed in an inimitable phrase: "Nothing can happen to *me!*" [3] It seems to me, however, that through this revealing characteristic or invulnerability we can immediately recognize His Majesty the Ego, the hero alike of every day-dream and of every story.

Other typical features of these egocentric stories point to the same

---

[3] *"Es kann mir nix g'schehen!"* This phrase from Anzengruber, the Viennese dramatist, was a favourite one of Freud's.

kinship. The fact that all the women in the novel invariably fall in love with the hero can hardly be looked on as a portrayal of reality, but it is easily understood as a necessary constituent of a day-dream. The same is true of the fact that the other characters in the story are sharply divided into good and bad, in defiance of the variety of human characters that are to be observed in real life. The "good" ones are the helpers, while the "bad" ones are the enemies and rivals, of the ego which has become the hero of the story.

We are perfectly aware that very many imaginative writings are far removed from the model of the naïve day-dream; and yet I cannot suppress the suspicion that even the most extreme deviations from that model could be linked with it through an uninterrupted series of transitional cases. It has struck me that in many of what are known as "psychological" novels only one person—once again the hero—is described from within. The author sits inside his mind, as it were, and looks at the other characters from outside. The psychological novel in general no doubt owes its special nature to the inclination of the modern writer to split up his ego, by self-observation, into many part-egos, and, in consequence, to personify the conflicting currents of his own mental life in several heroes. Certain novels, which might be described as "eccentric," seem to stand in quite special contrast to the type of the day-dream. In these, the person who is introduced as the hero plays only a very small active part; he sees the actions and sufferings of other people pass before him like a spectator. Many of Zola's later works belong to this category. But I must point out that the psychological analysis of individuals who are not creative writers, and who diverge in some respects from the so-called norm, has shown us analogous variations of the day-dream, in which the ego contents itself with the role of spectator.

If our comparison of the imaginative writer with the day-dreamer, and of poetical creation with the day-dream, is to be of any value, it must, above all, show itself in some way or other fruitful. Let us, for instance, try to apply to these authors' works the thesis we laid down earlier concerning the relation between phantasy and the three periods of time and the wish which runs through them; and, with its help, let us try to study the connections that exist between the life of the writer and his works. No one has known, as a rule, what expectations to frame in approaching this problem; and often the connection has been thought of in much too simple terms. In the light of the insight we have gained from phantasies, we ought to expect the following state of affairs. A strong experience in the present awakens in the creative writer a memory of an earlier experience (usually belonging to his childhood) from which there now proceeds a wish which finds its fulfilment in the creative work. The work itself exhibits elements of the recent provoking occasion as well as of the old memory.

Do not be alarmed at the complexity of this formula. I suspect that in fact it will prove to be too exiguous a pattern. Nevertheless, it may contain a first approach to the true state of affairs; and, from some experiments I have made, I am inclined to think that this way of looking at creative writings may turn out not unfruitful. You will not forget that the stress it lays on childhood memories in the writer's life —a stress which may perhaps seem puzzling—is ultimately derived from the assumption that a piece of creative writing, like a day-dream, is a continuation of, and a substitute for, what was once the play of childhood.

We must not neglect, however, to go back to the kind of imaginative works which we have to recognize, not as original creations, but as the refashioning of ready-made and familiar material. Even here, the writer keeps a certain amount of independence, which can express itself in the choice of material and in changes in it which are often quite extensive. In so far as the material is already at hand, however, it is derived from the popular treasure-house of myths, legends and fairy tales. The study of constructions of folk-psychology such as these is far from being complete, but it is extremely probable that myths, for instance, are distorted vestiges of the wishful phantasies of whole nations, the *secular dreams* of youthful humanity.

You will say that, although I have put the creative writer first in the title of my paper, I have told you far less about him than about phantasies. I am aware of that, and I must try to excuse it by pointing to the present state of our knowledge. All I have been able to do is to throw out some encouragements and suggestions which, starting from a study of phantasies, lead on to the problem of the writer's choice of his literary material. As for the other problem—by what means the creative writer achieves the emotional effects in us that are aroused by his creations—we have as yet not touched on it at all. But I should like at least to point out to you the path that leads from our discussion of phantasies to the problems of poetical effects.

You will remember how I have said that the day-dreamer carefully conceals his phantasies from other people because he feels he has reasons for being ashamed of them. I should now add that even if he were to communicate them to us he could give us no pleasure by his disclosures. Such phantasies, when we learn them, repel us or at least leave us cold. But when a creative writer presents his plays to us or tells us what we are inclined to take to be his personal day-dreams, we experience a great pleasure, and one which probably arises from the confluence of many sources. How the writer accomplishes this is his innermost secret; the essential *ars poetica* lies in the technique of overcoming the feeling of repulsion in us which is undoubtedly connected with the barriers that rise between each single ego and the others. We can guess two of the methods used by this technique. The writer softens the character of his egoistic day-dreams by altering and disguising it, and he bribes us by the purely formal—that is, aesthetic —yield of pleasure which he offers us in the presentation of his phantasies. We give the name of an *incentive bonus,* or a *fore-pleasure,* to a yield of pleasure such as this, which is offered to us so as to make possible the release of still greater pleasure arising from deeper psychical sources. In my opinion, all the aesthetic pleasure which a creative writer affords us has the character of a fore-pleasure of this kind, and our actual enjoyment of an imaginative work proceeds from a liberation of tensions in our minds. It may even be that not a little of this effect is due to the writer's enabling us thenceforward to enjoy our own day-dreams without self-reproach or shame. This brings us to the threshold of new, interesting and complicated enquiries; but also, at least for the moment, to the end of our discussion.

# T. S. ELIOT

# Tradition and
# the Individual Talent

## 1920

*The two apparently opposed terms in the title of Eliot's best-known essay immediately bring to mind an issue for critical debate that we have encountered many times before. Whether the opposing terms are ancients and moderns, or art and nature, or learning and genius, or rules and originality, the question has always been (and particularly for a critic who is also a poet), "Where and how does a new poet fit into the pantheon?" Differentiating mere novelty from the truly new, Eliot asks, in effect, how original can a poet ever be? Ralph Waldo Emerson's somewhat gnomic utterance was that "every new writer is only the crater of an old volcano." But Eliot redefines "old" and "new," and his apparently paradoxical conclusion rests upon a theory of literary history that is nonchronological. Starting with the commonplace that all art continues to live in a timeless present, he proposes a "simultaneous existence" and a "simultaneous order" of all the "existing monuments." The image of monuments may be unfortunate, for what Eliot stresses is their permanent vitality, so that the works of an earlier period are always being altered by the introduction of later works. (For example, our reading of Mark Twain today has been altered by our reading of Hemingway. Think of other instances to illustrate Eliot's thesis. What exactly does it mean to say that a work of art continues to grow in time?) Eliot's comparative approach, which is aesthetic and not merely historical, should be compared and con-*

From *Selected Essays* by T. S. Eliot, copyright 1950 by Harcourt Brace Jovanovich, Inc.; renewed 1978 by Esme Valerie Eliot. Reprinted by permission of the publisher. Reprinted by permission of Faber and Faber Ltd. from *Selected Essays* by T. S. Eliot.

*trasted with Arnold's "touchstone" method: do they start with the
same assumptions?*

*Stressing the poet's inevitable and necessary consciousness of history
leads Eliot to another formulation that has profoundly influenced
twentieth-century criticism—the theory of the depersonalization of art.
When he declares that poetry "is only a medium and not a personality," and that it "is not a turning loose of emotion, but an escape
from emotion," against what theories and what critics is he arguing?
Understanding why he rejects Wordsworth's definition of poetry as
"emotion recollected in tranquillity" will also enable you to grasp why
Eliot, in other essays, expresses unqualified enthusiasm for Keats as a
critic.*

*The theory of history and the theory of impersonality combined
have far-reaching implications for the practice of criticism. In this essay
Eliot succinctly states the critic's task: "to divert interest from the poet
to the poetry." With this phrase, Eliot is identified as one of the progenitors of the twentieth century's "New Criticism," which has as its
principal tenet the close examination of the poem as poem, without
regard for biographical, social, ethical, or other frames of reference
as sources of judgment; the poem has its own terminal value. That
this is not a totally new, exclusively modern approach, however, will
become apparent if you recall one of the oldest of the existing critical
monuments—Aristotle's "Poetics."*

IN ENGLISH writing we seldom speak of tradition, though we occasionally
apply its name in deploring its absence. We cannot refer to "the
tradition" or to "a tradition"; at most, we employ the adjective in saying
that the poetry of So-and-so is "traditional" or even "too traditional."
Seldom, perhaps, does the word appear except in a phrase of censure.
If otherwise, it is vaguely approbative, with the implication, as to the
work approved, of some pleasing archaeological reconstruction. You
can hardly make the word agreeable to English ears without this comfortable reference to the reassuring science of archaeology.

Certainly the word is not likely to appear in our appreciations of living
or dead writers. Every nation, every race, has not only its own creative,
but its own critical turn of mind; and is even more oblivious of the short-
comings and limitations of its critical habits than of those of its creative
genius. We know, or think we know, from the enormous mass of critical
writing that has appeared in the French language the critical method or
habit of the French; we only conclude (we are such unconscious people)
that the French are "more critical" than we, and sometimes even plume
ourselves a little with the fact, as if the French were the less spontaneous.

Perhaps they are; but we might remind ourselves that criticism is as inevitable as breathing, and that we should be none the worse for articulating what passes in our minds when we read a book and feel an emotion about it, for criticizing our own minds in their work of criticism. One of the facts that might come to light in this process is our tendency to insist, when we praise a poet, upon those aspects of his work in which he least resembles any one else. In these aspects or parts of his work we pretend to find what is individual, what is the peculiar essence of the man. We dwell with satisfaction upon the poet's difference from his predecessors, especially his immediate predecessors; we endeavour to find something that can be isolated in order to be enjoyed. Whereas if we approach a poet without this prejudice we shall often find that not only the best, but the most individual parts of his work may be those in which the dead poets, his ancestors, assert their immortality most vigorously. And I do not mean the impressionable period of adolescence, but the period of full maturity.

Yet if the only form of tradition, of handing down, consisted in following the ways of the immediate generation before us in a blind or timid adherence to its successes, "tradition" should positively be discouraged. We have seen many such simple currents soon lost in the sand; and novelty is better than repetition. Tradition is a matter of much wider significance. It cannot be inherited, and if you want it you must obtain it by great labour. It involves, in the first place, the historical sense, which we may call nearly indispensable to any one who would continue to be a poet beyond his twenty-fifth year; and the historical sense involves a perception, not only of the pastness of the past, but of its presence; the historical sense compels a man to write not merely with his own generation in his bones, but with a feeling that the whole of the literature of Europe from Homer and within it the whole of the literature of his own country has a simultaneous existence and composes a simultaneous order. This historical sense, which is a sense of the timeless as well as of the temporal and of the timeless and of the temporal together, is what makes a writer traditional. And it is at the same time what makes a writer most acutely conscious of his place in time, of his own contemporaneity.

No poet, no artist of any art, has his complete meaning alone. His significance, his appreciation is the appreciation of his relation to the dead poets and artists. You cannot value him alone; you must set him, for contrast and comparison, among the dead. I mean this as a principle of aesthetic, not merely historical, criticism. The necessity that he shall conform, that he shall cohere, is not one-sided; what happens when a new work of art is created is something that happens simultaneously to all the works of art which preceded it.    The existing monuments form an ideal order among themselves, which is modified by the introduction of the new (the really new) work of art among them.    The existing order is complete before the new work arrives; for order to persist after the supervention of novelty, the *whole* existing order must be, if ever so slightly, altered; and so the relations, proportions, values of each work of art toward the whole are readjusted; and this is conformity between the old and the new.    Whoever has approved this idea of order, of the form of European, of English literature will not find it preposterous that the past should be altered by the present as much as the present is directed by the past.    And the poet who is aware of this will be aware of great difficulties and responsibilities.

In a peculiar sense he will be aware also that he must inevitably be judged by the standards of the past.    I say judged, not amputated, by them; not judged to be as good as, or worse or better than, the dead; and certainly not judged by the canons of dead critics.    It is a judgment, a comparison, in which two things are measured by each other.    To conform merely would be for the new work not really to conform at all; it would not be new, and would therefore not be a work of art.    And we do not quite say that the new is more valuable because it fits in; but its fitting in is a test of its value—a test, it is true, which can only be slowly and cautiously applied, for we are none of us infallible judges of conformity.    We say: it appears to conform, and is perhaps individual, or it appears individual, and may conform; but we are hardly likely to find that it is one and not the other.

To proceed to a more intelligible exposition of the relation of the poet to the past: he can neither take the past as a lump, an indiscriminate bolus, nor can he form himself wholly on one or two private admirations, nor can he form himself wholly upon one preferred period.    The first course is inadmissible, the second is an important experience of youth, and the third is a pleasant and highly desirable supplement.    The poet must be very conscious of the main current, which does not at all flow invariably through the most distinguished reputations.    He must be quite aware of the obvious fact that art never improves, but that the material of art is never quite the same.    He must be aware that the mind of Europe—the mind of his own country—a mind which he learns in time to be much more important than his own private mind—is a mind which changes, and that this change is a development which abandons nothing *en route*, which does not superannuate either Shakespeare, or Homer, or the rock drawing of the Magdalenian draughtsmen.    That this development, refinement perhaps, complication certainly, is not, from the point of view of the artist, any improvement.    Perhaps not even an improvement from the point of view of the psychologist or not to the extent which we imagine; perhaps only in the end based upon a complication in economics and machinery.   But the difference between the present and the past is that the conscious present is an awareness of the past in a way and to an extent which the past's awareness of itself cannot show.

Some one said: "The dead writers are remote from us because we *know* so much more than they did."   Precisely, and they are that which we know.

I am alive to a usual objection to what is clearly part of my programme for the *métier* of poetry.   The objection is that the doctrine requires a ridiculous amount of erudition (pedantry), a claim which can be rejected by appeal to the lives of poets in any pantheon.   It will even be affirmed that much learning deadens or perverts poetic sensibility. While, however, we persist in believing that a poet ought to know as much as will not encroach upon his necessary receptivity and necessary laziness, it is not desirable to confine knowledge to whatever can be put into a useful shape for examinations, drawing-rooms, or the still more pretentious modes of publicity.   Some can absorb knowledge, the more tardy must sweat for it.   Shakespeare acquired more essential history from Plutarch than most men could from the whole British Museum. What is to be insisted upon is that the poet must develop or procure the consciousness of the past and that he should continue to develop this consciousness throughout his career.

What happens is a continual surrender of himself as he is at the moment to something which is more valuable.   The progress of an artist is a continual self-sacrifice, a continual extinction of personality.

There remains to define this process of depersonalization and its relation to the sense of tradition.   It is in this depersonalization that art may be said to approach the condition of science.   I, therefore, invite you to consider, as a suggestive analogy, the action which takes place when a bit of finely filiated platinum is introduced into a chamber containing oxygen and sulphur dioxide.

## II

Honest criticism and sensitive appreciation are directed not upon the poet but upon the poetry.   If we attend to the confused cries of the newspaper critics and the *susurrus* of popular repetition that follows, we shall hear the names of poets in great numbers; if we seek not Blue-book knowledge but the enjoyment of poetry, and ask for a poem, we shall seldom find it.   I have tried to point out the importance of the relation of the poem to other poems by other authors, and suggested the conception of poetry as a living whole of all the poetry that has ever been written.

The other aspect of this Impersonal theory of poetry is the relation of the poem to its author. And I hinted, by an analogy, that the mind of the mature poet differs from that of the immature one not precisely in any valuation of "personality," not being necessarily more interesting, or having "more to say," but rather by being a more finely perfected medium in which special, or very varied, feelings are at liberty to enter into new combinations.

The analogy was that of the catalyst. When the two gases previously mentioned are mixed in the presence of a filament of platinum, they form sulphurous acid. This combination takes place only if the platinum is present; nevertheless the newly formed acid contains no trace of platinum, and the platinum itself is apparently unaffected; has remained inert, neutral, and unchanged. The mind of the poet is the shred of platinum. It may partly or exclusively operate upon the experience of the man himself; but, the more perfect the artist, the more completely separate in him will be the man who suffers and the mind which creates; the more perfectly will the mind digest and transmute the passions which are its material.

The experience, you will notice, the elements which enter the presence of the transforming catalyst, are of two kinds: emotions and feelings. The effect of a work of art upon the person who enjoys it is an experience different in kind from any experience not of art. It may be formed out of one emotion, or may be a combination of several; and various feelings, inhering for the writer in particular words or phrases or images, may be added to compose the final result. Or great poetry may be made without the direct use of any emotion whatever: composed out of feelings solely. Canto XV of the *Inferno* (Brunetto Latini) is a working up of the emotion evident in the situation; but the effect, though single as that of any work of art, is obtained by considerable complexity of detail. The last quatrain gives an image, a feeling attaching to an image, which "came," which did not develop simply out of what precedes, but which was probably in suspension in the poet's mind until the proper combination arrived for it to add itself to. The poet's mind is in fact a receptacle for seizing and storing up numberless feelings, phrases, images, which remain there until all the particles which can unite to form a new compound are present together.

If you compare several representative passages of the greatest poetry you see how great is the variety of types of combination, and also how completely any semi-ethical criterion of "sublimity" misses the mark. For it is not the "greatness," the intensity, of the emotions, the components, but the intensity of the artistic process, the pressure, so to speak, under which the fusion takes place, that counts. The episode of Paolo and Francesca employs a definite emotion, but the intensity of the poetry is something quite different from whatever intensity in the supposed experience it may give the impression of. It is no more intense, further-more, than Canto XXVI, the voyage of Ulysses, which has not the direct dependence upon an emotion. Great variety is possible in the process of transmutation of emotion: the murder of Agamemnon, or the agony of Othello, gives an artistic effect apparently closer to a possible original than the scenes from Dante. In the *Agamemnon*, the artistic emotion approximates to the emotion of an actual spectator; in *Othello* to the emotion of the protagonist himself. But the difference between art and the event is always absolute; the combination which is the murder of Agamemnon is probably as complex as that which is the voyage of Ulysses. In either case there has been a fusion of elements. The ode of Keats contains a number of feelings which have nothing particular to do with the nightingale, but which the nightingale, partly, perhaps, because of its attractive name, and partly because of its reputation, served to bring together.

The point of view which I am struggling to attack is perhaps related to the metaphysical theory of the substantial unity of the soul: for my meaning is, that the poet has, not a "personality" to express, but a particular medium, which is only a medium and not a personality, in which impressions and experiences combine in peculiar and unexpected ways. Impressions and experiences which are important for the man may take no place in the poetry, and those which become important in the poetry may play quite a negligible part in the man, the personality.

I will quote a passage which is unfamiliar enough to be regarded with fresh attention in the light—or darkness—of these observations:

> *And now methinks I could e'en chide myself*
> *For doating on her beauty, though her death*
> *Shall be revenged after no common action.*
> *Does the silkworm expend her yellow labours*
> *For thee? For thee does she undo herself?*
> *Are lordships sold to maintain ladyships*
> *For the poor benefit of a bewildering minute?*
> *Why does yon fellow falsify highways,*
> *And put his life between the judge's lips,*
> *To refine such a thing—keeps horse and men*
> *To beat their valours for her? . . .*

In this passage (as is evident if it is taken in its context) there is a combina-tion of positive and negative emotions: an intensely strong attraction toward beauty and an equally intense fascination by the ugliness which is contrasted with it and which destroys it. This balance of contrasted emotion is in the dramatic situation to which the speech is pertinent, but that situation alone is inadequate to it. This is, so to speak, the structural emotion, provided by the drama. But the whole effect, the dominant tone, is due to the fact that a number of floating feelings, having an affinity to this emotion by no means superficially evident, have combined with it to give us a new art emotion.

It is not in his personal emotions, the emotions provoked by particular events in his life, that the poet is in any way remarkable or interesting. His particular emotions may be simple, or crude, or flat. The emotion in his poetry will be a very complex thing, but not with the complexity of the emotions of people who have very complex or unusual emotions in life. One error, in fact, of eccentricity in poetry is to seek for new human emotions to express; and in this search for novelty in the wrong place it discovers the perverse. The business of the poet is not to find new emotions, but to use the ordinary ones and, in working them up into poetry, to express feelings which are not in actual emotions at all. And emotions which he has never experienced will serve his turn as well as those familiar to him. Consequently, we must believe that "emotion recollected in tranquillity" is an inexact formula. For it is neither emotion, nor recollection, nor, without distortion of meaning, tranquillity. It is a concentration, and a new thing resulting from the concentration, of a very great number of experiences which to the practical and active person would not seem to be experiences at all; it is a concentration which does not happen consciously or of deliberation. These experiences are not "recollected," and they finally unite in an atmosphere which is "tranquil" only in that it is a passive attending upon the event. Of course this is not quite the whole story. There is a great deal, in the writing of poetry, which must be conscious and deliberate. In fact, the bad poet is usually unconscious where he ought to be conscious, and conscious where he ought to be unconscious. Both errors tend to make him "personal." Poetry is not a turning loose of emotion, but an escape from emotion; it is not the expression of personality, but an escape from personality. But, of course, only those who have personality and emotions know what it means to want to escape from these things.

### III

*ὁ δὲ νοῦς ἴσως Θειότερόν τι χαὶ ἀπαθές ἐστιν.*[1]

This essay proposes to halt at the frontier of metaphysics or mysticism, and confine itself to such practical conclusions as can be applied by the

[1] *O de nous isos Theioteron ti chai apathes estin.* For the mind is something both divine and impassive.

responsible person interested in poetry.   To divert interest from the poet
to the poetry is a laudable aim: for it would conduce to a juster estimation
of actual poetry, good and bad.   There are many people who appreciate
the expression of sincere emotion in verse, and there is a smaller number
of people who can appreciate technical excellence.   But very few know
when there is an expression of *significant* emotion, emotion which has its
life in the poem and not in the history of the poet.   The emotion of art is
impersonal.   And the poet cannot reach this impersonality without
surrendering himself wholly to the work to be done.   And he is not likely
to know what is to be done unless he lives in what is not merely the
present, but the present moment of the past, unless he is conscious, not of
what is dead, but of what is already living.

# Psychology and Form

## 1925

*Sophocles'* Oedipus Rex, *which was to Aristotle the perfect tragedy, has also been called the world's greatest detective story. By Aristotelian standards, it represents an organically unified whole, following the rule of probability and necessity and embodying the recognition and reversal that mark the complex plot. However, a well-made mystery novel also has these same attributes. Why, then, can we read* Oedipus Rex *repeatedly, even knowing in advance its resolution, with the same or even an intensified satisfaction—and why do we rarely re-read even the best detective novel? Another question: That a work of art must have organic unity seems to be a doctrine universally assumed, but what is the basis for such an assumption? Burke's essay on the meaning of form attempts to deal with these questions.*

*Shifting the discussion of form away from the elements in the work of art to how the human mind responds to those elements, Burke redefines literary form in psychological terms: Form is that which creates an expectation in the mind of the audience and then satisfies that expectation. Between the desire and the satisfaction falls the frustration—those delays, turns, and twists that only serve to make the final resolution richer and more rewarding. Our repeated pleasure in* Oedipus Rex *is due not to the surprise or suspense arising from the particulars of the story (or what Burke calls the "information") but to the formal excellence that creates an "emotional curve." In music, an unresolved chord calls for a resolution, satisfying an apparently basic human ap-*

---

*petite for completion and unity. Hence, for Burke, form is the essence
of all art and is identical with human psychology. Or is it biology?
Does Burke imply a correlation between our response to literature and
our very metabolic processes?*

*Thus the difference between* Oedipus Rex *and the mystery novel
is not one of kind but one of degree of intensity, or what Burke calls
"eloquence." It is important to grasp his somewhat special use of the
term, usually associated with ornamental, high-flown discourse ("plaster," he calls it). Eloquence here is synonymous with formal excellence;
it is the opposite of information, which can satisfy us only once. In
what terms can a painting by Cézanne be considered as a kind of state
forestry bulletin?*

*As a literary theorist examining the relationship between art and
psychology, Burke may usefully be compared and contrasted with
Freud. Burke is not concerned with the source or the process of creation
but with the effect of art; but how much does Burke owe to Freudian
theory?*

IT IS not until the fourth scene of the first act that Hamlet confronts
the ghost of his father. As soon as the situation has been made clear,
the audience has been, consciously or unconsciously, waiting for this
ghost to appear, while in the fourth scene this moment has been definitely promised. For earlier in the play Hamlet had arranged to come
to the platform at 'night with Horatio to meet the ghost, and it is now
night, he is with Horatio and Marcellus, and they are standing on the
platform. Hamlet asks Horatio the hour.

> "HOR. I think it lacks of twelve.
> MAR. No, it is struck.
> HOR. Indeed? I heard it not: then it draws near the season
>      Wherein the spirit held his wont to walk."

Promptly hereafter there is a sound off-stage. "A flourish of trumpets,
and ordnance shot off within." Hamlet's friends have established the
hour as twelve. It is time for the ghost. Sounds off-stage, and of course
it is not the ghost. It is, rather, the sound of the king's carousal, for
the king "keeps wassail." A tricky, and useful, detail. We have been
waiting for a ghost, and get, startlingly, a blare of trumpets. And, once
the trumpets are silent, we feel how desolate are these three men
waiting for a ghost, on a bare "platform," feel it by this sudden juxta-

position of an imagined scene of lights and merriment. But the trumpets announcing a carousal have suggested a subject of conversation. In the darkness Hamlet discusses the excessive drinking of his countrymen. He points out that it tends to harm their reputation abroad, since, he argues, this one showy vice makes their virtues "in the general censure take corruption." And for this reason, although he himself is a native of this place, he does not approve of the custom. Indeed, there in the gloom he is talking very intelligently on these matters, and Horatio answers, "Look, my Lord, it comes." All this time we had been waiting for a ghost, and it comes at the one moment which was not pointing towards it. This ghost, so assiduously prepared for, is yet a surprise. And now that the ghost has come, we are waiting for something further. Program: a speech from Hamlet. Hamlet must confront the ghost. Here again Shakespeare can feed well upon the use of contrast for his effects. Hamlet has just been talking in a sober, rather argumentative manner—but now the flood-gates are unloosed:

> "Angels and ministers of grace defend us!
> Be thou a spirit of health or goblin damn'd,
> Bring with thee airs from heaven or blasts from hell . . ."

and the transition from the matter-of-fact to the grandiose, the full-throated and full-voweled, is a second burst of trumpets, perhaps even more effective than the first, since it is the rich fulfilment of a promise. Yet this satisfaction in turn becomes an allurement, an itch for further developments. At first desiring solely to see Hamlet confront the ghost, we now want Hamlet to learn from the ghost the details of the murder—which are, however, with shrewdness and husbandry, reserved for "Scene V.—Another Part of the Platform."

I have gone into this scene at some length, since it illustrates so perfectly the relationship between psychology and form, and so aptly indicates how the one is to be defined in terms of the other. That is, the psychology here is not the psychology of the *hero,* but the psychology of the *audience.* And by that distinction, form would be the psychology of the audience. Or, seen from another angle, form is the creation of an appetite in the mind of the auditor, and the adequate satisfying of that appetite. This satisfaction—so complicated is the human mechanism—at times involves a temporary set of frustrations, but in the end these frustrations prove to be simply a more involved kind of satisfaction, and furthermore serve to make the satisfaction of fulfilment more intense. If, in a work of art, the poet says something, let us say, about a meeting, writes in such a way that we desire to observe that meeting, and then, if he places that meeting before us—that is form. While obviously, that is also the psychology of the audience, since it involves desires and their appeasements.

The seeming breach between form and subject-matter, between technique and psychology, which has taken place in the last century is the result, it seems to me, of scientific criteria being unconsciously introduced into matters of purely aesthetic judgment. The flourishing of science has been so vigorous that we have not yet had time to make a spiritual readjustment adequate to the changes in our resources of material and knowledge. There are disorders of the social system which are caused solely by our undigested wealth (the basic disorder being, perhaps, the phenomenon of overproduction: to remedy this, instead of having all workers employed on half time, we have half working full time and the other half idle, so that whereas overproduction could be the greatest reward of applied science, it has been, up to now, the most menacing condition our modern civilization has had to face). It would be absurd to suppose that such social disorders would not be paralleled by disorders of culture and taste, especially since science is so pronouncedly a spiritual factor. So that we are, owing to the sudden wealth science has thrown upon us, all *nouveaux-riches* in matters of culture, and most poignantly in that field where lack of native firmness is most readily exposed, in matters of æsthetic judgment.

One of the most striking derangements of taste which science has temporarily thrown upon us involves the understanding of psychology in art. Psychology has become a body of information (which is precisely what psychology in science should be, or must be). And similarly, in art, we tend to look for psychology as the purveying of information. Thus, a contemporary writer has objected to Joyce's *Ulysses* on the ground that there are more psychoanalytic data available in Freud. (How much more drastically he might, by the same system, have destroyed Homer's *Odyssey!*) To his objection it was answered that one might, similarly, denounce Cézanne's trees in favor of state forestry bulletins. Yet are not Cézanne's landscapes themselves tainted with the psychology of information? Has he not, by perception, *pointed out* how one object lies against another, *indicated* what takes place between two colors (which is the psychology of science, and is less successful in the medium of art than in that of science, since in art such processes are at best implicit, whereas in science they are so readily made explicit)? Is Cézanne not, to that extent, a state forestry bulletin, except that he tells what goes on in the eye instead of on the tree? And do not the true values of his work lie elsewhere—and precisely in what I distinguish as the psychology of form?

Thus, the great influx of information has led the artist also to lay his emphasis on the giving of information—with the result that art tends more and more to substitute the psychology of the hero (the subject) for the psychology of the audience. Under such an attitude, when form is preserved it is preserved as an annex, a luxury, or, as some feel, a downright affectation. It remains, though sluggish, like the human appendix, for occasional demands are still made upon it; but its true vigor is gone, since it is no longer organically required. Proposition: The hypertrophy of the psychology of information is accompanied by the corresponding atrophy of the psychology of form.

In information, the matter is intrinsically interesting. And by intrinsically interesting I do not necessarily mean intrinsically valuable, as witness the intrinsic interest of backyard gossip or the most casual newspaper items. In art, at least the art of the great ages (Æschylus, Shakespeare, Racine) the matter is interesting by means of an extrinsic use, a function. Consider, for instance, the speech of Mark Antony, the "Brutus is an honourable man." Imagine in the same place a very competently developed thesis on human conduct, with statistics, intelligence tests, definitions; imagine it as the finest thing of the sort ever written, and as really being at the roots of an understanding of Brutus. Obviously, the play would simply stop until Antony had finished. For in the case of Antony's speech, the value lies in the fact that his words are shaping the future of the audience's desires, not the desires of the Roman populace, but the desires of the pit. This is the psychology of form as distinguished from the psychology of information.

The distinction is, of course, absolutely true only in its non-existent extremes. Hamlet's advice to the players, for instance, has little of the quality which distinguishes Antony's speech. It is, rather, intrinsically interesting, although one could very easily prove how the play would benefit by some such delay at this point, and that anything which made this delay possible without violating the consistency of the subject would have, in this, its formal justification. It would, furthermore, be absurd to rule intrinsic interest out of literature. I wish simply to have it restored to its properly minor position, seen as merely one out of many possible elements of style. Goethe's prose, often poorly imagined, or neutral, in its line-for-line texture, especially in the treatment of romantic episode—perhaps he felt that the romantic episode in itself was enough?—is strengthened into a style possessing affirmative virtues by his rich use of aphorism. But this is, after all, but one of many possible facets of appeal. In some places, notably in *Wilhelm Meister's Lehrjahre* when Wilhelm's friends disclose the documents they have been collecting about his life unbeknown to him, the aphorisms are almost rousing in their efficacy, since they involve the story. But as a rule the appeal of aphorism is intrinsic: that is, it satisfies without being functionally related to the context.[1] . . . Also, to return to the matter of Hamlet, it must be observed that the style in this passage is no mere "information-giving" style; in its alacrity, its development, it really makes this one fragment into a kind of miniature plot.

One reason why music can stand repetition so much more sturdily than correspondingly good prose is that music, of all the arts, is by its nature least suited to the psychology of information, and has remained closer to the psychology of form. Here form cannot atrophy. Every dissonant chord cries for its solution, and whether the musician resolves or refuses to resolve this dissonance into the chord which the body cries for, he is dealing in human appetites. Correspondingly good prose, however, more prone to the temptations of pure information, cannot so much bear repetition since the æsthetic value of information is lost once that information is imparted. If one returns to such a work again it is purely because, in the chaos of modern life, he has been able to forget it. With a desire, on the other hand, its recovery is as agreeable as its discovery. One can memorize the dialogue between Hamlet and Guildenstern, where Hamlet gives Guildenstern the pipe to play on. For, once the speech is known, its repetition adds a new element to compensate for the loss of novelty. We cannot take a recurrent pleasure in the new (in information) but we can in the natural (in form). Already, at the moment when Hamlet is holding out the pipe to Guildenstern and asking him to play upon it, we "gloat over" Hamlet's triumphal descent upon Guildenstern, when, after Guildenstern has, under increasing embarrassment, protested three times that he cannot play the instrument, Hamlet launches the retort for which all this was preparation:

"Why, look you now, how unworthy a thing you make of me. You would play upon me, you would seem to know my stops; you would pluck out the heart of my mystery; you would sound me from my lowest note to the top of my compass; and there is much music, excel-

1 Similarly, the epigram of Racine is "pure art," because it usually serves to formulate or clarify some situation within the play itself. In Goethe the epigram is most often of independent validity, as in *Die Wahlverwandtschaften*, where the ideas of Ottilie's diary are obviously carried over bodily from the author's notebook. In Shakespeare we have the union of extrinsic and intrinsic epigram, the epigram growing out of its context and yet valuable independent of its context.

lent voice, in this little organ, yet cannot you make it speak. 'Sblood, do you think I am easier to be played on than a pipe? Call me what instrument you will, though you can fret me, you cannot play upon me." [2]

In the opening lines we hear the promise of the close, and thus feel the emotional curve even more keenly than at first reading. Whereas in most modern art this element is underemphasized. It gives us the gossip of a plot, a plot which too often has for its value the mere fact that we do not know its outcome.[3]

Music, then, fitted less than any other art for imparting information, deals minutely in frustrations and fulfilments of desire,[4] and for that reason more often gives us those curves of emotion which, because they are natural, can bear repetition without loss. It is for this reason that music, like folk tales, is most capable of lulling us to sleep. A lullaby is a melody which comes quickly to rest, where the obstacles are easily overcome—and this is precisely the parallel to those waking dreams of struggle and conquest which (especially during childhood) we permit ourselves when falling asleep or when trying to induce sleep. Folk tales are just such waking dreams. Thus it is right that art should be called a "waking dream." The only difficulty with this definition (indicated by Charles Baudouin in his *Psychoanalysis and Æsthetics*, a very valuable study of Verhaeren) is that today we understand it to mean art as a waking dream for the artist. Modern criticism, and psychoanalysis in particular, is too prone to define the essence of art in terms of the artist's weaknesses. It is, rather, the audience which dreams, while the artist oversees the conditions which determine this dream. He is the manipulator of blood, brains, heart, and bowels which, while we sleep, dictate the mould of our desires. This is, of course, the real meaning of artistic felicity—an exaltation at the correctness of the procedure, so that we enjoy the steady march of doom in a Racinian tragedy with exactly the same equipment as that which produces our

---

[2] One might indicate still further appropriateness here. As Hamlet finishes his speech, Polonius enters, and Hamlet turns to him, "God bless you, sir!" Thus, the plot is continued (for Polonius is always the promise of action) and a full stop is avoided: the embarrassment laid upon Rosencranz and Guildenstern is not laid upon the audience.

[3] Yet modern music has gone far in the attempt to renounce this aspect of itself. Its dissonances become static, demanding no particular resolution. And whereas an unfinished modulation by a classic musician occasions positive dissatisfaction, the refusal to resolve a dissonance in modern music does not dissatisfy us, but irritates or stimulates. Thus, "energy" takes the place of style.

[4] Suspense is the least complex kind of anticipation, as surprise is the least complex kind of fulfilment.

delight with Benedick's "Peace! I'll stop your mouth. (*Kisses her*)" which terminates the imbroglio of *Much Ado About Nothing*.

The methods of maintaining interest which are most natural to the psychology of information (as it is applied to works of pure art) are surprise and suspense. The method most natural to the psychology of form is eloquence. For this reason the great ages of Æschylus, Shakespeare, and Racine, dealing as they did with material which was more or less a matter of common knowledge so that the broad outlines of the plot were known in advance (while it is the broad outlines which are usually exploited to secure surprise and suspense) developed formal excellence, or eloquence, as the basis of appeal in their work.

Not that there is any difference in kind between the classic method and the method of the cheapest contemporary melodrama. The drama, more than any other form, must never lose sight of its audience: here the failure to satisfy the proper requirements is most disastrous. And since certain contemporary work is successful, it follows that rudimentary laws of composition are being complied with. The distinction is one of intensity rather than of kind. The contemporary audience hears the lines of a play or novel with the same equipment as it brings to reading the lines of its daily paper. It is content to have facts placed before it in some more or less adequate sequence. Eloquence is the minimizing of this interest in fact, *per se,* so that the "more or less adequate sequence" of their presentation must be relied on to a much greater extent. Thus, those elements of surprise and suspense are subtilized, carried down into the writing of a line or a sentence, until in all its smallest details the work bristles with disclosures, contrasts, restatements with a difference, ellipses, images, aphorism, volume, sound-values, in short all that complex wealth of minutiæ which in their line-for-line aspect we call style and in their broader outlines we call form.

As a striking instance of a modern play with potentialities in which the intensity of eloquence is missing, I might cite a recent success, Capek's *R.U.R.* Here, in a melodrama which was often astonishing in the rightness of its technical procedure, when the author was finished he had written nothing but the scenario for a play by Shakespeare. It was a play in which the author produced time and again the opportunity, the demand, for eloquence, only to move on. (At other times, the most successful moments, he utilized the modern discovery of silence, with moments wherein words could not possibly serve but to detract from the effect: this we might call the "flowering" of information.) The Adam and Eve scene of the last act, a "commission" which the Shakespeare of the comedies would have loved to fill, was in the verbal barrenness of Capek's play something shameless to the point of

blushing. The Robot, turned human, prompted by the dawn of love
to see his first sunrise, or hear the first bird-call, and forced merely to
say "Oh, see the sunrise," or "Hear the pretty birds"—here one could
do nothing but wring his hands at the absence of that æsthetic mould
which produced the overslung "speeches" of Romeo and Juliet.

Suspense is the concern over the possible outcome of some specific
detail of plot rather than for general qualities. Thus, "Will A marry B
or C?" is suspense. In *Macbeth,* the turn from the murder scene to the
porter scene is a much less literal channel of development. Here the
presence of one quality calls forth the demand for another, rather than
one tangible incident of plot awaking an interest in some other possible tangible incident of plot. To illustrate more fully, if an author
managed over a certain number of his pages to produce a feeling of
sultriness, or oppression, in the reader, this would unconsciously
awaken in the reader the desire for a cold, fresh northwind—and thus
some aspect of a northwind would be effective if called forth by some
aspect of stuffiness. A good example of this is to be found in a contemporary poem, T. S. Eliot's *The Waste Land,* where the vulgar, oppressively trivial conversation in the public house calls forth in the
poet a memory of a line from Shakespeare. These slobs in a public
house, after a desolately low-visioned conversation, are now forced
by closing time to leave the saloon. They say good-night. And suddenly
the poet, feeling his release, drops into another good-night, a good-
night with *désinvolture,* a good-night out of what was, within the conditions of the poem at least, a graceful and irrecoverable past.

> "Well that Sunday Albert was home, they had a hot gammon,
>   And they asked me in to dinner, to get the beauty of it hot"—
>   [at this point the bartender interrupts: it is closing time]
> "Goonight Bill. Goonight Lou. Goonight May. Goonight. Ta ta.
>   Goonight. Goonight.
> Good-night, ladies, good-night, sweet ladies, good-night, good-night."

There is much more to be said on these lines, which I have shortened
somewhat in quotation to make my issue clearer. But I simply wish to
point out here that this transition is a bold juxtaposition of one quality
created by another, an association in ideas which, if not logical, is
nevertheless emotionally natural. In the case of *Macbeth,* similarly,
it would be absurd to say that the audience, after the murder scene,
wants a porter scene. But the audience does want the quality which
this porter particularizes. The dramatist might, conceivably, have introduced some entirely different character or event in this place, pro-

vided only that the event produced the same quality of relationship and contrast (grotesque seriousness followed by grotesque buffoonery). . . . One of the most beautiful and satisfactory "forms" of this sort is to be found in Baudelaire's *Femmes Damnées,* where the poet, after describing the business of a Lesbian seduction, turns to the full oratory of his apostrophe:

> "*Descendez, descendez, lamentables victimes,*
> *Descendez le chemin de l'enfer éternel . . .*"

while the stylistic efficacy of this transition contains a richness which transcends all moral (or unmoral) sophistication: the efficacy of appropriateness, of exactly the natural curve in treatment. Here is morality even for the godless, since it is a morality of art, being justified, if for no other reason, by its paralleling of that staleness, that disquieting loss of purpose, which must have followed the procedure of the two characters, the *femmes damnées* themselves, a remorse which, perhaps only physical in its origin, nevertheless becomes psychic.[5]

But to return, we have made three terms synonymous: form, psychology, and eloquence. And eloquence thereby becomes the essence of art, while pity, tragedy, sweetness, humor, in short all the emotions which we experience in life proper, as non-artists, are simply the material on which eloquence may feed. The arousing of pity, for instance, is not the central purpose of art, although it may be an adjunct of artistic effectiveness. One can feel pity much more keenly at the sight of some actual misfortune—and it would be a great mistake to see art merely as a weak representation of some actual experience.[6] That artists today are content to write under such an æsthetic accounts in part for the inferior position which art holds in the community. Art, at least in the great periods when it has flowered, was the conversion, or transcendence, of emotion into eloquence, and was thus a factor added to life. I am reminded of St. Augustine's caricature of the theatre: that whereas we do not dare to wish people unhappy, we do want to feel sorry for them, and therefore turn to plays so that we

---

[5] As another aspect of the same subject, I could cite many examples from the fairy tale. Consider, for instance, when the hero is to spend the night in a bewitched castle. Obviously, as darkness descends, weird adventures must befall him. His bed rides him through the castle; two halves of a man challenge him to a game of nine-pins played with thigh bones and skulls. Or entirely different incidents may serve instead of these. The quality comes first, the particularization follows.

[6] Could not the Greek public's resistance to Euripides be accounted for in the fact that he, of the three great writers of Greek tragedy, betrayed his art, was guilty of æsthetic impiety, in that he paid more attention to the arousing of emotion *per se* than to the sublimation of emotion into eloquence?

can feel sorry although no real misery is involved. One might apply
the parallel interpretation to the modern delight in happy endings,
and say that we turn to art to indulge our humanitarianism in a well-
wishing which we do not permit ourselves towards our actual neighbors. Surely the catharsis of art is more complicated than this, and
more reputable.

Eloquence itself, as I hope to have established in the instance from
*Hamlet* which I have analyzed, is no mere plaster added to a framework of more stable qualities. Eloquence is simply the end of art, and
is thus its essence. Even the poorest art is eloquent, but in a poor way,
with less intensity, until this aspect is obscured by others fattening
upon its leanness. Eloquence is not showiness; it is, rather, the result
of that desire in the artist to make a work perfect by adapting it in
every minute detail to the racial appetites.

The distinction between the psychology of information and the
psychology of form involves a definition of æsthetic truth. It is here
precisely, to combat the deflection which the strength of science has
caused to our tastes, that we must examine the essential breach between
scientific and artistic truth. Truth in art is not the discovery of facts,
not an addition to human knowledge in the scientific sense of the
word.[7] It is, rather, the exercise of human propriety, the formulation
of symbols which rigidify our sense of poise and rhythm. Artistic truth
is the externalization of taste.[8] I sometimes wonder, for instance,

[7] One of the most striking examples of the encroachment of scientific truth into
art is the doctrine of "truth by distortion," whereby one aspect of an object is suppressed the better to emphasize some other aspect; this is, obviously, an attempt
to *indicate* by art some fact of knowledge, to make some implicit aspect of an
object as explicit as one can by means of the comparatively dumb method of art
(dumb, that is, as compared to the perfect ease with which science can indicate
its discoveries). Yet science has already made discoveries in the realm of this "factual truth," this "truth by distortion" which must put to shame any artist who
relies on such matter for his effects. Consider, for instance, the motion picture of a
man vaulting. By photographing this process very rapidly, and running the reel
very slowly, one has upon the screen the most striking set of factual truths to aid
in our understanding of an athlete vaulting. Here, at our leisure, we can observe
the contortions of four legs, a head and a butt. This squirming thing we saw
upon the screen showed up an infinity of factual truths anent the balances of an
athlete vaulting. We can, from this, observe the marvelous system of balancing
which the body provides for itself in the adjustments of movement. Yet, so far as
the æsthetic truth is concerned, this on the screen was not an athlete, but a
squirming thing, a horror, displaying every fact of vaulting except the exhilaration
of the act itself.

[8] The procedure of science involves the elimination of taste, employing as a
substitute the corrective norm of the pragmatic test, the empirical experiment,
which is entirely intellectual. Those who oppose the "intellectualism" of critics like
Matthew Arnold are involved in an hilarious blunder, for Arnold's entire approach
to the appreciation of art is through delicacies of taste intensified to the extent
almost of squeamishness.

whether the "artificial" speech of John Lyly might perhaps be "truer" than the revelations of Dostoevsky. Certainly at its best, in its feeling for a statement which returns upon itself, which attempts the systole to a diastole, it *could* be much truer than Dostoevsky.[9] And if it is not, it fails not through a mistake of Lyly's æsthetic, but because Lyly was a man poor in character, whereas Dostoevsky was rich and complex. When Swift, making the women of Brobdingnag enormous, deduces from this discrepancy between their size and Gulliver's that Gulliver could sit astride their nipples, he has written something which is æsthetically true, which is, if I may be pardoned, profoundly "proper," as correct in its Euclidean deduction as any corollary in geometry. Given the companions of Ulysses in the cave of Polyphemus, it is true that they would escape clinging to the bellies of the herd let out to pasture. St. Ambrose, detailing the habits of God's creatures, and drawing from them moral maxims for the good of mankind, St. Ambrose in his limping natural history rich in scientific inaccuracies that are at the very heart of emotional rightness, St. Ambrose writes "Of night-birds, especially of the nightingale which hatches her eggs by song; of the owl, the bat, and the cock at cock-crow; in what wise these may apply to the guidance of our habits," and in the sheer rightness of that program there is the truth of art.

In introducing this talk of night-birds, after many pages devoted to other of God's creatures, he says,

"What now! While we have been talking, you will notice how the birds of night have already started fluttering about you, and, in this same fact of warning us to leave off with our discussion, suggest thereby a further topic"—and this seems to me to contain the best wisdom of which the human frame is capable, an address, a discourse, which can make our material life seem blatant almost to the point of despair. And when the cock crows, and the thief abandons his traps, and the sun lights up, and we are in every way called back to God by the well-meaning admonition of this bird, here the very blindnesses of religion become the deepest truths of art.

9 As for instance, the "conceit" of Endymion's awakening, when he forgets his own name, yet recalls that of his beloved.

JOHN CROWE RANSOM

# Criticism as
# Pure Speculation

## 1941

*What may appear to be only a conventionally graceful personal tribute
in the first paragraphs of Ransom's essay is the real clue to his approach: if "the authority of criticism" rests upon a reconciliation of
criticism and philosophical aesthetics, Ransom's own critical theory is
to be grounded in certain assumptions about the nature of reality.
What Ransom means by his key term "ontology" is the nature of a
poem's being—namely, as a symbolic yet concrete representation of human experience, differing from scientific discourse in its avoidance of
and resistance to abstract concepts. The critic's task is to approach a
poem not in terms of its "meaning" but in terms of its "icons" or images
—"to attend to the poetic object." Recall, at this point, Eliot's influential statement of what he hoped his criticism would do: "to divert
interest from the poet to the poetry." As one of the main progenitors
of the New Criticism, Ransom distinguishes between science and
poetry, and then dismisses two traditional approaches to poetry, the
"psychologistic" and the "moralistic." On the basis of your familiarity
with preceding critics, are Ransom's comments accurate? Which particular critics might he have in mind in dealing with these critical
approaches? (Is his discussion of science and poetry like Wordsworth's,
in any respect?)*

*Ransom's insistence on "a structural understanding of poetry" de-*

*rives from his premise that poetry is not to be confused with the poet's biography or intentions, the audience response to the poem, or the uses to which it may be put. As an autonomous object, a poem is a special kind of nondiscursive verbal structure that must be read closely for the complex meaning that is there only because it is inherent in style, technique, and form. Despite some considerable differences in emphases, other New (or "formalist") Critics also take this as their starting point.*

*In order to solve the perplexing philosophical problem of how a poem can be both universal and concrete, Ransom formulates a distinction of great importance to him: the relationship between structure and texture, each having a particular function. Although he rejects the poetry of abstract ideas, to what extent does his concept of a "paraphrasable core" in a poem resemble what might also be thought of as the "content"? In this connection, study his own analogy of poetry with architecture: Is wallpaper organic?*

*Ransom's essays greatly influenced many younger New Critics. His book,* The New Criticism *(1941), even gave the name to this new way of studying and teaching literature, a mode which until fairly recently was the dominant critical approach of our time. The essay by Cleanth Brooks which follows this one (see p. 470) demonstrates the application of the theory to a particular poem and exemplifies the kind of analytical close reading that characterizes the New Criticism.*

# I

I WILL testify to the weight of responsibility felt by the critic who enters a serial discussion with such other lecturers as Mr. Wilson, Mr. Auden, and Mr. Foerster; and delivers his opinion to an audience at Princeton, where live at least two eminent critics, in Mr. Tate and Mr. Blackmur, and one eminent esthetician, in Mr. Greene.

Indeed, Mr. Blackmur and Mr. Greene have recently published books which bear on this discussion. Mr. Blackmur's essays are probably all that can be expected of a critic who has not explicitly submitted them to the discipline of general esthetics; but with that limitation the best critic in the world might expose himself to review and reproach. Mr. Greene's esthetic studies, in turn, may have wonderful cogency as philosophical discourse; but if throughout them he should fail to maintain intimate contact with the actual works of art he would invite damaging attentions from the literary critics. I am far from suggesting such proceedings against them. Mr. Blackmur has his native philosophical sense to keep his critical foundations from sliding into the sea. Mr. Greene is in a very strong position: recognizing the usual weakness of formal esthetics, he tries a device to secure his own studies against it; for when he needs them he uses reports from reputable actual critics upon the practices in the several arts. A chasm, perhaps an abyss, separates the critic and the esthetician ordinarily, if the books in the library are evidence. But the authority of criticism depends on its coming to terms with esthetics, and the authority of literary esthetics depends on its coming to terms with criticism. Mr. Greene is an esthetician, and his department is philosophy, but he has subscribed in effect to this thesis. I am a sort of critic, and my department is English poetry, so that I am very much in Mr. Blackmur's position: and I subscribe to the thesis, and am altogether disposed to solicit Mr. Greene's philosophical services.

When we inquire into the "intent of the critic," we mean: the intent of the generalized critic, or critic as such. We will concede that any professional critic is familiar with the technical practices of poets so long as these are conventional, and is expert in judging when they perform them brilliantly and when only fairly, or badly. We expect a critical discourse to cover that much, but we know that more is required. The most famous poets of our own time, for example, make wide departures from conventional practices: how are they to be judged? Innovations in poetry, or even conventions when pressed to their logical limits, cause the ordinary critic to despair. They cause the good critic to review his esthetic principles; perhaps to re-formulate his esthetic principles. He tries the poem against his best philosophical conception of the peculiar character that a poem should have.

Mr. T. S. Eliot is an extraordinarily sensitive critic. But when he discusses the so-called "metaphysical" poetry, he surprises us by refusing to study the so-called "conceit" which is its reputed basis; he observes instead that the metaphysical poets of the seventeenth century are more like their immediate predecessors than the latter are like the eighteenth and nineteenth century poets, and then he goes into a very broad philosophical comparison between two whole "periods" or types of poetry. I think it has come to be understood that his comparison is unsound; it has not proved workable enough to assist critics who have otherwise borrowed liberally from his critical principles. (It contains the famous dictum about the "sensibility" of the earlier poets, it imputes to them a remarkable ability to "feel their thought," and to have a kind of "experience" in which the feeling cannot be differentiated from the thinking.) Now there is scarcely another critic equal to Eliot at distinguishing the practices of two poets who are closely related. He is supreme as a comparative critic when the relation in question is delicate and subtle; that is, when it is a matter of close perception and not a radical difference in kind. But this line of criticism never goes far enough. In Eliot's own range of criticism the line does not always answer. He is forced by discontinuities in the poetic tradition into sweeping theories that have to do with esthetics, the philosophy of poetry; and his own philosophy probably seems to us insufficient, the philosophy of the literary man.

The intent of the critic may well be, then, first to read his poem sensitively, and make comparative judgments about its technical practice, or, as we might say, to emulate Eliot. Beyond that, it is to read and remark the poem knowingly; that is, with an esthetician's understanding of what a poem generically "is."

Before I venture, with inadequate argument, to describe what I take to be the correct understanding of poetry, I would like to describe two other understandings which, though widely professed, seem to me misunderstandings. First, there is a smart and bellettristic theory of poetry which may be called "psychologistic." Then there is an altogether staid and commonplace theory which is moralistic. Of these in their order.

## II

It could easily be argued about either of these untenable conceptions of poetry that it is an act of despair to which critics resort who cannot find for the discourse of poetry any precise differentia to remove it from the category of science. Psychologistic critics hold that poetry is addressed primarily to the feelings and motor impulses; they remind us frequently of its contrast with the coldness, the unemotionality, of science, which is supposed to address itself to the pure cognitive mind. Mr. Richards came out spectacularly for the doctrine, and furnished it with detail of the greatest ingenuity. He very nearly severed the dependence of poetic effect upon any standard of objective knowledge or belief. But the feelings and impulses which he represented as gratified by the poem were too tiny and numerous to be named. He never identified them; they seemed not so much psychological as infrapsychological. His was an esoteric poetic: it could not be disproved. But neither could it be proved, and I think it is safe at this distance to say that eventually his readers, and Richards himself, lost interest in it as being an improvisation, much too unrelated to the public sense of a poetic experience.

With other critics psychologism of some sort is an old story, and one that will probably never cease to be told. For, now that all of us know about psychology, there must always be persons on hand precisely conditioned to declare that poetry is an emotional discourse indulged in resentment and compensation for science, the bleak cognitive discourse in its purity. It becomes less a form of knowledge than a form of "expression." The critics are willing to surrender the honor of objectivity to science if they may have the luxury of subjectivity for poetry. Science will scarcely object. But one or two things have to be said about that. In every experience, even in science, there is feeling. No discourse can sustain itself without interest, which is feeling. The interest, or the feeling, is like an automatic index to the human value of the proceeding—which would not otherwise proceed. Mr. Eliseo Vivas is an esthetician who might be thought to reside in the camp of the enemy, for his affiliations are positivist; yet in a recent essay he writes about the "passion" which sustains the heroic labors of the scientist as one bigger and more intense than is given to most men.

I do not mean to differ with that judgment at all in remarking that we might very well let the passions and the feelings take care of themselves; it is precisely what we do in our pursuit of science. The thing to attend to is the object to which they attach. As between two similar musical phrases, or between two similar lines of poetry, we may often defy the most proficient psychologist to distinguish the one feeling—response from the other; unless we permit him to say at long last that one is the kind of response that would be made to the first line, and the other is the kind of response that would be made to the second line. But that is to do, after much wasted motion, what I have just suggested: to attend to the poetic object and let the feelings take care of themselves. It is their business to "respond." There may be a feeling correlative with the minutest alteration in an object, and adequate to it, but we shall hardly know. What we do know is that the feelings are grossly inarticulate if we try to abstract them and take their testimony in their own language. Since it is not the intent of the critic to be inarticulate, his discriminations must be among the objects. We understand this so well intuitively that the critic seems to us in possession of some esoteric knowledge, some magical insight, if he appears to be intelligent elsewhere and yet refers confidently to the "tone" or "quality" or "value" of the feeling he discovers in a given line. Probably he is bluffing. The distinctness resides in the cognitive or "semantical" ob-

jects denoted by the words. When Richards bewilders us by reporting
affective and motor disturbances that are too tiny for definition, and
other critics by reporting disturbances that are too massive and gross,
we cannot fail to grow suspicious of this whole way of insight as in-
competent.

Eliot has a special version of psychologistic theory which looks extremely fertile, though it is broad and nebulous as his psychologistic
terms require it to be. He likes to regard the poem as a structure of
emotion and feeling. But the emotion is singular, there being only one
emotion per poem, or at least per passage: it is the central emotion
or big emotion which attaches to the main theme or situation. The
feeling is plural. The emotion combines with many feelings; these are
our little responses to the single words and phrases, and he does not
think of them as being parts of the central emotion or even related
to it. The terminology is greatly at fault, or we should recognize at
once, I think, a principle that might prove very valuable. I would not
answer for the conduct of a technical philosopher in assessing this
theory; he might throw it away, out of patience with its jargon. But
a lay philosopher who respects his Eliot and reads with all his sympathy
might salvage a good thing from it, though I have not heard of anyone
doing so. He would try to escape from the affective terms, and translate
Eliot into more intelligible language. Eliot would be saying in effect
that a poem has a central logic or situation or "paraphrasable core" to
which an appropriate interest doubtless attaches, and that in this respect the poem is like a discourse of science behind which lies the
sufficient passion. But he would be saying at the same time, and this is
the important thing, that the poem has also a context of lively local
details to which other and independent interests attach; and that in this
respect it is unlike the discourse of science. For the detail of scientific
discourse intends never to be independent of the thesis (either objectively or affectively) but always functional, and subordinate to the
realization of the thesis. To say that is to approach to a structural
understanding of poetry, and to the kind of understanding that I wish
presently to urge.

### III

As for the moralistic understanding of poetry, it is sometimes the
specific moralists, men with moral axes to grind, and incidentally men
of unassailable public position, who cherish that; they have a "use"
for poetry. But not exclusively, for we may find it held also by critics
who are more spontaneous and innocent: apparently they fall back

upon it because it attributes some special character to poetry, which otherwise refuses to yield up to them a character. The moral interest is so much more frequent in poetry than in science that they decide to offer its moralism as a differentia.

This conception of poetry is of the greatest antiquity—it antedates the evolution of close esthetic philosophy, and persists beside it too. Plato sometimes spoke of poetry in this light—perhaps because it was recommended to him in this light—but nearly always scornfully. In the *Gorgias,* and other dialogues, he represents the poets as moralizing, and that is only what he, in the person of Socrates, is doing at the very moment, and given to doing; but he considers the moralizing of poets as mere "rhetoric," or popular philosophy, and unworthy of the accomplished moralist who is the real or technical philosopher. Plato understood very well that the poet does not conduct a technical or an original discourse like that of the scientist—and the term includes here the moral philosopher—and that close and effective moralizing is scarcely to be had from him. It is not within the poet's power to offer that if his intention is to offer poetry; for the poetry and the morality are so far from being identical that they interfere a little with each other.

Few famous estheticians in the history of philosophy have cared to bother with the moralistic conception; many critics have, in all periods. Just now we have at least two schools of moralistic critics contending for the official possession of poetry. One is the Neo-Humanist, and Mr. Foerster has identified himself with that. The other is the Marxist, and I believe it is represented in some degree and shade by Mr. Wilson, possibly by Mr. Auden. I have myself taken profit from the discussions by both schools, but recently I have taken more—I suppose this is because I was brought up in a scholastic discipline rather like the Neo-Humanist—from the writings of the Marxist critics. One of the differences is that the Neo-Humanists believe in the "respectable" virtues, but the Marxists believe that respectability is the greatest of vices, and equate respectable with "genteel." That is a very striking difference, and I think it is also profound.

But I do not wish to be impertinent; I can respect both these moralities, and appropriate moral values from both. The thing I wish to argue is not the comparative merits of the different moralities by which poetry is judged, but their equal inadequacy to the reading of the poet's intention. The moralistic critics wish to isolate and discuss the "ideology" or theme or paraphrase of the poem and not the poem itself. But even to the practitioners themselves, if they are sophisticated, comes sometimes the apprehension that this is moral rather than literary criticism. I have not seen the papers of my colleagues in this discussion, for that was against the rules, but it is reported to me that both Mr. Wilson and Mr. Foerster concede in explicit words that criticism has both the moral and the esthetic branches; Mr. Wilson may call them the "social" and esthetic branches. And they would hold the critical profession responsible for both branches. Under these circumstances the critics cease to be mere moralists and become dualists; that is better. My feeling about such a position would be that the moral criticism we shall have with us always, and have had always, and that it is easy—comparatively speaking—and that what is hard, and needed, and indeed more and more urgent after all the failures of poetic understanding, is a better esthetic criticism. This is the branch which is all but invariably neglected by the wise but morally zealous critics; they tend to forget their dual responsibility. I think I should go so far as to think that, in strictness, the business of the literary critic is exclusively with an esthetic criticism. The business of the moralist will naturally, and properly, be with something else.

If we have the patience to read for a little while in the anthology, paying some respect to the varieties of substance actually in the poems, we cannot logically attribute ethical character by definition to poetry; for that character is not universal in the poems. And if we have any faith in a community of character among the several arts, we are stopped quickly from risking such a definition for art at large. To claim a moral content for most of sculpture, painting, music, or architecture, is to plan something dialectically very roundabout and subtle, or else to be so arbitrary as to invite instant exposure. I should think the former alternative is impractical, and the latter, if it is not stupid, is masochistic.

The moralistic critics are likely to retort upon their accusers by accusing them in turn of the vapid doctrine known as Art for Art's Sake. And with frequent justice; but again we are likely. to receive the impression that it is first because Art for Art's Sake, the historic doctrine, proved empty, and availed them so little esthetically, like all the other doctrines that came into default, that they have fled to their moralism. Moralism does at least impute to poetry a positive substance, as Art for Art's Sake does not. It asserts an autonomy for art, which is excellent; but autonomy to do what? Only to be itself, and to reduce its interpreters to a tautology? With its English adherents in the 'nineties the doctrine seemed to make only a negative requirement of art, that is, that it should be anti-Victorian as we should say today, a little bit naughty and immoral perhaps, otherwise at least non-moral, or carefully squeezed dry of moral substance. An excellent example of how two doctrines, inadequate equally but in opposite senses, may keep themselves alive by abhorring each other's errors.

It is highly probable that the poem considers an ethical situation, and there is no reason why it should repel this from its consideration. But, if I may say so without being accused of verbal trifling, the poetic consideration of the ethical situation is not the same as the ethical consideration of it. The straight ethical consideration would be prose; it would be an act of interested science, or an act of practical will. The poetic consideration, according to Schopenhauer, is the objectification of this act of will; that is, it is our contemplation and not our exercise of will, and therefore qualitatively a very different experience; knowledge without desire. That doctrine also seems too negative and indeterminate. I will put the point as I see it in another way. It should be a comfort to the moralist that there is ordinarily a moral composure in the poem, as if the poet had long known good and evil, and made his moral choice between them once and for all. Art is post-ethical rather than unethical. In the poem there is an increment of meaning which is neither the ethical content nor opposed to the ethical content. The poetic experience would have to stop for the poet who is developing it, or for the reader who is following it, if the situation which is being poetically treated should turn back into a situation to be morally determined; if, for example, the situation were not a familiar one, and one to which we had habituated our moral wills; for it would rouse the moral will again to action, and make the poetic treatment impossible under its heat. Art is more cool than hot, and a moral fervor is as disastrous to it as a burst of passion itself. We have seen Marxists recently so revolted by Shakespeare's addiction to royal or noble personae that they cannot obtain esthetic experience from the plays; all they get is moral agitation. In another art, we know, and doubtless we approve, the scruple of the college authorities in not permitting the "department of fine arts" to direct the collegians in painting in the nude. Doctor Hanns Sachs, successor to Freud, in a recent number of his *American Imago,* gives a story from a French author as follows:

"He tells that one evening strolling along the streets of Paris he noticed a row of slot machines which for a small coin showed pictures of women in full or partial undress. He observed the leering interest with which men of all kind and description, well dressed and shabby, boys and old men, enjoyed the peep show. He remarked that they all avoided one of these machines, and wondering what uninteresting pictures it might show, he put his penny in the slot. To his great astonishment the generally shunned picture turned out to be the Venus of Medici. Now he begins to ponder: Why does nobody get excited about her? She is decidedly feminine and not less naked than the others which hold such strong fascination for everybody. Finally he finds a satisfactory answer: They fight shy of her because she is beautiful."

And Doctor Sachs, though in his own variety of jargon, makes a number of wise observations about the psychic conditions precedent to the difficult apprehension of beauty. The experience called beauty is beyond the powerful ethical will precisely as it is beyond the animal passion, and indeed these last two are competitive, and coordinate. Under the urgency of either we are incapable of appreciating the statue or understanding the poem.

## IV

The ostensible substance of the poem may be anything at all which words may signify: an ethical situation, a passion, a train of thought, a flower or landscape, a thing. This substance receives its poetic increment. It might be safer to say it receives some subtle and mysterious alteration under poetic treatment, but I will risk the cruder formula: the ostensible substance is increased by an x, which is an increment. The poem actually continues to contain its ostensible substance, which is not fatally diminished from its prose state: that is its logical core or paraphrase. The rest of the poem is x, which we are to find.

We feel the working of this simple formula when we approach a poetry with our strictest logic, provided we can find deliverance from certain inhibiting philosophical prepossessions into which we have been conditioned by the critics we have had to read. Here is Lady Macbeth planning a murder with her husband:

> When Duncan is asleep—
> Whereto the rather shall his hard day's journey
> Soundly invite him—his two chamberlains
> Will I with wine and wassail so convince,
> That memory, the warder of the brain,
> Shall be a fume, and the receipt of reason
> A limbec only; when in swinish sleep
> Their drenched natures lie as in a death,
> What cannot you and I perform upon
> The unguarded Duncan? what not put upon
> His spongy officers, who shall bear the guilt
> Of our great quell?

It is easy to produce the prose argument or paraphase of this speech; it has one upon which we shall all agree. But the passage is more than its argument. Any detail, with this speaker, seems capable of being expanded in some direction which is not that of the argument. For example, Lady Macbeth says she will make the chamberlains drunk so that they will not remember their charge, nor keep their wits about them. But it is indifferent to this argument whether memory according to the old psychology is located at the gateway to the brain, whether it is to be disintegrated into fume as of alcohol, and whether the whole receptacle of the mind is to be turned into a still. These are additions to the argument both energetic and irrelevant—though they do not quite stop or obscure the argument. From the point of view of the philosopher they are excursions into particularity. They give, in spite of the argument, which would seem to be perfectly self-sufficient, a sense of the real density and contingency of the world in which arguments and plans have to be pursued. They bring out the private character which the items of an argument can really assume if we look at them. This character spreads out in planes at right angles to the course of the argument, and in effect gives to the discourse another dimension, not present in a perfectly logical prose. We are expected to have sufficient judgment not to let this local character take us too far or keep us too long from the argument.

All this would seem commonplace remark, I am convinced, but for those philosophically timid critics who are afraid to think that the poetic increment is local and irrelevant, and that poetry cannot achieve its own virtue and keep undiminished the virtues of prose at the same time. But I will go a little further in the hope of removing the sense of strangeness in the analysis. I will offer a figurative definition of a poem.

A poem is, so to speak, a democratic state, whereas a prose discourse —mathematic, scientific, ethical, or practical and vernacular—is a totalitarian state. The intention of a democratic state is to perform the work of state as effectively as it can perform it, subject to one reservation of conscience; that it will not despoil its members, the citizens, of the free exercise of their own private and independent characters. But the totalitarian state is interested solely in being effective, and regards the citizens as no citizens at all; that is, regards them as functional members whose existence is totally defined by their allotted contributions to its ends; it has no use for their private characters, and therefore no provision for them. I indicate of course the extreme or polar opposition between two polities, without denying that a polity may come to us rather mixed up.

In this trope the operation of the state as a whole represents of course the logical paraphrase or argument of the poem. The private character of the citizens represents the particularity asserted by the parts in the poem. And this last is our x.

For many years I had seen—as what serious observer has not—that a poem as a discourse differentiated itself from prose by its particularity, yet not to the point of sacrificing its logical cogency or universality. But I could get no further. I could not see how real particularity could get into a universal. The object of esthetic studies became for me a kind of discourse, or a kind of natural configuration, which like any other discourse or configuration claimed universality, but which consisted actually, and notoriously, of particularity. The poem was concrete, yet universal, and in spite of Hegel I could not see how the two properties could be identified as forming in a single unit the "concrete universal." It is usual, I believe, for persons at this stage to assert that somehow the apparent diffuseness or particularity in the poem gets itself taken up or "assimilated" into the logic, to produce a marvellous kind of unity called a "higher unity," to which ordinary discourse is not eligible. The belief is that the "idea" or theme proves itself in poetry to be even more dominating than in prose by overcoming much more energetic resistance than usual on the part of the materials, and the resistance, as attested in the local development of detail, is therefore set not to the debit but to the credit of the unifying power of the poetic spirit. A unity of that kind is one which philosophers less audacious and more factual than Hegel would be loath to claim. Critics incline to call it, rather esoterically, an "imaginative" rather than a logical unity, but one supposes they mean a mystical, an ineffable, unity. I for one could neither grasp it nor deny it. I believe that is not an uncommon situation for poetic analysts to find themselves in.

It occurred to me at last that the solution might be very easy if looked for without what the positivists call "metaphysical preposses-sions." Suppose the logical substance remained there all the time, and was in no way specially remarkable, while the particularity came in by accretion, so that the poem turned out partly universal, and partly particular, but with respect to different parts. I began to remark the dimensions of a poem, or other work of art. The poem was not a mere moment in time, nor a mere point in space. It was sizeable, like a house. Apparently it had a "plan," or a central frame of logic, but it had also a huge wealth of local detail, which sometimes fitted the plan functionally or served it, and sometimes only subsisted comfortably under it; in either case the house stood up. But it was the political way of thinking which gave me the first analogy which seemed valid. The poem was like a democratic state, in action, and observed both macroscopically and microscopically.

The house occurred also, and provided what seems to be a more negotiable trope under which to construe the poem. A poem is a *logical structure* having a *local texture*. These terms have been actually though not systematically employed in literary criticism. To my imagination they are architectural. The walls of my room are obviously structural; the beams and boards have a function; so does the plaster, which is the visible aspect of the final wall. The plaster might have remained naked, aspiring to no character, and purely functional. But actually it has been painted, receiving color; or it has been papered, receiving color and design, though these have no structural value; and perhaps it has been hung with tapestry, or with paintings, for "decoration." The paint, the paper, the tapestry are texture. It is logically unrelated to structure. But I indicate only a few of the textural possibilities in architecture. There are not fewer of them in poetry.

The intent of the good critic becomes therefore to examine and define the poem with respect to its structure and its texture. If he has nothing to say about its texture he has nothing to say about it specifically as a poem, but is treating it only insofar as it is prose.

I do not mean to say that the good critic will necessarily employ my terms.

## V

Many critics today are writing analytically and with close intelligence, in whatever terms, about the logical substance or structure of the poem, and its increment of irrelevant local substance or texture. I believe that the understanding of the ideal critic has to go even further than that. The final desideratum is an ontological insight, nothing less. I am committed by my title to representation of criticism as, in the last resort, a speculative exercise. But my secret committal was to speculative in the complete sense of—ontological.

There is nothing especially speculative or ontological in reciting, or even appraising, the logical substance of the poem. This is its prose core—its science perhaps, or its ethics if it seems to have an ideology. Speculative interest asserts itself principally when we ask why we want the logical substance to be compounded with the local substance, the good lean structure with a great volume of texture that does not function. It is the same thing as asking why we want the poem to be what it is.

It has been a rule, having the fewest exceptions, for estheticians and great philosophers to direct their speculations by the way of overstating and overvaluing the logical substance. They are impressed by the apparent obedience of material nature, whether in fact or in art, to definable form or "law" imposed upon it. They like to suppose that in poetry, as in chemistry, everything that figures in the discourse means to be functional, and that the poem is imperfect in the degree that it contains items, whether by accident or intention, which manifest a private independence. It is a bias with which we are entirely familiar, and reflects the extent to which our philosophy hitherto has been impressed by the successes of science in formulating laws which would "govern" their objects. Probably I am here reading the state of mind of yesterday rather than of today. Nevertheless we know it. The worldview which ultimately forms itself in the mind so biassed is that of a world which is rational and intelligible. The view is sanguine, and naïve. Hegel's world-view, I think it is agreed, was a subtle version of this, and if so, it was what determined his view of art. He seemed to make the handsomest concession to realism by offering to knowledge a kind of universal which was not restricted to the usual abstracted aspects of the material, but included all aspects, and was a concrete universal. The concreteness in Hegel's handling was not honestly, or at any rate not fairly, defended. It was always represented as being in process of pointing up and helping out the universality. He could look at a work of art and report all its substance as almost assimilated to a ruling "idea." But at least Hegel seemed to distinguish what looked like two ultimate sorts of substance there, and stated the central esthetic problem as the problem of relating them. And his writings about art are speculative in the sense that he regarded the work of art not as of great intrinsic value necessarily, but as an object-lesson or discipline in the understanding of the world-process, and as its symbol.

I think of two ways of construing poetry with respect to its ultimate purpose; of which the one is not very handsome nor speculatively interesting, and the other will appear somewhat severe.

The first construction would picture the poet as a sort of epicure, and the poem as something on the order of a Christmas pudding, stuffed with what dainties it will hold. The pastry alone, or it may be the cake, will not serve; the stuffing is wanted too. The values of the poem would be intrinsic, or immediate, and they would include not only the value of the structure but also the incidental values to be found in the texture. If we exchange the pudding for a house, they would include not only the value of the house itself but also the value of the furnishings. In saying intrinsic or immediate, I mean that the poet is fond of the precise objects denoted by the words, and writes the poem for the reason that he likes to dwell upon them. In talking about the main value and the incidental values I mean to recognize the fact that the latter engage the affections just as truly as the former. Poetic discourse therefore would be more agreeable than prose to the epicure or the literally acquisitive man; for prose has but a single value, being about one thing only; its parts have no values of their own, but only instrumental values, which might be reckoned as fractions of the single value proportionate to their contributions to it. The prose is one-valued and the poem is many-valued. Indeed, there will certainly be poems whose texture contains many precious objects, and aggregates a greater value than the structure.

So there would be a comfortable and apparently eligible view that poetry improves on prose because it is a richer diet. It causes five or six pleasures to appear, five or six good things, where one had been before; an alluring consideration for robustious, full-blooded, bourgeois souls. The view will account for much of the poem, if necessary. But it does not account for all of it, and sometimes it accounts for less than at other times.

The most impressive reason for the bolder view of art, the speculative one, is the existence of the "pure," or "abstractionist," or non-representational works of art; though these will probably occur to us in other arts than poetry. There is at least one art, music, whose works are all of this sort. Tones are not words, they have no direct semantical function, and by themselves they mean nothing. But they combine to make brilliant phrases, harmonies, and compositions. In these compositions it is probable that the distinction between structure or functional content, on the one hand, and texture or local variation and departure, on the other, is even more determinate than in an impure art like poetry. The world of tones seems perfectly inhuman and impracticable; there is no specific field of experience "about which" music is telling us. Yet we know that music is powerfully affective. I take my own musical feelings, and those attested by other audients, as the sufficient index to some overwhelming human importance which the musical object has for us. At the same time it would be useless to ask the feelings precisely what they felt; we must ask the critic. The safest policy is to take the simplest construction, and try to improvise as little fiction as possible. Music is not music, I think, until we grasp its effects both in structure and in texture. As we grow in musical understanding the structures become always more elaborate and sustained, and the texture which interrupts them and sometimes imperils them becomes more bold and unpredictable. We can agree in saying about the works of music that these are musical structures, and they are richly textured; we can identify these elements, and perhaps precisely. To what then do our feelings respond? To music as structural composition itself; to music as manifesting the structural principles of the world; to modes of structure which we feel to be ontologically possible, or even probable. Schopenhauer construed music very much in that sense. Probably it will occur to us that musical compositions bear close analogy therefore to operations in pure mathematics. The mathematicians confess that their constructions are "nonexistential"; meaning, as I take it, that the constructions testify with assurance only to the structural principles, in the light of which they are possible but may not be actual, or if they are actual may not be useful. This would define the mathematical operations as speculative; as motivated by an interest so generalized and so elemental that no word short of ontological will describe it.

But if music and mathematics have this much in common, they differ sharply in their respective world-views or ontological biasses. That of music, with its prodigious display of texture, seems the better informed about the nature of the world, the more realistic, the less naïve. Perhaps the difference is between two ontological educations. But I should be inclined to imagine it as rising back of that point; in two ontological temperaments.

There are also, operating a little less successfully so far as the index-ical evidences would indicate, the abstractionist paintings, of many schools, and perhaps also works of sculpture; and there is architecture. These arts have tried to abandon direct representational intention almost as heroically as music. They exist in their own materials and indicate no other specific materials; structures of color, light, space, stone—the cheapest of materials. They too can symbolize nothing of value unless it is structure or composition itself. But that is precisely the act which denotes will and intelligence; which becomes the act of fuller intelligence if it carefully accompanies its structures. with their material textures; for then it understands better the ontological nature of materials.

Returning to the poetry. It is not all poems, and not even all "powerful" poems, having high index-ratings, whose semantical meanings contain situations important in themselves or objects precious in themselves. There may be little correlation between the single value of the poem and the aggregate value of its contents—just as there is no such correlation whatever in music. The "effect" of the poem may be astonishingly disproportionate to our interest in its materials. It is true, of course, that there is no art employing materials of equal richness with poetry, and that it is beyond the capacity of poetry to employ indifferent materials. The words used in poetry are the words the race has already formed, and naturally they call attention to things and events that have been thought to be worth attending to. But I suggest that any poetry which is "technically" notable is in part a work of abstractionist art, concentrating upon the structure and the texture, and the structure-texture relation, out of a pure speculative interest.

At the end of *Love's Labour's Lost* occurs a little diversion which seems proportionately far more effective than that laborious play as a whole. The play is over, but Armado stops the principals before they disperse to offer them a show:

ARM. But, most esteemed greatness, will you hear the dialogue that the two learned men have compiled in praise of the owl and the cuckoo? It should have followed in the end of our show.

KING. Call them forth quickly; we will do so.

ARM. Holla! approach.

*Re-enter Holofernes, etc.*

This side is Hiems, Winter, this Ver, the Spring; the one maintained by the owl, the other by the cuckoo. Ver, begin.

## THE SONG

SPRING.

When daisies pied and violets blue
And lady-smocks all silver-white
And cuckoo-buds of yellow hue
Do paint the meadows with delight,
The cuckoo then, on every tree,
Mocks married men; for thus sings he,
        Cuckoo;
Cuckoo, cuckoo: O word of fear,
Unpleasing to a married ear!

When shepherds pipe on oaten straws,
And merry larks are ploughmen's clocks,
When turtles tread, and rooks, and daws,
And maidens bleach their summer smocks,
The cuckoo then, on every tree,
Mocks married men; for thus sings he,
        Cuckoo;

Cuckoo, cuckoo: O word of fear,
Unpleasing to a married ear!

WINTER.

When icicles hang by the wall,
And Dick the shepherd blows his nail,
And Tom bears logs into the hall,
And milk comes frozen home in pail,
When blood is nipp'd and ways be foul,
Then nightly sings the staring owl,
    Tu-who;
Tu-whit, tu-who, a merry note,
While greasy Joan doth keel the pot.

When all aloud the wind doth blow,
And coughing drowns the parson's saw,
And birds sit brooding in the snow,
And Marian's nose looks red and raw,
When roasted crabs hiss in the bowl,
Then nightly sings the staring owl,
    Tu-who;
Tu-whit, tu-who, a merry note,
While greasy Joan doth keel the pot.

ARM. The words of Mercury are harsh after
the songs of Apollo. You that way,—we this way.
                      (Exeunt.)

The feeling-index registers such strong approval of this episode that a critic with ambition is obliged to account for it. He can scarcely account for it in terms of the weight of its contents severally.

At first glance Shakespeare has provided only a pleasant little carica-ture of the old-fashioned (to us, medieval) debate between personified characters. It is easygoing, like nonsense; no labor is lost here. Each party speaks two stanzas and concludes both stanzas with the refrain about his bird, the cuckoo or the owl. There is next to no generalized argument, or dialectic proper. Each argues by citing his characteristic exhibits. In the first stanza Spring cites some flowers; in the second stanza, some business by country persons, with interpolation of some birds that make love. Winter in both stanzas cites the country business of the season. In the refrain the cuckoo, Spring's symbol, is used to refer the love-making to more than the birds; and this repeats itself though it is naughty. The owl is only a nominal symbol for Winter, an "emblem" that is not very emblematic, but the refrain manages another reference to the kitchen, and repeats itself, as if Winter's pleasures focussed in the kitchen.

In this poem texture is not very brilliant, but it eclipses structure. The argument, we would say in academic language, is concerned with "the relative advantages of Spring and Winter." The only logical determinateness this structure has is the good coordination of the items cited by Spring as being really items peculiar to Spring, and of the Winter items as peculiar to Winter. The symbolic refrains look like summary or master items, but they seem to be a little more than summary and in fact to mean a little more than they say. The argument is trifling on the whole, and the texture from the point of view of felt human importance lacks decided energy; both which observations are to be made, and most precisely, of how many famous lyrics, especially those before that earnest and self-conscious nineteenth century! The value of the poem is greater than the value of its parts: that is what the critic is up against.

Unquestionably it is possible to assemble very fine structures out of ordinary materials. The good critic will study the poet's technique, in confidence that here the structural principles will be discovered at home. In this study he will find as much range for his activities as he desires.

Especially must he study the metrics, and their implications for structural composition. In this poem I think the critic ought to make good capital of the contrast between the amateurishness of the pleasant discourse as meaning and the hard determinate form of it phonetically. The meter on the whole is out of relation to the meaning of the poem or to anything else specifically; it is a musical material of low grade, but plastic and only slightly resistant material, and its presence in every poem is that of an abstractionist element that belongs to the art.

And here I will suggest another analogy, this one between Shakespeare's poem and some ordinary specimen of painting. It does not matter how old-fashioned or representational the painting is, we shall all, if we are instructed in the tradition of this art, require it to exhibit along with its represented object an abstract design in terms of pure physical balance or symmetry. We sense rather than measure the success of this design, but it is as if we had drawn a horizontal axis and a vertical axis through the center of the picture, and required the painted masses to balance with respect to each of these two axes. This is an over-simple statement of a structural requirement by which the same details function in two worlds that are different, and that do not correlate with each other. If the painting is of the Holy Family, we might say that this object has a drama, or an economy, of its own; but that the physical masses which compose it must enter also into another economy, that of abstract design; and that the value of any unit mass for the one economy bears no relation to its value for the other. The painting is of great ontological interest because it embodies this special dimension of abstract form. And turning to the poem we should find that its represented "meaning" is analogous to the represented object in the painting, while its meter is analogous to the pure design.

A number of fascinating speculative considerations must follow upon this discovery. They will have to do with the most fundamental laws of this world's structure. They will be profoundly ontological, though I do not mean that they must be ontological in some recondite sense; ontological in such a homely and compelling sense that perhaps a child might intuit the principles which the critic will arrive at analytically, and with much labor.

I must stop at this point, since I am desired not so much to anticipate the critic as to present him. In conclusion I will remark that the critic will doubtless work empirically, and set up his philosophy only as the drift of his findings compel him. But ultimately he will be compelled. He will have to subscribe to an ontology. If he is a sound critic his ontology will be that of his poets; and what is that? I suggest that the poetic world-view is Aristotelian and "realistic" rather than Platonic and "idealistic." He cannot follow the poets and still conceive himself as inhabiting the rational or "tidy" universe that is supposed by the scientists.

# Keats's Sylvan Historian: History Without Footnotes*

## 1942

*"It was possible to know everything about a literary work except why it was literature," an essayist once complained, reflecting on his university education in English. Indeed, until the early 1940's the typical academic approaches were historical, social, biographical, philosophical, psychological, mimetic, and moral, in any combination. The New Criticism seemed to be a liberation, a fresh new way of studying literature by returning to the words on the printed page, to the text itself. Although various of the New Critics differed from one another in particulars, the general direction was clear. The task of the critic and the teacher of literature was to analyze and describe objectively the formal properties of a literary text by a close, detailed reading, without regard to extrinsic considerations.*

*The principal exponents of this critical movement were American university professors such as John Crowe Ransom (see p. 450), Cleanth Brooks, Robert Penn Warren, W. K. Wimsatt, and Allen Tate, whose influential essays and books—including textbooks—redirected the study and teaching of literature for an entire generation. They rejected the idea of the work as an expression of a specific time and place; they rejected the idea of authorial intention, considered a Romantic fallacy; and they rejected the idea that a literary work was to be studied as an expression of its author's personality. As formalist critics, they were concerned only with the poem as poem, with an analysis of its form,*

---

From *The Well Wrought Urn,* copyright 1947, 1975 by Cleanth Brooks. Reprinted by permission of Harcourt Brace Jovanovich, Inc.

*structure, and imagery. The only relevant history was the historical meanings of words, including their connotations.*

*New terms were introduced into the critical vocabulary. By "structure," the New Critics referred to the interrelationships between the parts of a poem, how the complex organization of its parts created coherent meaning not of a logical kind, such as would be found in the propositions in expository writing, but of a kind peculiar to poems, thus distinguishing poems from other verbal structures. Unity, ambiguity, irony, integrity, and paradox were some of the new terms describing desirable literary qualities.*

*Eventually overcoming the entrenched opposition of the more traditional academics, by the fifties the New Criticism, although more fruitful in the analysis of poetry than of fiction and drama, had become the principal mode in American and British universities. Less interested in evaluation than in analysis and description, the New Critics nevertheless enunciated principles which purportedly distinguished good poetry from bad, and which brought about a revaluation of literary history by upgrading seventeenth-century metaphysical poetry and largely downgrading Romantic poetry. However, by the end of the 1960's, despite the significant change of direction it had given to the study of literature, the New Criticism was becoming old hat. It was to decline into over-ingenious, self-enclosed exercises in explication, as ambiguities, ironies, and paradoxes were discovered to flourish everywhere. But its influence is still strong today, and essays by some of its original practitioners retain their capacity to illuminate, as Brooks's exemplary article demonstrates.*

THERE IS much in the poetry of Keats which suggests that he would have approved of Archibald MacLeish's dictum, "A poem should not mean/ But be." There is even some warrant for thinking that the Grecian urn (real or imagined) which inspired the famous ode was, for Keats, just such a poem, "palpable and mute," a poem in stone. Hence it is the more remarkable that the "Ode" itself differs from Keats's other odes by culminating in a statement—a statement even of some sententiousness in which the urn itself is made to say that beauty is truth, and—more sententious still—that this bit of wisdom sums up the whole of mortal knowledge.*

* This essay had been finished some months before I came upon Kenneth Burke's brilliant essay on Keats's "Ode" ("Symbolic Action in a Poem by Keats," *Accent*, Autumn, 1943). I have decided not to make any alterations, though I have been

This is "to mean" with a vengeance—to violate the doctrine of the objective correlative, not only by stating truths, but by defining the limits of truth. Small wonder that some critics have felt that the unravished bride of quietness protests too much.

T. S. Eliot, for example, says that "this line ["Beauty is truth," etc.] strikes me as a serious blemish on a beautiful poem; and the reason must be either that I fail to understand it, or that it is a statement which is untrue." But even for persons who feel that they do understand it, the line may still constitute a blemish. Middleton Murry, who, after a discussion of Keats's other poems and his letters, feels that he knows what Keats meant by "beauty" and what he meant by "truth," and that Keats used them in senses which allowed them to be properly bracketed together, still, is forced to conclude: "My own opinion concerning the value of these two lines *in the context of the poem itself* is not very different from Mr. T. S. Eliot's." The troubling assertion is apparently an intrusion upon the poem—does not grow out of it—is not dramatically accommodated to it.

This is essentially Garrod's objection, and the fact that Garrod does object indicates that a distaste for the ending of the "Ode" is by no means limited to critics of notoriously "modern" sympathies.

But the question of real importance is not whether Eliot, Murry, and Garrod are right in thinking that "Beauty is truth, truth beauty" injures the poem. The question of real importance concerns beauty and truth in a much more general way: what is the relation of the beauty (the goodness, the perfection) of a poem to the truth or falsity of what it seems to assert? It is a question which has particularly vexed our own generation—to give it I. A. Richards' phrasing, it is the problem of belief.

The "Ode," by its bold equation of beauty and truth, raises this question in its sharpest form—the more so when it becomes apparent that the poem itself is obviously intended to be a parable on the nature of poetry, and of art in general. The "Ode" has apparently been an enigmatic parable, to be sure: one can emphasize *beauty* is

---

tempted to adopt some of Burke's insights, and, in at least one case, his essay has convinced me of a point which I had considered but rejected—the pun on "breed" and "Brede."

I am happy to find that two critics with methods and purposes so different should agree so thoroughly as we do on the poem. I am pleased, for my part, therefore, to acknowledge the amount of duplication which exists between the two essays, counting it as rather important corroboration of a view of the poem which will probably seem to some critics overingenious. In spite of the common elements, however, I feel that the emphasis of my essay is sufficiently different from Burke's to justify my going on with its publication.

truth and throw Keats into the pure-art camp, the usual procedure. But it is only fair to point out that one could stress *truth* is beauty, and argue with the Marxist critics of the 'thirties for a propaganda art. The very ambiguity of the statement, "Beauty is truth, truth beauty" ought to warn us against insisting very much on the statement in isolation, and to drive us back to a consideration of the context in which the statement is set.

It will not be sufficient, however, if it merely drives us back to a study of Keats's reading, his conversation, his letters. We shall not find our answer there even if scholarship does prefer on principle investigations of Browning's ironic question, "What porridge had John Keats?" For even if we knew just what porridge he had, physical and mental, we should still not be able to settle the problem of the "Ode." The reason should be clear: our specific question is not what did Keats the man perhaps want to assert here about the relation of beauty and truth; it is rather: was Keats the poet able to exemplify that relation in this particular poem? Middleton Murry is right: the relation of the final statement in the poem to the total context is all-important.

Indeed, Eliot, in the very passage in which he attacks the "Ode" has indicated the general line which we are to take in its defense. In that passage, Eliot goes on to contrast the closing lines of the "Ode" with a line from *King Lear*, "Ripeness is all." Keats's lines strike him as false; Shakespeare's, on the other hand, as not clearly false, and as possibly quite true. Shakespeare's generalization, in other words, avoids raising the question of truth. But is it really a question of truth and falsity? One is tempted to account for the difference of effect which Eliot feels in this way: "Ripeness is all" is a statement put in the mouth of a dramatic character and a statement which is governed and qualified by the whole context of the play. It does not directly challenge an examination into its truth because its relevance is pointed up and modified by the dramatic context.

Now, suppose that one could show that Keats's lines, *in quite the same way*, constitute a speech, a consciously riddling paradox, put in the mouth of a particular character, and modified by the total context of the poem. If we could demonstrate that the speech was "in character," was dramatically appropriate, was properly prepared for—then would not the lines have all the justification of "Ripeness is all"? In such case, should we not have waived the question of the scientific or philosophic truth of the lines in favor of the application of a principle curiously like that of dramatic propriety? I suggest that some such principle is the only one legitimately to be invoked in any case. Be this as it may, the "Ode on a Grecian Urn" provides us with as neat an instance as one could wish in order to test the implications of such a maneuver.

It has seemed best to be perfectly frank about procedure: the poem is to be read in order to see whether the last lines of the poem are not, after all, dramatically prepared for. Yet there are some claims to be made upon the reader too, claims which he, for his part, will have to be prepared to honor. He must not be allowed to dismiss the early characterizations of the urn as merely so much vaguely beautiful description. He must not be too much surprised if "mere decoration" turns out to be meaningful symbolism—or if ironies develop where he has been taught to expect only sensuous pictures. Most of all, if the teasing riddle spoken finally by the urn is not to strike him as a bewildering break in tone, he must not be too much disturbed to have the element of paradox latent in the poem emphasized, even in those parts of the poem which have none of the energetic crackle of wit with which he usually associates paradox. This is surely not too much to ask of the reader—namely, to assume that Keats meant what he said and that he chose his words with care. After all, the poem begins on a note of paradox, though a mild one: for we ordinarily do not expect an urn to speak at all; and yet, Keats does more than this: he begins his poem by emphasizing the apparent contradiction.

The silence of the urn is stressed—it is a "bride of quietness"; it is a "foster-child of silence," but the urn is a "historian" too. Historians tell the truth, or are at least expected to tell the truth. What is a "Sylvan historian"? A historian who is like the forest rustic, a woodlander? Or, a historian who writes histories of the forest? Presumably, the urn is sylvan in both senses. True, the latter meaning is uppermost: the urn can "express/ A flowery tale more sweetly than our rhyme," and what the urn goes on to express is a "leaf-fring'd legend" of "Tempe or the dales of Arcady." But the urn, like the "leaf-fring'd legend" which it tells, is covered with emblems of the fields and forests: "Overwrought,/ With forest branches and the trodden weed." When we consider the way in which the urn utters its history, the fact that it must be sylvan in both senses is seen as inevitable. Perhaps too the fact that it is a rural historian, a rustic, a peasant historian, qualifies in our minds the dignity and the "truth" of the histories which it recites. Its histories, Keats has already conceded, may be characterized as "tales"—not formal history at all.

The sylvan historian certainly supplies no names and dates—"What men or gods are these?" the poet asks. What it does give is action—of men *or* gods, of godlike men or of superhuman (though not daemonic) gods—action, which is not the less intense for all that the urn is cool marble. The words "mad" and "ecstasy" occur, but it is the quiet, rigid urn which gives the dynamic picture. And the paradox goes further: the scene is one of violent love-making, a Bacchanalian scene, but the urn itself is like a "still unravish'd bride," or like a child, a child "of silence and slow time." It is not merely like a child, but like a "foster-child." The exactness of the term can be defended. "Silence and slow time," it is suggested, are not the true parents, but foster-parents. They are too old, one feels, to have borne the child themselves. Moreover, they dote upon the "child" as grandparents do. The urn is fresh and unblemished; it is still young, for all its antiquity, and time which destroys so much has "fostered" it.

With Stanza II we move into the world presented by the urn, into an examination, not of the urn as a whole—as an entity with its own form—but of the details which overlay it. But as we enter that world, the paradox of silent speech is carried on, this time in terms of the objects portrayed on the vase.

The first lines of the stanza state a rather bold paradox—even the dulling effect of many readings has hardly blunted it. At least we can easily revive its sharpness. Attended to with care, it is a statement which is preposterous, and yet true—true on the same level on which the original metaphor of the speaking urn is true. The unheard music is sweeter than any audible music. The poet has rather cunningly enforced his conceit by using the phrase, "ye soft pipes." Actually, we might accept the poet's metaphor without being forced to accept the adjective "soft." The pipes might, although "unheard," be shrill, just as the action which is frozen in the figures on the urn can be violent and ecstatic as in Stanza I and slow and dignified as in Stanza IV (the procession to the sacrifice). Yet, by characterizing the pipes as "soft," the poet has provided a sort of realistic basis for his metaphor: the pipes, it is suggested, are playing very softly; if we listen carefully, we can hear them; their music is just below the threshold of normal sound.

The general paradox runs through the stanza: action goes on though the actors are motionless; the song will not cease; the lover cannot leave his song; the maiden, always to be kissed, never actually kissed, will remain changelessly beautiful. The maiden is, indeed, like the urn itself, a "still unravished bride of quietness"—not even ravished by a kiss; and it is implied, perhaps, that her changeless beauty, like that of the urn, springs from this fact.

The poet is obviously stressing the fresh, unwearied charm of the scene itself which can defy time and is deathless. But, at the same time, the poet is being perfectly fair to the terms of his metaphor. The beauty portrayed is deathless because it is lifeless. And it would be possible to shift the tone easily and ever so slightly by insisting more heavily on some of the phrasings so as to give them a darker implication. Thus, in the case of "thou canst not leave/ Thy song," one could interpret: the musician cannot leave the song even if he would: he is fettered to it, a prisoner. In the same way, one could enlarge on the hint that the lover is not wholly satisfied and content: "never canst thou kiss,/ . . . yet, do not grieve." These items are mentioned here, not because one wishes to maintain that the poet is bitterly ironical, but because it is important for us to see that even here the paradox is being used fairly, particularly in view of the shift in tone which comes in the next stanza.

This third stanza represents, as various critics have pointed out, a recapitulation of earlier motifs. The boughs which cannot shed their leaves, the unwearied melodist, and the ever-ardent lover reappear. Indeed, I am not sure that this stanza can altogether be defended against the charge that it represents a falling-off from the delicate but firm precision of the earlier stanzas. There is a tendency to linger over the scene sentimentally: the repetition of the word "happy" is perhaps symptomatic of what is occurring. Here, if anywhere, in my opinion, is to be found the blemish on the ode—not in the last two lines. Yet, if we are to attempt a defense of the third stanza, we shall come nearest success by emphasizing the paradoxical implications of the repeated items; for whatever development there is in the stanza inheres in the increased stress on the paradoxical element. For example, the boughs cannot "bid the Spring adieu," a phrase which repeats "nor ever can those trees be bare," but the new line strengthens the implications of speaking: the falling leaves are a gesture, a word of farewell to the joy of spring. The melodist of Stanza II played sweeter music because unheard, but here, in the third stanza, it is implied that he does not tire of his song for the same reason that the lover does not tire of his love—neither song nor love is consummated. The songs are "for ever new" because they cannot be completed.

The paradox is carried further in the case of the lover whose love is "For ever warm and still to be enjoy'd." We are really dealing with an ambiguity here, for we can take "still to be enjoy'd" as an adjectival phrase on the same level as "warm"—that is, "still virginal and warm." But the tenor of the whole poem suggests that the warmth of the love depends upon the fact that it has not been enjoyed—that is, "warm and still to be enjoy'd" may mean also "warm *because* still to be enjoy'd."

But though the poet has developed and extended his metaphors furthest here in this third stanza, the ironic counterpoise is developed furthest too. The love which a line earlier was "warm" and "panting" becomes suddenly in the next line, "All breathing human passion far above." But if it is *above* all breathing passion, it is, after all, outside the realm of breathing passion, and therefore, not human passion at all.

(If one argues that we are to take "All breathing human passion" as qualified by "That leaves a heart high-sorrowful and cloy'd"—that is, if one argues that Keats is saying that the love depicted on the urn is above only that human passion which leaves one cloyed and not above human passion in general, he misses the point. For Keats in the "Ode" is stressing the ironic fact that all human passion *does* leave one cloyed; hence the superiority of art.)

The purpose in emphasizing the ironic undercurrent in the foregoing lines is not at all to disparage Keats—to point up implications of his poem of which he was himself unaware. Far from it: the poet knows precisely what he is doing. The point is to be made simply in order to make sure that we are completely aware of what he *is* doing. Garrod, sensing this ironic undercurrent, seems to interpret it as an element over which Keats was not able to exercise full control. He says: "Truth to his main theme [the fixity given by art to forms which in life are impermanent] has taken Keats farther than he meant to go. The pure and ideal art of this 'cold Pastoral,' this 'silent form,' *has* a cold silentness which in some degree saddens him. In the last lines of the fourth stanza, especially the last three lines . . . every reader is conscious, I should suppose, of an undertone of sadness, of disappointment." The undertone is there, but Keats has not been taken "farther than he meant to go." Keats's attitude, even in the early stanzas, is more complex than Garrod would allow: it is more complex and more ironic, and a recognition of this is important if we are to be able to relate the stanza to the rest of the "Ode." Keats is perfectly aware that the frozen moment of loveliness is more dynamic than is the fluid world of reality *only* because it is frozen. The love depicted on the urn remains warm and young because it is not human flesh at all but cold, ancient marble.

With Stanza IV, we are still within the world depicted by the urn, but the scene presented in this stanza forms a contrast to the earlier scenes. It emphasizes, not individual aspiration and desire, but communal life. It constitutes another chapter in the history that the "Sylvan historian" has to tell. And again, names and dates have been omitted. We are not told to what god's altar the procession moves, nor the occasion of the sacrifice.

Moreover, the little town from which the celebrants come is unknown; and the poet rather goes out of his way to leave us the widest possible option in locating it. It may be a mountain town, or a river town, or a tiny seaport. Yet, of course, there is a sense in which the nature of the town—the essential character of the town—is actually suggested by the figured urn. But it is not given explicitly. The poet is willing to leave much to our imaginations; and yet the stanza in its organization of imagery and rhythm does describe the town clearly enough; it is small, it is quiet, its people are knit together as an organic whole, and on a "pious morn" such as this, its whole population has turned out to take part in the ritual.

The stanza has been justly admired. Its magic of effect defies reduction to any formula. Yet, without pretending to "account" for the effect in any mechanical fashion, one can point to some of the elements active in securing the effect: there is the suggestiveness of the word "green" in "green altar"—something natural, spontaneous, living; there is the suggestion that the little town is caught in a curve of the seashore, or nestled in a fold of the mountains—at any rate, is something secluded and something naturally related to its terrain; there is the effect of the phrase "peaceful citadel," a phrase which involves a clash between the ideas of war and peace and resolves it in the sense of stability and independence without imperialistic ambition—the sense of stable repose.

But to return to the larger pattern of the poem: Keats does something in this fourth stanza which is highly interesting in itself and thoroughly relevant to the sense in which the urn is a historian. One of the most moving passages in the poem is that in which the poet speculates on the strange emptiness of the little town which, of course, has not been pictured on the urn at all.

The little town which has been merely implied by the procession portrayed on the urn is endowed with a poignance beyond anything else in the poem. Its streets "for evermore/ Will silent be," its desolation forever shrouded in a mystery. No one in the figured procession will ever be able to go back to the town to break the silence there, not even one to tell the stranger there why the town remains desolate.

If one attends closely to what Keats is doing here, he may easily come to feel that the poet is indulging himself in an ingenious fancy, an indulgence, however, which is gratuitous and finally silly; that is, the poet has created in his own imagination the town implied by the procession of worshipers, has given it a special character of desolation and loneliness, and then has gone on to treat it as if it were a real town to which a stranger might actually come and be puzzled by its emptiness. (I can see no other interpretation of the lines, "and not a soul to tell/ Why thou art desolate can e'er return." But, actually, of course, no one will ever discover the town except by the very same process by which Keats has discovered it: namely, through the figured urn, and then, of course, he will not need to ask why it is empty. One can well imagine what a typical eighteenth-century critic would have made of this flaw in logic.

It will not be too difficult, however, to show that Keats's extension of the fancy is not irrelevant to the poem as a whole. The "reality" of the little town has a very close relation to the urn's character as a historian. If the earlier stanzas have been concerned with such paradoxes as the ability of static carving to convey dynamic action, of the soundless pipes to play music sweeter than that of the heard melody, of the figured lover to have a love more warm and panting than that of breathing flesh and blood, so in the same way the town implied by the urn comes to have a richer and more important history than that of actual cities. Indeed, the imagined town is to the figured procession as the unheard melody is to the carved pipes of the unwearied melodist. And the poet, by pretending to take the town as real—so real that he can imagine the effect of its silent streets upon the stranger who chances to come into it—has suggested in the most powerful way possible its essential reality for him—and for us. It is a case of the doctor's taking his own medicine: the poet is prepared to stand by the illusion of his own making.

With Stanza V we move back out of the enchanted world portrayed by the urn to consider the urn itself once more as a whole, as an object. The shift in point of view is marked with the first line of the stanza by the apostrophe, "O Attic shape . . ." It is the urn itself as a formed thing, as an autonomous world, to which the poet addresses these last words. And the rich, almost breathing world which the poet has conjured up for us contracts and hardens into the decorated motifs on the urn itself: "with brede/ Of marble men and maidens overwrought." The beings who have a life above life—"All breathing human passion far above"—are marble, after all.

This last is a matter which, of course, the poet has never denied. The recognition that the men and maidens are frozen, fixed, arrested, has, as we have already seen, run through the second, third, and fourth stanzas as an ironic undercurrent. The central paradox of the poem, thus, comes to conclusion in the phrase, "Cold Pastoral." The word "pastoral" suggests warmth, spontaneity, the natural and the informal as well as the idyllic, the simple, and the informally charming. What the urn tells is a "flowery tale," a "leaf-fring'd legend," but the "sylvan historian" works in terms of marble. The urn itself is cold, and the life beyond life which it expresses is life which has been formed, arranged. The urn itself is a "silent form," and it speaks, not by means of statement, but by "teasing us out of thought." It is as enigmatic as eternity is, for, like eternity, its history is beyond time, outside time, and for this very reason bewilders our time-ridden minds: it teases us.

The marble men and maidens of the urn will not age as flesh-and-blood men and women will: "When old age shall this generation waste." (The word "generation," by the way, is very rich. It means on one level "that which is generated"—that which springs from human loins—Adam's breed; and yet, so intimately is death wedded to men, the word "generation" itself has become, as here, a measure of time.) The marble men and women lie outside time. The urn which they adorn will remain. The "Sylvan historian" will recite its history to other generations.

What will it say to them? Presumably, what it says to the poet now: that "formed experience," imaginative insight, embodies the basic and fundamental perception of man and nature. The urn is beautiful, and yet its beauty is based—what else is the poem concerned with?—on an imaginative perception of essentials. Such a vision is beautiful but it is also true. The sylvan historian presents us with beautiful histories, but they are true histories, and it is a good historian.

Moveover, the "truth" which the sylvan historian gives is the only kind of truth which we are likely to get on this earth, and, furthermore, it is the only kind that we *have* to have. The names, dates, and special circumstances, the wealth of data—these the sylvan historian quietly ignores. But we shall never get all the facts anyway—there is no end to the accumulation of facts. Moreover, mere accumulations of facts—a point our own generation is only beginning to realize—are meaningless. The sylvan historian does better than that: it takes a few details and so orders them that we have not only beauty but insight into essential truth. Its "history," in short, is a history without footnotes. It has the validity of myth—not myth as a pretty but irrelevant make-believe, an idle fancy, but myth as a valid perception into reality.

So much for the "meaning" of the last lines of the "Ode." It is an interpretation which differs little from past interpretations. It is put forward here with no pretension to novelty. What is important is the fact that it can be derived from the context of the "Ode" itself.

And now, what of the objection that the final lines break the tone of the poem with a display of misplaced sententiousness? One can summarize the answer already implied thus: throughout the poem the poet has stressed the paradox of the speaking urn. First, the urn itself can tell a story, can give a history. Then, the various figures depicted upon the urn play music or speak or sing. If we have been alive to these items, we shall not, perhaps, be too much surprised to have the urn speak once more, not in the sense in which it tells a story—a metaphor which is rather easy to accept—but, to have it speak on a higher level, to have it make a commentary on its own nature. If the urn has been properly dramatized, if we have followed the development of the metaphors, if we have been alive to the paradoxes which work throughout the poem, perhaps then, we shall be prepared for the enigmatic, final paradox which the "silent form" utters. But in that case, we shall not feel that the generalization, unqualified and to be taken literally, is meant to march out of its context to compete with the scientific and philosophical generalizations which dominate our world.

"Beauty is truth, truth beauty" has precisely the same status, and the same justification as Shakespeare's "Ripeness is all." It is a speech "in character" and supported by a dramatic context.

To conclude thus may seem to weight the principle of dramatic propriety with more than it can bear. This would not be fair to the complexity of the problem of truth in art nor fair to Keats's little parable. Granted; and yet the principle of dramatic propriety may take us further than would first appear. Respect for it may at least insure our dealing with the problem of truth at the level on which it is really relevant to literature. If we can see that the assertions made in a poem are to be taken as part of an organic context, if we can resist the temptation to deal with them in isolation, then we may be willing to go on to deal with the world-view, or "philosophy," or "truth" of the *poem as a whole* in terms of its dramatic wholeness: that is, we shall not neglect the maturity of attitude, the dramatic tension, the emotional *and* intellectual coherence in favor of some statement of theme abstracted from it by paraphrase. Perhaps, best of all, we might learn to distrust our ability to represent any poem adequately by paraphrase. Such a distrust is healthy. Keats's sylvan historian, who is not above "teasing" us, exhibits such a distrust, and perhaps the point of what the sylvan historian "says" is to confirm us in our distrust.

# Why Write?

## 1949

*Two key terms in Sartre's essay that have distinct moral overtones should be noted in his opening paragraph: "choice" and "engagement." Other terms later in the essay—"freedom," "commitment," "responsibility," "faith"—also refer to the special relationship between writer and reader, for Sartre's concern is the obligation of one to the other and the result of their unique form of collaboration. The most widely known and influential of the French Existentialists who sprang into prominence after World War II, Sartre, a prolific philosopher, critic, playwright, and novelist, generally posits a point of view that denies traditional idealistic, religious, or psychological conceptions (for example, the existence of anything that might be called "human nature"). The famous formula "existence precedes essence" implies that man is nothing except what he makes of himself through a series of successive actions. In a universe to which he is bound but where he is nevertheless alone, each individual is responsible for the meaning of his own life. The consciousness of this freedom of choice creates a terrible burden, but the absurd situation is that the individual must always make choices in order to achieve the "authentic existence," for choice is both necessary and inevitable.*

*Sartre's version of existential thought has particular implications for the world of literature. The act of writing, like every other human act, involves choice as well as consequences; the act of reading involves the reader's temporary surrender of his freedom. Thus the transaction between writer and reader is an active collaboration: the work is both a tool for the reader in his search for freedom and a means of achieving freedom for the writer. The meaning of "engagement" may be grasped if one considers the "dialectical paradox" by which a work is created, according to Sartre. Since the writer does not write for himself alone, his own freedom is achieved in the relationship with his reader. It is worthwhile to analyze the basis for his statement: "the more we experience our freedom, the more we recognize that of the other; the more he demands of us, the more we demand of him."*

*In the light of this reciprocal relationship, Sartre's comments on other topics should also be noted. Why does he regard both "flight" and "conquering" as abuses of the nature of art? How do his statements on the dispassionate act of writing compare with Eliot's theory that, for the poet, poetry is an escape from emotion? Also, consider why Sartre rejects the concept of "gloomy literature." What is the basis for his distinction between good and bad novels? And what are the political implications of his philosophical theory of literature?*

EACH ONE has his reasons: for one, art is a flight; for another, a means of conquering. But one can flee into a hermitage, into madness, into death. One can conquer by arms. Why does it have to be *writing*, why does one have to manage his escapes and conquests by *writing*? Because, behind the various aims of authors, there is a deeper and more immediate choice which is common to all of us. We shall try to elucidate this choice, and we shall see whether it is not in the name of this very choice of writing that the engagement of writers must be required.

Each of our perceptions is accompanied by the consciousness that human reality is a "revealer," that is, it is through human reality that "there is" being, or, to put it differently, that man is the means by which things are manifested. It is our presence in the world which multiplies relations. It is we who set up a relationship between this tree and that bit of sky. Thanks to us, that star which has been dead for millennia, that quarter moon, and that dark river are disclosed in the unity of a landscape. It is the speed of our auto and our airplane which organizes the great masses of the earth. With each of our acts, the world reveals to us a new face. But, if we know that we are directors of being, we also know that we are not its producers. If we turn away from this landscape, it will sink back into its dark permanence. At least, it will sink back; there is no one mad enough to think that it is going to be annihilated. It is we who shall be annihilated, and the earth will remain in its lethargy until another consciousness comes along to awaken it. Thus, to our inner certainty of being "revealers" is added that of being inessential in relation to the thing revealed.

One of the chief motives of artistic creation is certainly the need of feeling that we are essential in relationship to the world. If I fix on canvas or in writing a certain aspect of the fields or the sea or a look on someone's face which I have disclosed, I am conscious of having produced them by condensing relationships, by introducing order where there was none, by imposing the unity of mind on the diversity of things. That is, I feel myself essential in relation to my creation. But this time it is the created object which escapes me; I can not reveal and produce at the same time. The creation becomes inessential in relation to the creative activity. First of all, even if it appears to others as definitive, the created object always seems to us in a state of suspension; we can always change this line, that shade, that word. Thus, it never *forces itself.* A novice painter asked his teacher, "When should I consider my painting finished?" And the teacher answered, "When you can look at it in amazement and say to yourself '*I'm* the one who did *that!*'"

Which amounts to saying "never." For it is virtually considering one's work with someone else's eyes and revealing what one has created. But it is self-evident that we are proportionally less conscious of the thing produced and more conscious of our productive activity. When it is a matter of pottery or carpentry, we work according to traditional norms, with tools whose usage is codified; it is Heidegger's famous "they" who are working with our hands. In this case, the result can seem to us sufficiently strange to preserve its objectivity in our eyes. But if we ourselves produce the rules of production, the measures, the criteria, and if our creative drive comes from the very depths of our heart, then we never find anything but ourselves in our work. It is we who have invented the laws by which we judge it. It is our history, our love, our gaiety that we recognize in it. Even if we should regard it without touching it any further, we never *receive* from it that gaiety or love. We put them into it. The results which we have obtained on canvas or paper never seem to us *objective.* We are too familiar with the processes of which they are the effects. These processes remain a subjective discovery; they are ourselves, our inspiration, our ruse, and when we seek to *perceive* our work, we create it again, we repeat mentally the operations which produced it; each of its aspects appears as a result. Thus, in the perception, the object is given as the essential thing and the subject as the inessential. The latter seeks essentiality in the creation and obtains it, but then it is the object which becomes the inessential.

This dialectic is nowhere more apparent than in the art of writing, for the literary object is a peculiar top which exists only in movement. To make it come into view a concrete act called reading is necessary, and it lasts only as long as this act can last. Beyond that, there are only black marks on paper. Now, the writer can not read what he writes, whereas the shoemaker can put on the shoes he has just made if they are his size, and the architect can live in the house he has built. In, reading, one foresees; one waits. He foresees the end of the sentence, the following sentence, the next page. He waits for them to confirm or disappoint his foresights. The reading is composed of a host of hypotheses, of dreams followed by awakenings, of hopes and deceptions. Readers are always ahead of the sentence they are reading in a merely probable future which partly collapses and partly comes together in proportion as they progress, which withdraws from one page to the next and forms the moving horizon of the literary object. Without waiting, without a future, without ignorance, there is no objectivity.

Now the operation of writing involves an implicit quasi-reading which makes real reading impossible. When the words form under his pen, the author doubtless sees them, but he does not see them as the reader does, since he knows them before writing them down. The function of his gaze is not to reveal, by stroking them, the sleeping words which are waiting to be read, but to control the sketching of the signs. In short, it is a purely regulating mission, and the view before him reveals nothing except for slight slips of the pen. The writer neither foresees nor conjectures; he *projects*. It often happens that he awaits, as they say, the inspiration. But one does not wait for himself the way he waits for others. If he hesitates, he knows that the future is not made, that he himself is going to make it, and if he still does not know what is going to happen to his hero, that simply means that he has not thought about it, that he has not decided upon anything. The future is then a blank page, whereas the future of the reader is two hundred pages filled with words which separate him from the end. Thus, the writer meets everywhere only *his* knowledge, *his* will, *his* plans, in short, himself. He touches only his own subjectivity; the object he creates is out of reach; he does not create it *for himself*. If he rereads himself, it is already too late. The sentence will never quite be a thing in his eyes. He goes to the very limits of the subjective but without crossing it. He appreciates the effect of a touch, of an epigram, of a well-placed adjective, but it is the effect they will have on others. He can judge it, not feel it. Proust never discovered the homosexuality of Charlus, since he had decided upon it even before starting on his book. And if a day comes when the book takes on for its author a semblance of objectivity, it is that years have passed, that he has forgotten it, that its spirit is quite foreign to him, and doubtless he is no longer capable of writing it. This was the case with Rousseau when he reread the *Social Contract* at the end of his life.

Thus, it is not true that one writes for himself. That would be the worst blow. In projecting his emotions on paper, one barely manages to give them a languishing extension. The creative act is only an incomplete and abstract moment in the production of a work. If the author existed alone he would be able to write as much as he liked; the work as *object* would never see the light of day and he would either have to put down his pen or despair. But the operation of writing implies that of reading as its dialectical correlative and these two connected acts necessitate two distinct agents. It is the conjoint effort of author and reader which brings upon the scene that concrete and imaginary object which is the work of the mind. There is no art except for and by others.

Reading seems, in fact, to be the synthesis of perception and creation.[1] It supposes the essentiality of both the subject and the object. The object is essential because it is strictly transcendent, because it imposes its own structures, and because one must wait for it and observe it; but the subject is also essential because it is required not only to disclose the object (that is, to make *there be* an object) but also so that this object might *be* (that is, to produce it). In a word, the reader is conscious of disclosing in creating, of creating by disclosing. In reality, it is not necessary to believe that reading is a mechanical operation and that signs make an impression upon him as light does on a photographic plate. If he is inattentive, tired, stupid, or thoughtless, most of the relations will escape him. He will never manage to "catch on" to the object (in the sense in which we see that fire "catches" or "doesn't catch"). He will draw some phrases out of the shadow, but they will seem to appear as random strokes. If he is at his best, he will project beyond the words a synthetic form, each phrase of which will be no more than a partial function: the "theme," the "subject," or the "meaning." Thus, from the very beginning, the meaning is no longer contained in the words, since it is he, on the contrary, who allows the signification of each of them to be understood; and the literary object,

---

[1] The same is true in different degrees regarding the spectator's attitude before other works of art (paintings, symphonies, statues, etc.).

though realized *through* language, is never given *in* language. On the contrary, it is by nature a silence and an opponent of the word. In addition, the hundred thousand words aligned in a book can be read one by one so that the meaning of the work does not emerge. Nothing is accomplished if the reader does not put himself from the very beginning and almost without a guide at the height of this silence; if, in short, he does not invent it and does not then place there, and hold on to, the words and sentences which he awakens. And if I am told that it would be more fitting to call this operation a re-invention or a discovery, I shall answer that, first, such a re-invention would be as new and as original an act as the first invention. And, especially, when an object has never existed before, there can be no question of re-inventing it or discovering it. For if the silence about which I am speaking is really the goal at which the author is aiming, he has, at least, never been familiar with it; his silence is subjective and anterior to language. It is the absence of words, the undifferentiated and lived silence of inspiration, which the word will then particularize, whereas the silence produced by the reader is an object. And at the very interior of this object there are more silences—which the author does not tell. It is a question of silences which are so particular that they could not retain any meaning outside of the object which the reading causes to appear. However, it is these which give it its density and its particular face.

To say that they are unexpressed is hardly the word; for they are precisely the inexpressible. And that is why one does not come upon them at any definite moment in the reading; they are everywhere and nowhere. The quality of the marvelous in *The Wanderer* (*Le Grand Meaulnes*), the grandiosity of *Armance,* the degree of realism and truth of Kafka's mythology, these are never given. The reader must invent them all in a continual exceeding of the written thing. To be sure, the author guides him, but all he does is guide him. The landmarks he sets up are separated by the void. The reader must unite them; he must go beyond them. In short, reading is directed creation.

On the one hand, the literary object has no other substance than the reader's subjectivity; Raskolnikov's waiting is *my* waiting which I lend him. Without this impatience of the reader he would remain only a collection of signs. His hatred of the police magistrate who questions him is my hatred which has been solicited and wheedled out of me by signs, and the police magistrate himself would not exist without the hatred I have for him via Raskolnikov. That is what animates him, it is his very flesh.

But on the other hand, the words are there like traps to arouse our feelings and to reflect them toward us. Each word is a path of transcendence; it shapes our feelings, names them, and attributes them to an imaginary personage who takes it upon himself to live them for us and who has no other substance than these borrowed passions; he confers objects, perspectives, and a horizon upon them.

Thus, for the reader, all is to do and all is already done; the work exists only at the exact level of his capacities; while he reads and creates, he knows that he can always go further in his reading, can always create more profoundly, and thus the work seems to him as inexhaustible and opaque as things. We would readily reconcile that "rational intuition" which Kant reserved to divine Reason with this absolute production of qualities, which, to the extent that they emanate from our subjectivity, congeal before our eyes into impermeable objectivities.

Since the creation can find its fulfillment only in reading, since the artist must entrust to another the job of carrying out what he has begun, since it is only through the consciousness of the reader that he can regard himself as essential to his work, all literary work is an appeal. To write is to make an appeal to the reader that he lead into objective existence the revelation which I have undertaken by means of language. And if it should be asked *to what* the writer is appealing, the answer is simple. As the sufficient reason for the appearance of the aesthetic object is never found either in the book (where we find merely solicitations to produce the object) or in the author's mind, and as his subjectivity, which he cannot get away from, cannot give a reason for the act of leading into objectivity, the appearance of the work of art is a new event which cannot *be explained* by anterior data. And since this directed creation is an absolute beginning, it is therefore brought about by the freedom of the reader, and by what is purest in that freedom. Thus, the writer appeals to the reader's freedom to collaborate in the production of his work.

It will doubtless be said that all tools address themselves to our freedom since they are the instruments of a possible action, and that the work of art is not unique in that. And it is true that the tool is the congealed outline of an operation. But it remains on the level of the hypothetical imperative. I may use a hammer to nail up a case or to hit my neighbor over the head. Insofar as I consider it in itself, it is not an appeal to my freedom; it does not put me face to face with it; rather, it aims at using it by substituting a set succession of traditional procedures for the free invention of means. The book does not serve my freedom; it requires it. Indeed, one cannot address himself to freedom as such by means of constraint, fascination, or entreaties. There is only one way of attaining it; first, by recognizing it, then, having confidence in it, and finally, requiring of it an act, an act in its own name, that is, in the name of the confidence that one brings to it.

Thus, the book is not, like the tool, a means for any end whatever; the end to which it offers itself is the reader's freedom. And the Kantian expression "finality without end" seems to me quite inappropriate for designating the work of art. In fact, it implies that the aesthetic object presents only the appearance of a finality and is limited to soliciting the free and ordered play of the imagination. It forgets that the imagination of the spectator has not only a regulating function, but a constitutive one. It does not play; it is called upon to recompose the beautiful object beyond the traces left by the artist. The imagination can not revel in itself any more than can the other functions of the mind; it is always on the outside, always engaged in an enterprise. There would be finality without end if some object offered such a set ordering that it would lead us to suppose that it has one even though we cannot ascribe one to it. By defining the beautiful in this way one can—and this is Kant's aim—liken the beauty of art to natural beauty, since a flower, for example, presents so much symmetry, such harmonious colors, and such regular curves, that one is immediately tempted to seek a finalist explanation for all these properties and to see them as just so many means at the disposal of an unknown end. But that is exactly the error. The beauty of nature is in no way comparable to that of art. The work of art *does not have* an end; there we agree with Kant. But the reason is that it is an end. The Kantian formula does not account for the appeal which resounds at the basis of each painting, each statue, each book. Kant believes that the work of art first exists as fact and that it is then seen. Whereas, it exists only if one *looks* at it and if it is first pure appeal, pure exigence to exist. It is not an instrument whose existence is manifest and whose end is undetermined. It presents itself as a task to be discharged; from the very beginning it places itself on the level of the categorical imperative. You are perfectly free to leave that book on the table. But if you open it, you assume responsibility for it. For freedom is not experienced by its enjoying its free subjective functioning, but in a creative act required by an imperative. This absolute end, this imperative which is transcendent yet acquiesced in, which freedom itself adopts as its own, is what we call a value. The work of art is a value because it is an appeal.

If I appeal to my readers so that we may carry the enterprise which I have begun to a successful conclusion, it is self-evident that I consider him as a pure freedom, as an unconditioned activity; thus, in no case can I address myself to his passivity, that is, try to *affect* him, to communicate to him, from the very first, emotions of fear, desire, or anger. There are, doubtless, authors who concern themselves solely with arousing these emotions because they are foreseeable, manageable, and because they have at their disposal sure-fire means for provoking them. But it is also true that they are reproached for this kind of thing, as Euripides has been since antiquity because he had children appear on the stage. Freedom is alienated in the state of passion; it is abruptly engaged in partial enterprises; it loses sight of its task which is to produce an absolute end. And the book is no longer anything but a means for feeding hate or desire. The writer should not seek to *overwhelm*; otherwise he is in contradiction with himself; if he wishes to *make demands* he must propose only the task to be fulfilled. Hence, the character of pure presentation which appears essential to the work of art. The reader must be able to make a certain aesthetic withdrawal. This is what Gautier foolishly confused with "art for art's sake" and the Parnassians with the imperturbability of the artist. It is simply a matter of precaution, and Genet more justly calls it the author's politeness toward the reader. But that does not mean that the writer makes an appeal to some sort of abstract and conceptual freedom. One certainly creates the aesthetic object with feelings; if it is touching, it appears through our tears; if it is comic, it will be recognized by laughter. However, these feelings are of a particular kind. They have their origin in freedom; they are loaned. The belief which I accord the tale is freely assented to. It is a Passion, in the Christian sense of the word, that is, a freedom which resolutely puts itself into a state of passivity to obtain a certain transcendent effect by this sacrifice. The reader renders himself credulous; he descends into credulity which, though it ends by enclosing him like a dream, is at every moment conscious of being free. An effort is sometimes made to force the writer into this dilemma: "Either one believes in your story, and it is intolerable, or one does not believe in it, and it is ridiculous." But the argument is absurd because the characteristic of aesthetic consciousness is to be a belief by means of engagement, by oath, a belief sustained by fidelity to one's self and to the author, a perpetually renewed choice to believe. I can awaken at every moment, and I know it; but I do not want to; reading is a free dream. So that all feelings which are exacted on the basis of this imaginary belief are like particular modulations of my freedom. Far from absorbing or masking it, they are so many different ways it has chosen to reveal itself to itself. Raskolnikov, as I have said, would only be a shadow, without the mixture of repulsion and friendship which I feel for him and which makes him live. But, by a reversal which is the characteristic of the imaginary object, it is not his behavior which excites my indignation or esteem, but my indignation and esteem which give consistency and objectivity to his behavior. Thus, the reader's feelings are never dominated by the object, and as no external reality can condition them, they have their permanent source in freedom; that is, they are all generous—for I call a feeling generous which has its origin and its end in freedom. Thus, reading is an exercise in generosity, and what the writer requires of the reader is not the application of an abstract freedom but the gift of his whole person, with his passions, his prepossessions, his sympathies, his sexual temperament, and his scale of values. Only this person will give himself generously; freedom goes through and through him and comes to transform the darkest masses of his sensibility. And as activity has rendered itself passive in order for it better to create the object, vice-versa, passivity becomes an act; the man who is reading has raised himself to the highest degree. That is why we see people who are known for their toughness shed tears at the recital of imaginary misfortunes; for the moment they have become what they would have been if they had not spent their lives hiding their freedom from themselves.

Thus, the author writes in order to address himself to the freedom of readers, and he requires it in order to make his work exist. But he does not stop there; he also requires that they return this confidence which he has given them, that they recognize his creative freedom, and that they in turn solicit it by a symmetrical and inverse appeal. Here there appears the other dialectical paradox of reading; the more we experience our freedom, the more we recognize that of the other; the more he demands of us, the more we demand of him.

When I am enchanted with a landscape, I know very well that it is not I who create it, but I also know that without me the relations which are established before my eyes among the trees, the foliage, the earth, and the grass would not exist at all. I know that I can give no reason for the appearance of finality which I discover in the assortment of hues and in the harmony of the forms and movements created by the wind. Yet, it exists; there it is before my eyes, and I can make *there be* being only if being already *is*. But even if I believe in God, I can not establish any passage, unless it be purely verbal, between the divine, universal solicitude and the particular spectacle which I am considering. To say that He made the landscape in order to charm me or that He made me the kind of person who is pleased by it is to take a question for an answer. Is the marriage of this blue and that green deliberate? How can I know? The idea of a universal providence is no guarantee of any particular intention, especially in the case under consideration, since the green of the grass is explained by biological laws, specific constants, and geographical determinism, while the reason for the blue of the water is accounted for by the depth of the river, the nature of the soil and the swiftness of the current. The assorting of the shades, if it is willed, can only be something *thrown into the bargain;* it is the meeting of two causal series, that is to say, at first sight, a fact of chance. At best, the finality remains problematic. All the relations we establish remain hypotheses; no end is proposed to us in the manner of an imperative, since none is expressly revealed as having been willed by a creator. Thus, our freedom is never *called forth* by natural beauty. Or rather, there is an appearance of order in the ensemble of the foliage, the forms, and the movements, hence, the illusion of a calling forth which seems to solicit this freedom and which disappears immediately when one regards it. Hardly have we begun to run our eyes over this arrangement, than the call disappears; we remain alone, free to tie up one color with another or with a third, to set up a relationship between the tree and the water or the tree and the sky, or the tree, the water and the sky. My freedom becomes caprice. To the extent that I establish new relationships, I remove myself further from the illusory objectivity which solicits me. I *muse* about certain motifs which are vaguely outlined by the things; the natural reality is no longer anything but a pretext for musing. Or, in that case, because I have deeply regretted that this arrangement which was momentarily perceived was not offered to me by somebody and consequently is not *real,* the result is that I fix my dream, that I transpose it to canvas or in writing. Thus, I interpose myself between the finality without end which appears in the natural spectacles and the gaze of other men. I transmit it to them. It becomes human by this transmission. Art here is a ceremony of the *gift* and the gift alone brings about the metamorphosis. It is something like the transmission of titles and powers in the matriarchate where the mother does not possess the names, but is the indispensable intermediary between uncle and nephew. Since I have captured this illusion in flight, since I lay it out for other men and have disengaged it and rethought it for them, they can consider it with confidence. It has become intentional. As for me, I remain, to be sure, at the border of the subjective and the objective without ever being able to contemplate the objective ordonnance which I transmit.

The reader, on the contrary, progresses in security. However far he may go, the author has gone farther. Whatever connections he may establish among the different parts of the book—among the chapters or the words—he has a guarantee, namely, that they have been expressly willed. As Descartes says, he can even pretend that there is a secret order among parts which seem to have no connection. The creator has preceded him along the way, and the most beautiful disorders are effects of art, that is, again order. Reading is induction, interpolation, extrapolation, and the basis of these activities rests on the reader's will, as for a long time it was believed that that of scientific induction rested on the divine will. A gentle force accompanies us and supports us from the first page to the last. That does not mean that we fathom the artist's intentions easily. They constitute, as we have said, the object of conjectures, and there is an *experience* of the reader; but these conjectures are supported by the great certainty we have that the beauties which appear in the book are never accidental. In nature, the tree and the sky harmonize only by chance; if, on the contrary, in the novel, the protagonists find themselves in a *certain* tower, in a *certain* prison, if they stroll in a *certain* garden, it is a matter both of the restitution of independent causal series (the character had a certain state of mind which was due to a succession of psychological and social events; on the other hand, he betook himself to a determined place and the layout of the city required him to cross a certain park) and of the expression of a deeper finality, for the park came into existence only *in order to* harmonize with a certain state of mind, to express it by means of things or to put it into relief by a vivid contrast, and the state of mind itself was conceived in connection with the landscape. Here it is causality which is appearance and which might be called "causality without cause," and it is the finality which is the profound reality. But if I can thus in all confidence put the order of ends under the order of causes, it is because by opening the book I am asserting that the object has its source in human freedom.

If I were to suspect the artist of having written out of passion and in passion, my confidence would immediately vanish, for it would serve no purpose to have supported the order of causes by the order of ends. The latter would be supported in its turn by a psychic causality and the work of art would end by re-entering the chain of determinism. Certainly I do not deny when I am reading that the author may be impassioned, nor even that he might have conceived the first plan of his work under the sway of passion. But his decision to write supposes that he withdraws somewhat from his feelings, in short, that he has transformed his emotions into free emotions as I do mine while reading him; that is, that he is in an attitude of generosity.

Thus, reading is a pact of generosity between author and reader. Each one trusts the other; each one counts on the other, demands of the other as much as he demands of himself. For this confidence is itself generosity. Nothing can force the author to believe that his reader will use his freedom; nothing can force the reader to believe that the author has used his. Both of them make a free decision. There is then established a dialectical going-and-coming; when I read, I make demands; if my demands are met, what I am then reading provokes me to demand more of the author, which means to demand of the author that he demand more of me. And, vice-versa, the author's demand is that I carry my demands to the highest pitch. Thus, my freedom, by revealing itself, reveals the freedom of the other.

It matters little whether the aesthetic object is the product of "realistic" art (or supposedly such) or "formal" art. At any rate, the natural relations are inverted; that tree on the first plane of the Cézanne painting first appears as the product of a causal chain. But the causality is an illusion; it will doubtless remain as a proposition as long as we look at the painting, but it will be supported by a deep finality; if the tree is placed in such a way, it is because the rest of the painting *requires* that this form and those colors be placed on the first plane. Thus, through the phenomenal causality, our gaze attains finality as the deep structure of the object, and, beyond finality, it attains human freedom as its source and original basis. Vermeer's realism is carried so far that at first it might be thought to be photographic. But if one considers the splendor of his texture, the pink and velvety glory of his little brick walls, the blue thickness of a branch of woodbine, the glazed darkness of his vestibules, the orange-colored flesh of his faces which are as polished as the stone of holy-water basins, one suddenly feels, in the pleasure that he experiences, that the finality is not so much in the forms or colors as in his material imagination. It is the very substance and temper of the things which here give the forms their reason for being. With this realist we are perhaps closest to absolute creation, since it is in the very passivity of the matter that we meet the unfathomable freedom of man.

The work is never limited to the painted, sculpted, or narrated object. Just as one perceives things only against the background of the world, so the objects represented by art appear against the background of the universe. On the background of the adventures of Fabrice are the Italy of 1820, Austria, France, the sky and stars which the Abbe Blanis consults, and finally the whole earth. If the painter presents us with a field or a vase of flowers, his paintings are windows which are open on the whole world. We follow the red path which is buried among the wheat much farther than Van Gogh has painted it, among other wheat fields, under other clouds, to the river which empties into the sea, and we extend to infinity, to the other end of the world, the deep finality which supports the existence of the field and the earth. So that, through the various objects which it produces or reproduces, the creative act aims at a total renewal of the world. Each painting, each book, is a recovery of the totality of being. Each of them presents this totality to the freedom of the spectator. For this is quite the final goal of art: to recover this world by giving it to be seen as it is, but as if it had its source in human freedom. But, since what the author creates takes on objective reality only in the eyes of the spectator, this recovery is consecrated by the ceremony of the spectacle—and particularly of reading. We are already in a better position to answer the question we raised a while ago: the writer chooses to appeal to the freedom of other men so that, by the reciprocal implications of their demands, they may re-adapt the totality of being to man and may again enclose the universe within man.

If we wish to go still further, we must bear in mind that the writer, like all other artists, aims at giving his reader a certain feeling that is customarily called aesthetic pleasure, and which I would very much rather call aesthetic joy, and that this feeling, when it appears, is a sign that the work is achieved. It is therefore fitting to examine it in the light of the preceding considerations. In effect, this joy, which is denied to the creator, insofar as he creates, becomes one with the aesthetic consciousness of the spectator, that is, in the case under consideration, of the reader. It is a complex feeling but one whose structures and condition are inseparable from one another. It is identical, at first, with the recognition of a transcendent and absolute end which, for a moment, suspends the utilitarian round of ends-means and means-ends,[2] that is, of an appeal or, what amounts to the same thing, of a value. And the positional consciousness which I take of this value is necessarily accompanied by the non-positional consciousness of my freedom, since my freedom is manifested to itself by a transcendent exigency. The recognition of freedom by itself is joy, but this structure of non-thetical consciousness implies another: since, in effect, reading is creation, my freedom does not only appear to itself as pure autonomy but as creative activity, that is, it is not limited to giving itself its own law but perceives itself as being constitutive of the object. It is on this level that the phenomenon specifically is manifested, that is, a creation wherein the created object is given *as object* to its creator. It is the sole case in which the creator gets any enjoyment out of the object he creates. And the word enjoyment which is applied to the positional consciousness of the work read indicates sufficiently that we are in the presence of an essential structure of aesthetic joy. This positional enjoyment is accompanied by the non-positional consciousness of being

[2] In *practical life* a means may be taken for an end as soon as one searches for it, and each end is revealed as a means of attaining another end.

essential in relation to an object perceived as essential. I shall call this aspect of aesthetic consciousness the feeling of security; it is this which stamps the strongest aesthetic emotions with a sovereign calm. It has its origin in the authentication of a strict harmony between subjectivity and objectivity. As, on the other hand, the aesthetic object is properly the world insofar as it is aimed at through the imaginary, aesthetic joy accompanies the positional consciousness that the world is a value, that is, a task proposed to human freedom. I shall call this the aesthetic modification of the human project, for, as usual, the world appears as the horizon of our situation, as the infinite distance which separates us from ourselves, as the synthetic totality of the given, as the undifferentiated ensemble of obstacles and implements— but never as a demand addressed to our freedom. Thus, aesthetic joy proceeds to this level of the consciousness which I take of recovering and internalizing that which is non-ego par excellence, since I transform the given into an imperative and the fact into a value. The world is *my task,* that is, the essential and freely accepted function of my freedom is to make that unique and absolute object which is the universe come into being in an unconditioned movement. And, thirdly, the preceding structures imply a pact between human freedoms, for, on the one hand, reading is a confident and exacting recognition of the freedom of the writer, and, on the other hand, aesthetic pleasure, as it is itself experienced in the form of a value, involves an absolute exigence in regard to others; every man, insofar as he is a freedom, feels the same pleasure in reading the same work. Thus, all mankind is present in its highest freedom; it sustains the being of a world which is both *its* world and the "external" world. In aesthetic joy the positional consciousness is an *image-making* consciousness of the world in its totality both as being and having to be, both as totally ours and totally foreign, and the more ours as it is the more foreign. The non-positional consciousness *really* envelops the harmonious totality of human freedoms insofar as it makes the object of a universal confidence and exigency.

To write is thus both to disclose the world and to offer it as a task to the generosity of the reader. It is to have recourse to the consciousness of others in order to make one's self be recognized as *essential* to the totality of being; it is to wish to live this essentiality by means of interposed persons; but, on the other hand, as the real world is revealed only by action, as one can feel himself in it only by exceeding it in order to change it, the novelist's universe would lack thickness if it were not discovered in a movement to transcend it. It has often been observed that an object in a story does not derive its density of existence from the number and length of the descriptions devoted to it, but from the complexity of its connections with the different characters. The more often the characters handle it, take it up, and put it down, in short, go beyond it toward their own ends, the more real will it appear. Thus, of the world of the novel, that is, the totality of men and things, we may say that in order for it to offer its maximum density the disclosure-creation by which the reader discovers it must also be an imaginary engagement in the action; in other words, the more disposed one is to change it, the more alive it will be. The error of realism has been to believe that the real reveals itself to contemplation, and that consequently one could draw an impartial picture of it. How could that be possible, since the very perception is partial, since by itself the naming is already a modification of the object? And how could the writer, who wants himself to be essential to this universe, want to be essential to the injustice which this universe comprehends? Yet, he must be; but if he accepts being the creator of injustices, it is in a movement which goes beyond them toward their abolition. As for me who read, if I create and keep alive an unjust world, I can not help making myself responsible for it. And the author's whole art is bent on obliging me to *create* what he *discloses*, therefore to compromise myself. So both of us bear the responsibility for the universe. And precisely because this universe is supported by the joint effort of our two freedoms, and because the author, with me as medium, has attempted to integrate it into the human, it must appear truly *in itself*, in its very marrow, as being shot through and through with a freedom which has taken human freedom as its end, and if it is not really the city of ends that it ought to be, it must at least be a stage along the way; in a word, it must be a becoming and it must always be considered and presented not as a crushing mass which weighs us down, but from the point of view of its going beyond toward that city of ends. However bad and hopeless the humanity which it paints may be, the work must have an air of generosity. Not, of course, that this generosity is to be expressed by means of edifying discourses and virtuous characters; it must not even be premeditated, and it is quite true that fine sentiments do not make fine books. But it must be the very warp and woof of the book, the stuff out of which the people and things are cut; whatever the subject, a sort of essential lightness must appear everywhere and remind us that the work is never a natural datum, but an *exigence* and a *gift*. And if I am given this world with its injustices, it is not so that I might contemplate them coldly, but that I might animate them with my indignation, that I might disclose them and create them with their nature as injustices, that is, as abuses to be suppressed. Thus, the

writer's universe will only reveal itself in all its depth to the examination, the admiration, and the indignation of the reader; and the generous love is a promise to maintain, and the generous indignation is a
promise to change, and the admiration a promise to imitate; although
literature is one thing and morality a quite different one, at the heart
of the aesthetic imperative we discern the moral imperative. For, since
the one who writes recognizes, by the very fact that he takes the trouble
to write, the freedom of his readers; and since the one who reads, by
the mere fact of his opening the book, recognizes the freedom of the
writer, the work of art, from whichever side you approach it, is an act
of confidence in the freedom of men. And since readers, like the author,
recognize this freedom only to demand that it manifest itself, the work
can be defined as an imaginary presentation of the world insofar as it
demands human freedom. The result of which is that there is no
"gloomy literature," since, however dark may be the colors in which
one paints the world, he paints it only so that free men may feel their
freedom as they face it. Thus, there are only good and bad novels. The
bad novel aims to please by flattering, whereas the good one is an
exigence and an act of faith. But above all, the unique point of view
from which the author can present the world to those freedoms whose
concurrence he wishes to bring about is that of a world to be impregnated always with more freedom. It would be inconceivable that this
unleashing of generosity provoked by the writer could be used to authorize an injustice, and that the reader could enjoy his freedom while
reading a work which approves or accepts or simply abstains from condemning the subjection of man by man. One can imagine a good novel
being written by an American Negro even if hatred of the whites were
spread all over it, because it is the freedom of his race that he demands
through this hatred. And, as he invites me to assume the attitude of
generosity, the moment I feel myself a pure freedom I can not bear
to identify myself with a race of oppressors. Thus, I require of all freedoms that they demand the liberation of colored people against the
white race and against myself insofar as I am a part of it, but nobody
can suppose for a moment that it is possible to write a good novel in
praise of anti-Semitism.[3] For, the moment I feel that my freedom is

---

[3] This last remark may arouse some readers. If so, I'd like to know a single good
novel whose express purpose was to serve oppression, a single good novel which has
been written against Jews, Negroes, workers, or colonial people. "But if there isn't
any, that's no reason why someone may not write one some day." But you then
admit that you are an abstract theoretician. You, not I. For it is in the name of
your abstract conception of art that you assert the possibility of a fact which has
never come into being, whereas I limit myself to proposing an explanation for a
recognized fact.

indissolubly linked with that of all other men, it can not be demanded of me that I use it to approve the enslavement of a part of these men. Thus, whether he is an essayist, a pamphleteer, a satirist, or a novelist, whether he speaks only of individual passions or whether he attacks the social order, the writer, a free man addressing free men, has only one subject—freedom.

Hence, any attempt to enslave his readers threatens him in his very art. A blacksmith can be affected by fascism in his life as a man, but not necessarily in his craft; a writer will be affected in both, and even more in his craft than in his life. I have seen writers, who before the war, called for fascism with all their hearts, smitten with sterility at the very moment when the Nazis were loading them with honors. I am thinking of Drieu la Rochelle [4] in particular; he was mistaken, but he was sincere. He proved it. He had agreed to direct a Nazi-inspired review. The first few months he reprimanded, rebuked, and lectured his countrymen. No one answered him because no one was free to do so. He became irritated; he no longer *felt* his readers. He became more insistent, but no sign appeared to prove that he had been understood. No sign of hatred, nor of anger either; nothing. He seemed disoriented, the victim of a growing distress. He complained bitterly to the Germans. His articles had been superb; they became shrill. The moment arrived when he struck his breast; no echo, except among the bought journalists whom he despised. He handed in his resignation, withdrew it, again spoke, still in the desert. Finally, he kept still, gagged by the silence of others. He had demanded the enslavement of others, but in his crazy mind he must have imagined that it was voluntary, that it was still free. It came; the man in him congratulated himself mightily, but the writer could not bear it. While this was going on, others, who, happily, were in the majority, understood that the freedom of writing implies the freedom of the citizen. One does not write for slaves. The art of prose is bound up with the only regime in which prose has meaning, democracy. When one is threatened, the other is too. And it is not enough to defend them with the pen. A day comes when the pen is forced to stop, and the writer must then take up arms. Thus, however you might have come to it, whatever the opinions you might have professed, literature throws you into battle. Writing is a certain way of wanting freedom; once you have begun, you are engaged, willy-nilly.

Engaged in what? Defending freedom? That's easy to say. Is it a matter of acting as guardian of ideal values like Benda's clerk before

[4] Pierre Drieu la Rochelle, editor of *Nouvelle Revue Française* during the German occupation of France, committed suicide in 1945.

the betrayal,[5] or is it concrete, everyday freedom which must be protected by our taking sides in political and social struggles? The question is tied up with another one, one very simple in appearance but which nobody ever asks himself: "For whom does one write?"

[5] The reference here is to Benda's *La Trahison des clercs,* translated into English as *The Treason of the Intellectuals.*—Translator's note.

# The Archetypes
# of Literature

## 1951

*To see and to study the principles of optics are obviously different kinds of experiences; to enjoy a novel and to criticize it are equally different. Seeing and enjoying cannot be taught, but physics and criticism can be. Nobody mistakes the expression "I feel cold" for a statement about the nature of heat, but similar statements applied to literature are called criticism. Literature, like the physical world, is "an inexhaustible source" of new discoveries; and criticism, like physics, can be assumed to be a "totally intelligible" science, an organized body of knowledge.*

*This basic assumption underlies Northrop Frye's prodigious output of essays and books; this early essay is representative of and wholly consistent with his theory of archetypes, dealt with more fully in his* Anatomy of Criticism *(1957). Like Aristotle, Frye is a supreme systematizer, attempting nothing less than the creation of a new and comprehensive poetics of criticism, "a systematic structure of knowledge" to replace the "leisure-class conversation" that passes for critical discourse. His intention is to supply the missing organizing principle for criticism, a "central hypothesis" that will put into perspective various partial or fragmentary critical approaches.*

*To study the principles of literary form, Frye relies heavily on both the insights and the methods of anthropology; indeed, he calls the search for archetypes "a kind of literary anthropology." As a literary anthropologist, he relates narrative to the creation of rituals, imagery*

*to moments of instantaneous insights, rhythm to natural cycles, and so
forth. The central myth of all literature he identifies as the quest-myth,
seen in four distinct phases that correspond to four aspects of cyclical
recurrence. In his reordering of all literature from epics to comic strips
according to this classification, Frye's system is clearly not bound by
any sense of historical continuity or development; his ideas on literary
history should be compared with those of Eliot, who also posits a nonchronological view of the "existing monuments" of literature.*

*Because Frye's attempts to organize a systematic and comprehensive
critical theory involve him in schematics, charts, and maps, with classifications and subclassifications that tend to get increasingly baroque, he
has himself been called a poetic myth-maker and not a scientist; and
indeed his work, which is both bold and imaginative, has had a strong
and continuing influence on criticism as much for the strikingly suggestive quality of his style as his ideas. A frequently voiced criticism of
the archetypal approach is that it ultimately tends to wash out the
specifics of individual works in favor of the universals charted in the
larger patterns. It is worth considering whether, in actual practice, his
classification does tend to stress the system at the expense of particular
uniquenesses.*

EVERY ORGANIZED body of knowledge can be learned progressively;
and experience shows that there is also something progressive about
the learning of literature. Our opening sentence has already got us
into a semantic difficulty. Physics is an organized body of knowledge
about nature, and a student of it says that he is learning physics, not
that he is learning nature. Art, like nature, is the subject of a systematic study, and has to be distinguished from the study itself,
which is criticism. It is therefore impossible to "learn literature": one
learns about it in a certain way, but what one learns, transitively, is
the criticism of literature. Similarly, the difficulty often felt in "teaching literature" arises from the fact that it cannot be done: the criticism of literature is all that can be directly taught. So while no one
expects literature itself to behave like a science, there is surely no
reason why criticism, as a systematic and organized study, should not
be, at least partly, a science. Not a "pure" or "exact" science, perhaps,
but these phrases form part of a nineteenth century cosmology which

is no longer with us. Criticism deals with the arts and may well be something of an art itself, but it does not follow that it must be unsystematic. If it is to be related to the sciences too, it does not follow that it must be deprived of the graces of culture.

Certainly criticism as we find it in learned journals and scholarly monographs has every characteristic of a science. Evidence is examined scientifically; previous authorities are used scientifically; fields are investigated scientifically; texts are edited scientifically. Prosody is scientific in structure; so is phonetics; so is philology. And yet in studying this kind of critical science the student becomes aware of a centrifugal movement carrying him away from literature. He finds that literature is the central division of the "humanities," flanked on one side by history and on the other by philosophy. Criticism so far ranks only as a subdivision of literature; and hence, for the systematic mental organization of the subject, the student has to turn to the conceptual framework of the historian for events, and to that of the philosopher for ideas. Even the more centrally placed critical sciences, such as textual editing, seem to be part of a "background" that recedes into history or some other non-literary field. The thought suggests itself that the ancillary critical disciplines may be related to a central expanding pattern of systematic comprehension which has not yet been established, but which, if it were established, would prevent them from being centrifugal. If such a pattern exists, then criticism would be to art what philosophy is to wisdom and history to action.

Most of the central area of criticism is at present, and doubtless always will be, the area of commentary. But the commentators have little sense, unlike the researchers, of being contained within some sort of scientific discipline: they are chiefly engaged, in the words of the gospel hymn, in brightening the corner where they are. If we attempt to get a more comprehensive idea of what criticism is about, we find ourselves wandering over quaking bogs of generalities, judicious pronouncements of value, reflective comments, perorations to works of research, and other consequences of taking the large view. But this part of the critical field is so full of pseudo-propositions, sonorous nonsense that contains no truth and no falsehood, that it obviously exists only because criticism, like nature, prefers a waste space to an empty one.

The term "pseudo-proposition" may imply some sort of logical positivist attitude on my own part. But I would not confuse the significant proposition with the factual one; nor should I consider it advisable to muddle the study of literature with a schizophrenic dichotomy between subjective-emotional and objective-descriptive aspects of meaning, considering that in order to produce any literary meaning at all one has to ignore this dichotomy. I say only that the principles by which one can distinguish a significant from a meaningless statement in criticism are not clearly defined. Our first step, therefore, is to recognize and get rid of meaningless criticism: that is, talking about literature in a way that cannot help to build up a systematic structure of knowledge. Casual value-judgments belong not to criticism but to the history of taste, and reflect, at best, only the social and psychological compulsions which prompted their utterance. All judgments in which the values are not based on literary experience but are sentimental or derived from religious or political prejudice may be regarded as casual. Sentimental judgments are usually based either on non-existent categories or antitheses ("Shakespeare studied life, Milton books") or on a visceral reaction to the writer's personality. The literary chit-chat which makes the reputations of poets boom and crash in an imaginary stock exchange is pseudo-criticism. That wealthy investor Mr. Eliot, after dumping Milton on the market, is now buying him again; Donne has probably reached his peak and will begin to taper off; Tennyson may be in for a slight flutter but the Shelley stocks are still bearish. This sort of thing cannot be part of any systematic study, for a systematic study can only progress: whatever dithers or vacillates or reacts is merely leisure-class conversation.

We next meet a more serious group of critics who say: the foreground of criticism is the impact of literature on the reader. Let us, then, keep the study of literature centripetal, and base the learning process on a structural analysis of the literary work itself. The texture of any great work of art is complex and ambiguous, and in unravelling the complexities we may take in as much history and philosophy as we please, if the subject of our study remains at the center. If it does not, we may find that in our anxiety to write about literature we have forgotten how to read it.

The only weakness in this approach is that it is conceived primarily as the antithesis of centrifugal or "background" criticism, and so lands us in a somewhat unreal dilemma, like the conflict of internal and external relations in philosophy. Antitheses are usually resolved, not by picking one side and refuting the other, or by making eclectic choices between them, but by trying to get past the antithetical way of stating the problem. It is right that the first effort of critical apprehension should take the form of a rhetorical or structural analysis of a work of art. But a purely structural approach has the same limitation in criticism that it has in biology. In itself it is simply a discreet series of analyses based on the mere existence of the literary structure, without developing any explanation of how the structure came to be what it was and what its nearest relatives are. Structural analysis brings rhetoric back to criticism, but we need a new poetics as well, and the attempt to construct a new poetics out of rhetoric alone can hardly avoid a mere complication of rhetorical terms into a sterile jargon. I suggest that what is at present missing from literary criticism is a co-ordinating principle, a central hypothesis which, like the theory of evolution in biology, will see the phenomena it deals with as parts of a whole. Such a principle, though it would retain the centripetal perspective of structural analysis, would try to give the same perspective to other kinds of criticism too.

The first postulate of this hypothesis is the same as that of any science: the assumption of total coherence. The assumption refers to the science, not to what it deals with. A belief in an order of nature is an inference from the intelligibility of the natural sciences; and if the natural sciences ever completely demonstrated the order of nature they would presumably exhaust their subject. Criticism, as a science, is totally intelligible; literature, as the subject of a science, is, so far as we know, an inexhaustible source of new critical discoveries, and would be even if new works of literature ceased to be written. If so, then the search for a limiting principle in literature in order to discourage the development of criticism is mistaken. The assertion that the critic should not look for more in a poem than the poet may safely be assumed to have been conscious of putting there is a common form of what may be called the fallacy of premature teleology. It corresponds to the assertion that a natural phenomenon is as it is because Providence in its inscrutable wisdom made it so.

Simple as the assumption appears, it takes a long time for a science to discover that it is in fact a totally intelligible body of knowledge. Until it makes this discovery it has not been born as an individual science, but remains an embryo within the body of some other subject. The birth of physics from "natural philosophy" and of sociology from "moral philosophy" will illustrate the process. It is also very approximately true that the modern sciences have developed in the order of their closeness to mathematics. Thus physics and astronomy assumed their modern form in the Renaissance, chemistry in the eighteenth century, biology in the nineteenth, and the social sciences in the twentieth. If systematic criticism, then, is developing only in our day, the fact is at least not an anachronism.

We are now looking for classifying principles lying in an area between two points that we have fixed. The first of these is the preliminary effort of criticism, the structural analysis of the work of art.

The second is the assumption that there is such a subject as criticism, and that it makes, or could make, complete sense. We may next proceed inductively from structural analysis, associating the data we collect and trying to see larger patterns in them. Or we may proceed deductively, with the consequences that follow from postulating the unity of criticism. It is clear, of course, that neither procedure will work indefinitely without correction from the other. Pure induction will get us lost in haphazard guessing; pure deduction will lead to inflexible and over-simplified pigeon-holing. Let us now attempt a few tentative steps in each direction, beginning with the inductive one.

## II

The unity of a work of art, the basis of structural analysis, has not been produced solely by the unconditioned will of the artist, for the artist is only its efficient cause: it has form, and consequently a formal cause. The fact that revision is possible, that the poet makes changes not because he likes them better but because they are better, means that poems, like poets, are born and not made. The poet's task is to deliver the poem in as uninjured a state as possible, and if the poem is alive, it is equally anxious to be rid of him, and screams to be cut loose from his private memories and associations, his desire for self-expression, and all the other navel-strings and feeding tubes of his ego. The critic takes over where the poet leaves off, and criticism can hardly do without a kind of literary psychology connecting the poet with the poem. Part of this may be a psychological study of the poet, though this is useful chiefly in analysing the failures in his expression, the things in him which are still attached to his work. More important is the fact that every poet has his private mythology, his own spectroscopic band or peculiar formation of symbols, of much of which he is quite unconscious. In works with characters of their own, such as dramas and novels, the same psychological analysis may be extended to the interplay of characters, though of course literary psychology would analyse the behavior of such characters only in relation to literary convention.

There is still before us the problem of the formal cause of the poem, a problem deeply involved with the question of genres. We cannot say much about genres, for criticism does not know much about them. A good many critical efforts to grapple with such words as "novel" or "epic" are chiefly interesting as examples of the psychology of rumor. Two conceptions of the genre, however, are obviously fallacious, and as they are opposite extremes, the truth must lie somewhere between them. One is the pseudo-Platonic conception of genres as existing prior to and independently of creation, which confuses them with mere conventions of form like the sonnet. The other is that pseudo-biological conception of them as evolving species which turns up in so many surveys of the "development" of this or that form.

We next inquire for the origin of the genre, and turn first of all to the social conditions and cultural demands which produced it—in other words to the material cause of the work of art. This leads us into literary history, which differs from ordinary history in that its containing categories, "Gothic," "Baroque," "Romantic," and the like are cultural categories, of little use to the ordinary historian. Most literary history does not get as far as these categories, but even so we know more about it than about most kinds of critical scholarship. The historian treats literature and philosophy historically; the philosopher treats history and literature philosophically; and the so-called "history of ideas" approach marks the beginning of an attempt to treat history and philosophy from the point of view of an autonomous criticism.

But still we feel there is something missing. We say that every poet has his own peculiar formation of images. But when so many poets use so many of the same images, surely there are much bigger critical problems involved than biographical ones. As Mr. Auden's brilliant essay *The Enchafèd Flood* shows, an important symbol like the sea cannot remain within the poetry of Shelley or Keats or Coleridge: it is bound to expand over many poets into an archetypal symbol of literature. And if the genre has a historical origin, why does the genre of drama emerge from medieval religion in a way so strikingly similar to the way it emerged from Greek religion centuries before? This is a problem of structure rather than origin, and suggests that there may be archetypes of genres as well as of images.

It is clear that criticism cannot be systematic unless there is a quality in literature which enables it to be so, an order of words corresponding to the order of nature in the natural sciences. An archetype should be not only a unifying category of criticism, but itself a part of a total form, and it leads us at once to the question of what sort of total form criticism can see in literature. Our survey of critical techniques has taken us as far as literary history. Total literary history moves from the primitive to the sophisticated, and here we glimpse the possibility of seeing literature as a complication of a relatively restricted and simple group of formulas that can be studied in primitive culture. If so, then the search for archetypes is a kind of literary anthropology, concerned with the way that literature is informed by pre-literary categories such as ritual, myth and folktale. We next realize that the relation between these categories and literature is by no means purely one of descent, as we find them reappearing in the greatest classics—in fact there seems to be a general tendency on the part of great classics to revert to them. This coincides with a feeling that we have all had: that the study of mediocre works of art, however energetic, obstinately remains a random and peripheral form of critical experience, whereas the profound masterpiece seems to draw us to a point at which we can see an enormous number of converging patterns of significance. Here we begin to wonder if we cannot see literature, not only as complicating itself in time, but as spread out in conceptual space from some unseen center.

This inductive movement towards the archetype is a process of backing up, as it were, from structural analysis, as we back up from a painting if we want to see composition instead of brushwork. In the foreground of the grave-digger scene in *Hamlet,* for instance, is an intricate verbal texture, ranging from the puns of the first clown to the *danse macabre* of the Yorick soliloquy, which we study in the printed text. One step back, and we are in the Wilson Knight and Spurgeon group of critics, listening to the steady rain of images of corruption and decay. Here too, as the sense of the place of this scene in the whole play begins to dawn on us, we are in the network of psychological relationships which were the main interest of Bradley. But after all, we say, we are forgetting the genre: *Hamlet* is a play, and an Elizabethan play. So we take another step back into the Stoll and Shaw group and see the scene conventionally as part of its dramatic context. One step more, and we can begin to glimpse the archetype of the scene, as the hero's *Liebestod* and first unequivocal declaration of his love, his struggle with Laertes and the sealing of his own fate, and the sudden sobering of his mood that marks the transition to the final scene, all take shape around a leap into and return from the grave that has so weirdly yawned open on the stage.

At each stage of understanding this scene we are dependent on a certain kind of scholarly organization. We need first an editor to clean up the text for us, then the rhetorician and philologist, then the literary psychologist. We cannot study the genre without the help of the literary social historian, the literary philosopher and the student of the "history of ideas," and for the archetype we need a literary anthropologist. But now that we have got our central pattern of criticism established, all these interests are seen as converging on literary criticism instead of receding from it into psychology and history and the rest. In particular, the literary anthropologist who chases the source of the Hamlet legend from the pre-Shakespeare play to Saxo, and from Saxo to nature-myths, is not running away from Shakespeare: he is drawing closer to the archetypal form which Shakespeare re-created. A minor result of our new perspective is that contradictions among critics, and assertions that this and not that critical approach is the right one, show a remarkable tendency to dissolve into unreality. Let us now see what we can get from the deductive end.

## III

Some arts move in time, like music; others are presented in space, like painting. In both cases the organizing principle is recurrence, which is called rhythm when it is temporal and pattern when it is spatial. Thus we speak of the rhythm of music and the pattern of painting; but later, to show off our sophistication, we may begin to speak of the rhythm of painting and the pattern of music. In other words, all arts may be conceived both temporally and spatially. The score of a musical composition may be studied all at once; a picture may be seen as the track of an intricate dance of the eye. Literature seems to be intermediate between music and painting: its words form rhythms which approach a musical sequence of sounds at one of its boundaries, and form patterns which approach the hieroglyphic or pictorial image at the other. The attempts to get as near to these boundaries as possible form the main body of what is called experimental writing. We may call the rhythm of literature the narrative, and the pattern, the simultaneous mental grasp of the verbal structure, the meaning or significance. We hear or listen to a narrative, but when we grasp a writer's total pattern we "see" what he means.

The criticism of literature is much more hampered by the representational fallacy than even the criticism of painting. That is why we are apt to think of narrative as a sequential representation of events in an outside "life," and of meaning as a reflection of some external "idea." Properly used as critical terms, an author's narrative is his linear movement; his meaning is the integrity of his completed form. Similarly an image is not merely a verbal replica of an external object, but any unit of a verbal structure seen as part of a total pattern or rhythm. Even the letters an author spells his words with form part of his imagery, though only in special cases (such as alliteration) would they call for critical notice. Narrative and meaning thus become respectively, to borrow musical terms, the melodic and harmonic contexts of the imagery.

Rhythm, or recurrent movement, is deeply founded on the natural

cycle, and everything in nature that we think of as having some analogy with works of art, like the flower or the bird's song, grows out of
a profound synchronization between an organism and the rhythms of
its environment, especially that of the solar year. With animals some
expressions of synchronization, like the mating dances of birds, could
almost be called rituals. But in human life a ritual seems to be something of a voluntary effort (hence the magical element in it) to recapture a lost rapport with the natural cycle. A farmer must harvest
his crop at a certain time of year, but because this is involuntary,
harvesting itself is not precisely a ritual. It is the deliberate expression
of a will to synchronize human and natural energies at that time
which produces the harvest songs, harvest sacrifices and harvest folk
customs that we call rituals. In ritual, then, we may find the origin of
narrative, a ritual being a temporal sequence of acts in which the
conscious meaning or significance is latent: it can be seen by an observer, but is largely concealed from the participators themselves. The
pull of ritual is toward pure narrative, which, if there could be such a
thing, would be automatic and unconscious repetition. We should
notice too the regular tendency of ritual to become encyclopedic. All
the important recurrences in nature, the day, the phases of the moon,
the seasons and solstices of the year, the crises of existence from birth
to death, get rituals attached to them, and most of the higher religions
are equipped with a definitive total body of rituals suggestive, if we
may put it so, of the entire range of potentially significant actions in
human life.

. Patterns of imagery, on the other hand, or fragments of significance,
are oracular in origin, and derive from the epiphanic moment, the
flash of instantaneous comprehension with no direct reference to time,
the importance of which is indicated by Cassirer in *Language and
Myth*. By the time we get them, in the form of proverbs, riddles, com-
mandments and etiological folktales, there is already a considerable
element of narrative in them. They too are encyclopedic in tendency,
building up a total structure of significance, or doctrine, from random
and empiric fragments. And just as pure narrative would be unconscious act, so pure significance would be an incommunicable state of
consciousness, for communication begins by constructing narrative.

The myth is the central informing power that gives archetypal significance to the ritual and archetypal narrative to the oracle. Hence
the myth *is* the archetype, though it might be convenient to say myth
only when referring to narrative, and archetype when speaking of
significance. In the solar cycle of the day, the seasonal cycle of the
year, and the organic cycle of human life, there is a single pattern of

significance, out of which myth constructs a central narrative around a figure who is partly the sun, partly vegetative fertility and partly a god or archetypal human being. The crucial importance of this myth has been forced on literary critics by Jung and Frazer in particular, but the several books now available on it are not always systematic in their approach, for which reason I supply the following table of its phases:

1. The dawn, spring and birth phase. Myths of the birth of the hero, of revival and resurrection, of creation and (because the four phases are a cycle) of the defeat of the powers of darkness, winter and death. Subordinate characters: the father and the mother. The archetype of romance and of most dithyrambic and rhapsodic poetry.

2. The zenith, summer, and marriage or triumph phase. Myths of apotheosis, of the sacred marriage, and of entering into Paradise. Subordinate characters: the companion and the bride. The archetype of comedy, pastoral and idyll.

3. The sunset, autumn and death phase. Myths of fall, of the dying god, of violent death and sacrifice and of the isolation of the hero. Subordinate characters: the traitor and the siren. The archetype of tragedy and elegy.

4. The darkness, winter and dissolution phase. Myths of the triumph of these powers; myths of floods and the return of chaos, of the defeat of the hero, and Götterdämmerung myths. Subordinate characters: the ogre and the witch. The archetype of satire (see, for instance, the conclusion of *The Dunciad*).

The quest of the hero also tends to assimilate the oracular and random verbal structures, as we can see when we watch the chaos of local legends that results from prophetic epiphanies consolidating into a narrative mythology of departmental gods. In most of the higher religions this in turn has become the same central quest-myth that emerges from ritual, as the Messiah myth became the narrative structure of the oracles of Judaism. A local flood may beget a folktale by accident, but a comparison of flood stories will show how quickly such tales become examples of the myth of dissolution. Finally, the tendency of both ritual and epiphany to become encyclopedic is realized in the definitive body of myth which constitutes the sacred scriptures of religions. These sacred scriptures are consequently the first documents that the literary critic has to study to gain a comprehensive view of his subject. After he has understood their structure, then he can descend from archetypes to genres, and see how the drama emerges from the ritual side of myth and lyric from the epiphanic or fragmented side, while the epic carries on the central encyclopedic structure.

Some words of caution and encouragement are necessary before literary criticism has clearly staked out its boundaries in these fields. It is part of the critic's business to show how all literary genres are derived from the quest-myth, but the derivation is a logical one within the science of criticism: the quest-myth will constitute the first chapter of whatever future handbooks of criticism may be written that will be based on enough organized critical knowledge to call themselves "introductions" or "outlines" and still be able to live up to their titles. It is only when we try to expound the derivation chronologically that we find ourselves writing pseudo-prehistorical fictions and theories of mythological contract. Again, because psychology and anthropology are more highly developed sciences, the critic who deals with this kind of material is bound to appear, for some time, a dilettante of those subjects. These two phases of criticism are largely undeveloped in comparison with literary history and rhetoric, the reason being the later development of the sciences they are related to. But the fascination which *The Golden Bough* and Jung's book on libido symbols have for literary critics is not based on dilettantism, but on the fact that these books are primarily studies in literary criticism, and very important ones.

In any case the critic who is studying the principles of literary form has a quite different interest from the psychologist's concern with states of mind or the anthropologist's with social institutions. For instance: the mental response to narrative is mainly passive; to significance mainly active. From this fact Ruth Benedict's *Patterns of Culture* develops a distinction between "Apollonian" cultures based on obedience to ritual and "Dionysiac" ones based on a tense exposure of the prophetic mind to epiphany. The critic would tend rather to note how popular literature which appeals to the inertia of the untrained mind puts a heavy emphasis on narrative values, whereas a sophisticated attempt to disrupt the connection between the poet and his environment produces the Rimbaud type of *illumination,* Joyce's solitary epiphanies, and Baudelaire's conception of nature as a source of oracles. Also how literature, as it develops from the primitive to the self-conscious, shows a gradual shift of the poet's attention from narrative to significant values, this shift of attention being the basis of Schiller's distinction between naive and sentimental poetry.

The relation of criticism to religion, when they deal with the same documents, is more complicated. In criticism, as in history, the divine is always treated as a human artifact. God for the critic, whether he finds him in *Paradise Lost* or the Bible, is a character in a human story; and for the critic all epiphanies are explained, not in terms of the riddle of a possessing god or devil, but as mental phenomena closely associated in their origin with dreams. This once established, it is then necessary to say that nothing in criticism or art compels the critic to take the attitude of ordinary waking consciousness towards the dream or the god. Art deals not with the real but with the conceivable; and criticism, though it will eventually have to have some theory of conceivability, can never be justified in trying to develop, much less assume, any theory of actuality. It is necessary to understand this before our next and final point can be made.

We have identified the central myth of literature, in its narrative aspect, with the quest-myth. Now if we wish to see this central myth as a pattern of meaning also, we have to start with the workings of the subconscious where the epiphany originates, in other words in the dream. The human cycle of waking and dreaming corresponds closely to the natural cycle of light and darkness, and it is perhaps in this correspondence that all imaginative life begins. The correspondence is largely an antithesis: it is in daylight that man is really in the power of darkness, a prey to frustration and weakness; it is in the darkness of nature that the "libido" or conquering heroic self awakes. Hence art, which Plato called a dream for awakened minds, seems to have as its final cause the resolution of the antithesis, the mingling of the sun and the hero, the realizing of a world in which the inner desire and the outward circumstance coincide. This is the same goal, of course, that the attempt to combine human and natural power in ritual has. The social function of the arts, therefore, seems to be closely connected with visualizing the goal of work in human life. So in terms of significance, the central myth of art must be the vision of the end of social effort, the innocent world of fulfilled desires, the free human society. Once this is understood, the integral place of criticism among the other social sciences, in interpreting and systematizing the vision of the artist, will be easier to see. It is at this point that we can see how religious conceptions of the final cause of human effort are as relevant as any others to criticism.

The importance of the god or hero in the myth lies in the fact that such characters, who are conceived in human likeness and yet have more power over nature, gradually build up the vision of an omnipotent personal community beyond an indifferent nature. It is this community which the hero regularly enters in his apotheosis. The world of this apotheosis thus begins to pull away from the rotary cycle of the quest in which all triumph is temporary. Hence if we look at the quest-myth as a pattern of imagery, we see the hero's quest first of all in terms of its fulfilment. This gives us our central pattern of archetypal images, the vision of innocence which sees the world in terms of total human intelligibility. It corresponds to, and is usually found in the form of, the vision of the unfallen world or heaven in religion. We may call it the comic vision of life, in contrast to the tragic vision, which sees the quest only in the form of its ordained cycle.

We conclude with a second table of contents, in which we shall attempt to set forth the central pattern of the comic and tragic visions. One essential principle of archetypal criticism is that the individual and the universal forms of an image are identical, the reasons being too complicated for us just now. We proceed according to the general plan of the game of Twenty Questions, or, if we prefer, of the Great Chain of Being:

1. In the comic vision the *human* world is a community, or a hero who represents the wish-fulfilment of the reader. The archetype of images of symposium, communion, order, friendship and love. In the tragic vision the human world is a tyranny or anarchy, or an individual or isolated man, the leader with his back to his followers, the bullying giant of romance, the deserted or betrayed hero. Marriage or some equivalent consummation belongs to the comic vision; the harlot, witch and other varieties of Jung's "terrible mother" belong to the tragic one. All divine, heroic, angelic or other superhuman communities follow the human pattern.

2. In the comic vision the *animal* world is a community of domesticated animals, usually a flock of sheep, or a lamb, or one of the gentler birds, usually a dove. The archetype of pastoral images. In the tragic vision the animal world is seen in terms of beasts and birds of prey, wolves, vultures, serpents, dragons and the like.

3. In the comic vision the *vegetable* world is a garden, grove or park, or a tree of life, or a rose or lotus. The archetype of Arcadian images, such as that of Marvell's green world or of Shakespeare's forest comedies. In the tragic vision it is a sinister forest like the one in *Comus* or at the opening of the *Inferno* or a heath or wilderness, or a tree of death.

4. In the comic vision the *mineral* world is a city, or one building or temple, or one stone, normally a glowing precious stone—in fact the whole comic series, especially the tree, can be conceived as luminous or fiery. The archetype of geometrical images: the "starlit dome" belongs here. In the tragic vision the mineral world is seen in terms of deserts, rocks and ruins, or of sinister geometrical images like the cross.

5. In the comic vision the *unformed* world is a river, traditionally

fourfold, which influenced the Renaissance image of the temperate body with its four humors. In the tragic vision this world usually becomes the sea, as the narrative myth of dissolution is so often a flood myth. The combination of the sea and beast images gives us the leviathan and similar water-monsters.

Obvious as this table looks, a great variety of poetic images and forms will be found to fit it. Yeats's "Sailing to Byzantium," to take a famous example of the comic vision at random, has the city, the tree, the bird, the community of sages, the geometrical gyre and the detachment from the cyclic world. It is, of course, only the general comic or tragic context that determines the interpretation of any symbol: this is obvious with relatively neutral archetypes like the island, which may be Prospero's island or Circe's.

Our tables are, of course, not only elementary but grossly oversimplified, just as our inductive approach to the archetype was a mere hunch. The important point is not the deficiencies of either procedure, taken by itself, but the fact that, somewhere and somehow, the two are clearly going to meet in the middle. And if they do meet, the ground plan of a systematic and comprehensive development of criticism has been established.

## ADRIENNE RICH

# When We Dead Awaken: Writing as Re-Vision

## 1971

*The title of Rich's essay, with its reference to Ibsen's play about the male domination of women and its pun relating revision to renewed insight, points to the very heart of modern feminist literary criticism. Frankly personal and openly political, Rich traces her intellectual development from acceptance of traditional male-centered critical principles to an increasingly radical advocacy of feminist ideology. Using herself as an example, she discusses the female writer's struggle to define her own reality through conventional societal and literary structures and the restrictions such structures impose upon women personally, professionally, and artistically. Her essay suggests some of the basic tenets of feminist belief: that traditionally accepted "truths" are simply myths based on codified expectations, that established political and social hierarchies do not exist as some Platonic ideal but are the creation of a male-centered culture, that individual experience—emotional and perceptual—is a legitimate means of achieving broader understanding.*

*Rich and other feminist poet-critics react against the idea of a universal poetic truth, arguing that what has been assumed to be "universal" is in fact an essentially male conception that trivializes, distorts, or simply ignores central concerns of the female experience and imagination. The goals of such critics are several: to nurture the development of authentic female expression based in individual ex-*

*perience and shared understanding, to question long-standing defini-*
*tions and systems of artistic value, to create new modes of artistic and*
*critical discourse. Like other late-twentieth-century critics, feminists*
*see form and content as interchangeable; indeed, from the most radical*
*perspective, art is a constant struggle not only with received cultural*
*and political formulations but with the very language that shapes our*
*perceptions of those formulations.*

*Feminist critical theory began to gain prominence around 1970,*
*when Kate Millett's* Sexual Politics, *a polemical study of male novelists,*
*defined gender as a major literary principle and criterion. Rich's*
*early work in fact predates Millett, and she continues to be in the*
*vanguard of the women's movement. In the meantime, the work of*
*feminist critics has led to interest in previously neglected women*
*authors, to a reexamination of well-known authors such as Emily*
*Dickinson and the Brontës, to revisions in the traditional literary*
*canon, and to new perceptions about how literature may be studied.*
*Feminist criticism today presents challenges to other critical ap-*
*proaches, demanding that assumptions unquestioned for centuries be*
*reconsidered and redefined.*

Ibsen's *When We Dead Awaken* is a play about the use that the male
artist and thinker—in the process of creating culture as we know it—
has made of women, in his life and in his work; and about a woman's
slow struggling awakening to the use to which her life has been put.
Bernard Shaw wrote in 1900 of this play:

> [Ibsen] shows us that no degradation ever devized or permitted is as
> disastrous as this degradation; that through it women can die into
> luxuries for men and yet can kill them; that men and women are
> becoming conscious of this; and that what remains to be seen as
> perhaps the most interesting of all imminent social developments is
> what will happen "when we dead awaken."[1]

It's exhilarating to be alive in a time of awakening consciousness; it
can also be confusing, disorienting, and painful. This awakening of
dead or sleeping consciousness has already affected the lives of millions of women, even those who don't know it yet. It is also affecting
the lives of men, even those who deny its claims upon them. The
argument will go on whether an oppressive economic class system is

---

[1] G. B. Shaw, *The Quintessence of Ibsenism* (New York: Hill & Wang, 1922), p. 139.

responsible for the oppressive nature of male/female relations, or whether, in fact, patriarchy—the domination of males—is the original model of oppression on which all others are based. But in the last few years the women's movement has drawn inescapable and illuminating connections between our sexual lives and our political institutions. The sleepwalkers are coming awake, and for the first time this awakening has a collective reality; it is no longer such a lonely thing to open one's eyes.

Re-vision—the act of looking back, of seeing with fresh eyes, of entering an old text from a new critical direction—is for women more than a chapter in cultural history: it is an act of survival. Until we can understand the assumptions in which we are drenched we cannot know ourselves. And this drive to self-knowledge, for women, is more than a search for identity: it is part of our refusal of the self-destructiveness of male-dominated society. A radical critique of literature, feminist in its impulse, would take the work first of all as a clue to how we live, how we have been living, how we have been led to imagine ourselves, how our language has trapped as well as liberated us, how the very act of naming has been till now a male prerogative, and how we can begin to see and name—and therefore live—afresh. A change in the concept of sexual identity is essential if we are not going to see the old political order reassert itself in every new revolution. We need to know the writing of the past, and know it differently than we have ever known it; not to pass on a tradition but to break its hold over us.

For writers, and at this moment for women writers in particular, there is the challenge and promise of a whole new psychic geography to be explored. But there is also a difficult and dangerous walking on the ice, as we try to find language and images for a consciousness we are just coming into, and with little in the past to support us. I want to talk about some aspects of this difficulty and this danger.

Jane Harrison, the great classical anthropologist, wrote in 1914 in a letter to her friend Gilbert Murray:

> By the by, about "Women," it has bothered me often—why do women never want to write poetry about Man as a sex—why is Woman a dream and a terror to man and not the other way around? . . . Is it mere convention and propriety, or something deeper?[2]

---

[2] J. G. Stewart, *Jane Ellen Harrison: A Portrait from Letters* (London: Merlin, 1959), p. 140.

I think Jane Harrison's question cuts deep into the myth-making tradition, the romantic tradition; deep into what women and men have been to each other; and deep into the psyche of the woman writer. Thinking about that question, I began thinking of the work of two twentieth-century women poets, Sylvia Plath and Diane Wakoski. It strikes me that in the work of both Man appears as, if not a dream, a fascination and a terror; and that the source of the fascination and the terror is, simply, Man's power—to dominate, tyrannize, choose, or reject the woman. The charisma of Man seems to come purely from his power over her and his control of the world by force, not from anything fertile or life-giving in him. And, in the work of both these poets, it is finally the woman's sense of *herself*—embattled, possessed—that gives the poetry its dynamic charge, its rhythms of struggle, need, will, and female energy. Until recently this female anger and this furious awareness of the Man's power over her were not available materials to the female poet, who tended to write of Love as the source of her suffering, and to view that victimization by Love as an almost inevitable fate. Or, like Marianne Moore and Elizabeth Bishop, she kept sexuality at a measured and chiseled distance in her poems.

One answer to Jane Harrison's question has to be that historically men and women have played very different parts in each others' lives. Where woman has been a luxury for man, and has served as the painter's model and the poet's muse, but also as comforter, nurse, cook, bearer of his seed, secretarial assistant, and copyist of manuscripts, man has played a quite different role for the female artist. Henry James repeats an incident which the writer Prosper Mérimée described, of how, while he was living with George Sand,

> he once opened his eyes, in the raw winter dawn, to see his companion, in a dressing-gown, on her knees before the domestic hearth, a candlestick beside her and a red *madras* round her head, making bravely, with her own hands the fire that was to enable her to sit down betimes to urgent pen and paper. The story represents him as having felt that the spectacle chilled his ardor and tried his taste; her appearance was unfortunate, her occupation an inconsequence, and her industry a reproof—the result of all which was a lively irritation and an early rupture.[3]

---

[3] Henry James, "Notes on Novelists," in *Selected Literary Criticism of Henry James*, Morris Shapira, ed. (London: Heinemann, 1963), pp. 157–58.

The specter of this kind of male judgment, along with the misnaming and thwarting of her needs by a culture controlled by males, has created problems for the woman writer: problems of contact with herself, problems of language and style, problems of energy and survival.

In rereading Virginia Woolf's *A Room of One's Own* (1929) for the first time in some years, I was astonished at the sense of effort, of pains taken, of dogged tentativeness, in the tone of that essay. And I recognized that tone. I had heard it often enough, in myself and in other women. It is the tone of a woman almost in touch with her anger, who is determined not to appear angry, who is *willing* herself to be calm, detached, and even charming in a roomful of men where things have been said which are attacks on her very integrity. Virginia Woolf is addressing an audience of women, but she is acutely conscious—as she always was—of being overheard by men: by Morgan and Lytton and Maynard Keynes and for that matter by her father, Leslie Stephen.[4] She drew the language out into an exacerbated thread in her determination to have her own sensibility yet protect it from those masculine presences. Only at rare moments in that essay do you hear the passion in her voice; she was trying to sound as cool as Jane Austen, as Olympian as Shakespeare, because that is the way the men of the culture thought a writer should sound.

No male writer has written primarily or even largely for women, or with the sense of women's criticism as a consideration when he chooses his materials, his theme, his language. But to a lesser or greater extent, every woman writer has written for men even when, like Virginia Woolf, she was supposed to be addressing women. If we have come to the point when this balance might begin to change, when women can stop being haunted, not only by "convention and propriety" but by internalized fears of being and saying themselves, then it is an extraordinary moment for the woman writer—and reader.

I have hesitated to do what I am going to do now, which is to use myself as an illustration. For one thing, it's a lot easier and less dangerous to talk about other women writers. But there is something else. Like Virginia Woolf, I am aware of the women who are not with us here because they are washing the dishes and looking after

---

4 *A. R., 1978:* This intuition of mine was corroborated when, early in 1978, I read the correspondence between Woolf and Dame Ethel Smyth (Henry W. and Albert A. Berg Collection, The New York Public Library, Astor, Lenox and Tilden Foundations); in a letter dated June 8, 1933, Woolf speaks of having kept her own personality out of *A Room of One's Own* lest she not be taken seriously: ". . . how personal, so will they say, rubbing their hands with glee, women always are; *I even hear them as I write.*" (Italics mine.)

the children. Nearly fifty years after she spoke, that fact remains largely unchanged. And I am thinking also of women whom she left out of the picture altogether—women who are washing other people's dishes and caring for other people's children, not to mention women who went on the streets last night in order to feed their children. We seem to be special women here, we have liked to think of ourselves as special, and we have known that men would tolerate, even romanticize us as special, as long as our words and actions didn't threaten their privilege of tolerating or rejecting us and our work according to *their* ideas of what a special woman ought to be. An important insight of the radical women's movement has been how divisive and how ultimately destructive is this myth of the special woman, who is also the token woman. Every one of us here in this room has had great luck—we are teachers, writers, academicians; our own gifts could not have been enough, for we all know women whose gifts are buried or aborted. Our struggles can have meaning and our privileges—however precarious under patriarchy—can be justified only if they can help to change the lives of women whose gifts—and whose very being—continue to be thwarted and silenced.

My own luck was being born white and middle-class into a house full of books, with a father who encouraged me to read and write. So for about twenty years I wrote for a particular man, who criticized and praised me and made me feel I was indeed "special." The obverse side of this, of course, was that I tried for a long time to please him, or rather, not to displease him. And then of course there were other men—writers, teachers—the Man, who was not a terror or a dream but a literary master and a master in other ways less easy to acknowledge. And there were all those poems about women, written by men: it seemed to be a given that men wrote poems and women frequently inhabited them. These women were almost always beautiful, but threatened with the loss of beauty, the loss of youth—the fate worse than death. Or, they were beautiful and died young, like Lucy and Lenore. Or, the woman was like Maud Gonne, cruel and disastrously mistaken, and the poem reproached her because she had refused to become a luxury for the poet.

A lot is being said today about the influence that the myths and images of women have on all of us who are products of culture. I think it has been a peculiar confusion to the girl or woman who tries to write because she is peculiarly susceptible to language. She goes to poetry or fiction looking for *her* way of being in the world, since she too has been putting words and images together; she is looking eagerly for guides, maps, possibilities; and over and over in the "words' masculine persuasive force" of literature she comes up against something that negates everything she is about: she meets the image of Woman in books written by men. She finds a terror and a dream, she finds a beautiful pale face, she finds La Belle Dame Sans Merci, she finds Juliet or Tess or Salomé, but precisely what she does not find is that absorbed, drudging, puzzled, sometimes inspired creature, herself, who sits at a desk trying to put words together.

So what does she do? What did I do? I read the older women poets with their peculiar keenness and ambivalence: Sappho, Christina Rossetti, Emily Dickinson, Elinor Wylie, Edna Millay, H. D. I discovered that the woman poet most admired at the time (by men) was Marianne Moore, who was maidenly, elegant, intellectual, discreet. But even in reading these women I was looking in them for the same things I had found in the poetry of men, because I wanted women poets to be the equals of men, and to be equal was still confused with sounding the same.

I know that my style was formed first by male poets: by the men I was reading as an undergraduate—Frost, Dylan Thomas, Donne, Auden, MacNiece, Stevens, Yeats. What I chiefly learned from them was craft.[5] But poems are like dreams: in them you put what you don't know you know. Looking back at poems I wrote before I was twenty-one, I'm startled because beneath the conscious craft are glimpses of the split I even then experienced between the girl who wrote poems, who defined herself in writing poems, and the girl who was to define herself by her relationships with men. "Aunt Jennifer's Tigers" (1951), written while I was a student, looks with deliberate detachment at this split.[6]

> Aunt Jennifer's tigers stride across a screen,
> Bright topaz denizens of a world of green.
> They do not fear the men beneath the tree;
> They pace in sleek chivalric certainty.
>
> Aunt Jennifer's fingers fluttering through her wool
> Find even the ivory needle hard to pull.
> The massive weight of Uncle's wedding band
> Sits heavily upon Aunt Jennifer's hand.

[5] *A. R., 1978:* Yet I spent months, at sixteen, memorizing and writing imitations of Millay's sonnets; and in notebooks of that period I find what are obviously attempts to imitate Dickinson's metrics and verbal compression. I knew H. D. only through anthologized lyrics; her epic poetry was not then available to me.

[6] *A. R., 1978:* Texts of poetry quoted herein can be found in A. R., *Poems Selected and New: 1950–1974* (New York: Norton, 1975).

When Aunt is dead, her terrified hands will lie
Still ringed with ordeals she was mastered by.
The tigers in the panel that she made
Will go on striding, proud and unafraid.

In writing this poem, composed and apparently cool as it is, I thought I was creating a portrait of an imaginary woman. But this woman suffers from the opposition of her imagination, worked out in tapestry, and her life-style, "ringed with ordeals she was mastered by." It was important to me that Aunt Jennifer was a person as distinct from myself as possible—distanced by the formalism of the poem, by its objective, observant tone—even by putting the woman in a different generation.

In those years formalism was part of the strategy—like asbestos gloves, it allowed me to handle materials I couldn't pick up bare-handed. A later strategy was to use the persona of a man, as I did in "The Loser" (1958):

*A man thinks of the woman he once loved: first, after her wedding, and then nearly a decade later.*

I
I kissed you, bride and lost, and went
home from that bourgeois sacrament,
your cheek still tasting cold upon
my lips that gave you benison
with all the swagger that they knew—
as losers somehow learn to do.

Your wedding made my eyes ache; soon
the world would be worse off for one
more golden apple dropped to ground
without the least protesting sound,
and you would windfall lie, and we
forget your shimmer on the tree.

Beauty is always wasted: if
not Mignon's song sung to the deaf,
at all events to the unmoved.
A face like yours cannot be loved
long or seriously enough.
Almost, we seem to hold it off.

II

Well, you are tougher than I thought.
Now when the wash with ice hangs taut
this morning of St. Valentine,
I see you strip the squeaking line,
your body weighed against the load,
and all my groans can do no good.

Because you are still beautiful,
though squared and stiffened by the pull
of what nine windy years have done.
You have three daughters, lost a son.
I see all your intelligence
flung into that unwearied stance.

My envy is of no avail.
I turn my head and wish him well
who chafed your beauty into use
and lives forever in a house
lit by the friction of your mind.
You stagger in against the wind.

I finished college, published my first book by a fluke, as it seemed to me, and broke off a love affair. I took a job, lived alone, went on writing, fell in love. I was young, full of energy, and the book seemed to mean that others agreed I was a poet. Because I was also determined to prove that as a woman poet I could also have what was then defined as a "full" woman's life, I plunged in my early twenties into marriage and had three children before I was thirty. There was nothing overt in the environment to warn me: these were the fifties, and in reaction to the earlier wave of feminism, middle-class women were making careers of domestic perfection, working to send their husbands through professional schools, then retiring to raise large families. People were moving out to the suburbs, technology was going to be the answer to everything, even sex; the family was in its glory. Life was extremely private; women were isolated from each other by the loyalties of marriage. I have a sense that women didn't talk to each other much in the fifties—not about their secret emptinesses, their frustrations. I went on trying to write; my second book and first child appeared in the same month. But by the time that book came out I was already dissatisfied with those poems, which seemed to me mere exercises for poems I hadn't written. The book was praised, however, for its "gracefulness"; I had a marriage and a child. If there were doubts, if there were periods of null depression or active despairing, these could only mean that I was ungrateful, insatiable, perhaps a monster.

About the time my third child was born, I felt that I had either to consider myself a failed woman and a failed poet, or to try to find some synthesis by which to understand what was happening to me. What frightened me most was the sense of drift, of being pulled along on a current which called itself my destiny, but in which I seemed to be losing touch with whoever I had been, with the girl who had experienced her own will and energy almost ecstatically at times, walking around a city or riding a train at night or typing in a student room. In a poem about my grandmother I wrote (of myself): "A young girl, thought sleeping, is certified dead" ("Halfway"). I was writing very little, partly from fatigue, that female fatigue of suppressed anger and loss of contact with my own being; partly from the discontinuity of female life with its attention to small chores, errands, work that others constantly undo, small children's constant needs. What I did write was unconvincing to me; my anger and frustration were hard to acknowledge in or out of poems because in fact I cared a great deal about my husband and my children. Trying to look back and understand that time I have tried to analyze the real nature of the conflict. Most, if not all, human lives are full of fantasy—passive day-dreaming which need not be acted on. But to write poetry or fiction, or even to think well, is not to fantasize, or to put fantasies on paper. For a poem to coalesce, for a character or an action to take shape, there has to be an imaginative transformation of reality which is in no way passive. And a certain freedom of the mind is needed— freedom to press on, to enter the currents of your thought like a glider pilot, knowing that your motion can be sustained, that the buoyancy of your attention will not be suddenly snatched away. Moreover, if the imagination is to transcend and transform experience it has to question, to challenge, to conceive of alternatives, perhaps to the very life you are living at that moment. You have to be free to play around with the notion that day might be night, love might be hate; nothing can be too sacred for the imagination to turn into its opposite or to call experimentally by another name. For writing is re-naming. Now, to be maternally with small children all day in the old way, to be with a man in the old way of marriage, requires a holding-back, a putting-aside of that imaginative activity, and demands instead a kind of conservatism. I want to make it clear that I am *not* saying that in order to write well, or think well, it is necessary to become unavailable to others, or to become a devouring ego. This has been the myth of the masculine artist and thinker; and I do not accept it. But to be a female human being trying to fulfill traditional female functions in a traditional way *is* in direct conflict with the subversive function of the imagination. The word traditional is important here. There must be ways, and we will be finding out more and more about them, in which the energy of creation and the energy of relation can be united. But in those years I always felt the conflict as a failure of love in myself. I had thought I was choosing a full life: the life available to most men, in which sexuality, work, and parenthood could coexist. But I felt, at twenty-nine, guilt toward the people closest to me, and guilty toward my own being.

I wanted, then, more than anything, the one thing of which there was never enough: time to think, time to write. The fifties and early sixties were years of rapid revelations: the sit-ins and marches in the South, the Bay of Pigs, the early antiwar movement, raised large questions—questions for which the masculine world of the academy around me seemed to have expert and fluent answers. But I needed to think for myself—about pacifism and dissent and violence, about poetry and society, and about my own relationship to all these things. For about ten years I was reading in fierce snatches, scribbling in notebooks, writing poetry in fragments; I was looking desperately for clues, because if there were no clues then I thought I might be insane. I wrote in a notebook about this time:

> Paralyzed by the sense that there exists a mesh of relationships—e.g., between my anger at the children, my sensual life, pacifism, sex (I mean sex in its broadest significance, not merely sexual desire)—an interconnectedness which, if I could see it, make it valid, would give me back myself, make it possible to function lucidly and passionately. Yet I grope in and out among these dark webs.

I think I began at this point to feel that politics was not something "out there" but something "in here" and of the essence of my condition.

In the late fifties I was able to write, for the first time, directly about experiencing myself as a woman. The poem was jotted in fragments during children's naps, brief hours in a library, or at 3:00 A.M. after rising with a wakeful child. I despaired of doing any continuous work at this time. Yet I began to feel that my fragments and scraps had a common consciousness and a common theme, one which I would have been very unwilling to put on paper at an earlier time because I had been taught that poetry should be "universal," which meant, of course, nonfemale. Until then I had tried very much *not* to identify myself as a female poet. Over two years I wrote a ten-part poem called "Snapshots of a Daughter-in-Law" (1958–1960), in a longer looser mode than I'd ever trusted myself with before. It was an extraordinary relief to write that poem. It strikes me now as too literary, too dependent on allusion; I hadn't found the courage yet to do without authorities, or even to use the pronoun "I"—the woman in the poem is always "she." One section of it, No. 2, concerns a woman who thinks she is going mad; she is haunted by voices telling her to resist and rebel, voices which she can hear but not obey.

2.
Banging the coffee-pot into the sink
she hears the angels chiding, and looks out
past the raked gardens to the sloppy sky.
Only a week since They said: *Have no patience.*

The next time it was: *Be insatiable.*
Then: *Save yourself; others you cannot save.*
Sometimes she's let the tapstream scald her arm,
a match burn to her thumbnail,

or held her hand above the kettle's snout
right in the woolly steam. They are probably angels,
since nothing hurts her anymore, except
each morning's grit blowing into her eyes.

The poem "Orion," written five years later, is a poem of reconnection with a part of myself I had felt I was losing—the active principle, the energetic imagination, the "half-brother" whom I projected, as I had for many years, into the constellation Orion. It's no accident that the words "cold and egotistical" appear in this poem, and are applied to myself.

For back when I went zig-zagging
through tamarack pastures
you were my genius, you
my cast-iron Viking, my helmed
lion-heart king in prison.
Years later now you're young

my fierce half-brother, staring
down from that simplified west

your breast open, your belt dragged down
by an oldfashioned thing, a sword
the last bravado you won't give over
though it weighs you down as you stride

and the stars in it are dim
and maybe have stopped burning.
But you burn, and I know it;
as I throw back my head to take you in
an old transfusion happens again:
divine astronomy is nothing to it.

Indoors I bruise and blunder,
break faith, leave ill enough
alone, a dead child born in the dark.
Night cracks up over the chimney,
pieces of time, frozen geodes
come showering down in the grate.

A man reaches behind my eyes
and finds them empty
a woman's head turns away
from my head in the mirror
children are dying my death
and eating crumbs of my life.

Pity is not your forte.
Calmly you ache up there
pinned aloft in your crow's nest,
my speechless pirate!
You take it all for granted
and when I look you back

it's with a starlike eye
shooting its cold and egotistical spear
where it can do least damage.
Breathe deep!  No hurt, no pardon
out here in the cold with you
you with your back to the wall.

The choice still seemed to be between "love"—womanly, maternal
love, altruistic love—a love defined and ruled by the weight of an entire culture; and egotism—a force directed by men into creation,
achievement, ambition, often at the expense of others, but justifiably

so. For weren't they men, and wasn't that their destiny as womanly, selfless love was ours? We know now that the alternatives are false ones—that the word "love" is itself in need of re-vision.

There is a companion poem to "Orion," written three years later, in which at last the woman in the poem and the woman writing the poem become the same person. It is called "Planetarium," and it was written after a visit to a real planetarium, where I read an account of the work of Caroline Herschel, the astronomer, who worked with her brother William, but whose name remained obscure, as his did not.

*Thinking of Caroline Herschel, 1750–1848, astronomer, sister of William; and others*

A woman in the shape of a monster
a monster in the shape of a woman
the skies are full of them

a woman        "in the snow
among the Clocks and instruments
or measuring the ground with poles"

in her 98 years to discover
8 comets

she whom the moon ruled
like us
levitating into the night sky
riding the polished lenses

Galaxies of women, there
doing penance for impetuousness
ribs chilled
in those spaces        of the mind

An eye,
        "virile, precise and absolutely certain"
        from the mad webs of Uranisborg
                                encountering the NOVA

every impulse of light exploding
from the core
as life flies out of us
        Tycho whispering at last
        "Let me not seem to have lived in vain"

What we see, we see
and seeing is changing

the light that shrivels a mountain
and leaves a man alive

Heartbeat of the pulsar
heart sweating through my body

The radio impulse
pouring in from Taurus

     I am bombarded yet     I stand

I have been standing all my life in the
direct path of a battery of signals
the most accurately transmitted most
untranslateable language in the universe
I am a galactic cloud so deep     so invo-
luted that a light wave could take 15
years to travel through me     And has
taken     I am an instrument in the shape
of a woman trying to translate pulsations
into images     for the relief of the body
and the reconstruction of the mind.

In closing I want to tell you about a dream I had last summer. I dreamed I was asked to read my poetry at a mass women's meeting, but when I began to read, what came out were the lyrics of a blues song. I share this dream with you because it seemed to me to say something about the problems and the future of the woman writer, and probably of women in general. The awakening of consciousness is not like the crossing of a frontier—one step and you are in another country. Much of woman's poetry has been of the nature of the blues song: a cry of pain, of victimization, or a lyric of seduction.[7] And today, much poetry by women—and prose for that matter—is charged with anger. I think we need to go through that anger, and we will betray our own reality if we try, as Virginia Woolf was trying, for an objectivity, a detachment, that would make us sound more like Jane Austen or Shakespeare. We know more than Jane Austen or Shakespeare knew: more than Jane Austen because our lives are more

---

[7] *A. R., 1978:* When I dreamed that dream, was I wholly ignorant of the tradition of Bessie Smith and other women's blues lyrics which transcended victimization to sing of resistance and independence?

complex, more than Shakespeare because we know more about the lives of women—Jane Austen and Virginia Woolf included.

Both the victimization and the anger experienced by women are real, and have real sources, everywhere in the environment, built into society, language, the structures of thought. They will go on being tapped and explored by poets, among others. We can neither deny them, nor will we rest there. A new generation of women poets is already working out of the psychic energy released when women begin to move out towards what the feminist philosopher Mary Daly has described as the "new space" on the boundaries of patriarchy.[8] Women are speaking to and of women in these poems, out of a newly released courage to name, to love each other, to share risk and grief and celebration.

To the eye of a feminist, the work of Western male poets now writing reveals a deep, fatalistic pessimism as to the possibilities of change, whether societal or personal, along with a familiar and threadbare use of women (and nature) as redemptive on the one hand, threatening on the other; and a new tide of phallocentric sadism and overt woman-hating which matches the sexual brutality of recent films. "Political" poetry by men remains stranded amid the struggles for power among male groups; in condemning U.S. imperialism or the Chilean junta the poet can claim to speak for the oppressed while remaining, as male, part of a system of sexual oppression. The enemy is always outside the self, the struggle somewhere else. The mood of isolation, self-pity, and self-imitation that pervades "nonpolitical" poetry suggests that a profound change in masculine consciousness will have to precede any new male poetic—or other—inspiration. The creative energy of patriarchy is fast running out; what remains is its self-generating energy for destruction. As women, we have our work cut out for us.

[8] Mary Daly, *Beyond God the Father: Towards a Philosophy of Women's Liberation* (Boston: Beacon, 1973).

## TERRY EAGLETON

# *Marxism and Literary Criticism* (Chapters 1-2)

## 1976

*In the preface to his book, Eagleton writes ironically: "No doubt we shall soon see Marxist criticism comfortably wedged between Freudian and mythological approaches to literature, as yet one more stimulating academic 'approach,' one more well-tilled field of inquiry for students to tramp." He urges against such an attitude, believing it "dangerous" to the centrality of Marxism as an agent of social change. Despite his warning, however, and because of his claims for the significance of Marxist criticism, Eagleton's opening chapters, dealing with two topics central to literary criticism, are here presented for some thoughtful "tramping."*

*"Marxism," which in some quarters remains a pejorative term, is in fact an indispensable concern in modern intellectual history. Developed primarily as a way of examining historical, economic, and social issues, Marxist doctrine does not deal explicitly with theories of literature; consequently, there is no one orthodox Marxist school (as there is an orthodox Freudianism), but rather a diversity of Marxist readings. Eagleton's own discussion partly illustrates this diversity: he uses the familiar derogatory term "vulgar Marxism" to refer to the simplistic deterministic notion that a literary work is nothing more than the direct product of its socio-economic base. Aware also of how Marxist theory can be perverted, Eagleton in another chapter is scornful of such politically motivated corruptions as the Stalinist doctrine*

of "socialist realism," an extension of statist propaganda that has had chilling effects upon art and artists.

Like many sophisticated Marxist critics, Eagleton stresses the complicated interrelationships between the socio-economic base and the institutions and values (including literature) which comprise the superstructure. But precisely because those relationships are so complex, a wide variety of critical thought has been brought to bear upon them. Thus, Eagleton takes as his starting point an analysis of how various Marxist critics have addressed themselves to particular questions of literary analysis; subsequent chapters of his book, for example, explore the role that the writer plays in advancing the cause of the proletariat and the extent to which literature is a commodity, as much the product of economic activity as the automobile.

Other problems central to Marxist critical discussions include questions such as: What is the relationship between literature and ideology? How does literature develop out of the life of a society? Are there formal laws of literature which serve to distance it from the forms of the material world? Is the primary function of criticism to describe, to explain, to interpret, or to evaluate? To what extent is language separable from society, and is ideology separable from language? To what extent has Marxism, itself a body of theory, been influenced by other modern intellectual currents such as psychoanalysis, existentialism, structuralism, and semiotics? Far from being the monolithic dogma its detractors suggest, Marxism is a living body of thought, seeking to answer questions such as these, which are often ignored in other approaches to literature.

# 1: Literature and history

## Marx, Engels and Criticism

IF KARL MARX and Frederick Engels are better known for their political and economic rather than literary writings, this is not in the least because they regarded literature as insignificant. It is true, as Leon Trotsky remarked in *Literature and Revolution* (1924), that 'there are many people in this world who think as revolutionists and feel as philistines'; but Marx and Engels were not of this number. The writ-

ings of Karl Marx, himself the youthful author of lyric poetry, a fragment of verse-drama and an unfinished comic novel much influenced
by Laurence Sterne, are laced with literary concepts and allusions; he
wrote a sizeable unpublished manuscript on art and religion, and
planned a journal of dramatic criticism, a full-length study of Balzac
and a treatise on aesthetics. Art and literature were part of the very
air Marx breathed, as a formidably cultured German intellectual in
the great classical tradition of his society. His acquaintance with literature, from Sophocles to the Spanish novel, Lucretius to potboiling
English fiction, was staggering in its scope; the German workers' circle
he founded in Brussels devoted an evening a week to discussing the
arts, and Marx himself was an inveterate theatre-goer, declaimer of
poetry, devourer of every species of literary art from Augustan prose
to industrial ballads. He described his own works in a letter to Engels
as forming an 'artistic whole', and was scrupulously sensitive to questions of literary style, not least his own; his very first pieces of journal-
ism argued for freedom of artistic expression. Moreover, the pressure
of aesthetic concepts can be detected behind some of the most crucial
categories of economic thought he employs in his mature work.

Even so, Marx and Engels had rather more important tasks on their
hands than the formulation of a complete aesthetic theory. Their comments on art and literature are scattered and fragmentary, glancing
allusions rather than developed positions. This is one reason why
Marxist criticism involves more than merely re-stating cases set out by
the founders of Marxism. It also involves more than what has become
known in the West as the 'sociology of literature'. The sociology of
literature concerns itself chiefly with what might be called the means of
literary production, distribution and exchange in a particular society—
how books are published, the social composition of their authors and
audiences, levels of literacy, the social determinants of 'taste'. It also
examines literary texts for their 'sociological' relevance, raiding literary
works to abstract from them themes of interest to the social historian.
There has been some excellent work in this field, and it forms one
aspect of Marxist criticism as a whole; but taken by itself it is neither
particularly Marxist nor particularly critical. It is, indeed, for the most
part a suitably tamed, degutted version of Marxist criticism, appropriate for Western consumption.

Marxist criticism is not merely a 'sociology of literature', concerned
with how novels get published and whether they mention the working
class. Its aim is to *explain* the literary work more fully; and this means
a sensitive attention to its forms, styles and meanings. But it also means
grasping those forms, styles and meanings as the products of a par-

ticular history. The painter Henri Matisse once remarked that all art bears the imprint of its historical epoch, but that great art is that in which this imprint is most deeply marked. Most students of literature are taught otherwise: the greatest art is that which timelessly transcends its historical conditions. Marxist criticism has much to say on this issue, but the 'historical' analysis of literature did not of course begin with Marxism. Many thinkers before Marx had tried to account for literary works in terms of the history which produced them; and one of these, the German idealist philosopher G.W.F. Hegel, had a profound influence on Marx's own aesthetic thought. The originality of Marxist criticism, then, lies not in its historical approach to literature, but in its revolutionary understanding of history itself.

## Base and Superstructure

The seeds of that revolutionary understanding are planted in a famous passage in Marx and Engels's *The German Ideology* (1845-6):

> The production of ideas, concepts and consciousness is first of all directly interwoven with the material intercourse of man, the language of real life. Conceiving, thinking, the spiritual intercourse of men, appear here as the direct efflux of men's material behaviour . . . we do not proceed from what men say, imagine, conceive, nor from men as described, thought of, imagined, conceived, in order to arrive at corporeal man; rather we proceed from the really active man . . . Consciousness does not determine life: life determines consciousness.

A fuller statement of what this means can be found in the Preface to *A Contribution to the Critique of Political Economy* (1859):

> In the social production of their life, men enter into definite relations that are indispensable and independent of their will, *relations of production* which correspond to a definite stage of development of their material productive *forces*. The sum total of these relations of production constitutes the economic structure of society, the real foundation, on which rises a legal and political superstructure and to which correspond definite forms of social consciousness. The mode of production of material life conditions the social, political and intellectual life process in general. It is not the consciousness of men that determines their being, but on the contrary, their social being that determines their consciousness.

The social relations between men, in other words, are bound up with the way they produce their material life. Certain 'productive forces'—say, the organisation of labour in the middle ages—involve the social relations of villein to lord we know as feudalism. At a later stage, the development of new modes of productive organisation is based on a changed set of social relations—this time between the capitalist class who owns those means of production, and the proletarian class whose labour-power the capitalist buys for profit. Taken together, these 'forces' and 'relations' of production form what Marx calls 'the economic structure of society', or what is more commonly known by Marxism as the economic 'base' or 'infrastructure'. From this economic base, in every period, emerges a 'superstructure'—certain forms of law and politics, a certain kind of state, whose essential function is to legitimate the power of the social class which owns the means of economic production. But the superstructure contains more than this: it also consists of certain 'definite forms of social consciousness' (political, religious, ethical, aesthetic and so on), which is what Marxism designates as *ideology*. The function of ideology, also, is to legitimate the power of the ruling class in society; in the last analysis, the dominant ideas of a society are the ideas of its ruling class.

Art, then, is for Marxism part of the 'superstructure' of society. It is (with qualifications we shall make later) part of a society's ideology—an element in that complex structure of social perception which ensures that the situation in which one social class has power over the others is either seen by most members of the society as 'natural', or not seen at all. To understand literature, then, means understanding the total social process of which it is part. As the Russian Marxist critic Georgy Plekhanov put it: 'The social mentality of an age is conditioned by that age's social relations. This is nowhere quite as evident as in the history of art and literature'. Literary works are not mysteriously inspired, or explicable simply in terms of their authors' psychology. They are forms of perception, particular ways of seeing the world; and as such they have a relation to that dominant way of seeing the world which is the 'social mentality' or ideology of an age. That ideology, in turn, is the product of the concrete social relations into which men enter at a particular time and place; it is the way those class-relations are experienced, legitimized and perpetuated. Moreover, men are not free to choose their social relations; they are constrained into them by material necessity—by the nature and stage of development of their mode of economic production.

To understand *King Lear, The Dunciad* or *Ulysses* is therefore to do more than interpret their symbolism, study their literary history and add footnotes about sociological facts which enter into them. It is first of all to understand the complex, indirect relations between those works and the ideological worlds they inhabit—relations which emerge not just in 'themes' and 'preoccupations', but in style, rhythm, image, quality and (as we shall see later) *form*. But we do not understand ideology either unless we grasp the part it plays in the society as a whole—how it consists of a definite, historically relative structure of perception which underpins the power of a particular social class. This is not an easy task, since an ideology is never a simple reflection of a ruling class's ideas; on the contrary, it is always a complex phenomenon, which may incorporate conflicting, even contradictory, views of the world. To understand an ideology, we must analyse the precise relations between different classes in a society; and to do that means grasping where those classes stand in relation to the mode of production.

All this may seem a tall order to the student of literature who thought he was merely required to discuss plot and characterization. It may seem a confusion of literary criticism with disciplines like politics and economics which ought to be kept separate. But it is, nonetheless, essential for the fullest explanation of any work of literature. Take, for example, the great Placido Gulf scene in Conrad's *Nostromo*. To evaluate the fine artistic force of this episode, as Decoud and Nostromo are isolated in utter darkness on the slowly sinking lighter, involves us in subtly placing the scene within the imaginative vision of the novel as a whole. The radical pessimism of that vision (and to grasp it fully we must, of course, relate *Nostromo* to the rest of Conrad's fiction) cannot simply be accounted for in terms of 'psychological' factors in Conrad himself; for individual psychology is also a *social* product. The pessimism of Conrad's world view is rather a unique transformation into art of an ideological pessimism rife in his period— a sense of history as futile and cyclical, of individuals as impenetrable and solitary, of human values as relativistic and irrational, which marks a drastic crisis in the ideology of the Western bourgeois class to which Conrad allied himself. There were good reasons for that ideological crisis, in the history of imperialist capitalism throughout this period. Conrad did not, of course, merely anonymously reflect that history in his fiction; every writer is individually placed in society, responding to a general history from his own particular standpoint, making sense of it in his own concrete terms. But it is not difficult to see how Conrad's personal standing, as an 'aristocratic' Polish exile deeply committed to English conservatism, intensified for him the crisis of English bourgeois ideology.

It is also possible to see in these terms why that scene in the Placido

Gulf should be artistically fine. To write well is more than a matter of 'style'; it also means having at one's disposal an ideological perspective which can penetrate to the realities of men's experience in a certain situation. This is certainly what the Placido Gulf scene does; and it can do it, not just because its author happens to have an excellent prose-style, but because his historical situation allows him access to such insights. Whether those insights are in political terms 'progressive' or 'reactionary' (Conrad's are certainly the latter) is not the point—any more than it is to the point that most of the agreed major writers of the twentieth century—Yeats, Eliot, Pound, Lawrence—are political conservatives who each had truck with fascism. Marxist criticism, rather than apologising for the fact, explains it—sees that, in the absence of genuinely revolutionary art, only a radical conservatism, hostile like Marxism to the withered values of liberal bourgeois society, could produce the most significant literature.

## Literature and Superstructure

It would be a mistake to imply that Marxist criticism moves mechanically from 'text' to 'ideology' to 'social relations' to 'productive forces'. It is concerned, rather, with the *unity* of these 'levels' of society. Literature may be part of the superstructure, but it is not merely the passive reflection of the economic base. Engels makes this clear, in a letter to Joseph Bloch in 1890:

> According to the materialist conception of history, the determining element in history is *ultimately* the production and reproduction in real life. More than this neither Marx nor I have ever asserted. If therefore somebody twists this into the statement that the economic element is the *only* determining one, he transforms it into a meaningless, abstract and absurd phrase. The economic situation is the basis, but the various elements of the superstructure—political forms of the class struggle and its consequences, constitutions established by the victorious class after a successful battle, etc.—forms of law—and then even the reflexes of all these actual struggles in the brains of the combatants: political, legal, and philosophical theories, religious ideas and their further development into systems of dogma— also exercise their influence upon the course of the historical struggles and in many cases preponderate in determining their *form*.

Engels wants to deny that there is any mechanical, one-to-one correspondence between base and superstructure; elements of the superstructure constantly react back upon and influence the economic base. The materialist theory of history denies that art can *in itself* change the course of history; but it insists that art can be an active element in such change. Indeed, when Marx came to consider the relation between base and superstructure, it was art which he selected as an instance of the complexity and indirectness of that relationship:

> In the case of the arts, it is well known that certain periods of their flowering are out of all proportion to the general development of society, hence also to the material foundation, the skeletal structure, as it were, of its organisation. For example, the Greeks compared to the moderns or also Shakespeare. It is even recognised that certain forms of art, e.g. the epic, can no longer be produced in their world epoch-making, classical stature as soon as the production of art, as such, begins; that is, that certain significant forms within the realm of the arts are possible only at an undeveloped stage of artistic development. If this is the case with the relation between different kinds of art within the realm of art, it is already less puzzling that it is the case in the relation of the entire realm to the general development of society. The difficulty consists only in the general formulation of these contradictions. As soon as they have been specified, they are already clarified.

Marx is considering here what he calls 'the unequal relationship of the development of material production . . . to artistic production'. It does not follow that the greatest artistic achievements depend upon the highest development of the productive forces, as the example of the Greeks, who produced major art in an economically undeveloped society, clearly evidences. Certain major artistic forms like the epic are only *possible* in an undeveloped society. Why then, Marx goes on to ask, do we still respond to such forms, given our historical distance from them?:

> But the difficulty lies not in understanding that the Greek arts and epic are bound up with certain forms of social development. The difficulty is that they still afford us artistic pleasure and that in a certain respect they count as a norm and as an unattainable model.

Why does Greek art still give us aesthetic pleasure? The answer which Marx goes on to provide has been universally lambasted by unsympathetic commentators as lamely inept:

A man cannot become a child again, or he becomes childish. But does he not find joy in the child's naiveté, and must he himself not strive to reproduce its truth at a higher stage? Does not the true character of each epoch come alive in the nature of its children? Why should not the historic childhood of humanity, its most beautiful unfolding, as a stage never to return, exercise an eternal charm? There are unruly children and precocious children. Many of the old peoples belong in this category. The Greeks were normal children. The charm of their art for us it not in contradiction to the undeveloped stage of society on which it grew. (It) is its result, rather, and is inextricably bound up, rather, with the fact that the unripe social conditions under which it arose, and could alone rise, can never return.

So our liking for Greek art is a nostalgic lapse back into childhood—a piece of unmaterialist sentimentalism which hostile critics have gladly pounced on. But the passage can only be treated thus if it is rudely ripped from the context to which it belongs—the draft manuscripts of 1857, known today as the *Grundrisse*. Once returned to that context, the meaning becomes instantly apparent. The Greeks, Marx is arguing, were able to produce major art not *in spite of* but *because of* the undeveloped state of their society. In ancient societies, which have not yet undergone the fragmenting 'division of labour' known to capitalism, the overwhelming of 'quality' by 'quantity' which results from commodity-production and the restless, continual development of the productive forces, a certain 'measure' or harmony can be achieved between man and Nature—a harmony precisely dependent upon the *limited* nature of Greek society. The 'childlike' world of the Greeks is attractive because it thrives within certain measured limits—measures and limits which are brutally overridden by bourgeois society in its limitless demand to produce and consume. Historically, it is essential that this constricted society should be broken up as the productive forces expand beyond its frontiers; but when Marx speaks of 'striv(ing) to reproduce its truth at a higher stage', he is clearly speaking of the communist society of the future, where unlimited resources will serve an unlimitedly developing man.

   Two questions, then, emerge from Marx's formulations in the *Grundrisse*. The first concerns the relation between 'base' and 'superstructure'; the second concerns our own relation in the present with past art. To take the second question first: how can it be that we moderns still find aesthetic appeal in the cultural products of past, vastly different societies? In a sense, the answer Marx gives is no different from the answer to the question: How is it that we moderns still respond to the exploits of, say, Spartacus? We respond to Spartacus or Greek sculpture because our own history links us to those ancient societies; we find in them an undeveloped phase of the forces which condition us. Moreover, we find in those ancient societies a primitive image of 'measure' between man and Nature which capitalist society necessarily destroys, and which socialist society can reproduce at an incomparably higher level. We ought, in other words, to think of 'history' in wider terms than our own contemporary history. To ask how Dickens relates to history is not just to ask how he relates to Victorian England, for that society was itself the product of a long history which includes men like Shakespeare and Milton. It is a curiously narrowed view of history which defines it merely as the 'contemporary moment' and relegates all else to the 'universal'. One answer to the problem of past and present is suggested by Bertolt Brecht, who argues that 'we need to develop the historical sense . . . into a real sensual delight. When our theatres perform plays of other periods they like to annihilate distance, fill in the gap, gloss over the differences. But what comes then of our delight in comparisons, in distance, in dissimilarity—which is at the same time a delight in what is close and proper to ourselves?'

The other problem posed by the *Grundrisse* is the relation between base and superstructure. Marx is clear that these two aspects of society do not form a *symmetrical* relationship, dancing a harmonious minuet hand-in-hand throughout history. Each element of a society's superstructure—art, law, politics, religion—has its own tempo of development, its own internal evolution, which is not reducible to a mere expression of the class struggle or the state of the economy. Art, as Trotsky comments, has 'a very high degree of autonomy'; it is not tied in any simple one-to-one way to the mode of production. And yet Marxism claims too that, in the last analysis, art is determined by that mode of production. How are we to explain this apparent discrepancy?

Let us take a concrete literary example. A 'vulgar Marxist' case about T.S. Eliot's *The Waste Land* might be that the poem is directly determined by ideological and economic factors—by the spiritual emptiness and exhaustion of bourgeois ideology which springs from that crisis of imperialist capitalism known as the First World War. This is to explain the poem as an immediate 'reflection' of those conditions; but it clearly fails to take into account a whole series of 'levels' which 'mediate' between the text itself and capitalist economy. It says nothing, for instance, about the social situation of Eliot himself—a writer living an ambiguous relationship with English society,

as an 'aristocratic' American expatriate who became a glorified City
clerk and yet identified deeply with the conservative-traditionalist,
rather than bourgeois-commercialist, elements of English ideology. It
says nothing about that ideology's more general forms—nothing of its
structure, content, internal complexity, and how all these are produced
by the extremely complex class-relations of English society at the time.
It is silent about the form and language of *The Waste Land*—about
why Eliot, despite his extreme political conservatism, was an *avant-
garde* poet who selected certain 'progressive' experimental techniques
from the history of literary forms available to him, and on what ideological basis he did this. We learn nothing from this approach about
the social conditions which gave rise at the time to certain forms of
'spirituality', part-Christian, part-Buddhist, which the poem draws on;
or of what role a certain kind of bourgeois anthropology (Fraser) and
bourgeois philosophy (F.H. Bradley's idealism) used by the poem fulfilled in the ideological formation of the period. We are unilluminated
about Eliot's social position as an artist, part of a self-consciously
erudite, experimental élite with particular modes of publication (the
small press, the little magazine) at their disposal; or about the kind
of audience which that implied, and its effect on the poem's styles and
devices. We remain ignorant about the relation between the poem
and the aesthetic theories associated with it—of what role that aesthetic
plays in the ideology of the time, and how it shapes the construction of
the poem itself.

Any complete understanding of *The Waste Land* would need to
take these (and other) factors into account. It is not a matter of
*reducing* the poem to the state of contemporary capitalism; but neither
is it a matter of introducing so many judicious complications that
anything as crude as capitalism may to all intents and purposes be forgotten. On the contrary: all of the elements I have enumerated (the
author's class-position, ideological forms and their relation to literary
forms, 'spirituality' and philosophy, techniques of literary production, aesthetic theory) are directly relevant to the base/superstructure
model. What Marxist criticism looks for is the unique *conjuncture* of
these elements which we know as *The Waste Land*. No one of these
elements can be conflated with another: each has its own relative independence. *The Waste Land* can indeed be explained as a poem
which springs from a crisis of bourgeois ideology, but it has no simple
correspondence with that crisis or with the political and economic
conditions which produced it. (As a poem, it does not of course *know
itself* as a product of a particular ideological crisis, for if it did it
would cease to exist. It needs to translate that crisis into 'universal'

terms—to grasp it as part of an unchanging human condition, shared alike by ancient Egyptians and modern man.) *The Waste Land*'s relation to the real history of its time, then, is highly *mediated*; and in this it is like all works of art.

## Literature and Ideology

Friedrich Engels remarks in *Ludwig Feuerbach and the End of Classical German Philosophy* (1888) that art is far richer and more 'opaque' than political and economic theory because it is less purely ideological. It is important here to grasp the precise meaning for Marxism of 'ideology'. Ideology is not in the first place a set of doctrines; it signifies the way men live out their roles in class-society, the values, ideas and images which tie them to their social functions and so prevent them from a true knowledge of society as a whole. In this sense *The Waste Land* is ideological: it shows a man making sense of his experience in ways that prohibit a true understanding of his society, ways that are consequently false. All art springs from an ideological conception of the world; there is no such thing, Plekhanov comments, as a work of art entirely devoid of ideological content. But Engels' remark suggests that art has a more complex relationship to ideology than law and political theory, which rather more transparently embody the interests of a ruling class. The question, then, is what relationship art has to ideology.

This is not an easy question to answer. Two extreme, opposite positions are possible here. One is that literature is *nothing but* ideology in a certain artistic form—that works of literature are just expressions of the ideologies of their time. They are prisoners of 'false consciousness', unable to reach beyond it to arrive at the truth. It is a position characteristic of much 'vulgar Marxist' criticism, which tends to see literary works merely as reflections of dominant ideologies. As such, it is unable to explain, for one thing, why so much literature actually *challenges* the ideological assumptions of its time. The opposite case seizes on the fact that so much literature challenges the ideology it confronts, and makes this part of the definition of literary art itself. Authentic art, as Ernst Fischer argues in his significantly entitled *Art Against Ideology* (1969), always transcends the ideological limits of its time, yielding us insight into the realities which ideology hides from view.

Both of these cases seem to me too simple. A more subtle (although still incomplete) account of the relationship between literature and ideology is provided by the French Marxist theorist Louis Althusser.

Althusser argues that art cannot be reduced to ideology: it has, rather, a particular *relationship* to it. Ideology signifies the imaginary ways in which men experience the real world, which is, of course, the kind of experience literature gives us too—what it feels like to live in particular conditions, rather than a conceptual analysis of those conditions. However, art does more than just passively reflect that experience. It is held within ideology, but also manages to distance itself from it, to the point where it permits us to 'feel' and 'perceive' the ideology from which it springs. In doing this, art does not enable us to *know* the truth which ideology conceals, since for Althusser 'knowledge' in the strict sense means *scientific* knowledge—the kind of knowledge of, say, capitalism which Marx's *Capital* rather than Dickens's *Hard Times* allows us. The difference between science and art is not that they deal with different objects, but that they deal with the same objects in different ways. Science gives us conceptual knowledge of a situation; art gives us the experience of that situation, which is equivalent to ideology. But by doing this, it allows us to 'see' the nature of that ideology, and thus begins to move us towards that full understanding of ideology which is scientific knowledge.

How literature can do this is more fully developed by one of Althusser's colleagues, Pierre Macherey. In his *Pour Une Théorie de la Production Littéraire* (1966), Macherey distinguishes between what he terms 'illusion' (meaning essentially, ideology), and 'fiction'. Illusion— the ordinary ideological experience of men—is the material on which the writer goes to work; but in working on it he transforms it into something different, lends it a shape and structure. It is by giving ideology a determinate form, fixing it within certain fictional limits, that art is able to distance itself from it, thus revealing to us the limits of that ideology. In doing this, Macherey claims, art contributes to our deliverance from the ideological illusion.

I find the comments of both Althusser and Macherey at crucial points ambiguous and obscure; but the relation they propose between literature and ideology is nonetheless deeply suggestive. Ideology, for both critics, is more than an amorphous body of free-floating images and ideas; in any society it has a certain structural coherence. Because it possesses such relative coherence, it can be the object of scientific analysis; and since literary texts 'belong' to ideology, they too can be the object of such scientific analysis. A scientific criticism would seek to explain the literary work in terms of the ideological structure of which it is part, yet which it transforms in its art: it would search out the principle which both ties the work to ideology and distances it from it. The finest Marxist criticism has indeed done precisely that;

Macherey's starting-point is Lenin's brilliant analyses of Tolstoy. To do this, however, means grasping the literary work as a *formal* structure; and it is to this question that we can now turn.

# 2: Form and content

## History and Form

IN HIS EARLY essay *The Evolution of Modern Drama* (1909), the Hungarian Marxist critic Georg Lukács writes that 'the truly social element in literature is the form'. This is not the kind of comment which has come to be expected of Marxist criticism. For one thing, Marxist criticism has traditionally opposed all kinds of literary formalism, attacking that inbred attention to sheerly technical properties which robs literature of historical significance and reduces it to an aesthetic game. It has, indeed, noted the relationship between such critical technocracy and the behaviour of advanced capitalist societies. For another thing, a good deal of Marxist criticism has in practice paid scant attention to questions of artistic form, shelving the issue in its dogged pursuit of political content. Marx himself believed that literature should reveal a unity of form and content, and burnt some of his own early lyric poems on the grounds that their rhapsodic feelings were dangerously unrestrained; but he was also suspicious of excessively formalistic writing. In an early newspaper article on Silesian weavers' songs, he claimed that mere stylistic exercises led to 'perverted content', which in turn impresses the stamp of 'vulgarity' on literary form. He shows, in other words, a *dialectical* grasp of the relations in question: form is the product of content, but reacts back upon it in a double-edged relationship. Marx's early comment about oppressively formalistic law in the *Rheinische Zeitung*—'form is of no value unless it is the form of its content'—could equally be applied to his aesthetic views.

In arguing for a unity of form and content, Marx was being faithful to the Hegelian tradition he inherited. Hegel had argued in the *Philosophy of Fine Art* (1835) that 'every definite content determines a form suitable to it'. 'Defectiveness of form', he maintained, 'arises from defectiveness of content'. Indeed for Hegel the history of art can be written in terms of the varying relations between form and content. Art manifests different stages in the development of what Hegel calls the 'World-Spirit', the 'Idea' or the 'Absolute'; this is the 'content' of art, which successively strives to embody itself adequately in artistic form. At an early stage of historical development, the World-Spirit can find no adequate formal realization: ancient sculpture, for example, reveals how the 'Spirit' is obstructed and overwhelmed by an excess of sensual material which it is unable to mould to its own purposes. Greek classical art, on the other hand, achieves an harmonious unity between content and form, the spiritual and the material: here, for a brief historical moment, 'content' finds its entirely appropriate embodiment. In the modern world, however, and most typically in Romanticism, the spiritual absorbs the sensual, content overwhelms form. Material forms give way before the highest development of the Spirit, which like Marx's productive forces have outstripped the limited classical moulds which previously contained them.

It would be mistaken to think that Marx adopted Hegel's aesthetic wholesale. Hegel's aesthetic is idealist, drastically oversimplifying and only to a limited extent dialectical; and in any case Marx disagreed with Hegel over several concrete aesthetic issues. But both thinkers share the belief that artistic form is no mere quirk on the part of the individual artist. Forms are historically determined by the kind of 'content' they have to embody; they are changed, transformed, broken down and revolutionized as that content itself changes. 'Content' is in this sense prior to 'form', just as for Marxism it is changes in a society's material 'content', its mode of production, which determine the 'forms' of its superstructure. 'Form itself', Fredric Jameson has remarked in his *Marxism and Form* (1971), 'is but the working out of content in the realm of the superstructure'. To those who reply irritably that form and content are inseparable anyway—that the distinction is artificial—it is as well to say immediately that this is of course true *in practice*. Hegel himself recognized this: 'Content', he wrote, 'is nothing but the transformation of form into content, and form is nothing but the transformation of content into form'. But if form and content are inseparable in practice, they are theoretically distinct. This is why we can talk of the varying *relations* between the two.

Those relations, however, are not easy to grasp. Marxist criticism sees form and content as dialectically related, and yet wants to assert in the end the primacy of content in determining form. The point is put, tortuously but correctly, by Ralph Fox in his *The Novel and the People* (1937), when he declares that 'Form is produced by content, is identical and one with it, and, though the primacy is on the side of content, form reacts on content and never remains passive.' This dialectical conception of the form-content relationship sets itself against two opposed positions. On the one hand, it attacks that formalist school (epitomized by the Russian Formalists of the 1920s) for whom content is merely a function of form—for whom the content of a poem is selected merely to reinforce the technical devices the poem deploys. But it also criticizes the 'vulgar Marxist' notion that artistic form is merely an artifice, externally imposed on the turbulent content of history itself. Such a position is to be found in Christopher Caudwell's *Studies in a Dying Culture* (1938). In that book, Caudwell distinguishes between what he calls 'social being'—the vital, instinctual stuff of human experience—and a society's forms of consciousness. Revolution occurs when those forms, having become ossified and obsolete, are burst asunder by the dynamic, chaotic flood of 'social being' itself. Caudwell, in other words, thinks of 'social being' (*content*) as inherently formless, and of forms as inherently restrictive; he lacks, that is to say, a sufficiently dialectical understanding of the relations at issue. What he does not see is that 'form' does not merely process the raw material of 'content', because that content (whether social or literary) is for Marxism already *informed*; it has a significant structure. Caudwell's view is merely a variant of the bourgeois critical commonplace that art 'organizes the chaos of reality'. (What is the ideological significance of seeing reality as chaotic?) Fredric Jameson, by contrast, speaks of the 'inner logic of content', of which social or literary forms are transformative products.

Given such a limited view of the form-content relationship, it is not surprising that English Marxist critics of the 1930s fall often enough into the 'vulgar Marxist' mistake of raiding literary works for their ideological content and relating this directly to the class-struggle or the economy. It is against this danger that Lukács's comment is meant to warn: the true bearers of ideology in art are the very forms, rather than abstractable content, of the work itself. We find the impress of history in the literary work precisely *as literary*, not as some superior form of social documentation.

## Form and Ideology

What does it mean to say that literary form is ideological? In a suggestive comment in *Literature and Revolution*, Leon Trotsky maintains that 'The relationship between form and content is determined by the fact that the new form is discovered, proclaimed and evolved under the pressure of an inner need, of a collective psychological de-

mand which, like everything else . . . has its social roots.' Significant
developments in literary form, then, result from significant changes in
ideology. They embody new ways of perceiving social reality and (as
we shall see later) new relations between artist and audience. This is
evident enough if we look at well-charted examples like the rise of the
novel in eighteenth-century England. The novel, as Ian Watt has
argued, reveals in its very *form* a changed set of ideological interests.
No matter what content a particular novel of the time may have, it
shares certain formal structures with other such works: a shifting of
interest from the romantic and supernatural to individual psychology
and 'routine' experience; a concept of life-like, substantial 'character';
a concern with the material fortunes of an individual protagonist who
moves through an unpredictably evolving, linear narrative and so on.
This changed form, Watt claims, is the product of an increasingly confident bourgeois class, whose consciousness has broken beyond the
limits of older, 'aristocratic' literary conventions. Plekhanov argues
rather similarly in *French Dramatic Literature and French 18th Century Painting* that the transition from classical tragedy to sentimental
comedy in France reflects a shift from aristocratic to bourgeois values.
Or take the break from 'naturalism' to 'expressionism' in the European
theatre around the turn of the century. This, as Raymond Williams
has suggested, signals a breakdown in certain dramatic conventions
which in turn embody specific 'structures of feeling', a set of received
ways of perceiving and responding to reality. Expressionism feels the
need to transcend the limits of a naturalistic theatre which assumes the
ordinary bourgeois world to be solid, to rip open that deception and
dissolve its social relations, penetrating by symbol and fantasy to the
estranged, self-divided psyches which 'normality' conceals. The transforming of a stage convention, then, signifies a deeper transformation
in bourgeois ideology, as confident mid-Victorian notions of selfhood
and relationship began to splinter and crumble in the face of growing
world capitalist crises.

    There is, needless to say, no simple, symmetrical relationship be-
tween changes in literary form and changes in ideology. Literary form,
as Trotsky reminds us, has a high degree of autonomy; it evolves partly
in accordance with its own internal pressures, and does not merely
bend to every ideological wind that blows. Just as for Marxist economic theory each economic formation tends to contain traces of older,
superseded modes of production, so traces of older literary forms sur-
vive within new ones. Form, I would suggest, is always a complex
unity of at least three elements: it is partly shaped by a 'relatively
autonomous' literary history of forms; it crystallizes out of certain

dominant ideological structures, as we have seen in the case of the novel; and as we shall see later, it embodies a specific set of relations between author and audience. It is the dialectical unity between these elements that Marxist criticism is concerned to analyse. In selecting a form, then, the writer finds his choice already ideologically circumscribed. He may combine and transmute forms available to him from a literary tradition, but these forms themselves, as well as his permutation of them, are ideologically significant. The languages and devices a writer finds to hand are already saturated with certain ideological modes of perception, certain codified ways of interpreting reality; and the extent to which he can modify or remake those languages depends on more than his personal genius. It depends on whether at that point in history, 'ideology' is such that they must and can be changed.

## Lukács and Literary Form

It is in the work of Georg Lukács that the problem of literary form has been most thoroughly explored. In his early, pre-Marxist work, *The Theory of the Novel* (1920), Lukács follows Hegel in seeing the novel as the 'bourgeois epic', but an epic which unlike its classical counterpart reveals the homelessness and alienation of man in modern society. In Greek classical society man is at home in the universe, moving within a rounded, complete world of immanent meaning which is adequate to his soul's demands. The novel arises when that harmonious integration of man and his world is shattered; the hero of fiction is now in search of a totality, estranged from a world either too large or too narrow to give shape to his desires. Haunted by the disparity between empirical reality and a vanished absolute, the novel's form is typically *ironic*; it is 'the epic of a world abandoned by God'.

Lukács rejected this cosmic pessimism when he became a Marxist; but much of his later work on the novel retains the Hegelian emphases of *The Theory of the Novel*. For the Marxist Lukács of *Studies in European Realism* and *The Historical Novel*, the greatest artists are those who can recapture and recreate a harmonious totality of human life. In a society where the general and the particular, the conceptual and the sensuous, the social and the individual are increasingly torn apart by the 'alienations' of capitalism, the great writer draws these dialectically together into a complex totality. His fiction thus mirrors, in microcosmic form, the complex totality of society itself. In doing this, great art combats the alienation and fragmentation of capitalist society, projecting a rich, many-sided image of human wholeness. Lukács names such art 'realism', and takes it to include the Greeks and

Shakespeare as much as Balzac and Tolstoy; the three great periods of historical 'realism' are ancient Greece, the Renaissance, and France in the early nineteenth century. A 'realist' work is rich in a complex, comprehensive set of relations between man, nature and history; and these relations embody and unfold what for Marxism is most 'typical' about a particular phase of history. By the 'typical' Lukács denotes those latent forces in any society which are from a Marxist viewpoint most historically significant and progressive, which lay bare the society's inner structure and dynamic. The task of the realist writer is to flesh out these 'typical' trends and forces in sensuously realized individuals and actions; in doing so he links the individual to the social whole, and informs each concrete particular of social life with the power of the 'world-historical'—the significant movements of history itself.

Lukács's major critical concepts—'totality', 'typicality', 'world-historical'—are essentially Hegelian rather than directly Marxist, although Marx and Engels certainly use the notion of 'typicality' in their own literary criticism. Engels remarked in a letter to Lassalle that true character must combine typicality with individuality; and both he and Marx thought this a major achievement of Shakespeare and Balzac. A 'typical' or 'representative' character incarnates historical forces without thereby ceasing to be richly individualized; and for a writer to dramatize those historical forces he must, for Lukács, be 'progressive' in his art. All great art is socially progressive in the sense that, whatever the author's conscious political allegiance (and in the case of Scott and Balzac it is overtly reactionary), it realizes the vital 'world-historical' forces of an epoch which make for change and growth, revealing their unfolding potential in its fullest complexity. The realist writer, then, penetrates through the accidental phenomena of social life to disclose the essences or essentials of a condition, selecting and combining them into a total form and fleshing them out in concrete experience.

Whether or not a writer can do this depends for Lukács not just on his personal skill but on his position within history. The great realist writers arise from a history which is visibly in the making; the historical novel, for example, appears as a *genre* at a point of revolutionary turbulence in the early nineteenth century, where it was possible for writers to grasp their own present as *history*—or, to put it in Lukács's phrase, to see past history as 'the pre-history of the present'. Shakespeare, Scott, Balzac and Tolstoy can produce major realist art because they are present at the tumultuous birth of an historical epoch, and so are dramatically engaged with the vividly exposed 'typical' conflicts and dynamics of their societies. It is this historical 'content' which lays the basis for their formal achievement; 'richness and profundity of created characters', Lukács claims, 'relies upon the richness and profundity of the total social process'. For the successors of the realists— for, say, Flaubert who follows Balzac—history is already an inert object, an externally given fact no longer imaginable as men's dynamic product. Realism, deprived of the historical conditions which gave it birth, splinters and declines into 'naturalism' on the one hand and 'formalism' on the other.

The crucial transition here for Lukács is the failure of the European revolutions of 1848—a failure which signals the defeat of the proletariat, seals the demise of the progressive, heroic period of bourgeois power, freezes the class-struggle and cues the bourgeoisie for its proper, sordidly unheroic task of consolidating capitalism. Bourgeois ideology forgets its previous revolutionary ideals, dehistoricizes reality and accepts society as a natural fact. Balzac depicts the last great struggles against the capitalist degradation of man, while his successors passively register an already degraded capitalist world. This draining of direction and meaning from history results in the art we know as naturalism. By naturalism Lukács means that distortion of realism epitomized by Zola, which merely photographically reproduces the surface phenomena of society without penetrating to their significant essences. Meticulously observed detail replaces the portrayal of 'typical' features; the dialectical relations between men and their world give way to an environment of dead, contingent objects disconnected from characters; the truly 'representative' character yields to a 'cult of the average'; psychology or physiology oust history as the true determinant of individual action. It is an alienated vision of reality, transforming the writer from an active participant in history to a clinical observer. Lacking an understanding of the typical, naturalism can create no significant totality from its materials; the unified epic or dramatic actions launched by realism collapse into a set of purely private interests.

'Formalism' reacts in an opposite direction, but betrays the same loss of historical meaning. In the alienated worlds of Kafka, Musil, Joyce, Beckett, Camus, man is stripped of his history and has no reality beyond the self; character is dissolved to mental states, objective reality reduced to unintelligible chaos. As with naturalism, the dialectical unity between inner and outer worlds is destroyed, and both individual and society consequently emptied of meaning. Individuals are gripped by despair and *angst,* robbed of social relations and so of authentic selfhood; history becomes pointless or cyclical, dwindled to mere duration. Objects lack significance and become merely contingent; and so symbolism gives way to allegory, which rejects the idea of immanent meaning. If naturalism is a kind of abstract objectivity, formalism is an abstract subjectivity; both diverge from that genuinely dialectical art-form (realism) whose form mediates between concrete and general, essence and existence, type and individual.

## Goldmann and Genetic Structuralism

George Lukács's chief disciple, in what has been termed the 'neo-Hegelian' school of Marxist criticism, is the Rumanian critic Lucien Goldmann. Goldmann is concerned to examine the structure of a literary text for the degree to which it embodies the structure of thought (or 'world vision') of the social class or group to which the writer belongs. The more closely the text approximates to a complete, coherent articulation of the social class's 'world vision', the greater is its validity as a work of art. For Goldmann, literary works are not in the first place to be seen as the creation of individuals, but of what he calls the 'trans-individual mental structures' of a social group—by which he means the structure of ideas, values and aspirations that group shares. Great writers are those exceptional individuals who manage to transpose into art the world vision of the class or group to which they belong, and to do this in a peculiarly unified and translucent (although not necessarily conscious) way.

Goldmann terms his critical method 'genetic structuralism', and it is important to understand both terms of that phrase. *Structuralism*, because he is less interested in the contents of a particular world vision than in the structure of categories it displays. Two apparently quite different writers may thus be shown to belong to the same collective mental structure. *Genetic*, because Goldmann is concerned with how such mental structures are historically produced—concerned, that is to say, with the relations between a world vision and the historical conditions which give rise to it.

Goldmann's work on Racine in *The Hidden God* is perhaps the most exemplary model of his critical method. He discerns in Racine's drama a certain recurrent structure of categories—God, World, Man—which alter in their 'content' and interrelations from play to play, but which disclose a particular world vision. It is the world vision of men who are lost in a valueless world, accept this world as the only one there is (since God is absent), and yet continue to protest against it—to justify themselves in the name of some absolute value which is always hidden from view. The basis of this world vision Goldmann finds in the French religious movement known as Jansenism; and he explains Jansenism, in turn, as the product of a certain displaced social group in seventeenth-century France—the so-called *noblesse de robe*, the court officials who were economically dependent on the monarchy and yet becoming increasingly powerless in the face of that monarchy's growing absolutism. The contradictory situation of this group, needing the Crown but politically opposed to it, is expressed in Jansenism's refusal both of the world and of any desire to change it historically. All of this has a 'world-historical' significance: the *noblesse de robe*, themselves recruited from the bourgeois class, represent the failure of the bourgeoisie to break royal absolutism and establish the conditions for capitalist development.

What Goldmann is seeking, then, is a set of structural relations between literary text, world vision and history itself. He wants to show how the historical situation of a social group or class is transposed, by the mediation of its world vision, into the structure of a literary work. To do this it is not enough to begin with the text and work outwards to history, or vice versa; what is required is a dialectical method of criticism which moves constantly between text, world vision and history, adjusting each to the others.

Interesting as it is, Goldmann's critical enterprise seems to me marred by certain major flaws. His concept of social consciousness, for example, is Hegelian rather than Marxist: he sees it as the direct expression of a social class, just as the literary work then becomes the direct expression of this consciousness. His whole model, in other words, is too trimly symmetrical, unable to accommodate the dialectical conflicts and complexities, the unevenness and discontinuity, which characterize literature's relation to society. It declines, in his later work *Pour une Sociologie du Roman* (1964), into an essentially mechanistic version of the base-superstructure relationship.

## Pierre Macherey and 'Decentred' Form

Both Lukács and Goldmann inherit from Hegel a belief that the literary work should form a unified totality; and in this they are close to a conventional position in non-Marxist criticism. Lukács sees the work as a *constructed* totality rather than a natural organism; yet a vein of 'organistic' thinking about the art object runs through much of his criticism. It is one of the several scandalous propositions which Pierre Macherey throws out to bourgeois and neo-Hegelian criticism alike that he rejects this belief. For Macherey, a work is tied to ideology not so much by what it says as by what it does not say. It is in the significant *silences* of a text, in its gaps and absences, that the presence of ideology can be most positively felt. It is these silences which the critic must make 'speak'. The text is, as it were, ideologically forbidden to say certain things; in trying to tell the truth in his own way, for example, the author finds himself forced to reveal the limits of the ideology within which he writes. He is forced to reveal its gaps and silences, what it is unable to articulate. Because a text contains these gaps and silences, it is always *incomplete*. Far from constituting a rounded, coherent whole, it displays a conflict and contradiction of meanings; and the significance of the work lies in the difference rather than unity between these meanings. Whereas a critic like Goldmann finds in the work a central structure, the work for Macherey is always *'de-centred'*; there is no central essence to it, just a continuous conflict and disparity of meanings. 'Scattered', 'dispersed', 'diverse', 'irregular': these are the epithets which Macherey uses to express his sense of the literary work.

When Macherey argues that the work is 'incomplete', however, he does not mean that there is a piece missing which the critic could fill in. On the contrary, it is in the nature of the work to be incomplete, tied as it is to an ideology which silences it at certain points. (It is, if you like, complete in its incompleteness.) The critic's task is not to fill the work in; it is to seek out the principle of its conflict of meanings, and to show how this conflict is produced by the work's relation to ideology.

To take a fairly obvious example: in *Dombey and Son* Dickens uses a number of mutually conflicting languages—realist, melodramatic, pastoral, allegorical—in his portrayal of events; and this conflict comes to a head in the famous railway chapter, where the novel is ambiguously torn between contradictory responses to the railway (fear, protest, approval, exhilaration etc.), reflecting this in a clash of styles and symbols. The ideological basis of this ambiguity is that the novel is divided between a conventional bourgeois admiration of industrial progress and a petty-bourgeois anxiety about its inevitably disruptive effects. It sympathizes with whose washed-up minor characters whom the new world has superannuated at the same time as it celebrates the progressive thrust of industrial capitalism which has made them obsolete. In discovering the principle of the work's conflict of meanings, then, we are simultaneously analysing its complex relationship to Victorian ideology. . . .

## ROLAND BARTHES

# Introduction to the
# Structuralist Analysis
# of Narratives

## 1966

*Roland Barthes' essay demonstrates the Structuralist approach to litera-*
*ture that assumed widespread importance from the 1950's through the*
*early 1970's. As a critical doctrine, Structuralism developed from ex-*
*tending the language theories of the Swiss linguist Ferdinand de*
*Saussure beyond the analysis of the sentence to a systematic method*
*for the study of anthropology, folklore and mythology, the fine arts,*
*literature, and even popular culture and fashion.*

*Several principles of Saussurean linguistics are essential to an under-*
*standing of Structuralism. Saussure posited that a language (*langage*)*
*consists of a collection of arbitrarily devised signifiers (words) that*
*represent mental concepts (signifieds). Through a complex code system*
*—or grammar—literate speakers of a language are able at an uncon-*
*scious level to interpret the signifieds represented by the signifiers of*
*either oral or written utterances, which Saussure called* paroles. *The*
*code system, consisting basically of phonology and syntax, Saussure*
*called* langue. *The combined unit of signifier and signified is called a*
*sign. Thus, speakers of a given language (*langage*) share an implicit*
*understanding of a code system (*langue*) that enables them to create*
*meaning from a set of signals (*paroles*), i.e., that allows them to make*

*appropriate connections between signifieds and signifiers in their interpretation of signs. (Translating* langue *and* langage *into English may result in confusion because English has only one word—"language" —for the two words that have specialized meanings in Structuralist nomenclature. In the translation that follows, each use of the English word is followed by the French original in brackets.)*

*Structuralism attempts to articulate the codes that govern various kinds of communication. Saussure himself had imagined an extension of his analytic method beyond the level of the sentence and had invented the term* semiology, *the "science of signs," to describe such a field of study; thus the terms Structuralism, Semiology, and Semiotics are roughly synonyms in that they all refer to the analysis of code systems by which signifiers represent signifieds.*

*Barthes' essay on Structuralism and narrative treats narrative not merely as a genre but rather as a species of discourse. For Barthes, the* langue *of narrative can be deduced from an analysis of a limited number of examples of narratives, just as the grammar of a language can be deduced from an analysis of a limited number of sentences. The* langue *of narrative will involve elements analogous to the elements of grammar in sentences. In his investigation, Barthes posits that this "grammar" will include concepts of a general language of narrative, with attention to the levels of meaning; a system of functional units higher than the sentence, with attention to the classes of such units; a system of "indices" that link the atmosphere of the story; a structural status of characters in the action; and levels in a system of narration.*

*How do these concepts of analysis differ from traditional notions of the analysis of plot, character, and style? Structuralism attempts a bolder scheme of systematizing literary analysis within the entire domain of language and sees analytic concepts as derived from, and part of, a universal code.*

THE NARRATIVES of the world are numberless. Narrative is first and foremost a prodigious variety of genres, themselves distributed amongst different substances—as though any material were fit to receive man's stories. Able to be carried by articulated language, spoken or written, fixed or moving images, gestures, and the ordered mixture of all these substances; narrative is present in myth, legend, fable, tale, novella, epic, history, tragedy, drama, comedy, mime, painting (think of Carpaccio's *Saint Ursula*), stained glass windows, cinema, comics, news item, conversation. Moreover, under this almost infinite diversity of forms, narrative is present in every age, in every place, in every society; it begins with the very history of mankind and there nowhere is nor has been a people without narrative. All classes, all human groups, have their narratives, enjoyment of which is very often shared by men with different, even opposing,[1] cultural backgrounds. Caring nothing for the division between good and bad literature, narrative is international, transhistorical, transcultural: it is simply there, like life itself.

Must we conclude from this universality that narrative is insignificant? Is it so general that we can have nothing to say about it except for the modest description of a few highly individualized varieties, something literary history occasionally undertakes? But then how are we to master even these varieties, how are we to justify our right to differentiate and identify them? How is novel to be set against novella, tale against myth, drama against tragedy (as has been done a thousand times) without reference to a common model? Such a model is implied by every proposition relating to the most individual, the most historical, of narrative forms. It is thus legitimate that, far from the abandoning of any idea of dealing with narrative on the grounds of its universality, there should have been (from Aristotle on) a periodic interest in narrative form and it is normal that the newly developing structuralism should make this form one of its first concerns—is not structuralism's constant aim to master the infinity of utterances [*paroles*] by describing the 'language' ['*langue*'] of which they are the products and from which they can be generated. Faced with the infinity of narratives, the multiplicity of standpoints—historical, psychological, ethnological, aesthetic, etc.—from which they can be studied, the analyst finds himself in more or less the same situation as Saussure confronted by the heterogeneity of language [*langage*] and seeking to extract a principle of classification and a central focus for description from the apparent confusion of the individual messages. Keeping simply to modern times, the Russian Formalists, Propp and Lévi-Strauss have taught us to recognize the following dilemma: either a narrative is merely a rambling collection of events, in which case nothing can be said about it other than by referring back to the storyteller's (the author's) art, talent or genius—all mythical forms of

---

[1] It must be remembered that this is not the case with either poetry or the essay, both of which are dependent on the cultural level of their consumers.

chance[2]—or else it shares with other narratives a common structure which is open to analysis, no matter how much patience its formulation requires. There is a world of difference between the most complex randomness and the most elementary combinatory scheme, and it is impossible to combine (to produce) a narrative without reference to an implicit system of units and rules.

Where then are we to look for the structures of narrative? Doubtless, in narratives themselves. *Each and every* narrative? Many commentators who accept the idea of a narrative structure are nevertheless unable to resign themselves to dissociating literary analysis from the example of the experimental sciences; nothing daunted, they ask that a purely inductive method be applied to narrative and that one start by studying all the narratives within a genre, a period, a society. This commonsense view is utopian. Linguistics itself, with only some three thousand languages to embrace, cannot manage such a programme and has wisely turned deductive, a step which in fact marked its veritable constitution as a science and the beginning of its spectacular progress, it even succeeding in anticipating facts prior to their discovery.[3] So what of narrative analysis, faced as it is with millions of narratives? Of necessity, it is condemned to a deductive procedure, obliged first to devise a hypothetical model of description (what American linguists call a 'theory') and then gradually to work down from this model towards the different narrative species which at once conform to and depart from the model. It is only at the level of these conformities and departures that analysis will be able to come back to, but now equipped with a single descriptive tool, the plurality of narratives, to their historical, geographical and cultural diversity.[4]

Thus, in order to describe and classify the infinite number of narratives, a 'theory' (in this pragmatic sense) is needed and the immediate task is that of finding it, of starting to define it. Its development

[2] There does, of course, exist an 'art' of the storyteller, which is the ability to generate narratives (messages) from the structure (the code). This art corresponds to the notion of *performance* in Chomsky and is far removed from the 'genius' of the author, romantically conceived as some barely explicable personal secret.

[3] See the history of the Hittite *a*, postulated by Saussure and actually discovered fifty years later, as given in Emile Benveniste, *Problèmes de linguistique générale*, Paris 1966, p. 35 [*Problems of General Linguistics*, Coral Gables, Florida 1971, p. 32].

[4] Let us bear in mind the present conditions of linguistic description: '. . . linguistic "structure" is always relative not just to the data or corpus but also to the grammatical theory describing the data' E. Bach, *An Introduction to Transformational Grammars*, New York 1964, p. 29; 'it has been recognized that language must be described as a formal structure, but that the description first of all necessitates specification of adequate procedures and criteria and that, finally, the reality of the object is inseparable from the method given for its description', Benveniste, op. cit., p. 119 [trans. p. 101].

can be greatly facilitated if one begins from a model able to provide it with its initial terms and principles. In the current state of research, it seems reasonable[5] that the structural analysis of narrative be given linguistics itself as founding model.

## I. The Language of Narrative

### 1. Beyond the sentence

As we know, linguistics stops at the sentence, the last unit which it considers to fall within its scope. If the sentence, being an order and not a series, cannot be reduced to the sum of the words which compose it and constitutes thereby a specific unit, a piece of discourse, on the contrary, is no more than the succession of the sentences composing it. From the point of view of linguistics, there is nothing in discourse that is not to be found in the sentence: 'The sentence,' writes Martinet, 'is the smallest segment that is perfectly and wholly representative of discourse.'[6] Hence there can be no question of linguistics setting itself an object superior to the sentence, since beyond the sentence are only more sentences—having described the flower, the botanist is not to get involved in describing the bouquet.

And yet it is evident that discourse itself (as a set of sentences) is organized and that, through this organization, it can be seen as the message of another language, one operating at a higher level than the language of the linguists.[7] Discourse has its units, its rules, its 'grammar': beyond the sentence, and though consisting solely of sentences, it must naturally form the object of a second linguistics. For a long time indeed, such a linguistics of discourse bore a glorious name, that of Rhetoric. As a result of a complex historical movement, however, in which Rhetoric went over to belles-lettres and the latter was divorced from the study of language, it has recently become necessary to take up the problem afresh. The new linguistics of discourse has still to be developed, but at least it is being postulated, and by the linguists

---

5 But not imperative: see Claude Bremond, 'La logique des possibles narratifs', *Communications* 8, 1966, which is more logical than linguistic. [Bremond's various studies in this field have now been collected in a volume entitled, precisely, *Logique du récit*, Paris 1973; his work consists in the analysis of narrative according to the pattern of possible alternatives, each narrative moment—or function—giving rise to a set of different possible resolutions, the actualization of any one of which in turn produces a new set of alternatives.]

6 André Martinet, 'Réflexions sur la phrase', in *Language and Society* (Studies presented to Jansen), Copenhagen 1961, p. 113.

7 It goes without saying, as Jakobson has noted, that between the sentence and what lies beyond the sentence there are transitions; co-ordination, for instance, can work over the limit of the sentence.

themselves.[8] This last fact is not without significance, for, although constituting an autonomous object, discourse must be studied from the basis of linguistics. If a working hypothesis is needed for an analysis whose task is immense and whose materials infinite, then the most reasonable thing is to posit a homological relation between sentence and discourse insofar as it is likely that a similar formal organization orders all semiotic systems, whatever their substances and dimensions. A discourse is a long 'sentence' (the units of which are not necessarily sentences), just as a sentence, allowing for certain specifications, is a short 'discourse'. This hypothesis accords well with a number of propositions put forward in contemporary anthropology. Jakobson and Lévi-Strauss have pointed out that mankind can be defined by the ability to create secondary—'self-multiplying'—systems (tools for the manufacture of other tools, double articulation of language, incest taboo permitting the fanning out of families) while the Soviet linguist Ivanov supposes that artificial languages can only have been acquired after natural language: what is important for men is to have the use of several systems of meaning and natural language helps in the elaboration of artificial languages. It is therefore legitimate to posit a 'secondary' relation between sentence and discourse—a relation which will be referred to as homological, in order to respect the purely formal nature of the correspondences.

The general language [langue[ of narrative is one (and clearly only one) of the idioms apt for consideration by the linguistics of discourse[9] and it accordingly comes under the homological hypothesis. Structurally, narrative shares the characteristics of the sentence without ever being reducible to the simple sum of its sentences: a narrative is a long sentence, just as every constative sentence is in a way the rough outline of a short narrative. Although there provided with different signifiers (often extremely complex), one does find in narrative, expanded and transformed proportionately, the principal verbal categories: tenses, aspects, moods, persons. Moreover the 'subjects' themselves, as opposed to the verbal predicates, readily yield to the sentence model; the actantial typology proposed by A. J. Greimas[10] discovers in the

[8] See especially: Benveniste, op. cit., Chapter 10; Z. S. Harris, 'Discourse Analysis', *Language* 28, 1952, pp. 18–23 & 474–94; N. Ruwet, 'Analyse structurale d'un poème français', *Linguistics* 3, 1964, pp. 62–83.

[9] One of the tasks of such a linguistics would be precisely that of establishing a typology of forms of discourse. Three broad types can be recognized provisionally: metonymic (narrative), metaphoric (lyric poetry, sapiential discourse), enthymematic (intellectual discourse).

[10] See below III.1. [Also, section II of 'The struggle with the angel' in the present volume. Greimas's own account can be found in *Sémantique structurale*, Paris 1966, Chapter 10.]

multitude of narrative characters the elementary functions of grammatical analysis. Nor does the homology suggested here have merely a heuristic value: it implies an identity between language and literature (inasmuch as the latter can be seen as a sort of privileged vehicle of narrative). It is hardly possible any longer to conceive of literature as an art that abandons all further relation with language the moment it has used it as an instrument to express ideas, passion or beauty: language never ceases to accompany discourse, holding up to it the mirror of its own structure—does not literature, particularly today, make a language of the very conditions of language?[11]

## 2. Levels of meaning

From the outset, linguistics furnishes the structural analysis of narrative with a concept which is decisive in that, making explicit immediately what is essential in every system of meaning, namely its organization, it allows us both to show how a narrative is not a simple sum of propositions and to classify the enormous mass of elements which go to make up a narrative. This concept is that of *level of description*.[12]

A sentence can be described, linguistically, on several levels (phonetic, phonological, grammatical, contextual) and these levels are in a hierarchical relationship with one another, for, while all have their own units and correlations (whence the necessity for a separate description of each of them), no level on its own can produce meaning. A unit belonging to a particular level only takes on meaning if it can be integrated in a higher level; a phoneme, though perfectly describable, means nothing in itself: it participates in meaning only when integrated in a word, and the word itself must in turn be integrated in a sentence.[13] The theory of levels (as set out by Benveniste) gives two types of relations: distributional (if the relations are situated on the

11 Remember Mallarmé's insight at the time when he was contemplating a work of linguistics: 'Language appeared to him the instrument of fiction: he will follow the method of language (determine it). Language self-reflecting. So fiction seems to him the very process of the human mind—it is this that sets in play all method, and man is reduced to will' Œuvres complètes, Bibliothèque de la Pléiade, Paris 1961, p. 851. It will be recalled that for Mallarmé 'Fiction' and 'Poetry' are taken synonymously (cf. ibid., p. 335).

12 'Linguistic descriptions are not, so to speak, monovalent. A description is not simply "right" or "wrong" in itself . . . it is better thought of as more useful or less', M. A. K. Halliday, 'General linguistics and its application to language teaching', *Patterns of Language*, London 1966, p. 8.

13 The levels of integration were postulated by the Prague School (vid. J. Vachek, *A Prague School Reader in Linguistics*, Bloomington 1964, p. 468) and have been adopted since by many linguists. It is Benveniste who, in my opinion, has given the most illuminating analysis in this respect; op. cit., Chapter 10.

same level) and integrational (if they are grasped from one level to the next); consequently, distributional relations alone are not sufficient to account for meaning. In order to conduct a structural analysis, it is thus first of all necessary to distinguish several levels or instances of description and to place these instances within a hierarchical (integrationary) perspective.

The levels are operations.[14] It is therefore normal that, as it progresses, linguistics should tend to multiply them. Discourse analysis, however, is as yet only able to work on rudimentary levels. In its own way, rhetoric had assigned at least two planes of description to discourse: *dispositio* and *elocutio*.[15] Today, in his analysis of the structure of myth, Lévi-Strauss has already indicated that the constituent units of mythical discourse (mythemes) acquire meaning only because they are grouped in bundles and because these bundles themselves combine together.[16] As too, Tzvetan Todorov, reviving the distinction made by the Russian Formalists, proposes working on two major levels, themselves subdivided: *story* (the argument), comprising a logic of actions and a 'syntax' of characters, and *discourse*, comprising the tenses, aspects and modes of the narrative.[17] But however many levels are proposed and whatever definition they are given, there can be no doubt that narrative is a hierarchy of instances. To understand a narrative is not merely to follow the unfolding of the story, it is also to recognize its construction in 'storeys', to project the horizontal concatenations of the narrative 'thread' on to an implicitly vertical axis; to read (to listen to) a narrative is not merely to move from one word to the next, it is also to move from one level to the next. Perhaps I may be allowed to offer a kind of apologue in this connection. In *The Purloined Letter*, Poe gives an acute analysis of the failure of the chief commissioner of the Paris police, powerless to find the letter. His investigations, says Poe, were perfect '*within the sphere of his specialty*',[18] he searched everywhere, saturated entirely the level of the 'police search', but in order to find the letter, protected by its conspicuous-

---

[14] 'In somewhat vague terms, a level may be considered as a system of symbols, rules, and so on, to be used for representing utterances', Bach, op. cit., p. 57.

[15] The third part of rhetoric, *inventio*, did not concern language—it had to do with *res*, not with *verba*.

[16] Claude Lévi-Strauss, *Anthropologie structurale*, Paris 1958, p. 233 [*Structural Anthropology*, New York and London 1963, p. 211].

[17] See T. Todorov, 'Les catégories du récit littéraire', *Communications* 8, 1966 [Todorov's work on narrative is now most easily accessible in two books, *Littérature et Signification*, Paris 1967; *Poétique de la prose*, Paris 1972. For a short account in English, see 'Structural analysis of narrative', *Novel* I, 3, 1969, pp. 70–6].

[18] [This in accordance with the Baudelaire version of the Poe story from which Barthes quotes; Poe's original reads: 'so far as his labours extended'.]

ness, it was necessary to shift to another level, to substitute the con-
cealer's principle of relevance for that of the policeman. Similarly, the
'search' carried out over a horizontal set of narrative relations may
well be as thorough as possible but must still, to be effective, also operate 'vertically': meaning is not 'at the end' of the narrative, it runs
across it; just as conspicuous as the purloined letter, meaning eludes
all unilateral investigation.

A great deal of tentative effort is still required before it will be possible to ascertain precisely the levels of narrative. Those that are suggested in what follows constitute a provisional profile whose merit
remains almost exclusively didactic; they enable us to locate and group
together the different problems, and this without, I think, being at
variance with the few analyses so far.[19] It is proposed to distinguish
three levels of description in the narrative work: the level of *'functions'*
(in the sense this word has in Propp and Bremond), the level of *'actions'*
(in the sense this word has in Greimas when he talks of characters as
actants) and the level of *'narration'* (which is roughly the level of 'discourse' in Todorov). These three levels are bound together according
to a mode of progressive integration: a function only has meaning
insofar as it occupies a place in the general action of an actant, and
this action in turn receives its final meaning from the fact that it is
narrated, entrusted to a discourse which possesses its own code.

## II. Functions

### 1. The determination of the units

Any system being the combination of units of known classes, the
first task is to divide up narrative and determine the segments of narrative discourse that can be distributed into a limited number of
classes. In a word, we have to define the smallest narrative units.

Given the integrational perspective described above, the analysis
cannot rest satisfied with a purely distributional definition of the
units. From the start, meaning must be the criterion of the unit: it is
the functional nature of certain segments of the story that makes them
units—hence the name 'functions' immediately attributed to these first
units. Since the Russian Formalists,[20] a unit has been taken as any seg-

---

[19] I have been concerned in this introduction to impede research in progress as
little as possible.

[20] See especially B. Tomachevski, 'Thématique' (1925), in *Théorie de la littérature*,
ed. T. Todorov, Paris 1965, pp. 263–307. A little later, Propp defined the function
as 'an act of a character, defined from the point of view of its significance for the
course of the action', *Morphology of the Folktale*, Austin and London 1968, p. 21.

ment of the story which can be seen as the term of a correlation. The essence of a function is, so to speak, the seed that it sows in the narrative, planting an element that will come to fruition later—either on the same level or elsewhere, on another level. If in *Un Cœur simple* Flaubert at one point tells the reader, seemingly without emphasis, that the daughters of the Sous-Préfet of Pont-l'Evêque owned a parrot, it it because this parrot is subsequently to have a great importance in Félicité's life; the statement of this detail (whatever its linguistic form) thus constitutes a function, or narrative unit.

Is everything in a narrative functional? Does everything, down to the slightest detail, have a meaning? Can narrative be divided up entirely into functional units? We shall see in a moment that there are several kinds of functions, there being several kinds of correlations, but this does not alter the fact that a narrative is never made up of anything other than functions: in differing degrees, everything in it signifies. This is not a matter of art (on the part of the narrator), but of structure; in the realm of discourse, what is noted is by definition notable. Even were a detail to appear irretrievably insignificant, resistant to all functionality, it would nonetheless end up with precisely the meaning of absurdity or uselessness: everything has a meaning, or nothing has. To put it another way, one could say that art is without noise (as that term is employed in information theory):[21] art is a system which is pure, no unit ever goes wasted,[22] however long, however loose, however tenuous may be the thread connecting it to one of the levels of the story.[23]

From the linguistic point of view, the function is clearly a unit of content: it is 'what it says' that makes of a statement a functional unit,[24] not the manner in which it is said. This constitutive signified may have a number of different signifiers, often very intricate. If I am

[21] This is what separates art from 'life', the latter knowing only 'fuzzy' or 'blurred' communications. 'Fuzziness' (that beyond which it is impossible to see) can exist in art, but it does so as a coded element (in Watteau for example). Even then, such 'fuzziness' is unknown to the written code: writing is inescapably distinct.

[22] At least in literature, where the freedom of notation (in consequence of the abstract nature of articulated language) leads to a much greater responsibility than in the 'analogical' arts such as cinema.

[23] The functionality of a narrative unit is more or less immediate (and hence apparent) according to the level on which it operates: when the units are situated on the same level (as for instance in the case of suspense), the functionality is very clear; it is much less so when the function is saturated on the narrational level—a modern text, weakly signifying on the plane of the anecdote, only finds a full force of meaning on the plane of the writing.

[24] 'Syntactical units beyond the sentence are in fact units of content', A. J. Greimas, *Cours de sémantique structurale* (roneoed), 1964, VI, 5 [cf. *Sémantique structurale*, pp. 116f.]. The exploration of the functional level is thus part of general semantics.

told (in *Goldfinger*) that *Bond saw a man of about fifty*, the piece of information holds simultaneously two functions of unequal pressure: on the one hand, the character's age fits into a certain description of the man (the 'usefulness' of which for the rest of the story is not nil, but diffuse, delayed); while on the other, the immediate signified of the statement is that Bond is unacquainted with his future interlocutor, the unit thus implying a very strong correlation (initiation of a threat and the need to establish the man's identity). In order to determine the initial narrative units, it is therefore vital never to lose sight of the functional nature of the segments under consideration and to recognize in advance that they will not necessarily coincide with the forms into which we traditionally cast the various parts of narrative discourse (actions, scenes, paragraphs, dialogues, interior monologues, etc.) still less with 'psychological' divisions (modes of behaviour, feelings, intentions, motivations, rationalizations of characters).

In the same way, since the 'language' ['*langue*'] of narrative is not the language [*langue*] of articulated language [*langage articulé*]—though very often vehicled by it—narrative units will be substantially independent of linguistic units; they may indeed coincide with the latter, but occasionally, not systematically. Functions will be represented sometimes by units higher than the sentence (groups of sentences of varying lengths, up to the work in its entirety) and sometimes by lower ones (syntagm, word and even, within the word, certain literary elements only[25]). When we are told that—the telephone ringing during night duty at Secret Service headquarters—*Bond picked up one of the four receivers*, the moneme *four* in itself constitutes a functional unit, referring as it does to a concept necessary to the story (that of a highly developed bureaucratic technology). In fact, the narrative unit in this case is not the linguistic unit (the word) but only its connoted value (linguistically, the word/four/never means 'four'); which explains how certain functional units can be shorter than the sentence without ceasing to belong to the order of discourse: such units then extend not beyond the sentence, than which they remain materially shorter, but beyond the level of denotation, which, like the sentence, is the province of linguistics properly speaking.

## 2. *Classes of units*

The functional units must be distributed into a small number of classes. If these classes are to be determined without recourse to the sub-

---

[25] 'The word must not be treated as an indivisible element of literary art, like a brick in building. It can be broken down into much finer "verbal elements"', J. Tynianov, quoted by T. Todorov in *Langages* 6, 1971, p. 18.

stance of content (psychological substance for example), it is again necessary to consider the different levels of meaning: some units have as correlates units on the same level, while the saturation of others requires a change of levels; hence, straightaway, two major classes of functions, distributional and integrational. The former correspond to what Propp and subsequently Bremond (in particular) take as functions but they will be treated here in a much more detailed way than is the case in their work. The term *'functions'* will be reserved for these units (though the other units are also functional), the model of description for which has become classic since Tomachevski's analysis: the purchase of a revolver has for correlate the moment when it will be used (and if not used, the notation is reversed into a sign of indecision, etc.); picking up the telephone has for correlate the moment when it will be put down; the intrusion of the parrot into Félicité's home has for correlate the episode of the stuffing, the worshipping of the parrot, etc. As for the latter, the integrational units, these comprise all the *'indices'* (in the very broad sense of the word[26]), the unit now referring not to a complementary and consequential act but to a more or less diffuse concept which is nevertheless necessary to the meaning of the story: psychological indices concerning the characters, data regarding their identity, notations of 'atmosphere', and so on. The relation between the unit and its correlate is now no longer distributional (often several indices refer to the same signified and the order of their occurrence in the discourse is not necessarily pertinent) but integrational. In order to understand what an indicial notation 'is for', one must move to a higher level (characters' actions or narration), for only there is the indice clarified: the power of the administrative machine behind Bond, indexed by the number of telephones, has no bearing on the sequence of actions in which Bond is involved by answering the call; it finds its meaning only on the level of a general typology of the actants (Bond is on the side of order). Indices, because of the, in some sort, vertical nature of their relations, are truly semantic units: unlike 'functions' (in the strict sense), they refer to a signified, not to an 'operation'. The ratification of indices is 'higher up', sometimes even remaining virtual, outside any explicit syntagm (the 'character' of a narrative agent may well never be explicitly named while yet being constantly indexed), is a paradigmatic ratification. That of functions, by contrast, is always 'further on', is a syntagmatic ratification.[27] *Functions* and *indices* thus

---

[26] These designations, like those that follow, may all be provisional.

[27] Which does not mean that the syntagmatic setting out of functions may not *finally* hold paradigmatic relations between separate functions, as is recognized since Lévi-Strauss and Greimas.

overlay another classic distinction: functions involve metonymic relata, indices metaphoric relata; the former correspond to a functionality of doing, the latter to a functionality of being.[28]

These two main classes of units, functions and indices, should already allow a certain classification of narratives. Some narratives are heavily functional (such as folktales), while others on the contrary are heavily indicial (such as 'psychological' novels); between these two poles lies a whole series of intermediary forms, dependent on history, society, genre. But we can go further. Within each of the two main classes it is immediately possible to determine two sub-classes of narrative units. Returning to the class of functions, its units are not all of the same 'importance': some constitute real hinge-points of the narrative (or of a fragment of the narrative); others merely 'fill in' the narrative space separating the hinge functions. Let us call the former *cardinal functions* (or *nuclei*) and the latter, having regard to their complementary nature, *catalysers*. For a function to be cardinal, it is enough that the action to which it refers open (or continue, or close) an alternative that is of direct consequence for the subsequent development of the story, in short that it inaugurate or conclude an uncertainty. If, in a fragment of narrative, *the telephone rings*, it is equally possible to answer or not answer, two acts which will unfailingly carry the narrative along different paths. Between two cardinal functions however, it is always possible to set out subsidiary notations which cluster around one or other nucleus without modifying its alternative nature: the space separating *the telephone rang* from *Bond answered* can be saturated with a host of trivial incidents or descriptions—*Bond moved towards the desk, picked up one of the receivers, put down his cigarette*, etc. These catalysers are still functional, insofar as they enter into correlation with a nucleus, but their functionality is attenuated, unilateral, parasitic; it is a question of a purely chronological functionality (what is described is what separates two moments of the story), whereas the tie between two cardinal functions is invested with a double functionality, at once chronological and logical. Catalysers are only consecutive units, cardinal functions are both consecutive and consequential. Everything suggests, indeed, that the mainspring of narrative is precisely the confusion of consecution and consequence, what comes *after* being read in narrative as what is *caused by*; in which case narrative would be a systematic application of the logical fallacy denounced by Scholasticism in the formula *post*

---

[28] Functions cannot be reduced to actions (verbs), nor indices to qualities (adjectives), for there are actions that are indicial, being 'signs' of a character, an atmosphere, etc.

*hoc, ergo propter hoc*—a good motto for Destiny, of which narrative all things considered is no more than the 'language'.

It is the structural framework of cardinal functions which accomplishes this 'telescoping' of logic and temporality. At first sight, such functions may appear extremely insignificant; what defines them is not their spectacularity (importance, volume, unusualness or force of the narrated action), but, so to speak, the risk they entail: cardinal functions are the risky moments of a narrative. Between these points of alternative, these 'dispatchers', the catalysers lay out areas of safety, rests, luxuries. Luxuries which are not, however, useless: it must be stressed again that from the point of view of the story a catalyser's functionality may be weak but not nil. Were a catalyser purely redundant (in relation to its nucleus), it would nonetheless participate in the economy of the message; in fact, an apparently merely expletive notation always has a discursive function: it accelerates, delays, gives fresh impetus to the discourse, it summarizes, anticipates and sometimes even leads astray.[29] Since what is noted always appears as being notable, the catalyser ceaselessly revives the semantic tension of the discourse, says ceaselessly that there has been, that there is going to be, meaning. Thus, in the final analysis, the catalyser has a constant function which is, to use Jakobson's term, a phatic one:[30] it maintains the contact between narrator and addressee. A nucleus cannot be deleted without altering the story, but neither can a catalyst without altering the discourse.

As for the other main class of units, the indices, an integrational class, its units have in common that they can only be saturated (completed) on the level of characters or on the level of narration. They are thus part of a *parametrical* relation[31] whose second—implicit—term is continuous, extended over an episode, a character or the whole work. A distinction can be made, however, between *indices* proper, referring to the character of a narrative agent, a feeling, an atmosphere (for example suspicion) or a philosophy, and *informants*, serving to identify, to locate in time and space. To say that through the window of the office where Bond is on duty the moon can be seen half-hidden by thick

[29] Valéry spoke of 'dilatory signs'. The detective novel makes abundant use of such 'confusing' units.

[30] [For the scheme of the six factors of verbal communication and their corresponding linguistic functions—emotive, conative, referential, phatic, metalinguistic and poetic—see R. Jakobson, 'Linguistics and Poetics' in *Style in Language*, ed. T. A. Sebeok, New York 1960, pp. 350–77.]

[31] N. Ruwet calls 'parametrical' an element which remains constant for the whole duration of a piece of music (for instance, the tempo in a Bach allegro or the monodic character of a solo).

billowing clouds, is to index a stormy summer night, this deduction in turn forming an index of atmosphere with reference to the heavy, anguish-laden climate of an action as yet unknown to the reader. Indices always have implicit signifieds. Informants, however, do not, at least on the level of the story: they are pure data with immediate signification. Indices involve an activity of deciphering, the reader is to learn to know a character or an atmosphere; informants bring ready-made knowledge, their functionality, like that of catalysers, is thus weak without being nil. Whatever its 'flatness' in relation to the rest of the story, the informant (for example, the exact age of a character) always serves to authenticate the reality of the referent, to embed fiction in the real world. Informants are realist operators and as such possess an undeniable functionality not on the level of the story but on that of the discourse.[32]

Nuclei and catalysers, indices and informants (again, the names are of little importance), these, it seems, are the initial classes in which the functional level units can be divided. This classification must be completed by two remarks. Firstly, a unit can at the same time belong to two different classes: to drink a whisky (in an airport lounge) is an action which can act at a catalyser to the (cardinal) notation of *waiting*, but it is also, and simultaneously, the indice of a certain atmosphere (modernity, relaxation, reminiscence, etc.). In other words, certain units can be mixed, giving a play of possibilities in the narrative economy. In the novel *Goldfinger*, Bond, having to search his adversary's bedroom, is given a master-key by his associate: the notation is a pure (cardinal) function. In the film, this detail is altered and Bond laughingly takes a set of keys from a willing chamber-maid: the notation is no longer simply functional but also indicial, referring to Bond's character (his easy charm and success with women). Secondly, it should be noted (this will be taken up again later) that the four classes just described can be distributed in a different way which is moreover closer to the linguistic model. Catalysers, indices and informants have a common characteristic: in relation to nuclei, they are *expansions*. Nuclei (as will be seen in a moment) form finite sets grouping a small number of terms, are governed by a logic, are at once necessary and sufficient. Once the framework they provide is given, the other units fill it out according to a mode of proliferation in prin-

---

[32] In 'Frontières du récit', *Communications* 8, 1966 [reprinted in *Figures II*, Paris 1969], Gérard Genette distinguishes two types of description: ornamental and significant. The second clearly relates to the level of the story; the first to that of the discourse, which explains why for a long time it formed a perfectly coded rhetorical 'piece': *descriptio* or *ekphrasis*, a very highly valued exercise in neo-rhetoric.

ciple infinite. As we know, this is what happens in the case of the sentence, which is made up of simple propositions endlessly complicated with duplications, paddings, embeddings and so on. So great an importance did Mallarmé attach to this type of structure that from it he constructed *Jamais un coup de dés*, a poem which with its 'nodes' and 'loops', its 'nucleus-words' and its 'lace-words', can well be regarded as the emblem of every narrative—of every language.

### 3. Functional syntax

How, according to what 'grammar', are the different units strung together along the narrative syntagm? What are the rules of the functional combinatory system? Informants and indices can combine freely together: as for example in the portrait which readily juxtaposes data concerning civil status and traits of character. Catalysers and nuclei are linked by a simple relation of implication: a catalyser necessarily implies the existence of a cardinal function to which it can connect, but not vice-versa. As for cardinal functions, they are bound together by a relation of solidarity: a function of this type calls for another function of the same type and reciprocally. It is this last relation which needs to be considered further for a moment—first, because it defines the very framework of the narrative (expansions can be deleted, nuclei cannot); second, because it is the main concern of those trying to work towards a structure of narrative.

It has already been pointed out that structurally narrative institutes a confusion between consecution and consequence, temporality and logic. This ambiguity forms the central problem of narrative syntax. Is there an atemporal logic lying behind the temporality of narrative? Researchers were still quite recently divided on this point. Propp, whose analytic study of the folktale paved the way for the work going on today, is totally committed to the idea of the irreducibility of the chronological order: he sees time as reality and for this reason is convinced of the necessity for rooting the tale in temporality. Yet Aristotle himself, in his contrast between tragedy (defined by the unity of action) and historical narrative (defined by the plurality of actions and the unity of time), was already giving primacy to the logical over the chronological.[33] As do all contemporary researchers (Lévi-Strauss, Greimas, Bremond, Todorov), all of whom (while differing on other points) could subscribe to Lévi-Strauss's proposition that 'the order of chronological succession is absorbed in an atemporal matrix struc-

[33] *Poetics*, 1459a.

ture'.[34] Analysis today tends to 'dechronologize' the narrative continuum and to 'relogicize' it, to make it dependent on what Mallarmé called with regard to the French language *'the primitive thunderbolts of logic'*;[35] or rather, more exactly (such at least is our wish), the task is to succeed in giving a structural description of the chronological illusion—it is for narrative logic to account for narrative time. To put it another way, one could say that temporality is only a structural category of narrative (of discourse), just as in language [*langue*] temporality only exists in the form of a system; from the point of view of narrative, what we call time does not exist, or at least only exists functionally, as an element of a semiotic system. Time belongs not to discourse strictly speaking but to the referent; both narrative and language know only a semiotic time, 'true' time being a 'realist', referential illusion, as Propp's commentary shows. It is as such that structural analysis must deal with it.[36]

What then is the logic which regulates the principal narrative functions? It is this that current work is actively trying to establish and that has so far been the major focus of debate. Three main directions of research can be seen. The first (Bremond) is more properly logical in approach: it aims to reconstitute the syntax of human behaviour utilized in narrative, to retrace the course of the 'choices' which inevitably face[37] the individual character at every point in the story and so to bring out what could be called an energetic logic,[38] since it grasps the characters at the moment when they choose to act. The second (Lévi-Strauss, Jakobson) is linguistic: its essential concern is to demonstrate paradigmatic oppositions in the functions, oppositions which, in accordance with the Jakobsonian definition of the 'poetic',[39] are 'ex-

---

[34] Quoted by Claude Bremond, 'Le message narratif', *Communications* 4, 1964 [Claude Lévi-Strauss, 'La structure et la forme', *Cahiers de l'Institut de Science Economique Appliquée* 99, March 1960 (Série M, No. 7), p. 29; article reprinted in *Anthropologie structurale II*, Paris 1974].

[35] *Œuvres complètes*, p. 386.

[36] In his own way—as always perspicacious but left undeveloped—Valéry well expressed the status of narrative time: 'The belief in time as agent and guiding thread is based on *the mechanism of memory and on that of combinatory discourse'*, *Tel Quel*, *Œuvres* Vol. II, Bibliothèque de la Pléiade, Paris 1957, p. 348 (my italics); the illusion is precisely produced by the discourse itself.

[37] This idea recalls Aristotle: *proairesis*, the rational choice of actions to be undertaken, is the foundation of *praxis*, the practical science which, contrary to *poiesis*, produces no object-work distinct from its agent. Using these terms, one can say that the analyst tries to reconstitute the praxis inherent in narrative.

[38] Such a logic, based on alternatives (*doing this or that*), has the merit of accounting for the process of dramatization for which narrative is usually the occasion.

[39] ['The poetic function projects the principle of equivalence of the axis of selection on to the axis of combination.' Jakobson, 'Linguistics and Poetics', p. 3.]

tended' along the line of the narrative (new developments in Greimas's work correct or complete the conception of the paradigmatic nature of functions[40]). The third (Todorov) is somewhat different in that it sets the analysis at the level of the 'actions' (that is to say, of the characters), attempting to determine the rules by which narrative combines, varies and transforms a certain number of basic predicates.

There is no question of choosing between these working hypotheses; they are not competitive but concurrent, and at present moreover are in the throes of elaboration. The only complement we will attempt to give them here concerns the dimensions of the analysis. Even leaving aside the indices, informants and catalysers, there still remains in a narrative (especially if it is a novel and no longer a tale) a very large number of cardinal functions and many of these cannot be mastered by the analyses just mentioned, which until now have worked on the major articulations of narrative. Provision needs to be made, however, for a description sufficiently close as to account for *all* the narrative units, for the smallest narrative segments. We must remember that cardinal functions cannot be determined by their 'importance', only by the (doubly implicative) nature of their relations. A 'telephone call', no matter how futile it may seem, on the one hand itself comprises some few cardinal functions (telephone ringing, picking up the receiver, speaking, putting down the receiver), while on the other, taken as a whole, it must be linkable—at the very least proceeding step by step—to the major articulations of the anecdote. The functional covering of the narrative necessitates an organization of relays the basic unit of which can only be a small group of functions, hereafter referred to (following Bremond) as a *sequence*.

A sequence is a logical succession of nuclei bound together by a relation of solidarity:[41] the sequence opens when one of its terms has no solidary antecedent and closes when another of its terms has no consequent. To take a deliberately trivial example, the different functions order a drink, obtain it, drink it, pay for it, constitute an obviously closed sequence, it being impossible to put anything before the order or after the payment without moving out of the homogenous group '*Having a drink*'. The sequence indeed is always nameable. Determining the major functions of the folktale, Propp and subsequently Bremond have been led to name them (*Fraud, Betrayal, Struggle, Contract, Seduction*, etc.); the naming operation is equally

[40] See A. J. Greimas, 'Eléments pour une théorie de l'interprétation du récit mythique', *Communications* 8, 1966 [article reprinted in *Du Sens*, Paris 1970].
[41] In the Hjelmslevian sense of double implication: two terms presuppose one another.

inevitable in the case of trivial sequences, the 'micro-sequences' which often form the finest grain of the narrative tissue. Are these namings solely the province of the analyst? In other words, are they purely metalinguistic? No doubt they are, dealing as they do with the code of narrative. Yet at the same time they can be imagined as forming part of an inner metalanguage for the reader (or listener) who can grasp every logical succession of actions as a nominal whole: to read is to name; to listen is not only to perceive a language, it is also to construct it. Sequence titles are similar enough to the *cover-words* of translation machines which acceptably cover a wide variety of meanings and shades of meaning. The narrative language [*la langue du récit*] within us comprises from the start these essential headings: the closing logic which structures a sequence is inextricably linked to its name; any function which initiates a *seduction* prescribes from the moment it appears, in the name to which it gives rise, the entire process of seduction such as we have learned it from all the narratives which have fashioned in us the language of narrative.

However minimal its importance, a sequence, since it is made up of a small number of nuclei (that is to say, in fact, of 'dispatchers'), always involves moments of risk and it is this which justifies analysing it. It might seem futile to constitute into a sequence the logical succession of trifling acts which go to make up the offer of a cigarette (*offering, accepting, lighting, smoking*), but precisely, at every one of these points, an alternative—and hence a freedom of meaning—is possible. Du Pont, Bond's future partner, offers him a light from his lighter but Bond refuses; the meaning of this bifurcation is that Bond instinctively fears a booby-trapped gadget.[42] A sequence is thus, one can say, a *threatened logical unit*, this being its justification *a minimo*. It is also founded *a maximo*: enclosed on its function, subsumed under a name, the sequence itself constitutes a new unit, ready to function as a simple term in another, more extensive sequence. Here, for example, is a micro-sequence: *hand held out, hand shaken, hand released*. This *Greeting* then becomes a simple function: on the one hand, it assumes the role of an indice (flabbiness of Du Pont, Bond's distaste); on the other, it forms globally a term in a larger sequence, with the name *Meeting*, whose other terms (*approach, halt, interpellation, sitting down*) can themselves be micro-sequences. A whole network of

[42] It is quite possible to identify even at this infinitesimal level an opposition of paradigmatic type, if not between two terms, at least between two poles of the sequence: the sequence *Offer of a cigarette* spreads out, by suspending it, the paradigm *Danger/Safety* (demonstrated by Cheglov in his analysis of the Sherlock Holmes cycle), *Suspicion/Protection, Aggressiveness/Friendliness*.

subrogations structures the narrative in this way, from the smallest matrices to the largest functions. What is in question here, of course, is a hierarchy that remains within the functional level: it is only when it has been possible to widen the narrative out step by step, from Du Pont's cigarette to Bond's battle against Goldfinger, that functional analysis is over—the pyramid of functions then touches the next level (that of the Actions.) There is both a syntax within the sequences and a (subrogating) syntax between the sequences together. The first episode of *Goldfinger* thus takes on a 'stemmatic' aspect:

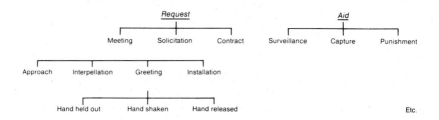

Obviously this representation is analytical; the reader perceives a linear succession of terms. What needs to be noted, however, is that the terms from several sequences can easily be imbricated in one another: a sequence is not yet completed when already, cutting in, the first term of a new sequence may appear. Sequences move in counter-point;[43] functionally, the structure of narrative is fugued: thus it is this that narrative at once 'holds' and 'pulls on'. Within the single work, the imbrication of sequences can indeed only be allowed to come to a halt with a radical break if the sealed-off blocks which then compose it are in some sort recuperated at the higher level of the Actions of the characters). *Goldfinger* is composed of three functionally independent episodes, their functional stemmas twice easing to inter-communicate: there is no sequential relation between the swimming-pool episode and the Fort Knox episode; but there remains an actantial relation, for the characters (and consequently the structure of their relations) are the same. One can recognize here the epic pattern (a 'whole made of multiple fables'): the epic is a narrative broken at the functional level but unitary at the actantial level (something which can be verified in the *Odyssey* or in Brecht's plays). The level of functions (which provides the major part of the narrative syntagm) must

---

[43] This counterpoint was recognized by the Russian Formalists who outlined its typology; it is not without recalling the principal 'intricate' structures of the sentence.

thus be capped by a higher level from which, step by step, the first level units draw their meaning, the level of actions.

## III. Actions

### 1. Towards a structural status of characters

In Aristotelian poetics, the notion of character is secondary, entirely subsidiary to the notion of action: there may be actions without 'characters', says Aristotle, but not characters without an action; a view taken over by classical theoreticians (Vossius). Later the character, who until then had been only a name, the agent of an action,[44] acquired a psychological consistency, became an individual, a 'person', in short a fully constituted 'being', even should he do nothing and of course even before acting.[45] Characters stopped being subordinate to the action, embodied immediately psychological essences; which essences could be drawn up into lists, as can be seen in its purest form in the list of 'character parts' in bourgeois theatre (the coquette, the noble father, etc.). From its very outset, structural analysis has shown the utmost reluctance to treat the character as an essence, even merely for purposes of classification; Tomachevski went so far as to deny the character any narrative importance, a point of view he subsequently modified. Without leaving characters out of the analysis altogether, Propp reduced them to a simple typology based not on psychology but on the unity of the actions assigned them by the narrative *(Donor of a magical agent, Helper, Villain,* etc.).

Since Propp, the character has constantly set the structural analysis of narrative the same problem. On the one hand, the characters (whatever one calls them—*dramatis personae* or *actants*) form a necessary plane of description, outside of which the slightest reported 'actions' cease to be intelligible; so that it can be said that there is not a single narrative in the world without 'characters',[46] or at least without agents.

---

[44] It must not be forgotten that classical tragedy as yet knows only 'actors', not 'characters'.

[45] The 'character-person' reigns in the bourgeois novel; in *War and Peace*, Nikolay Rostov is from the start a good fellow, loyal, courageous and passionate, Prince Andrey a disillusioned individual of noble birth, etc. What happens illustrates them, it does not form them.

[46] If one section of contemporary literature has attacked the 'character', it is not in order to destroy it (which is impossible) but to depersonalize it, which is quite different. A novel seemingly devoid of characters, such as *Drame* by Philippe Sollers, gets rid of the person to the benefit of language but nonetheless retains a fundamental play of actants confronting the very action of discourse. There is still a 'subject' in this literature, but that 'subject' is henceforth that of language.

Yet on the other hand, these—extremely numerous—'agents' can be neither described nor classified in terms of 'persons'—whether the 'person' be considered as a purely historical form, limited to certain genres (those most familiar to us it is true), in which case it is necessary to leave out of account the very large number of narratives (popular tales, modern texts) comprising agents but not persons, or whether the 'person' is declared to be no more than a critical rationalization foisted by our age on pure narrative agents. Structural analysis, much concerned not to define characters in terms of psychological essences, has so far striven, using various hypotheses, to define a character not as a 'being' but as a 'participant'. For Bremond, every character (even secondary) can be the agent of sequences of actions which belong to him (*Fraud, Seduction*); when a single sequence involves two characters (as is usual), it comprises two perspectives, two names (what is *Fraud* for the one is *Gullibility* for the other); in short, every character (even secondary) is the hero of his own sequence. Todorov, analysing a 'psychological' novel (*Les Liaisons dangereuses*), starts not from the character-persons but from the three major relationships in which they can engage and which he calls base predicates (love, communication, help). The analysis brings these relationships under two sorts of rules: rules of *derivation*, when it is a question of accounting for other relationships, and rules of *action*, when it is a question of describing the transformation of the major relationships in the course of the story. There are many characters in *Les Liaisons dangereuses* but 'what is said of them' (their predicates) can be classified. Finally, Greimas has proposed to describe and classify the characters of narrative not according to what they are but according to what they do (whence the name *actants*), inasmuch as they participate in three main semantic axes (also to be found in the sentence: subject, object, indirect object, adjunct) which are communication, desire (or quest) and ordeal.[47] Since this participation is ordered in couples, the infinite world of characters is, it too, bound by a paradigmatic structure *(Subject/ Object, Donor/Receiver, Helper/Opponent)* which is projected along the narrative; and since an actant defines a class, it can be filled by different actors, mobilized according to rules of multiplication, substitution or replacement.

These three conceptions have many points in common. The most important, it must be stressed again, is the definition of the character according to participation in a sphere of actions, these spheres being few in number, typical and classifiable; which is why this second level

---

[47] *Sémantique structurale*, pp. 129f.

of description, despite its being that of the characters, has here been called the level of Actions: the word *actions* is not to be understood in the sense of the trifling acts which form the tissue of the first level but in that of the major articulations of *praxis* (desire, communication, struggle).

## 2. The problem of the subject

The problems raised by a classification of the characters of narrative are not as yet satisfactorily resolved. Certainly there is ready agreement on the fact that the innumerable characters of narrative can be brought under rules of substitution and that, even within the one work, a single figure can absorb different characters.[48] Again, the actantial model proposed by Greimas (and adopted by Todorov in another perspective) seems to stand the test of a large number of narratives. Like any structural model, its value lies less in its canonic form (a matrix of six actants) than in the regulated transformations (replacements, confusions, duplications, substitutions) to which it lends itself, thus holding out the hope of an actantial typology of narratives.[49] A difficulty, however, is that when the matrix has a high classificational power (as is the case with Greimas's actants) it fails adequately to account for the multiplicity of participations as soon as these are analysed in terms of perspectives and that when these perspectives are respected (as in Bremond's description) the system of characters remains too fragmented. The reduction proposed by Todorov avoids both pitfalls but has so far only been applied to one narrative. All this, it seems, can be quickly and harmoniously resolved. The real difficulty posed by the classification of characters is the place (and hence the existence) of the *subject* in any actantial matrix, whatever its formulation. *Who* is the subject (the hero) of a narrative? Is there—or not—a privileged class of actors? The novel has accustomed us to emphasize in one way or another—sometimes in a devious (negative) way—one character in particular. But such privileging is far from extending over the whole of narrative literature. Many narratives, for example, set two adversaries in conflict over some stake; the subject

---

[48] Psychoanalysis has widely accredited these operations of condensation. Mallarmé was saying already, writing of *Hamlet*: 'Supernumeraries, necessarily! for in the ideal painting of the stage, everything moves according to a symbolic reciprocity of types amongst themselves or relatively to a single figure.' *Crayonné au théâtre, Œuvres complètes*, p. 301.

[49] For example: narratives where object and subject are confounded in a single character, that is narratives of the search for oneself, for one's own identity (*The Golden Ass*); narratives where the subject pursues successive objects (*Madame Bovary*), etc.

is then truly double, not reducible further by substitution. Indeed, this is even perhaps a common archaic form, as though narrative, after the fashion of certain languages, had also known a *dual* of persons. This dual is all the more interesting in that it relates narrative to the structures of certain (very modern) games in which two equal opponents try to gain possession of an object put into circulation by a referee; a schema which recalls the actantial matrix proposed by Greimas, and there is nothing surprising in this if one is willing to allow that a game, being a language, depends on the same symbolic structure as is to be found in language and narrative: a game too is a sentence.[50] If therefore a privileged class of actors is retained (the subject of the quest, of the desire, of the action), it needs at least to be made more flexible by bringing that actant under the very categories of the grammatical (and not psychological) person. Once again, it will be necessary to look towards linguistics for the possibility of describing and classifying the personal (*je/tu*, first person/second person) or apersonal (*il*, third person), singular, dual or plural, instance of the action. It will—perhaps—be the grammatical categories of the person (accessible in our pronouns) which will provide the key to the actional level; but since these categories can only be defined in relation to the instance of discourse, not to that of reality,[51] characters, as units of the actional level, find their meaning (their intelligibility) only if integrated in the third level of description, here called the level of Narration (as opposed to Functions and Actions).

## IV. Narration

### 1. Narrative communication

Just as there is within narrative a major function of exchange (set out between a donor and a beneficiary), so, homologically, narrative as object is the point of a communication: there is a donor of the narrative and a receiver of the narrative. In linguistic communication, *je* and *tu* (*I* and *you*) are absolutely presupposed by one another; similarly, there can be no narrative without a narrator and a listener (or reader). Banal perhaps, but still little developed. Certainly the role of the sender has been abundantly enlarged upon (much study of the 'author' of a novel, though without any consideration of whether

---

[50] Umberto Eco's analysis of the James Bond cycle ('James Bond: une combinatoire narrative', *Communications* 8, 1966) refers more to game than to language.

[51] See the analyses of person given by Benveniste in *Problèmes de linguistique générale*.

he really is the 'narrator'); when it comes to the reader, however, literary theory is much more modest. In fact, the problem is not to introspect the motives of the narrator or the effects the narration produces on the reader, it is to describe the code by which narrator and reader are signified throughout the narrative itself. At first sight, the signs of the narrator appear more evident and more numerous than those of the reader (a narrative more frequently says *I* than *you*); in actual fact, the latter are simply more oblique than the former. Thus, each time the narrator stops 'representing' and reports details which he knows perfectly well but which are unknown to the reader, there occurs, by signifying failure, a sign of reading, for there would be no sense in the narrator giving himself a piece of information. *Leo was the owner of the joint*,[52] we are told in a first-person novel: a sign of the reader, close to what Jakobson calls the conative function of communication. Lacking an inventory however, we shall leave aside for the moment these signs of reception (though they are of equal importance) and say a few words concerning the signs of narration.[53]

Who is the donor of the narrative? So far, three conceptions seem to have been formulated. The first holds that a narrative emanates from a person (in the fully psychological sense of the term). This person has a name, the author, in whom there is an endless exchange between the 'personality' and the 'art' of a perfectly identified individual who periodically takes up his pen to write a story: the narrative (notably the novel) then being simply the expression of an *I* external to it. The second conception regards the narrator as a sort of omniscient, apparently impersonal, consciousness that tells the story from a superior point of view, that of God:[54] the narrator is at once inside his characters (since he knows everything that goes on in them) and outside them (since he never identifies with any one more than another). The third and most recent conception (Henry James, Sartre) decrees that the narrator must limit his narrative to what the characters can observe or know, everything proceeding as if each of the characters in turn were the sender of the narrative. All three conceptions are equally difficult in that they seem to consider narrator and

52 *Double Bang à Bangkok* [secret agent thriller by Jean Bruce, Paris 1959]. The sentence functions as a 'wink' to the reader, as if he was being turned towards. By contrast, the statement '*So Leo had just left*' is a sign of the narrator, part of a process of reasoning conducted by a 'person'.

53 In 'Les catégories du récit littéraire' Todorov deals with the images of narrator and reader.

54 'When will someone write from the point of view of a *superior joke*, that is as God sees things from above?' Flaubert, *Préface à la vie d'écrivain*, ed. G. Bollème, Paris 1965, p. 91.

characters as real—'living'—people (the unfailing power of this literary
myth is well known), as though a narrative were originally determined
at its referential level (it is a matter of equally 'realist' conceptions).
Narrator and characters, however, at least from our perspective, are
essentially 'paper beings'; the (material) author of a narrative is in no
way to be confused with the narrator of that narrative.[55] The signs
of the narrator are immanent to the narrative and hence readily accessible to a semiological analysis; but in order to conclude that the
author himself (whether declared, hidden or withdrawn) has 'signs' at
his disposal which he sprinkles through his work, it is necessary to
assume the existence between this 'person' and his language of a
straight descriptive relation which makes the author a full subject
and the narrative the instrumental expression of that fullness. Structural analysis is unwilling to accept such an assumption: *who speaks*
(in the narrative) is not *who writes* (in real life) and *who writes* is not
*who is*.[56]

   In fact, narration strictly speaking (the code of the narrator), like
language, knows only two systems of signs: personal and apersonal.
These two narrational systems do not necessarily present the linguistic
marks attached to person (*I*) and non-person (*he*): there are narratives
or at least narrative episodes, for example, which though written in
the third person nevertheless have as their true instance the first person. How can we tell? It suffices to rewrite the narrative (or the passage) from *he* to *I*: so long as the rewriting entails no alteration of the
discourse other than this change of the grammatical pronouns, we can
be sure that we are dealing with a personal system. The whole of the
beginning of *Goldfinger*, though written in the third person, is in fact
'spoken' by James Bond. For the instance to change, rewriting must
become impossible; thus the sentence 'he saw a man in his fifties, still
young looking . . .' is perfectly personal despite the *he* ('I, James Bond,
saw . . .'), but the narrative statement 'the tinkling of the ice against
the glass appeared to give Bond a sudden inspiration' cannot be personal on account of the verb 'appeared', it (and not the *he*) becoming
a sign of the apersonal. There is no doubt that the apersonal is the
traditional mode of narrative, language having developed a whole
tense system peculiar to narrative (based on the aorist[57]), designed to

---

[55] A distinction all the more necessary, given the scale at which we are working,
in that historically a large mass of narratives are without authors (oral narratives,
folktales, epics entrusted to bards, reciters, etc.).

[56] J. Lacan: 'Is the subject I speak of when I speak the same as the subject who
speaks?'

[57] E. Benveniste, op. cit. [especially Chapter XIX].

wipe out the present of the speaker. As Benveniste puts it: 'In narrative, no one speaks.' The personal instance (under more or less disguised forms) has, however, gradually invaded narrative, the narration being referred to the *hic et nunc* of the locutionary act (which is the definition of the personal system). Thus it is that today many narratives are to be found (and of the most common kinds) which mix together in extremely rapid succession, often within the limits of a single sentence, the personal and the apersonal; as for instance this sentence from *Goldfinger*:

| | |
|---|---|
| His eyes, | *personal* |
| grey-blue, | *apersonal* |
| looked into those of Mr Du Pont who did | |
| not know what face to put on | *personal* |
| for this look held a mixture of candour, | |
| irony and self-deprecation. | *apersonal* |

The mixing of the systems is clearly felt as a facility and this facility can go as far as trick effects. A detective novel by Agatha Christie (*The Sittaford Mystery*) only keeps the enigma going by cheating on the person of the narration: a character is described from within when he is already the murderer[58]—as if in a single person there were the consciousness of a witness, immanent to the discourse, and the consciousness of a murderer, immanent to the referent, with the dishonest tourniquet of the two systems alone producing the enigma. Hence it is understandable that at the other pole of literature the choice of a rigorous system should have been made a necessary condition of a work—without it always being easy fully to meet that condition.

Rigour of this kind—the aim of certain contemporary writers—is not necessarily an aesthetic imperative. What is called the psychological novel usually shows a mixture of the two systems, successively mobilizing the signs of non-person and those of person; 'psychology', that is, paradoxically, cannot accommodate itself to a pure system, for by bringing the whole narrative down to the sole instance of the discourse—or, if one prefers, to the locutionary act—it is the very content of the person which is threatened: the psychological person (of referential order) bears no relation to the linguistic person, the latter never defined by states of mind, intentions or traits of character but

---

[58] Personal mode: 'It even seemed to Burnaby that nothing looked changed . . .' The device is still more blatant in *The Murder of Roger Ackroyd*, since there the murderer actually says *I*.

only by its (coded) place in discourse. It is this formal person that writers today are attempting to speak and such an attempt represents an important subversion (the public moreover has the impression that 'novels' are no longer being written) for it aims to transpose narrative from the purely constative plane, which it has occupied until now, to the performative plane, whereby the meaning of an utterance is the very act by which it is uttered:[59] today, writing is not 'telling' but saying that one is telling and assigning all the referent ('what one says') to this act of locution; which is why part of contemporary literature is no longer descriptive, but transitive, striving to accomplish so pure a present in its language that the whole of the discourse is identified with the act of its delivery, the whole *logos* being brought down—or extended—to a *lexis*.[60]

## 2. Narrative situation

The narrational level is thus occupied by the signs of narrativity, the set of operators which reintegrate functions and actions in the narrative communication articulated on its donor and its addressee. Some of these signs have already received study; we are familiar in oral literatures with certain codes of recitation (metrical formulae, conventional presentation protocols) and we know that here the 'author' is not the person who invents the finest stories but the person who best masters the code which is practised equally by his listeners: in such literatures the narrational level is so clearly defined, its rules so binding, that it is difficult to conceive of a 'tale' devoid of the coded signs of narrative (*'once upon a time'*, etc.). In our written literatures, the 'forms of discourse' (which are in fact signs of narrativity) were early identified: classification of the modes of authorial intervention (outlined by Plato and developed by Diomedes[61]), coding of the beginnings and endings of narratives, definition of the different styles of representation (*oratio directa, oratio indirecta* with its *inquit, oratio tecta*),[62] study of 'points of view' and so on. All these elements form part of the narrational level, to which must obviously be added the

---

[59] On the performative, see Todorov's 'Les catégories du récit littéraire'. The classic example of a performative is the statement *I declare war* which neither 'constates' nor 'describes' anything but exhausts its meaning in the act of its utterance (by contrast to the statement *the king declared war*, which constates, describes).

[60] For the opposition logos/lexis, see Genette, 'Frontières du récit'.

[61] *Genus activum vel imitativum* (no intervention of the narrator in the discourse: as for example theatre); *genus ennarativum* (the poet alone speaks: sententiae, didactic poems); *genus commune* (mixture of the two kinds: epic poems).

[62] H. Sorensen in *Language and Society* (Studies presented to Jansen), p. 150.

writing as a whole, its role being not to 'transmit' the narrative but to display it.

It is indeed precisely in a display of the narrative that the units of the lower levels find integration: the ultimate form of the narrative, as narrative, transcends its contents and its strictly narrative forms (functions and actions). This explains why the narrational code should be the final level attainable by our analysis, other than by going outside of the narrative-object, other, that is, than by transgressing the rule of immanence on which the analysis is based. Narration can only receive its meaning from the world which makes use of it: beyond the narrational level begins the world, other systems (social, economic, ideological) whose terms are no longer simply narratives but elements of a different substance (historical facts, determinations, behaviours, etc.). Just as linguistics stops at the sentence, so narrative analysis stops at discourse—from there it is necessary to shift to another semiotics. Linguistics is acquainted with such boundaries which it has already postulated—if not explored—under the name of *situations*. Halliday defines the 'situation' (in relation to a sentence) as 'the associated non-linguistic factors',[63] Prieto as 'the set of facts known by the receiver at the moment of the semic act and independently of this act'.[64] In the same way, one can say that every narrative is dependent on a 'narrative situation', the set of protocols according to which the narrative is 'consumed'. In so-called 'archaic' societies, the narrative situation is heavily coded;[65] nowadays, avant-garde literature alone still dreams of reading protocols—spectacular in the case of Mallarmé who wanted the book to be recited in public according to a precise combinatory scheme, typographical in that of Butor who tries to provide the book with its own specific signs. Generally, however, our society takes the greatest pains to conjure away the coding of the narrative situation: there is no counting the number of narrational devices which seek to naturalize the subsequent narrative by feigning to make it the outcome of some natural circumstance and thus, as it were, 'disinaugurating' it: epistolary novels, supposedly rediscovered manuscripts, author who met the narrator, films which begin the story before the credits. The reluctance to declare its codes characterizes bourgeois society and the mass culture issuing from it: both demand signs which do not look like signs. Yet this is only, so to speak, a structural epiphenomenon: however familiar, however causal may today be the

---

[63] M. A. K. Halliday, op. cit., p. 4.

[64] L. J. Prieto, *Principes de noologie*, Paris and The Hague 1964, p. 36.

[65] A tale, as Lucien Sebag stressed, can be told anywhere anytime, but not a mythical narrative.

act of opening a novel or a newspaper or of turning on the television,
nothing can prevent that humble act from installing in us, all at once
and in its entirety, the narrative code we are going to need. Hence
the narrational level has an ambiguous role: contiguous to the narrative situation (and sometimes even including it), it gives on to the
world in which the narrative is undone (consumed), while at the same
time, capping the preceding levels, it closes the narrative, constitutes
it definitively as utterance of a language [*langue*] which provides for
and bears along its own metalanguage.

## V. The System of Narrative

Language [*langue*] proper can be defined by the concurrence of two
fundamental processes: articulation, or segmentation, which produces
units (this being what Benveniste calls *form*), and integration, which
gathers these units into units of a higher rank (this being *meaning*).
This dual process can be found in the language of narrative [*la langue
du récit*] which also has an articulation and an integration, a form
and a meaning.

### 1. Distortion and expansion

The form of narrative is essentially characterized by two powers:
that of distending its signs over the length of the story and that of
inserting unforeseeable expansions into these distortions. The two
powers appear to be points of freedom but the nature of narrative is
precisely to include these 'deviations' within its language.[66]
The distortion of signs exists in linguistic language [*langue*] and
was studied by Bally with reference to French and German.[67] Dystaxia
occurs when the signs (of a message) are no longer simply juxtaposed,
when the (logical) linearity is disturbed (predicate before subject for
example). A notable form of dystaxia is found when the parts of one
sign are separated by other signs along the chain of the message (for
instance, the negative *ne jamais* and the verb *a pardonné* in *elle ne nous
a jamais pardonné*): the sign split into fractional parts, its signified is
shared out amongst several signifiers, distant from one another and
not comprehensible on their own. This, as was seen in connection
with the functional level, is exactly what happens in narrative: the
units of a sequence, although forming a whole at the level of that

[66] Valéry: 'Formally the novel is close to the dream; both can be defined by consideration of this curious property: *'all their deviations form part of them.'*
[67] Charles Bally, *Linguistique générale et linguistique française*, Paris 1932.

very sequence, may be separated from one another by the insertion of units from other sequences—as was said, the structure of the functional level is fugued.[68] According to Bally's terminology, which opposes synthetic languages where dystaxia is predominant (such as German) and analytic languages with a greater respect for logical linearity and monosemy (such as French), narrative would be a highly synthetic language, essentially founded on a syntax of embedding and enveloping: each part of the narrative radiates in several directions at once. When Bond orders a whisky while waiting for his plane, the whisky as indice has a polysemic value, is a kind of symbolic node grouping several signifieds (modernity, wealth, leisure); as a functional unit, however, the ordering of the whisky has to run step by step through numerous relays (consumption, waiting, departure, etc.) in order to find its final meaning: the unit is 'taken' by the whole narrative at the same time that the narrative only 'holds' by the distortion and irradiation of its units.

This generalized distortion is what gives the language of narrative its special character. A purely logical phenomenon, since founded on an often distant relation and mobilizing a sort of confidence in intellective memory, it ceaselessly substitutes meaning for the straightforward copy of the events recounted. On meeting in 'life', it is most unlikely that the invitation to take a seat would not immediately be followed by the act of sitting down; in narrative these two units, contiguous from a mimetic point of view, may be separated by a long series of insertions belonging to quite different functional spheres. Thus is established a kind of *logical time* which has very little connection with real time, the apparent pulverization of units always being firmly held in place by the logic that binds together the nuclei of the sequence. 'Suspense' is clearly only a privileged—or 'exacerbated' —form of distortion: on the one hand, by keeping a sequence open (through emphatic procedures of delay and renewal), it reinforces the contact with the reader (the listener), has a manifestly phatic function; while on the other, it offers the threat of an uncompleted sequence, of an open paradigm (if, as we believe, every sequence has two poles), that is to say, of a logical disturbance, it being this disturbance which is consumed with anxiety and pleasure (all the more so because it is always made right in the end). 'Suspense', therefore, is a game with structure, designed to endanger and glorify it, constituting a veritable 'thrilling' of intelligibility: by representing order (and no longer series) in its fragility, 'suspense' accomplishes the very idea of language: what

---

68 Cf. Lévi-Strauss: 'Relations pertaining to the same bundle may appear diachronically at remote intervals' *Anthropologie structurale*, p. 234 [trans. p. 211]. A. J. Greimas has emphasized the spacing out of functions.

seems the most pathetic is also the most intellectual—'suspense' grips you in the 'mind', not in the 'guts'.[69]

What can be separated can also be filled. Distended, the functional nuclei furnish intercalating spaces which can be packed out almost infinitely; the interstices can be filled in with a very large number of catalysers. Here, however, a new typology comes in, for the freedom to catalyse can be regulated according both to the content of the functions (certain functions are more apt than others for catalysing—as for example *Waiting*[70]) and to the substance of the narrative (writing contains possibilities of diaeresis—and so of catalysing—far superior to those of film: a gesture related linguistically can be 'cut up' much more easily than the same gesture visualized[71]). The catalytic power of narrative has for corollary its elliptic power. Firstly, a function (*he had a good meal*) can economize on all the potential catalysers it covers over (the details of the meal)[72]; secondly, it is possible to reduce a sequence to its nuclei and a hierarchy of sequences to its higher terms without altering the meaning of the story: a narrative can be identified even if its total syntagm be reduced to its actants and its main functions as these result from the progressive upwards integration of its functional units.[73] In other words, narrative lends itself to *summary* (what used to be called the *argument*). At first sight this is true of any discourse, but each discourse has its own kind of summary. A lyric poem, for example, is simply the vast metaphor of a signified[74] and to summarize it is thus to give this signified, an operation so drastic that it eliminates the poem's identity (summarized, lyric poems come down to the signifieds *Love* and *Death*)—hence the conviction that poems

[69] J. P. Faye, writing of Klossowski's *Baphomet*: 'Rarely has fiction (or narrative) so clearly revealed what it always is, necessarily: an experimentation of "thought" on "life".' *Tel Quel* 22, p. 88.

[70] Logically *Waiting* has only two nuclei: 1. the wait established 2. the wait rewarded or disappointed; the first, however, can be extensively catalysed, occasionally even indefinitely (*Waiting for Godot*): yet another game—this time extreme—with structure.

[71] Valéry: 'Proust divides up—and gives us the feeling of being able to divide up indefinitely—what other writers are in the habit of passing over.'

[72] Here again, there are qualifications according to substance: literature has an unrivalled elliptic power—which cinema lacks.

[73] This reduction does not necessarily correspond to the division of the book into chapters; on the contrary, it seems that increasingly chapters have the role of introducing breaks, points of suspense (serial technique).

[74] N. Ruwet: 'A poem can be understood as the outcome of a series of transformations applied to the proposition "I love you".' 'Analyse structurale d'un poème français', *Linguistics* 3, 1964, p. 82. Ruwet here refers precisely to the analysis of paranoiac delirium given by Freud in connection with President Schreber ('Psychoanalytic Notes on an Autobiographical Account of a Case of Paranoia', *Standard Edition* Vol. 12).

cannot be summarized. By contrast, the summary of a narrative (if conducted according to structural criteria) preserves the individuality of the message; narrative, in other words, is *translatable* without fundamental damage. What is untranslatable is determined only at the last, narrational, level. The signifiers of narrativity, for instance, are not readily transferable from novel to film, the latter utilizing the personal mode of treatment only very exceptionally;[75] while the last layer of the narrational level, namely the writing, resists transference from one language to another (or transfers very badly). The translatability of narrative is a result of the structure of its language, so that it would be possible, proceeding in reverse, to determine this structure by identifying and classifying the (varyingly) translatable and untranslatable elements of narrative. The existence (now) of different and concurrent semiotics (literature, cinema, comics, radio-television) would greatly facilitate this kind of analysis.

## 2. Mimesis and meaning

The second important process in the language of narrative is integration: what has been disjoined at a certain level (a sequence for example) is most often joined again at a higher level (a hierarchically important sequence, the global signified of a number of scattered indices, the action of a class of characters). The complexity of a narrative can be compared to that of an organization profile chart, capable of integrating backwards and forwards movements; or, more accurately, it is integration in various forms which compensates for the seemingly unmasterable complexity of units on a particular level. Integration guides the understanding of the discontinuous elements, simultaneously contiguous and heterogeneous (it is thus that they appear in the syntagm which knows only one dimension—that of succession). If, with Greimas, we call *isotopy* the unity of meaning (that, for instance, which impregnates a sign and its context), then we can say that integration is a factor of isotopy: each (integrational) level gives its isotopy to the units of the level below, prevents the meaning from 'dangling'—inevitable if the staggering of levels were not perceived. Narrative integration, however, does not present itself in a serenely regular manner like some fine architectural style leading by symmetrical chicaneries from an infinite variety of simple elements to a few complex masses.

---

[75] Once again, there is no relation between the grammatical 'person' of the narrator and the 'personality' (or subjectivity) that a film director puts into his way of presenting a story: the *camera-I* (continuously identified with the vision of a particular character) is exceptional in the history of cinema.

Very often a single unit will have two correlates, one on one level (function of a sequence), the other on another (indice with reference to an actant). Narrative thus appears as a succession of tightly inter-locking mediate and immediate elements; dystaxia determines a 'hor-izontal' reading, while integration superimposes a 'vertical' reading: there is a sort of structural 'limping', an incessant play of potentials whose varying falls give the narrative its dynamism or energy: each unit is perceived at once in its surfacing and in its depth and it is thus that the narrative 'works'; through the concourse of these two move-ments the structure ramifies, proliferates, uncovers itself—and recovers itself, pulls itself together: the new never fails in its regularity. There is, of course, a freedom of narrative (just as there is a freedom for every speaker with regard to his or her language), but this freedom is lim-ited, literally *hemmed in*: between the powerful code of language [*langue*] and the powerful code of narrative a hollow is set up—the sentence. If one attempts to embrace the whole of a written narrative, one finds that it starts from the most highly coded (the phonematic, or even the merismatic, level), gradually relaxes until it reaches the sentence, the farthest point of combinatorial freedom, and then begins to tighten up again, moving progressively from small groups of sen-tences (micro-sequences), which are still very free, until it comes to the main actions, which form a strong and restricted code. The creativity of narrative (at least under its mythical appearance of 'life') is thus situated *between two codes*, the linguistic and the translinguistic. That is why it can be said paradoxically that *art* (in the Romantic sense of the term) is a matter of statements of detail, whereas *imagination* is mastery of the code: 'It will be found in fact,' wrote Poe, 'that the ingenious are always fanciful, and the *truly* imaginative never other-wise than analytic . . .'[76]

Claims concerning the 'realism' of narrative are therefore to be dis-counted. When a telephone call comes through in the office where he is on duty, Bond, so the author tells us, reflects that 'Communications with Hong-Kong are as bad as they always were and just as difficult to obtain'. Neither Bond's 'reflection' nor the poor quality of the telephone call is the real piece of information; this contingency per-haps gives things more 'life' but the true information, which will come to fruition later, is the localization of the telephone call, Hong-Kong. In all narrative imitation remains contingent.[77] The function of nar-

[76] *The Murders in the Rue Morgue.*

[77] G. Genette rightly reduces *mimesis* to passages of directly reported dialogue (cf. 'Frontières du récit'); yet even dialogue always contains a function of intelligi-bility, not of mimesis.

rative is not to 'represent', it is to constitute a spectacle still very enigmatic for us but in any case not of a mimetic order. The 'reality' of a sequence lies not in the 'natural' succession of the actions composing it but in the logic there exposed, risked and satisfied. Putting it another way, one could say that the origin of a sequence is not the observation of reality, but the need to vary and transcend the first *form* given man, namely repetition: a sequence is essentially a whole within which nothing is repeated. Logic has here an emancipatory value—and with it the entire narrative. It may be that men ceaselessly reinject into narrative what they have known, what they have experienced; but if they do, at least it is in a form which has vanquished repetition and instituted the model of a process of becoming. Narrative does not show, does not imitate; the passion which may excite us in reading a novel is not that of a 'vision' (in actual fact, we do not 'see' anything). Rather it is that of meaning, that of a higher order of relation which also has its emotions, its hopes, its dangers, its triumphs. 'What takes place' in a narrative is from the referential (reality) point of view literally *nothing*;[78] 'what happens' is language alone, the adventure of language, the unceasing celebration of its coming. Although we know scarcely more about the origins of narrative than we do about the origins of language, it can reasonably be suggested that narrative is contemporaneous with monologue, a creation seemingly posterior to that of dialogue. At all events, without wanting to strain the phylogenetic hypothesis, it may be significant that it is at the same moment (around the age of three) that the little human 'invents' at once sentence, narrative, and the Oedipus.

[78] Mallarmé: 'A dramatic work displays the succession of exteriors of the act without any moment retaining reality and, in the end, anything happening.' *Crayonné au théâtre, Œuvres complètes*, p. 296.

# Of Grammatology
# (From Part I)

## 1967

*Jacques Derrida became instantly famous, even infamous, in American academic circles with his presentation of a paper, "Structure, Sign, and Play in the Discourse of the Human Sciences," at a symposium held at Johns Hopkins University in 1966. More a philosopher than a literary critic, Derrida's theories of language and culture have been developed, sometimes by himself and sometimes by followers, and applied to literature under the enigmatic term "Deconstruction," which, because initially a reaction to Structuralism, is often also referred to as Post-structuralism.*

*Deconstruction has at least two meanings. First, the term describes the process of "taking apart" necessary in each reader's individual reading of a text. Second, it is a confrontative skepticism that challenges certain constructs of western civilization which Derrida identifies as errors central also to structuralism. One of these, which he terms logocentrism, refers to the assumption pervasive since Aristotle that the spoken word, the uttered sound, is the purest representation of the essential truth of mind. Derrida rejects this notion as outmoded Platonism and naive positivism. Instead, he asserts that language is not a simple and reliable matching of signified with signifier; it may be that language controls us instead of our controlling language.*

*The following selection from the first chapter of his book,* Of Grammatology, *shows the philosophical attitude of Deconstruction*

*as a challenge to such traditional constructs. Derrida proposes an
alternate science, grammatology, or the science of writing. "Writing"
means more than marks on the page, certainly more than writing as
mere representation of sounds. Because he includes creativity in his
discussion of writing, as in "writing a symphony," "writing" (écriture)
means the mental production of language, or language as mental
process. He draws an important distinction between book and text,
to develop his position that writing is not a static construct (like a
book) but an active process, involving the writer's mental creation—
as well as the reader's individual deconstruction—of a text.*

*Deconstruction has not formulated a clearcut methodological ap-
proach to literature. The approach Derrida takes with a text, however,
has a basis in his approach to logocentrism. He organizes his perceptions of a literary text into a scheme of binary oppositions, such as
"male/female," "nature/culture," "writing/speaking," "absence/pres-
ence," etc. Thus part of his program is to attempt to rescue the lost
half of the dialectic that will be found in a complete reading, or
deconstruction, of a text. At times, although his interpretations seem
perverse and based on seemingly minor, even irrelevant, aspects of a
text, the intention is actually the quest for balance and completeness.
Unfortunately, because Derrida's style and method cannot be readily
imitated, some of his followers have given him a worse name than he
perhaps deserves. The elegance and clarity, however, of the essay by
Paul de Man, which follows Derrida's, shows American Deconstruc-
tionist criticism at its best.*

Socrates, he who does not write—*Nietzsche*

HOWEVER THE topic is considered, the *problem of language* has never
been simply one problem among others. But never as much as at present has it invaded, *as such*, the global horizon of the most diverse
researches and the most heterogeneous discourses, diverse and heterogeneous in their intention, method, and ideology. The devaluation of
the word "language" itself, and how, in the very hold it has upon us,
it betrays a loose vocabulary, the temptation of a cheap seduction, the
passive yielding to fashion, the consciousness of the avant-garde, in
other words—ignorance—are evidences of this effect. This inflation of
the sign "language" is the inflation of the sign itself, absolute inflation,
inflation itself. Yet, by one of its aspects or shadows, it is itself still a
sign: this crisis is also a symptom. It indicates, as in spite of itself,

that a historico-metaphysical epoch *must* finally determine as language
the totality of its problematic horizon. It must do so not only because
all that desire had wished to wrest from the play of language finds
itself recaptured within that play but also because, for the same
reason, language itself is menaced in its very life, helpless, adrift in the
threat of limitlessness, brought back to its own finitude at the very
moment when its limits seem to disappear, when it ceases to be self-
assured, contained, and *guaranteed* by the infinite signified which
seemed to exceed it.

## The Program

By a slow movement whose necessity is hardly perceptible, everything
that for at least some twenty centuries tended toward and finally succeeded in being gathered under the name of language is beginning to
let itself be transferred to, or at least summarized under, the name of
writing. By a hardly perceptible necessity, it seems as though the concept of writing—no longer indicating a particular, derivative, auxiliary
form of language in general (whether understood as communication,
relation, expression, signification, constitution of meaning or thought,
etc.), no longer designating the exterior surface, the insubstantial
double of a major signifier, *the signifier of the signifier*—is beginning to
go beyond the extension of language. In all senses of the word, writing
thus *comprehends* language. Not that the word "writing" has ceased
to designate the signifier of the signifier, but it appears, strange as it
may seem, that "signifier of the signifier" no longer defines accidental
doubling and fallen secondarity. "Signifier of the signifier" describes
on the contrary the movement of language: in its origin, to be sure,
but one can already suspect that an origin whose structure can be
expressed as "signifier of the signifier" conceals and erases itself in its
own production. There the signified always already functions as a
signifier. The secondarity that it seemed possible to ascribe to writing
alone affects all signifieds in general, affects them always already, the
moment they *enter the game*. There is not a single signified that
escapes, even if recaptured, the play of signifying references that constitute language. The advent of writing is the advent of this play; today such a play is coming into its own, effacing the limit starting from
which one had thought to regulate the circulation of signs, drawing
along with it all the reassuring signifieds, reducing all the strongholds,
all the out-of-bounds shelters that watched over the field of language.
This, strictly speaking, amounts to destroying the concept of "sign" and

its entire logic. Undoubtedly it is not by chance that this *overwhelming* supervenes at the moment when the extension of the concept of language effaces all its limits. We shall see that this overwhelming and this effacement have the same meaning, are one and the same phenomenon. It is as if the Western concept of language (in terms of what, beyond its plurivocity and beyond the strict and problematic opposition of speech [*parole*] and language [*langue*], attaches it *in general* to phonematic or glossematic production, to language, to voice, to hearing, to sound and breadth, to speech) were revealed today as the guise or disguise of a primary writing:[1] more fundamental than that which, before this conversion, passed for the simple "supplement to the spoken word" (Rousseau). Either writing was never a simple "supplement," or it is urgently necessary to construct a new logic of the "supplement." It is this urgency which will guide us further in reading Rousseau.

These disguises are not historical contingencies that one might admire or regret. Their movement was absolutely necessary, with a necessity which cannot be judged by any other tribunal. The privilege of the *phonè* does not depend upon a choice that could have been avoided. It responds to a moment of *economy* (let us say of the "life" of "history" or of "being as self-relationship"). The system of "hearing (understanding)-oneself-speak" through the phonic substance—which *presents itself* as the nonexterior, nonmundane, therefore nonempirical or noncontingent signifier—has necessarily dominated the history of the world during an entire epoch, and has even produced the idea of the world, the idea of world-origin, that arises from the difference between the worldly and the non-worldy, the outside and the inside, ideality and nonideality, universal and nonuniversal, transcendental and empirical, etc.[2]

With an irregular and essentially precarious success, this movement would apparently have tended, as toward its *telos*, to confine writing to a secondary and instrumental function: translator of a full speech

---

[1] To speak of a primary writing here does not amount to affirming a chronological priority of fact. That debate is well-known; is writing, as affirmed, for example, by Metchaninov and Marr, then Loukotka, "anterior to phonetic language?" (A conclusion assumed by the first edition of the Great Soviet Encyclopedia, later contradicted by Stalin. On this debate, cf. V. Istrine, "Langue et écriture," *Linguistique,* op. cit., pp. 35, 60. This debate also forms around the theses advanced by P. van Ginneken. On the discussion of these propositions, cf. James Février, *Histoire de l'écriture* (Payot, 1948–50), pp. 5 ff.). I shall try to show below why the terms and premises of such a debate are suspicious.

[2] I shall deal with this problem more directly in *La voix et le phénomène* (Paris, 1967).

that was fully *present* (present to itself, to its signified, to the other, the very condition of the theme of presence in general), technics in the service of language, *spokesman*, interpreter of an originary speech itself shielded from interpretation.

Technics in the service of language: I am not invoking a general essence of technics which would be already familiar to us and would help us in *understanding* the narrow and historically determined concept of writing as an example. I believe on the contrary that a certain sort of question about the meaning and origin of writing precedes, or at least merges with, a certain type of question about the meaning and origin of technics. That is why the notion of technique can never simply clarify the notion of writing.

It is therefore as if what we call language could have been in its origin and in its end only a moment, an essential but determined mode, a phenomenon, an aspect, a species of writing. And as if it had succeeded in making us forget this, and *in wilfully misleading us*, only in the course of an adventure: as that adventure itself. All in all a short enough adventure. It merges with the history that has associated technics and logocentric metaphysics for nearly three millennia. And it now seems to be approaching what is really its own *exhaustion*; under the circumstances—and this is no more than one example among others of this death of the civilization of the book, of which so much is said and which manifests itself particularly through a convulsive proliferation of libraries. All appearances to the contrary, this death of the book undoubtedly announces (and in a certain sense always has announced) nothing but a death of speech (of a *so-called* full speech) and a new mutation in the history of writing, in history as writing. Announces it at a distance of a few centuries. It is on that scale that we must reckon it here, being careful not to neglect the quality of a very heterogeneous historical duration: the acceleration is such, and such its qualitative meaning, that one would be equally wrong in making a careful evaluation according to past rhythms. "Death of speech" is of course a metaphor here: before we speak of disappearance, we must think of a new situation for speech, of its subordination within a structure of which it will no longer be the archon.

To affirm in this way that the concept of writing exceeds and comprehends that of language, presupposes of course a certain definition of language and of writing. If we do not attempt to justify it, we shall be giving in to the movement of inflation that we have just mentioned, which has also taken over the word "writing," and that not fortuitously. For some time now, as a matter of fact, here and there, by a gesture and for motives that are profoundly necessary, whose degradation is easier to denounce than it is to disclose their origin, one says "language" for action, movement, thought, reflection, consciousness, unconsciousness, experience, affectivity, etc. Now we tend to say "writing" for all that and more: to designate not only the physical gestures of literal pictographic or ideographic inscription, but also the totality of what makes it possible; and also, beyond the signifying face, the signified face itself. And thus we say "writing" for all that gives rise to an inscription in general, whether it is literal or not and even if what it distributes in space is alien to the order of the voice: cinematography, choreography, of course, but also pictorial, musical, sculptural "writing." One might also speak of athletic writing, and with even greater certainty of military or political writing in view of the techniques that govern those domains today. All this to describe not only the system of notation secondarily connected with these activities but the essence and the content of these activities themselves. It is also in this sense that the contemporary biologist speaks of writing and *pro-gram* in relation to the most elementary processes of information within the living cell. And, finally, whether it has essential limits or not, the entire field covered by the cybernetic *program* will be the field of writing. If the theory of cybernetics is by itself to oust all metaphysical concepts—including the concepts of soul, of life, of value, of choice, of memory—which until recently served to separate the machine from man,[3] it must conserve the notion of writing, trace, grammè [written mark], or grapheme, until its own historico-metaphysical character is also exposed. Even before being determined as human (with all the distinctive characteristics that have always been attributed to man and the entire system of significations that they imply) or nonhuman, the *grammè*—or the *grapheme*—would thus name the element. An element without simplicity. An element, whether it is understood as the medium or as the irreducible atom, of the arche-synthesis in general, of what one must forbid oneself to define within the system of oppositions of metaphysics, of what consequently one should not even call *experience* in general, that is to say the origin of *meaning* in general.

This situation has always already been announced. Why is it today in the process of making itself known *as such* and *after the fact*? This

---

3 Wiener, for example, while abandoning "semantics," and the opposition, judged by him as too crude and too general, between animate and inanimate etc., nevertheless continues to use expressions like "organs of sense," "motor organs," etc. to qualify the parts of the machine.

question would call forth an interminable analysis. Let us simply
choose some points of departure in order to introduce the limited remarks to which I shall confine myself. I have already alluded to
*theoretical* mathematics; its writing—whether understood as a sensible
*graphie* [manner of writing] (and that already presupposes an identity,
therefore an ideality, of its form, which in principle renders absurd
the so easily admitted notion of the "sensible signifier"), or understood as the ideal synthesis of signifieds or a trace operative on another
level, or whether it is understood, more profoundly, as the *passage* of
the one to the other—has never been absolutely linked with a phonetic
production. Within cultures practicing so-called phonetic writing,
mathematics is not just an enclave. That is mentioned by all historians
of writing; they recall at the same time the imperfections of alphabetic
writing, which passed for so long as the most convenient and "the most
intelligent"[4] writing. This enclave is also the place where the practice
of scientific language challenges intrinsically and with increasing profundity the ideal of phonetic writing and all its implicit metaphysics
(metaphysics *itself*), particularly, that is, the philosophical idea of the
*epistémè*; also of *istoria*, a concept profoundly related to it in spite
of the dissociation or opposition which has distinguished one from
the other during one phase of their common progress. History and
knowledge, *istoria* and *epistémè* have always been determined (and not
only etymologically or philosophically) as detours *for the purpose of*
the reappropriation of presence.

   But beyond theoretical mathematics, the development of the *practical methods* of information retrieval extends the possibilities of the
"message" vastly, to the point where it is no longer the "written"
translation of a language, the transporting of a signified which could
remain spoken in its integrity. It goes hand in hand with an extension
of phonography and of all the means of conserving the spoken language, of making it function without the presence of the speaking
subject. This development, coupled with that of anthropology and
of the history of writing, teaches us that phonetic writing, the medium
of the great metaphysical, scientific, technical, and economic adventure
of the West, is limited in space and time and limits itself even as it is
in the process of imposing its laws upon the cultural areas that had
escaped it. But this nonfortuitous conjunction of cybernetics and the
"human sciences" of writing leads to a more profound reversal.

---

   [4] Cf., e.g., *EP*, pp. 126, 148, 355, etc. From another point of view, cf. Roman
Jakobson, *Essais de linguistique générale* (tr. fr. [Nicolas Ruwet, Paris, 1963], p. 116)
[Jakobson and Morris Halle, *Fundamentals of Language* (the Hague, 1956), p. 16].

## The Signifier and Truth

The "rationality"—but perhaps that word should be abandoned for reasons that will appear at the end of this sentence—which governs a writing thus enlarged and radicalized, no longer issues from a logos. Further, it inaugurates the destruction, not the demolition but the de-sedimentation, the de-construction, of all the significations that have their source in that of the logos. Particularly the signification of *truth*. All the metaphysical determinations of truth, and even the one beyond metaphysical onto-theology that Heidegger reminds us of, are more or less immediately inseparable from the instance of the logos, or of a reason thought within the lineage of the logos, in whatever sense it is understood: in the pre-Socratic or the philosophical sense, in the sense of God's infinite understanding or in the anthropological sense, in the pre-Hegelian or the post-Hegelian sense. Within this logos, the original and essential link to the *phonè* has never been broken. It would be easy to demonstrate this and I shall attempt such a demonstration later. As has been more or less implicitly determined, the essence of the *phonè* would be immediately proximate to that which within "thought" as logos relates to "meaning," produces it, receives it, speaks it, "composes" it. If, for Aristotle, for example, "spoken words (ta en tē phonē) are the symbols of mental experience (pathēmata tes psychēs) and written words are the symbols of spoken words" (*De interpretatione*, 1, 16a 3) it is because the voice, producer of *the first symbols*, has a relationship of essential and immediate proximity with the mind. Producer of the first signifier, it is not just a simple signifier among others. It signifies "mental experiences" which themselves reflect or mirror things by natural resemblance. Between being and mind, things and feelings, there would be a relationship of translation or natural signification; between mind and logos, a relationship of conventional symbolization. And the *first* convention, which would relate immediately to the order of natural and universal signification, would be produced as spoken language. Written language would establish the conventions, interlinking other conventions with them.

> Just as all men have not the same writing so all men have not the same speech sounds, but mental experiences, of which these are the *primary symbols (semeîa prótos)*, are the same for all, as also are those things of which our experiences are the images (*De interpretatione*, 1, 16a. Italics added).

The feelings of the mind, expressing things naturally, constitute a sort of universal language which can then efface itself. It is the stage of transparence. Aristotle can sometimes omit it without risk.[5] In every case, the voice is closest to the signified, whether it is determined strictly as sense (thought or lived) or more loosely as thing. All signifiers, and first and foremost the written signifier, are derivative with regard to what would wed the voice indissolubly to the mind or to the thought of the signified sense, indeed to the thing itself (whether it is done in the Aristotelian manner that we have just indicated or in the manner of medieval theology, determining the *res* as a thing created from its *eidos*, from its sense thought in the logos or in the infinite understanding of God). The written signifier is always technical and representative. It has no constitutive meaning. This derivation is the very origin of the notion of the "signifier." The notion of the sign always implies within itself the distinction between signifier and signified, even if, as Saussure argues, they are distinguished simply as the two faces of one and the same leaf. This notion remains therefore within the heritage of that logocentrism which is also a phonocentrism: absolute proximity of voice and being, of voice and the meaning of being, of voice and the ideality of meaning. Hegel demonstrates very clearly the strange privilege of sound in idealization, the production of the concept and the self-presence of the subject.

> This ideal motion, in which through the sound what is as it were the simple subjectivity [*Subjektivität*], the soul of the material thing expresses itself, the ear receives also in a theoretical [*theoretisch*] way, just as the eye shape and colour, thus allowing the interiority of the object to become interiority itself [*läßt dadurch das Innere der Gegenstände für das Innere selbst werden*] (*Esthétique*, III. I tr. fr. p. 16). . . . The ear, on the contrary, perceives [*vernimmt*] the result of that interior vibration of material substance without placing itself in a practical relation toward the objects, a result by means of which it is no longer the material form [*Gestalt*] in its repose, but the first, more ideal activity of the soul itself which is manifested [*zum Vorschein kommt*] (p. 296).

[5] This is shown by Pierre Aubenque (*Le problème de l'être chez Aristotle* [Paris, 1966], pp. 106 f.). In the course of a provocative analysis, to which I am here indebted, Aubenque remarks: "In other texts, to be sure, Aristotle designates as symbol the relationship between language and things: 'It is not possible to bring the things themselves to the discussion, but, instead of things, we can use their names as symbols.' The intermediary constituted by the mental experience is here suppressed or at least neglected, but this suppression is legitimate, since, mental experiences behaving like things, things can be substituted for them immediately. On the other hand, one cannot by any means substitute names for things" (pp. 107–08).

What is said of sound in general is a fortiori valid for the *phonè* by which, by virtue of hearing (understanding)-oneself-speak—an indissociable system—the subject affects itself and is related to itself in the element of ideality.

We already have a foreboding that phonocentrism merges with the historical determination of the meaning of being in general as *presence*, with all the subdeterminations which depend on this general form and which organize within it their system and their historical sequence (presence of the thing to the sight as *eidos*, presence as substance/essence/existence [*ousia*], temporal presence as point [*stigmè*] of the now or of the moment [*nun*], the self-presence of the cogito, consciousness, subjectivity, the co-presence of the other and of the self, intersubjectivity as the intentional phenomenon of the ego, and so forth). Logocentrism would thus support the determination of the being of the entity as presence. To the extent that such a logocentrism is not totally absent from Heidegger's thought, perhaps it still holds that thought within the epoch of onto-theology, within the philosophy of presence, that is to say within philosophy *itself*. This would perhaps mean that one does not leave the epoch whose closure one can outline. The movements of belonging or not belonging to the epoch are too subtle, the illusions in that regard are too easy, for us to make a definite judgment.

The epoch of the logos thus debases writing considered as mediation of mediation and as a fall into the exteriority of meaning. To this epoch belongs the difference between signified and signifier, or at least the strange separation of their "parallelism," and the exteriority, however extenuated, of the one to the other. This appurtenance is organized and hierarchized in a history. The difference between signified and signifier belongs in a profound and implicit way to the totality of the great epoch covered by the history of metaphysics, and in a more explicit and more systematically articulated way to the narrower epoch of Christian creationism and infinitism when these appropriate the resources of Greek conceptuality. This appurtenance is essential and irreducible; one cannot retain the convenience or the "scientific truth" of the Stoic and later medieval opposition between *signans* and *signatum* without also bringing with it all its metaphysico-theological roots. To these roots adheres not only the distinction between the sensible and the intelligible—already a great deal—with all that it controls, namely, metaphysics in its totality. And this distinction is generally accepted as self-evident by the most careful linguists and semiologists, even by those who believe that the scientificity of their work begins where metaphysics ends. Thus, for example:

As modern structural thought has clearly realized, language is a system of signs and linguistics is part and parcel of the science of signs, or *semiotics* (Saussure's *sémiologie*). The mediaeval definition of sign—"*aliquid stat pro aliquo*"—has been resurrected and put forward as still valid and productive. Thus the constitutive mark of any sign in general and of any linguistic sign in particular is its twofold character: every linguistic unit is bipartite and involves both aspects—one sensible and the other intelligible, or in other words, both the *signans* "signifier" (Saussure's *significant*) and the *signatum* "signified" (*signifié*). These two constituents of a linguistic sign (and of sign in general) necessarily suppose and require each other.[6]

But to these metaphysico-theological roots many other hidden sediments cling. The semiological or, more specifically, linguistic "science" cannot therefore hold on to the difference between signifier and signified—the very idea of the sign—without the difference between sensible and intelligible, certainly, but also not without retaining, more profoundly and more implicitly, and by the same token the reference to a signified able to "take place" in its intelligibility, before its "fall," before any expulsion into the exteriority of the sensible here below. As the face of pure intelligibility, it refers to an absolute logos to which it is immediately united. This absolute logos was an infinite creative subjectivity in medieval theology: the intelligible face of the sign remains turned toward the word and the face of God.

Of course, it is not a question of "rejecting" these notions; they are necessary and, at least at present, nothing is conceivable for us without them. It is a question at first of demonstrating the systematic and historical solidarity of the concepts and gestures of thought that one often believes can be innocently separated. The sign and divinity have the same place and time of birth. The age of the sign is essentially theological. Perhaps it will never *end*. Its historical *closure* is, however, outlined.

Since these concepts are indispensable for unsettling the heritage to which they belong, we should be even less prone to renounce them. Within the closure, by an oblique and always perilous movement, constantly risking falling back within what is being deconstructed, it is necessary to surround the critical concepts with a careful and thor-

---

[6] Roman Jakobson, *Essais de linguistique générale*, tr. fr., p. 162 ["The Phonemic and Grammatical Aspects of Language in their Interrelations," *Proceedings of the Sixth International Congress of Linguistics* (Paris, 1949), p. 6]. On this problem, on the tradition of the concept of the sign, and on the originality of Saussure's contribution within this continuity, cf. Ortigues, op. cit., pp. 54 f.

ough discourse—to mark the conditions, the medium, and the limits of their effectiveness and to designate rigorously their intimate relationship to the machine whose deconstruction they permit; and, in the same process, designate the crevice through which the yet unnameable glimmer beyond the closure can be glimpsed. The concept of the sign is here exemplary. We have just marked its metaphysical appurtenance. We know, however, that the thematics of the sign have been for about a century the agonized labor of a tradition that professed to withdraw meaning, truth, presence, being, etc., from the movement of signification. Treating as suspect, as I just have, the difference between signified and signifier, or the idea of the sign in general, I must state explicitly that it is not a question of doing so in terms of the instance of the present truth, anterior, exterior or superior to the sign, or in terms of the place of the effaced difference. Quite the contrary. We are disturbed by that which, in the concept of the sign—which has never existed or functioned outside the history of (the) philosophy (of presence)—remains systematically and genealogically determined by that history. It is there that the concept and above all the work of deconstruction, its "style," remain by nature exposed to misunderstanding and nonrecognition.

The exteriority of the signifier is the exteriority of writing in general, and I shall try to show later that there is no linguistic sign before writing. Without that exteriority, the very idea of the sign falls into decay. Since our entire world and language would collapse with it, and since its evidence and its value keep, to a certain point of derivation, an indestructible solidity, it would be silly to conclude from its placement within an epoch that it is necessary to "move on to something else," to dispose of the sign, of the term and the notion. For a proper understanding of the gesture that we are sketching here, one must understand the expressions "epoch," "closure of an epoch," "historical genealogy" in a new way; and must first remove them from all relativism.

Thus, within this epoch, reading and writing, the production or interpretation of signs, the text in general as fabric of signs, allow themselves to be confined within secondariness. They are preceded by a truth, or a meaning already constituted by and within the element of the logos. Even when the thing, the "referent," is not immediately related to the logos of a creator God where it began by being the spoken/thought sense, the signified has at any rate an immediate relationship with the logos in general (finite or infinite), and a mediated one with the signifier, that is to say with the exteriority of writing. When it seems to go otherwise, it is because a metaphoric mediation

has insinuated itself into the relationship and has simulated imme-
diacy; the writing of truth in the soul, opposed by *Phaedrus* (278a) to
bad writing (writing in the "literal" [*propre*] and ordinary sense,
"sensible" writing, "in space"), the book of Nature and God's writing,
especially in the Middle Ages; all that functions as *metaphor* in these
discourses confirms the privilege of the logos and founds the "literal"
meaning then given to writing: a sign signifying a signifier itself signifying an eternal verity, eternally thought and spoken in the proximity of a present logos. The paradox to which attention must be
paid is this: natural and universal writing, intelligible and nontem-
poral writing, is thus named by metaphor. A writing that is sensible,
finite, and so on, is designated as writing in the literal sense; it is thus
thought on the side of culture, technique, and artifice; a human procedure, the ruse of a being accidentally incarnated or of a finite creature. Of course, this metaphor remains enigmatic and refers to a
"literal" meaning of writing as the first metaphor. This "literal" meaning is yet unthought by the adherents of this discourse. It is not,
therefore, a matter of inverting the literal meaning and the figurative
meaning but of determining the "literal" meaning of writing as
metaphoricity itself.

In "The Symbolism of the Book," that excellent chapter of *European
Literature and the Latin Middle Ages*, E. R. Curtius describes with
great wealth of examples the evolution that led from the *Phaedrus* to
Calderon, until it seemed to be "precisely the reverse" (tr. fr. p. 372)
by the "newly attained position of the book" (p. 374) [p. 306]. But
it seems that this modification, however important in fact it might be,
conceals a fundamental continuity. As was the case with the Platonic
writing of the truth in the soul, in the Middle Ages too it is a writing
understood in the metaphoric sense, that is to say a *natural*, eternal,
and universal writing, the system of signified truth, which is recognized in its dignity. As in the *Phaedrus*, a certain fallen writing continues to be opposed to it. There remains to be written a history of
this metaphor, a metaphor that systematically contrasts divine or
natural writing and the human and laborious, finite and artificial inscription. It remains to articulate rigorously the stages of that history,
as marked by the quotations below, and to follow the theme of God's
book (nature or law, indeed natural law) through all its modifications.

Rabbi Eliezer said: "If all the seas were of ink, and all ponds planted
with reeds, if the sky and the earth were parchments and if all human
beings practised the art of writing—they would not exhaust the
Torah I have learned, just as the Torah itself would not be dimin-

ished any more than is the sea by the water removed by a paint brush dipped in it."[7]

Galileo: "It [the book of Nature] is written in a mathematical language."

Descartes: ". . . to read in the great book of Nature . . ."

Demea, in the name of natural religion, in the *Dialogues*, . . . of Hume: "And this volume of nature contains a great and inexplicable riddle, more than any intelligible discourse or reasoning."

Bonnet: "It would seem more philosophical to me to presume that our earth is a book that God has given to intelligences far superior to ours to read, and where they study in depth the infinitely multiplied and varied characters of His adorable wisdom."

G. H. von Schubert: "This language made of images and hieroglyphs, which supreme Wisdom uses in all its revelations to humanity—which is found in the inferior [*nieder*] language of poetry —and which, in the most inferior and imperfect way [*auf der allerniedrigsten und unvollkommensten*], is more like the metaphorical expression of the dream than the prose of wakefulness, . . . we may wonder if this language is not the true and wakeful language of the superior regions. If, when we consider ourselves awakened, we are not plunged in a millennial slumber, or at least in the echo of its dreams, where we only perceive a few isolated and obscure words of God's language, as a sleeper perceives the conversation of the people around him."

Jaspers: "The world is the manuscript of an other, inaccessible to a universal reading, which only existence deciphers."

Above all, the profound differences distinguishing all these treatments of the same metaphor must not be ignored. In the history of this treatment, the most decisive separation appears at the moment when, at the same time as the science of nature, the determination of absolute presence is constituted as self-presence, as subjectivity. It is the moment of the great rationalisms of the seventeenth century. From then on, the condemnation of fallen and finite writing will take another form, within which we still live: it is non-self-presence that will be denounced. Thus the exemplariness of the "Rousseauist" moment, which we shall deal with later, begins to be explained. Rousseau

---

[7] Cited by Emmanuel Levinas, in *Difficile liberté* [Paris, 1963], p. 44.

repeats the Platonic gesture by referring to another model of presence: self-presence in the senses, in the sensible cogito, which simultaneously carries in itself the inscription of divine law. On the one hand, *representative*, fallen, secondary, instituted writing, writing in the literal and strict sense, is condemned in *The Essay on the Origin of Languages* (it "enervates" speech; to "judge genius" from books is like "painting a man's portrait from his corpse," etc.). Writing in the common sense is the dead letter, it is the carrier of death. It exhausts life. On the other hand, on the other face of the same proposition, writing in the metaphoric sense, natural, divine, and living writing, is venerated; it is equal in dignity to the origin of value, to the voice of conscience as divine law, to the heart, to sentiment, and so forth.

> The Bible is the most sublime of all books, . . . but it is after all a book. . . . It is not at all in a few sparse pages that one should look for God's law, but in the human heart where His hand deigned to write (*Lettre à Vernes*).

> If the natural law had been written only in the human reason, it would be little capable of directing most of our actions. But it is also engraved in the heart of man in ineffacable characters. . . . There it cries to him (*L'état de guerre.*)

Natural writing is immediately united to the voice and to breath. Its nature is not grammatological but pneumatological. It is hieratic, very close to the interior holy voice of the *Profession of Faith*, to the voice one hears upon retreating into oneself: full and truthful presence of the divine voice to our inner sense: "The more I retreat into myself, the more I consult myself, the more plainly do I read these words written in my soul: be just and you will be happy. . . . I do not derive these rules from the principles of the higher philosophy, I find them in the depths of my heart written by nature in characters which nothing can efface."

There is much to say about the fact that the native unity of the voice and writing is *prescriptive*. Arche-speech is writing because it is a law. A natural law. The beginning word is understood, in the intimacy of self-presence, as the voice of the other and as commandment.

There is therefore a good and a bad writing: the good and natural is the divine inscription in the heart and the soul; the perverse and artful is technique, exiled in the exteriority of the body. A modification well within the Platonic diagram: writing of the soul and of the body, writing of the interior and of the exterior, writing of conscience and of the passions, as there is a voice of the soul and a voice of the body. "Conscience is the voice of the soul, the passions are the voice of the body" [p. 249]. One must constantly go back toward the "voice of nature," the "holy voice of nature," that merges with the divine inscription and prescription; one must encounter oneself within it, enter into a dialogue within its signs, speak and respond to oneself in its pages.

> It was as if nature had spread out all her magnificence in front of our eyes to offer its text for our consideration. . . . I have therefore closed all the books. Only one is open to all eyes. It is the book of Nature. In this great and sublime book I learn to serve and adore its author.

The good writing has therefore always been *comprehended*. Comprehended as that which had to be comprehended: within a nature or a natural law, created or not, but first thought within an eternal presence. Comprehended, therefore, within a totality, and enveloped in a volume or a book. The idea of the book is the idea of a totality, finite or infinite, of the signifier; this totality of the signifier cannot be a totality, unless a totality constituted by the signified preexists it, supervises its inscriptions and its signs, and is independent of it in its ideality. The idea of the book, which always refers to a natural totality, is profoundly alien to the sense of writing. It is the encyclopedic protection of theology and of logocentrism against the disruption of writing, against its aphoristic energy, and, as I shall specify later, against difference in general. If I distinguish the text from the book, I shall say that the destruction of the book, as it is now under way in all domains, denudes the surface of the text. That necessary violence responds to a violence that was no less necessary. . . .

## PAUL DE MAN

# Semiology and Rhetoric

## 1979

*Paul de Man examines issues of interpretation common to New Criti-
cism, Structuralism, and Deconstruction. The New Criticism he sees
as reductive and compromised by inherent fallacies; and although
French Semiology is in his view an advance over New Criticism, de
Man believes that the Semiologists (or Structuralists) have not been
rigorous enough in their analysis of Rhetoric. Because Rhetoric is
essential to the study of literature, he delineates an approach to Rhetoric that will be appropriate to the grammatical foundations of
Semiology.*

   *He defines Rhetoric by alluding to Charles Sanders Peirce's distinc-
tion between grammar and rhetoric: while grammar suggests a system
in which signs have a stable and explicit meaning, rhetoric requires an
interpretant who reads a sign so that "one sign gives birth to another."
De Man also refers to Monroe Beardsley's idea that both literary and
rhetorical language are characterized by a concentrated use of implicit
meanings. Finally he mentions Austin's theory of the "illocutionary
act," the primary concern of which is analyzing the effect a speaker intends to achieve with a given utterance. The problem for criticism is
in devising a Semiology of Rhetoric that will yield an instrument of
investigation that is rigorous because based on grammar. Deconstruction will provide the means of devising such a Rhetoric.*

   *De Man demonstrates his Deconstructive approach in seeking the
oppositions contained in literary passages. Deconstruction is appropriate as an approach to Rhetoric, he argues, because Rhetoric itself de-*

constructs, or undermines, the grammatical stability and reliability of language. In rhetorical questions, for example, grammatical and rhetorical forms are exactly congruent; the literal and figurative meanings derived from them, however, diverge into opposites.

De Man's deconstruction of the oppositions of literal/figurative and grammatical/rhetorical leads him to discover two semiological categories of rhetoric. First is the rhetorization of grammar, as in the rhetorical question. (His example is the famous question at the end of Yeats's "Among School Children.") Secondly, de Man finds a grammatization of rhetoric in a passage from Proust's Swann's Way. The analysis of Proust's rhetoric reveals that the oppositions of inner/outer, reading/living, presence/absence, and so forth, apparently develop a literary statement of the superiority of metaphor (a whole equals another whole) through a strategy of metonymy and synecdoche (a part equals a whole). Deconstruction thrives on the sort of unresolved oppositions that are anathema to logocentrism.

De Man's argument moves in deliberate indirection, never forcing certainties but discovering and maintaining multiple possibilities. He concludes that Deconstruction must ultimately merge with psycholinguistics, so that our perceptions about literature will join with our understanding of the processes of language and mind.

To JUDGE from various recent publications, the spirit of the times is not blowing in the direction of formalist and intrinsic criticism. We may no longer be hearing too much about relevance but we keep hearing a great deal about reference, about the nonverbal "outside" to which language refers, by which it is conditioned and upon which it acts. The stress falls not so much on the fictional status of literature— a property now perhaps somewhat too easily taken for granted—but on the interplay between these fictions and categories that are said to partake of reality, such as the self, man, society, "the artist, his culture and the human community," as one critic puts it. Hence the emphasis on hybrid texts considered to be partly literary and partly referential, on popular fictions deliberately aimed towards social and psychological gratification, on literary autobiography as a key to the understanding of the self, and so on. We speak as if, with the problems of literary form resolved once and forever, and with the techniques of structural analysis refined to near-perfection, we could now move "beyond formalism" towards the questions that really interest us and reap, at last, the fruits of the ascetic concentration on techniques that prepared us for this decisive step. With the internal law and order of literature well policed, we can now confidently devote ourselves to the foreign affairs, the external politics of literature. Not only do we feel able to do so, but we owe it to ourselves to take this step: our moral conscience would not allow us to do otherwise. Behind the assurance that valid interpretation is possible, behind the recent interest in writing and reading as potentially effective public speech acts, stands a highly respectable moral imperative that strives to reconcile the internal, formal, private structures of literary language with their external, referential, and public effects.

I want, for the moment, to consider briefly this tendency in itself, as an undeniable and recurrent historical fact, without regard for its truth or falseness or for its value as desirable or pernicious. It is a fact that this sort of thing happens, again and again, in literary studies. On the one hand, literature cannot merely be received as a definite unit of referential meaning that can be decoded without leaving a residue. The code is unusually conspicuous, complex, and enigmatic; it attracts an inordinate amount of attention to itself, and this attention has to acquire the rigor of a method. The structural moment of concentration on the code for its own sake cannot be avoided, and literature necessarily breeds its own formalism. Technical innovations in the methodical study of literature only occur when this kind of attention predominates. It can legitimately be said, for example, that, from a technical point of view, very little has happened in American criticism since the innovative works of New Criticism. There certainly have been numerous excellent books of criticism since, but in none of them have the techniques of description and interpretation evolved beyond the techniques of close reading established in the thirties and the forties. Formalism, it seems, is an all-absorbing and tyrannical muse; the hope that one can be at the same time technically original and discursively eloquent is not borne out by the history of literary criticism.

On the other hand—and this is the real mystery—no literary formalism, no matter how accurate and enriching in its analytic powers, is ever allowed to come into being without seeming reductive. When form is considered to be the external trappings of literary meaning or content, it seems superficial and expendable. The development of intrinsic, formalist criticism in the twentieth century has changed this model: form is now a solipsistic category of self-reflection, and the referential meaning is said to be extrinsic. The polarities of inside and outside have been reversed, but they are still the same polarities that are at play: internal meaning has become outside reference, and the outer form has become the intrinsic structure. A new version of reductiveness at once follows this reversal: formalism nowadays is mostly described in an imagery of imprisonment and claustrophobia: the "prison house of language," "the impasse of formalist criticism," etc. Like the grandmother in Proust's novel ceaselessly driving the young Marcel out into the garden, away from the unhealthy inwardness of his closeted reading, critics cry out for the fresh air of referential meaning. Thus, with the structure of the code so opaque, but the meaning so anxious to blot out the obstacle of form, no wonder that the reconciliation of form and meaning would be so attractive. The attraction of reconciliation is the elective breeding-ground of false models and metaphors; it accounts for the metaphorical model of literature as a kind of box that separates an inside from an outside, and the reader or critic as the person who opens the lid in order to release in the open what was secreted but inaccessible inside. It matters little whether we call the inside of the box the content or the form, the outside the meaning or the appearance. The recurrent debate opposing intrinsic to extrinsic criticism stands under the aegis of an inside/outside metaphor that is never being seriously questioned.

Metaphors are much more tenacious than facts, and I certainly don't expect to dislodge this age-old model in one short try. I merely wish to speculate on a different set of terms, perhaps less simple in their differential relationships than the strictly polar, binary opposition between inside and outside and therefore less likely to enter into the easy play of chiasmic reversals. I derive these terms (which are as old as the hills) pragmatically from the observation of developments and debates in recent critical methodology.

One of the most controversial among these developments coincides with a new approach to poetics or, as it is called in Germany, poetology, as a branch of general semiotics. In France, a semiology of literature comes about as the outcome of the long-deferred but all the more explosive encounter of the nimble French literary mind with the category of form. Semiology, as opposed to semantics, is the science or study of signs as signifiers; it does not ask what words mean but how they mean. Unlike American New Criticism, which derived the internalization of form from the practice of highly self-conscious modern writers, French semiology turned to linguistics for its model and adopted Saussure and Jakobson rather than Valéry or Proust for its masters. By an awareness of the arbitrariness of the sign (Saussure) and of literature as an autotelic statement "focused on the way it is expressed" (Jakobson) the entire question of meaning can be bracketed, thus freeing the critical discourse from the debilitating burden of paraphrase. The demystifying power of semiology, within the context of French historical and thematic criticism, has been considerable. It demonstrated that the perception of the literary dimensions of language is largely obscured if one submits uncritically to the authority of reference. It also revealed how tenaciously this authority continues to assert itself in a variety of disguises, ranging from the crudest ideology to the most refined forms of aesthetic and ethical judgment. It especially explodes the myth of semantic correspondence between sign and referent, the wishful hope of having it both ways, of being, to paraphrase Marx in the German Ideology, a formalist critic in the morning and a communal moralist in the afternoon, of serving both the technique of form and the substance of meaning. The results, in the practice of French criticism, have been as fruitful as they are irreversible. Perhaps for the first time since the late eighteenth century, French critics can come at least somewhat closer to the kind of linguistic awareness that never ceased to be operative in its poets and novelists and that forced all of them, including Sainte Beuve, to write their main works "contre Sainte Beuve." The distance was never so considerable in England and the United States, which does not mean, however, that we may be able, in this country, to dispense altogether with some preventative semiological hygiene.

One of the most striking characteristics of literary semiology as it is practiced today, in France and elsewhere, is the use of grammatical (especially syntactical) structures conjointly with rhetorical structures, without apparent awareness of a possible discrepancy between them. In their literary analyses, Barthes, Genette, Todorov, Greimas, and their disciples all simplify and regress from Jakobson in letting grammar and rhetoric function in perfect continuity, and in passing from grammatical to rhetorical structures without difficulty or interruption. Indeed, as the study of grammatical structures is refined in contemporary theories of generative, transformational, and distributive grammar, the study of tropes and of figures (which is how the term *rhetoric* is used here, and not in the derived sense of comment or of eloquence or persuasion) becomes a mere extension of grammatical models, a particular subset of syntactical relations. In the recent *Dictionnaire encyclopédique des sciences du langage*, Ducrot and Todorov write that rhetoric has always been satisfied with a paradigmatic view over words (words substituting for each other), without questioning their syntagmatic relationship (the contiguity of words to each other). There ought to be another perspective, complementary to the first, in which metaphor, for example, would not be defined as a substitution but as a particular type of combination. Research inspired by linguistics or, more narrowly, by syntactical studies, has begun to reveal this possibility—but it remains to be explored. Todorov, who calls one of his books a *Grammar of the Decameron*, rightly thinks of his own work and that of his associates as first explorations in the elaboration of a systematic grammar of literary modes, genres, and also of literary figures. Perhaps the most perceptive work to come out of this school, Genette's studies of figural modes, can be shown to be assimilations of rhetorical transformations or combinations to syntactical, grammatical patterns. Thus a recent study, now printed in *Figures III* and entitled *Metaphor and Metonymy in Proust*, shows the combined presence, in a wide and astute selection of passages, of paradigmatic, metaphorical figures with syntagmatic, metonymic structures. The combination of both is treated descriptively and nondialectically without considering the possibility of logical tensions.

One can ask whether this reduction of figure to grammar is legitimate. The existence of grammatical structures, within and beyond the unit of the sentence, in literary texts is undeniable, and their description and classification are indispensable. The question remains if and how figures of rhetoric can be included in such a taxonomy. This question is at the core of the debate going on, in a wide variety of apparently unrelated forms, in contemporary poetics. But the historical picture of contemporary criticism is too confused to make the mapping out of such a topography a useful exercise. Not only are these questions mixed in and mixed up within particular groups or local trends, but they are often co-present, without apparent contradiction, within the work of a single author.

Neither is the theory of the question suitable for quick expository treatment. To distinguish the epistemology of grammar from the epistemology of rhetoric is a redoubtable task. On an entirely naïve level, we tend to conceive of grammatical systems as tending towards universality and as simply generative, i.e., as capable of deriving an infinity of versions from a single model (that may govern transformations as well as derivations) without the intervention of another model that would upset the first. We therefore think of the relationship between grammar and logic, the passage from grammar to propositions, as being relatively unproblematic: no true propositions are conceivable in the absence of grammatical consistency or of controlled deviation from a system of consistency no matter how complex. Grammar and logic stand to each other in a dyadic relationship of unsubverted support. In a logic of acts rather than of statements, as in Austin's theory of speech acts, that has had such a strong influence on recent American work in literary semiology, it is also possible to move between speech acts and grammar without difficulty. The performance of what is called illocutionary acts such as ordering, questioning, denying, assuming, etc., within the language is congruent with the grammatical structures of syntax in the corresponding imperative, interrogative, negative, optative sentences. "The rules for illocutionary acts," writes Richard Ohman in a recent paper, "determine whether performance of a given act is well-executed, in just the same way as *grammatical* rules determine whether the product of a locutionary act —a sentence—is well formed. . . . But whereas the rules of grammar concern the relationships among sound, syntax, and meaning, the rules of illocutionary acts concern relationships among people."[1] And since rhetoric is then conceived exclusively as persuasion, as actual action upon others (and not as an intralinguistic figure or trope), the continuity between the illocutionary realm of grammar and the perlocutionary realm of rhetoric is self-evident. It becomes the basis for a new rhetoric that, exactly as is the case for Todorov and Genette, would also be a new grammar.

Without engaging the substance of the question, it can be pointed out, without having to go beyond recent and American examples, and without calling upon the strength of an age-old tradition, that the continuity here assumed between grammar and rhetoric is not borne out by theoretical and philosophical speculation. Kenneth Burke mentions *deflection* (which he compares structurally to Freudian displacement), defined as "any slight bias or even unintended error," as the rhetorical basis of language, and deflection is then conceived as a dialectical subversion of the consistent link between sign and meaning that operates within grammatical patterns; hence Burke's well-known insistence on the distinction between grammar and rhetoric. Charles Sanders Peirce, who, with Nietzsche and Saussure, laid the philosophical foundation for modern semiology, stressed the distinction between grammar and rhetoric in his celebrated and so suggestively unfathomable definition of the sign. He insists, as is well known, on the necessary presence of a third element, called the interpretant, within any relationship that the sign entertains with its object. The sign is to be interpreted if we are to understand the idea it is to convey, and this is so because the sign is not the thing but a meaning derived from the thing by a process here called representation that is not simply generative, i.e., dependent on a univocal origin. The interpretation of the sign is not, for Peirce, a meaning but another sign; it is a reading, not a decodage, and this reading has, in its turn, to be inter-

[1] "Speech, Literature, and the Space in Between," *New Literary History* 4 (Autumn 1972): 50.

preted into another sign, and so on *ad infinitum*. Pierce calls this process by means of which "one sign gives birth to another" pure rhetoric, as distinguished from pure grammar, which postulates the possibility of unproblematic, dyadic meaning, and pure logic, which postulates the possibility of the universal truth of meanings. Only if the sign engendered meaning in the same way that the object engenders the sign, that is, by representation, would there be no need to distinguish between grammar and rhetoric.

These remarks should indicate at least the existence and the difficulty of the question, a difficulty which puts its concise theoretical exposition beyond my powers. I must retreat therefore into a pragmatic discourse and try to illustrate the tension between grammar and rhetoric in a few specific textual examples. Let me begin by considering what is perhaps the most commonly known instance of an apparent symbiosis between a grammatical and a rhetorical structure, the so-called rhetorical question, in which the figure is conveyed directly by means of a syntactical device. I take the first example from the sub-literature of the mass media: asked by his wife whether he wants to have his bowling shoes laced over or laced under, Archie Bunker answers with a question: "What's the difference?" Being a reader of sublime simplicity, his wife replies by patiently explaining the difference between lacing over and lacing under, whatever this may be, but provokes only ire. "What's the difference" did not ask for difference but means instead "I don't give a damn what the difference is." The same grammatical pattern engenders two meanings that are mutually exclusive: the literal meaning asks for the concept (difference) whose existence is denied by the figurative meaning. As long as we are talking about bowling shoes, the consequences are relatively trivial; Archie Bunker, who is a great believer in the authority of origins (as long, of course, as they are the right origins) muddles along in a world where literal and figurative meanings get in each other's way, though not without discomforts. But suppose that it is a *de*-bunker rather than a "Bunker," and a de-bunker of the arche (or origin), an archie Debunker such as Nietzsche or Jacques Derrida for instance, who asks the question "What is the Difference"—and we cannot even tell from his grammar whether he "really" wants to know "what" difference is or is just telling us that we shouldn't even try to find out. Confronted with the question of the difference between grammar and rhetoric, grammar allows us to ask the question, but the sentence by means of which we ask it may deny the very possibility of asking. For what is the use of asking, I ask, when we cannot even authoritatively decide whether a question asks or doesn't ask?

The point is as follows. A perfectly clear syntactical paradigm (the question) engenders a sentence that has at least two meanings, of which the one asserts and the other denies its own illocutionary mode. It is not so that there are simply two meanings, one literal and the other figural, and that we have to decide which one of these meanings is the right one in this particular situation. The confusion can only be cleared up by the intervention of an extra-textual intention, such as Archie Bunker putting his wife straight; but the very anger he displays is indicative of more than impatience; it reveals his despair when confronted with a structure of linguistic meaning that he cannot control and that holds the discouraging prospect of an infinity of similar future confusions, all of them potentially catastrophic in their consequences. Nor is this intervention really a part of the mini-text constituted by the figure which holds our attention only as long as it remains suspended and unresolved. I follow the usage of common speech in calling this semiological enigma "rhetorical." The grammatical model of the question becomes rhetorical not when we have, on the one hand, a literal meaning and on the other hand a figural meaning, but when it is impossible to decide by grammatical or other linguistic devices which of the two meanings (that can be entirely incompatible) prevails. Rhetoric radically suspends logic and opens up vertiginous possibilities of referential aberration. And although it would perhaps be somewhat more remote from common usage, I would not hesitate to equate the rhetorical, figural potentiality of language with literature itself. I could point to a great number of antecedents to this equation of literature with figure; the most recent reference would be to Monroe Beardsley's insistence in his contribution to the *Essays* to honor William Wimsatt, that literary language is characterized by being "distinctly above the norm in ratio of implicit [or, I would say rhetorical] to explicit meaning."[2]

Let me pursue the matter of the rhetorical question through one more example. Yeats's poem "Among School Children" ends with the famous line: "How can we know the dancer from the dance?" Although there are some revealing inconsistencies within the commentaries, the line is usually interpreted as stating, with the increased emphasis of a rhetorical device, the potential unity between form and experience, between creator and creation. It could be said that it denies the discrepancy between the sign and the referent from which we started out. Many elements in the imagery and the dramatic devel-

[2] "The Concept of Literature," in *Literary Theory and Structure: Essays in Honor of William K. Wimsatt,* ed. Frank Brady, John Palmer, and Martin Price (New Haven, 1973), p. 37.

opment of the poem strengthen this traditional reading; without having to look any further than the immediately preceding lines, one finds powerful and consecrated images of the continuity from part to whole that makes synecdoche into the most seductive of metaphors: the organic beauty of the tree, stated in the parallel syntax of a similar rhetorical question, or the convergence, in the dance, of erotic desire with musical form:

> O chestnut-tree, great-rooted blossomer,
> Are you the leaf, the blossom or the bole?
> O body swayed to music, O brightening glance,
> How can we know the dancer from the dance?

A more extended reading, always assuming that the final line is to be read as a rhetorical question, reveals that the thematic and rhetorical grammar of the poem yields a consistent reading that extends from the first line to the last and that can account for all details in the text. It is equally possible, however, to read the last line literally rather than figuratively, as asking with some urgency the question we asked earlier within the context of contemporary criticism: *not* that sign and referent are so exquisitely fitted to each other that all difference between them is at times blotted out but, rather, since the two essentially different elements, sign and meaning, are so intricately intertwined in the imagined "presence" that the poem addresses, how can we possibly make the distinctions that would shelter us from the error of identifying what cannot be identified? The clumsiness of the paraphrase reveals that it is not necessarily the literal reading which is simpler than the figurative one, as was the case in our first example; here, the figural reading, which assumes the question to be rhetorical, is perhaps naïve, whereas the literal reading leads to greater complication of theme and statement. For it turns out that the entire scheme set up by the first reading can be undermined, or deconstructed, in the terms of the second, in which the final line is read literally as meaning that, since the dancer and the dance are not the same, it might be useful, perhaps even desperately necessary—for the question can be given a ring of urgency, "Please tell me, how *can* I know the dancer from the dance"—to tell them apart. But this will replace the reading of each symbolic detail by a divergent interpretation. The oneness of trunk, leaf, and blossom, for example, that would have appealed to Goethe, would find itself replaced by the much less reassuring Tree of Life from the Mabinogion that appears in the poem "Vacillation," in which the fiery blossom and the earthly leaf are held together, as well as apart, by the crucified and castrated God Attis, of whose body it can hardly be said that it is "not bruised to pleasure soul." This hint should suffice to suggest that two entirely coherent but entirely incompatible readings can be made to hinge on one line, whose grammatical structure is devoid of ambiguity, but whose rhetorical mode turns the mood as well as the mode of the entire poem upside down. Neither can we say, as was already the case in the first example, that the poem simply has two meanings that exist side by side. The two readings have to engage each other in direct confrontation, for the one reading is precisely the error denounced by the other and has to be undone by it. Nor can we in any way make a valid decision as to which of the readings can be given priority over the other; none can exist in the other's absence. There can be no dance without a dancer, no sign without a referent. On the other hand, the authority of the meaning engendered by the grammatical structure is fully obscured by the duplicity of a figure that cries out for the differentiation that it conceals.

Yeats's poem is not explicitly "about" rhetorical questions but about images or metaphors, and about the possibility of convergence between experiences of consciousness such as memory or emotions— what the poem calls passion, piety, and affection—and entities accessible to the senses such as bodies, persons, or icons. We return to the inside/outside model from which we started out and which the poem puts into question by means of a syntactical device (the question) made to operate on a grammatical as well as on a rhetorical level. The couple grammar/rhetoric, certainly not a binary opposition since they in no way exclude each other, disrupts and confuses the neat antithesis of the inside/outside pattern. We can transfer this scheme to the act of reading and interpretation. By reading we get, as we say, *inside* a text that was first something alien to us and which we now make our own by an act of understanding. But this understanding becomes at once the representation of an extra-textual meaning; in Austin's terms, the illocutionary speech act becomes a perlocutionary actual act—in Frege's terms, *Bedeutung* becomes *Sinn*. Our recurrent question is whether this transformation is semantically controlled along grammatical or along rhetorical lines. Does the metaphor of reading really unite outer meaning with inner understanding, action with reflection, into one single totality? The assertion is powerfully and suggestively made in a passage from Proust that describes the experience of reading as such a union. It describes the young Marcel, near the beginning of Combray, hiding in the closed space of his room in order to read. The example differs from the earlier ones in that we are not dealing with a grammatical structure that also functions rhetorically but have instead the representation, the dramatization, in terms of the experience of a subject, of a rhetorical structure—just as, in many other passages, Proust dramatizes tropes by means of land-scapes or descriptions of objects. The figure here dramatized is that of metaphor, an inside/outside correspondence as represented by the act of reading. The reading scene is the culmination of a series of ac-tions taking place in enclosed spaces and leading up to the "dark cool-ness" of Marcel's room.

I had stretched out on my bed, with a book, in my room which sheltered, tremblingly, its transparent and fragile coolness from the afternoon sun behind the almost closed blinds through which a glimmer of daylight had nevertheless managed to push its yellow wings, remaining motionless between the wood and the glass, in a corner, poised like a butterfly. It was hardly light enough to read, and the sensation of the light's splendor was given me only by the noise of Camus . . . hammering dusty crates; resounding in the sonorous atmosphere that is peculiar to hot weather, they seemed to spark off scarlet stars; and also by the flies executing their little concert, the chamber music of summer: evocative not in the man-ner of a human tune that, heard perchance during the summer, afterwards reminds you of it but connected to summer by a more necessary link: born from beautiful days, resurrecting only when they return, containing some of their essence, it does not only awaken their image in our memory; it guarantees their return, their actual, persistent, unmediated presence.
  The dark coolness of my room related to the full sunlight of the street as the shadow relates to the ray of light, that is to say it was just as luminous and it gave my imagination the total spec-tacle of the summer, whereas my senses, if I had been on a walk, could only have enjoyed it by fragments; it matched my repose which (thanks to the adventures told by my book and stirring my tranquility) supported, like the quiet of a motionless hand in the middle of a running brook the shock and the motion of a torrent of activity. [*Swann's Way*. Paris: Pléiade, 1954, p. 83.]

For our present purpose, the most striking aspect of this passage is the juxtaposition of figural and metafigural language. It contains seductive metaphors that bring into play a variety of irresistible ob-jects: chamber music, butterflies, stars, books, running brooks, etc., and it describes these objects within dazzling fire- and water-works of figuration. But the passage also comments normatively on the best way to achieve such effects; in this sense, it is metafigural: it writes figuratively about figures. It contrasts two ways of evoking the natural experience of summer and unambiguously states its preference for one of these ways over the other: the "necessary link" that unites the buzzing of the flies to the summer makes it a much more effective symbol than the tune heard "perchance" during the summer. The preference is expressed by means of a distinction that corresponds to the difference between metaphor and metonymy, necessity and chance being a legitimate way to distinguish between analogy and contiguity. The inference of identity and totality that is constitutive of metaphor is lacking in the purely relational metonymic contact: an element of truth is involved in taking Achilles for a lion but none in taking Mr. Ford for a motor car. The passage is *about* the aesthetic superiority of metaphor over metonymy, but this aesthetic claim is made by means of categories that are the ontological ground of the metaphysical system that allows for the aesthetic to come into being as a category. The metaphor for summer (in this case, the synesthesia set off by the "chamber music" of the flies) guarantees a presence which, far from being contingent, is said to be essential, permanently recurrent and unmediated by linguistic representations or figurations. Finally, in the second part of the passage, the metaphor of presence not only appears as the ground of cognition but as the performance of an action, thus promising the reconciliation of the most disruptive of contradictions. By then, the investment in the power of metaphor is such that it may seem sacrilegious to put it in question.

Yet, it takes little perspicacity to show that the text does not practice what it preaches. A rhetorical reading of the passage reveals that the figural praxis and the metafigural theory do not converge and that the assertion of the mastery of metaphor over metonymy owes its persuasive power to the use of metonymic structures. I have carried out such an analysis in a somewhat more extended context; at this point, we are more concerned with the results than with the procedure. For the metaphysical categories of presence, essence, action, truth, and beauty do not remain unaffected by such a reading. This would become clear from an inclusive reading of Proust's novel or would become even more explicit in a language-conscious philosopher such as Nietzsche who, as a philosopher, has to be concerned with the epistemological consequences of the kind of rhetorical seductions exemplified by the Proust passage. It can be shown that the systematic critique of the main categories of metaphysics undertaken by Nietzsche in his late work, the critique of the concepts of causality, of the subject, of identity, of referential and revealed truth, etc., occurs along the same pattern of deconstruction that was operative in Proust's text; and it can also be shown that this pattern exactly corresponds to Nietzsche's description, in texts that precede *The Will to Power* by more than fifteen years, of the structure of the main rhetorical tropes. The key to this critique of metaphysics, which is itself a recurrent gesture throughout the history of thought, is the rhetorical model of the trope or, if one prefers to call it that, literature. It turns out that in these innocent-looking didactic exercises we are in fact playing for very sizeable stakes.

It is therefore all the more necessary to know what is linguistically involved in a rhetorically conscious reading of the type here undertaken on a brief fragment from a novel and extended by Nietzsche to the entire text of post-Hellenic thought. Our first examples dealing with the rhetorical questions were rhetorizations of grammar, figures generated by syntactical paradigms, whereas the Proust example could be better described as a grammatization of rhetoric. By passing from a paradigmatic structure based on substitution, such as metaphor, to a syntagmatic structure based on contingent association such as metonymy, the mechanical, repetitive aspect of grammatical forms is shown to be operative in a passage that seemed at first sight to celebrate the self-willed and autonomous inventiveness of a subject. Figures are assumed to be inventions, the products of a highly particularized individual talent, whereas no one can claim credit for the programmed pattern of grammar. Yet, our reading of the Proust passage shows that precisely when the highest claims are being made for the unifying power of metaphor, these very images rely in fact on the deceptive use of semi-automatic grammatical patterns. The deconstruction of metaphor and of all rhetorical patterns such as mimesis, paranomasis, or personification that use resemblance as a way to disguise differences, takes us back to the impersonal precision of grammar and of a semiology derived from grammatical patterns. Such a reading puts into question a whole series of concepts that underlie the value judgments of our critical discourse: the metaphors of primacy, of genetic history, and, most notably, of the autonomous power to will of the self.

There seems to be a difference, then, between what I called the rhetorization of grammar (as in the rhetorical question) and the grammatization of rhetoric, as in the readings of the type sketched out in the passage from Proust. The former end up in indetermination, in a suspended uncertainty that was unable to choose between two modes of reading, whereas the latter seems to reach a truth, albeit by the negative road of exposing an error, a false pretense. After the rhetorical reading of the Proust passage, we can no longer believe the assertion made in this passage about the intrinsic, metaphysical superiority of metaphor over metonymy. We seem to end up in a mood of negative assurance that is highly productive of critical discourse. The further text of Proust's novel, for example, responds perfectly to an extended application of this pattern: not only can similar gestures be repeated throughout the novel, at all the crucial articulations or all passages where large aesthetic and metaphysical claims are being made—the scenes of involuntary memory, the workshop of Elstir, the septette of Vinteuil, the convergence of author and narrator at the end of the novel—but a vast thematic and semiotic network is revealed that structures the entire narrative and that remained invisible to a reader caught in naïve metaphorical mystification. The whole of literature would respond in similar fashion, although the techniques and the patterns would have to vary considerably, of course, from author to author. But there is absolutely no reason why analyses of the kind here suggested for Proust would not be applicable, with proper modifications of technique, to Milton or to Dante or to Hölderlin. This will in fact be the task of literary criticism in the coming years.

It would seem that we are saying that criticism is the deconstruction of literature, the reduction to the rigors of grammar of rhetorical mystifications. And if we hold up Nietzsche as the philosopher of such a critical deconstruction, then the literary critic would become the philosopher's ally in his struggle with the poets. Criticism and literature would separate around the epistemological axis that distinguishes grammar from rhetoric. It is easy enough to see that this apparent glorification of the critic-philosopher in the name of truth is in fact a glorification of the poet as the primary source of this truth; if truth is the recognition of the systematic character of a certain kind of error, then it would be fully dependent on the prior existence of this error. Philosophers of science like Bachelard or Wittgenstein are notoriously dependent on the aberrations of the poets. We are back at our unanswered question: does the grammatization of rhetoric end up in negative certainty or does it, like the rhetorization of grammar, remain suspended in the ignorance of its own truth or falsehood?

Two concluding remarks should suffice to answer the question. First of all, it is not true that Proust's text can simply be reduced to the mystified assertion (the superiority of metaphor over metonymy) that our reading deconstructs. The reading is not "our" reading, since it uses only the linguistic elements provided by the text itself; the distinction between author and reader is one of the false distinctions that the reading makes evident. The deconstruction is not something we have added to the text but it constituted the text in the first place. A literary text simultaneously asserts and denies the authority of its own rhetorical mode, and by reading the text as we did we were only trying to come closer to being as rigorous a reader as the author had to be in order to write the sentence in the first place. Poetic writing is the most advanced and refined mode of deconstruction; it may differ from critical or discursive writing in the economy of its articulation, but not in kind.

But if we recognize the existence of such a moment as constitutive of all literary language, we have surreptitiously reintroduced the categories that this deconstruction was supposed to eliminate and that have merely been displaced. We have, for example, displaced the question of the self from the referent into the figure of the narrator, who then becomes the *signifié* of the passage. It becomes again possible to ask such naïve questions as what Proust's, or Marcel's motives may have been in thus manipulating language: was he fooling himself, or was he represented as fooling himself and fooling us into believing that fiction and action are as easy to unite, by reading, as the passage asserts? The pathos of the entire section, which would have been more noticeable if the quotation had been a little more extended, the constant vacillation of the narrator between guilt and well-being, invites such questions. They are absurd questions, of course, since the reconciliation of fact and fiction occurs itself as a mere assertion made in a text, and is thus productive of more text at the moment when it asserts its decision to escape from textual confinement. But even if we free ourselves of all false questions of intent and rightfully reduce the narrator to the status of a mere grammatical pronoun, without which the narrative could not come into being, this subject remains endowed with a function that is not grammatical but rhetorical, in that it gives voice, so to speak, to a grammatical syntagm. The term *voice*, even when used in a grammatical terminology as when we speak of the passive or interrogative voice, is, of course, a metaphor inferring by analogy the intent of the subject from the structure of the predicate. In the case of the deconstructive discourse that we call literary, or rhetorical, or poetic, this creates a distinctive complication illustrated by the Proust passage. The reading revealed a first paradox: the passage valorizes metaphor as being the "right" literary figure, but then proceeds to constitute itself by means of the epistemologically incompatible figure of metonymy. The critical discourse reveals the presence of this delusion and affirms it as the irreversible mode of its truth. It cannot pause there however. For if we then ask the obvious and simple next question, whether the rhetorical mode of the text in question is that of metaphor or metonymy, it is impossible to give an answer. Individual metaphors, such as the chiaroscuro effect or the butterfly, are shown to be subordinate figures in a general clause whose syntax is metonymic; from this point of view, it seems that the rhetoric is superseded by a grammar that deconstructs it. But this metonymic clause has as its subject a voice whose relationship to this clause is again metaphorical. The narrator who tells us about the impossibility of metaphor is himself, or itself, a metaphor, the metaphor of a grammatical syntagm whose meaning is the denial of metaphor stated, by antiphrasis, as its priority. And this subject-metaphor is, in its turn, open to the kind of deconstruction to the second degree, the rhetorical deconstruction of psycholinguistics, in which the more advanced investigations of literature are presently engaged, against considerable resistance.

We end up therefore, in the case of the rhetorical grammatization of semiology, just as in the grammatical rhetorization of illocutionary phrases, in the same state of suspended ignorance. Any question about the rhetorical mode of a literary text is always a rhetorical question which does not even know whether it is really questioning. The resulting pathos is an anxiety (or bliss, depending on one's momentary mood or individual temperament) of ignorance, not an anxiety of reference—as becomes thematically clear in Proust's novel when reading is dramatized, in the relationship between Marcel and Albertine, not as an emotive reaction to what language does, but as an emotive reaction to the impossibility of knowing what it might be up to. Literature as well as criticism—the difference between them being delusive—is condemned (or privileged) to be forever the most rigorous and, consequently, the most unreliable language in terms of which man names and transforms himself.

## STANLEY FISH

# Is There a Text in This Class?

## 1980

*Critics since Plato have concerned themselves with the relationship between writer and reader or with the effects of literature upon its readers. As examples, recall Aristotle's definition of tragedy partly in terms of the special emotions it evokes; Longinus' definition of sublimity in terms of its unique effect upon the reader; Horace's awareness of audience response as an actual determinant upon composition; Wordsworth's characterization of the poet as "a man speaking to men"; and the many critics who have dealt with the function of poetry. Implicit throughout is a communication model of inter-subjectivity; that is, the writer's subjectivity speaks to the reader's subjectivity through the medium of a fixed and determinate text.*

*Beginning in the late 1960's a number of American scholars and critics began to reexamine that communication model and to propose a closer scrutiny of what actually happens to readers, who are, after all, not merely passive receptacles. What is the reader's role in this "transaction" (as one scholar calls it)? The "reader-response" theorists may differ from one another in assumptions, methods, terminology, or conclusions, but they all deny the New Critical implication that analyses of the formal properties of a literary work ("the work itself") result in similar responses and interpretations. Indeed the history of contradiction among contending explicators tends to support that denial.*

*The teacher and writer who has become best known as a reader-response critic is Stanley Fish, who since 1967 has been gradually evolving in public his own theory of interpretation. His essay, originally delivered as part of a lecture series in 1979, represents the latest, but clearly not the final, stage in the development of his new model. Fish argues against the doctrine of the integrity of the text, and regards readers as actively participating in the construction of meaning. Reading is an activity, a process; therefore the critic's task is to analyze "the developing responses of the reader in relation to the words as they succeed one another in time." For him, the key word is "experience"; the subtitle of his* Self-Consuming Artifacts *(1970) is "The Experience of Seventeenth-Century Literature." In later works his discovery and rejection of the hidden formalism in his own earlier essays leads him to argue that any recognition of formal units depends on the interpretive model the reader is already familiar with; formal units are not found in the text itself. Against the argument that the reader-response theory is solipsistic and invites anarchy, that it abandons literature to idiosyncratic and irresponsible interpretations, Fish develops the concept of interpretive communities: "The meanings and texts produced by an interpretive community are not subjective because they do not proceed from an isolated individual but from a public and conventional point of view."*

*In his "Introduction, or How I Stopped Worrying and Learned to Love Interpretation" (1980), an explanation and defense of his position as well as a rebuttal to attacks upon it, Fish describes the evolution of his theory, which now subsumes both reader and text "under the larger category of interpretation." But having created a new model, he grants that the theory is still in the process of transformation, that there are many other problems yet to be dealt with. Reader-response theory is today still developing, but represents a potentially compelling new emphasis in criticism.*

ON THE first day of the new semester a colleague at Johns Hopkins University was approached by a student who, as it turned out, had just taken a course from me. She put to him what I think you would agree is a perfectly straightforward question: "Is there a text in this class?" Responding with a confidence so perfect that he was unaware of it (although in telling the story, he refers to this moment as "walking into the trap"), my colleague said, "Yes; it's the *Norton Anthology of Literature,*" whereupon the trap (set not by the student but by the infinite capacity of language for being appropriated) was sprung: "No, no," she said, "I mean in this class do we believe in poems and things, or is it just us?" Now it is possible (and for many tempting) to read this anecdote as an illustration of the dangers that follow upon listening to people like me who preach the instability of the text and the unavailability of determinate meanings; but in what follows I will try to read it as an illustration of how baseless this fear of these dangers finally is.

Of the charges levied against what Meyer Abrams has recently called the New Readers (Derrida, Bloom, Fish) the most persistent is that these apostles of indeterminacy and undecidability ignore, even as they rely upon, the "norms and possibilities" embedded in language, the "linguistic meanings" words undeniably have, and thereby invite us to abandon "our ordinary realm of experience in speaking, hearing, reading and understanding" for a world in which "no text can mean anything in particular" and where "we can never say just what anyone means by anything he writes." The charge is that literal or normative meanings are overriden by the actions of willful interpreters. Suppose we examine this indictment in the context of the present example. What, exactly, is the normative or literal or linguistic meaning of "Is there a text in this class?"

Within the framework of contemporary critical debate (as it is reflected in the pages, say, of *Critical Inquiry*) there would seem to be only two ways of answering this question: either there *is* a literal meaning of the utterance and we should be able to say what it is, or there are as many meanings as there are readers and no one of them is literal. But the answer suggested by my little story is that the utterance has *two* literal meanings: within the circumstances assumed by my colleague (I don't mean that he took the step of assuming them, but that he was already stepping within them) the utterance is obviously a question about whether or not there is a required textbook in this particular course; but within the circumstances to which he was alerted by his student's corrective response, the utterance is just as obviously a question about the instructor's position (within the range of positions available in contemporary literary theory) on the status of the text. Notice that we do not have here a case of indeterminacy or undecidability but of a determinacy and decidability that do not always have the same shape and that can, and in this instance do, change. My colleague was not hesitating between two (or more) possible meanings of the utterance; rather, he immediately apprehended what seemed to be an inescapable meaning, given his prestructured understanding of the situation, and then he immediately apprehended another inescapable meaning when that understanding was altered. Neither meaning was imposed (a favorite word in the anti–new-reader polemics) on a more normal one by a private, idiosyncratic interpretive act; both interpretations were a function of precisely the public and constituting norms (of language and understanding) invoked by Abrams. It is just that these norms are not embedded in the language (where they may be read out by anyone with sufficiently clear, that is, unbiased, eyes) but inhere in an institutional structure within which one hears utterances as already organized with reference to certain assumed purposes and goals. Because both my colleague and his student are situated in that institution, their interpretive activities are not free, but what constrains them are the understood practices and assumptions of the institution and not the rules and fixed meanings of a language system.

Another way to put this would be to say that neither reading of the question—which we might for convenience's sake label as "Is there a text in this class?"$_1$ and "Is there a text in this class?"$_2$—would be immediately available to any native speaker of the language. "Is there a text in this class?"$_1$ is interpretable or readable only by someone who already knows what is included under the general rubric "first day of class" (what concerns animate students, what bureaucratic matters must be attended to before instruction begins) and who therefore hears the utterance under the aegis of that knowledge, which is not applied after the fact but is responsible for the shape the fact immediately has. To someone whose consciousness is not already informed by that knowledge, "Is there a text in this class?"$_1$ would be just as unavailable as "Is there a text in this class?"$_2$ would be to someone who was not already aware of the disputed issues in contemporary literary theory. I am not saying that for some readers or hearers the question would be wholly unintelligible (indeed, in the course of this essay I will be arguing that unintelligibility, in the strict or pure sense, is an impossibility), but that there are readers and hearers for whom the intelligibility of the question would have neither of the shapes it had, in a temporal succession, for my colleague. It is possible, for example, to imagine someone who would hear or intend the question as an inquiry about the location of an object, that is, "I think I left my text in this class; have you seen it?" We would then have an "Is there a text in this class?"$_3$ and the possibility, feared by the defenders of the normative and determinate, of an endless succession of numbers, that is, of a world in which every utterance has an infinite plurality of meanings. But that is not what the example, however it might be extended, suggests at all. In any of the situations I have imagined (and in any that I might be able to imagine) the meaning of the utterance would be severely constrained, not after it was heard but in the ways in which it *could*, in the first place, be heard. An infinite plurality of meanings would be a fear only if sentences existed in a state in which they were not already embedded, and had come into view as a function of, some situation or other. That state, if it could be located, would be the normative one, and it would be disturbing indeed if the norm were free-floating and indeterminate. But there is no such state; sentences emerge only in situations, and within those situations, the normative meaning of an utterance will always be obvious or at least accessible, although within another situation that same utterance, no longer the same, will have another normative meaning that will be no less obvious and accessible. (My colleague's experience is precisely an illustration.) This does not mean that there is no way to discriminate between the meanings an utterance will have in different situations, but that the discrimination will already have been made by virtue of our being in a situation (we are never not in one) and that in another situation the discrimination will also have already been made, but differently. In other words, while at any one point it is always possible to order and rank "Is there a text in this class?"$_1$ and "Is there a text in this class?"$_2$ (because they will always have already been ranked), it will never be possible to give them an immutable once-and-for-all ranking, a ranking that is independent of their appearance or nonappearance in situations (because it is only in situations that they do or do not appear).

Nevertheless, there is a distinction to be made between the two that allows us to say that, in a limited sense, one is more normal than the other: for while each is perfectly normal in the context in which their literalness is immediately obvious (the successive contexts occupied by my colleague), as things stand now, one of those contexts is surely more available, and therefore more likely to be the perspective within which the utterance is heard, than the other. Indeed, we seem to have here an instance of what I would call "institutional nesting": if "Is there a text in this class?"$_1$ is hearable only by those who know what is included under the rubric "first day of class," and if "Is there a text in this class?"$_2$ is hearable only by those whose categories of understanding include the concerns of contemporary literary theory, then it is obvious that in a random population presented with the utterance, more people would "hear" "Is there a text in this class?"$_1$ than "Is there a text in this class?"$_2$; and, moreover, that while "Is there a text in this class?"$_1$ could be immediately hearable by someone for whom "Is there a text in this class?"$_2$ would have to be laboriously explained, it is difficult to imagine someone capable of hearing "Is there a text in this class?"₂ who was not already capable of hearing "Is there a text in this class."₁ (One is hearable by anyone in the profession and by most students and by many workers in the book trade, and the other only by those in the profession who would not think it peculiar to find, as I did recently, a critic referring to a phrase "made popular by Lacan.") To admit as much is not to weaken my argument by reinstating the category of the normal, because the category as it appears in that argument is not transcendental but institutional; and while no institution is so universally in force and so perdurable that the meanings it enables will be normal for ever, some institutions or forms of life are so widely lived in that for a great many people the meanings they enable seem "naturally" available and it takes a special effort to see that they are the products of circumstances.

The point is an important one, because it accounts for the success with which an Abrams or an E. D. Hirsch can appeal to a shared understanding of ordinary language and argue from that understanding to the availability of a core of determinate meanings. When Hirsch offers "The air is crisp" as an example of a "verbal meaning," that is, accessible to all speakers of the language, and distinguishes what is sharable and determinate about it from the associations that may, in certain circumstances, accompany it (for example, "I should have eaten less at supper," "Crisp air reminds me of my childhood in Vermont"), he is counting on his readers to agree so completely with his sense of what that shared and normative verbal meaning is that he does not bother even to specify it; and although I have not taken a survey, I would venture to guess that his optimism, with respect to this particular example, is well founded. That is, most, if not all, of his readers immediately understand the utterance as a rough meteorological description predicting a certain quality of the local atmosphere. But the "happiness" of the example, far from making Hirsch's point (which is always, as he has recently reaffirmed, to maintain "the stable determinacy of meaning") makes mine. The obviousness of the utterance's meaning is not a function of the values its words have in a linguistic system that is independent of context; rather, it is because the words are heard as already embedded in a context that they have a meaning that Hirsch can then cite as obvious. One can see this by embedding the words in another context and observing how quickly another "obvious" meaning emerges. Suppose, for example, we came upon "The air is crisp" (which you are even now hearing as Hirsch assumes you hear it) in the middle of a discussion of music ("When the piece is played correctly the air is crisp"); it would immediately be heard as a comment on the performance by an instrument or instruments of a musical air. Moreover, it would *only* be heard that way, and to hear it in Hirsch's way would require an effort on the order of a strain. It could be objected that in Hirsch's text "The air is crisp"₁ has no contextual setting at all; it is merely presented, and therefore any agreement as to its meaning must be because of the utterance's acontextual properties. But there *is* a contextual setting and the sign of its presence is precisely the absence of any reference to it. That is, it is impossible even to think of a sentence independently of a context, and when we are asked to consider a sentence for which no context has been specified, we will automatically hear it in the context in which it has been most often encountered. Thus Hirsch invokes a context by not invoking it; by not surrounding the utterance with circumstances, he directs us to imagine it in the circumstances in which it is most likely to have been produced; and to so imagine it is already to have given it a shape that seems at the moment to be the only one possible.

What conclusions can be drawn from these two examples? First of all, neither my colleague nor the reader of Hirsch's sentence is constrained by the meanings words have in a normative linguistic system; and yet neither is free to confer on an utterance any meaning he likes. Indeed, "confer" is exactly the wrong word because it implies a two stage procedure in which a reader or hearer first scrutinizes an utterance and *then* gives it a meaning. The argument of the preceding pages can be reduced to the assertion that there is no such first stage, that one hears an utterance within, and not as preliminary to determining, a knowledge of its purposes and concerns, and that to so hear it is already to have assigned it a shape and given it a meaning. In other words, the problem of how meaning is determined is only a problem if there is a point at which its determination has not yet been made, and I am saying that there is no such point.

I am *not* saying that one is never in the position of having to self-consciously figure out what an utterance means. Indeed, my colleague is in just such a position when he is informed by his student that he has not heard her question as she intended it ("No, No, I mean in this class do we believe in poems and things, or is it just us?") and therefore must now figure it out. But the "it" in this (or any other) case is not a collection of words waiting to be assigned a meaning but an utterance whose already assigned meaning has been found to be inappropriate. While my colleague has to begin all over again, he does not have to begin from square one; and indeed he never was at square one, since from the very first his hearing of the student's question was informed by his assumption of what its concerns could possibly be. (That is why he is not "free" even if he is unconstrained by determinate meanings.) It is that assumption rather than his performance within it that is challenged by the student's correction. She tells him that he has mistaken her meaning, but this is not to say that he has made a mistake in combining her words and syntax into a meaningful unit; it is rather that the meaningful unit he immediately discerns is a function of a mistaken identification (made before she speaks) of her intention. He was prepared as she stood before him to hear the kind of thing students ordinarily say on the first day of class, and therefore that is precisely what he heard. He has not misread the text (his is not an error in calculation) but mis*pre*read the text, and if he is to correct himself he must make another (pre)determination of the structure of interests from which her question issues. This, of course, is exactly what he does and the question of how he does it is a crucial one, which can best be answered by first considering the ways in which he *didn't* do it.

He didn't do it by attending to the literal meaning of her response. That is, this is not a case in which someone who has been misunderstood clarifies her meaning by making more explicit, by varying or adding to her words in such a way as to render their sense inescapable. Within the circumstances of utterance as he has assumed them her words are perfectly clear, and what she is doing is asking him to imagine other circumstances in which the same words will be equally, but differently, clear. Nor is it that the words she does add ("No, No, I mean . . .") direct him to those other circumstances by picking them out from an inventory of all possible ones. For this to be the case there would have to be an inherent relationship between the words she speaks and a particular set of circumstances (this would be a higher level literalism) such that any competent speaker of the language hearing those words would immediately be referred to that set. But I have told the story to several competent speakers of the language who simply didn't get it, and one friend—a professor of philosophy—reported to me that in the interval between his hearing the story and my explaining it to him (and just how I was able to do that is another crucial question) he found himself asking "What kind of joke is this and have I missed it?" For a time at least he remained able only to hear "Is there a text in this class" as my colleague first heard it; the student's additional words, far from leading him to another hearing, only made him aware of his distance from it. In contrast, there are those who not only get the story but get it before I tell it; that is, they know in advance what is coming as soon as I say that a colleague of mine was recently asked, "Is there a text in this class?" Who are these people and what is it that makes their comprehension of the story so immediate and easy? Well, one could say, without being the least bit facetious, that they are the people who come to hear me speak because they are the people who already know my position on certain matters (or know that I will *have* a position). That is, they hear, "Is there a text in this class?" even as it appears at the beginning of the anecdote (or for that matter as a title of an essay) in the light of their knowledge of what I am likely to do with it. They hear it coming from *me*, in circumstances which have committed me to declaring myself on a range of issues that are sharply delimited.

My colleague was finally able to hear it in just that way, as coming from me, not because I was there in his classroom, nor because the words of the student's question pointed to me in a way that would have been obvious to any hearer, but because he was able to think of me in an office three doors down from his telling students that there are no determinate meanings and that the stability of the text is an illusion. Indeed, as he reports it, the moment of recognition and comprehension consisted of his saying to himself, "Ah, there's one of Fish's victims!" He did not say this because her words identified her as such but because his ability to see her as such informed his perception of her words. The answer to the question "How did he get from her words to the circumstances within which she intended him to hear them?" is that he must already be thinking within those circumstances in order to be able to hear her words as referring to them. The question, then, must be rejected, because it assumes that the construing of sense leads to the identification of the context of utterance rather than the other way around. This does not mean that the context comes first and that once it has been identified the construing of sense can begin. This would be only to reverse the order of precedence, whereas precedence is beside the point because the two actions it would order (the identification of context and the making of sense) occur simultaneously. One does not say "Here I am in a situation; now I can begin to determine what these words mean." To be in a situation is to see the words, these or any other, as already meaningful. For my colleague to realize that he may be confronting one of my victims is *at the same time* to hear what she says as a question about his theoretical beliefs.

But to dispose of one "how" question is only to raise another: if her words do not lead him to the context of her utterance, how does he get there? Why did he think of me telling students that there were no determinate meanings and not think of someone or something else? First of all, he might well have. That is, he might well have guessed that she was coming from another direction (inquiring, let us say, as to whether the focus of this class was to be the poems and essays or our responses to them, a question in the same line of country as hers but quite distinct from it) or he might have simply been stymied, like my philosopher friend, confined, in the absence of an explanation, to his first determination of her concerns and unable to make any sense of her words other than the sense he originally made. How, then, did he do it? In part, he did it because he *could* do it; he was able to get to this context because it was already part of his repertoire for organizing the world and its events. The category "one of Fish's victims" was one he already had and didn't have to work for. Of course, *it* did not always have *him*, in that his world was not always being organized by it, and it certainly did not have him at the beginning of the conversation; but it was available to him, and he to it, and all he had to do was to recall it or be recalled to it for the meanings it subtended to emerge. (Had it not been available to him, the career of his comprehension would have been different and we will come to a consideration of that difference shortly.)

This, however, only pushes our inquiry back further. How or why was he recalled to it? The answer to this question must be probabilistic and it begins with the recognition that when something changes, not everything changes. Although my colleague's understanding of his circumstances is transformed in the course of this conversation, the circumstances are still understood to be academic ones, and within that continuing (if modified) understanding, the directions his thought might take are already severely limited. He still presumes, as he did at first, that the student's question has something to do with university business in general, and with English literature in particular, and it is the organizing rubrics associated with these areas of experience that are likely to occur to him. One of those rubrics is "what-goes-on-in-the-other-classes" and one of those other classes is mine. And so, by a route that is neither entirely unmarked nor wholly determined, he comes to me and to the notion "one of Fish's victims" and to a new construing of what his student has been saying.

Of course that route would have been much more circuitous if the category "one of Fish's victims" was not already available to him as a device for producing intelligibility. Had that device not been part of his repertoire, had he been incapable of being recalled to it because he never knew it in the first place, how would he have proceeded? The answer is that he could not have proceeded at all, which does not mean that one is trapped forever in the categories of understanding at one's disposal (or the categories at whose disposal one is), but that the introduction of new categories or the expansion of old ones to include new (and therefore newly seen) data must always come from the outside or from what is perceived, for a time, to be the outside. In the event that he was unable to identify the structure of her concerns because it had never been his (or he its), it would have been her obligation to explain it to him. And here we run up against another instance of the problem we have been considering all along. She could not explain it to him by varying or adding to her words, by being more explicit, because her words will only be intelligible if he already has the knowledge they are supposed to convey, the knowledge of the assumptions and interests from which they issue. It is clear, then, that she would have to make a new start, although she would not have to start from scratch (indeed, starting from scratch is never a possibility); but she would have to back up to some point at which there was a shared agreement as to what was reasonable to say so that a new and wider basis for agreement could be fashioned. In this particular case, for example, she might begin with the fact that her interlocutor already knows what a text is; that is, he has a way of thinking about it that is responsible for his hearing of her first question as one about bureaucratic classroom procedures. (You will remember that "he" in these sentences is no longer my colleague but someone who does not have his special knowledge.) It is that way of thinking that she must labor to extend or challenge, first, perhaps, by pointing out that there are those who think about the text in other ways, and then by trying to find a category of his own understanding which might serve as an analogue to the understanding he does not yet share. He might, for example, be familiar with those psychologists who argue for the constitutive power of perception, or with Gombrich's theory of the beholder's share, or with that philosophical tradition in which the stability of objects has always been a matter of dispute. The example must remain hypothetical and skeletal, because it can only be fleshed out after a determination of the particular beliefs and assumptions that would make the explanation necessary in the first place; for whatever they were, they would dictate the strategy by which she would work to supplant or change them. It is when such a strategy has been successful that the import of her words will become clear, not because she has reformulated or refined them but because they will now be read or heard within the same system of intelligibility from which they issue.

In short, this hypothetical interlocutor will in time be brought to the same point of comprehension my colleague enjoys when he is able to say to himself, "Ah, there's one of Fish's victims," although pre-

sumably he will say something very different to himself if he says anything at all. The difference, however, should not obscure the basic
similarities between the two experiences, one reported, the other imagined. In both cases the words that are uttered are immediately heard
within a set of assumptions about the direction from which they could
possibly be coming, and in both cases what is required is that the hearing occur within another set of assumptions in relation to which the
same words ("Is there a text in this class?") will no longer be the same.
It is just that while my colleague is able to meet that requirement by
calling to mind a context of utterance that is already a part of his
repertoire, the repertoire of his hypothetical stand-in must be expanded to include that context so that should he some day be in an
analogous situation, he would be able to call it to mind.

The distinction, then, is between already having an ability and
having to acquire it, but it is not finally an essential distinction, because the routes by which that ability could be exercised on the one
hand, and learned on the other, are so similar. They are similar first
of all because they are similarly *not* determined by words. Just as the
student's words will not direct my colleague to a context he already
has, so will they fail to direct someone not furnished with that context
to its discovery. And yet in neither case does the absence of such a
mechanical determination mean that the route one travels is randomly
found. The change from one structure of understanding to another
is not a rupture but a modification of the interests and concerns that
are already in place; and because they are already in place, they constrain the direction of their own modification. That is, in both cases
the hearer is already in a situation informed by tacitly known purposes and goals, and in both cases he ends up in another situation
whose purposes and goals stand in some elaborated relation (of contrast, opposition, expansion, extension) to those they supplant. (The
one relation in which they could not stand is no relation at all.) It is
just that in one case the network of elaboration (from the text as an
obviously physical object to the question of whether or not the text is
a physical object) has already been articulated (although not all of its
articulations are in focus at one time; selection is always occurring),
while in the other the articulation of the network is the business of
the teacher (here the student) who begins, necessarily, with what is
already given.

The final similarity between the two cases is that in neither is success assured. It was no more inevitable that my colleague tumble to
the context of his student's utterance than it would be inevitable that
she could introduce that context to someone previously unaware of

it; and, indeed, had my colleague remained puzzled (had he simply not thought of me), it would have been necessary for the student to bring him along in a way that was finally indistinguishable from the way she would bring someone to a new knowledge, that is, by beginning with the shape of his present understanding.

I have lingered so long over the unpacking of this anecdote that its relationship to the problem of authority in the classroom and in literary criticism may seem obscure. Let me recall you to it by recalling the contention of Abrams and others that authority depends upon the existence of a determinate core of meanings because in the absence of such a core there is no normative or public way of construing what anyone says or writes, with the result that interpretation becomes a matter of individual and private construings none of which is subject to challenge or correction. In literary criticism this means that no interpretation can be said to be better or worse than any other, and in the classroom this means that we have no answer to the student who says my interpretation is as valid as yours. It is only if there is a shared basis of agreement at once guiding interpretation and providing a mechanism for deciding between interpretations that a total and debilitating relativism can be avoided.

But the point of my analysis has been to show that while "Is there a text in this class?" does not have a determinate meaning, a meaning that survives the sea change of situations, in any situation we might imagine the meaning of the utterance is either perfectly clear or capable, in the course of time, of being clarified. What is it that makes this possible, if it is not the "possibilities and norms" already encoded in language? How does communication ever occur if not by reference to a public and stable norm? The answer, implicit in everything I have already said, is that communication occurs within situations and that to be in a situation is already to be in possession of (or to be possessed by) a structure of assumptions, of practices understood to be relevant in relation to purposes and goals that are already in place; and it is within the assumption of these purposes and goals that any utterance is *immediately* heard. I stress immediately because it seems to me that the problem of communication, as someone like Abrams poses it, is a problem only because he assumes a distance between one's receiving of an utterance and the determination of its meaning—a kind of dead space when one has only the words and then faces the task of construing them. If there were such a space, a moment before interpretation began, then it would be necessary to have recourse to some mechanical and algorithmic procedure by means of which meanings could be calculated and in relation to which one could recognize mis-

takes. What I have been arguing is that meanings come already calculated, not because of norms embedded in the language but because
language is always perceived, from the very first, within a structure
of norms. That structure, however, is not abstract and independent
but social; and therefore it is not a single structure with a privileged
relationship to the process of communication as it occurs in any situation but a structure that changes when one situation, with its assumed
background of practices, purposes, and goals, has given way to another.
In other words, the shared basis of agreement sought by Abrams and
others is never not already found, although it is not always the same
one.

Many will find in this last sentence, and in the argument to which
it is a conclusion, nothing more than a sophisticated version of the
relativism they fear. It will do no good, they say, to speak of norms
and standards that are context specific, because this is merely to authorize an infinite plurality of norms and standards, and we are still left
without any way of adjudicating between them and between the competing systems of value of which they are functions. In short, to have
many standards is to have no standards at all.

On one level this counterargument is unassailable, but on another
level it is finally beside the point. It is unassailable as a general and
theoretical conclusion: the positing of context- or institution-specific
norms surely rules out the possibility of a norm whose validity would
be recognized by everyone, no matter what his situation. But it is beside the point for any particular individual, for since everyone is
situated somewhere, there is no one for whom the absence of an asitua-
tional norm would be of any practical consequence, in the sense that
his performance or his confidence in his ability to perform would be
impaired. So that while it is generally true that to have many standards
is to have none at all, it is not true for anyone in particular (for there
is no one in a position to speak "generally"), and therefore it is a truth
of which one can say "it doesn't matter."

In other words, while relativism is a position one can entertain, it
is not a position one can occupy. No one can *be* a relativist, because
no one can achieve the distance from his own beliefs and assumptions
which would result in their being no more authoritative *for him* than
the beliefs and assumptions held by others, or, for that matter, the
beliefs and assumptions he himself used to hold. The fear that in
a world of indifferently authorized norms and values the individual is
without a basis for action is groundless because no one is indifferent
to the norms and values that enable his consciousness. It is in the
name of personally held (in fact they are doing the holding) norms

and values that the individual acts and argues, and he does so with the full confidence that attends belief. When his beliefs change, the norms and values to which he once gave unthinking assent will have been demoted to the status of opinions and become the objects of an analytical and critical attention; but that attention will itself be enabled by a new set of norms and values that are, for the time being, as unexamined and undoubted as those they displace. The point is that there is never a moment when one believes nothing, when consciousness is innocent of any and all categories of thought, and whatever categories of thought are operative at a given moment will serve as an undoubted ground.

Here, I suspect, a defender of determinate meaning would cry "solipsist" and argue that a confidence that had its source in the individual's categories of thought would have no public value. That is, unconnected to any shared and stable system of meanings, it would not enable one to transact the verbal business of everyday life; a shared intelligibility would be impossible in a world where everyone was trapped in the circle of his own assumptions and opinions. The reply to this is that an individual's assumptions and opinions are not "his own" in any sense that would give body to the fear of solipsism. That is, *he* is not their origin (in fact it might be more accurate to say that they are his); rather, it is their prior availability which delimits in advance the paths that his consciousness can possibly take. When my colleague is in the act of construing his student's question ("Is there a text in this class?"), none of the interpretive strategies at his disposal are uniquely his, in the sense that he thought them up; they follow from his preunderstanding of the interests and goals that could possibly animate the speech of someone functioning within the institution of academic America, interests and goals that are the particular property of no one in particular but which link everyone for whom their assumption is so habitual as to be unthinking. They certainly link my colleague and his student, who are able to communicate and even to reason about one another's intentions, not, however, because their interpretive efforts are constrained by the shape of an independent language but because their shared understanding of what could possibly be at stake in a classroom situation results in language appearing to them in the same shape (or successions of shapes). That shared understanding is the basis of the confidence with which they speak and reason, but its categories are their own only in the sense that as actors within an institution they automatically fall heir to the institution's way of making sense, its systems of intelligibility. That is why it is so hard for someone whose very being is defined by his position within an institution (and if not this one, then some other) to explain to someone outside it a practice or a meaning that seems to him to require no explanation, because he regards it as natural. Such a person, when pressed, is likely to say, "but that's just the way it's done" or "but isn't it obvious" and so testify that the practice of meaning in question is community property, as, in a sense, he is too.

We see then that (1) communication does occur, despite the absence of an independent and context-free system of meanings, that (2) those who participate in this communication do so confidently rather than provisionally (they are not relativists), and that (3) while their confidence has its source in a set of beliefs, those beliefs are not individual-specific or idiosyncratic but communal and conventional (they are not solipsists).

Of course, solipsism and relativism are what Abrams and Hirsch fear and what lead them to argue for the necessity of determinate meaning. But if, rather than acting on their own, interpreters act as extensions of an institutional community, solipsism and relativism are removed as fears because they are not possible modes of being. That is to say, the condition required for someone to be a solipsist or relativist, the condition of being independent of institutional assumptions and free to originate one's own purposes and goals, could never be realized, and therefore there is no point in trying to guard against it. Abrams, Hirsch, and company spend a great deal of time in a search for the ways to limit and constrain interpretation, but if the example of my colleague and his student can be generalized (and obviously I think it can be), what they are searching for is never not already found. In short, my message to them is finally not challenging, but consoling—not to worry.

# Further Readings

## GENERAL

Abrams, M. H., *The Mirror and the Lamp*, 1953.

Adams, Hazard, *The Interests of Criticism*, 1969.

Atkins, J. W. H., *English Literary Criticism* (3 vols.), 1943–1951.

Auerbach, Erich, *Mimesis*, 1953.

Beardsley, Monroe, *Aesthetics: Problems in the Philosophy of Criticism*, 1958.

Boas, George, *A Primer for Critics*, 1937.

Buckley, Vincent, *Poetry and Morality*, 1959.

Collingwood, R. G., *The Principles of Art*, 1938.

Crane, Ronald S., ed., *Critics and Criticism: Ancients and Moderns*, 1952.

Crane, Ronald S., *The Languages of Criticism and the Structure of Poetry*, 1953.

Daiches, David, *Critical Approaches to Literature*, 1956.

Foerster, Norman, *American Criticism: A Study of Literary Theory from Poe to the Present*, 1962.

Gardner, Helen, *The Business of Criticism*, 1959.

Goodman, Paul, *The Structure of Literature*, 1954.

Greene, Theodore M., *The Arts and the Art of Criticism*, 1940.

Hall, Vernon, Jr., *A Short History of Literary Criticism*, 1963.

Langer, Suzanne K., *Feeling and Form*, 1953.

Levin, Harry, *The Contexts of Criticism*, 1963.

Muller, Herbert, *Science and Criticism: The Humanist Tradition*, 1943.

Pepper, Stephen C., *The Basis of Criticism in the Arts*, 1945.

Pritchard, John P., *Criticism in America*, 1956.

Shipley, Joseph T., *Quest for Literature: A Survey of Literary Criticism and the Theories of the Literary Forms*, 1931.

Shumaker, Wayne, *Elements of Critical Theory*, 1952.

Thorpe, James, ed., *Relations of Literary Study*, 1967.

Trilling, Lionel, *The Liberal Imagination*, 1953.

Warren, Alba, Jr., *English Poetic Theory, 1825–1865*, 1950.

Watson, George, *The Literary Critics*, 1962.

Wellek, Rene, *Concepts of Criticism*, 1963.

Wellek, Rene, *A History of Modern Criticism, 1700–1950* (4 vols.), 1955–1965.

640    CRITICISM: THE MAJOR STATEMENTS

Wellek, Rene, and Austin Warren, *Theory of Literature*, 1949.
Wimsatt, William K., and Cleanth Brooks, *Literary Criticism: A Short History*, 1957.

## PLATO

Adamson, John E., *The Theory of Education in Plato's "Republic,"* 1903.
Grene, David, *Greek Political Theory*, 1965.
Grube, G. M. A., *Plato's Thought*, 1935.
Gulley, Norman, *Plato's Theory of Knowledge*, 1962.
Havelock, Eric, *Preface to Plato*, 1963.
Lodge, Rupert C., *Plato's Theory of Art*, 1953.
Oates, Whitney J., *Plato's View of Art*, 1972.
Randall, John H., *Plato: Dramatist of the Life of Reason*, 1970.
Shorey, Paul, *What Plato Said*, 1933.
Taylor, A. E., *Plato*, 1929.

## ARISTOTLE

Butcher, S. H., *Aristotle's Theory of Poetry and Fine Art* (4th ed.), 1923.
Cooper, Lane, *The Poetics of Aristotle, Its Meaning and Influence*, 1923.
Else, Gerald, *Aristotle's Poetics: The Argument*, 1957.
Fergusson, Francis, *The Idea of a Theatre*, 1953.
Herrick, Marvin T., *The Poetics of Aristotle in England*, 1930.
House, Humphrey, *Aristotle's Poetics* (rev. ed.), 1966.
Lucas, F. L., *Tragedy in Relation to Aristotle's "Poetics,"* 1928.
McKeon, Richard, "Literary Criticism and the Concept of Imitation in Antiquity," in *Critics and Criticism*, edited by R. S. Crane, 1952.
Olson Elder, ed., *Aristotle's Poetics and English Literature*, 1965.

## LONGINUS

Atkins, J. W. H., *Literary Criticism in Antiquity*, vol. II, 1934.
Brody, Jules, *Boileau and Longinus*, 1958.
Grube, G. M. A., *The Greek and Roman Critics*, 1965.
Henn, T. R., *Longinus and English Criticism*, 1934.
Monk, Samuel H., *The Sublime: A Study of Critical Theories in Eighteenth-Century England*, 1935.
Tate, Allen, "Longinus and the New Criticism," in *Lectures in Criticism*, edited by Elliott Coleman, 1949.

## HORACE

Blakeney, E. H., *Horace on the Art of Poetry*, 1928.
Costa, Charles D. N., *Horace*, 1973.

D'Alton, J. F., *Horace and His Age*, 1917.
Fiske, George C., *Lucilius and Horace, a Study in the Classical Theory of Imitation*, 1966.
Goad, Caroline, *Horace in the English Literature of the Eighteenth Century*, 1918.
Herrick, Marvin T., *The Fusion of Horatian and Aristotelian Literary Criticism*, 1946.
Showerman, Grant, *Horace and His Influence*, 1922.

## SIDNEY

Atkins, J. W. H., *English Literary Criticism: The Renascence*, 1951.
Baldwin, C. S., *Renaissance Literary Theory and Practice*, 1939.
Clark, Donald L., *Rhetoric and Poetic in the Renaissance*, 1922.
Hall, Vernon, Jr., *Renaissance Literary Criticism: A Study of Its Social Content*, 1959.
Hathaway, Baxter, *Marvels and Commonplaces: Renaissance Literary Criticism*, 1958.
Spingarn, Joel E., *A History of Literary Criticism in the Renaissance*, 1908.

## DRYDEN

Bredvold, Louis I., *The Intellectual Milieu of John Dryden*, 1934.
Eliot, T. S., *John Dryden, the Poet, the Dramatist, the Critic*, 1966.
Frye, Prosser H., *Dryden and the Critical Canons of the Eighteenth Century*, 1907.
Hume, Robert D., *Dryden's Criticism*, 1970.
Huntley, Frank L., *The Unity of Dryden's Dramatic Criticism*, 1944.
Smith, D. N., *John Dryden*, 1950.
Swedenberg, H. T., *The Theory of the Epic in England, 1650–1800*, 1944.

## POPE

Crane, Ronald S., "English Neo-Classical Criticism: An Outline Sketch," in *Critics and Criticism*, edited by R. S. Crane, 1952.
Dennis, John, *The Age of Pope*, 1928.
Edwards, Thomas R., *This Dark Estate: A Reading of Pope*, 1963.
Quennell, Peter, *Alexander Pope: The Education of Genius, 1688–1728*, 1968.
Root, Robert K., *The Poetical Career of Pope*, 1938.
Sherburn, George, *The Early Career of Alexander Pope*, 1934.
Tillotson, Geoffrey, *On the Poetry of Pope*, 1938.
Warren, Austin, *Alexander Pope as Critic and Humanist*, 1929.

# JOHNSON

Bate, Walter J., *The Achievement of Samuel Johnson*, 1955.
Bosker, A., *Literary Criticism in the Age of Johnson*, 1930.
Brown, Joseph E., *The Critical Opinions of Samuel Johnson*, 1926.
Hagstrum, Jean, *Samuel Johnson's Literary Criticism*, 1952.
Houston, Percy H., *Doctor Johnson: A Study in Eighteenth-Century Humanism*, 1923.
Keast, W. R., "The Theoretical Foundations of Johnson's Criticism," in *Critics and Criticism*, edited by R. S. Crane, 1952.
Sherbo, Arthur, *Johnson, Editor of Shakespeare*, 1956.

# WORDSWORTH

Barstow, Marjorie L., *Wordsworth's Theory of Poetic Diction*, 1917.
Beatty, Arthur, *William Wordsworth: His Doctrine and Art in Their Historical Relations*, 1922.
Heffernan, J. A., *Wordsworth's Theory of Poetry*, 1969.
Jones, H. J. F., *The Egotistical Sublime: A History of Wordsworth's Imagination*, 1954.
Lucas, F. L., *The Decline and Fall of the Romantic Ideal*, 1936.
Peacock, Markham L., Jr., *Critical Opinions of William Wordsworth*, 1950.

# COLERIDGE

Fogle, Richard H., *The Idea of Coleridge's Criticism*, 1962.
Fruman, Norman, *Coleridge: The Damaged Archangel*, 1971.
George, Andrew J., ed., *Coleridge's Principles of Criticism*, 1897.
Lowes, John Livingston, *The Road to Xanadu*, 1927.
McKenzie, Gordon, *Organic Unity in Coleridge*, 1939.
Muirhead, J. H., *Coleridge as Philosopher*, 1930.
Read, Herbert, *The True Voice of Feeling*, 1953.
Richards, I. A., *Coleridge on Imagination*, 1950.
Sherwood, Margaret, *Coleridge's Imaginative Conception of the Imagination*, 1937.

# KEATS

Bate, Walter J., *Negative Capability*, 1939.
Caldwell, J. R., *John Keats' Fancy*, 1945.
D'Avanzo, Mario L., *Keats' Metaphors for the Poetic Imagination*, 1967.
Gittings, Robert, *John Keats: The Living Year*, 1954.
Thorpe, Clarence D., *The Mind of John Keats*, 1926.
Trilling, Lionel, ed., *The Selected Letters of John Keats*, 1951.
Ward, Aileen, *John Keats: The Making of a Poet*, 1963.

## SHELLEY

Barrell, Joseph, *Shelley and the Thought of His Time*, 1967.
Grabo, Carl H., *The Magic Plant: The Growth of Shelley's Thought*, 1936.
Notopoulos, James A., *The Platonism of Shelley*, 1969.
Schulze, Earl J., *Shelley's Theory of Poetry: A Reappraisal*, 1966.
Shawcross, John, ed., *Shelley's Literary and Philosophical Criticism*, 1909.
Solve, Melvin T., *Shelley: His Theory of Poetry*, 1927.
White, Newman I., *The Unextinguished Hearth*, 1938.
Wright, John W., *Shelley's Myth of Metaphor*, 1970.


## POE

Alterton, Margaret, *Origins of Poe's Critical Theory*, 1925.
Campbell, Killis, *The Mind of Poe and Other Studies*, 1933.
Davidson, Edward H., *Poe: A Critical Study*, 1957.
Fagin, N. Bryllion, *The Histrionic Mr. Poe*, 1949.
Jacobs, R. D., *Poe: Journalist and Critic*, 1969.
Moss, Sidney P., *Poe's Literary Battles*, 1963.
Parks, Edd W., *Edgar Allan Poe as Literary Critic*, 1964.


## ARNOLD

Anderson, W. D., *Matthew Arnold and the Classical Tradition*, 1965.
Brown, E. K., *Arnold: A Study in Conflict*, 1948.
Eells, J. S., *The Touchstones of Matthew Arnold*, 1955.
Harvey, Charles H., *Matthew Arnold: A Critic of the Victorian Period*, 1931.
Robbins, William, *The Ethical Idealism of Matthew Arnold*, 1959.
Trilling, Lionel, *Matthew Arnold*, 1955.


## PATER

Child, Ruth C., *The Aesthetic of Walter Pater*, 1940.
Crinkley, Richmond, *Walter Pater: Humanist*, 1970.
Eliot, T. S., "Arnold and Pater," in *Selected Essays*, 1932.
Hough, Graham, *The Last Romantics*, 1949.
McKenzie, Gordon, *The Literary Character of Walter Pater*, 1967.
Ward, Anthony, *Walter Pater: The Idea in Nature*, 1966.
Young, Helen H., *The Writings of Walter Pater*, 1933.


## JAMES

Andreas, Osborn, *Henry James and the Expanding Horizon*, 1948.
Beach, Joseph Warren, *The Method of Henry James* (enlarged ed.), 1954.
Dupee, F. W., *Henry James*, 1951.

Edel, Leon, ed., *The Prefaces of James*, 1931.
Hughes, Herbert L., *Theory and Practice in Henry James*, 1969.
Matthiessen, F. O., and Kenneth B. Murdock, eds., *The Notebooks of Henry James*, 1947.
Miller, James E., Jr., *Theory of Fiction: Henry James*, 1972.
Roberts, Morris, *Henry James' Criticism*, 1929.
Sears, Sallie, *The Negative Imagination: Form and Perspective in the Novels of Henry James*, 1968.

## TOLSTOY

Duffield, Holley Gene, and Manuel Bilsky, eds., *Tolstoy and the Critics*, 1965.
Farrell, James T., *Literature and Morality*, 1947.
Flaccus, Louis W., *Artists and Thinkers*, 1967.
Maude, Aylmer, *Tolstoy on Art and Its Critics*, 1925.
Simmons, Ernest J., *Leo Tolstoy*, 1946.
Spence, Gordon W., *Tolstoy the Ascetic*, 1968.
Steiner, George, *Tolstoy or Dostoevsky, an Essay in the Old Criticism*, 1959.

## FREUD

Basler, Roy P., *Sex, Symbolism, and Psychology in Literature*, 1948.
Bergler, Edmund, *The Writer and Psychoanalysis*, 1950.
Fraiberg, Louis, *Psychoanalysis and American Literary Criticism*, 1960.
Hoffman, Frederick J., *Freudianism and the Literary Mind*, 1959.
Holland, Norman, *The Dynamics of Literary Response*, 1968.
Kris, Ernst, *Psychoanalytical Explorations in Art*, 1952.
Lesser, Simon O., *Fiction and the Unconscious*, 1957.
Lucas, F. L., *Literature and Psychology*, 1957.
Trilling, Lionel, "Freud and Literature," in *The Liberal Imagination*, 1953.

## ELIOT

Eliot, T. S., *Selected Essays*, 1932.
Eliot, T. S., *The Use of Poetry and the Use of Criticism*, 1933.
Freed, Lewis, *T. S. Eliot: Aesthetics and History*, 1962.
Frye, Northrop, *T. S. Eliot*, 1963.
Kenner, Hugh, *The Invisible Poet*, 1959.
Lucy, Seán, *T. S. Eliot and the Idea of Tradition*, 1960.
Matthiessen, F. O., *The Achievement of T. S. Eliot* (3rd ed.), 1958.
Stead, C. K., *The New Poetic*, 1964.

# BURKE

Brown, Merle E., *Kenneth Burke*, 1969.
Burke, Kenneth, *The Philosophy of Literary Form*, 1941.
Frank, Armin P., *Kenneth Burke*, 1969.
Hyman, Stanley Edgar, *The Armed Vision*, 1948.
Knox, George A., *Critical Moments: Kenneth Burke's Categories and Critiques*, 1957.
Rueckert, William H., *Kenneth Burke and the Drama of Human Relations*, 1963.

# RANSOM

Brooks, Cleanth, *Modern Poetry and the Tradition*, 1939.
Krieger, Murray, *The New Apologists for Poetry*, 1956.
Magner, James E., *John Crowe Ransom: Critical Principles and Preoccupations*, 1971.
O'Connor, William Van, *An Age of Criticism, 1900–1950*, 1952.
Ransom, John Crowe, *The World's Body*, 1938.
Ransom, John Crowe, *The New Criticism*, 1941.
Stewart, John L., *John Crowe Ransom*, 1962.
Young, Thomas D., ed., *John Crowe Ransom: Critical Essays and a Bibliography*, 1968.

# BROOKS

Brooks, Cleanth, *The Well Wrought Urn*, 1947.
Brooks, Cleanth, *Modern Poetry and the Tradition*, 1939.
Krieger, Murray, *The New Apologists for Poetry*, 1956.
Ransom, John Crowe, *The New Criticism*, 1941.
Richards, I. A., *Principles of Literary Criticism*, 1924.
Tate, Allen, *The Man of Letters in the Modern World*, 1955.
Wimsatt, W. K., *The Verbal Icon*, 1954.

# SARTRE

Barnes, Hazel E., *The Literature of Possibility: Studies in Humanistic Existentialism*, 1959.
Barrett, William, *Irrational Man*, 1958.
Bauer, George H., *Sartre and the Artist*, 1969.
Brée, Germaine, *Camus and Sartre: Crisis and Commitment*, 1972.
Camus, Albert, *The Myth of Sisyphus*, 1955.

Grene, Marjorie, *Sartre*, 1973.
Kaelin, Eugene F., *An Existentialist Aesthetic*, 1962.
Murdoch, Iris, *Sartre, Romantic Rationalist*, 1953.
Suhl, Benjamin, *Jean-Paul Sartre: The Philosopher as Literary Critic*, 1973.

## FRYE

Bodkin, Maud, *Archetypal Patterns in Poetry*, 1963.
Campbell, Joseph, *The Hero with a Thousand Faces*, 1949.
Frye, Northrop, *Anatomy of Criticism*, 1957.
Kermode, Frank, *Puzzles and Epiphanies*, 1962.
Krieger, Murray, ed., *Northrop Frye in Modern Criticism: Selected Papers from the English Institute*, 1966.
Murray, Henry A., ed., *Myth and Myth-Making*, 1960.
Seboek, Thomas, ed., *Myth, A Symposium*, 1955.
Slote, Bernice, ed., *Myth and Symbol*, 1963.
Wheelwright, Philip, *The Burning Fountain*, 1954.

## RICH

Auerbach, Nina, *Communities of Women*, 1978.
Bernikow, Louise, *Among Women*, 1980.
Daly, Mary, *Beyond God the Father*, 1973.
Gilbert, Sandra and Gubar, Susan, *Madwoman in the Attic*, 1979.
Millett, Kate, *Sexual Politics*, 1969.
Moers, Ellen, *Literary Women*, 1976.
Rich, Adrienne, *On Lies, Secrets, and Silence*, 1979.
Showalter, Elaine, *A Literature of Their Own*, 1976.
Woolf, Virginia, *A Room of One's Own*, 1929.

## EAGLETON

Arvon, Henri, *Marxist Aesthetics*, 1970.
Baxandall, Lee, *Marxism and Aesthetics*, 1968.
Caudwell, Christopher, *Illusion and Reality*, 1947.
Demetz, Peter, *Marx, Engels and the Poets*, 1967.
Eagleton, Terry, *Criticism and Ideology*, 1976.
Jameson, Fredric, *Marxism and Form*, 1971.
Lukács, Georg, *Studies in European Realism*, 1964.
Williams, Raymond, *Marxism and Literature*, 1977.

## BARTHES

Barthes, Roland, *Critical Essays*, 1972.
Barthes, Roland, *S/Z*, 1974.

Barthes, Roland, *Writing Degree Zero*, 1968.
Culler, Jonathan, *Structuralist Poetics: Structuralism, Linguistics, and the Study of Literature*, 1975.
Lentricchia, Frank, *After the New Criticism*, 1980.
Petit, Philip, *The Concept of Structuralism: A Critical Analysis*, 1977.
Scholes, Robert, *Structuralism in Literature: An Introduction*, 1974.

## DERRIDA

Culler, Jonathan, *On Deconstruction: Theory and Criticism in the 1970's*, 1982.
Derrida, Jacques, *Of Grammatology*, 1976.
Derrida, Jacques, "Structure, Sign, and Play in the Discourse of the Human Sciences," in *The Structuralist Controversy: The Languages of Criticism and the Sciences of Man* (ed. Richard Macksey and Eugenio Donato), 1972.
Derrida, Jacques, *Writing and Difference*, 1978.
Hartman, Geoffrey, *Saving the Text: Literature/Derrida/Philosophy*, 1981.
Leitch, Vincent B., *Deconstructive Criticism: An Advanced Introduction*, 1983.
Norris, Christopher, *Deconstruction, Theory and Practice*, 1982.

## DE MAN

Bloom, Harold, *A Map of Misreading*, 1975.
Bloom, Harold, *Agon: Towards a Theory of Revisionism*, 1982.
Bloom, Harold, *Deconstruction and Criticism*, 1979.
de Man, Paul, *Allegories of Reading*, 1979.
de Man, Paul, *Blindness and Insight: Essays in the Rhetoric of Contemporary Criticism*, 1971.
Lentricchia, Frank, "Paul de Man," in *After the New Criticism*, 1980.

## FISH

Bleich, David, *Readings and Feelings: An Introduction to Subjective Criticism*, 1975.
Fish, Stanley, *Surprised by Sin*, 1967.
Fish, Stanley, *Self-Consuming Artifacts*, 1972.
Holland, Norman L., *Poems in Persons*, 1973.
Iser, Wolfgang, *The Act of Reading*, 1978.
McGuire, Richard L., *Passionate Attention*, 1973.
Rosenblatt, Louise, *The Reader, The Text, The Poem*, 1978.
Slatoff, Walter J., *With Respect to Readers*, 1970.

# Index